DEDICATED
TO
OUR
UNFORGOTTEN
DEAD
COMRADES

THE LEIBSTANDARTE III

By Rudolf Lehmann
Translated by Nick Olcott

J.J. Fedorowicz Publishing

THE LEIBSTANDARTE III

By Rudolf Lehmann
An English translation by Nick Olcott

Originally published in German
As DIE LEIBSTANDARTE III, by
Munin Verlag, in Osnabruck, West Germany

Published by
J.J. Fedorowicz Publishing
267 Whitegates Crescent
Winnipeg, Manitoba
Canada R3K 1L2
(204) 837-6080

Printed in the USA
ISBN 0-921991-05-3

Typesetting—The JADA Group
Printed by—Publishers Press

MAPBOOK

THE LIEBSTANDARTE III

Dear Friend:

In this volume there are references to maps and sketches. When volume II of THE LIEBSTANDARTE was published a separate map booklet was enclosed with maps from vols. II and III. If you did not buy volume II, you can obtain the map booklet by buying volume II. A limited number of map booklets is available, ask the dealer from whom you bought this book. If your dealer does not carry it, you can order it directly from myself. The cost is: $5.00 US plus $1.00 for shipping.

John Fedorowicz

PUBLISHER'S ACKNOWLEDGEMENTS

I wish to thank the following individuals who have contributed to the publishing of this book.

Nick Olcott — Translation
Miles Krogfus — Proofreading
George Rugenius — Proofreading
Konrad Gunzel — Donation of LAH cuffband

I also wish to thank you the reader for purchasing this book, and all those of you who have purchased my other books, and have written me with your kind words of praise and encouragement. It gives me impetus to continue to publish translations of the best German books, as you can see by the additional books which are in preparation for publication in the near future. Other titles are either being negotiated or seriously contemplated, many as a result of your helpful proposals. Such proposals have also motivated me to pursue the start of serious military art print series, focusing on the Waffen-SS and German armor. More on these in the near future, further suggestions are always welcome.

John Fedorowicz

Books published by J.J. Fedorowicz Publishing

THE LEIBSTANDARTE I (1 SS Panzer Division)
THE LEIBSTANDARTE II
THE LEIBSTANDARTE III
EUROPEAN VOLUNTEERS (5 SS Panzer Division)
DAS REICH I (2 SS Panzer Division) a 5 Vol set
OTTO WEIDINGER (W-SS Knight's Cross Winner, A Biography)
OTTO KUMM (W-SS Knight's Cross Winner, A Biography)
MANHAY, THE ARDENNES; CHRISTMAS 1944
ARMOR BATTLES OF THE WAFFEN-SS 1943-45
TIGER; THE HISTORY OF A LEGENDARY WEAPON 1942-45

In preparation for publication in the near future (1991 and 1992)

THE LEIBSTANDARTE IV/1
THE LEIBSTANDARTE IV/2
DAS REICH II
DAS REICH III
HISTORY OF THE PANZERKORPS GROSSDEUTSCHLAND I, a 3 Vol set.
HISTORY OF THE 12 SS PANZER DIVISION HITLERJUGEND
PANZER ACES
TIGERS IN THE MUD
HITLER MOVES EAST (deluxe reprint of Paul Carrell's classic)
SCORCHED EARTH (deluxe reprint of Paul Carrell's classic)
EAST FRONT DRAMA 1944

J.J. Fedorowicz Publishing

CONTENTS

Appendix 8

Appendix 9

Appendix 10

Appendix 10a

Appendix 11

FOREWORD
from
THE HISTORIAN

More than two years were needed to assemble this material, not only the documents, but also the reports from survivors. The latter seem to be especially important. In the present book, Volume III of the division history of the *Leibstandarte*, we seek to present not just facts, figures, and accurate descriptions of the war's events.

Historical truth only shines through such data when the "unknown soldier," too, is allowed to speak. His descriptions, whether from journals or from reminiscences, are of incomparable worth, especially the further we travel into World War II. Interested historians have advised me to neglect not the smallest detail I have discovered, no matter how insignificant it may appear. The result is a thick book.

The preparations for Volumes IV/1 and IV/2 will require a fairly long time because descriptions of the battles under consideration there exist only in documents about the larger groupings, such as Armee or Heeresgruppe, and they have little to say, naturally enough, about an individual Division.

I appeal therefore once more for the cooperation of all survivors from our brave division. Please assist me with reports, sketches, maps, photos, in short, with all important sources of information. My intent is to include all the additions and corrections to the previously written combat reports, officer rosters, and troop histories in an appendix to the last volume. The author therefore asks everyone concerned to make full use of this opportunity to correct or amend.

The unit designations changed during the period covered by this volume. To maintain authenticity, I have used the unit designation which was valid at the time.

With this renewed call for help from my comrades, I must include my thanks for the extensive assistance of all kinds so generously given so far. It has achieved such an extent that it would explode the framework of this foreword to list all the names individually as I would wish. I therefore extend my heartfelt gratitude in representative fashion to all my helpers by thanking the unit association of the I. Panzerkorps and its president, Albert Stenwedel. I am also indebted to the German and foreign historians who have taken this work under serious and critical consideration and have given me valuable advice on its continuation. The gentlemen of the federal military archieves in Freiburg, especially Herr Oberarchivrat Meyer and his indefatigable colleagues, have contributed significantly to the completeness of this work. In the final stages of preparation, my old comrades and friends Otto Baum and Dr. Bernhard Frank provided excellent support as readers, while Horst Hütten and Ralf Tiemann prepared the sketches. To them, too, I owe special gratitude.

There is a tendency to assume that a former soldier always wants to glorify the war, and journalistic critics have raised that objection. This author's intention is rather to present the much-maligned men of our unit, men who were damned to service in the war in their early youth. I hope I have managed to show how they coped with that fate. The respect they gained for the young men of our former enemy who suffered the same fate is part of that story. To suppress the darker hours of that time would make the entire effort worthless. "A people is only able to act when it is in a position to tell its history and find its identity in that history and through that history." (Notes from the Carl-Siemens-Stiftung, Volume 3. Ullstein Verlag, 1980.)

For those of us lucky enough to have survived, this chronicle should serve as a reminder of those comrades who fought and suffered beside us, to whom we perhaps owe our lives in time of danger or whose lives we may have saved. Our second Divisional commander, Brigadeführer and Generalmajor der Waffen-SS, Theodor Wisch, wrote about my work: "We thank our comrade Rudolf Lehmann for taking over the task of writing the history of the *Leibstandarte*. Thanks goes, too, to the comrades who contributed their documents and knowledge. That thereby do a great service to our fallen and living men and to their families. The unimaginable feats of all soldiers deserve to be retained for posterity. They were performed out of patriotism, comradeship, and sense of duty. We now face the question: how did we see ourselves? There are many answers. One of them is that we saw ourselves as the ones from whom the world expected success. Everyone, from commander to last private, acted accordingly, just as in all other divisions. I remember the words of our former commander, Sepp Dietrich, who used to give an attack order and follow it with the warning, "Bring my boys back!' We led the unit with this spirit."

In presenting this third volume, the author once again hopes to occasion serious consideration on the part of young and old. Please regard it as his modest contribution to the better understanding of the recent history of our German people.

signed, Rudolf Lehmann

INTRODUCTION

The summer offensive of 1942 on the southern Russian front, an offensive which had begun successfully, came to a virtual standstill at the end of August because of a fateful splitting of the forces between the Caucasus, Stalingrad, and Leningrad. In the extreme south, the units of Heeresgruppe A, including the SS-Division *Wiking*, were able to capture only the northern edge of the Caucasus and occupy the first, rather small, oilfield near Maikop. After the heroic, but militarily rather senseless, raising of the flag on Mount Elbrus, the thrust toward the Black Sea harbors of Tuapse, Anapa, and Batus died in the fighting for the passes through the Caucasus, a death due largely to the supply difficulties. After the departure of Generalfeldmarschall List, Heeresgruppe A, then under the command of Generaloberst Kleist, dug in hard on the Terek river in late summer. On the Volga, the 4. Panzerarmee and the 6. Armee had reached Stalingrad. There the offensive concentrated on this huge industrial city, stretching for kilometers along the bank of the Volga. The advantages of mobile combat were exchanged for grinding, crushing siege warfare. The flanks, bent back far to the rear, were covered in the south by the 4. Panzerarmee and the newly introduced 4th Rumanian Army and in the north by the 3rd Rumanian Army, 8th Italian Army, and German 2. Armee, with some Hungarian units.

The shape of the advance bulwark near Stalingrad invited a pincer attack. On November 19, 1942, strong Soviet tank and infantry units broke through the 3rd Rumanian Army in the north. The following day, they reached the 4. Panzerarmee and broke through the 4th Rumanian Army. On November 22 and 23, the ring around Stalingrad was closed.

> "As soon as the Russians recognized that the 6. Armee was stuck, they devoted all their resources to winning as much ground as possible as quickly as possible in the gap which had been opened up south and southwest of Stalingrad and to preventing any front from forming in the vicinity of the surrounded Armee. Depite this, the German forces did manage, by bringing up their weak reserves, by pulling together men separated from their units and placing them under the command of particularly effective officers, and by other means, to form a loose defensive front between the mouth of the Tschir and that of the Weschenskaja into the Don, thus virtually along the course of the Tschir. This new front provided the first check to the Russians' hitherto unencumbered advance," explains General Tippelskirch in "Geschichte des 2. Weltkriegs" (page 271).

Generalfeldmarschall von Manstein was brought in from Leningrad, and a new *Heeresgruppe Don* was formed under him. This army group had as its mission the closing of the torn front and the preparation of a relief attack on Stalingrad. The 4. Panzerarmee was reinforced with troops brought from the Caucasus, from Woronesch, and from Orel. Under Generaloberst Hoth, it assembled as a new attack group in the Kotelnikowo area. Setting out on December 10, it came to within fifty kilometers of the encirclement front by December 21.

The Russians started their next thrust on December 16, this time along the Don and the Tschir simultaneously. The thrust first hit the 8th Italian Army, which formed the right wing of Heeresgruppe B. This fact was decisive for the suspension of the 4. Panzerarmee's relief attack.

After a few days, the entire front of the 8th Italian Army, in which stood seven Italian divisions and one German Division, was torn apart, and the Army found itself on December 18 in an insupportable retreat. By then, the Russians were moving through a gap more than a hundred kilometers wide and were proceeding south on Rostow. A premature loss of this city would have cut off Heeresgruppe A in the Caucasus, as well as the 4. Panzerarmee and all the forces situated to the east, from supply lines and retreat routes. In mid- December, 1942, the Stab of the XXX. Armeekorps was moved up to join Heeresgruppe B. It received orders to form "Armeeabteilung Fretter-Pico" in order to close up the hole, by then grown to almost two hundred kilometers wide, between Heeresgruppe Don and Heeresgruppe B. The forces standing at the Armeeabteilung's disposal were scattered over three areas. In Woroschilowgrad stood a field training Regiment, some marching Bataillone, and a Turkbataillon under the able leadership of Oberst i.G. Nagel. In Donskoj waited the severely weakened Gruppe von der Lancken, which still possessed a few tanks. Elements of the 3. Gebirgsdivision under command of Generalmajor Kreysing were spread between Millerowo and Meschkoff (about ninety kilometers). The 304. Infanteriedivision, completely lacking in experience on the eastern front, was brought up from the coastal defenses in France. East of the Kalitwa sector, in a line with Millerowo, the remains of the XXIX. AK and the 298. Infanteriedivision pushed their way through. They were also subordinated to the Armeeabteilung. In addition, the Armeeabteilung was to receive the yet-to- be-assembled Kampfgruppe Schuldt, toward which the Wachbataillon Berlin of the *Leibstandarte* was to push its way.[1]

Part 5
DEPLOYMENT OF THE WACHBATAILLON BERLIN (Continuation)

Section II
THE VII. (WACH)/*LSSAH* IN THE DEFENSIVE FIGHTING IN THE DONEZ AREA (KAMPFGRUPPE SCHULDT) 18.12.1942 - 15.3.1943

In the course of the expansion of the *LSSAH* to a Panzergrenadierdivision, a process which began in February of 1942, the Führungshauptamt issued orders on 14.2.1942 for the establishment of the VII. Bataillon/*LAH* in Berlin-Lichterfelde. It was to be structured into a Stab, a Stabskompanie, and three Schützenkompanien.

On December 4, 1942, the following order was issued by the Kommandoamt of the Waffen-SS, renaming the unit:

> "The VII. Bataillon/*LSSAH*, headquartered in Berlin-Lichterfelde, which is intended for use at the front, is redesignated 'Wachbataillon Berlin *LSSAH*' effective 1.12.1942.
>
> The elements of the Bataillon remaining in Berlin are to be restructured on 1.12.1942 into a Wachkompanie according to KStN and KAN 4136 (Schützenkompanie/Wachbataillon Berlin)."[2]

On the same date, 4.12.1942, the Kommandoamt of the Waffen-SS also issued orders establishing a heavy Kompanie for the Wachbataillon and a Regimentsstab and Stabskompanie for a new Infanterie-Regiment (mot.) in Berlin-Lichterfelde. Standartenführer Schuldt was named commander of the Regiment, and Obersturmführer Drescher was named leader of the heavy Kompanie of the Wachbataillon/*LSSAH*.[3]

As early as 6.12.1942, the Wachbataillon and probably the Regimentsstab embarked for the front. The reconstruction of the officer roster is difficult because so many documents are missing. An attempt will be made to impose some order on the sometimes contradictory memories of the survivors:

Stab of the Brigade Schuldt

Commander: Standartenführer Schuldt
Adjutant: Hauptsturmführer Molt
Ordonnanz-Offizier: Obersturmführer Vogel
Administrative officer: ?
Doctor: ?
TFK: ?

Stab of the VII./*LAH* in Lichterfelde

	Former commander: Sturmbannführer Ernst Meyer (not able to serve on the front because of severe war wounds)

Commander of the Wachbataillon Berlin/*LAH*

	At time of transport: Hauptsturmführer Beutler (?) Shortly after arrival in Russia: Hauptsturmführer Ott After about 31.12.1942: Hauptsturmführer Lantscher
1. Kompanie	Hauptsturmführer Ott, later Obersturmführer Horvath Zugführer: Untersturmführer Deistung, wounded 12.1 and 18.1.1943
2. Kompanie	Obersturmführer Leiteritz, wounded while getting off the train 18.12.1943 Successor: Obersturmführer Knösel
3. Kompanie	Obersturmführer Blunck
4. (heavy) Kompanie	Obersturmführer Drescher Infanteriegeschützzug (from the commander of the Waffen-SS in the Netherlands) Pakzug (also from the Netherlands) Pionierzug (from the Pionier-Ersatzbataillon Dresden)

Other officers mentioned in a casualty list are:
- Untersturmführer J. Friedrichs of the 1./*LAH*, killed
- Untersturmführer Herbert Deistung of the 1./*LAH*, wounded
- Obersturmführer Hemsiecke, insignia of 7./*LAH*, killed 11.1.1943

The Kampfgruppe of Polizei-Infanterie-Regiment 1
  Commander: Sturmbannführer Wilhelm Dietrich
Stab of the I./Polizei-Infanterie-Regiment 1
  Untersturmführer Kersten
  Oberjunker Schröter
Elements of the 1./Polizei-Infanterie-Regiment 1
  Obersturmführer Tigge
  (not part of Kampfgruppe Dietrich)
2./Polizei-Infanterie-Regiment 1
  Obersturmführer Waldmann
  Obersturmführer Drieske
Elements of the 3./Polizei-Infanterie-Regiment 1
  Obersturmführer Schneider
Elements of the 4./Polizei-Infanterie-Regiment 1
  Hauptsturmführer Schwarting
  (not part of Kampfgruppe Dietrich)

The Stabskompanie of the Regimentsstab Schuldt was structured as follows under the establishment order:

Kradmeldezug from the Kradschützen-Ersatzbataillon Ellwangen
Panzerjägerzug from the commander of the Waffen-SS in the Netherlands
Infanterie-Pionierzug from the Pionier-Ersatzbataillon Dresden
Nachrichtenzug from the headquarters of the Stab of the Reichsführer-SS.

On 16.12.1942, the first transport trains, carrying the Regimentsstab, Stabskompanie, and probably the 1. Kompanie and elements of the 4. (heavy) Kompanie of the Wachbataillon, arrived in Millerowo. They were subordinated to the Armeeabteilung Fretter-Pico.[4] Standartenführer Schuldt received orders to assemble his Kampfgruppe in the Meschkoff area and to move forward on both sides of Meschkoff toward the hills north of the Tschaja against the Soviet breakthrough point. In addition to the Wachbataillon, the I. Bataillon of the Polizei-Infanterie-Regiment 1 (under Sturmbannführer Dietrich) and the Führer-Flakabteilung were to belong to the Kampfgruppe. There was also talk in the Führer's headquarters of a strong Panzerjäger unit, but nothing was ever seen of one. From the Führer-Flakabteilung, only a few guns reached Brigade Schuldt, and those not until February. From the I. Bataillon of the Polizei-Infanterie-Regiment 1, only the Bataillonsstab, the 2. and 3. Kompanie and small parts of the 1. and 4. Kompanie were actually moved up after being unloaded in Tschertkowo on 18.12. They came in an overland march, some forces in vehicles belonging to the Wachbataillon/*LAH*. From then on, the Kampfgruppe bore the name of the Bataillon commander, Kampfgruppe Dietrich. The other half of the I. Bataillon of the Polizei-Infanterie-Regiment 1, which included the bulk of the 1. and 4. Kompanie with the 2. Staffel of the Bataillonsstab, was deployed directly from the transport train to provide temporary defense against a Russian tank breakthrough in Zschertkowo. From there it fought its way, first as part of Kampfgruppe Göhler (19. Panzerdivision), alone toward the west. In the beginning of February, 1943, the remainders of the 1. and 4. Kompanien pulled back into the Charkow combat area under covering fire from the Sturmgeschütze of the *LSSAH* under command of Hauptsturmführer Schwarting east of Skripai.[5]

On 17.12 shortly before midnight, the Bataillonsstab of the Wachbataillon *LAH* arrived at a little railway station in the southern part of Meschkoff with the 2., 3., and most of the 4. (heavy) Kompanie. Hardly any of the vehicles would start because of the cold and the long railway journey. Almost all of them had to be pushed off the train cars on ramps. As a result, when daylight came, the vehicles were standing too close together, and before long Russian planes arrived and dropped their bombs. The first casualties resulted, including the leader of the 2. Kompanie, Obersturmführer Leiteritz and possibly the Bataillon leader, Hauptsturmführer Beutler, for the next day, Hauptsturmführer Ott is listed as holding that post.[6]

On the evening of 18.12, Kampfgruppe Dietrich reached Brigade Schuldt in the Meschkoff area. It was moved up farther to Nasaroff, about six kilometers west of Meschkoff, and billeted there.[7]

On 18.12, the Wachbataillon moved in closed formation from the basin north of Meschkoff in an attack on the hills three kilometers northwest of the town.[8] It must have been against a relief attack waged by elements of the retreating Italian 8th Army, for at midnight the Bataillon got free of the enemy and moved back, while containing the action, to the northern edge of Meschkoff. Kampgruppe Dietrich was added to the defensive front around Meschkoff on 19.12. Around midday, there was a Russian tank attack from the west around Nasaroff, and it was repulsed with at least four enemy tanks hit. Combat reconnaissance reported preparations underway by motorized Russian infantry forces in captured Italian vehicles to the southwest of the town.[9] In the night between 19.12 and 20.12, two Russian tanks managed to break into the town and blow up three trucks containing wounded men.[10]

Armeeabteilung Fretter-Pico, with which contact was still being maintained at this time, issued orders in the evening for the Brigade to move out of Meschkoff starting at midnight.[11]

20.12.1942: At 00.00 hours, a well-ordered pullback from the enemy line began. As the rearguard was moving back, a Russian tank unit met them on the road between Meschkoff and Millerowo and split the Wachbataillon *LAH* in two.[12] The first grouping resulting from the split contained the 1. Kompanie, most of the 2. Kompanie, and elements of the 4. (heavy) Kompanie. This group was able to fight its way through to Millerowo, where the 3. Gebirgsdivision took charge of it. The 3. Gebirgsdivision placed it under the command of Obersturmführer Dahl, an officer of the Polizeidivision who had been separated from his unit and had ended up with the Gebirgsdivision. The resulting Kampgruppe Dahl, with a strength of about two Kompanien, remained in Millerowo as the only counterattack reserve for the 3. Gebirgsdivision until it broke out on 15.1.1943.[13] On 19.1.1943, the group reached Woroschilowgrad. General der Infanterie Tippelskirch described this breakout on page 273 of his "Geschichte des 2. Weltkriegs" in connection with the order later issued in mid-November to the 6. Armee in Stalingrad for its breakout:

> "No situation left the Russian lower-level and mid-level officers more helpless than a surprise storm attack by desperate German soldiers under effective command. Only a few weeks earlier, 4,000 Germans and the 12,000 Italians they pulled along, forces which had been trapped in Millerowo for weeks, had managed to break through the surrounding Russian forces by night. They plowed through snow with only a few Sturmgeschütze blazing the trail more than twenty kilometers to reach the German lines, and their losses only amounted to ten percent. The deployment of strong air units, which held back the Russians (especially their artillery) facing us across the front, was enough to blaze a trail for the last heavy unit of the escaping Kolonne."

Kampgruppe Dahl finally came under the command of Kampgruppe Schuldt (see the entries for 15.1. - 19.1.1943 below) on 20.1.1943. The second group that resulted from the splitting of the Wachbataillon consisted of the Regimentsstab of Kampfgruppe Schuldt, the Bataillonsstab of the Wachbataillon, the 3. Kompanie, the Pionierzug, several heavy Granatwerfer from the 4. (heavy) Kompanie, elements of the 2. Kompanie of the Wachbataillon, and most of Kampfgruppe Dietrich, to which the units of the Wachbataillon were subordinated in Donskoj.[14] This town was reached on 20.12 at 04.00 hours. The troops moved from there to the southeast by way of the Jablonowaja and Bolschoja sector to Ssmolin on the Metschettka river. After a strenuous journey of about seventy kilometers, the group reached its objective at 14.30 hours on 20.12. It could finally get some rest. (See Sketch 1)

On 21.12.1942, at about 18.00 hours, the combat units' march continued, after several false alarms, to the west toward Kijewskij, while the supply train stayed behind in Ssmolin. The Kampfgruppe was to set up defensive positions in Kijewskij toward the west and southwest.[15] Oberschütze Robert Krötz described the march in a report written at the time:

> "A small column, close to physical collapse and oppressed by the psychological burden of a hopeless mission, but unshaken in their determination to defend themselves, marched through night and fog far from the train tracks, with no contact to German units or the German front, through snow and biting cold all the way to Kijewskij."

In the night between 21.12 and 22.12, the designated positions were assumed. They were improved in the course of the day and in part advanced to the west. Artillery men, Panzerjäger, and one entire marching Bataillon, all of which had become separated from their units, were found and added to Kampfgruppe Dietrich.[16]

In the early afternoon, a Russian tank assault was repulsed and four of their tanks destroyed. In the evening, the Italians were sent to relieve Kampfgruppe Schuldt, but their forces were absolutely inadequate. Only eighty men were available to take over the sector held by Kampfgruppe Dietrich.1[17]

On 23.12, the Armeeabteilung Fretter-Pico ordered the closing of the Russian supply route in the sector Ssweschnikowo — Roshek, about ten kilometers south of the former defensive position. Elements of Kampfgruppe Dietrich moved just north of Ssweschnikowo and elements of the *LAH* moved into position near Roshek. Most of the Kampfgruppe remained in Metschetka. Roshek had to be captured for this move to take place.[18]

Standartenführer Schuldt led his men in an assault on the town on 24.12.[19] The enemy was thrown out, one T-34 was captured, two more were blown up, and a number of prisoners were taken.

In the evening, Standartenführer Schuldt restructured the units belonging to his Kampfgruppe. Gruppe Dietrich was numbered the 1. Kompanie, the elements of the Wachbataillon *LAH* named the 2. Kompanie, Marschbataillon 179 designated the 3. Kompanie, and the heavy weapons were assigned to stand at the disposal of the Kampfgruppe command.

The Kriegstagebuch of Armeeabteilung Fretter-Pico reveals that Gruppe Schuldt, together with the Korpsstab of the XXIX. Armeekorps (under General Geier), was surrounded by enemy tanks at 09.00 hours on 26.12.1942 in Krassnojarowka. It received orders to fight its way back to the Shassyrskaja bridgehead.

On Christmas Day, the Russians renewed their attacks. At about noon on 25.12.1942, several tanks and armoured reconnaissance vehicles launched an attack. The vehicle in front was destroyed, but the second broke through and tore through the town, firing to all sides. Our Pak, which had moved into position on the edge of town, did manage to score a hit and do the driver some damage. A T-34 broke through the wall of a house where the supply train of the 3. Kompanie of Polizei-Infanterie-Regiment 1 was enjoying its Christmas dinner.[20] Husemann, the author of the Divisional history of the Polizeidivision, reported that a self-propelled gun finished off this tank, while Krötz reported:

> "Before the tank could maneuver itself free, Ritterkreuz-decorated warrior Sturmbannführer Dietrich jumped up on the colossus and gunned down its crew through the open turret hatch."

The accompanying Russian infantry did not enter the attack initially. During the morning, the Kampfgruppe received supplies via air drops. During the attack on Roshek described above, the Stäbe had hastily retreated to Krassnojarowka. In the Kriegstagebuch of Armeeabteilung Fretter-Pico, our information about the enemy on 25.12 was given as follows:

> "Strong enemy tank forces have broken through the Armeeabteilung's sector to the southeast and have been engaged since yesterday in combat with our Panzer forces of the XXXXVIII. Panzerkorps' 6. and 11. Panzerdivision near Gruppe Hollidt on the left wing of Heeresgruppe Don. The enemy appears to be holding steady along the line north of Millerowo-Woloschino and to be making preparations to break through our strong points there in order to continue his thrust to the south in the direction of Rostow. The strength of the enemy is estimated to be two tank corps on both sides of Millerowo."

The XXIX. Armeekorps ordered our forces to move to Krassnojarowka during the night between 25.12 and 26.12. While Gruppe Dietrich reached the town in a motorized march, elements of the Wachbataillon/*LAH* had to trudge through on foot. (See sketch 2.)

On 26.12, according to the Kriegstagebuch of Armeeabteilung Fretter-Pico, Kampfgruppe Schuldt and the Korpsstab of the XXIX. Armeekorps were once again surrounded by tanks. The Kampfgruppe repulsed several tank attacks and destroyed two enemy tanks. It was able to continue its march to the southeast, via Wodjanyj, toward Romanowskij. After a brief regrouping, the march was continued toward Pritschenskij at the edge of the Beresowka sector. Before the units set out, however, three German planes appeared and dropped eleven supply crates, "...after we had identified ourselves as the proper recipients by use of the correct recognition signals."[21]

The Kampfgruppe reached Pritschenskij by nightfall and was given emergency billets in a town already filled to overflowing with Italians and Rumanians.[22]

For 27.12, the XXIX. Armeekorps received orders from Armeeabteilung Fretter-Pico to fight its way back toward the German bridgehead near Skassyrskaja to the southwest. There the Korps was to establish contact with Armeeabteilung Hollidt. During the entire morning, the Kampfgruppe had to fight off heavy attacks, but these abated in the afternoon. The rest of the day was used to reorganize the troops.[23]

On 28.12, at 03.00 hours, the Kampfgruppe started its march. Soon after daybreak, the Kampfgruppe had its first contact with the enemy. Shortly thereafter, a reconnaissance plane dropped a road map containing a new march objective. The Kampfgruppe was to move toward Skassyrskaja in the Bystria sector.

After a fairly long rest, the Kampfgruppe continued its march just before nightfall. During this rest period, two Panzerspäwagen from outside joined the unit, to the great joy of all. Their arrival signalled contact, however, tenuous, to the outside world.[24] Sturmmann Miehe described this march's difficulty and its end as follows:

> "On the last day when we were cut off and alone, we had just paused for a short rest before nightfall. We were physically at the end of our ropes, for we had had nothing to eat for several days. Suddenly the cry rang out: 'Tanks!' We quickly took cover, but soon recognized to our exceeding delight that they were two German Panzerspähwagen. These vehicles accompanied us under the cover of darkness about ten or fifteen kilometers farther to the German positions. We had with us only a radio car and two self-propelled guns from the Heer. Without these, we probably never would have broken out of the pocket. But the next morning, we presented a kind of review march to a Heer General, who made a speech thanking us for providing cover for him and his Korpsstab."

Schütze Krötz reported the event as follows:

> "With only a few vehicles (the rest had been destroyed long ago) in which to transport our severely wounded comrades, worn down by the ceaseless combat, the Kompanien of the Kampfgruppen disengaged themselves from the enemy and marched out into the icy desert. Soon, the first exhausted men sank into the snow. With kind words, but iron fists, the Standartenführer pulled them to their feet one by one and forced them to be stronger than their weakened bodies. Felt boots, heavy winter clothing, weapons, and munitions hung like lead weights on tired limbs, which refused to obey even the strongest-willed. But just when a few men seemed on the verge of falling asleep and freezing to death, the Standartenführer made the Kampfgruppe stand in march formation and mercilessly forced them to goosestep past their General in strictest discipline. It was the General of the XXIX. Armeekorps, who had pushed his way through with his Stab to join the Kampfgruppe, the last assembled, combat-ready unit."

According to this report, Standartenführer Schuldt was still with the Kampfgruppe as late as the morning of 29.12. The Kampfgruppe had been subordinated to the XXIX. AK as part of Heeresgruppe Don since 27.12. In the Kriegstagebuch of Armeeabteilung Fretter-Pico, his name also appears in the entry for 29.12, where mention is made of an "SS-Gruppe Sculdt," which was to be formed in Donskoj. It is possible that Standartenführer Schuldt, after capturing the designated line in Skassyrskaja, handed over the command of the Kampfgruppe to Sturmbannführer Dietrich and went to Donskoj upon orders from higher up to form another Kampfgruppe under the command of Armee-abteilung Fretter-Pico. The fate of this Gruppe Schuldt will be reported with the events affecting Kampfgruppe Dietrich when our chronicle reaches the point at which Kampfgruppe Dietrich joined Gruppe Schuldt (see below, entry for 19.2.1943). A visit by Standartenführer Schuldt to the Führer's headquarters between Christmas and New Year, as Husemann reports took place, is not remembered by any of the surviving members of the Adjutant staff of the Führer.

29.12.1942: Kampfgruppe Dietrich received emergency billets in Skassyrskaja after a march of over fifty kilometers. After one false alarm, the unit was finally granted ten field kitchens and informed, to everyone's great joy, that it would be transferred to a rest area the following day.[25]

30.12.1942: The advance command was sent ahead in vehicles to the Alexejew rest area, and the bulk of the Kampfgruppe set out on foot. After some difficulties, the twenty-kilometer march came to an end by evening. The last men to arrive brought news with them that Skassyrskaja had come under heavy artillery fire in the course of the day.[26]

31.12.1942: The Kampfgruppe was finally able to enjoy its well-deserved rest. It was subordinated to the 6. Panzerdivision under Generalleutnant Raus as part of the XVII. AK (Armeeabteilung Hollidt) on 1.1.1943. In the meantime, Standartenführer Schuldt had attempted to get Kampfgruppe Dietrich added to the structure of his newly-formed Kampfgruppe. A partial victory was granted him when orders arrived to move the unit to Kamensk. A vehicle column was indeed dispatched and reached Kampfgruppe Dietrich on 2.1.1943, but the changing situation forced the column to return empty on 3.1.1943.[27]

3.1.1943: Kampfgruppe Dietrich was subordinated to the I./Panzergrenadier-Regiment 114 (6. Panzerdivision) and deployed in the sector Makejew — Alexejew — Kowylkin — Bakowa and assigned to establish a new rear position. (See sketch 3.)

The situation:
Armeeabteilung Hollidt on the left wing of Heeresgruppe Don was to prevent the enemy, who was advancing from the north, from making it to the lower Don (the rear of the 4. Panzerarmee) and above all from breaking through to Rostow. This was its mission as long as the 4. Panzerarmee and Heeresgruppe A remained in the region south of the lower Don. Hollidt was also to prevent the enemy from breaking through his left wing toward the crossings over the Don between Forchstadt and Woroschilowgrad, where he would attempt to open a road for himself to Rostow from the northwest. At the same time, however, Armeeabteilung Hollidt was being threatened on both flanks. On its western flank, the Italians were disappearing from the battlefield, and Gruppe Fretter-Pico was only slowly fighting its way back into the position from the area around Millerowo toward the Donez. The 6. Panzerdivision had orders to close up the hole at the front by launching a counterattack with the reinforced Panzer-Aufklärungsabteilung 6 north of Tazinskaja and thus to provide a retreat route for the Garde-Panzerkorps under General Badanow. It was also to use the rest of the Division to hold the line Morosowskaja — Tazinskaja. The 11. Panzerdivision under General Balck was to attack and destroy the enemy forces which had broken through near Tazinskaja. The two Panzerdivisionen fulfilled their

missions with speed and élan. The Russian XXIVth Tank Corps was surrounded, and the enemy forces which had broken through were finally destroyed.[28]

On 31.12.1942, Kampfgruppe Dietrich was structured as follows:

Stab I./Polizei-Infanterie-Regiment 1
2. Kompanie/Polizei-Infanterie-Regiment 1
3. Kompanie/Polizei-Infanterie-Regiment 1
one Kompanie/Wachbataillon Berlin *LAH*
Pionierzug/4. Kompanie/Wachbataillon Berlin *LAH*
light Infanteriegeschützzug/4. Kompanie/Wachbataillon Berlin *LAH*
elements of the Stabskompanie/Wachbataillon Berlin *LAH* under Hauptsturmführer Lantscher (This name appears in Husemann only. No other source gives this name.)
518. Panzerjägerkompanie under Oberleutnant Wilde.[29]

Kampfgruppe Dietrich was therefore assigned to be deployed in the defensive front to cooperate in this fighting.

As a first step, the sick were sent back on 3.1.1943, and equipment was augmented.[30]

On 4.1, Kampfgruppe Dietrich was added to Kampfgruppe Unrein (under Oberst Unrein, part of the Panzergrenadier-Regiment 4, II. Panzerregiment 11 under Major Dr. Bäke) in the sector Werchne — Obljswkij. It had first to win its position, which was only achieved by a concerted attack by all Kompanien with Panzer support ending on the evening of 5.1.[31]

On 6.1, the Artillerie assigned to cooperate with the units was able to provide some perceptible relief. After a period of indecision, orders finally arrived for Kampfgruppe Dietrich to be relieved. It was to be transferred initially to Kowytkin and from there it was to assume a rear position in the Alexjew sector. At 18.30 hours the loading of men and munitions into vehicles began. The Kampfgruppe's dead were taken along to be buried in Kowytkin. Available for the move were four trucks belonging to the *LAH* and two from the Bataillonsstab and the 2./Polizei-Infanterie-Regiment 1. The 3./Polizei-Infanterie-Regiment was loaded into Panzers and heavy Panzerwagens for the twelve-kilometer journey to Lugowoj. From there, the trucks from the Kampfgruppe took them on to Kowytkin. The elements of Wachbataillon/*LAH* moved into position before Alexejew, along the railway line toward Stalingrad (about two hundred and fifty kilometers away), while the 518. Panzerjägerkompanie assumed a position to the left of them.[32]

On 7.1, the Kampfgruppe was subordinated to Panzergrenadier-Regiment 114 (under Oberst Zollenkopf). Three self-propelled guns from the Heer were brought to the Kampfgruppe and subordinated to it. In the evening, Russian assault forces managed to push their way through into the northernmost buildings of Alexejew. They were pushed back in a counterthrust, whereby they suffered bloody losses. Twenty Russian dead were counted.

Up until 8.1, Armeeabteilung Hollidt had to let the front west of Morosoff swing back to the southwest. That meant that the positions of Wachbataillon/*LAH* before Alexejew were suddenly the closest to Stalingrad.[33]

The day of 9.1 passed with our reconnaissance troops actively engaged, while the Russians saved their heavy attacks for the early morning hours of 10.1. By midday, the enemy had been repulsed. (See sketch 3.)

In order to cut off the forces positioned west of Morosoff, the Soviets moved their tank forces between the Kalitwa and Bistraja rivers to the southwest, thus into the flank and rear of the German units standing before Rostow. The 7. Panzerdivision was able to bring this enemy move to a standstill on 7.1 in the line from the hills west of Nadeschowka — just south of Petrowskij — Kononoff.[34]

Most of the 7. Panzerdivision had to be hastily pulled out from these positions, however, on 8.1 in order to be deployed against a potential Russian breakthrough eighty kilometers to the south. The remaining Panzergrenadier-Regiment 7 under Oberst Steinkeller faced heavy fighting in the positions between the Kalitwa and Bistraja rivers.[35] For that reason, Kampfgruppe Dietrich was relieved on 11.1 from its positions on both sides of Alexejew with orders to march "as quickly as possible" via Tazinskaja and Massloff toward Krassny Gornjak, six kilometers west of Massloff. There the Kampfgruppe, subordinated to Panzergrenadier-Regiment 7, was to reinforce the front on both sides of Krassny Gornjak.[36] According to the notations for close-range combat in the pay book of Sturmmann Miehe, the Kampfgruppe held the positions near Krassny Gornjak until 13.1, despite heavy attacks on 12.1 and the following night.

On 13.1, elements of the 2. Panzerdivision, after exhaustive preparations, launched a relief attack to the east on Massloff, but it was unsuccessful.[37]

14.1 was a day of rest.

On 15.1 and 16.1, the Kampfgruppe pulled back about eight kilometers south to Karpowo-Obrywskij, according to the combat days entered in the pay book mentioned above.[38]

The Kampfgruppe was transferred on 17.1 via Forchstadt to Olchowskij. Subordinated to the 6. Panzerdivision, its orders were:

"1. Constant reconnaissance by patrols between the adjacent units to the left and right while maintaining contact on both sides; reconnaissance, especially at night, also on the far side of the Donez to spot any enemy approaches.
2. Establishment of all-around defenses in case of a breakthrough. Kampfgruppe Dietrich is to hold the sector to the west and southwest as far as electrical conduit 5 and the Koksofen (Kossowyj) part of the town and as far as the embankments between the railway line and the Donez. Kampfgruppe Dietrich is the left wing of Regiment Zollenkopf. Unit adjacent to the right: Gruppe Oberleutnant Franke (Nebelwerfer-abteilung and furloughed men, insufficient weapons, a motley crew). Unit adjacent to the left: Regiment Hünersdorff."[39]

Generfeldmarschall von Manstein described the situation on this left wing of his Heeresgruppe as follows: "The situation on the left wing of the Heeresgruppe is growing considerably more serious. East of Woroschilowgrad, the 6. Panzer-division, which was deployed under orders from the Heeresgruppe on 14.1 to move from Armeeabteilung Hollidt and to attack the middle Don, was unable to push the enemy back over the Donez. We were only able to pin him down on the bridgehead he had established."[40]

Kampfgruppe Dietrich found itself in the position on the western edge of Olchowskij until 3.2. During this period, only 27.1 was designated a day of close combat. On that day, our forces drove a Russian combat force from its position. During this period, too, the light Infanteriegeschütz of the 4. Wachbataillon/*LAH* was manned and deployed.[41] On 20.1, two enemy army corps moved against the Donez north of Kamensk and were only held back by a concerted effort of all our forces, including elements of the 7. Panzerdivision. When Woroschilowgrad appeared to be threatened on 24.1, the 7. Panzerdivision was moved from its adjacent position into the area northwest of Woroschilowgrad.[42]

The 6. Armee, deployed in Stalingrad, transmitted the following desperate message to the Oberkommando des Heeres on 24.1:

> "On the basis of such reports from the Korps and personal messages from the commanding generals as are available, the Armee provides the following evaluation of the situation: Force lacking ammunition or supplies, only some elements of six Divisionen still contactable. Signs of disintegration on the southern, northern, and western fronts. Uniform command no longer possible. Eastern front little changed. 18,000 wounded without even basic care, medical supplies, or medicine. The 44., 76., 100., 305., and 384. Infanteriedivision destroyed. Front torn apart by numerous breakthroughs. Support points and cover possible only in the cities. Other defense meaningless. Collapse of the front inevitable. Armee requests immediate permission to surrender in order to save remaining lives. Signed Paulus."

The Führer's headquarters registered receipt of the message at 11.16 hours, without giving an answer.

An excerpt from Generalfeldmarschall von Manstein's description of the situation:

> "The northern wing of Heeresgruppe A was 150 to 200 kilometers southeast of Rostow. The withdrawal of the 1. Panzerarmee, with most of the force moving via Rostow, had finally been approved by the OKH. From the Heeresgruppe Don, the 4. Panzerarmee was engaged in desperate fighting east of Rostow to hold the crossing over the Don open for the 1. Panzerarmee, which I intended to move onto the left wing of the Heeresgruppe on the Donez from Woroschilowgrad up. Armeeabteilung Hollidt was defending the Donez from its confluence with the Don to upstream of Forschstadt. Gruppe Fretter-Pico (two Divisionen), subordinated in the meantime to the Heeresgruppe, was securing the Donez on both sides of Kamensk.

Since 19.1, with the disintegration of the Italian Army and the overunning of the Hungarian Army on the Don, there had been a gaping hole from Woroschilowgrad on the Donez to Woronesch on the Don (about 320 kilometers).

On 23.1, the 'front' as far as Starobjelsk was subordinated to Heeresgruppe Don. Along it was already the 19. Panzerdivision, practically destroyed, which had surrendered Starobjelsk to three enemy corps. When the last resistance of the 6. Armee finally fell apart on February 1, the enemy was in a position to threaten a crossing over the Donez in the Woroschilowgrad area with a force of three tank corps, one mechanized corps, and one rifle corps, in addition to having apparently another force of three or four tank corps and a rifle corps deployed along the Donez line from Lissitschansk to Slawiansk. It is unnecessary to describe how the situation would have progressed between January 9 and February 1, or how it could have developed afterwards, if the heroic resistance of the 6. Armee had not kept the enemy's strong forces locked up near Stalingrad for so long!"

On 3.2, Kampfgruppe Dietrich was relieved by the III./Infanterie-Regiment 129 (306. Infanteriedivision) and newly subordinated to the 22. Panzerdivision about fifteen kilometers farther west in the sector Lipoff — Ssasonoff. The Divisionsführer was Oberst Rodt, the Ia was Oberstleutnant i.G. Estor.[43]

The following were deployed on 4.2: to the right *LAH* Kompanie Knösel one-and-a-half kilometers north-northwest of Werch. Ssasonoff as far as the eastern edge of Werch. Ssasonoff; Polizeikompanie under Schneider from the western edge of Nishe Ssasonoff as far as the Boganoff gorge. The line was occupied only by support points, and a 2-centimeter-Flakzug (under Leutnant Bogatny) was subordinated to provide reinforcement. The adjacent unit to the right was Schützenbataillon 24.[44]

In the days leading up to 8.2, there was lively reconnaissance activity both on our side and on the enemy's across the Donez in both directions. A deep Russian thrust about fifty kilometers farther to the northwest forced another withdrawal of the front. From the position held by Kampfgruppe Dietrich, it was now to bend to the south. As the front was being altered, the Kampfgruppe had to hold the hinge of the positions for almost an entire day.

In the late afternoon of 9.2, the Kampfgruppe was relieved by the II. and III./Infanterie-Regiment 581 and moved in vehicles from the Korps supply column to the area just east of Swerdlowsk. The vehicles remaining in the Kampfgruppe's motor pool at that point (3.2.1943) consisted of seven trucks, four cars of the type 15, one motorcycle with side-car, and several motorcycle without. The trucks consisted of kitchen and ammunition trucks, supply-train trucks, and no personnel trucks.[45]

On 10.2, there were rumors of a new transfer, "either to the 6. Panzerdivision or to Kampfgruppe Schuldt."[46]

On 11.2, several trucks arrived from Kampfgruppe Schuldt (this for the second time) to pick up Kampfgruppe Dietrich and transport it to Krassnodonsk. Once again, however, a Russian breakthrough, this time south of Woroschilowgrad, forced a change in the orders. The planned relief of the 22. Panzerdivision did not take place; the unit instead received orders to move forward with the newly-subordinated Kampfgruppe Dietrich along the line Wolnuchino — Kruglik — Malaja — Nikolajewka in order to prevent another Russian advance and in order to conduct reconnaissance to the north.[47]

Obergruppenführer und General der Waffen-SS Paul Hausser.
Born 7.10.1880
Died 21.12.1972
Commanding general of the II. SS-Panzerkorps

Obergruppenführer und General der Waffen-SS Sepp Dietrich
Born 28.5.1892
Died 22.4.1966
Twenty-sixth soldier to receive the Schwerter [swords] on 16.3.1943 as the commander of SS-Panzergrenadierdivison LSSAH.

The Kampfgruppe moved on 12.2 toward Rebrikowo and conducted reconnaissance from there towards Wolnuchino, Orechowo, Kruglik, and Malaja-Nikolajewka. Because of heavy snowstorms, this reconnaissance work had to be done on foot. All towns were clear of enemy troops. (See sketch 4.)

On 13.2, the Kampfgruppe secured the designated line and conducted reconnaissance on 14.2 farther to the southwest, west, and northwest. While they did find that the towns of Schterowka, Petro Krassnossnelje (held by Kompanie Schneider), and Malo Jurjewka were clear of enemy forces when they entered them, they learned that enemy cavalry had moved through to the west and northwest on the previous day.[48]

On 15.2, the 22. Panzerdivision ordered the unit transferred to Woroschilowa. Practically directly from their march the Kampfgruppe was sent to push back an enemy incursion near Gebirgsjägerregiment 114 on Hills 220.5 and 199. With support from three Sturmgeschütze, Kompanie Schneider and Kompanie Knösel restored the situation by nightfall. The Kampfgruppe found billets in Woroschilowa.

On 16.2, a so-called day of rest could not be used as such because of the uncertain situation and the constant state of alert.

On 17.2, the Kampfgruppe was once again called upon to iron out a small breakthrough in the hills north of Woroschilowa. In the evening, the Kampfgruppe was designated as a rearguard for the retreat, which was accomplished without the enemy giving pursuit.

In the early morning hours of 18.2, the Kampfgruppe finally reached its billets in Petro Krassnosselje. Orders reached the unit there that its subordination to the 22. Panzerdivision was to end at midnight on 18.2 and that it would be moved to join Kampfgruppe Schuldt in Dekoljewo on 19.2 and subordinated to it.[49]

At noon on 19.2, Gruppe Dietrich moved to Utkino and met the Kampfgruppe under Standartenführer Schuldt. "Käptn" Schuldt, as his men called him, was last mentioned in our entry for 29.12. He had come in 1934 from the Kriegsmarine as a Kapitänleutnant to the *LAH* and had become Kompaniechef of the 3. Friedenskompanie [peacetime company] during the long years of peace.

We will now attempt to piece together from the few remaining sources his route to the reunion with Kampfgruppe Dietrich on 19.2. In addition, the actions of Kampfgruppe Dahl, which was surrounded in Millerowo on 20.12, will be mentioned at the proper juncture.

As expected, on 27.12.1942, at 06.00 hours, the Russians attacked the positions of Gruppe Kreysing (3. Gebirgsdivision) around Millerowo on all sides with strong tank support. A few individual tanks were able to push their way into Millerowo, but they were destroyed by our fire. There for the first time, Gruppe Dahl, consisting of men separated from the Wachbataillon/*LAH* and the I./Polizei-Infanterie-Regiment 1 organized into two Kompanien under the command of Obersturmführer Dahl (probably from the I./Polizei-Infanterie-Regiment 1), proved its worth in battle.[50]

The enemy continued his attacks until 08.00 hours on 28.12, when it grew somewhat quieter.

The Russians then attempted to attack again, this time just at nightfall and with strong artillery support. The attack came this time from the west, north, and east simultaneously. The Armeeabteilung was of the opinion that the enemy had deployed a total of three corps (the XVIIIrd and the XVIIth Tank Corps and the VIth Guard Corps) just for the capture of Millerowo. But our Division support point at Millerowo was tying up considerable numbers of enemy forces which would otherwise have been available for the push on Rostow. Farther to the south, the Armeeabteilung was making efforts to push the front of the 304. Infanteriedivision as far as the Kalitwa sector southeast of Millerowo. North of Millerowo, the 19. Panzerdivision (fighting under the command of the Italian Army High Command 8) had captured the Kamyschnaja valley. It was to move from there to the southeast and to attack the enemy in the rear around Millerowo. In the entry for 29.12, the Kriegstagebuch of the Armeeabteilung mentions SS-Gruppe Schuldt in connection with the fact that the arriving Flak forces (possibly the Führer-Flakabteilung) were not added to Gruppe Schuldt as intended, but instead to the 304. Infanteriedivision in the Kalitwa sector.

During the entire night from 29. - 30.12, the attacks on Millerowo continued. The assault Kompanien under Dahl were, however, not permitted to attack.[51]

In the course of 30.12, the attacks on Millerowo subsided. The 19. Panzerdivision's attack from the north was supposed to provide support, but it failed. Three and a half Russian divisions stopped it in its tracks. There were conferences held in Millerowo between the Chef of the Generalstab of the Armeeabteilung Fretter-Pico and Generalleutnant Kreysing about the conduct of the battle. Kreysing reported that he would be able at short notice (within three hours) to ready an assault force of two Kompanien (read: Gruppe Dahl).[52]

31.12.1942 passed without incident. On 1.1.1943, Kampfgruppe Schuldt reported to Brigade Nagel that the Stabskompanie Schuldt, the 4. (heavy)/Wachbataillon/*LAH* with two light Infanteriegeschütze and six heavy Pak, had arrived in Donskoj and that the Polizei-Granatwerferbataillon 15 with twelve heavy Granatwerfer and four Pak was arriving at the moment. As mentioned in the earlier entry for 2.1 (see above), Standartenführer Schuldt had tried in vain to bring Kampfgruppe Dietrich into his unit. From a report from Kampfgruppe Nagel of 4.1.1943, we learn that there was combat-strength reconnaissance conducted in the direction of Woloschino on that day. The report is not explicit as to whether Kampfgruppe Schuldt was part of that action.[53]

On 5.1, Armeeabteilung Fretter-Pico reported under paragraph 3:

> "Gruppe Schuldt is to be formed anew on 7.1.1943 at 00.00 hours. The structure will be as reported in the daily report of 6.1.1943."

Armeeabteilung
Fretter-Pico
Ia Number 25/43 geh.

Headquarters, 5.1.1943

Structure of Kampfgruppe Schuldt.

1.) Effective 00.00 hours on 7.1.1943, the following restructuring of the command structure is in effect:

a) *SS-Standartenführer Schuldt* is to assume command of the Armeeabteilung's mobile attack group and of the Donskoj Krassnowka tactical strong point. The headquarters of Abteilung Schuldt are to to be hooked up to the telephone network in Tarassowo.
Abteilung Schuldt is to report directly to the Armeeabteilung. A temporary subordination to the 304. Infanteriedivision will be ordered from time to time if the situation demands it.

b) *Oberst i.G. Nagel* is to assume command over all elements previously subordinated to Gruppe Schramm.

Boundary between Gruppe Schuldt and Gruppe Nagel:
The confluence of the Derkul and the Donez — Jelan (to Nagel) — Prognoj (to Nagel) — Blagoschweschtschenka (to Schuldt) — Rognalik stream.

Composition *of Gruppe Schuldt:*

a) Stab with Stabskompanie and Nachrichtenzug
Supply of additional communications materiel is to be arranged with the Korps signals officer immediately.
Aerial signals liaison force Leutnant Schreiber

b) Luftwaffe-Feld-Bataillon with 4. heavy SS-Kompanie and
Polizei-Granatwerferkompanie 15
6./Flak 43 (8.8-centimeter)
4./Flakabteilung 100 (2-centimeter)
one emergency heavy Feldhaubitze-Batterie
one Bataillon of men separated from their units.
All the above at the Donskoj tactical support point.

c) Mobile Kampfgruppe:
one Infanterie Bataillon from the 304. Infanteriedivision (with emergency motor capabilities)
Panzerabteilung 138
Stab of the Flakabteilung 100 with the 3./Flak 100
Führer-Flakabteilung as soon as it is assembled.
Additional forces will be added as their arrival permits and the situation demands.

The commanding general
Signed Fretter-Pico

Distributor:
(only on draft)

For 9.1, the Armeeabteilung ordered a relief attack from Tarasowo along the march route toward Millerowo.

The Kampfgruppe reported that the first attack objective, the bend in the road two kilometers west of Turoweroff (six kilometers south of Millerowo), was captured, with the enemy suffering considerable losses. The enemy deserted his positions west of Millerowo along the line Dolokin — Shurawka — Grekowo.

In a report to the Armeeabteilung, the Kampfgruppe complained about the lack of combat experience in the Infanterie-Bataillon, which had just arrived from the west, and in the Führer-Flakabteilung. A request was also made for all SS units in Gruppe Kreysing in Millerowo, in the 6. Panzerdivision (Gruppe Dietrich), and in Tschertkowo (remains of the I./Polizei-Infanterie-Regiment 1) to be moved up to join the Kampfgruppe. In a letter dated 12.1 from the Armeeabteilung to Gruppe Schuldt we read, among other passages:

> "After heavy fighting, all attacks in Millerowo have been repulsed in the night between 10.1 and 11.1 by using the last reserve (Dahl), and the enemy has been thrown back from the point of his breakthrough."

The Armeeabteilung used that as a justification for refusing the Gruppe Schuldt's request for the additional SS units.

The Armeeabteilung issued the following orders of 11.1:

> "Gruppe Schuldt, to which Gruppe Ehrenkrook is hereby subordinated, is to take Matwejewka on 11.1 and hold it. After capture of Matwejewka, reconnaissance is to be conducted to the southeast and the basis laid for another thrust on 11.1 or 12.1. Favorable conditions for pushing the enemy out of the area Romanowka — Pogorelowka must be exploited while they exist. Relief of the units deployed in Matwejewka by Gruppe Ehrenkrook is to be prepared. The march of a three-hundred-sixty-man replacement force for Gruppe Kreysing from Ssutormino to Tarassowo is to be given protection in the form of an accompanying force (Pak and some MG) and reconnaissance to the west and northwest. Gruppe Schuldt is to report its intent to attack and the time of the attack's beginning."

Gruppe Schuldt reported on 12.1 that it had accomplished its Rososch — Matwejewka mission as ordered, that the town of Matwejewka and Hill 201.3 had been captured. The Kampfgruppe turned back to Tarassowo.

On 12.1, reconnaissance forces went out the entire day all around Tarassowo and Donskoj — Krossnowka. They determined that the enemy was steadily gaining reinforcements. The losses reported for 11.1 and 12.1 were as follows:

Dead

Four officers

Obersturmführer Hemsiecke, H.O., 7./*LAH*
Untersturmführer Friedrichs, J., 1./*LAH*
Oberleutnant Vorgel, H. II./575
Oberleutnant Finster, Gottfried, II./575

Thirty-eight non-commissioned officers and men

Wounded

Four officers

Untersturmführer Deistung, 1./*LAH*
Hauptmann Blumgartel, Helmut, II./575
Leutnant Seifert, Günter, II./575
Leutnant Kleinert, Ernst, II,./575

One hundred fourteen non-commissioned officers and men

Missing

Sixteen non-commissioned officers and men

For 13.1, the Armeeabteilung issued the following orders:

1) Strong enemy forces in the Litwinow — Dubowoi area and to the southeast have taken Djadin on the Donez on 12.1 with tanks and motorized forces.

The XXXXVIII. Panzerkorps intends to launch a counterattack to the northwest on 13.1.1943 from the Krutenskij area with an assault group consisting of Panzers and Infanterie.

2) Kampfgruppe Schuldt is to set out at daybreak on 13.1 and reach Nowyi Jerochin in order to provide cover for the deep right flank of the Armeeabteilung. The Kampfgruppe is to block the roads leading to the Kalitwenez sector around Krassnyj-Jar and all the crossings over the river there; only the crossing at Oreschkin is to be kept open. Reconnaissance should be conducted to the south, east, and northeast as far as the line Djadin — Olchowskij — Dubowoj — Demischoff.

Contact is to be established and maintained with the right wing of the 304. Infanteriedivision near Ostaschkin and with the units posted in Gruzynoff and Gussew.

3) Supply and repair equipment belonging to Gruppe Schuldt is to be sent to Kamensk.

4) The Donskoj tactical strong point is subordinated to Gruppe Nagel effective 00.00 hours on 13.1.[54]

According to the daily report of Gruppe Schuldt, the designated areas were reached by 20.30 hours on 13.1. The town of Oreschkin, still occupied by the enemy, was captured. The enemy lost thirty men, and our forces captured one anti-tank gun and two men. The Kampfgruppe set up its headquarters there.

For this period, Kampfgruppe Dietrich was on the left wing of Armeeabteilung Hollidt, and Kampfgruppe Schuldt was on the right wing of Armeeabteilung Fretter-Pico, so for the first time these two units came within forty kilometers of each other.

Because the orders for 14.1 included holding Kaltiwenskaja and Now. Jeroschin on the Kalitwinez sector, we can assume that the enemy was expected to continue his attack there.

The heavy Polizei Granatwerferkompanie 15 was subordinated to the Donskoj tactical support post.

A deep enemy thrust through the lines farther to the north caused the elements of the Kampfgruppe remaining in Kamensk to be subordinated to Gruppe Baer on 15.1; this entailed chiefly the supply train.

On 15.1, Stoßgruppe [assault force] Dahl joined with the surrounded elements of the 3. Gebirgsdivision and of the Italian Army to break out of their encirclement. In heavy fighting in extreme cold, many men froze, but the break-out was successful. Stoßgruppe Dahl, consisting of two Kompanien of SS and Polizei troops (the 1. and 2. Kompanie of the Wachbataillon/*LAH* and elements of the I./Polizei-Infanterie-Regiment 1), the 4./Flakabteilung 100, and the Panzerjägerzug of the 4./Wachbataillon/*LAH*, was still part of the newly-formed defensive front of Gruppe Kreysing on both sides of Petrowa on 21.1. There attack preparations for a campaign on Woroschilowgrad were underway.

In the southern part of Woroschilowgrad on 23.1, Kampfgruppe Schuldt stood as the reserve unit for the Armeeabteilung. It consisted at this point of the Panzerabteilung 138 and the arriving Führer-Flakabteilung (one Batterie of six 8.8-centimeter Geschütze, one Batterie of five 3.7-centimeter Geschütze, and one Batterie of nine self-propelled 2-centimeter Geschütze). The I. SS-Panzer-Grenadierregiment *DF* with the 14./*DF* and the 3./Flakabteilung 2 under Hauptsturmführer Opificius, expected to arrive on 22.1, was to be subordinated to Kampfgruppe Schuldt. According to Weidinger's "Division *Das Reich*" (Volume III, page 461), the Bataillon was also to be reinforced by one Zug from the 16. (Pioniere)/*DF* and two Batterien from the SS-Artillerie-Regiment *Das Reich*. It can be assumed that Stoßgruppe Dahl also joined Gruppe Schuldt on this day.

Armeeabteilung Fretter-Pico issued the following order for 24.1:

To Gruppe Schuldt

1) *Gruppe Schuldt* is to move upon arrival of orders on 24.1 from the line 165.1 — 164.7 (northwest of Podgornoje) to the northwest, then to destroy the enemy forces which have pushed across the Donez to the south, and to capture the Sslawjanosserbsk — Ssmelyj — Nowo-Grigorjewka area. Defenses should be set up against the weak enemy forces standing in Sheltoje and Dolgoje.

   Combat-strength reconnaissance forces should set out at daybreak and move as far as the line Krassnyj — Liman — Krymskaja, especially investigating possibilities for moving Panzers and motorized units across the Donez in this sector.

   Contact is to be established with the security forces stationed near Nishnoje.

   The boundary between Gruppe Kreysing and Gruppe Schuldt: Alexandrowka (to Kreysing) — Lobytschew (Schuldt) — Gretschinschkino.

2) The Armeeabteilung headquarters will be in Woroschilowgrad on 24.1. Brief reports should be made hourly to the Armeeabteilung by radio.

The commander signed Fretter-Pico

According to the daily report from Brigade Schuldt for 24.1, the attack just north of hill 168.1 (northwest of Podgornoje) met with little resistance. After smashing what resistance there was, the attack Bataillon, the reinforced I./*DF* (Panzerabteilung 138), came under heavy artillery fire there but was able to continue the attack immediately, and its leading elements captured Hill 174.5. The attack was impeded by enemy flank attacks from Sheltoje and Dolgoje, but it was never stopped. The following losses were listed for the enemy forces: about one hundred men, four anti-tank guns, and two 7.5-centimeter artillery pieces. Our losses amounted to only one man killed and six wounded. For the night between 24.1 and 25.1, Brigade Schuldt set up the following defenses: the reinforced I./*DF* on Hills 168.7 — 158.8 — 116, Panzerabteilung 138 with its subordinated Flak combat unit in Podgornoje, the Führer-Flakabteilung in Alexandrowka, Stoßgruppe Dahl as defensive force on Hill 165.1 and around Rodakowo. In Rodakowo itself stood a Schützenzug [rifle platoon] and the Polizei-Panzerjäger-Kompanie under Weise. The Brigade headquarters was in Alexandrowka.

The following is an excerpt from Weidinger's "Division *Das Reich*" (Volume III, page 462):

> "In the night between 24.1.1943 and 25.1.1943, there was another surprising drop in temperature. The thermometer suddenly plummeted to twenty-eight degrees below zero! Because the daytime weather had been warm, some of the men had left their winter clothing in the vehicles. The cold and the icy wind were hard on them. It was a torture for those wearing felt boots, which would get saturated with water and freeze to the men's legs at night. All those men had to drop out of their units because of severe frostbite. In these crazy temperature variations, the good old jackboot proved itself once again to be disaster-proof and reliable footwear."

The Bataillon commander of the I./*DF* reported that he wanted to continue the attack by placing the riflemen on top of the Panzers assigned to cooperate with his unit. This request was denied and the Panzers called back during the night. The I./*DF* was left to hold the positions captured on this high plateau. The number of men who became unfit for combat because of frostbite grew shockingly high, and the fighting strength of the Bataillon was reduced by fifty percent in this one night.[55]

The orders for 25.1.1943 read as follows:

> "On 25.1, moving via Skeltoje and Dolgoje, Kampfgruppe Schuldt is to push back the enemy forces which have crossed the Donez and to capture those towns. Gruppe Schuldt is to relieve its own elements by deploying the III./Grenadier-Regiment 682, presently in Alexandrowka.
> The III./Grenadier-Regiment 682 is subordinated to Gruppe Schuldt and will come under the command of Gruppe Kreysing after its deployment on the Donez. Gruppe Schuldt is to assemble in the southern part of Woroschilowgrad after completion of its mission and to stand at the disposal of the Armeeabteilung."

The commander
Signed, Fretter-Pico

The attack did not gain much ground. In the course of the day on 25.1, the newly-won defensive positions on the hills southeast of Sheltoje were pushed back, but a counterthrust recaptured them.

For 26.1 - 27.1, the Brigade reported expansion of its positions and the repulsing of isolated enemy forces up to company strength.

On 27.1, eighty prisoners were taken, and the enemy suffered over one hundred deaths. The following were destroyed: seven 7.62-centimeter anti-tank guns, three 4.7-centimeter anti-tank guns, two light infantry guns, two anti-tank rifles, six heavy machine guns and six heavy trench mortars.

The Brigade reported that it had ready for action: eleven Panzer IV's, one Panzer III, and three Befehlspanzer [command tanks]. The I./Artillerie-Regiment 335 was subordinated to the Brigade.[56]

On 27.1.1943, Standartenführer Schuldt finally received an answer from Armeeabteilung Fretter-Pico to his repeated requests for the reunification of all the elements intended for his Brigade:

The Chef of the Generalstab — 27.1.1943
Armeeabteilung Fretter-Pico

To *Standartenführer Schuldt*

I return once more in writing to our frequent conversations regarding the assembly of the elements belonging to your Gruppe. I know that you have explored all approaches to get your Gruppe unified in your hands. The Armeeabteilung did all it could immediately upon assuming command to bring together those elements which were separated upon being unloaded from transport. If that goal has eluded both you and the Armeeabteilung, the cause can be traced to the tactical situation, which prohibits the withdrawal of the elements in question. No one regrets this more than the Armeeabteilung, which so highly values having your combat-strength force united under your command for mobile attack and battle.

The Armeeabteilung will continue its efforts to collect your Abteilung into its originally-intended composition whenever the situation stops demanding another composition.

Heil Hitler
Signature

Let us note here, incidentally, that the first transport trains of the Panzergrenadierdivision *LAH* and the Panzergrenadierdivision *DR* were being unloaded during these same days in the Charkow area, about three hundred kilometers to the northwest.

By 20.00 hours on 28.1, Kampfgruppe Schuldt was relieved from its positions by the Grenadier-Regiment 684. With that, the III./682 and the I./Artillerie-Regiment 335 ended their subordination to the unit. Panzerabteilung 138 and the two Flak combat units of the Führer-Flakabteilung came under the direct command of the Armeeabteilung. The Brigade readied itself in Alexandrovka and Rodakowo for the march out.[57]

On 29.1, the Armeeabteilung ordered Gruppe Schuldt to set off at daybreak on 30.1 for Woroschiloff. It was to establish close contact with the 304. Infanteriedivision and to prepare itself for an attack on Bolschoj Ssuchodol.
There, according to air reconnaissance, the enemy was building an ice bridge over the Donez. He was reported to have established a small bridgehead there already.

On 30.1, Brigade Schuldt was subordinated to the 304. Infanteriedivision upon arrival in Woroschiloff. The I./*DF* was reinforced by bringing up Feldersatzbataillon without its staff or supply train.[58]

On 31.1.1943, the planned attack did not occur. Kampfgruppe Schuldt, especially the reinforced I./*DF* and the subordinated Stoßgruppe Dahl, managed to hold Woroschiloff in heavy fighting and to intercept an enemy attack to the northwest, aimed at Petrowka, near Shiroki.[59]

On 1.2, Shiroki had to be abandoned, but the forces of the reinforced I./*DF* (under Hauptsturmführer Opificius) held on tenaciously. Woroschiloff was defended by Stoßgruppe Dahl, the reinforced 3./*DF* (under Hauptsturmführer Lex), and the Pionierzug of the 16./*DF* under Oberscharführer von Eberstein. In Petrowka, the reinforced 1./*DF* (one Zug of the 14./*DF* and elements of the 3./SS-Flakabteilung 2) repulsed all attacks. Rottenführer Heider hit five tanks with his Pak alone; he was awarded the Eisernes Kreuz I [Iron Cross First Class] on the battlefield.[60]
Because the enemy had broken through farther to the north, the Brigade had to pull back the Bataillon to Wodjanoj in the night between 1.2 and 2.2.

On 2.2, there was an attack by two enemy companies along the railway line toward the station at Wernji Duwannyi. Brigade Schuldt left Armeeabteilung Fretter-Pico with the 304. Infanteriedivision and was subordinated to the XXXXVIII. Panzerkorps of Armeeabteilung Hollidt.

On 3.2, the Brigade was subordinated to the 6. Panzerdivision.

> "The enemy was putting more and more pressure on our positions with concentrated artillery and mortar fire, with tank and fighter plane support. Despite these hostile conditions, our Panzergrenadiere dug themselves into the houses, trenches, and foxholes and repulsed every enemy attack. Special thanks must go to the crews of the Panzers of the Heer's 6. Panzerdivision and to our Stuka pilots, who brought relief and help in this most dangerous situation. During this fighting, we lost the Chef of the 4./*DF*, Hauptsturmführer Hocke, to a shell falling on the Bataillon headquarters," writes Weidinger in "Division *Das Reich*" (Volume III, page 464).

On 4.2, Brigade Schuldt and the Panzergrenadiere of the 6. Panzerdivision undertook a joint assault on Popowka on the Donez and another on Woroschiloff on 5.2. The latter was cleared of enemy troops on 6.2 and the former on 7.2. Elements from Brigade Schuldt established a defensive line north of Popowka and held it until 12.2.[61]

On 12.2, the enemy moved again, this time just south of Woroschilowgrad. In the course of the regrouping which the enemy move required, the Brigade was once again subordinated to the 304. Infanteriedivision and therefore belonged to the XXI. Armeekorps. Armeeabteilung Fretter-Pico ordered trucks to be sent to pick up Kampfgruppe Dietrich, but once again they returned empty.

On 14.2, the Brigade was assembled in Krassnoskij to stand at the disposal of the XXI. Armeekorps. On 15.2, it was subordinated to the 22. Panzerdivision and set on the march toward Uspenka.

There it was set up in a defensive position on 15.2 in the hills two kilometers northwest of Lutogino, where it was able to hold its position in heavy fighting until 18.2. Then the 304. Infanteriedivision ordered the position to be abandoned and moved the unit to the Krassnaja Sweska area. On 18.2, all the forces subordinated to the 304. Infanteriedivision once again returned with the Division to the command of Armeeabteilung Fretter-Pico. The Armeeabteilung finally allowed the reunification of Kampfgruppe Schuldt in the Adrianopol area on 19.2.1943. With Kampfgruppe Dietrich once again part of the structure of the unit, our chronicle of events can continue for all the elements of Brigade Schuldt together.[62]

The reunited Brigade Schuldt was structured as follows:

Brigadestab:	Commander Standartenführer Schuldt Adjutant Hauptsturmführer Molt
Truppe:	Bataillonsstab of Bataillon Dietrich, Commander Sturmbannführer Dietrich from 23.1, Hauptsturmführer Lex Adjutant Obersturmführer Winter
1. Kompanie	Schützenkompanie *DF* Hauptsturmführer Lex
2. Kompanie	former Kampfgruppe Dietrich Obersturmführer Knösel (elements of the *LAH* and elements of the I./Polizei-Infanterie-Regiment 1) Zugführer Untersturmführer Schneider
3. Kompanie	former Stoßgruppe Dahl (elements of the *LAH* and SS-Polizei)
4. Kompanie	heavy Kompanie I./*DF* Hauptsturmführer Repplinger

Panzerkompanie 138
2. Batterie/SS-Artillerie-Regiement *DR*
3. SS-Flakabteilung *DR*
Führer-Flakabteilung or Batterie (?)

It is unknown whether the other elements (6./Flak 43, 4./Flak 100, Feldersatzbataillon/304. Infanteriedivision), originally subordinated to the Brigade, were still part of it.[63]

The restructuring had to be completed by 22.2, because the Brigade was to be placed on readiness alert on that day. Enemy forces had broken through and dug themselves in in the three-pronged gorge north of Utkino; an attack from the north was to drive them out.

The Brigade was moved via the Parishkaja Kommuna into the assembly area at Sselesnewka. From there, the 1. and 2. Kompanie were to attack from the north, while the 3. Kompanie was to move to Baschtewitsch to prevent the enemy's escape to the east.

It was known that the enemy had troops of approximately one batallion's strength and many heavy weapons.

At nightfall, Bataillon Dietrich set out, but was stopped after a short time; three hours later, it received orders to march to Baschtewitsch. (See sketch 4.)

In the morning of 22.2, the march objective was finally reached after the Bataillon had overcome drifting snow and straggling enemy units. Its new orders were to destroy the enemy troops which had pushed their way into the Wassjukowa gorge. The attack objective was the demolished village at the end of the gorge between Jelisawetowka and Schterowka. The following were involved in the attack: adjacent to the right, Gruppe Siewert (the remainder of Panzerjäger 611), and adjacent to the left a Bataillon from the Gebirgsjäger-Regiment 144. Fighting with tough and stubborn enemy forces, our troops did not manage to push them back until nightfall, and that was with good support from the heavy Infanterie weapons. The gorge was a deeply-fissured terrain, and the enemy had to be thrown out of the cracks in the rocks practically one by one. There were heavy losses on both sides. Sturmbannführer Dietrich was wounded in the course of the afternoon, but remained with the unit until Sturmbannführer Schuldt finally ordered him behind the lines in the evening. The command of the Bataillon was taken over by Hauptsturmführer Lex.[64]

The Kriegstagebuch of the 1. Panzerarmee (under Generaloberst von Mackensen, with Oberst Wenck as Chef of Stab; the Armeeoberkommando had returned from the Caucasus by this time and Armeeabteilung Fretter-Pico was once again operating as the XXX. Armeekorps) contains the following entry for 24.2 (excerpt):

> "In the area held by the XXX. Armeekorps, the enemy is using strong infantry forces supported by many tanks to expand his breakthrough west of Jelisawetowka to the north and west. The enemy forces moving as far forward as the area Anissimowka — Baschtewitsch must be stopped by concentrating and regrouping all our forces, and the breakthrough must be closed off by emergency measures. A tank-supported enemy push has taken Kamyschewacha. Reconnaissance moves towards Illirija by enemy forces in company strength have been pushed back. Newly-recognized preparations in front of the Jelisawetowka breakthrough point, in the Olchowka valley, and near Kamyschewacha leave no doubt as to the enemy's intention to continue the attacks with strong forces, especially at the points of breakthrough, in order to achieve a path through to the industrial area.[65]

Bataillon Dietrich reported on 24.2 the continuous addition of strong enemy forces moving from the direction of Wodino through the Olchowka valley. On orders from the Brigade, the units assumed defensive posture, and they had to repulse numerous enemy reconnaissance sorties on 24.2 and 25.2, some with tank support. Two or three Russian tanks were destroyed. The defensive fighting received excellent Stuka support.[66]

In the course of the day on 25.2, a Regiment of the 62. Infanteriedivision arrived as reinforcement. The entry for 24.1 in the Kriegstagebuch of the Panzerarmee Oberkommando 1 provides an explanation for this "unexpected blessing":

> "The numerous telephone reports on the situation received in the course of the day clearly showed that the forces assigned to clearing the area around Jelisawetowka, especially Kampfgruppe Schuldt, were insufficient for the job and that the enemy incursion moving to the northwest could only be halted by implementation of exceptional measures. In a Sonderbefehl to the XXX. Armeekorps and the 62. Infanteriedivision, the Armee subordinated a Regimentsgruppe from the 62. Infanteriedivision under the XXX. Armeekorps to be used in clearing away the incursion near Jelisawetowka. These elements of the 62. Infanteriedivision were at that time in the Petrowo — Krassnosselje — Fedorowka — Schewtschenko area; they were moved up immediately to join the Korps. The second Regimentsgruppe of the Division was still in action at the time on the northern wing of Armeeabteilung Hollidt. That unit was expected to be relieved on 25.2. It is not expected that this Regimentsgruppe will also be released for deployment with the XXX. Armeekorps."[67]

For 25.2, the reinforced Brigade (Regimentsgruppe of the 62. Infanteriedivision, Sturmgeschützabteilung of the 19. Panzerdivision) was ordered to attack the points of enemy breakthrough around Jelisawetowka and to clear away the enemy forces. The attack objective was the hills east of Jelisawetowka. The Korps pointed out that the clearing up of the situation around Jelisawetowka was urgent, because the subordinated Regimentsgruppe was needed immediately to reinforce the attack of the XI. Panzerkorps on the western wing of the Panzerarmee. This was the attack which was waged jointly with the attack of the SS-Panzerkorps (see entry for 20.2.1943 and those following).

The carefully planned attack was initiated on 26.2 at 07.00 hours by a Stuka attack. It made good progress under the personal command of Standartenführer Schuldt. Schuldt returned to the headquarters at about 09.00 hours with a slight wound and received a visit at about 10.15 from the commanding general of the XXX. Armeekorps, General Fretter-Pico, who offered him his congratulations for the brilliant success. Around noon, the designated attack objective, the old main battle line on the hills east of Jelisawetowka, was captured, and the forces were in pursuit of the retreating enemy. The commanding general was forced, nevertheless, to order the rapid relief of the Regimentsgruppe of the 62. Infanteriedivision for the reasons given above.[68] (See sketch 4.)

In the following days, Brigade Schuldt was transferred to the Debalzewo area. The Brigade maintained contact between the XXX. Armeekorps (front to the east) and the III. Panzerkorps (front to the north) by means of several small actions.

On 7.3, the commander of the I./*DF*, Hauptsturmführer Opificius, came from Panzergrenadierdivision *DR* with orders for the Bataillon to return to the Regiment immediately via Pawlograd.[69]

On 15.3, the remainder of Wachbataillon/*LAH* and the remainder of the I./Polizei-Infanterie-Regiment 1 were loaded on a train in Woroschilowsk and transported to the drill grounds at Debica. For the remaining elements of the

Wachbataillon/*LAH*, one railway car was enough, as was true for the I./Polizei-Infanterie-Regiment 1.[70]

Those who managed to live through this battle against the enemy and against nature will always in quiet hours turn inward and hear the howling of the wind over the steppe, the crunching of the snow, and the groaning of their dying comrades. They will not forget them.

Standartenführer Hugo Kraas.
Received Ritterkreuz on 28.3.1943 as commander of the I./2 LSSAH.
Received Eichenlaub on 24.1.1944 as Obersturmbannführer and commander of SS-Panzergrenadier-Regiment 2 LSSAH.

Sturmbannführer Jochen Peiper.
Received Ritterkreuz on 9.3.1943 as commander of the III. (armoured)/2. LSSAH.
Received Eichenlaub on 27.1.1944 as Sturmbannführer and Regimental commander of SS-Panzergrenadier-Regiment 1 LSSAH
Murdered 14.7.1976 in France.

Brigadeführer und Generalmajor der Waffen-SS Theodor Wisch.
Three hundred ninety-third soldier to receive the Eichenlaub on 12.2.1944 as Oberführer and commander of the 1. SS-Panzerdivision LSSAH.

Obersturmführer Helmut Wendorff.
Received Ritterkreuz on 12.2.1944 as Untersturmführer in the 13. (heavy) SS-Panzerregiment 1 LSSAH.
Killed 6.8.1944 in Normandy

Obersturmführer Michael Wittman.
Received Ritterkreuz on 14.1.1944 as Untersturmführer in the 13. (heavy) SS-Panzerregiment 1. Received Eichenlaub on 30.1.1944 as Untersturmführer in the same unit.
Killed 8.8.1944 at Normandy.

Rottenführer Balthasar Woll.
Received Ritterkreuz 16.1.1944 as gunner in Michael Wittmann's Tiger.

Unterscharführer Alfred Schneidereit.
Received Ritterkreuz on 20.12.1943 as Rottenführer and anti-tank rifle leader in the 8./SS-Panzergrenadier-Regiment 1 LSSAH.

Syurmbannführer Karl Rettlinger.
Received Ritterkreuz on 20.12.1943 as Kompaniechef of the 3./SS-Sturmgeschützabteilung 1 LSSAH.

Part 6

THE SS-PANZER-GRENADIER-DIVISION *LSSAH* IN THE UKRAINE 22.1. - 23.3.1943

Section I
THE ABANDONMENT OF CHARKOW TRANSFER TO AND DEFENSE OF THE DONEZ 22.1. - 9.2.1943

a) 22.1. - 3.2.1943: Establishment of defenses on the Donez

The advance personnel (VP) of the Division under the command of the 1. Generalstabsoffizier, Sturmbannführer Lehmann, arrived at the Tschugujew railway station after a railway journey of twelve days. There an order was waiting for the Ia to report immediately to the "German general at the Italian 8th Army High Command" in Tschugujew.[1] Generalmajor Dr. Speidel, the Chef of the Generalstab of that German general, briefed him on the situation and his unit's mission.

> Panzer-Grenadier-Division *LAH* is to be unloaded from the train southeast of Charkow and is to assemble and stand at the disposal of the OKH such that it can be deployed on short notice to secure the Donez sector between Smijew and Chotomlja should the need arise.[2]

23.1.1943: After establishing contact with the transport officer in charge, who designated the railway stations to be used and the areas in which to assemble, the advance commands of each individual unit involved received their orders.

24.1.1943: The Ia scouted the area and used his maps to determine the location of the main line of battle along and to the east of the Donez. Because the Divisional headquarters were set up in the same building complex as those of the Italian 8th Army High Command, there was close contact to the Command's staff. General von Tippelskirch was the "German general at the Italian 8th Army High Command."
Upon request from the Ia/*LAH*, the Chef of the Generalstab had the Feldgendarmerie leave the town of Malinowka. This town, situated east of the sector in the bend of the Donez, was viewed by the Division as being the lynch pin of the battle line. East of it, the reinforced Aufklärungsabteilung was to set up its positions, which could then be flanked by the 1. Regiment to the north. From the Malinowka bridgehead, Panzer attacks could be launched if needed.

25.1. - 28.1.1943: The advance commands made all the preparations for the expected arrival of the units.

28.1.1943: The Stab of the 1. Panzer-Grenadier-Regiment *LAH* and the 1. Kompanie of the 1. Panzer-Grenadier-Regiment *LAH* arrived at the Tschugujew railway station. They were briefed on their mission by the Ia and set on the march route to Petschenegi. A snowstorm and the bitter cold took care of briefing them on the "local conditions."

29.1.1943: The following units arrived: the Aufklärungsabteilung/*LAH* (minus the heavy Kompanie), most of the I./1. Panzer-Grenadier-Regiment *LAH*, the 1. and 4. Batterie of the Artillerie-Regiment *LAH*, the 1. Flakabteilung *LAH*, the 2./Panzerjägerabteilung *LAH*, and one-half of each of the Fernsprechkompanie [telephone communications company] and the Funkkompanie [radio communications company] of the Nachrichtenabteilung *LAH*. All these elements were sent immediately from the railway station to their positions along the main battle line. This step was necessary because rapid march maneuvers from the arrival points to the defensive sector were impossible in the continuing cold and snowfall and because the construction of the positions was extraordinarily difficult in the frozen ground. The greatest difficulties were in unloading the vehicles, which simply would not start after ten to fourteen days in icy wind on open railway cars. (See sketch 5)

Because over two hundred trains were used to transport this large number of troops, some of the trains travelled in a great detour through the Ruhr valley — Hamburg — Güstrow — Pasewalk — Stettin — Dirschau — Marienburg — Königsberg — Eydkau — Wilna — Minsk — Bobruisk — Gomel — Brjansk — west of Kursk to Charkow. The Panzerspähkompanie survived two separate track demolitions by partisans outside of Minsk and Brjansk. The men were also able to observe a bomber attack on Brjansk from a distance. In spite of all that, the transport detour took only eleven days.

The Division learned from the "German general" that the remainder of the SS-Kampfgruppe Fegelein was being brought to Tschugujew under the command of Standartenführer Döffler-Schuband of the *LAH*. It was assembled in Charkow and sent back to the homeland. The 1. (8.8-centimeter)/Flakabteilung *LAH* under the command of Hauptsturmführer Dr. Loenicker was moved into position on the steep bank of the Donez such that it could both protect the vital crossing over the Donez at Malinowka from air attacks and take aim at tanks in the open terrain in front of the battle line held by the Aufklärungsabteilung and the I./2. Panzer-Grenadier-Regiment *LAH*. Sturmbannführer Kraas arrived to become commander of the I./2. Panzer-Grenadier-Regiment *LAH*. He reported to the Division and received orders to set up defenses with his Bataillon in the sector bounded on the right by the gorge on the southeast edge of Skripai (including the town) and on the left by the Tschugujew — Kupjansk railway line (excluding the line itself).

The Division was subordinated at 12.00 hours on 29.1.1943 to the Generalkommando of the SS-Panzerkorps under commanding general Obergruppenführer Hausser, with Standartenführer Ostendorf as his Chef of Generalstab. Also subordinated to this Generalkommando were the SS-Panzer-Grenadier-Division *DR* and the 298. Infanteriedivision. The SS-Panzer-

Grenadier-Division *T* was still in transport to the area, but it was subordinated to the Generalkommando at the same time.[3]

30.1.1943: The Stab of the I./2. Panzer-Grenadier-Regiment, elements of the 2. Kompanie/2. Panzer-Grenadier-Regiment, the 3./2. Panzer-Grenadier-Regiment, the 1./Panzerjägerabteilung, the 1./Pionier-Bataillon, and the 2./Flakabteilung were unloaded from trains. The 3. Kompanie/2. Panzer-Grenadier-Regiment came under a bomber attack on the Orel railway station and suffered three dead and twenty-six wounded.

On orders from the Korps, the reinforced 2./Aufklärungsabteilung *LAH* was put on the march to join the 298. Infanterie-Division and to provide support for it. It was ordered to watch over the terrain between Kupjansk and Dwuretschnaja on the Oskol. Permission to enter battle had to be given by the SS-Panzerkorps through the 298. Infanteriedivision.[4] The 2. and 3. Zug of the 2./Aufklärungsabteilung *LAH* started their march to Kupjansk, seventy kilometers away, at 17.00 hours. Untersturmführer Maurer, given command of this group, reported as follows:

> "The 2. Zug under Untersturmführer Mauthe and my own 3. Zug set out shortly before dark and arrived seventy kilometers later in Kupjansk, frozen through and through. I reported to the Ia of the 298. Infanteriedivision at 22.00 hours. Both of the Züge were billeted in the collective farm Kutscherowka on the northern edge of the city. Our orders were: 'Take over the sector from the northern edge of Kupjansk as far as Dwuretschnaja and establish contact with the 15./Regiment *D*. The tactical support point is to be maintained.'"

The Generalkommando of the SS-Panzerkorps provided the following description of the situation at this point:

> "With their 69th Army and 3rd Tank Army, the Russians have reached the upper Oskol and Waluiki, and their 6th Army is pressing hard on Kupjansk and Sswatowo. The Popow Army is also approaching Slawiansk. The German 320. Infanteriedivision finds itself near Sswatowo locked in bitter defensive fighting. The 298. Infanteriedivision is assembling in Kupjansk as it fights its way back under heavy attack.
> West of Waluiki, elements of the Panzer-Grenadier-Division *Großdeutschland* are engaged in combat, and the Generalkommando z.b.V. [special-services general command] under Cramer is pulling together the elements of the German and Hungarian units retreating from the upper Don. Between the units, there are gaping holes. The OKH's intention to deploy the SS-Panzerkorps after its arrival from the Charkow area in one concentrated counterattack will be defeated if the Soviets manage a rapid advance. They must be prevented from making their thrust into the Korps' very assembly area. The city of Charkow, important for the roads it controls, for its economic base, and for its political significance, may under no circumstances be lost. Elements of the Division *DR* must therefore be moved forward on 30.1 to defend the area west of Waluiki (northeast of the *LAH*)."[5]

31.1.1943: The 2./Aufklärungsabteilung *LAH* made contact with elements of the Division *DR* and the 15./Regiment *Deutschland* on 31.1. and 1.2 south of Dwuretschnaja. Untersturmführer Maurer, the commander of this Kampfgruppe, reported:

> "Shortly after daybreak, we swept the terrain for mines. Two Kradschützenzüge with a force of only fifty-two men could not be expected to hold a sector of about seventeen kilometers in a normal fashion. We decided therefore to use each of the two Züge as liaison reconnaissance forces to travel the road to Dwuretschnaja. I took the first trip there with my Zug. The road was clear of the enemy. In Dwuretschnaja, the enemy gave us harassing fire with his anti-tank weapons and heavy trench mortars. In the afternoon, the second Zug set out to establish contact. Untersturmführer Mauthe reported no change in the situation."

The first squadron of the Divisionstab arrived with the 4. and 5. Kompanie of the 2. Panzer-Grenadier-Regiment *LAH*. Because the Divisional commander, Obergruppenführer Sepp Dietrich was still at the Führer's headquarters, the Ia requested the commander of the 1. Panzer-Grenadier-Regiment *LAH*, Standartenführer Witt, who had already arrived, to take temporary command of the Division. At 19.00 hours, the Korps ordered a Pionier obstacle-construction unit to be assigned and subordinated to the town Kommandant in Isjum. The Division ordered the 1./Pionier-Bataillon *LAH* to send one Zug under the leadership of Untersturmführer Taubert to Isjum. He reported to the town Kommandant. The Zug made it to Isjum without coming into contact with the enemy, and one group from it was assigned to protect the railway bridges, while another defended the road bridges. The Zug was relieved by Pioniere from the 320. Infanteriedivision under Armeeabteilung Lanz on orders from the Heeresgruppe at 20.00 hours on 1.2.1943 and returned to its unit in Smijew on 2.2. An order from the Führer forbade splitting up SS units.

1.2.1943 - 3.2.1943: In Stalingrad, the German 6. Armee had surrendered on 31.1.1943 after suffering serious losses in heavy fighting. The last desperate battles lasted until 2.2.1943. The Italian 8th Army High Command vacated the command, and the former duty post "German general with the Italian 8th Army High Command" was restructured as the Oberkommando of Armeeabteilung Lanz under General der Gebirgstruppen Lanz. The arriving Divisional units, which were being reinforced daily, worked uninterruptedly during those days to expand their positions, sometimes with the help of the civilian population. While the work was complicated by the frozen ground, an existing former Russian installation on the spot made it somewhat easier. Thus, in a relatively short time, a defense system relying on tactical support points was constructed, especially in the middle section held by the I./2. Panzer-Grenadier-Regiment. The section held by the 2. Panzer-Grenadier-Regiment *LAH* was about twenty-two kilometers long. The reinforced Pionier-Bataillon *LAH*, posted to the right in front of Smijew, was responsible for about ten kilometers of the front. The reinforced Aufklärungsabteilung *LAH*, left of the 2. Panzer-Grenadier-Regiment, provided defense from its position in front of Malinowka for a stretch fourteen kilometers long, and the reinforced 1. Panzer-Grenadier-Regiment *LAH*, deployed to the north, held positions on the elevated western bank of the Donez with outposts east of the river along a section forty-five kilometers in length. The total defensive front amounted to about one hundred kilometers, and it was to be held by an incomplete Division.

The terrain across from the defense sections to the right and the center was cut by long, deep gorges, or Balkas. The enemy therefore had the opportunity to approach our positions under cover and unnoticed. We were positioned either on the eastern edges of the Balkas or in entirely open, level terrain. Behind the section to the right, there was a large forest, which provided good location for supply points, vehicle parking, and so forth. In front of the left-hand section, there were streams running through valleys to the Donez, with the villages of Balabajewka, Artemowka, Martowaja, and Chotomlja nestled in them. These valleys provided the enemy good opportunities of approach. The towns named above were secured by combat posts of the I. and II./1. Panzer-Grenadier-Regiment. The Donez itself was frozen solid and posed no obstacle to enemy forces equipped with sled-equipped vehicles.

Untersturmführer Maurer, commander of the Kampfgruppe with the 298. Infanteriedivision, reported:

> "In the morning of 1.2.1943 the 3. Zug went out once more as liaison reconnaissance force . Combat alert was declared in Dwuretschnaja. There was anti-tank fire, heavy mortar shelling, and scattered machine gun fire. I left the Zug behind the last hill and went on alone to the Kompanie headquarters of the 15./Regiment *Deutschland*. The enemy had in the meantime worked its way forward closer to the edge of town. The 15. was nevertheless in complete control of the situation. During our march back to Kupjansk, we encountered a single passenger car just about at the half-way point. I stopped it because I thought it had probably crossed our thin defensive line by mistake. A voice from the back seat boomed, 'Calm down, young man, I know that already.' It was our commanding general, Papa Hausser. I made my apologies and learned that the General was on the way to the 15./*Deutschland* in Dwuretschnaja. I still hadn't learned my lesson, and I tried to inform him that the enemy fire on the road into town would prevent his reaching it. His answer: 'Will you kindly leave that decision to me?' My men, fortunately, did not hear that. My offer to travel along to provide protection was refused. Since the General did not specifically order us to continue our march back, we stayed in the rolling terrain just out of his sight. We did not take our eye off him as he travelled to Dwuretschnaja and back to Kupjansk.
>
> At 06.30 hours on 2.2.1943, Russian artillery fire on the northern edge of Kupjansk awakened us. Shortly thereafter, the first mortar shells hit the billeting area. Alarm! The vehicles would not start and had to be towed by tractor. Individual infantrymen from the 298. Infanteriedivision returned with the news that the Russians had come within one or two kilometers.
>
> While a force from the 2. Zug provided defense, I raced to the Divisional headquarters to get our orders, but I found that headquarters had been moved during the night. Because we were unable to establish contact with the Division, I decided to move the Abteilung back to Malinowka. Before setting off, we stopped at the supply depot to stock up on preserves, meat, butter and cigarettes, and we were still there when Ivan came within a rifle shot's range of us. One group, the one under Ampletzer, took my order to

skip the alcohol and to load up on high-fat-content food too literally. Two barrels of butter are just too much for the rear axle of a VW! We reported back to the Kompanie at 16.00 hours."

On 2.2.1943, the Division issued Divisionsbefehl No. 1 for the defense of the Donez (see Appendix No. 4).

The commander of the 2. Panzer-Grenadier-Regiment *LAH*, Standartenführer Wisch, arrived with his Stab and was briefed by the Ia at Divisional headquarters. In the course of the day on 3.2, land reconnaissance determined that weak enemy forces were present in Nowy Burluk and that the enemy defensive line had been moved up to Jurtschenkowo — Bogoroditschnoje.

Enemy reconnaissance was sending out feelers along our defenses held by the 7./(under Denecke) and the 6./(under Weither). The 1. Panzer-Grenadier-Regiment was on the eastern edges of Martowaja and Chotomlja. The Division determined that the enemy forces consisted of two Russian rifle regiments reinforced by tanks preparing for an attack on our positions in the bend of the Donez on both sides of Petschenegi.[6] Because only weak elements had arrived from the 1. Regiment, the Division moved up the reinforced II./2. Panzer-Grenadier-Regiment *LAH* (minus the 1. Kompanie) behind the threatened sector and placed it under the command of the 1. Regiment. The commander of this force was Hauptsturmführer Scappini. The Division formed a reserve force for its own use in the Kotschelok area consisting of one Zug each from the 1./Panzerjägerabteilung, the 2./Panzerjägerabteilung, and the 1./Sturmgeschützabteilung. The reinforced Aufklärungsabteilung received orders to secure the crossings over the Burluk at Balabajewka, Wassilenkowo, and Otradnoje. It was to pull back to the main line of battle only in the event of strong enemy pressure, and it was to blow up the bridges before pulling back. This mission was not accomplished, because the crossings were found to be occupied by enemy forces as the Abteilung approached them.

Untersturmführer Maurer reported:

"At about 17.00 hours, Meinig arrived with the order: 'The 2. and 3. Zug are to prepare for march; both Zugführer are to report to the commander!' There, we were briefed quickly about the situation. Our orders were: 'Reconnaissance force with combat mission to be sent toward Wassilenkowo (about thirty kilometers). The town is to be captured if it is enemy-held and the bridge to the east is to be held open until the Division *Das Reich* arrives for the attack in about two days. At the end, report to the Chef of the 3./Aufklärungsabteilung (Knittel) in Schewtschenkowo.' We moved out shortly after 19.00 hours. The Zug under Maurer was the leading element. As soon as we left the main highway, we marched over practically nothing but snow-covered country roads. Visibility was reasonable. About eight kilometers before Wassilenkowo, the road led steeply down to an extensive patch of forest which did not appear on the maps. Halt! We suddenly saw flares in the forest and Russian ground signals behind it. This did not make me happy. After consulting briefly with Kurt Mauthe, who held as low an opinion as I of night fighting in forests, we decided to go around the forest to the southeast. We pushed the vehicles silently around. We were only about three hundred meters away when the fire broke loose, but we were no longer there, thank God. Our instincts had been right, and I suspect that these were advance security forces, indicating that the town was already occupied by sufficient forces to render an attack by two Züge fruitless. Taking our short distance from the Kompanie headquarters of the 3./Aufklärungsabteilung into account, I decided to have Knittel fill me in on the situation."

The 3./Aufklärungsabteilung (under Knittel) was moved up along the road from Kupjansk toward Schewtschenkowo. It was there to cover the 298. Infanteriedivision as it retreated from Kupjansk. In the evening of 3.2, we gained the following information about the enemy: several enemy divisions were proceeding to the west between Dwuretschnaja and Waluiki, and our advance combat units had already encountered their leading elements. They belonged to the 3rd Soviet Tank Army, which was intending to move five to seven divisions on Charkow, perhaps across our left wing.

b) 4.2.1943 - 10.2.1943: Defensive fighting on the Donez (see sketch 6)

4.2.1943: The advance combat units of the 7. and 1./1. Panzer-Grenadier-Regiment were pulled back from Boroditschnoje and Martowaja-Artemowka to the main line of battle in the face of the attacking enemy forces.[7]

In the course of the day, the Soviets attacked repeatedly, especially the positions near Petschenegi. Hauptsturmführer Springer, the Chef of the 1. Kompanie of the 1. Panzer-Grenadier-Regiment, which was stationed there, reported:

> "On 4.2 the Russians appeared in front of our positions. They attempted several times to cross the frozen Donez and break through our positions, but they were unsuccessful. In the first place, there was behind us a sufficiently large counterthrust reserve force (thin, it is true, but in deeply echeloned positions) capable of throwing back any Russian forces that made it through. In the second place, we had two MG 42's assigned to each group; this was the first time we had used them, and they were tremendously effective. On one of these days, Papa Hausser showed up at my Kompanie headquarters to observe the MG 42's effect himself. A large number of Russian dead lay on the ice of the Donez in front of our position. He praised our well-designed installation."

At 11.00 hours, the 3. (armoured)/Aufklärungsabteilung (under Knittel), reinforced with Sturmgeschütze, launched an attack on the town of Korobotschkino, which was enemy-occupied. The Kompanie drove the enemy out about 12.00 hours and started its thrust on Schewtschenkowo. This thrust failed because of road congestion caused by our own sleighs, columns of retreating Italian soldiers from the 8th Army, and groups of German soldiers cut off from their units. While the Kompanie was attempting to make way through these obstacles, it was attacked from the north by several tanks with infantrymen manning anti-tank guns mounted on them. Our Kompanie was able, despite the heavy losses it suffered, to get free of this attack. Before this Kompanie had begun its thrust, the group under Maurer, consisting of the two Züge of the

2./Aufklärungsabteilung *LAH*, had already made it that far. In fighting its way back along the road, which the enemy had blocked, the Kompanie under Knittel encountered an enemy battery and freed about one hundred men from the 298. Infanteriedivision. The rest of this Division had set up all around defenses near Schewtschenkowo. Untersturmführer Maurer reported on this fighting as follows:

> "I reported at 02.30 hours on 4.2 to Hauptsturmführer Knittel, Chef of the 3./Aufklärungsabteilung. He had us find billets while waiting for the early report. We received it dropped from a plane: 'Road to Malinowka blocked by weak enemy calvalry forces. Road to Isjum unpassable due to drifting snow.' Knittel decided to risk making a breakthrough to Malinowka. Two groups from the 3./Aufklärungsabteilung *LAH* took over the spearhead of the force with their armoured personnel cars, then came the 3. Zug. The 2. Zug travelled in the formation of the 3. Kompanie. At first all went splendidly. After the first volleys fired by the leading Zug, volleys which caused noticeable damage, Russian cavalry started running away to the right and left of the road. The enemy resistance grew and grew as Russian infantry units marched toward us on the same road. Firing in all directions, we roared through a column of Russian soldiers. There were dead Russians on the road, the bodies of horses twitched, ammunition sleds were flying into the air, and we tore through the middle of it all. All of a sudden there were grey uniforms amidst the Russians: our comrades from the Heer who had been taken prisoner. We pulled them into the moving vehicles; I have seldom seen happier faces. And then came the bend in the road before Korobotschkino. There the Russians had, without our seeing it, set up a roadblock, and Russian anti-tank guns were waiting right around the bend. Machine gun fire and hand grenades turned it into an inferno. It was too late to dismount. Only constant speed could save us. Three vehicles ahead of me, Unterscharführer Moosmann, the leader of my third group, jumped out right beside an enemy anti-tank gun and finished off its crew with his submachine gun at close range. Then he stood in the middle of the road and roared: 'Speed, speed!' Men from vehicles which had been hit were pulled on board the armoured vehicles as they passed. All of a sudden, we were through. The 1./Aufklärungsabteilung found us just outside of Korobotschkino. But the bitter pill was yet to be swallowed: who was missing? Unterscharführer Moosmann and Sturmmann Vollert had been killed; Rottenführer Broöcker, Rottenführer Neustedt, and Rottenführer Andree were wounded; three men were missing. Lampert and Kahler, whose vehicle had taken a direct hit from the anti-tank guns, made it back to us, thank God. In the 2. Zug, which was riding behind us, things looked terrible. Kurt Mauthe sat as if paralyzed. 'Where are my comrades?' he kept asking us. Unterscharführer Krüger had managed, despite serious wounds, to crawl aboard a sled and come through.
> In a counterthrust, the 1./Aufklärungsabteilung *LAH* managed to pick up our dead and collect the vehicles which had been hit. Both Züge lost almost a third of their combat strength."

In the early afternoon, the 1./Aufklärungsabteilung *LAH* (under Bremer) waged a successful attack on Annowka in the bend of the Donez. The attack received effective support from the I./Artillerie-Regiment *LAH* and the 4./Artillerie-Regiment *LAH*. The attacking force was pulled back at nightfall.

From the elevated Donez bank, the 1. (8.8-centimer)/Flakabteilung *LAH* (under Dr. Loenicker) used its 8.8-centimeter Flak guns and its heavy range finder to achieve targeted firing on the Russian tanks from a distance of between six and nine kilometers. The Kompanie was able to set nine tanks on fire and drive the rest back into the Balkas. It must have given the Russian tank crews, so certain of their victory, panic attacks to be shot at from an unknown location.

The enemy had not yet attacked the defensive sector of the 2. Panzer-Grenadier-Regiment, situated to the right farther to the south. He appeared to be assembling in the larger villages about fifteen kilometers away. The Division therefore undertook reconnaissance on the right wing along the road to Isjum. Schütze Borchers remembered the action as follows:

> "With our Bataillon commander, Sturmbannführer Kraas, we reconnoitered toward Isjum. The remains of the *Herz-Division* (the 320. Infanteriedivision) were supposed to be fighting their way back from there. As far as Alexandrowka, about fifteen kilometers from our position, everything was clear of enemy forces. There was sometimes a house burning on the side of the road, and we occasionally received light mortar fire. On we rolled. After another five kilometers, driving snow began to fall. We drove in deep echelon formation. To the front were the motorcycles, a hundred meters later the riflemen in two Volkswagens, then one self-propelled Pak and an armoured personnel carrier. Russian civilians with red armbands disappeared from the streets as we approached. The Russians with tanks, infantry on sleds, and horse-drawn artillery popped up to the left of our march route, northwest of Balakeja. There was at least a regiment. With that, our mission was fulfilled, and we hightailed it back. But the Russian cavalry had already blocked off our route. The MG riflemen in the motorcycle sidecards opened fire as we drove across the fields through the deep snow back to the Bataillon headquarters to report. Racing at full throttle over the open terrain demanded the last ounce from our machines, and the exhaust pipes were red-hot. We hoped that Ivan would not reach us quickly, for our Artillerie and heavy weapons were still on the way. The Russian wedge was moving directly on our Bataillon. Pity the poor Infanterie if the heavy weapons did not get here from France as soon as possible."

Because of this reconnaissance information, the Ia ordered the 18. (Panzerjäger)/2. Panzer-Grenadier-Regiment and the 6./2. Panzer-Grenadier-Regiment *LAH* under the command of Hauptsturmführer Linden to move into position next to the reinforced I./2. Panzer-Grenadier-Regiment along the road to Scheludowka immediately upon arrival.

Hauptsturmführer Linden reported:

> "We had to hack fox holes out of the ice-hard ground as our first task; even the Russian civilians helped us at it. In little groups, exhausted and half-frozen comrades separated from their Heer units kept arriving. By night it was difficult to tell whether they were Russians or our wounded comrades. I had first to order and finally to compel these men to join the defensive

line in order to provide Infanterie cover for our heavy weapons. In order to make these soldiers ready for combat again, I used our one-tonne tractor to bring them tea, soup, and supplies through the night."

The positions of the 2. Panzer-Grenadier-Regiment remained unmolested during the entire night.

Information about the enemy: In his attempt to fulfill his mission of taking Charkow, the enemy was sending out feelers all along the Donez from north to south. The Division expected a continuation of the enemy attack on 5.2, this time with the main point of concentration near the Aufklärungsabteilung and the 2. Panzer-Grenadier-Regiment.[8]

In the late evening, the Division commander, Obergruppenführer Sepp Dietrich arrived in Tschugujew. He was coming from the Führer's Headquarters.

5.2.1943: At dawn, the enemy moved from Annowka and Bogoroditschnoje and attacked the positions of the reinforced Aufklärungsabteilung *LAH* in Malinowka and in front of Petschenegi. The Aufklärungsabteilung was able to reinforce itself by taking on ten 7.5-centimeter Pak guns and six heavy Infanteriegeschütze which happened to be standing on an out-of-use train in the Malinowka station. The crews for the weapons came from the 298. Infanteriedivision.[9]

At 07.05 hours, the advance combat units of the 2./2. Panzer-Grenadier-Regiment (under Hauptsturmführer Becker) encountered the enemy east of Gniliza for the first time.

At 07.35 hours, a report was dropped from a plane to the commander of the I./2. Panzer-Grenadier-Regiment: "Russian cavalry is in Novo Gniliza at the head of the chain of villages stretching all the way to Gniliza. Force strength of 800 to 1,000 men."

The Russian attack collapsed under concentrated fire from our Artillerie, Flak, and heavy Infanterie weapons in front of the positions of our advance detachments. The enemy pulled back along the Balka to Grakowo. Untersturmführer Tack, a Zugführer in the 2. Kompanie, was killed in this fighting. The 1./Sturmgeschützabteilung *LAH* under Obersturmführer Heimann and the 10. (Werfer)/Artillerie-Regiment *LAH* under Obersturmführer Bartels were moved up to join the I./2. Panzer-Grenadier-Regiment, to which they were subordinated.

At 08.05 hours, the 2. Regiment reported that Kampfgruppe Linden had taken on about two hundred men from the 298. Infanteriedivision and had stationed them as reinforcements along the main battle line. At 13.10 hours, the enemy launched an attack along a broad front against the following positions: the advance detachments of the I./2. Panzer-Grenadier-Regiment on the eastern edge of Gniliza, the reinforced Aufklärungsabteilung *LAH* on the eastern edge of Gniliza, and the reinforced Aufklärungsabteilung *LAH* on the eastern edge of Malinowka. The attack also hit the entire front of the I. and II./1. Panzer-Grenadier-Regiment on the Donez. These attacks lasted with varying intensity until nightfall. The 2. Panzer-Grenadier-Regiment *LAH* suffered the following casualties on 5.2:

one officer and one enlisted man killed, two officers and eighteen enlisted men wounded, one enlisted man missing.

In the 1. Panzer-Grenadier-Regiment *LAH*'s sector, the hill southeast of Kizewka, defended by the 3. Kompanie, changed hands many times in the course of the fighting. In this bitter, close-range combat, the Kompanieführer, Obersturmführer Gessner, and all the Kompanie's Zugführer were killed.

The Divisional observation post on the elevated Donez bank near Tschugujew could see that the attacking enemy forces were no longer receiving constant reinforcement, but that reserve troops were moving to the southwest in long sled columns and in single tanks. A strong column seemed to be heading for the enemy unit which was attacking our left wing. The Division requested and got a Stuka attack on the column at 15.30 hours. The III./1. Panzer-Grenadier-Regiment (under Sturmbannführer Weidenhaupt) arrived in the afternoon and was posted in Tschugujew as Divisional reserve.

The elements of the II./2. Panzer-Grenadier-Regiment subordinated to the 1. Panzer-Grenadier-Regiment were taken back to their Regiment and deployed on its right wing. The Division assumed that the enemy would continue to attack along the former front and would attempt to determine the position of our wings and flanks to the south in order to go around them. For this reason, the Division requested of the Korps that a mobile winter unit be deployed in front of the right wing.[10]

6.2.1943: The Oberkommando of Heeresgruppe B under Generalfeldmarschall von Weichs was removed from the command structure of the Eastern Front. Armeeabteilung Lanz and the Generalkommando of the SS-Panzerkorps came under the command of Heeresgruppe Süd under Generalfeldmarschall von Manstein. From then on, Armeeabteilung Lanz was designated Heeresgruppe Don. Hitler paid the unit a visit on 6.2.1943 in their headquarters at Saporoshje. In the course of the visit, Hitler agreed to von Manstein's proposals for the further conduct of the battle. The Heeresgruppe received permission to abandon Rostow, a move which brought about a considerable shortening of the front.

Von Manstein hoped to stop the Russian offensive by positioning to the south the 1. and 4. Panzerarmee, which had arrived in the meantime on the northern bank of the Don, and to the north the SS-Panzerkorps and Heeresdivision *Großdeutschland*, which were just assembling their forces around Charkow.[11]

Starting at midnight, there were constant attacks from enemy forces ranging in size from company to battalion in the Skripai sector (held by the 2. Panzer-Grenadier-Regiment) and Petschenegi (held by the 1. Panzer-Grenadier-Regiment). The attacks were repulsed, sometimes by means of counteroffensives, and the enemy suffered serious losses. In front of the Aufklärungsabteilung *LAH* alone, three hundred and sixty Russians died, including five officers. A sudden Russian artillery barrage killed Untersturmführer Klingner of the Pionier-Bataillon, whose Pionierzug had been subordinated to the Aufklärungsabteilung.

In the forest west of Martowaja, held by the I./1. Panzer-Grenadier-Regiment, enemy forces managed to sneak through, but they were caught and destroyed at dawn.

At 12.35 hours, the enemy's fourth thrust against the I./2. Panzer-Grenadier-Regiment's position at the bridge succeeded in forcing its way into Skripai. An immediate counterthrust by the 2. Kompanie (under Hauptsturmführer Becker) with support from the 1./Sturmgeschützabteilung *LAH* (under Obersturmführer

Heimann) and from the 16. Kompanie and elements of the 5./Flakabteilung *LAH* pushed the enemy forces back.

In the afternoon, elements of the Regiments-Stabskompanie, with the 11., 13. and 15. Kompanie of the 2. Panzer-Grenadier-Regiment and the 5./Flakabteilung *LAH* under the command of the Regiments-Adjutant, Obersturmführer Diefenthal, cleared away an enemy incursion in Gniliza.

At 08.30 hours, a large number of German soldiers spotted moving from Korobotschkino and along the railway line Kupjansk — Tschugujew were freed from captivity by a counterthrust of the 3./2. Panzer-Grenadier-Regiment (under Hauptsturmführer Beutler) from Skripai and the 2./Aufklärungsabteilung (under Obersturmführer Weiser) from Malinowka with support from the Sturmgeschütze. The 3./2. Panzer-Grenadier-Regiment liberated, among others, about five men from the I./Polizei-Infanterie-Regiment 1 under Hauptsturmführer Schwarting (see list of officers at beginning of Part 5, Section II), about one hundred men of the 298. Infanteriedivision, and men separated from the 320. Infanteriedivision. The 2./Aufklärungsabteilung *LAH* freed eight hundred men under the command of Oberst Michaelis. On orders from the Armeeabteilung, they were initially subordinated to the *LAH*. The 2. Regiment and the Aufklärungsabteilung made great efforts to supply them with food and care.

The 2. Panzer-Grenadier-Regiment received orders at 14.00 hours to extend its battle front nine kilometers farther to Lake Liman and to send a Schützenpanzerwagenkompanie reinforced with Sturmgeschütze to Andrejewka to serve as a strong defensive force along the road to Isjum. The reinforced 11. (armoured)/2. Panzer-Grenadier-Regiment (under Obersturmführer Guhl) was assigned this mission. At 21.15 hours, it reported that Andrejewka was clear of enemy forces.

In the late afternoon, a second, heavier enemy attack in front of Petschenegi (I./1. Panzer-Grenadier-Regiment) collapsed under defensive fire about one hundred meters in front of the battle line. The Russians were successful, however, in making an incursion into the forest north of that spot. The 1. Panzer-Grenadier-Regiment intended to push back these enemy forces on the morning of 7.2 by systematically combing the forest.

According to statements from prisoners, there were 3,000 - 4,000 Russian soldiers and many tanks in Korobotschkino. A Stuka attack was requested immediately, but it was not deemed possible to launch one that day. It was promised as the first action for 7.2. A serious confrontation arose between the Chef of the Generalstab of the Korps, Standartenführer Ostendorf, and the Ia of the *LAH*, Sturmbannführer Lehmann, about a Panzer attack which the Armeeabteilung requested be launched from Petschenegi on Artemowsk. When the Korps finally came around to the Division's rejection of the plan, the commanding general, Obergruppenführer Hausser, was able to convince the Armee that such an attack would be senseless.

Information about the enemy: in the opinion of the Korps, SS-Panzer-Grenadier-Division *Das Reich*, deployed to the left of us, was being outflanked in the north just as the *LAH* was in the south.

The only solution was for the 320. Infanteriedivision, currently fighting its way back along the road from Isjum to Smijew, to join us as quickly as possible on the right wing in order to extend our front to the south. The mission of the 11./2.

Panzer-Grenadier-Regiment, providing defense in Andrejewka, was therefore especially important.

7.2.1943: Erwin Jäckel, at the time commander of a Sturmgeschütz, recalls the action in Andrejewka as follows:

> "The next morning, a German close-range reconnaissance plane flew over us a couple of times. At about noon, it returned from the east and dropped a message container with a smoke flare. My crew and I received orders to recover the container, which lay about a hundred meters in front of our battle line. It contained the following message: 'Column on the march from the northeast. Presumably one of ours.' We immediately moved to meet this column. It really was German troops, elements of the 298. Infanteriedivision. But what shape they were in! They were coming from the great bend in the Don, where they had been deployed as 'corset stay' between Italian divisions. As the Russians were sweeping away the Italians and Hungarians, these brave doughboys had marched hundreds of kilometers up hill and down dale, through meadow and forest, constantly under enemy threat, sometimes in a moving pocket, until they met up with us. The joy was enormous on both sides. What these men had had to endure is indescribable. We provided our comrades from the Heer with everything that we could spare in our efforts to make their long period of suffering a forgotten memory. They were moved back on the same day."

Early on the morning of 7.2, the reserves of the 1. Panzer-Grenadier-Regiment *LAH* started out to perform the planned mop-up operation in the forest northwest of Petschenegi. By 11.00 hours, the enemy forces were either destroyed (with about two hundred twenty dead) or pushed back across the Donez. The reconnaissance thrusts which the enemy made throughout the day into the Division's entire sector were also pushed back, and the enemy suffered heavy losses. The advance unit, the 11./2. Panzer-Grenadier-Regiment, reported at 12.30 hours that there were significant enemy forces seven kilometers east of Andrejewka. At 15.00 hours the unit reported that two large enemy columns were marching on Andrejewka from the northeast and southeast. The Kompanie moved to confront the column from the southeast and destroyed one or two enemy squads.

At about noon, Generalmajor Postel, the commander of the 320. Infanteriedivision, known as the *Berliner Herz-Division* [Berlin Heart Division] because of its Divisional insignia, landed in a Fieseler Storch in Tschugujew. We provided him with a hot bath and fresh underwear from Obergruppenführer Dietrich's stock of it. After telephone conversations with the Korps and the Armee, Generalmajor Postel arranged with the Ia of the *LAH* for his Division to fight its way through to the *LAH*. It was expected that this would not take place on 9.2, as the 320. Infanteriedivision thought, but on 12.2 when the situation had changed completely.

The Division ordered the 2. Panzer-Grenadier-Regiment *LAH* to hold Andrejewka because the 320. Infanteriedivision was assembling in Ssawinzy (thirty kilometers southeast of Andrejewka) and was to move through Balakleja. The town of Andrejewka, which had been temporarily abandoned, was captured again in a counterthrust by the 12. and 13./2. Panzer-Grenadier-Regiment and

Oberscharführer Fritz Henke
Received Ritterkreuz on 12.2.1944 as a Zugführer in the 3./SS-Sturmgeschütz-abteilung 1 *LSSAH*

Obersturmbannführer Rudolf Lehmann
Received Ritterkreuz 23.2.1944 as 1. Generalstabsoffizier of the 1. SS-Panzer-division *LSSAH*

Strumbannführer Heinrich Heimann
Received Ritterkreuz on 23.2.1944 as Hauptsturmführer and commander of the SS-Strumgeschützabteilung 1 *LSSAH* Killed 20.8.1944 in Normandy.

Sturmbannführer Herbert Kuhlmann
Received Ritterkreuz on 13.2.1944 as commander of the I./Panzerregiment 1 *LSSAH*

Sturmbannführer Max Hansen
Received Ritterkreuz on 28.3.1943 as commander of the II./Panzer-grenadier-Regiment 1 *LSSAH*

Sturmbannführer Rudolf Sandig
Received Ritterkreuz on 5.5.1943 as commander of the II./Panzer-grenadier-Regiment 2 *LSSAH*

Hauptsturmführer Hermann Weiser
Received Rittenkreuz on 28.3.1943 as Obersturmführer and Kompanieführer of the 2./Auflärungsabteilung *LSSAH*

Hauptsturmführer Hans Becker
Received the Ritterkreuz on 28.3.1943 as Chef of the 2./2. Panzergrenadier-Regiment.

elements of the 3./Sturmgeschützabteilung *LAH* (under Hauptsturmführer Rettlinger). At 21.55 hours, the 1. Panzer-Grenadier-Regiment reported that strong enemy forces had appeared at the seam between that unit and Pionier-Bataillon *Das Reich* near Chotomlja.

There was heavy fighting once again around Skripai, too, but the town was back securely in the hands of the 2. Panzer-Grenadier-Regiment by evening.

At 22.00 hours, Obersturmführer Guhl requested his Kampfgruppe be reinforced in Andrejewka. He also transmitted a warning for the supply vehicles which he assumed were on their way to him. He suspected that enemy forces could have filtered through the lines and be on their way to the south, and the supply vehicles were to watch out for them. In the course of the day, Pionier-Bataillon *LAH* was given responsibility for blowing up the railway bridges at Smijew and Tschugujew; the bridges had already been prepared for demolition.

8.2.1943: After a peaceful day, marked only by reconnaissance activity on both sides and the knocking out of a T-34 by Kampfgruppe Guhl near Andrejewka, the enemy attacked at dawn along the entire front held by the Division. The point of concentration proved initially to be the town of Gniliza, held by the I./2. Panzer-Grenadier-Regiment (under Sturmbannführer Kraas). The enemy suffered heavy losses and pulled back under our concentrated fire. A Pionier force supported by Sturmgeschütze moved forward from Kampfgruppe Linden and cleared the valley of enemy troops. In doing so, it took eighteen prisoners, captured several machine guns and trench mortars, and found eighty Russian dead in front of its positions. At 06.30 hours, Kampfgruppe Linden defeated an attack by an enemy battalion.[12]

At 08.30 hours, the enemy once again attempted an attack on Gniliza, but his effort was in vain. Between 10.00 hours and 14.45 hours, an enemy regiment launched attacks in repeated waves on the positions of the I./2. Panzer-Grenadier-Regiment, especially those of the 2. Kompanie. Only a counterthrust with Sturmgeschütze from the 1. Batterie/Sturmgeschützabteilung *LAH* and the Zug under Armberger of the 3. (3.7-centimeter)/Flakabteilung *LAH* could stop this mass attack. Two Russian tanks were destroyed in the counterthrust.

Kampfgruppe Guhl (11./2. Panzer-Grenadier-Regiment) reported at 12.35 hours that it had been forced to pull back under overwhelming enemy pressure to the western section in front of Andrejewka. The unit was then under heavy artillery fire and was being attacked by tanks on three sides. After conferring with the Division, Obersturmführer Guhl received orders to retreat fighting to Liman and from there to seek a way of joining the right wing of the II./2. Panzer-Grenadier-Regiment (under Sturmbannführer Sandig).

Up until midday, the enemy attempted to free the key position at Petschenegi from the 1. Panzer-Grenadier-Regiment *LAH* by waging a pincer attack from Annowka on Kizewka and from Martowaja on Pjatnizkoje. The I./1. Panzer-Grenadier-Regiment (under Sturmbannführer Frey) and the right wing of the II./1. Panzer-Grenadier-Regiment (under Sturmbannführer Max Hansen), especially the 7. Kompanie, pushed the enemy back again in bitter defensive fighting. The reinforced III./1. Panzer-Grenadier-Regiment (under Sturmbannführer Weidenhaupt) finally launched a well-placed counterattack from Kizewka and threw the enemy back across the Donez.

Heinz Schmolke, at that time a Zugführer in the 1. Kompanie/1. Panzer-Grenadier-Regiment *LAH*, wrote the following about the broad defensive sectors each unit was forced to hold in this fighting:

> "My sector was much too wide to be covered by one Zug. I managed to bring ten vehicle drivers to the front each night, and I also had a Zug of Ukrainian volunteers. Despite that, my messenger and I had to swing in and out of the gaps all night long and shoot off ground signals at different spots in order to give the impression of a larger force."

The information from the combat reconnaissance forces sent out ahead of the right wing confirmed what aerial reconnaissance had reported. The enemy was in the process of attempting to move considerable forces around our right wing. Across from the 2. Panzer-Grenadier-Regiment was the Soviet 111th Rifle Division with Regiments 399, 468, and 532 and Artillery Regiment 286.

The 320. Infanteriedivision was moving its leading elements, which were cut off from contact with any other unit, east of Balakleja to provide cover for our right flank, but the move did not have the desired result. Between the southern wing of the *LAH* and the 320. Infanteriedivision, a gap of forty kilometers opened up.

An assault group consisting of the I./Panzerregiment *LAH* (under Sturmbannführer Groß) and Kradschützen-Bataillon 2 (under Sturmbannführer Fick) assembled in Merefa (south of Charkow) with orders from the Korps to attack the enemy forces streaming through this gap in their flank. The attack was to begin on 9.2 and was to destroy the enemy.

Division *Das Reich* was pulled back to the Donez and deployed next to the *LAH* near Stary Ssaltow.

But farther to the north, the enemy began once again to outflank our weak Korps under Cramer. This move indicated an operational encirclement of the city of Charkow. Our leadership was therefore faced with the decision whether to begin the abandonment of this large city or to allow it to be surrounded. On top of that, the Soviets also initiated a thrust from the north on the Donez basin, which was cutting off the defensive front on the Mius from its supply lines. If the Soviets were to succeed in their operation, most of Heeresgruppe Süd would be cut off from their communications to the rear. There would be no German forces of any consequence opposing the Russians, and the Eastern Front would become an unmanagable situation. The Korps evaluated it thus: "The situation is very serious!"[13]

9.2.1943: During the night, the enemy continued his attacks against the Division's entire front, but all attacks were repulsed.

At 07.00 hours, new enemy attacks commenced, especially against the sectors held by the I./2. Panzer-Grenadier-Regiment, the Aufklärungsabteilung, and the right wing of the I./1. Panzer-Grenadier-Regiment, thus against Gniliza, Malinowka, and Petschenegi. Near Malinowka, two KV I's were hit and destroyed.

At about midday, the Chef of the Generalstab of the Korps, Standartenführer Ostendorf, informed the Ia of the *LAH*, Sturmbannführer Lehmann, that the OKH had ordered the Korps to form a strong attack force in the Merefa area. To make this possible, the front was to be pulled back to a shortened line in the coming night. The *LAH*'s line stretched from Mirgorod — Konstantowka —

Lisogubowka — Rogan, including the towns. It there joined the sector held by Regiment *Deutschland* of the Division *Das Reich*. The Division *LAH* was to make its reinforced Aufklärungsabteilung and a Regimental force available for the thrust to the south.

The Division issued the following order:

> "*The reinforced Pionier-Bataillon* is to use one Kompanie to hold the sector Mirgorod — Timtschenko (excluding the towns) and is to assemble most of its forces in Merefa. *The reinforced 2. Panzer-Grenadier-Regiment* is to use two Bataillone to hold the line Timtschenko (including the town) — Wodjanoje (including the town); the III. (armoured)/2. Panzer-Grenadier-Regiment is to be sent to Podolchow to stand at the disposal of the Division. *The reinforced 1. Panzer-Grenadier-Regiment* is to use two Bataillone to hold the line Wodjanoje (excluding the town) — Rogan (including the town). There, one reinforced Kompanie is to serve as contact command to the Division *Das Reich*."

At 16.00 hours, the Division ordered conclusively the formation of a new battle line. A short counterthrust at 24.00 hours started our disengagement from the enemy.

Kampfgruppe Guhl was to remain in Smijew to provide cover for the 320. Infanteriedivision.

In the course of the afternoon, there were a number of enemy attacks to repulse, particularly in the Division's center section. The elements of the 298. Infanteriedivision deployed with the Division were pulled out under orders from the Korps and put on the march to Ljubotin.

At nightfall, the Divisional headquarters were moved to Wyssokij. The leader of the Divison's map unit reported on the events in the Divisional headquarters as follows:

> "We heard the nervous steps of the Ia in the room above us as he tensely worked. Special-duty officers and messengers came and went. There was no rest for us, either, for motorcycle messengers were constantly arriving from the units picking up the maps we had bundled up only the evening before. In between, we were drawing and pasting up new maps. Through the night, there were columns passing on the road without pause.
>
> In order to be more mobile, the Divisionsstab's supply train was moved to Rogan. Then, because the enemy had moved around us to the north and south and was making a thrust on our supply route to Rogan, the supply train was moved back to Poltawa. Of the map unit's vehicles, only the transport truck, the passenger car, and the map truck were still at the Divisional headquarters. Our work did not abate, for new maps were constantly needed.
>
> The first prisoners were brought in and interrogated by the Ic in the room next to us. To our rear, the road to Charkow had been captured by the enemy near Rogan. In the night between February 9 and 10, we escaped from the noose which had been laid around us. The order to move the Divisional headquarters came on the evening of February 9, and we made the perilous trip to Wyssokij by night. This trip, across the country roads and fields, through snowstorms, over frozen streams, will probably always

stay in our memories. Despite our good winter equipment, we froze mercilessly. Many vehicles were put out of service by the cold and had to be towed. We took turns pulling each other. Our passenger car would not start after it had made a short stop. The battery had frozen, and the steering column was full of ice and would not work anymore. Jupp Hocke, who had a little more experience, pulled us out of it. Just before Wyssokij, we had the bad luck to run into another vehicle standing on the road. The windows of our car were coated thick with ice, and our driver was only steering by feel. The collision luckily only cost us our bumper and a fender. After driving for twelve hours to travel forty-five kilometers, we arrived in our new location on the morning of February 10."

10.2.1943: (See sketch 7) The move ordered for the Division was successful despite the difficulties presented by the driving snow and the bitter cold. The 2. Panzer-Grenadier-Regiment, deployed in the southern sector, was able to make the ordered counterthrust and to pull back to the new battle line without coming into contact with the enemy. It established a defensive position there.

The reinforced Aufklärungsabteilung, too, succeeded in disengaging from the enemy without being noticed. In the grey of dawn, it pulled back to Merefa. The 1. Panzer-Grenadier-Regiment *LAH*, on the other hand, was forced to pull back under pressure from the enemy. The III./1. Panzer-Grenadier-Regiment (under Weidenhaupt), which was stationed in reserve, was able to establish a covering position on both sides of the Tschugujew — Charkow road near Kammenaja Jaruga on the morning of 10.2. Subsequently, this Bataillon's pullback was covered by the reinforced 1./1. Panzer-Grenadier-Regiment (one Zug of four-barrelled, self-propelled Flak) under Hauptsturmführer Springer in Rogan. South of the road, the Bataillon assumed positions which extended to within about one kilometer south of the Rogan railway station. There it was adjacent to the II./1. Panzer-Grenadier-Regiment (under Max Hansen), which was seeking to establish contact with the unit on the left wing of the 2. Panzer-Grenadier-Regiment, the I. Bataillon (under Kraas).

The I./1. Panzer-Grenadier-Regiment (minus the 1. Kompanie) was on the march to Merefa on the afternoon of 10.2. The road Charkow — Merefa was carrying too much traffic, for the remains of Kradschützen-Bataillon 2, the reinforced Regiment *DF*, and the II./Panzer-Regiment *LAH* were also moving along it. For this reason, the *LAH*'s attack group could not be assembled until the morning of 11.2.

At 15.30 hours, a reconnaissance unit from the 2. Panzer-Grenadier-Regiment under the command of Untersturmführer Reif was destroyed by enemy tanks.

At 17.00 hours, an enemy company attacked Lisogubowka and was repulsed by a counterattack from a Zug of the 12./2. Panzer-Grenadier-Regiment under the command of Untersturmführer Westrup. On urgent orders from the Korps, a thrust was made from Merefa to the south by the Aufklärungsabteilung/*LAH* reinforced by the I./Panzer-Regiment *LAH*. Deep snow brought it to a halt, however. This Kampfgruppe was able, nevertheless, to establish an extended bridgehead south of Merefa, which made it possible to conduct the attack planned for 11.2 along a broad front.[15]

At 14.30 hours, the Korps issued orders for the *LAH* Divisionkommando to assume command over the Korps attack wing consisting of elements from both Divisionen (Angriffsgruppe SS-Panzerkorps [attack force of the SS-Panzerkorps]) and for the forces fighting on the Korps' eastern and northern fronts (Deckungsgruppe SS-Panzerkorps [cover force of the SS-Panzerkorps]) to be subordinated to Division *Das Reich*.

With that order, the following came under the command of Divison *Das Reich*: the reinforced 2. Panzer-Grenadier-Regiment *LAH*, the 1./Sturmgeschützabteilung *LAH*, elements of the Artillerie-Regiment *LAH*, elements of the Flakabteilung *LAH*, one Kompanie of the Pionier-Bataillon *LAH*, the 1. Kompanie of the 1. Panzer-Grenadier-Regiment with its Regimentsstab, and the III. Bataillon of the 1. Panzer-Grenadier-Regiment.

The Angriffsgruppe under the command of the *LAH* consisted of:

The reinforced Panzer-Grenadier-Regiment *DF* (minus the I. Bataillon) commanded by Obersturmführer Kumm,
the Regimentsstab of the 1. Panzer-Grenadier-Regiment *LAH* (minus the Stabskompanie),
the I./1. Panzer-Grenadier-Regiment (minus the 1. Kompanie),
the Pionier-Bataillon *LAH* (minus one Kompanie),
the Panzer-Regiment *LAH*, the Sturmgeschützabteilung *LAH* (minus one Batterie),
the Flakabteilung *LAH* (minus elements which were with the 2. Regiment), and
most of the Artillerie-Regiment *LAH*.

At 14.45 hours, the 2. Panzer-Grenadier-Regiment *LAH* received orders to assume the responsibility for command of the *LAH* elements deployed on the defensive front. The Regiment, subordinated to the Panzer-Grenadier-Division, reported that it was unable to assume command of Kampfgruppe Weidenhaupt, consisting of the reinforced III./1. Panzer-Grenadier-Regiment deployed all the way out on the left flank, because of the great extent of the front and its meager communications resources. Division *Das Reich* took direct command of this Kampfgruppe itself.

At 17.00 hours, an order reached the 2. Panzer-Grenadier-Regiment: the reinforced III. (armoured)/ 2. (consisting of two Züge of Sturmgeschütze) was to break through to Smijew with a sixty-vehicle ambulance column on the night between 10.2 and 11.2, establish contact there with the 320. Infanteriedivision, and cover the 320.'s retreat and the transport of the wounded. This action required the 13. (armoured)/ 2. Panzer-Grenadier-Regiment to be pulled out, which created a gap in the Regiment's defensive front. This hole was closed by moving over from the left flank the groups of vehicle drivers, writers, etc. under the command of Hauptsturmführer Linden. Kampfgruppe Linden was subordinated to the I./2. Panzer-Grenadier-Regiment (under Kraas).

At 21.00 hours, two enemy companies attacked Kampfgruppe Linden in Krissanowka and Ternowoje, but they were repulsed. A T-34 was destroyed in the fighting. The enemy stayed hard on the heels of the reinforced 1./1. Panzer-Grenadier-Regiment and the III./1. Panzer-Grenadier-Regiment as they retreated along the road from Tschugujew to Charkow. The sector held by the III. Bataillon and the 1. Kompanie were under constant pressure from the enemy. After the covering forces had been pulled back from the eastern edge of Rogan, the bridge in the middle of town was blown up by the Pionierzug of the I./1. Panzer-Grenadier-Regiment. In the night, the Chef of the 5. (heavy)/1. Panzer-

Grenadier-Regiment, Hauptsturmführer Besch, traveling on skis made from planks, paid a visit to the Kampfgruppe's positions.

The 15./1. Panzer-Grenadier-Regiment, deployed to the north of town, fired on Russian soldiers on the ground floor of the school and flushed them out in order to save the German soldiers trapped on the top floor. A survivor of this fighting remembers that the cold was so severe that the sausage given the men had to be cut with an ax and the bread had to be thawed over the soldering gun. The positions on both sides of the march route were under constant artillery and mortar fire.

In the following section, the defensive fighting engaged in by the elements of the *LAH* deployed with Division *Das Reich* will be described.

c) 11.2. - 17.2.1943: Defensive fighting by Kampfgruppe Wisch and Kampfgruppe Weidenhaupt as elements of the Deckungsgruppe SS-Panzerkorps east of Charkow and the abandonment of Charkow (see sketch 8)

The Armee order from Armeeabteilung Lanz on 10.3.1943 read as follows (excerpt):

1. Four enemy armies at the Armee's front are pushing their southern wing across the Donez to the southwest and moving a strong northern force toward Charkow through Woltschansk and Belgorod.
2. The Armee's mission is to hold fast in the area around Charkow while preventing the enemy from advancing on the northern flank of Heeresgruppe Don. The success of the Armee in fulfilling this mission will determine the success of the entire campaign.
3. For this action, I order the following:
   a) [Applies to Angriffsgruppe SS-Panzerkorps; see section Id, following.]
   b) Deckungsgruppe SS-Panzerkorps is to hold the line Smijew (which is to be recaptured by the morning of 11.2 at the latest) — Rogan (including the road from Tschugujew to Charkow); the attack reserve and the main focus of the Panzer defense are to be on the Tschugujew road.
   c) The reinforced Regiment *Deutschland* of SS-Panzer-Grenadier-Division *Das Reich* is to assemble as soon as possible on 11.2 in the region of the northern Charkow airstrip in order to stand at the disposal of the Armeeabteilung.
   d) The Korps under Cramer with Panzer-Grenadier-Division *Großdeutschland* and the occupying forces in Charkow are to delay the enemy's advance and to defend the eastern and northern fronts in the line Roganj [sic] (exclusive of it) — Lipzy — Solotschew. The 168. Infanteriedivision is to move up to Bogoduchoff via Graiworon.
4. ...
5. The 320. Infanteriedivision has orders to move forward on 11.2 across Liman to Smijew. The SS-Panzerkorps is to provide cover.
6. The Luftwaffe command on the Don is requested to:

a) destroy the enemy forces, particularly those facing the Angriffsgruppe SS-Panzerkorps.
b) provide supplies to the 320. Infanteriedivision.[16]

11.2.1943: At 02.00 hours, the enemy launched a new attack on Ternowoje and was successful in breaking through the front held by Kampfgruppe Linden. A counterattack by the newly-formed 19. (Aufklärung)/2. Panzer-Grenadier-Regiment (under Dix), supported by the Sturmgeschütze from the 1. Batterie of the Sturmgeschützabteilung (under Heimann), threw the enemy back and restored the old battle line.

In the course of the night, the 1./1., under Hauptsturmführer Springer, had repulsed attacks by two batallions with tank support moving on Rogan. The 1. Kompanie had established its battle line at the Balka which divides the town down the middle from northeast to southwest. Hauptsturmführer Springer reported at 13.00 hours that since 06.00 hours there had been constant arrivals of new Russian troops on trucks, along with accompanying tanks. He emphasized that his own forces had suffered losses and that the situation was grave. He finally requested reinforcements, claiming that he would not be able to hold his position until evening without them.[17] In this heavy fighting, Untersturmführer Wolf Berger,son of Obergruppenführer Berger, was killed. Two T-34's were destroyed by the Geschütz commanded by Weber of the 5./1. The Geschütz under Seigies received a direct hit.

The leading elements of the 320. Infanteriedivision reached N. Grigorijewka that afternoon. The Armee commanded it to push through on 12.2 by 06.00 hours toward Sidki on both sides of the road, where it would receive cover from Kampfgruppe Peiper, the reinforced III. (armoured)/ 2. Panzer-Grenadier-Regiment.

In the middle of the defensive front, the day passed quietly. Information about the enemy: his forces had closed ranks along the entire front and would probably continue strong attacks on the following day.

In the course of 11.2, the Divisional headquarters were moved to Merefa.

12.2.1943: At 04.30 hours, Kampfgruppe Peiper set out from Podolchow.

The following report on the relief of the 320. Infanteriedivison by the reinforced III. (armoured)/2. Panzer-Grenadier-Regiment *LAH* (Kampfgruppe Peiper) relies primarily on entries in the Kriegstagebuch of the I./2. Panzer-Grenadier-Regiment, of the 2. Panzer-Grenadier-Regiment, and of the Generalkommando of the SS-Panzerkorps.

On 12.2.1943 at 05.15 hours, Kampfgruppe Peiper crossed the German line in the section held by the I. Bataillon, destroyed the enemy forces on the bridge to Krassnaja Poljana and gained control of the road, making it available to the vehicle column. Late-arriving elements of the vehicle column were attacked by enemy forces, however, and six vehicles were destroyed.

At 06.40 hours, Kampfgruppe Peiper captured Smijew without enemy resistance. The Ia of the *LAH* informed the unit that a pilot had reported the leading elements of the 320. Infanteriedivision to be near Liman.

At 08.00 hours, Kampfgruppe Peiper received orders to conduct reconnaissance toward Liman and to establish contact there with the 320. Infanteriedivision.

Untersturmführer Hermann Dahlke
Received Ritterkreuz on 28.3.1943 as Oberscharführer and Kompanieführer of the 3./SS-Panzergrenadier-Regiment 1.

Oberscharführer Hans Reimling
Received Ritterkreuz on 28.2.1943 as Oberscharführer and a Zugführer in the 2./SS-Panzerregiment 1.

Hauptscharführer Alfred Günther
Received Ritterkreuz on 3.3.1943 as Oberscharführer and a Zugführer in the 1./Sturmgeschützabteilung *LSSAH*
Killed August, 1944, in Normandy.

Haupsturmführer Wilhelm Beck
Received Ritterkreuz on 8.3.1943 as Obersturmführer and Kompanieführer of the 2./Panzerregiment 1 *LSSAH*
Killed 10.6.1944 in Normandy

In memory of Hauptsturmführer Gerhard Grebarsche.
Received Ritterkreuz on 24.1.1944 as a Zugführer in the 3./Panzergrenadier-Regiment 2 LAH.
(Unfortunately, no picture available.

In memory of Hauptsturmführer Emil Wiesemann.
Received Ritterkreuz on 20.12.1943 as Chef of the 2./SS-Sturmgeschützabteilung 1 LAH.
Killed 14.11.1943
(Unfortunately no picture available)

Left: Obersturmbannführer George Schönberger. Received Ritterkreuz on 20.12.1943 posthumously as commander of the SS-Panzerregiment 1 LSSAH. Killed 20.11.1943 in the Ukraine.

Middle: Sturmbannführer Gustav Knittel. Received Ritterkreuz on 4.6.1944 as commander of SS-Panzer-Aufklärungsabteilung 1 LSSAH.

Right: Obersturmbannführer Albert Frey. Was three hundred fifty-ninth soldier to receive the Eichenlaub as commander of SS-Panzergrenadier-Regiment 1 LSSAH on 20.12.1943

At 14.00 hours, the contact was established. Under orders from the 320. Infanteriedivision, the Kampfgruppe provided cover for the Division's assembly area near Tscheremuschnaja — Sidki — Samostje — Butowka.

13.2.1943: In the early morning hours, Kampfgruppe Peiper set out to provide cover for the vehicle column moving out from Sidki and reached Wodjanoje at 11.50 hours. The enemy had set the bridge on fire from his side in an attempt to cut off the retreat of the 320. Infanteriedivision and Kampfgruppe Peiper. The Kampfgruppe cleared Krassnaja Poljana of enemy forces and drove them east. In doing so, it came smack up against a Soviet battalion on skis. In the western part of the town, a Zug from the 2./2. Panzer-Grenadier-Regiment moved forward to hold the western flank so the wounded could be brought over and to allow the 320. Infanteriedivision to cross. The bridge was repaired sufficiently to allow ambulances over it.

At 16.00 hours, all the ambulances with their wounded were brought behind German lines. The condition of the bridges in Wodjanoje forced the Schützenpanzerwagen of Kampfgruppe Peiper to take a detour through Butowka, Sidki, Artjueschewka, and Mirgorod in enemy territory. A reinforced Kompanie was left behind at the Sidki railway station as rear guard.

14.2.1943: At 07.00 hours, the last elements of the 320. Infanteriedivision finally crossed the bridge. In the course of the day, the enemy assembled his forces and attacked the Sidki and Borowoje railway stations at 20.00 hours. The attacks collapsed under concentrated artillery fire. At 03.00 hours, the Schützenpanzerwagen-Bataillon (Kampfgruppe Peiper) received its supply train in Charkow and started its march toward Merefa at 07.00 hours through the burning city of Charkow. On the afternoon of 15.2, the Korps ordered Kampfgruppe Peiper, reinforced by one Sturmgeschützkompanie, to launch a counterattack against the enemy forces which had forced their way into Ossnowa (a section of Charkow). The Kampfgruppe set out at 14.30 hours from Merefa and was able to reach the railway line southwest of Ossnowa by 18.00 hours. Because darkness had fallen, the reinforced Bataillon Peiper was ordered to pull back.

The above information was gleaned from the entries in the Kriegtagebuch of the units listed above. A very personal report comes from then-Sturmbannführer Peiper. Dated 10.4.1976, this excerpt sheds some light on the dry formulations of the war logs:

> "The III. (armoured)/2. Panzer-Grenadier-Regiment *LAH* had orders to move forward to the German battle line at Smijew and to cover the pull-back by the remnants of the 320. Infanteriedivision. We were to drag back the 1,500 wounded men from this Division. For this purpose, the Bataillon received all the available ambulance vehicles and a considerable number of other vehicles not being used. Our battle line was along a stream (the Udy), over which there was a long wooden bridge. On the other side was a village (Krassnaja Poljana), which was occupied by a weak enemy force. Unexpectedly, we were able to move on Smijew without serious trouble with the enemy. There we stood on the bank of a river (the Donez) and waited for the leading group of the 320. Infanteriedivision under its commander, Postel. We could see it approaching us. A little later, General Postel

appeared with a great formation of vehicles and officers. I was first asked why we had not crossed the river. Our objection that the ice was not strong enough to hold us was dismissed by the General, but an Ordonnanz-Offizier confirmed it at the same moment, saying: 'Herr General, the ice is not holding and the first Sturmgeschütz has just fallen through.' General Postel was in a temper and declared that he would get a billet here and that we were to take over providing cover. He got very excited by how far back the battle line still lay, and then he disappeared. After a long pause, in which we sat silently in our Schützenpanzerwagen feeling uncomfortable, the Division arrived. We all had the same impression: Beresina! This must be what Napoleon's retreat looked like. In front came those able to walk, then the wounded, with the seriously wounded at the rear. A parade of misery on sleighs and sleds. These were so full that some unfortunates were tied on and carried underneath the sleighs. Our doctors and medics had set up emergency facilities to receive them. The wounded first got something to eat, hot drinks, and first aid. I remember well that my Bataillon doctor, Dr. Brüstle, complained to me the next morning. He and his colleague had operated the entire night (because of all the frostbitten limbs), and no one from the 320. Infanteriedivision had helped. We provided the watch, looking out with hollow cheeks into the ghostly night, convinced that it would not go well for long.
The next day (14.2), we got underway with an endless column. The Division proceeded along the road with the wounded, and our combat elements fanned out on both sides as cover for the flank. When we finally reached the stream, we discovered that the long wooden bridge spanning it was now nothing but some smoking posts. A Russian ski battalion was in possession of the town and had massacred many German medics and drivers (stragglers from the day before) and had mutilated their bodies. These Russians now fired on the Division's column from all sides. My Bataillon finally captured the town after vicious house-to-house combat, established a bridgehead, dragged our rescued comrades over the ice, and secured the hurriedly repaired bridge. When the last vehicle finally made it to the other side, my Schützenpanzerwagen-Bataillon turned around and raced back to Smijew in order to reach the German lines again by sneaking along parallel to the Russians.
According to General Postel's telling of it, the German troops experienced no 'uninterrupted fighting to break through'; instead, they marched relatively unmolested behind the Russians the whole way. The factors which made their situation so critical were their decreasing mobility, the growing number of men unable to walk, and the crisis of morale which hit as the German front, instead of growing closer, began to retreat away in front of them."

On 14.2 at 08.25 hours, the commander of the 320. Infanteriedivision reported to the Armeeabteilung by radio as follows:

"Arrival of the last rear guard, Bataillon 585. With that arrival, the entire 320. Infanteriedivision, missing only those men and that equipment lost in battle, was finally massed at the German lines after heavy, uninterrupted fighting to break through. From 26.1 to 14.2, it had been forced to rely completely on itself through a wide expanse of territory while surrounded by enemy forces of at least battalion strength. Now, after meeting its most pressing needs, it stood ready for new deployment."[18]

With this angry report from Peiper and the optimistic report of the 320. Infanteriedivision, we close our description of the liberation of this Division and turn to the defensive fighting engaged in by the elements of the *Leibstandarte* under the command of the 2. SS-Panzer-Grenadier-Division *Das Reich*.

On 12.2.1943 at 06.45 hours, the I./2. Panzer-Grenadier-Regiment reported that the enemy had succeeded in infiltrating our territory by taking advantage of the night and the light morning fog and had moved unnoticed through the deep gullies in the Udy river terrain. At daybreak, our concentrated mortar and Artillerie fire managed to destroy part of these forces. While some of our troops pulled back to the north, most of them remained in Borowoje. Recognizing the threat this posed to our rear, elements from the 3./2. Panzer-Grenadier-Regiment (under Becker) and from the 1./2. Panzer-Grenadier-Regiment (under Hausdorf) left our own line undefended and launched a counterattack in the afternoon. The 7. Kompanie (under Bormann), meanwhile, flanked and attacked the enemy from the forest near the western part of Temnowka. Elements from the 1. and 2. Kompanie spent the entire day fighting numerically superior, well camouflaged, and well oriented enemy forces, often in bitter house-to-house fighting, and were able to throw them back by evening as far as the church in Borowoje. The 7. Kompanie's attack got caught in heavy infantry fire, especially from the heavy trench mortars, on an open piece of terrain. The Kompanie was finally pulled back to Borowoje and stationed at the church; facing north, it was to provide cover in that direction. The elements of the 1. and 3. Kompanie assumed their old positions in the battle line. At 14.10 hours, the enemy took possession of the hills south of Krassnaja Poljana and deployed about a regiment to launch continual attacks on the sector Wodjanoje — Kirssanowka — Lisogubowka. All the attacks were repulsed, and all enemy forces which did manage to break through were pushed back in counterattacks. Two T-34's were hit in the fighting.

At 17.00 hours, there was a heavy enemy attack on the boundary between the II./1. Panzer-Grenadier-Regiment (under Hansen) and the III./1. Panzer-Grenadier-Regiment (under Weidenhaupt) near the Rogan station. Because there was no contact with the enemy in the sector held by the 2. Panzer-Grenadier-Regiment, Standartenführer Wisch moved the 8. and 9. Kompanie of his Regiment from Hf. Timtschenko and Hf. Mirgorod to Besljudowka in order to have them available as attack reserve for the left flank.

At 18.00 hours, a second attack on the Rogan station was repulsed by the II./1., but contact was lost between the 7. and 8. Kompanie of the 1. Panzer-Grenadier-Regiment. A gap opened up there.

At 19.30 hours, there was a renewed attack on Ternowo, and an attack on the bridge on the edge of Kirssanowka followed at 21.00 hours. Both attacks were repulsed in several hours of heavy close-range fighting, and our troops pursued the enemy forces into the forests south of Panskaja — Ternowka. At 22.00 hours, the enemy sent strong forces to put pressure on the Rogan station. A counterattack under the command of Sturmbannführer Max Hansen, the commander of the II./1., pushed the enemy infantry back. The Bataillon assumed a switch position one kilometer west of the Rogan station.

At 11.00 hours, the town of Rogan itself had to be abandoned by Kampfgruppe Weidenhaupt (III./1. and 1./1.), deployed farther to the north on both sides of the Tschugujew — Charkow road. In the withdrawal, however, Unterscharführer Lohr picked off another T-34 with his Pak.

A report prepared by Traugott Schmidt on the action of the 2. Panzer-Grenadier-Regiment *LAH*'s Stabskompanie follows:

> "We, i.e. the Kradzug under Oberscharführer Ladinger, occupied the right-hand sector of the town, to the right of the road, behind and in houses, behind hedges and manure piles. The Pionierzug occupied the outer left-hand section, thus the western part of Rogan. On the first day (10.2), it was beastly cold, and we mourned the death of Sturmmann Köhler. The enemy attacked in vain with machine guns and rifles. His assault forces were repulsed. In the evening, an order arrived (I do not know to this day from whom) for us to abandon the town and to assume a new position to the left of the Pionierzug. It was a road flanked by two rows of townhouses to the right and left. The first group was stationed behind the stairways and behind the right-hand block of houses under the command of Unterscharführer Henke. (He was wounded the next day, but reportedly is still alive and living in the Rheinland.) The second group, under Unterscharführer Dragan (an Italian by birth) was in front of the left-hand block of houses, and the third group under Unterscharführer Schmidt (from Speyer) was adjacent to it on the left. About fifty meters ahead of us, the Russian sharpshooters lay well disguised; their well-aimed shots at us did some 'mopping up.' I lay with Schütze Richter behind the stairs on the first-floor landing. The Pionierzug under Untersturmführer Kureth launched a relief attack, but it got caught in the rain of fire. In the meantime, Unterscharführer Schmidt and Unterscharführer Dragan had been killed. The enemy increased his attacks, shooting with mortars and ratschbums. The sounds of massive tank movements were audible. Oberscharführer Ladinger ordered a fifty-meter withdrawal to better cover behind the rows of houses. By this time of the morning (dawn on 11.2), the two Züge were practically destroyed. Richter, right next to me, took a shot in the head and died. I grabbed the MG 42 and the two magazines and was pulling back when Ivan's shells hit, and the red dust of the crumbling roof tiles cut off my visibility. Moving anywhere was fatal, for the enemy could see into everything. About ten men assembled behind the right-hand block of houses; that was all the men left over from both Züge. I noticed that Ladinger was wounded.
>
> Untersturmführer Kureth ran across the open area to the rear in order to see if there was a better spot to offer some defense. He came back and set us running with a quick 'March, march!' We ran just as if in a drill to the last house, where there stood a Pak with a gun crew. Oberscharführer Ladinger was not to be seen. Untersturmführer Kureth took a shot in his belly (and lived through it!).
>
> Today it sounds theatrical and ridiculous that I said to the few remaining men: 'Wait for the word of command!' I was the only MG-Schütze 1 left and still had my weapon. All the other MG 42's, a total of eight in the two Züge, were gone. We set up all-around defenses circling the house. Raging machine gun and rifle fire rained down upon us, and more men were killed.

To our great misfortune, three T-34's then attacked. The commander of the Pak crew, whose gunstand was frozen solid in the ground, uneasily requested us to help him turn the gun. We succeeded at the last second. I was wounded, but not seriously, in doing so. The Pak shot at and hit the first T-34 at a range of about twenty-five meters. Curiously, and I still do not understand to this day why, the two other tanks turned around and left. There were a few moments of peace. Suddenly, the Pak's prime mover arrived and hooked up the gun. We all jumped on and raced back to the tractor factory, or to put it more precisely, to the railway embankment. Untersturmführer Kuretch asked us to go without taking him along. We loaded him into the vehicle and took him away.
In the following night (from 13.2 to 14.2), the motorcycles and their drivers moved up from their post in the tractor factory. They told us to hold the airstrip. This was to be done with only twelve men?! A new order came for Charkow to be abandoned, but only after another well-known order had been issued. The motorcycles were destroyed before we got to them. We proceeded on foot.
This was the end of the Kradzug and the Pionierzug. I was awarded the Eisernes Kreuz II."

A telegram from the Oberfehlshaber of Armeeabteilung Lanz to Generalfeldmarschall von Manstein of Heeresgruppe B clearly demonstrates that the time had come for a clear decision on the part of the Armee and Korps: was Charkow to be held at the possible expense of an entire Korps, or was the mobile conduct of the campaign to be continued? The telegram reads as follows:

"10.2.1943, 18.00 hours
The order No. 654/43 g.Kdos. from the Oberkommando of Heeresgruppe B, just received, assigns the Armeeabteilung two missions:

1) Conducting an attack with the strongest forces possible from the SS-Panzerkorps to prevent the enemy from piercing the northern flank of Heeresgruppe Don and making it to Nowomoskowsk. This means launching an attack as far as the Losowaja area across a snow field over about one-hundred kilometers breadth as the crow flies.

2) Holding the Charkow area with crucial defense along a line of about one-hundred kilometers length as the crow flies.
The Armeeabteilung has for all practical purposes three Divisionen available to it for this mission (the *Leibstandarte*, Division *Das Reich*, Division *Großdeutschland*).
The 169. and 320. Division are so weakened in number and fighting ability that it would be best for the men to fight their way back through the enemy to save at least a part of their men. They must thereafter receive rest.
The leading elements of SS-Division *Totenkopf* are arriving near Poltawa. The entire Division will not be in place for another ten days.
It is unknown whether the intention exists to send more forces to the Charkow area. Opposing our three available Divisionen stand four

enemy armies. The new 69th Army had shown itself particularly powerful today, and its attack is already aimed at Charkow.
Given the current condition of our forces, the double mission assigned the Armeeabteilung is extremely difficult.
After waging tomorrow's attack, I will report whether I am able to accomplish this double task.

signed Lanz."

It is well known that under these circumstances the commanding general of the SS-Panzerkorps, Obergruppenführer Hausser, acted against a repeated, urgent order from the Führer and abandoned Charkow. In doing so he created the chance for the Oberkommando of Heeresgruppe B to give the enemy a "backhand slap" and wage the last great offensive success of the war. We will not go into it in detail here. My comrade Otto Weidinger has thoroughly handled this singular and monumental decision by the unforgettable Obergruppenführer Hausser in Volume III of his work "Division *Das Reich*." The Bundesverband der Soldaten der ehemaligen Waffen-SS e.V. (The Association of Soldiers of the Former Waffen-SS), moreover, has documented the sequence of events in their publication of the faithfully reproduced Armee and Korps combat journals in "Befehl des Gewissens" ["Command of Conscience"].

This author has therefore limited himself to providing the orders and reports between the Oberkommandos of the Heeresgruppe, the Armeeabteilung, and Korps from the end of that day. It is interesting to note how united all parties were in their evaluation of the situation, but that the Armee and the Heeresgruppe could not bring themselves to make the necessary decision. Our revered commanding general, Obergruppenführer Hausser, at first received no recognition, even though his decision created the basis for the subsequent successes, ultimately crowned by the recapture of Charkow. It was not until 1.7.1943 that Hitler at a speech to the commanders and generals who took part in operation "Zitadelle" finally awarded Hausser the golden party insignia. That was in the eyes of the Führer a high honor, to be sure. It is not known today how Obergruppenführer Hausser felt about the honor. My former commander, Obergruppenführer Sepp Dietrich, when the award was reported to him, is said to have remarked in laconic Bavarian dialect, "Der wird a Freid' ham" ["That will be a joy for him"].

In order to avoid more interruption in the narration of events, the author will not undertake here a correction of General Dr. Hans Speidel's erroneous presentation of the fighting for Charkow in his book "Aus unserer Zeit." Please refer to Appendix No. 5, where Dr. Speidel's work is discussed briefly.

13.2.1943: The I./2. sent out assault troops from the 1. and 3. Kompanie to clear away the remaining enemy support points in Borowoje. After the last men of the 320. Infanteriedivision had been gathered up, the enemy attacked again. He succeeded in breaking through into Lisogubowka at about 14.00 hours. A counterthrust was mounted immediately, involving elements of the 320. Infanteriedivision as well, and the situation was restored. Across from the 2. Panzer-Grenadier-Regiment, the enemy's attacks subsided in the late afternoon, and by nightfall they slacked off entirely.

The 8./2. (under Junge) was moved into the gap next to the II./1. (under Max Hansen), but the Kompanie was unable to establish direct contact. A Zug from the 9./2. (under Weitzel) was deployed farther to the north, but it, too, was unable to restore the contact. After conferring with the Division *Das Reich*, Standartenführer Wisch moved his line back to the eastern edge of Kirssanowka — eastern edge of Lisogubowka — Hp. Wassitschewo — Rogan railway station. The II./1. (under Hansen) was near Wassitschewo and the Rogan railway station.

The 10. (Werfer)/Artillerie-Regiment *LAH* under Obersturmführer Bartels served there as a considerable support to the defensive fighting.

North of there, Kampfgruppe Weidenhaupt held the railway embankment as far as the tractor factory near Lossewo.

Orders and reports from the command offices in charge on 12.2.1943 and 13.2.1943:

The Oberbefehlshaber of the Armeeabteilung, General der Gebirgstruppen Lanz, reported to the Heeresgruppe on 12.2.1943 at 21.25 hours as follows:

> "My impression on the battlefield of the enemy's situation and our own troops' combat worthiness compel me again today to give the following report:
>
> 1) The enemy today attacked our Charkow defensive front heavily from the east and the north. While local incursions on the eastern front and on both sides of the road to Belgorod could still be counterbalanced by the deployment of our last reserves, enemy forces supported by tanks late this afternoon made a thrust against the weak Aufklärungsabteilung *Großdeutschland* and pushed through as far as Dergatschi. Countermeasures are underway.
> Under the pressure created by this situation, the defensive ring around the city must be pulled in closer tomorrow.
> I consider it my duty to report that if the concentrated attacks from the superior enemy forces continue, particularly from the northwest, the city can only be held for a few more days, even if the forces in place for decisive defense (the Infanteriedivision *Großdeutschland* and elements of the SS-Panzerkorps) are sacrificed.
> Soon I will be forced to make use of the authority given me to begin the destruction and blasting of the roads and other installations in the city."

From the Generalkommano of the SS-Panzerkorps to Armeeabteilung Lanz on 13.2.1943:

> "The heaviest attacks, supported by tanks, are hitting the SS-Division *Das Reich* in the sector Rogan — Bjrak with the intention of making a deep breakthrough north of Rogan near Satische. The forces on hand to prevent it are entirely insufficient. An incursion into the tractor factory during the night between 13.2 and 14.2 is possible. The Korps expects that even after pulling back the defensive front it will be able to hold the designated line until the evening of 14.2 at the latest. Thereafter, an orderly retreat can no longer be guaranteed. Heavy losses of men and materiel can be expected.

An immediate order to abandon Charkow on the evening of 14.2 and to begin the blasting on the morning of 14.2 is unconditionally necessary."

Excerpts from the Kriegstagebuch of Armeeabteilung Lanz, dated 13.2:

"At 12.30 hours, General Lanz said in a telephone conversation to Obergruppenführer Hausser:

'Defense must be offered; orders to that effect have come from the highest level."

At 16.50 hours, the Ia of the SS-Panzerkorps reported to the Armee:
'In Rogan and northwest of there, there has been a deep incursion almost as far as the tractor factory. Forces not available to close it off.'

At 18.00 hours, the SS-Panzerkorps reported to the Armee:
'The heaviest attacks are hitting the SS-Division *Das Reich*; breakthrough near Rogan and Satische. The forces to prevent it are insufficient. Holding the line, even pulled back as ordered, is possible until the evening of 14.2 at the latest. Thereafter, heavy losses of men and materiel resulting from a major incursion into the city can be expected. An immediate order to abandon Charkow on the evening of 14.2 and to begin the blasting on the morning of 14.2 is unconditionally necessary.'
(This report was passed along to the OKH in this formulation.)

At 19.00 hours, the Oberbefehlshaber informed Obergruppenführer Hausser:
'I agree that

1. the defensive line be pulled in tighter,

2. blasting be allowed to begin,

3. all the vehicles not required for conduct of the battle be pulled out.

With that, your requests are granted.

The mission for tomorrow is defense of the closer line and continuation of the attack to the south.'"

Transcript of message from the Generalkommando of the SS-Panzerkorps No. 136/43 g.Kdos. of 13.2.1943, received 14.2.1943 at 02.55 hours to Armeeabteilung Lanz:

For the further conduct of the battle, the Generalkommando proposes:

1) In the night between 14.2 and 15.2, withdrawal to behind the Udy sector, with the following deployments:

   a) the 320. Infanteriedivision in the sector from the Charkow road in Wodjanoje to Merefa (exclusive of it)

b) the reinforced SS-"D" in the sector from the Charkow road — Merefa (inclusive of it) — Korotitsch (inclusive of it)

c) contact with Korps Krauss near Korotitsch

d) withdrawal of Gruppe Wisch to the area around and southwest of Merefa; preparation of a covering position on both sides of Merefa

e) relief of elements of Sicherungsdivision 213 and preparation of a covering position on the Merefa on both sides of Ljubotin.

2) In the night between 15.2 and 16.2, withdrawal to behind the Merefa sector, with the following deployments

a) a withdrawal of the 320. Infanteriedivision to the Merefa sector on both sides of Merefa to the Gruppe Wisch covering position

b) withdrawal of Gruppe Wisch and move to join the attack to the south

d) [sic]connection of Korps Krauss to the 320. Infanteriedivision on the Merefa southeast of Ljubotin

e) assumption of command over the 320. Infanteriedivision by Korps Krauss.

A quick decision is requested, because the roads must be reconnoitered, the snow cleared, and the traffic patterns arranged by the morning of 14.2.

Chef

14.2.1943: At 03.00 hours, there were attacks by enemy batallions on the positions of Kampfgruppe Linden near Lisogubowka and Kirssanowka. The Kampfgruppe, ably supported by the Flakzüge of the 4./Flakabteilung *LAH* under Untersturmführer Armberger and Untersturmführer Kunde, threw the enemy back out of our positions.

At 03.30 hours, an Ordonnanzoffizier was ordered to go to the headquarters of the Division *Das Reich* and receive the preliminary orders for moving to an assembly area near Nowaja Wodolaga (south of Merefa).

At 11.10 hours, the enemy made an incursion near Kampfgruppe Weidenhaupt north of the Rogan railway station and started marching toward Ossnowa. The Regiment's commander, Standartenführer Wisch, deployed the remaining elements of the 9. Kompanie, reinforced by the Sturmgeschütze from the 2. Sturmgeschützabteilung *LAH* (under Rettlinger) to wage a counterattack at the enemy flank under the commander of the II./2. (Sturmbannführer Sandig). This action succeeded in pushing the enemy back as far as the airstrip. The elements involved remained there as a covering force to keep the rear open for the Regiment.

At 16.50 hours, there was an enemy attack on Lisogubowka (held by the Kampfgruppe Linden), but it was repulsed and four T-34's were hit.

At 20.00 hours, there was a Soviet attack on the Sidki railway station and on the southern edge of Borowoje, in the area held by the I./2. It collapsed under concentrated fire from all the heavy weapons. A KV I was destroyed in the action. By evening, the eastern front held by the *LAH* elements ran from Mirgorod — Sidki railway station — Borowoje — Lisogubowka East — Hp. Wossytschewo — the hills 1.5 kilometers west of Rogan — Losewo East.

Orders and reports from the command authorities on 14.2:

At 05.10 hours, an order from Heeresgruppe Süd to the Armee:

"The Führer has ordered that all positions around Charkow are to be held under all circumstances, even if that means that the SS-Panzerkorps' thrust to the south must be temporarily halted. Localized incursions in the Charkow area are to be brought under control by mobile combat actions."

At 07.20 hours, the Oberbefehlshaber ordered the subordinated Korps to hold all the positions around Charkow in accordance with the Führer's order. An attempt was made to make forces available from the SS-Panzerkorps attack troops in order to counterbalance any enemy incursion into Charkow. The streets and bridges could not yet be blown up because our own troops still had to travel over them.

At 08.00 hours, the Oberfehlshaber flew to the SS-Panzerkorps in Merefa, where he was briefed on the situation and conferred repeatedly with the commanding general about the Führer's order.

At 08.20 hours, the Korps sent the Armee the following message by radio:

A decision about pulling back must be made by 12.00 hours.

At 09.15 hours, there was a telephone conversation between the Chef of the Generalstab of the Armeeabteilung and the Chef of the Generalstab of the Heeresgruppe, General Schulz:

Chef of the Armee:

The Führer's instructions are clear. The danger of being surrounded is, however, acute.

Orientation: the enemy is moving wide to the west, and his leading elements are on both sides of Olschany and Bogoduchow. We have only small forces there. The arc is stretched too far. There has already been contact with the enemy near Krassnograd, albeit with weak forces. Krassnograd must remain firmly in our hands as a supply base.

General Schulz agreed.

Chef of the Armee:

Intention: assemble the bulk of the SS "T" around Poltawa. The 320. Infanteriedivision must be moved north. Request permission from the Oberbefehlshaber to move the Armee Stab quarters to Poltawa and the advance headquarters to Walki.

General Schulz: No objections.

At 10.50 hours, there was a written Armee order, the first paragraph of which read:

> Our positions around Charkow are to be held, on orders from the Führer, under all conditions.

At 13.30 hours, the O1 of the Armee transmitted another written order to the SS-Panzerkorps that the positions around Charkow were to be held and that the Gruppe Dietrich was to continue its attack.

At 16.20 hours, there was a telephone conversation between the Chef of the Armee and Generalmajor Kinzel (Chef of the Korps Raus). Obergruppenführer Hausser had the information transmitted to him, because he was without telephone lines:

1. The situation on the eastern front of Charkow near Division *Das Reich* has developed so unfavorably under the heavy enemy pressure that the city and our forces will be lost if no order to pull back the present line is given by 16.30.

2. In Charkow itself there is unrest among the civilian population, which has begun to arm itself, and there have already been deaths.

3. If the order to pull back the line is not given by 16.00 hours, Obergruppenführer Hausser will do it himself.

The Chef of the Generalstab of Armeeabteilung Lanz repeated the order from the Oberbefehlshaber, that all positions around Charkow were to be held, in accordance with the Führer's orders, under all circumstances.

At 16.45 hours, there was a radio message from the Generalkommando of the SS-Panzerkorps to Armeeabteilung Lanz:

> At 16.45 hours on 14.2, I gave orders to abandon Charkow and at the same time for Korps Raus to move behind the Udy sector in the night between 14.2 and 15.2. Evaluation of the situation to follow in writing.

At 17.25 hours, there was a radio message from Armeeabteilung Lanz to the Generalkommando of the SS-Panzerkorps:

> In accordance with the Führer's orders, the Panzerkorps is to hold its present position on the eastern front of Charkow to the last man. Signed, Lanz.

At 18.00 hours, there was a telephone conversation between the Oberbefehlshaber and Obergruppenführer Hausser:

OB:	Inquiry as to situation.
Hausser:	Strong preparations underway for a breakthrough onto the southern airstrip, which is in the enemy's hands.
OB:	Whether the positions were held today?
Hausser:	At the moment, yes, but the order to retreat was given a half hour ago.
OB:	This order contradicts the Führer's order, and it is therefore to be rescinded.
Hausser:	Doubt whether this order can be rescinded.

OB:	The Führer's order is to be executed. The 320. Infanteriedivision is to be deployed in a counterattack.
Hausser:	Division is still in Smijew and unavailable.
OB:	The Division is to be brought up immediately.
Hausser:	There are no forces available to fight their way forward. The horses themselves are too weak even to march.

At 21.00 hours, the daily report from the SS-Panzerkorps and Korps Raus read as follows (excerpt):

On the defensive front, the enemy has succeeded in occupying the southern airstrip and in breaking into Ossnowa.

Mopping up the situation is not possible with the small number of forces available. In the city, there is unrest and activity by armed groups of civilian bandits.

Korps Raus: In the area held by Infanteriedivision *Großdeutschland*, the enemy has managed to break into the forest region south of Dergatschi and south of Olschany despite heroic defensive fighting. The fighting is, however, tearing our forces to pieces...

Intention for 15.2:

1. Continuation of the defense of Charkow in accordance with the Führer's orders.

2. Attack by Stoßgruppe Dietrich (*LAH*) must be suspended temporarily and the terrain already captured must be held. Elements from Stoßgruppe Dietrich and from SS-"T" must be used to wage a counterattack from Walki against the enemy forces which have crossed the line Olschany-Bogoduchoff.

The wording of the evening report ended by accepting the order issued by the Generalkommando of the SS-Panzerkorps:

The Oberbefehlshaber once again points out that, despite repeated express orders to hold the Charkow positions in accordance with the Führer's wishes, the commanding general of the SS-Panzerkorps has given orders to retreat behind the Udy sector. In repeated attempts expressly to reiterate the order, the Oberbefehlshaber received from General Hausser an expression of doubt that his order could effectively be rescinded. At present, an inquiry into the matter is underway. The Oberbefehlshaber declares in closing that he requests a decree from the Führer; in the face of failure to follow clearly given orders, he is no longer in a position to command the Armeeabteilung.

At 21.30 hours, the SS-Panzerkorps reported its intended action for 15.2:

To hold Charkow to the last man...

At 22.30 hours, the SS-Panzerkorps in its written evaluation of the situation (considerable enemy incursion, insufficient forces to mop up the area, threat to the supply roads, danger of being surrounded) requested a decree from the Führer as to whether Charkow was to be held to the last man.

At 23.00 hours, Standartenführer Ostendorf confirmed that the line designated on 14.2 was to be held on 15.2.

15.2.1943: At 05.30 hours the enemy attacked the eastern edge of Lisogubowka (held by Kampfgruppe Linden) and was able to break through at that point. The enemy was thrown back in a counterattack and the original battle line reestablished.

At 07.10 hours, a reconnaissance probe by a weak enemy force on the Sidki railway station was repulsed.

At 11.00 hours, the Regiment's commander, Standartenführer Wisch, launched a counterattack from the south on Ossnowa using forces from the 15./1. Panzer-Grenadier-Regiment (under Hauptsturmführer Pinter). The enemy suffered bloody losses. On our side, the second Kompanieführer, Hauptsturmführer Pinter, was killed. The Panzer-Grenadier-Division *Das Reich* requested an attack by the III. (armoured)/2. Panzer-Grenadier-Regiment *LAH* under Sturmbannführer Peiper, which was successful in penetrating Ossnowa from the west, but a Schützenpanzerwagen fell victim to close-range Russian anti-tank fighters (Molotov cocktails). After conferring with the Ia of the *LAH*, the Ia of the *DR*, Sturmbannführer Max Schulz called off the attack, and the Bataillon was called back to Artemowka (just north of Merefa) in the early morning hours on 16.2. Obersturmführer Döhring was badly wounded in the action.

At 15.30 hours, the Panzer-Grenadier-Division *Das Reich* ordered that the battle line be pulled back starting at 00.00 hours to the line Lisogubowka — loading ramp — point 146.8 — two kilometers northwest of Besljudowka. Along the railway embankment and at the tractor factory held by Kampfgruppe Weidenhaupt and the 1./1. Panzer-Grenadier-Regiment *LAH*, there was heavy fighting the entire day, just as there had been on the previous day. In the course of the day on 15.2, Hauptsturmführer Hubert Meyer took over the command of this Kampfgruppe. Untersturmführer Schmolke, at the time a Zugführer in the 1./1., provided the following summary of the fighting around Rogan:

> "We had hardly reached Rogan on 10.2. I had just gotten a bucket of water to give myself a thorough cleaning. There I stood half-naked when a messenger found me. 'The Russians are on the eastern edge of town!' They had followed us faster than expected. Shortly thereafter the fighting for this town began, fighting which lasted until 12.2. I had command of the Infanterie in the center of town, while the Zug of the 5. (heavy) Kompanie under Untersturmführer Troschier was stationed on a hill just north of town. The Russian forces were clearly numerically superior; one could see with the naked eye how they streamed over the hill on the east side of town, their officers high on their horses. The fighting brought us continual losses, particularly men being shot in the head because they were always caught if they so much as looked out from their cover to observe or to shoot. At the time I calculated that we suffered a casualty every quarter hour. In rapid order fell Untersturmführer Berger, commander of the Zug next to mine, Unterscharführer Spandack, an experienced non-commissioned officer from the same Zug, and a great number of men. Finally, the first Gruppe of my Zug consisted of only one man. In the night between 13.2 and 14.2, I had Gruppe Kenngott in reserve. The continuing casualty rate made reinforcements necessary, so the Regiment's Kradzug (under Oberscharführer Ladinger) and finally the Regiment's Pionierzug (under Untersturmführer Kureth) were put into action. I had planned an assault

force action for 13.2 to capture a large building from which the enemy had a clear shot at us. I had received a promise of Pak and Infanteriegeschütz for the action and had made all the necessary preparations when a report came that a Russian force had broken through on my right wing. Among other things, there was an enemy tank in an orchard. I launched a counterthrust with my reserve, the Gruppe Kenngott, threw the Russians back, and occupied our former positions. Even the tank must have felt a little uncomfortable in the middle of town, for it abandoned the orchard in short order."

At 16.00 hours, the Korps ordered the Pionierzug of the II./2. Panzer-Grenadier-Regiment be deployed near Timtschenkow in order to prevent the Russians from moving into the Msha valley.

At 17.30 hours, the enemy broke into Kirssanowka and was pushed back by a counterthrust by Kampfgruppe Linden. Untersturmführer Semmelrock was badly wounded in the fighting. At 22.30 hours, a new battle line was established starting from the left wing (II./1. under Sturmbannführer Max Hansen) because the enemy was attempting to go around the left wing by moving through the gap near the southern airstrip.

At 23.30 hours, there was a heavy enemy attack on the pivot point of the 2. Panzer-Grenadier-Regiment *LAH*, Lisogubowka, but it was repulsed by the 6./1. (under Hauptsturmführer Weiher).

Orders and reports from the command authorities on 15.2.1943:

At 02.41 hours, Heeresgruppe Süd reported via radio that the Führer, upon the inquiry of Generalfeldmarschall von Manstein, had decided that Charkow must be held under all circumstances, but that the combat in the Charkow area was to be structured to be mobile in order to prevent the city from being surrounded.

At 06.40 hours, the SS-Panzerkorps reported via radio:

In front of the eastern front heavy enemy preparations near Bobrow. Unsuccessful in clearing Ossnowa of enemy forces. Since 04.15 hours, heavy enemy attack with tank support on the northern wing and on the road west of Rogan.

At 09.30 hours, a telephone conversation between the Oberbefehlshaber and the Chef of Heeregruppe Süd:

OB: In accordance with new orders, the Armeeabteilung has as its sole mission the holding of Charkow, for the order to attack to the south is now rescinded. Its continuation is to be stopped. The principal threat at the moment is in the northwest.... The intention is to form two sectors to the southeast and northwest, with mobile combat in the area between the front line and the edge of the city.

Chef: Agreed with the measures taken and the intention.

At 09.43 hours, radio message from Korps Raus:

The enemy has moved more than a batallion into the northwest part of Charkow, with more troops following. The forces are not available to clear the enemy away from our defenses on the western edge. The orders given by the Führer could not be carried out. In order to save at least part of the Division *Großdeutschland* and SS-Division *Das Reich*, we once again request orders to fight our way to the southwest.

At 11.00 hours, the Oberbefehlshaber, after presenting the desperate situation, gave Heeresgruppe Süd a new evaluation in a telegram:

> If the battle is continued, heavy losses of both men and materiel are to be expected to the north and east of the city. Therefore, a suggestion: pull back the front to a line from Smijew — Merefa — western edge of Ljubotin — Boguduchoff — Kirikowka. Decision requested.

At 11.25 hours, there was a call from the Chef of the Generalstab of the Heer, General der Infanterie Zeitzler. The Oberbefehlshaber briefed him about the heavy enemy attacks against the Charkow front, which had been underway for four days already, and about the pullback of the troops from the defensive front, as had been ordered, for the attack to the south. The attack to the south had come to a temporary conclusion on the previous day after three days of fighting with the destruction of most of the Russian VIth Guard Cavalry Corps. The Oberbefehlshaber went on to describe the weakened defensive forces, the enemy's ten-fold numerical superiority, the fighting in Charkow, the enemy incursions resulting from this superiority, and the danger of the forces in the east being surrounded. A decision was urgently requested as to whether the eastern front was still to held.

The Chef of the Generalstab of the Heer asked whether troops could be moved up from the south. The Oberfehlshaber responded:

> Perhaps a Regiment, but not yet available for action in city because it must first clear the road Walki — Ljubotin — Charkow. Therefore suggest you pull back this evening behind the Merefa sector, since the unit would be lost with continued waiting.

The Chef of the Generalstab of the Heer asked why the SS-Panzerkorps had been pulled back to Charkow so quickly.

> The Oberbefehlshaber responded that Division *Das Reich* had to be pulled back to the Donez because it was already surrounded, and the Division's thrust could not be supported by the *LSSAH*. This Division was already stretched along a front eighty kilometers long. If he himself had not arranged for the Division to be pulled back during his last visit, it would have been destroyed in its position before the Don in the opinion of the Korps.

The Chef of the Generalstab of the Heer offered assurances that the Führer's decision would be issued soon.

At 11.30 hours, a new Armeebefehl was issued, based on the Führer's command, for the defense of Charkow. At 13.15 hours, the Führer's decision arrived:

1) The western front of Charkow is to be held.

2) The arriving SS units are to be used to fight the road to Charkow free and to destroy the enemy forces pressing in on Charkow from the northwest.

This decree from the Führer was transmitted immediately to the SS-Panzerkorps and confirmed there at 15.07 hours.

At 13.32 hours a radio message arrived from Korps Raus; it had been sent at 12.40 hours. It reported that the front had been penetrated in several places and that strong enemy forces were flowing from the northwest toward Charkow. The situation had grown so critical that escape from some parts of Charkow was possible only if immediate orders were given to do so. The city was no longer to be held. The Korps headquarters was moved to Merefa.

At 13.40 hours, a radio message (sent at 13.05 hours) arrived from Obergruppenführer Hausser:

> At 13.00 hours, orders given to fight the way through to the Udy sector. Korps Raus informed. At 14.33 hours, a radio message (sent at 13.32 hours) arrived from the SS-Panzerkorps:
>
> The enemy in the western and southwestern sections of Charkow, and new enemy forces now in Bogdanowka-Andrejewka. Intended action for 16.2: pull back to the south behind the Msha — Merefa line.

At 15.15 hours, the Ia of Armeeabteilung Lanz called the Ia of Heeresgruppe Süd to transmit the radio messages from Korps Raus and the SS-Panzerkorps and to report that the Führer's decree had been transmitted to both Korps and that the Oberbefehlshaber himself had flown to visit both.

The Chef of the Heeresgruppe demanded that the Armee take a position as to whether Obergruppenführer Hausser's course of action could be approved in the face of the fact that execution of the Führer's decree was no longer possible, or whether, in the event that the Obergruppenführer's actions were not approved, the SS-Obergruppenführer would be asked to offer a request to be relieved of duty.

The Ia of the Armeeabteilung reported that no position could be taken until the Oberbefehlshaber could return and give his personal impressions of the situation.

At 15.50 hours, Infanteriedivision *Großdeutschland* reported by radio that there were deep breakthroughs in two places on the northern front in the western part of Charkow. The Division was retreating to the south and holding open the march route to the west. The Division had begun to disengage from the enemy at 14.00 hours. Rear guard groups were holding the northern and northwestern edge of Charkow. The intended action: withdrawal to behind the Udy sector.

At 16.50 hours, the Oberbefehlshaber announced in a radio message to SS-Obergruppenführer Hausser that, in order to prevent at the last minute the forces fighting on the northern and eastern edges of Charkow from being surrounded and lost, as desired in the Führer's decree, the Oberbefehlshaber was in agreement with the new battle line at the Udy sector, as envisioned by Obergruppenführer Hausser.

In a second radio message, the Oberbefehlshaber offered Obergruppenführer Dietrich sincere congratulations on his victory over the Russian VIth Cavalry Corps.

Telegram KR

Secret (after arrival to be treated as top secret document)
15.2.1943 24.00 hours

To

1) OKH Generalstab of the Heer/Operationsabteilung (Ia)

2) Oberkommando of Heeresgruppe Süd/Ia

Concerning:
Communication from OKH Generalstab of the Army/Operationsabteilung (Ia) of 15.2.1943 at 20.54 hours

To augment my telegram of 15.2 at 17.00 hours to Heeresgruppe Süd, I report the following:

In my reports of 11.2, 12.2, and 13.2 to Heeresgruppe B, I referred to the fact that if both missions were insisted upon, i.e. attack to the south and defense to the north, the city could not be held later than 15.2.

Our observations at the time indicated only eighteen enemy units before Charkow with a combined strength of one division. Since the morning of 15.2, twenty rifle divisions, four rifle brigades, ten tank brigades, two tank regiments, two motorized brigades and two cavalry divisions have been discerned. Our Armeeabteilung, on the other hand, has now only two Divisionen, one of which (*Großdeutschland*) is severely weakened.

The enemy had succeeded in breaking through into the northwestern and southeastern parts of the city on 14.2, and even using our last reserves in a counterthrust, we were only partially successful in pushing him back. In the morning on 15.2, three enemy divisions penetrated the northwestern and western sections of the city so deeply that they threatened to cut off our forces fighting in the east and north. Other localized incursions, particularly the expansion of the deep thrust into the southeastern front, threatened to surround us completely. Forces were no longer available to expand or even to hold open our corridor, only two kilometers in width.

In this situation, Obergruppenführer Hausser reached his decision, transmitted by radio, to pull back behind the Udy. At the headquarters of the SS-Panzerkorps, I reviewed the combat conditions in and around Charkow shortly after his radio message had been sent and had the situation explained to me. In light of the estimate of enemy forces facing our men, I was forced to approve his decision. I thereby acted in accordance with the Führer's orders to prevent the troops fighting on the eastern and northern fronts from being surrounded and destroyed.

signed, Lanz.

With that, a temporary conclusion was reached concerning the abandonment of Charkow.

16.2.1943: In the middle sector occupied by the 2. Panzer-Grenadier-Regiment, Kampfgruppe Linden, the II./2. Panzer-Grenadier-Regiment, and the right wing of the II./1. Panzer-Grenadier-Regiment disengaged from the enemy without being observed at 00.00 hours, and by 05.00 hours had occupied the new battle line northwest of Besljudowka. The new headquarters of the 2. Panzer-Grenadier-Regiment *LAH* was in Corecho. Contact had not yet been established to the north with the 7./1. Panzer-Grenadier-Regiment (under Obersturmführer Denecke). This Kompanie had subordinated itself in the meantime to the III./1. Panzer-Grenadier-Regiment. At 06.00 hours, the enemy broke through into Krissanowka and was thrown back in a counterthrust by Kampfgruppe Linden.

At about noon, the III. (armoured)/2. Panzer-Grenadier-Regiment (under Sturmbannführer Peiper) reported that it had assumed billets in Komarowka. On the left wing of the eastern front, held by the reinforced III./1. Panzer-Grenadier-Regiment, the Chef of the 1. Kompanie, Hauptsturmführer Springer, was wounded as he left his Kompanie headquarters. He was succeeded by Untersturmführer Schmolke. He wrote in his report:

> I assumed command of the Kompanie. As we were moving up a hill, Untersturmführer Troschier with his Zug came toward us from the north, and he subordinated his unit to me on the spot. It was an impossible situation: lacking heavy weapons, I requested the only self-propelled Pak we had to cover our retreat, and I pulled back the Kompanie onto both sides of the road Tschugujew — Charkow. In an attempt to gain control of the forces, I ordered them to move into position halfway up the hill on both sides of the road. It took some time for my order to be passed on correctly, for the Russians kept shooting at us with Ratschbums and machine guns, and that held up the equipment. My messenger got his eye shot out. He was whisked away in a motorcycle, and I did not see him again until much later in Berlin. The men, totally apathetic and exhausted from the sleepless nights of the preceding days, were toiling up the next hill and at first did not react to my order. Infuriated, I issued the word: 'Any man retreating farther will be shot.' That worked; the men stopped and the non-commissioned officers began to reorder their groups. An Untersturmführer unknown to me raced up to the leading elements and hit the men in front with his ski poles, shouting: 'Didn't you hear the order from your Chef down below?' We finally succeeded in bringing the Kompanie into position on both sides of the road, which meant at first that every man lay there devoid of cover. We were just readying our front to face the enemy when three T-34's pulled up from the town. I was lying in the ditch beside the road and could just get out the order: 'Open fire on the pursuing infantry!' Then the first T-34 was upon us. But it rode right on by. The next tank stopped a few meters in front of us and a couple of Russians jumped out. One of them was immediately shot and killed. While that was going on, the third tank rolled on past us, too. The front T-34 knocked off a Pak gun which was trying to move into position down the hill. A Sturmgeschütz, however, hit the T-34 shortly thereafter. The second tank turned around and drove back down the hill at top speed. The tank right in front of us sat there with no discernible damage, but it did not move. As soon as things had settled down a little, I attempted late in the afternoon to establish contact to the left (thus, the north), where as far as I knew the 4. (MG) Kompanie was in position (it was the Regiment's Pionierzug). Only a few

meters from the position held by the unit adjacent to the left, I came under machine gun fire from in front, crashing my vehicle, and received a severe wound to my head. The nearest soldier was a young Pionier in battle for the first time. He bandaged my head according to my instructions, and I was taken to Untersturmführer Troschier, to whom I gave command of the Kompanie of about eighty men. A motorcycle was called, which took me to the medical clearing station, where I received my first medical attention from Hauptsturmführer Dr. Klein, the Regiment's dentist. The Kompanie was deployed on 16.2 under Untersturmführer Troschier by the III./1. Panzer-Grenadier-Regiment *LAH* to clear enemy forces from the tractor factory, but it was unable to make it through. After that, the Kompanie vanished without a trace. Heinz Troscher was listed as missing on 16.2.1943. From this proud Kompanie, four men, including the brave Kompanie medic Halder, managed to make it back to Merefa in a captured T-34. The Chef of the Replacement Office of the Waffen-SS, Obergruppenführer Berger, whose son was killed in this Kompanie, sent up a new Kompanie, composed entirely of ethnic Germans from Siebenbürgen, in the pause before Operation Zitadelle. This Kompanie was under the command of Obersturmführer von Christen."

At 15.00 hours, the orders arrived for Division *Das Reich* to pull back to the Udy sector starting at 00.00 hours on 17.2. The reinforced III./1. with the remaining elements of the 1./1. and the 7./1. were relieved and moved back to join the 1. Panzer-Grenadier-Regiment.

The new battle line was held by the following units:

There was a support point (Stützpunkt Scappini held by the 6./2. Panzer-Grenadier-Regiment) in Konstantowka with its front to the south and southeast; adjoining it was the I./2. Panzer-Grenadier-Regiment (under Sturmbannführer Kraas) with Kampfgruppe Linden, stretching all the way to Hp. Wassitschewo on the Udy; there the adjacent unit was the I./1. Panzer-Grenadier-Regiment (under Sturmbannführer Max Hansen); the left wing of the Hansen force was at the Stichow railway station, where the II./2. Panzer-Grenadier-Regiment (under Sturmbannführer Sandig) adjoined it and extended to the northern corner of Choroschewo; there Panzer-Grenadier-Regiment *Deutschland* joined on. At 22.00 hours, another attack on Lisogubowka had to be repulsed, and another attack followed at 23.00 hours, this time extending to Kirssanowka, as well. In this attack, the headquarters of Kampfgruppe Linden was destroyed in shelling, and about ten motorcycles parked on the road were flattened. A Russian tank collapsed the rough-hewn bridge which the Pioniere had constructed.

Our counterthrust was successful in clearing these towns, and Kampfgruppe Linden and the reinforced I./2. (under Kraas) were able to withdraw unmolested.

Elements of the Kaschula reserve force, sent to provide cover for the withdrawal, were absorbed into the new battle line. The move back across the Udy terrain, deeply cut by gorges and gullies, was made even more difficult by the icy roads. The kinds of obstacles which had to be overcome are apparent in the description provided by the Kommandant of a Sturmgeschütz, Erwin Jäckel:

"In the night, the last elements began to move back. It was bitterly cold. The whole night through, it was wait, drive, wait, drive. We finally came to a straight piece of road with the forest to the right, open terrain to the left, and the frozen Udy about two hundred meters ahead. On the other side, there was a railway line running along the hill. We could hear the dull sound of blasting. Suddenly a group of Landsers appeared at the side of the road, shouting wildly and waving their arms. I stopped my Sturmgeschütz and asked what the matter was. They said that the prime mover pulling their 10-centimeter Kanone was broken down and had already been towed away. The recovery vehicle was unable, however, to pull the gun. Could we tow it and take them along? Sure, we said, hitch the thing up, jump aboard my Panzer, and off we go. Everything went just fine as long as the road was level. But things changed as we approached the crossing over the Udy. There was a sharp drop down to the bridge and a steep climb up the other side. Our little procession of Sturmgeschütz and 10-centimeter Kanone drove down the incline slowly in first gear. But the Kanone pushed so hard from behind that the Sturmgeschütz's right track ended up in the ditch beside the road. Attempts to get back up on the road bore no fruit, so the whole procession had to travel all the way down in the ditch. At a flat spot on the bottom we got out of the ditch. It went all right across the bridge, but how were we going to get up that steep bank? The road had been worn down smooth as glass. Off we went. We took a run at it, shifted down, and everyone jumped out. Whether a Kanonier or a Sturmgeschützmann, everyone pushed: twenty-four tonnes of Sturmgeschütz, an attached 10-centimeter Kanone, and the mounting. No flyweight, to be sure. Almost at the top, the tracks started turning without biting into anything. Damned nuisance! But other comrades ran to us and pushed with all their might. We made it! We dropped the Kanone off beside a wall in the next village and received the thanks of its crew. We finally reached our Batterie. The next day, the commander of the Artillerie-Regiment thanked us by telegram for saving his men and gun."

The reinforced III./1. (1./1., 7./1., Regiment-Pionierzug and Kradzug), positioned at the tractor factor, also received orders the next morning to disengage from the enemy at midnight and to march to Merefa, where it was to come under the command of the 1. Panzer-Grenadier-Regiment (under Standartenführer Witt) once more.

The Kampfgruppe's commander decided to use the 7./1. (under Obersturmführer Denecke) as rear guard and to begin withdrawing the bulk of his Kampfgruppe at nightfall.

The Kompanieführer of the 7./1. Panzer-Grenadier-Regiment *LAH*, Obersturmführer Denecke, reported on his unit's fighting as follows:

"While all the other units were set on the march to the rear, I received orders to use a Kampfgruppe consisting of the remaining men of the 7. Kompanie, one Pionierzug, and three self-propelled Pak to hold the road on the eastern edge of Charkow and about three hundred meters on each side of it open until 24.00 hours. We were also to prevent the enemy from making pursuit too early. The order continued: 'After a green flare is fired at 24.00 hours, pull back and march on foot to march route marker 21, moving to the southwest past the edge of Charkow to the rear position near Merefa on the Udy sector.' Seldom had we counted the hours and minutes as we did then, for the enemy had been pressing in on the city

Obersturmbannführer Kurt Meyer.
Was one hundred ninety-fifth soldier
to receive the Eichenlaub on23.2.1943
as commander of the
Aufklärungsabteilung/LSSAH.

Sturmbannführer Max Wünsche.
Received Ritterkreuz on 28.2.1943 as
commander of the I./SS-Panzer-
regiment 1.

Hauptsturmführer Heinz Kling
Received Ritterkreuz on 23.2.1944 as Chef of the 13. (heavy) /SS-Panzerregiment 1 LSSAH.

Hauptsturmführer Erich Grätz.
Received Ritterkreuz on 14.5.1944 as leader of an LSSAH combat force.

Obersturmführer Heinz Nowotnik.
Received Ritterkreuz on 14.5.1944 as Untersturmführer and Kompanieführer of the 14. (MG) /SS-Panzergrenadier-Regiment 1 LSSAH.

Unterscharführer Hans Dauser.
Received Ritterkreuz on 4.6.1944 as Oberscharführer and a Zugführer in the 2./SS-Panzerregiment 1 LSSAH.

north of us since the last afternoon; by evening it was somewhat quieter. Combat alert condition was relaxed, and it appeared that for the most part the city had already been abandoned.

Finally I was able to fire the green flare. Our group, consisting of about seventy men from the 7. Kompanie, about fifteen men of the subordinated Pionierzug, and the three self-propelled Pak, started its march. The Pak had to leave us after only a short time. They would have gotten stuck in the difficult snowy terrain. They were going to attempt to break through across the city, and we learned later that they in fact succeeded.

In a seemingly endless row, the exhausted men in their snow smocks tramped one behind the other through snow up to their knees. The fog kept us from seeing our surroundings. I kept having the march route markers checked. I sent Spiekhoven to the end of the column. He spoke a little Russian and was to attempt, in the event of contact with pursuing Russian reconnaissance troops, to fool them. From the beginning, this march seemed horrible and the decision to make it seemed impossible to defend. The deep snow, the rolling terrain with its poor visibility, and the level of exhaustion among all the men left us no other choice. So we trudged silently along one behind the other for about five hours without coming into contact with the enemy; later we discovered that in five hours we had barely left the suburbs of Charkow. Suddenly, the group in front saw a group of five houses spring up before them out of the fog. Behind these typical thatched-roof clay cottages, we saw about one hundred meters from us the road leading to Smijew, and on it an endless column of Russian infantry clad in long coats silently marching toward Charkow. Marching foot soldiers in tight ranks alternated with a few horse-drawn wagons. There must have been thousands of them, stretching from the horizon on our left to far in the direction of Charkow. At first we were frozen to the spot with fear; they had not seen us yet. I signalled for the troops to lie down. My messenger, Sepp Tellerfuß, who was with me at the front of the column, carefully brought his machine gun into position. Several comrades fanned out to the right and used the houses for cover. We had to attempt to make it across the road before it grew lighter. But one of our men lost his nerve. Shots rang out. Some of our men ran forward, but the Russians moved into position on the road with lightning speed. Russian commands could be heard. Tellerfuß fired with all his machine gun's might, but I was not able to tell whether our comrades made it across the road; deadly rifle and machine gun fire forced us to take cover.

Our long marching column now become our doom. Another attempt to break through could not be undertaken; it would be destined to fail, for the terrain on the other side of the road was wide open, with good visibility and no cover. Most of the men from our Kampfgruppe had now crawled up from behind. We used the five houses as cover; we stood not a chance of moving back. The Russians began to move out from the road in a wide arc in order to surround us, while their machine guns pinned us down behind our snow drifts. Sharpshooters fired on individual comrades lying between the houses or running toward them. I saw that the march column started moving again. Apparently a force of about one hundred and fifty Russian infantrymen had received orders to hold us in check and eventually destroy us. My fear that tanks would be coming up in the march was fortunately not realized until the evening. We divided up our men quickly among the five houses. Tellerfuß, Spiekhoven, and twelve other men crawled with me into the house situated farthest to the left. It consisted of just one big room and a small added stall built of planks. We saw a Russian woman crouching in the corner. She was holding a small child, about a year old, on her lap and trembled with fear. I quickly sent two men to each side. They punched firing holes through the walls. The machine gun could no longer be used; we had to save our ammunition. The ammunition belts were emptied for the rifles. The rifle fire was constantly building in intensity. Shots hissed through the thin clay walls. Four men were badly wounded, two of them taking shots to the stomach. The others, myself included, were grazed by bullets. We had no contact with our comrades in the other houses. Tellerfuß wanted to drag his friend inside, who was lying about ten meters from the door crying with pain. About halfway to his friend, my trusty messenger doubled over from a lethal shot to the head. The Russian sharpshooters were letting no one out of the houses. The Russian woman's little child was grazed on the leg by a bullet. Spiekhoven bandaged it from his first-aid kit. The mood was oppressive. I knew, as did we all, that we were facing certain death if a miracle did not occur. I tried to comfort my comrades. Darkness could save us, but it was still morning. Could we hold out that long? With a roar, the Russians stormed first one, then a second, and later a third house. We tried to help as much as possible with our flank fire, but they made their way into the houses. Shots were heard; they were taking no prisoners. It was now 15.00 hours. Aside from ours, there was only one other house still occupied by our comrades, and it was about forty meters away from us. We saw Russian infantrymen crawling toward it. We fired as if possessed. Suddenly, about fifty or sixty Russians jumped up and stormed the doors front and back. There were individual shots, then silence. Soon it would be our turn. Toni, stationed on the side facing the road, fired through his hole in the wall on the Russians working outside to spread tents or canvas over our wounded comrades in order to overpower them. We could see the columns marching by. A few trucks began to appear.

Spiekhoven gave me a signal. With his bayonet, he had made a large hole in the wall behind the sofa. He showed me that the little stall was behind it. We could hide there until darkness, but what would we do about our wounded comrades? One of them appointed himself spokesmen: 'Forget about us! You can't take us along, but we can still help you. Drag us over to the firing holes and we'll take over the defense. Just leave us all the grenades.'

There was no other choice. With a handshake, we said good-bye to them. We told the woman to hide behind the hearth in case there was a grenade explosion. Then we crawled through the little hole into the stall, and the sofa was pushed in front of it. The hole was closed. Our comrades fired, then there was silence. Suddenly, after about fifteen minutes, we heard the typical cry of 'Urräh.' The Russians attacked the house. Our comrades opened fire. These four men, severely wounded, defended themselves to the end. Then we heard the door being broken down. There were pistol shots. A terrible explosion shook the whole house and the stall. We knew the battle was over. We heard Russian words, then there was silence. We could peek outside through the cracks in our stall. In the twilight, we could see a Russian field kitchen drive up. Only ten meters from our stall, it began to distribute food. Several Russians stood in a line before it. We held our breath as two Russian headed straight for our stall. But they only came there to do their business, and then they headed back. By 19.30 hours, it had grown darker. Then we heard tanks on the road, rumbling toward Charkow. I gave a sign to move out. Every man knew that rapid movement or running would mean certain death. We had to act like Russians. Spiekhoven slowly opened the door. Standing straight and tall, we walked slowly through the chatting Russians right past the field kitchen, through a gap in the march column and across the road. Ten meters, fifteen meters, fifty meters, about two hundred meters with calm steps through the deep snow. Just get away from the road! Then our nerves let loose. We ran, storming away into the dark night. Then the Russians noticed something. There were rifle shots, shots from machine guns. One or two tanks moved into position. Grenades were thrown. We ran for half an hour before collapsing in exhaustion. They had apparently lost our track. The rifle fire stopped, but when we looked around, Spiekhoven was missing. There were only ten of us. I sent two men back. They returned fifteen minutes later, out of breath. No trace of him. Spikhoven fulfilled his mission with his life. As always, he had brought up the rear so that he could give answers in Russian if required. We remembered our wounded comrades, who had sacrificed themselves for us. The Russians must have believed that those men were the only defenders of that house and therefore did not look any further. We travelled two days and nights, avoiding all houses and villages, and finally, with our last ounce of energy, reached German troops at Merefa. We received fire from our own forces several times. They no longer expected to see us. We were guided for the last piece through the dense forest by a Ukrainian peasant who appeared to want nothing to do with the Soviets.

During the fighting to recapture Charkow, I was wounded in the calf right at the start and had to be hospitalized in Poltawa. Later I learned that our comrades had been thrown naked into a trench. At the Charkow cemetary, we could hardly recognize them, since the Russians had even torn off the dog tags. The Russian woman had not betrayed us because we had bandaged her child. Perhaps because she spent the last minutes of the battle with our wounded comrades, she used her silence to assure that their sacrifice would not be in vain."

17.2.1943: At 05.00 hours, the left wing of the 2. Panzer-Grenadier-Regiment *LAH* reached the installations on the Udy sector and installed itself in them. Starting at 07.00 hours, the 7./2. (under Hauptsturmführer Röhwer) on the northeastern edge of Borowoje was under constant attack from a regiment-strength force. All the attacks were repulsed in hours of fighting. Counterthrusts by groups of three or four men against forces of forty to fifty Russians were successful again and again. At 10.15 hours, the Division *Das Reich* ordered the force to disengage itself from the enemy. The new line was to be Mirgorod — Axjutowka — Choroschewo. The II./2. (under Scappini) was in Konstantowka, where orders from the Regiment reached it instructing a foot march to Merefa. From there, the march continued in vehicles to Starowerowka. The commander was to travel ahead to the Regimental headquarters in Starowerowka.

The situation on the left wing has already been described in the report from Obersturmführer Denecke.

At 11.10 hours, the 2. Panzer-Grenadier-Regiment received information that strong enemy forces with tank support had already broken through south of the Udy sector and were proceeding on Merefa from Ssokolowa. The III. (armoured)/2. (under Sturmbannführer Peiper) was deployed from Komarowka against this enemy force. The II./1. (under Max Hansen) received orders to assume a covering position on the eastern edge of Merefa.

When the new battle was assumed, the elements previously subordinated to Panzer-Grenadier-Division *Das Reich* were placed once more under the command of Panzer-Grenadier-Division *LAH.*

With this restoration of the normal structure, we can conclude the presentation of the defensive fighting by Kampfgruppe Wisch and Kampfgruppe Weidenhaupt as parts of the *Deckungsgruppe SS-Panzerkorps* east of Charkow.

In the following section, the fighting by *Angriffsgruppe SS-Panzerkorps* will be presented, beginning with 11.2.1943.

d) 11.2.1943 - 17.2.1943: The attack of *Angriffsgruppe SS-Panzerkorps*

(*Angriffsgruppe SS-Panzerkorps* consisted of the Regimentsstab of the Panzergrenadier-Regiment 1 *LAH*, the I./1. Panzergrenadier-Regiment minus the 1. and 5. Kompanie, elements of the Artillerie-Regiment *LAH*, the Pionier-Bataillon *LAH* minus one Kompanie, and the Panzergrenadier-Regiment *Der Führer*. Kampfgruppe Meyer consisted of the Aufklärungsabteilung *LAH*, the I./Panzerregiment *LAH*, and the 3./Artillerie-Regiment *LAH*. See sketch 9.)

Paragraph 3 of the Armeebefehl from Armeeabteilung Lanz contains the orders governing this attack; it reads as follows:

3. I hereby order
   a) *Angriffsgruppe SS-Panzerkorps* is to set off from the Merefa region starting at 08.00 hours on 11.2.1943 and head south, crossing the line Starowerowka — Taranowka, and is to destroy enemy forces in the region Bereka — Alexejewka. Day's objective: Alexejewka.
4. ...
5. ...
6. The Luftwaffe command for the Don is asked:
   a) to concentrate its bombing on the enemy forces facing Stoßgruppe SS-Panzerkorps.

This initial thrust to the south was ordered with such urgency because the enemy forces had pursued the retreat from Oskol closely across a wide area. The enemy was making a large enveloping movement from the north to surround Charkow, and he was putting considerable pressure on the Donez front. Then, in addition, strong enemy forces from the left wing of the Soviet 6th Army were not only threatening Charkow from the south, but were also threatening to move through the gap between Armeeabteilung Lanz and Armeeabteilung Fretter-Pico to the southwest toward the Black Sea, thereby cutting off Heeresgruppe Don.

The events of 10.2.1943 (a continuation of Part 6, Section Ib):

In the evening of 10.2.1943, the commanding general, Obergruppenführer Hausser, arrived by motorcycle at the Divisional headquarters of Panzergrenadierdivision *LAH* to discuss the continued conduct of the fighting with the Divisional commanders of the *LAH* and *Das Reich*.

The Ia of the *LAH* gave a presentation on the planned conduct of the battle for *Angriffsgruppe SS-Panzerkorps*, which ran as follows: *The Stoßgruppe to the right:*

Leader: Sturmbannführer Meyer, commander of the Aufklärungsabteilung *LAH*

Force: Aufklärungsabteilung/*LAH*
6./Panzerregiment *LAH* (under Obersturmführer Astheger)
3./Artillerie-Regiment *LAH* (under Obersturmführer Haack)
I./Panzerregiment *LAH* (under Sturmbannführer Wünsche)

This force was to move out of the assembly area south of Merefa, which had already been captured, starting at 08.00 hours on 11.2 and was to proceed via Nowaja Wodolaga, Stanitschnyij, Starowerowka, and Paraskoweja toward Alexejewka. There it was to attack the flank of the enemy forces moving toward the west.

The breakthrough force

Leader: Obersturmbannführer Kumm, commander of the SS-Panzergrenadier-Regiment *DF*

Force: SS-Panzergrenadier-Regiment *DF* (minus the I. Bataillon)
II./Panzerregiment *LAH* (under Sturmbannführer Groß and minus the 6. Kompanie)
One Batterie of the Artillerie-Regiment *DR*

This force was to set out on 11.2 from Merefa behind the Aufklärungsabteilung *LAH* and to proceed via the Borki railway station, the town of Borki, and Rjabuchino toward Ochotschaje.

Kampfgruppe Witt:

Leader: Obersturmbannführer Witt, commander of the 1. Panzergrenadier-Regiment *LAH*

Force: Stab of the 1. Panzergrenadier-Regiment (minus the Kradzug and the Pionierzug)
I./1. Panzergrenadier-Regiment (minus the 1. and 5. Kompanie)
11. and 13./1. Panzergrenadier-Regiment *LAH*
elements of the Sturmgeschützabteilung *LAH*
elements of the Artillerie-Regiment *LAH*
Pionier-Bataillon *LAH* (minus one Kompanie)

This force was to have orders to launch an attack from the area southeast of Merefa across Golubow, along the Taranowka—Bereka railway line, and on toward Alexejewka in order to provide cover for the eastern flank of the force at the center of the attack.[19]

The attack waged by the reinforced Aufklärungsabteilung and the I./Panzerregiment *LAH* on the morning of 10.2.1943 had shown that the snow conditions made the use of Panzers ineffective in this terrain. The snow was one or two meters deep and was only frozen on the surface. It held infantrymen well enough, and in some places amphibious Volkswagens and Schützenpanzerwagen could cross it. Under the weight of the Panzers, however, the snow gave way. The body of the Panzer would push up a mounting wall of snow before it, until the wall grew too big and brought the Panzer to a halt. For this reason, classic Panzer warfare was an impossibility. The Panzers were therefore to be used in Abteilungen to support the force at the center of the attack and the Stoßgruppe to the right.

Kradschüten-Bataillon 2 under Sturmbannführer Fick, which was not scheduled to arrive until the afternoon, was to be moved up behind the Stoßgruppe to the right and was to be used either to reinforce the Aufklärungsabteilung or to fill up any gaps that might appear. The rough terrain and the unfavorable weather made it extremely likely that the three forces would have to narrow their formations as they moved forward on increasingly unplowed roads, and that gaps would therefore appear.

The presentation of the plan of attack by the 1. Generalstabsoffizier of the *LAH* ended with that. The commanding general approved the plan; he explained at the same time the situation on the Korps' defensive front and indicated that Charkow could be held no longer.

The commander of the reinforced Aufklärungsabteilung (Sturmbannführer Meyer) arranged with the commander of the I./Panzerregiment *LAH* (Sturmbannführer Wünsche) that the Aufklärungsabteilung would attempt to break through to its attack objective (Alexejewka, about eight-five kilometers away) as quickly as possible, while the slower-moving Panzerabteilung would hold the march and supply route open until Kradschüten-Bataillon 2 could assume that duty.

11.2.1943 (see sketch 10): At 08.00 hours, the reinforced Aufklärungsabteilung started its attack in initially moderate snowfall. The leading Zug of the Abteilung, under Obersturmführer Schulz of the 2./Aufklärungsabteilung, reinforced by the 6./Panzerregiment *LAH*, with Untersturmführer von Ribbentrop as Zugführer, encountered little trouble from the surprised Russians and was able to push through to Nowaja Wodolaga. Obersturmführer Schulz, however, was killed by a shot to his chest. The surprised Russian columns were driven apart southwest of Nowaja Wodolaga by our ground fire and by the low-flying attacks from our bombers. The thrust of the reinforced Aufklärungsabteilung succeeded in cutting off the tip of the Soviet VIth Guard Cavalry Corps' attack. In the early afternoon, a heavy snowstorm began, and the drifts made the road almost unpassable.

At 13.35 hours, the leading elements of the German force arrived in Starowerowka. At 14.00 hours, they set off again and fought their way through both the enemy forces and the snowstorm until they reached Jefremowka at 18.00 hours. There they dug in. The drifting snow had broken the force's march formation. That night, individual groups from the I./Panzerregiment, elements of the 5. (heavy)/Aufklärungsabteilung, and the supply vehicles of the Aufklärungsabteilung dug in in Stanitschnyi, Starowerowka, and Paraskoweja.[20]

The attack by Kumm's center group, which had set out shortly before 09.00 hours, encountered tough resistance. A Panzer attack on the town of Borki was repulsed by heavy enemy anti-tank fire. The Kampfgruppe from the reinforced

Panzergrenadier-Regiment *DF* fought for the line Nowyi—Borki railway station, and it was captured by evening.[21]

Kampfgruppe Witt overcame considerable difficulties with the terrain and broke the enemy resistance, particularly at the bend in the railway line near Kononenkow, to capture the patches of forest northeast of Perwomajskij.

Kradschützen-Bataillon 2, which had set out at 16.00 hours on the right-hand march route with orders to defend Starowerowka, encountered the enemy just north of Novaja Wodolaga. The enemy troops were marching from Borki to the west, and they had once again blocked the road behind the Kampfgruppe to the right.[22]

Orders for 12.2.1943:

The reinforced Aufklärungsabteilung *LAH* was to capture and hold Alexejewka.

Kampfgruppe Kumm was to continue its attack across Borki toward Ochotschaje.

Kampfgruppe Witt was to continue its attack across Taranowka toward Bereka.

Kradschüten-Bataillon 2, with support from elements of the II./Panzerregiment *LAH*, was to open up the march route to the right in the night between 11.2 and 12.2, take Nowaja Wodolaga, and to clear the town just to the east of the road of all enemy troops.

12.2.1943: The Kradschüten-Bataillon 2, reinforced by elements of the II./Panzerregiment *LAH*, launched its attack against Nowaja Wodolaga in the night along the road and east of it. Even with Panzer support, the attack won ground only very slowly against a numerically superior enemy force offering tough resistance. By noon, the attack had succeeded in pushing the enemy back to the northern edge of Posselok and in capturing the commanding hills northeast of Nowaja Wodolaga. Nowaja Wodolaga was taken three times in the course of the day, and three times the enemy recaptured it. Three German Panzers were destroyed in the fighting.

Kampfgruppe Kumm continued its attack at 08.00 hours and captured the northwestern edge of Borki by 10.00 hours. The enemy evaded our forces there. The deep ravines which cut through the terrain made it difficult to get a clear view of the area. (Characteristic of the Ukraine, these ravines are called "Balkas.") Enemy elements also moved into the forests to the south and southwest. Stuka-Geschwader 77, whose leading officer accompanied the attack of *DF*, provided excellent support for this attack.

Kampfgruppe Witt succeeded in breaking through weak enemy resistance to capture the sprawling town of Taranowka, which stretched six kilometers from north to south on both sides of the railway line. The Kampfgruppe set out to continue its attack to the south at 10.30 hours. A Sturmgeschützbatterie reinforced with mounted Pionier troops from the 1./Pionier-Bataillon, which had been deployed to provide cover for the left flank, was able to clear Bespalowka of enemy troops. It left a force from the 1./Pionier-Bataillon *LAH* there under the command of Unterscharführer Wolfgang Meiser as a standing reconnaissance unit, but the unit was wiped out by a Russian regiment which stormed the town.

Six badly wounded Pioniere were able to make it through on their own to Taranowka.

The reinforced Aufklärungsabteilung fought its way to the east through the raging storm starting at daybreak. Russian forces and our Kampfgruppe passed each other in the storm without seeing each other. At about noon, a reconnaissance plane flew over the Abteilung. The men spelled the word "Gasoline" on the roofs of the houses to ask for the much-needed fuel. At 14.00 hours, the reinforced Aufklärungsabteilung assembled near Oktjabrskij at the road junction seven kilometers west of Alexejewka. Obersturmführer von Ribbentrop was wounded that morning. Untersturmführer Maurer of the Aufklärungsabteilung told the story:

> "Ribbentrop, who was with his Panzer IV Zug providing defense at the edge of town that evening, climbed out of the tank just as two sleighs approached out of the darkness. He recognized too late that these were not civilians, but Russian infantrymen. In hand-to-hand combat, for he had left his pistol in the turret of his Panzer, he received two knife wounds in the shoulder. The following day, he refused to allow himself to be flown out. Instead, he sent one of his wounded men."

The elements of the Aufklärungsabteilung *LAH* and the I./Panzerregiment *LAH* which had remained along the road finally closed rank in the course of the day at Paraskoweja. The supplies were loaded off the half-track vehicles onto the trucks of the Aufklärungsabteilung's supply train. These supplies were to reach the reinforced Aufklärungsabteilung the next day or the day after, depending on the truck's success in moving forward.

According to the daily report from the Ia dated 12.2.1943, the front line ran as follows: Point 189 just east of Nowaja Wodolaga (Kradschüten-Bataillon 2) — hills south of Borki (*DF*) — one kilometer north of Bereka (Witt). There were tactical support points in Starowerowka and Paraskowega (I./ Panzerregiment), and the reinforced Aufklärungsabteilung *LAH* was holding the northern and eastern edges of Jefremowka, the Bereka train station, and Oktjabrskij. The enemy forces fighting in front of the Division consisted of the Russian VIth Guard Cavalry Corps with the 11th and 83rd Cavalry Divisions. These cavalry units were extremely mobile and were not forced to use the roads. They had many tanks and sleighs. Our forces lost five Panzers.

Losses for the Division up to 10.2.1943:
- 43 dead (four of them officers)
- 118 wounded (seven of them officers), including twenty-four cases of frostbite
- 43 missing

The Armee's intention for 13.2 was to destroy the enemy forces surrounded by our units southeast of Nowaja Wodolaga and then to continue the attack with Krassnopawlowka as the point of main concentration.

Orders for 13.2.1943:

Kradschützen-Bataillon 2, subordinated to the Regiment *DF* for the Nowaja Wodolaga mission, was to capture Nowaja Wodolaga once again and to clear it of enemy forces. It was then to hold the advance march route open in conjunction with the Stanitschnji support point. Contact was to be established to Regiment *Thule* of the SS-Panzergrenadierdivision *T*, which had orders to take and hold Krassnograd. The time for the start was 05.00 hours.

Kampfgruppe Kumm was to use some of its elements to support the attack by Kradschüten-Bataillon 2 on Nowaja Wodolaga. The line captured south of Borki was to be held. After capturing Nowaja Wodolaga, the thrust toward Ochotschaje was to be continued.

Kampfgruppe Witt was to take Bereka by an attack from the north and was to establish contact to the reinforced Aufklärungsabteilung *LAH* in Oktjabrskij.

The reinforced Aufklärungsabteilung LAH was to take Alexejewka and to move from the south and southwest, across from the Kampfgruppe, toward Bereka.

The I./Panzerregiment LAH was to move forward in order to break through to join the reinforced Aufklärungsabteilung as soon as possible.

13.2.1943: At 05.00 hours, Kradschüten-Bataillon 2 and elements of Kampfgruppe Kumm (the III./*DF*) started their attack on Nowaja Wodolaga. The enemy retreated to the southeast after Nowaja Wodolaga was captured and the town cleared of enemy forces. After regrouping their units, Kradschüten-Bataillon 2 and Kampfgruppe Kumm continued the attack to the south around noon. By nightfall, Kradschüten-Bataillon 2 had reached the Stanitschnji junction, and the Regiment *DF* was able to capture Rjabuchino in heavy fighting.

Kradschüten-Bataillon 2 had orders to move the bulk of its forces to Starowerowka and to leave a security force at the Stanitschnji junction.

Kampfgruppe Witt had to defend itself against heavy attacks with tank support from the east and southeast as it moved into its assembly area. The defensive fighting lasted the entire day. The Kampfgruppe thereby fulfilled its primary mission: providing cover for the eastern flank of the center attack group.

An assault unit of the 13./1, under Unterscharführer Hahn, succeeded in moving along the railway line and establishing temporary contact with a reconnaissance unit from the Aufklärungsabteilung *LAH*.[24]

The reinforced Aufklärungsabteilung *LAH* set off at dawn and managed to capture Alexejewka. There it set up all-around defenses, because the unit was without fuel and had only small supplies of ammunition left and could therefore not continue its forward thrust. After the arrival of the Kradschüten-Bataillon 2 in Stanitschnji, the I./Panzerregiment *LAH* moved the elements of the 3./Artillerie-Regiment and of the Aufklärungsabteilung's supply train which had remained there as security forces and brought them by evening as far as Jefremowka. The town of Paraskoweja, under attack from all sides, had to be abandoned in the course of the day.[25]

By evening, the units standing under the command of the *LAH* were holding the following line: Stanitschnji (Kradschüten-Bataillon 2) — Rjabuchino (*DF*) — hills north of Bereka (Kampfgruppe Witt) — eastern edge of Taranowka (Pionier *LAH*). There were advance detachments set up for all-around defense in Jefremowka (I./Panzerregiment *LAH*) and Alexejewka (Aufklärungsabteilung *LAH*).

The situation in the *LAH* as regards armor-piercing weapons on 13.2.1943:

5	3.7-cm Pak	12	Panzer II
10	3.7-cm Pak (self-propelled)	12	Panzer III
31	5-cm Pak 38	41	Panzer IV
9	7.5-cm Pak 40	21	Sturmgeschütze (7.5-cm long)
12	Kampfwagenkanonen (5 cm) [=tank gun]	8	8.8-cm Flak

For 14.2, the Division had orders to destroy the enemy forces in the Bereka — Ochotschaje — Paraskoweja area.

Starting at 00.00 hours on 14.2, Armeeabteilung Lanz, which included the SS-Panzerkorps and the *LAH*, was subordinated to Heeresgruppe Süd (formerly Heeresgruppe Don) under Generalfeldmarschall von Manstein. The Oberkommando of the former Heeresgruppe Süd under Generalfeldmarschall von Weichs was pulled out of the field.

Orders for 14.2.1943:

Kradschützen-Bataillon 2 was to hold onto Starowerowka and to clear the towns of Melechowka and Paraskoweja of enemy troops while seeking to establish contact with the *LAH* elements in Jefremowka.

Kampfgruppe Kumm was to take Ochotschaje in order to move via Jefremowka farther to the south.

Kampfgruppe Witt was to take Bereka and to establish contact with the reinforced Aufklärungsabteilung in Alexewjewka.

The reinforced Aufklärungsabteilung was to hold Alexejewka and to attack to the north in an attempt to establish contact with Kampfgruppe Witt in Bereka.

The I./Panzerregiment LAH was to move through Alexejewka with the Aufklärungsabteilung's combat supply train. The SS-Panzerkorps was asked to take care of providing supplies to the Aufklärungsabteilung in Alexejewka by air.

14.2.1943 (see sketch 11):

The situation: On the SS-Panzerkorps' defensive front, the enemy was able in the early morning hours to penetrate our weak lines, held only by support points north of the Rogan railway station and north of Satischje. (In Part 6, Section Ic, see the entry for 14.2.1943.) Until the afternoon, enemy forces were streaming through into the Ossnowa section of the town.

South of the *LAH* attack force, there was a gap about two hundred kilometers wide between it and the bulk of Heeresgruppe Süd. At that point, tightly concentrated enemy tank and rifle divisions under General Popow had succeeded in outflanking the bulk of Heeresgruppe Süd on the northern edge of the Donez basin and were proceeding quickly toward the Dnieper. The Soviet 6th Army was covering this thrust, and the *LAH* found itself locked in battle with that Army's left wing, the VIth Guard Cavalry Corps. While the *LAH* was preparing to move farther to the south, it had to deal with the fact that the defensive front at its back could no longer stand the overwhelming enemy pressure. The collapse of that front would have meant that while its forces were committed to an attack to the south, it had to expect an enemy thrust into its back. The SS-Panzerkorps took steps against this danger by issuing at just the right moment the order to pull the front back to the Udy sector.

At 01.00 hours, Kradschüten-Bataillon 2 encountered enemy forces west of Paraskoweja. In the course of the day, it cleared the towns of Paraskoweja and Melechowka of enemy forces, sometimes in close-range combat, and a reinforced Kompanie established temporary contact with the I./Panzerregiment *LAH* in Jefremowka. There, the I./Panzerregiment *LAH* had made preparations to break through to the reinforced Aufklärungsabteilung in Alexejewka. The Adjutant of this Abteilung, Obersturmführer Isecke, reported:

> "Three Panzer III's and three Panzer IV's set out with twelve prime movers full of fuel and ammunition. Five heavy personnel cars from the 5. (heavy) Aufklärungsabteilung were taken along as valuable support. Late in the morning, we found ourselves about four kilometers from Alexejewka. About two kilometers to one side of us, we spotted enemy movement in a section of the town. We received scattered mortar fire from the right. Sturmbannführer Wünsche ordered once again: 'Don't get involved in fighting to the right. Drive on to Alexejewka and deal with the situation there!' The tension mounted. We stepped on the gas. The first houses came into view. We were on the last section of straight road. Figures waved at us and came running toward us. Sturmbannführer Wünsche halted; he recognized Sturmbannführer Meyer. I jumped from my Panzer. The two commanders embraced: 'Max, my man, you have come at just the right moment!' There was a short conference on the road: 'The Russians are sure to attack at any moment from the east. In one last effort we have driven them back out of the town. Let us face them jointly and concentrate all our forces on this attack!' Thus it happened that soon we (the I./Panzerabteilung reinforced by Kradschützen) were leaving the last houses of the town behind and setting out across the wide fields of snow. At first there was quiet, but then the machine gun and mortar fire started up. There were also Russian Ratschbums. Our tanks, behind their walls of snow, opened fire on them. Then shots from anti-tank rifles began to ring on our armour. Up ahead to the right, I spotted Panzermeyer in his four-wheeled Panzerspähwagen. Suddenly, three men fell into the snow: the anti-tank rifles had hit us. All three wounded men were picked up by a Schützenpanzerwagen. The attack rolled on. The Russians suffered losses. Some of them attempted to abandon their camouflaged positions and became the victims of our machine gun fire. After one hour, we turned back. Thanks be to God, we had only a few wounded men."

In the early morning, the reinforced Aufklärungsabteilung *LAH* received the requested supply delivery by air. The commander, Sturmbannführer Meyer, related the event as follows in his book "Grenadiere":

> "The clouds hung heavy in the sky. We heard the sounds of motors. From the droning, we could tell that we were being looked for. Suddenly, we recognized the silouhette of an He 111. Would it be our salvation? After several minutes, the shadow once again passed over us and dipped low over Alexejewka. Supply cannisters fell from the sky. Unfortunately,

however, little remained intact for us. Most of the crates burst under the impact of the fall."

The attack by Kampfgruppe Witt on Bereka could not take place because of chest-high snowdrifts on the road to the assembly area. The Aufklärungsabteilung was informed by radio that the thrust on Bereka would not take place until 15.2.

Kampfgruppe Kumm, in particular the III./*DF* reinforced with one Kompanie of Panzers (the II./Panzerregiment *LAH*), took up a position in the forest about 4.5 kilometers north of Ochotschaje in the night of 13.2/14.2 and prepared itself for the attack. Obersturmbannführer Kumm reported on the preparations, as quoted in Weidinger's "Kameraden bis zum Ende," (Plesse Verlag, Göttingen, page 127):

"Marching along the road from Rjabuchino to Ochotschaje with the 10. and 11. Kompanie side-by-side, the III. Bataillon quickly reached the first houses of the town; they lay just west of the stream, which ran north. The Panzer crews and the artillerymen had scored direct hits and flushed out one mortar nest after another, thereby providing excellent support for our attack. Unfortunately, both ran out of ammunition quickly and could offer no help in the main phase of the battle, which then began to assume full intensity. The 9. Kompanie, still mounted in its vehicles, had fought its way to within about one kilometer of Ochotschaje, with orders to continue its thrust through the town and across the Berestowaja river to the south. Just as the 9. Kompanie arrived and ventured out onto the gigantic open field, an extraordinarily heavy volley of enemy machine gun, anti-tank, mortar, and tank fire hit. The Kompanien, especially the 9. Kompanie, suffered considerable losses. The rear elements of the Kompanie pulled back, while the front Züge sought cover in the buildings and took up fighting from there. Upon receiving the report that the Bataillon's commander, Sturmbannführer Horn, had been wounded and that the Chef of the 9. Kompanie, Haupsturmführer Schober, had taken over command of the Bataillon, the Regiment's commander moved up to the edge of the town and saw that our troops, under pressure from the numerically vastly superior enemy force, were ready to give up. If the Bataillon were to suspend its combat in the gathering darkness, it would hardly be able to withstand another enemy attack against it. The Regiment's Adjutant, Hauptsturmführer Holzer, assumed command of the III. Bataillon with orders from the Regiment's commander to renew our attack and to continue it at all costs. At the same time, the II./*DF* under Hauptsturmführer Stadler, mounted on the Schützenpanzerwagens of the III./*DF*, were deployed against Ochotschaje from the east via Popowka. It was determined that the enemy had set up in the town about thirty tanks and some anti-tank guns, carefully disguised as haystacks, and that they were firing from all their barrels. The fighting lasted until late in the night, but finally the enemy was pushed back, and Ochotschaje fell into the Regiment's hands. Unfortunately, most of the enemy's tanks escaped."

Because of the development of the situation in Charkow, Armeeabteilung Lanz issued the following order at 17.30 hours: "Force under Dietrich suspend attack. Hold current position. Put a Spähwagenbataillon [Author's note: a Schützenpanzerwagenbataillon is meant], a Kradschützenbataillon, and a Panzer-

Unterscharführer Franz Staudegger.
Received Ritterkreuz on 10.7.1943 as commander in the 13. (heavy) /Panzerregiment LSSAH.

Obersturmführer Rudolf von Rippentrop.
Received Ritterkreuz on 15.7.1943 as leader of the 6./Panzerregiment LSSAH.

Sturmbannführer Martin Groß.
Received Ritterkreuz on 22.7.1943 as commander of the II./Panzerregiment LSSAH.

Oberscharführer Kurt Sammetreiter.
Received Ritterkreuz on 31.7.1943 as gun commander in the 3./Panzerjägerabteilung LSSAH.

Obersturmführer der Reserve
Georg (Oschi) Karck.
Received Ritterkreuz on 3.8.1943 as leader of the 9./Panzergrenadier-Regiment 2 LSSAH.
Killed in accident on 3.7.1944 in Normandy.

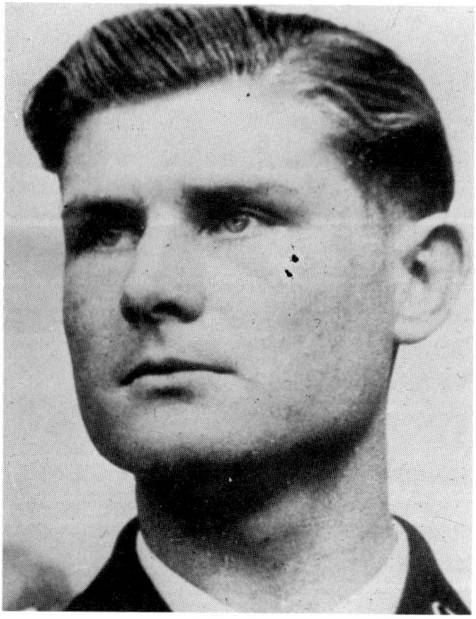

Obersturmführer Werner Wolff.
Received Ritterkreuz on 7.8.1943 as Untersturmführer and Adjutant in the III. (armoured)/Panzergrenadier-Regiment 2.
Killed in March, 1945 in Hungary.

Hauptsturmführer Paul Guhl.
Received Ritterkreuz on 4.6.1944 as Bataillon commander of the III. (armoured) /SS-Panzergrenadier-Regiment 2 LSSAH.

Sturmbannführer Gustav Knittel.
Received Ritterkreuz on 4.6.1944 as commander of SS-Panzer-Aufklärungsabteilung 1 LSSAH.

abteilung on the march to Walki immediately. From there, conduct the attack to free the main road toward Oltschany under unified command!"

This order could not be carried out because all our forces were engaged in combat with the enemy. Because of the road conditions, bringing up the forces would have taken two days, without even taking into account the time needed to get free of the enemy.

After a long dispute between the Chef of the Generalstab and the Ia of the *LAH*, the Korps ordered the former positions to be held in aggressive defense.

Orders for 15.2.1943:

Kradschützen-Bataillon 2 and Kampfgruppe Kumm were to make small thrusts in order to hold the line Paraskoweja — Melechowka — Ochotschaje and were to establish contact with the reinforced Aufklärungsabteilung in Jefremowka.

Kampfgruppe Witt was to take and hold Bereka. It was to establish contact with the reinforced Aufklärungsabteilung in Jefremowka or Alexejewka.

The reinforced Aufklärungsabteilung and the I./Panzerregiment LAH were to hold Alexejewka and to conduct a fighting reconnaissance to the south and east. A reinforced Kompanie was to be sent to establish contact with Kampfgruppe Witt in Bereka.

The Divisional headquarters were to be moved that evening to Stanitschnji.

15.2.1943: The entire day, Kradschüten-Bataillon 2 had to defend itself against enemy attacks on Paraskoweja and Melechowka from the south and east. The Bataillon maintained contact with the support point of the I./Panzerregiment *LAH* in Jefremowka by means of shuttling reconnaissance forces. In the night between 14.2 and 15.2, Kradschüten-Bataillon 2 gave effective support for the capture of Ochotschaje by launching an attack from the southwest.

On the morning of 15.2, Kampfgruppe Kumm pursued the enemy forces retreating after the capture of Ochotschaje as far as the railway line between Taranowka and Bereka. There, the commander of the Regiment *DF*, Obersturmbannführer Kumm, suspended his unit's attack because his men were exhausted. On orders from the Division, the Regiment was pulled back to the southeastern and eastern edges of Ochotschaje.[26]

The attack by Kampfgruppe Witt, after initial success, got stuck in the intensifying enemy fire on both sides of the church in the center of Bereka. This attack was continued past the village by the Bataillon under Frey on the right and the reinforced Pionier-Bataillon on the left. After reaching the middle of the town, the forces were to turn their flank on the rest of the town. A tank-supported attack from the east on the flank was repulsed. Artillery support was, however, impossible on that day because of the thick fog. In this attack, the Kompanieführer of the 3./1. was killed, and all the Zugführer were put out of action either by death or wounding. The Kompanie-Truppführer, Oberscharführer Dahlke, assumed command of the Kompanie and moved it forward in a spirited attack. In close-range fighting, the Kompanie forced its way into Bereka. Dahlke was awarded the Ritterkreuz for his brave action.

Unterscharführer Karl Hahn of the 13./1., subordinated for this attack to the I./1., wrote about it in his diary:

> "We lay the whole night in the snow and froze terribly. At 04.00 hours on 15.2, the Kompanien arrived in the assembly area. At 07.00 hours, the

attack began. It moved forward quickly at the beginning, even though some Russian Ratschbum shells hit us right at the start. We pushed our way past Bereka on the right and got as far as the other side of the village, where heavy infantry, mortar, and artillery fire hit us. Oberscharführer Vogelauer took a direct hit and was killed. The 4. Zug was moved up to be at the personal disposal of the Bataillon commander. We cleared the western approaches to the town of enemy forces and took up quarters there for about two hours. My men cooked three chickens for themselves, which they greedily devoured just before our departure. The whole Kompanie was to defend the right flank. The entire night, there was incredible noise. Tracer shells whizzed past our ears. Under the cover of darkness, the Russians had once again set up their positions in the town and were shooting at anything that moved, whether soldier or civilian. We froze miserably in the night once again."

The Schütze 1 of the third gun in the heavy MG-Zug of the *LAH* Pionier-Bataillon's heavy Kompanie offered the following description:

"On the left wing, the 1. Pionierkompanie, supported by three or four Sturmgeschütze, joined us in the attack. In the morning at 07.00 hours, with twenty to thirty centimeters of crusty snow on the ground and a temperature of about fifteen degrees below zero, the attack began. We moved across an open area for several kilometers without anything happening. Then suddenly the first shots hissed toward us, and the first mortar shells darkened the snow here and there. The first wounded men, too, began to call for the medics. But a few shots from our Sturmgeschütz proved that Ivan could not hold his position. We saw them jump out of their trenches and disappear from view. That spurred us on, of course, and before they could reach the first buildings of the village lying in the valley (Bereka), the first bursts of our machine gun fire were already rat-tat-tatting after them. In my first attempt to move into position in front of the enemy, I failed! Assuming a position on a slope had never been part of our training program, and we soon learned how dangerous it is to lie out on a platter like that. In the excitement, I fooled around with the legs of my gun mount and did not get it set up properly. Only after my squad leader, Willi Bolz, gave me a hand, meanwhile covering me in a barrage of abuse, did I get it right. A couple of shots from us, and our targets disappeared into the buildings. They then began to make life miserable for us with mortar fire on our slope. We moved quickly to capture the edge of town which was, God be praised, free of the enemy. There we could recover our balance and get our breath back. Our Zugführer was wounded, but not seriously, and two squad leaders and one rifleman were wounded. A short time later, squad leader Fritz Chemnitzer lay at our feet, shot through the heart by a sharpshooter. He had tried to jump from one house to the next. Bereka was a long, skinny village (nine kilometers long). On our side, the east, almost at the bottom of the valley, there was a street with houses. On the small slope across from us, about two hundred meters away, there was a second row of houses. The town seemed completely deserted. The only civilian life to be seen was a shaggy old horse, which was fated later to pull our ammunition wagon. Our first task, however, was to make our 'colleagues' on the other side be quiet. We suddenly noticed that there was one particular house into which Ivan kept disappearing. We brought our gun into position behind a dung heap between two houses and aimed at this little cottage (there was a heart on the door). We knocked a few of the Ivans out, and their comrades dragged them to cover. But this place provided us with unpleasantness for some time to come. We could clearly hear the shot leave the mortar and even more clearly hear it falling. Full cover! The first landed just in front of our dung heap, the second just behind. We took only seconds to vanish behind the house, but could just observe how the third hit in the center of our position and knocked over the machine gun. We dragged it to cover. The middle leg of the mount was bent. Right after this little interlude, someone appeared, leaned his submachine gun against the wall of our house, took a sharpshooter's rifle from one of our wounded comrades, and set himself up at the corner of our house to take aim at our old target. After a couple of rounds of fire, it got to be too much for us: 'You stupid dog, get out of here! Your noise is drawing Ivan's fire right onto us!' With careful steps, Obersturmführer Taubert of the 1. Pionierkompanie turned and came toward us, informing us who he was. For our part, we told him what had just happened, and he grinned as he noted our excitement. While the Schütze 3 and Schütze 4 stayed nearby, holding off the enemy with their carbine fire, we tried to dislodge the empty shells which were jammed tight in the machine gun's mechanism, using oil and sulphur to get it working again. We did not stay long at any house corner or window. After a few rounds had been fired, the Russians shot a flare and set our roof on fire. We were forced to shift positions. We could just make out a few figures of the men of the Aufklärungsabteilung at the northern road out of the village. As night fell, the noise of the battle subsided. At about 22.00 hours, I made my way with six mess kits to the place where the food was being handed out. Hannes Eggers was supposed to be standing with the field kitchen about two hundred meters to the rear behind a house. I had to crawl most of the way, but I got there and back in one piece in that manner, and the mess kits were even about three-quarters full. How my comrades crowded around! It was the first food of the day."

The reinforced Aufklärungsabteilung used the bulk of its forces to repulse an attack on Alexejewka from the north and, in an immediate counterthrust to the east, destroyed a Russian battalion. The 2./Aufklärungsabteilung *LAH*, deployed against Bereka, pushed its way two kilometers into the town but was pulled back to Alexejewka in the course of the night. In this thrust, the Kompanie destroyed several enemy anti-tank guns and dealt the enemy infantry some serious losses. Obersturmführer Weiser, the Kompanieführer of the 2./Aufklärungsabteilung *LAH*, was wounded for the third time in this fighting. In the night between 15.2 and 16.2, the enemy forced his way into Alexejewka and pushed Kampfgruppe Meyer back to the center of town. Kurt Meyer described the event in "Grenadiere" (page 173) as follows:

"The battle had reached its climax. The Grenadiere fought courageously against their desperate plight. But in the very midst of this seemingly hopeless situation, the tables were turned with breath-taking speed. The

Panzerspähwagen, forced into close concentration, formed an unbelievable fire power force, able to contain the attacking Soviets with high-explosive shells and to set the thatched-roof houses on fire. We sat in the middle of a ring of fire and shot from the darkness into the brightly lighted ranks of the Russians. Their attack momentum was broken. Our counterthrust, undertaken immediately, repulsed them completely from Alexejewka and brought us back to our old positions."

The SS-Panzerkorps reported in its evening report of 15.2.1943 to Armee-abteilung Lanz the following:

"On 15.2, the southern front at Ochotschaje was taken. We have penetrated Bereka, which will certainly be cleared of enemy troops on 15.2 [author's note: this must mean 16.2]. Heavy losses for the enemy. The VIth Cavalry Corps has been reduced to scattered remains between 10.2. and 15.2.1943."

The Armee radioed back to the SS-Panzerkorps:

"With gratitude and admiration, I ask that you express my sincere congratulations to Obergruppenführer Dietrich for his victory over the Russian VIth Cavalry Corps. Signed, Lanz."

The numerical measure of the destruction wreaked upon the VIth Guard Cavalry Corps (11th and 83rd Cavalry Divisions and the 201st Tank Brigade): troop strength at the beginning of the fighting was about seven thousand men with sixteen tanks; there were about three thousand men wounded, six tanks destroyed, four more probably destroyed, and four hundred prisoners taken. The rest of the Corps was broken down into scattered groups.

At 22.05 hours, the Heeresgruppe issued orders by radio:

Armeeabteilung Lanz was given as its mission keeping the Russian 6th Army (moving from Stalino to Pawlowgrad), the 3rd Tank Army under Popow (moving south of Charkow via Krassnograd toward Saporoshje and Dnjepropetrowsk), the 69th Army (in Charkow), and the 40th Army (moving on Bjelgorod and Poltawa) engaged at all costs. At first, the Armeeabteilung was to hold the Udy sector. Offensive defense and renewed assaults against the tip of the Russian attack were ordered. In particular, the Russian 6th Army was to be prevented from making a swing into the deep flank of our 1. Panzerarmee (in the Slawjansk area).

The missions alloted for 16.2.1943 demonstrate the Korps' intention, after the completion of the southern thrust toward Bereka, to establish a solid and lasting defensive line across a broad sector.

The *LAH* received the following orders to 16.2.1943:

Kradschützen-Bataillon 2 was to stand at the disposal of the Division in the area Paraskoweja — Melechowka and to send combat-strength reconnaissance forces to establish contact with Kradschützenregiment *Thule* in Krassnograd. The Bataillon was to prepare itself to be deployed as reinforcement on the endangered eastern flank in the Bereka — Taranowka area.

Kampfgruppe Kumm was to hold Ochotschaje and to use some of its forces to destroy the enemy units between Ochotschaje and the Paraskoweja — Jefremowka road.
Kampfgruppe Witt was to capture and hold Bereka. Taranowka was also to be held.
The reinforced Aufklärungsabteilung and I./Panzerregiment LAH were to make a localized counterattack against Alexejewka and Oktjabrskij and then to set themselves up in Alexejewka as a defensive force.

16.2.1943: At 04.00 hours, Standartenführer Witt ordered his Kampfgruppe to suspend the attack. In the night, the enemy had succeeded in penetrating the town of Taranowka, which had only a weak defense provided by the supply trains. The Kampfgruppe was ordered to clear this town of enemy forces.

In order to prevent further enemy advance to the west, Kradschüten-Bataillon 2 received orders to capture and hold Rjabuchino (five kilometers west of Taranowka). Unterscharführer Karl Hahn of the 13./1. provided information about the retreat from Bereka and the attack on Taranowka in his diary:

"Toward morning, the order to retreat arrived. In the night, a Russian regiment had attacked our supply train in Taranowka and had captured some of the vehicles. I was terribly tired and so *kaputt* my legs would barely carry me. My old wound announced its presence once again. On a hill, a messenger stopped and told me that the men from my Gruppe were stuck in a ravine with a sleigh full of ammunition. When I reached them, I found Speer, Brausewetter, and Späth sitting by their sleigh, completely exhausted. Despite my own condition, I gave them a tremendous pep-talk, and we managed to cover the eight kilometers to Taranowka in one-hundred-meter stretches. As we climbed back up the slope, day was breaking. We could see right into Bereka. The Russians were not moving. They were probably just as worn out as we were. When I reported in with my three men, the Chef was astounded that we still existed. We had already been reported missing. We had had a short rest and something to eat in a Russian cottage when the alarm sounded. Our supply train, six to eight kilometers away in Taranowka, was in extreme danger. It could no longer withstand the Russian onslaught. We marched forward with security forces around us. The 13. Kompanie was at the head. My Gruppe was with the 2. Zug, which was at the head of the Infanterie. A Sturmgeschütz accompanied us. We came as far as the edge of the town, where we met some of our supply train drivers, some of them with their vehicles, others without. The first shots whizzed past our ears here. A shell scored a direct hit on one of our ammunition vehicles, and there were mighty explosions. A fuel wagon, right next to it, immediately caught fire. My Gruppe and I struck out to the left, moved into position in the open field, and opened fire on the Russians we could see moving along the edge of the town. The ammunition supply system worked exceedingly well. Oskar Speer had managed to capture two Russian horses, and he used them to provide ammunition to the immediate vicinity. With courage and true enthusiasm, Späth, Brausewetter, and Kugler, all barely eighteen years old, ran back and forth between the firing positions and the sleigh. Even after we changed position, everything was once again there: ammunition and clean machine gun barrels. Two Kompanien moved in and cleared the section of town to the left of the railroad tracks of enemy forces. The town was about twelve to fifteen kilometers long. I was able to move with my Gruppe toward the tracks because the second Zug had already gained considerable ground. With that move, I ended up in the sector held by the third Zug, and I received orders from Obersturmführer Fürbringer to move into position such that I could support the attack on the railway line. This attack got stuck under the fire from the sharpshooters in the buildings on the other side of the railway embankment. Unterscharführer Traub and Unterscharführer Paul Maurer were killed by shots to their heads. Darkness began to fall. For the night, we established individual support points within the 13. Kompanie, from which we exchanged fire with the Russians all night long."

Those were the events west of the railway line. The MG-Schütze 1 of the third gun of the heavy MG-Zug of the 4. (heavy) Pioniere *LAH* described what was going on east of there:

"In Taranowka, the Russians had let their tanks rage. None of our 5-centimeter Geschütze were in operation anymore. They had been mowed down by the Russian tanks. Altogether, there must have been some goings-on during our absence, as proved by the number of wounded and dead men lying in the medical station of our Bataillon doctor, Hauptsturmführer Dr. Kayser. All the usable vehicles were loaded with the wounded men from the Pionier-Bataillon. The three self-propelled Feldhaubitzen from the III./Artillerie-Regiment, now assigned to the Kampfgruppe, had driven the tanks away during the night. Now they were set in motion. They were to use their caterpillar tracks to make a road through the snow for our trucks. Our heavy MG-Zug took over flank defense for this force accompanying the wounded. We set up our heavy MG on a captured sleigh, pulled by the horse confiscated the previous day. Miraculously in one piece, we reached the combat outpost of Kradschüten-Bataillon 2 near Rjabuchino as darkness fell."

The Adjutant of the Panzerabteilung, Obersturmführer Isecke, provided a description of the events affecting those forces deployed ahead of the position, the reinforced Aufklärungsabteilung and the I./Panzerregiment *LAH*:

"During the evening and into the night, the reinforced Aufklärungsabteilung and the I./Panzerregiment *LAH* made all the preparations for the breakthrough to the west. The Panzers, the 3./Artillerie-Regiment, the Kradschützenkompanien, and the Panzerspähkompanien filled their fuel tanks and loaded up with ammunition. The wounded, including Obersturmführer von Ribbentrop, were put on the prime movers and the few remaining trucks. Panzers provided security to the front, while the troops marched in echelon formation to the left and rear. What would the Russians sitting in the roads out of the town to our left do? Had they received sufficient reinforcements to outflank us and cut our column off? We could spot some movement, but outside of some mortar fire, all was calm. In the early morning hours on 16.2, we reached Jefremowka. First, we refueled; the Aufklärungsabteilung took over our defense. Then we all fell asleep.

Otherwise, the day passed quietly.

17.2.1943: The Generalkommando of the SS-Panzerkorps issued the following daily orders:

> "Since 30.1.1943, the SS-Panzerkorps has been engaged in alternating offensive and defensive fighting in an attempt to stop the advance of three Russian armies. The enemy's losses have been heavy. One cavalry corps was shattered to pieces.
> For the first time, Panzergrenadierdivisionen *LSSAH* and *DR*, to which Panzergrenadierdivision *Totenkopf* now belongs, were able to fight side-by-side. Every unit gave its all during these weeks, and, despite the complications in the command process caused by mixing of the units, decisive defensive successes were achieved.
> Fighting alongside the old, proven Regimenter and Bataillone, the newly-formed units, especially the Panzerregimenter and Sturmgeschützabteilungen, passed their trial by fire under the most difficult terrain conditions imaginable. The Panzergrenadiere once again bore the brunt of the battle.
> Elements of the 209. Infanteriedivision and the 213. Sicherungsdivision, added to the ranks of the SS men, participated in the success.
> The 320. Infanteriedivision, subordinated to the Korps for the first time, provided vital relief on the southern flank in ten days of brave perseverance under conditions of hard deprivation.
> I offer my deepest respect to the officers and men of all the subordinated units for their performance and conduct in these difficult weeks.
>
> signed, Hausser.

Early the next morning, the Aufklärungsabteilung observed several enemy columns moving from the east toward Jefremowka. The two commanders, Sturmbannführer Meyer and Sturmbannführer Wünsche, conferred and agreed to move the reinforced Aufklärungsabteilung into position on the edge of the town and to let it confront the enemy. The Panzerabteilung was to make a large enveloping movement in an attempt to exploit the rolling terrain, to move with the Kompanien stationed in Paraskoweja against the flank and rear of the enemy columns, and to destroy them. The Kompanie stationed in Paraskoweja received the order by radio. The tactic worked. One hour after the order had been issued, the reinforced 2./Panzerregiment (under Obersturmführer Beck) reported contact with the enemy. With over twenty Panzers, the unit broke through the Russians' flank and rear across a wide front. The Russian anti-tank guns, caught completely off guard, were unable to move into position. They were hit and destroyed. The infantry columns were destroyed and driven into disarray. The ox-drawn artillery was also caught in this attack. The Russian units involved were Infantry Regiment 747 and the 172nd Rifle Division. The day was marked by about 1,200 enemy casualties and the capture of eight artillery pieces.[27]

Kampfgruppe Witt did not succeed in capturing the entire town of Taranowka on 17.2. It even had to repulse several Russian counterattacks by forces up to battalion strength. Finally, Sturmbannführer Frey reported from the western section of Taranowka that he was unable to disengage from the enemy because of the large number of wounded men he had (over one hundred) and because of the impossibility of transporting them, caused by the drifting snow and the lack of vehicles. The Ia held a short conference with Obersturmbannführer Kumm, and the latter sent the armoured personnel carriers from one Kompanie of the III./*DF* to Taranowka to pick up the wounded. Kampfgruppe Witt then was able to pull back from Taranowka. It provided defense with its front to the east and northeast from the northern part of Rjabuchino via Borki, the Borki railway station, and Nowaja as far as northern Wodolaga. The 320. Infanteriedivision was to take over the positions from Borki on in the course of the day on 18.2. At the time, it was assembling in Merefa.

The III. (armoured)/2. Panzergrenadier-Regiment *LAH* received orders to prevent the enemy from moving through the Msha valley to the west near Kolessnikow in the night and to stand ready to capture and hold Ziglerowka on the morning of 18.2. Following a report on the situation, we come now to a description of the defensive fighting south of Charkow.

Section II

THE RECAPTURE OF CHARKOW 18.2.1943 - 18.3.1943

1) DEFENSIVE FIGHTING SOUTH OF CHARKOW 18.2.1943 - 4.3.1943

a) 18.2.1943 - 1.3.1943: Aggressive defense to prop up the northern wing of Heeresgruppe Süd southwest of Charkow (see sketch 12)

The situation: Armeeabteilung Hollidt occupied the Mius position on 17.2 under heavy pressure from the enemy. The 1. Panzerarmee (under General von Mackensen) was able to stop the enemy advance near Grischino, but it did not have sufficient forces to destroy him. Near Kramatorskaja, the heavy fighting against the enemy troops attacking from Lissitschansk and Slawijansk was still continuing. Armeeabteilung Lanz, as previously mentioned, had abandoned Charkow and was retreating toward the Msha sector to the southwest.

On 17.2.1943, Adolf Hitler, together with the Chef of the Generalstab of the Heer, General Zeitzler, and General Jodl, arrived at the headquartes of Heeresgruppe Süd in Saporoshje. There, the Oberbefehlshaber of Heeresgruppe Süd, Generalfeldmarschall von Manstein, presented his plans to free up all the units of the SS-Panzerkorps from Charkow and to leave only the remaining elements of Armeeabteilung Lanz. The Generalfeldmarschall continued in his presentation of the situation as follows, according to his recounting of it in "Verlorene Siege":

> "The SS-Panzerkorps was to move forward from the Krassnograd area to the southwest in the general direction of Pawlograd and thereby to enter into cooperation with the 4. Panzerarmee, already on the march. These forces were to attack the enemy moving into the wide gap between the 1. Panzerarmee and Armeeabteilung Lanz. When that move had been completed, and thereby the danger avoided of Armeeabteilung Hollidt and the 1. Panzerarmee being surrounded and cut off, we would be able to make a large enveloping movement and launch an attack in the Charkow area.

The Division received the following orders for the next day:

> "The *LAH* and the elements subordinated to it are to disengage from the line Jefremowka — east Ochotschaje — Taranowka and to occupy the line Beresowka (inclusive of it) — Melechowka — hill north of Ochotschaje — eastern edge of Rjabuchino — hills south of Borki."

18.2.1943: The 2. Panzergrenadier-Regiment (under Standartenführer Wisch), once again under the command of the Division, assembled in Starowerowka during the day in order to relieve Regiment *DF*, which was leaving the formation of the *LAH*. The *DF* was to be replaced in its positions west of Ochotschaje by the II./2. (under Sandig). The I./2. (under Kraas) was to assume an adjoining position farther to the south, starting at the western edge of Losowaja. The III. (armoured)/2. (under Peiper) was to stand ready in Krassnograd for mobile combat at the front. The 1. Panzergrenadier-Regiment (under Standartenführer Witt), which the II./1. (under Hansen) had once again joined, assembled in Nowowaja Wodolaga, and three of its Bataillone assumed positions in the front line.

The Artillerie-Regiment *LAH* ordered the following to work in conjunction with each other:

the I. Abteilung and 9. (heavy Feldhaubitze) with the 2. Panzergrenadier-Regiment;

the II. Abteilung and III. Abteilung (minus one Batterie) with the 1. Panzergrenadier-Regiment.

The IV. Abteilung was to move into position such that it could reinforce the barrage fire of the I. and III. Abteilung.

The following line was designated as the main battle line: Beresowka (inclusive of it) — Melechowka (the 2.) — hill north of Ochotschaje — eastern edge of Rjabuchino — hills south of Borki (for the 1. Panzergrenadier-Regiment). By 20.00 hours, all elements had assumed their assigned positions.

The following assembled in the course of the day to stand at the disposal of the Division:

The Aufklärungsabteilung in eastern Starowerowka.

The I. Abteilung of Panzergrenadier-Regiment 1 in Starowerowka, the II. in Nowaja Wodolaga.

The Pionier-Bataillon in Knjashnoje with orders to reconnoiter the possibilities for action at the boundary held by the 320. Infanterie-Division (southern edge of Borki). This Division's sector was initially over sixty kilometers wide.

Divisionsbefehl No. 5 provided information about the deployment of the other units:

Leibstandarte SS Adolf Hitler	Divisional headquarters
Abteilung of the Ia Le./Ga.	17.2.1943, 13.00 hours

Divisionsbefehl No. 5
(Map scale 1 : 300,000)
(essential points have been issued orally in advance)

1) The *LSSAH* and the elements subordinated to it are to pull back on 17.2.1943 from the line Jefremowka — eastern Ochotschaje — Taranowka and are to assume and hold the line Beresowka (inclusive of it) — Melechowka — hill north of Ochotschaje — eastern edge of Rjabuchino — hills south of Borki.

2) Dividing line:

between the LSSAH and Division DR:

Krestischtsche (*DR*) — Berestowenka (*DR*) — Petrowka (*DR*);
between DF and Kampfgruppe Witt:
(later the 2. Panzergrenadier-Regiment and the 1. Panzergrenadier-Regiment)
junction of the road and railway six kilometers north of Starowerowka — north of Melechowka (*DF*) — Rostow Rostanja (Witt);
between the LSSAH and the 320. Infanterie Division:
southern edge of Nowaja Wodolaga — southeastern edge of Borki.

Start of the move back from the line: 17.2.1943, 16.30 hours.

3) *To this end I order the following:*

a) The SS-*DF* is to pull back from the enemy beginning with its left wing, then it is to provide cover for the assembly of the Aufklärungsabteilung/*LSSAH* in the hills east of Paraskoweja and to hold the Paraskoweja sector. It will be relieved by the reinforced 2. Panzergrenadier-Regiment *LSSAH* in the night between 17.2 and 18.2; the *DF* is then to assemble in Berestowenka.
b) *Kampfgruppe Witt* is to disengage from the enemy in Taranowka and then move back via Ochotschaje and assume the designated line. The elements of the 1. Panzergrenadier-Regiment *LSSAH* travelling with Kampfgruppe Wisch are to be moved to Nowaja Wodolaga on 18.2.1943; they are to relieve the Pionier-Bataillon/*LSSAH*, which is to assemble in Knjashnoje to stand at the disposal of the Division.
c) *The reinforced Aufklärungsabteilung/LSSAH* is to hold Jefremowka until the southern wing of *DF* has disengaged from the enemy. It is then to stand at the Division's disposal in the eastern section of Starowerowka. Its arrival in Paraskoweja is to be covered by the *DF* and the III./Artillerie-Regiment *LSSAH*.
d) *The SS-Kradschützen-Bataillon 2* (after the arrival of Kampfgruppe Witt) is to be put on the march toward Krassnograd, where it will stand at the disposal of the Generalkommando of the SS-Panzerkorps. A Sturmgeschützbatterie from the *DR* will be moved there and subordinated.
e) *The 1. Panzergrenadier-Regiment LSSAH* (minus the elements deployed with Kampfgruppe Witt) are to be moved to Nowaja Wodolaga in the night between 17.2 and 18.2 and are to be detailed by Kampfgruppe Witt.
f) *The 2. Panzergrenadier-Regiment LSSAH* is to reach Starowerowka in the night between 17.2 and 18.2 and to relieve the reinforced *DF* from the main battle line.
g) *The Artillerie-Regiment LSSAH* is to leave its subordinated elements with their former Kampfgruppen. In the course of the day on 17.2.1943, it is to reconnoiter possible artillery action to concentrate our fire on the march route and the towns in front of the battle line.
h) *Panzerregiment LSSAH* is to assemble one Abteilung in Starowerowka and one in the southern section of Nowaja Wodolaga to stand at the Division's disposal.
i) *The Sturmgeschützabteilung/LSSAH* is to leave with the Kampfgruppen Geschütze capable of firing and is to establish full combat readiness in Karawanksoje (six kilometers northeast of Starowerowka).

k) *The Panzerjägerabteilung/LSSAH* is to station the bulk of its forces in Starowerowka at the disposal of the Division. It should leave the subordinated Geschütze with the Kampfgruppen and establish full combat readiness.
l) *The Pionier-Bataillon/LSSAH* is to be relieved by the 1. Panzergrenadier-Regiment in Knjashnoje and is to stand at the Division's disposal.
m) *The Flakabteilung/LSSAH* with the Stab, 3., 4., and 6. Batterie is to stay with the supply trains. It is to leave one Batterie subordinated to the 1. Panzergrenadier-Regiment, the 1. Batterie at the disposal of the Division, and the 5. Batterie subordinated to the 2. Panzergrenadier-Regiment.

4) *The Nachrichtenabteilung of the LSSAH* is to establish:
Telephone communications with the fighting units and the Division's reserves and
Radio communications as before.

5) *The Sanitätsabteilung/LSSAH/ is to set up:*
a) *Main medical station* in Nowaja Wodolaga,
b) *Field hospital* in Krassnograd.

6) *The Feldgendarmeriekompanie/LSSAH* is responsible for directing traffic from *Merefa* to *Paraskoweja*. That is the focal point.

7) *Signal flares*:
Green = *We are here!*
Red = *Move the fire further forward!*
White = *The enemy is attacking!*

8) *Ammunition may be picked up* from the Ib starting on 17.2.1943 in Stanitschnoje
Fuel may be obtained from the Ib starting on 17.2.1943 in Stanitschnoje
Bread may be picked up from the Ib starting on 17.2.1943 in Stanitschnoje

9) *Instandesetzungabteilung/LSSAH* and
Wirtschaft-Bataillon/LSSAH in Poltawa.

10) *Divisional headquarters* Stanitschnoje.

signed Dietrich
SS-Obergruppenführer
and General of the Waffen-SS

At 20.30 hours, the commander of the *DF*, Obersturmbannführer Kumm, and the commander of Kradschüten-Bataillon 2, Sturmbannführer Fick, reported their withdrawal.

During the entire day, the enemy sent out feelers along the Division's front with forces up to battalion size. Reconnaissance revealed enemy movements of considerable magnitude near Alexejewka and Bereka and columns, each of regimental size, moving from Alexejewka toward Krassnograd.

On the left wing near Borki and in the patches of forest to the north, where our forces had been unable to move into position adjoining the 320. Infanterie-Division, the enemy moved in a battalion and established his position. As a result, the SS-Panzerkorps ordered a new dividing line between our unit and the 320. Infanterie-Division. It was to be the southern edge of Nowaja Wodolaga — southeastern edge of Borki. At 03.00 hours, the Generalkommando of the SS-Panzerkorps received an Armeebefehl subordinating the 320. Infanterie-Division to Korps Raus starting on 18.2.1943 and moving the Korps boundary to Staraja Wodolaga — Borki railway station — Sanki railway station. This order did not reach the Division until 08.40 hours on 18.2.1943, so the gap created by the move was not occupied during the night. The Korps ordered that, upon the decision from the Armee, the gap should be closed by the Panzergrenadier-Regiment *LAH* with the III./Infanterie-Regiment 586, subordinated to it for this purpose. Cooperation among the III./Infanterie-Regiment 586, the 1./Pioniere *LAH*, and the 2./Sturmgeschützabteilung *LAH* made the capture of the town of Borki by the late afternoon possible. The enemy in the patches of forest to the north and northwest of the town offered tough resistance and could not be pushed back. Responsibility for holding Borki was given to the Pionier-Bataillon *LAH*. The III./Infanterie-Regiment 586 was moved into position west of the forest.

Orders for 19.2.1943:

> "The *LAH* is to move combat-strength reconnaissance forces to the southeast in order to provide a screen across the northern wing of Panzergrenadier-Regiment *DR*, which is setting off to the southeast. To this end, the 2. Panzergrenadier-Regiment with the III. (armoured)/2. (under Peiper), supported by the I./2., is to capture Ziglerowka, move forward over Partssjesda toward Jeremejewka, capture Jeremejewka, and then set up an aggressive defense in front of its position to the south, the east, and the southeast. The Division is also to make a thrust across the Berestowaja section, recapture Jefremowka and Ochotschaje, and together with the 320. Infanterie-Division take the Borki railway station. To this end, the 1. Panzergrenadier-Regiment *LAH*, together with elements of the Pionier-Bataillon *LAH* and the III./586 are to capture and hold the Borki railway station."

19.2.1943: In the southern sector, the 2. Kompanie and elements from the 4. Kompanie of the 2. Panzergrenadier-Regiment had first captured Beresowka and were setting up defensive positions on the eastern edge of the town. With that move, the conditions were created for a successful envelopment of and attack on Ziglerowka with the III. (armoured)/2. moving in from the northwest and elements of the I./2. moving in from the northeast.

At 16.50 hours, the 13./2. (under Peiper) received orders to move forward with the entire Bataillon on two separate roads toward Jeremejewka. At 00.50 hours, Sturmbannführer Peiper reported the capture of Kasatschij Maidan. In the fighting, a Soviet battalion (of about seven hundred fifty men) with eleven

7.62-centimter guns, three tanks, and fifteen mortars was destroyed southeast of Ziglerowka.

Untersturmführer Gührs, Zugführer of the Kraftwagenkanonenzug of the 14. (heavy)/2., reported:

> "With one Geschütz, I accompanied the 13. Kompanie's attack. Our thrust achieved surprising success. The night came, and the moon was very bright. Our first night attack! We felt our way forward very slowly. At 23.30 hours, we arrived at out first attack objective: a village occupied by Russians. The Bataillon spread out. I stood with my Kraftwagenkanonenzug on the right wing. A heavenly sight in the moonlight. We opened fire at a range of eight hundred meters. There was weak counterfire from two Russian guns. One vehicle after another from our Zug moved forward into the village. In an hour, we were through it. It was just 00.30 hours."

In the center sector, the enemy in Ochotschaje was being harrassed by concentrated Artillerie fire in a surprise attack. In the northern sector, the reinforced III./1. was occupied repulsing several Russian attacks on its positions east of Rjabuchino. A dangerous attack north of Rjabuchino was finally repulsed with our last forces, including the vehicle drivers.

The reinforced I./1. (under Frey) and elements of the Pionier-Bataillon *LAH*, together with the 2./Sturmgeschützabteilung *LAH*, were able to capture the Borki railway station by 18.00 hours.

The reinforced II./1. (under Hansen) had moved into position north of Bulachi and offered support fire for the attack of the I./1. against the Borki railway station.

The orders for 20.2.1943 remained unchanged except those for the reinforced Aufklärungsabteilung and the I./Panzerregiment *LAH*, which received orders to proceed via Krassnograd and Ziglerowka toward Jeremejewka, where it was to relieve the Bataillon under Peiper and to conduct mobile combat to prevent any further advance to the west by enemy forces.

The III. (armoured)/2. was to launch one more attack and then move to the northern section of Krassnograd, where it was to stand at the disposal of the Division.

It may be noted at this point that the *LAH*'s butchering Kompanie under the command of Hauptsturmführer Zander had, under orders from the Oberquartiermeister of the Armeeabteilung, occupied the slaughterhouse in Poltwa. The Russian civilian administration had abandoned it. Haupsturmführer Zander had taken over the operation with its entire staff, including eight Russian veterinarians. He reported good cooperation with the Russian prisoner volunteers.

20.2.1943 (see sketch 13): Heeresgruppe Süd intended to use the newly-formed 4. Panzerarmee (under Generaloberst Hoth) to attack the enemy in the gap between Armeeabteilung Lanz and the 1. Panzerarmee (under General von Mackensen). Armeeabteilung Lanz, together with the SS-Panzerkorps (minus the *LAH*), conducted the attack as ordered against Nowomoskowsk until command was assumed by Panzerarmee-Oberkommando 4. The SS-Panzergrenadier-Division *T* was to be moved forward to Krassnograd, and from here it was to be moved up by the 4. Panzerarmee.

Armeeabteilung Lanz with the *LAH* was assigned the task of holding the enemy forces directly opposite it under all circumstances and to conduct the battle for as long as possible from the positions held at the time.

In the night of 19.2/20.2, the SS-Panzergrenadierdivision *DR*, together with the reinforced III./*D*, had attacked from Otrada to the south and by 05.30 hours had captured Pereschtschepino.

After a brief reorganization, the III. (armoured)/2. (under Peiper) set out once again at 04.00 hours, heading east from Ziglerowka, and by 06.30 hours had taken Jeremejewka and the Leninskij factory. After pursuing the retreating enemy forces a short way (about five kilometers), the Bataillon set up defenses in Jeremejewka. Untersturmführer Gührs reported on this nocturnal attack as follows:

> "The Bataillon assembled behind the village. As it started to grow light in the east, we attacked again. We barely felt the bitter cold. Before the next village, we paused only briefly to prepare ourselves. There was reported to be a Russian regiment there, armed with heavy weapons. We attacked at high speed. Our Schützenpanzerwagens made it easily through the snow. The enemy fled; we pursued and moved far past our original goal. Suddenly, a Schützenpanzerwagen beside me was hit by an anti-tank shell fired from close range. Unterscharführer Hesse was killed. Sturmbannführer Peiper gave the order to halt. We had taken two towns, advanced twenty kilometers and destroyed a Russian regiment. Now all we wanted to do was sleep."

The successes of this attack were reported as follows: two T-34's, one light tank, twelve 2.62-centimeter guns, one light infantry gun, fifteen heavy mortars, eight heavy machine guns, and three hundred rifles destroyed; two trucks captured; seven hundred fifty Russians killed.

In the course of the morning, the 2./2. (under Hauptsturmführer Becker) cleared Ziglerowka of enemy forces and set up defensive positions on the eastern edge of the town.

At 08.00 hours, the II./2. (under Sandig) repulsed an enemy attack from Ochotschaje against the left wing of the 2. Panzergrenadier-Regiment.

In the right-hand sector, the 1. Panzergrenadier-Regiment, situated near Melchowka — Rjabuchino, was forced to defend itself against constant attack by forces up to battalion strength. In addition, there was a tank attack with about two companies of enemy infantry at 14.00 hours. It was repulsed with the support of the 10. (Werfer)/Artillerie-Regiment (under Obersturmführer Bartels). Obersturmführer Schmaloer, the Regiment's Nachrichtenführer, was badly wounded in the fighting. Oberscharführer Günther, a Zugführer in the 2./Sturmgeschützabteilung *LAH*, single-handedly destroyed five enemy tanks and was rewarded for his valiant action with the Ritterkreuz. The II./1. (under Max Hansen) was able to launch a counterattack to push back enemy breakthroughs into Hf. Podgopai and Klijutschewodsk.

The II./1. reported that the III./Infanterie-Regiment 586 had been pulled back without warning, with the result that the enemy immediately surged into the gap, occupied the northwestern section of Borki, and was launching constant attacks from there. A request from the Regiment for support from the Division was initially turned down because of the lack of resources in the face of the assigned task of offensive fighting on the right wing. As soon as the III. (armoured)/2. could be freed up, it was to be moved to join the 1. Panzergrenadier-Regiment and temporarily subordinated to it.

The reinforced Aufklärungsabteilung and the I./Panzerregiment *LAH* received orders in the course of the morning to relieve the III. (armoured)/2. in Jeremejewka and to move immediately in offensive fighting against the enemy forces moving east of Krassnograd to the west.

At about 15.00 hours, the reinforced Aufklärungsabteilung and the I./Panzerregiment *LAH* arrived in Jeremejewka. After a briefing from Sturmbannführer Peiper, Jeremejewka was set up as a support point. A Panzerkompanie, reinforced by mounted Kradschützen, launched an attack against an enemy column of battalion strength which was moving to the west about five kilometers south of our position; the column was destroyed.

At noon, the SS-Panzerkorps informed the leadership that four 7.5-centimeter self-propelled Paks, intended for the *LAH*, had been subordinated temporarily to the 168. Infanterie-Division immediately upon being unloaded near Achtyrka. The fate of these four guns after that is unknown.

The III. (armoured)/2. received orders to make an enveloping movement to the south via Woroschilowa and Rossochowatyi toward Krassnograd. There, it was to stock up on ammunition and then to march to the 1. Panzergrenadier-Regiment's headquarters, where it was to be deployed to mop up the situation near Borki.

Orders for 21.2.1943:

> The reinforced III. (armoured)/2. was to be subordinated to the 1. Panzergrenadier-Regiment *LAH* in order to mop up the situation near Borki. It stood at the Regiment's disposal only for 21.2 and 22.2 and was to assemble on 22.2 at 20.00 hours in Krassnograd to stand at the Division's disposal once again. The main task assigned the Division remained the conduct of offensive fighting in the rear of the SS-Panzerkorps, which was attacking to the south.

The right wing of the Division was to be moved up as far as Kegitschewka. The reinforced Aufklärungsabteilung and the I./Panzerregiment *LAH* received orders to this end.

21.2.1943 (see sketch 14): In the course of the day, General der Panzertruppen Kempf assumed command over the Armeeabteilung, which thereby changed its name to Armeeabteilung Kempf. (For an examination of the personality of General der Panzertrupper Kempf, see "Die Leibstandarte," Volume II, pages 88 ff.)

At dawn, the thrust of the I./Panzerregiment *LAH* and the reinforced Aufklärungsabteilung (minus the 3./Artillerie-Regiment and Panzerjäger, which were engaged in holding the Jeremejewka support point) continued to the south via Kegitschewka, Rojakowka, Gurjewka, and Krutojarowka, distance of fifty kilometers. This attack destroyed nineteen 7.62-centimeter guns, four 4.5-centimeter anti-tank guns, seven heavy mortars and an unknown number of infantry weapons. The enemy also suffered bloody personnel losses. An attack by an enemy battalion moving from Paraskowejewskie toward Jeremejewka was destroyed by a Panzer counterthrust.

The armoured thrust to the south is described by the commander of the reinforced Aufklärungsabteilung, Sturmbannführer Meyer in his book "Grenadiere" (page 180 ff.) as follows:

> "We left our support point unnoticed by the enemy. The weather was favorable to our plan. The Artillerie provided harassing fire on the known preparation positions east of Jeremejewka, which fooled the enemy as to our intentions. Our marching unit could hardly be spotted in the snow. Every vehicle was painted with white camouflage, and the men wore snow smocks or white winter clothing. We snaked our way quickly through the rolling terrain.
>
> The Kampfgruppe halted behind a small hill.
>
> Enemy columns were moving steadily toward the west. A rambling town absorbed the Soviet troops and hid them from our view. We were only about a thousand meters from the Soviets. Should we dare it and storm down the gently sloping road? Red Army soldiers had been marching by to the west for twenty-four hours. Weren't they numerically too superior? Weren't we running right into a deadly wall of anti-tank fire? I stood with the commander of the Panzerabteilung, Wünsche, and the Kompanie commanders of the Aufklärungsabteilung at the head of the Kampfgruppe to discuss the suitable form of attack. As usual, I held speed to be the best weapon. It was my intention to move one Kompanie of the Aufklärungsabteilung into the very middle of the Soviet force under the cover of fire from our Panzers, cut their march formation in half and then to move to the west.
>
> A group of amphibious vehicles reported themselves as volunteers to lead the spearhead of the attack. The boys knew what to expect. It was certain that the flank of the enemy march formation would be protected with mines. In just a few minutes, everything was ready to roll. The wheels ground into the snow and gradually made traction. They moved faster and faster, finally moving into high gear, and they bore down on the town at full tilt. The open terrain had to be covered as quickly as possible, so that the enemy had no time to take countermeasures. The vehicles raced down the slope like an unleashed storm. Panzers moved left and right of the road on the hill and fired their shells into the Soviet mass. Heavy mortar fire intensified the effect of the Panzers. I found myself in the spearhead Kompanie hanging off the side of a jeep when the first amphibious vehicle flew into the air, and my comrades were thrown to the ground with their limbs smashed. Without braking for even a second, the second vehicle took over the lead spot, and it was torn apart in the next moment. The Kompanie flew over the breach like an arrow. In the truest sense of the word, our comrades blazed a trail. The mine barrier had been broken through. The shattered limbs of the two drivers and a few wounded riflemen lay in the snow. The Gruppenführer had lost both legs. We could not help, but the Kompanie following behind up took care of them.
>
> The Soviets took hasty flight away from the main street of the town and dashed into houses or sought to save themselves by fleeing to the south. They were mowed down on the white snowfields by our machine guns. Artillery pieces they tried to take along were rolled over by our Panzers, which pushed them off the road or shoved them together into a tangled

mass. The destruction we wreaked was indescribable. Some Panzers fired shell after shell into the troops retreating to the east, forcing them to take wild flight, which the advance of our Panzers only helped to accelerate. The Soviet march was smashed by our raging Panzers as if by a giant fist. Speed showed itself once again to be a mighty weapon. Hardly a single Soviet anti-tank gun was able to unlimber and move into position. They were mostly pulverized by the grinding tracks and weight of our Panzers. Within just a few minutes, we had moved through the long town and transformed their march route into a street of misery. Shrapnel was mixed with the flesh of Siberian oxen which had served as the draft animals for the anti-tank guns. From the edge of the town, the chase continued to the west. The Soviets had been completely surprised. They could not understand how death could spur them on from behind. The column fell victim to our onslaught virtually without resistance. Between the last buildings of the town, there was one damaged Panzer, which had been hit by a Russian anti-tank gun standing about one hundred fifty meters to the rear in an orchard. Our infantrymen were just moving in to destroy the anti-tank gun when a spray of machine-gun fire hit us. With lightning speed, we took cover on the other side of the Panzer. Only Franz Roth, the ever-eager war correspondent, did not make it. He took a shot to the chest. We pulled him to cover and moved him into a little house, where he received immediate attention from Dr. Gatternig. Roth died several days later in the field hospital. He had been one of our best correspondents. Our tracer shells set fire to the next town. There, too, the Red Army men ran for their lives and died in the fire of our machine guns. The chase continued into the next town after that, scattering the Soviets in wild flight. Equipment and weapons lay like detritus on the road back. The danger to our southern flank had been temporarily eliminated. At nightfall, we tiredly turned back to our support point. The destruction of the Russian force had cost us two dead and several heavy wounds. The speed of our action, the free use of our mobility, and the application of our firepower brought about this triumph."

For this deed, the commander of the Aufklärungsabteilung *LAH*, Sturmbannführer Kurt Meyer, was awarded the oak leaves to his Ritterkruez. In the middle sector, on the boundary between the 2. and 1. Panzergrenadier-Regiment *LAH*, enemy thrusts from Ochotschaje and Taranowka had to be repulsed the entire day.

Starting at 12.00 hours, the Panzergrenadier-Regiment *LAH* was directly subordinated to Armeeabteilung Kempf. With that, a time of harmonious cooperation began. The Oberbefehlshaber was well known and respected by the Division from the time when he was commanding general of the III. Panzerkorps. Between his Chef of the Generalstab, Generalmajor Dr. Speidel, and our Divisional commander, there was a relationship which was almost a friendship, and toward the Ia of the *LAH*, the Chef of the Generalstab showed a paternal good will. In the first telephone conversation between the Chef of the Generalstab of the Armeeabteilung and the 1. Generalstabsoffizer of the *LAH*, it was mentioned that the Armeeabteilung had made a request to the Heeresgruppe to pull back our line from the middle of the *LAH*'s front. The Division was able to prepare itself to pull back the left wing in the night between 21.2 and 22.2.

For this reason, the planned counterattack of the 1. Panzergrenadier-Regiment on Kljiutschewodsk was never carried out.

The III. (armoured)/2., reinforced with the 1./Pionier-Bataillon *LAH*, had in the meanwhile set up. By 16.30 hours, when night was already beginning to fall, it had crossed through Borki and replaced the 1./Pionier-Bataillon *LAH* on the northwestern edge of the town. The Bataillon was once again back behind the main battle line by the morning of 22.2. Untersturmführer Gührs had to remain with his Kraftwagenkanonenzug for technical reasons, and he later sought to reestablish contact with the Bataillon. He vividly described what can happen to a vehicle left behind:

> "It was 03.00 hours and dark as pitch. Columns were rolling to the rear. What was that supposed to mean? Sturmgeschütze, too, with mounted infantrymen on them turned back. Then there was nothing more. I increased my speed in my attempt to find the Bataillon, and suddenly I found myself in front of Rjabuchino. The town was on fire. Dead men lay all around. Ammunition, abandoned guns, dead horses, broken wagons. There was not a sound in the whole town. There were tank tracks in the snow. I suspected that the Bataillon had passed through. Beside the road stood Russian anti-tank guns with their crews dead, to the right was a Russian tank. It had certainly been put out of commission already. There was not much to see. In front of me was another village, and a few of its houses were burning. By then it was 04.00 hours. There was a noise, and my vehicle stopped and tipped to one side. We had been hit. Before the next shell could hit, I ordered the men to dismount to the right. Unterscharführer Mewes, Siart, Krell, Eberhard, and I. There were five of us, we had only two pistols, and the Russians had us. It was still dark, and Eberhard had suffered something of a shock. I held him by the wrist as the machine gun fire whistled around us. I was completely calm and felt that this was not the end. We crept into the village in front of us. By then it was 05.00 hours. I carefully approached the first house and asked an old Russian about German soldiers. He said that they had been forced out on the previous evening by assault guns. It became clear to me that our lines had been pulled back and no one had stopped us! As I was having a look at the village, Russian soldiers appeared. I pulled my men into the next piece of low ground in order to avoid any contact with the enemy. I tried to return to the disabled tank in order to get some weapons. But the Russians had already taken possession of it. The anti-tank gun which had hit us was standing in front of it. We had to get out of there! They spotted us and watched. We all had on snow jackets, however, so I waved, pretending that we belonged with them, and we marched on. The sun was at our backs, so we were heading west. Two Russian sleighs came over toward us. We kept our heads and disappeared into the next bit of low-lying ground. Behind us were more Russians, individual riders moving across the terrain. Things were getting risky. I tried to make it to the forest lying in front of us. Eight hundred meters to our left, an entire Russian battalion passed on skis. The prospects for our coming through this grew worse. After three hours of strenuous marching, we reached the road on which we had approached the previous night. We passed several abandoned installations, but we saw no Russians. There was a German plane overhead.

He dropped bombs on us! But nothing happened. Suddenly, there stood before me a Russian sleigh column. We took cover behind a snow drift. To our left, too, troops were passing in an open skirmish line. What could we do? Either dig in and wait out the night or risk it all by pretending to join the attack? But they spotted us and came our way. We turned off immediately and joined the attackers. The Russians began to take cover. I acted as if we were just a particularly brave band of soldiers and simply kept going. Thankfully, no one shot from behind. In front of us, through the binoculars, I spotted a new group which we had no hope of avoiding. They were also wearing snow jackets. Friend and foe were impossible to tell apart. As we came within sixty meters, I waved in any event. A little closer, and I suddenly found myself face-to-face with Sturmbannführer Frey. We had made it!"

After nightfall on 21.2, the 1. Panzergrenadier-Regiment shortened its front by pulling back to the line from the northeastern edge of Nowaja Wodolaga to the eastern edge of Knjatschnoj.

The 1./Pioniere *LAH*, left behind in Borki, was cut off. The Kompanieführer for this Pionier-Kompanie, Obersturmführer Taubert, reported on the consequences of the III./Infanterie-Regiment 586's retreat without notification:

"In the night, at 02.00 hours, the reconnaissance liaison officer reported to me that he had received fire from the Kompanie headquarters of the unit adjacent to the left. Our comrades, it seemed, had pulled back without conferring with us, and Ivan had broken through. We confirmed that suspicion the next morning when we received fire from the rear, and we set up all-around defenses. Our contact with Regiment Witt, which had always been weak, was entirely broken. We were completely surrounded, and Ivan was moving in on us from all sides, covering us with artillery and mortar fire. By the evening of the following day, we already had suffered three fatalities and forty-five woundings at headquarters. The medics had their hands full. My radio officer, Unterscharführer Stemmermann, had been grazed by a bullet to his head, but he stayed at his post by the radio. The next day, I notified the Regiment by radio: 'If we are not relieved by this evening, it is all over; our ammunition will be spent by then.' We were saved that evening by a Kompanie from the Panzerregiment. We took along our wounded and dead, naturally."

At about noon, the new Oberbefehlshaber, General der Panzertruppen Kempf, paid a visit to the *LAH*.

The spearhead unit of the SS-Panzerkorps reached Pawlograd with Division *DR* and, already subordinated to the 4. Panzerarmee, continued its thrust farther to the southwest.

The *LAH* at this point had the following Panzers: six Panzer VI's, forty-nine Panzer IV's, twenty-one Sturmgeschütze.

Orders for the *LAH* for 22.2.1943:

The northern wing of the *LAH* was to capture the line Melechowka — eastern edge of Nowaja Wodolaga, enabling a mobile attack force to be withdrawn.

The reinforced Aufklärungsabteilung *LAH* and the III. (armoured)/2. were to stand ready to serve as the mobile attack force.

22.2.1943: In the course of the retreat to the new battle line, the reinforced II./1. (under Sturmbannführer M. Hansen) had carried out a nighttime attack against Klijutschewodsk. The move had cost us many casualties, but it prevented the enemy's immediate pursuit.

At 05.30 hours, the reinforced 1. Panzergrenadier-Regiment Kampfgruppe reported that it had assumed the designated battle line with the I. Bataillon (under Sturmbannführer Frey) in the sector Melechowka — Knjashnoj and the reinforced II. Bataillon (under Max Hansen) in the sector Podkopai — Bulachi — Nowaja Wodolaga. The III./1. (under Weidenhaupt) remained in Karawanskoje at the disposal of the Regiment.

At 06.00 hours, there was an attack by an enemy company against the strong point at Melechowka (II.2.). It was repulsed.

In the sector held by the I./1. (under Frey), there were several reconnaissance thrusts by forces up to company strength.

At about 16.00 hours, there was an attack by an enemy battalion on the advance strong point at Podkopai (II./1.), which was also repulsed.

At 17.00 hours, the II./1. reported that, with the support of the Sturmgeschütze, a localized enemy breakthrough between Hf. Chomenki and Ordiwka had been cleared away.

At the same time, there was an attack by a force of at least battalion strength from Ochotschaje on the eastern edge of Melechowka, which was repulsed by the II./2. (under Sturmbannführer Sandig). The enemy suffered bloody losses in the fighting.

The enemy force of company strength found in Paraskowejewskije was not attacked on that day, because the reinforced Aufklärungsabteilung and I./Panzerregiment, functioning as the mobile attack force, were in urgent need of a pause for repairs. In addition, the enemy was moving more and more forces into the town, and it would make a more rewarding target on 23.2. A reconnaissance force under the command of Oberscharführer Bügelsack had been able to establish contact with the *T* Division in Alexandrowka. The reinforced III. (armoured)/2. had orders to seek and maintain contact from Natalino to the *T* Division in Otrada and, in cooperation with the reinforced Aufklärungsabteilung and the I./Panzerregiment *LAH*, to destroy any enemy troop build-up west of the Orels.

The *LAH* passed along to Armeeabteilung Kempf its evaluation of the situation, which was that the enemy was moving hesitantly because of the hard blows he had taken in this terrain, so suited to Panzers, on both sides of the Jefremowka — Paraskoweja road. In the terrain east and southeast of Nowaja Wodolaga, which was deeply creased with ravines and occupied by only our strong points, he would renew his attemps to apply pressure with strong attacks on the eastern front of our Armee along its northern wing.

As night fell, Major i.G. Heidenreich transmitted a written order from the Armeeabteilung which "demanded with emphasis that the principle of offensive combat finally prevail with this strong and mobile unit."

This order, which was incomprehensible to us in the face of the aggressively conducted defense we had in fact been waging, was finally explained in the exchange of telegrams between the Armee and Heeregruppe cited below:

With telegram 714/43, dated 22.2, 11.28 hours, Generalfeldmarschall von Manstein asked the Armee "emphatically to bear responsibility that the principle of offensive combat prevail."

Armeeabteilung Kempf responded on 22.2 at 18.10 hours:

"1.) An order corresponding to the telegram from the Ia of the Heeresgruppe (714/43 g.Kdos. dated 22.2 at 11.28 hours) has been transmitted to the *Leibstandarte* by the Generalstabsoffizier.

2.) In respect to the order from Herr Oberbefehlshaber of the Heeresgruppe, I feel obliged to offer the following report in the interest of the *Leibstandarte SS-AH*, which is fighting so valiantly under such capable command:

The *Leibstandarte* has carried out its mission according to orders in offensive combat on the southern wing of its eighty-kilometer-wide defensive sector.

In the last few days, it has achieved the following successes:

On 17.2, the Aufklärungsabteilung and the 1. Panzerabteilung destroyed 1,200 men (Soviet Rifle Regiment 747 of the 172nd Rifle Division) and eight 7.62-centimeter guns.

In the night between 19.2 and 20.2, one reinforced Grenadier-Bataillon destroyed seven hundred fifty men, eleven 7.62-centimeter guns, three tanks, and fifteen mortars southeast of Ziglerowka. Four additional artillery pieces were destroyed near Borki.

On 21.2, the reinforced Aufklärungsabteilung smashed four enemy columns near Jeremejewka and destroyed seventeen 7.62-centimeter guns (Soviet Artillery Regiment 131 of the 6th Rifle Division).

In the night between 21.2 and 22.2, the reinforced Aufklärungsabteilung launched a surprise attack and broke an enemy troop assembly near Rossochowatij.

The Panzerregiment was successfully deployed in the night between 21.2 and 22.2 in a mobile attack to free the Pionier-Bataillon which was surrounded in Borki.

No. 266/43 g.Kdos.

Kempf."

The response from Generalfeldmarschall von Manstein was as follows:

"In answer to telegram no. 266/43 g.Kdos. dated 22.2:

1.) From the above-mentioned telegram I infer that Herr Oberbefehlshaber is of the opinion that my telegram Ia no. 714/43 g.Kdos. dated 22.2 placed an unreasonable demand on the *Leibstandarte SS-Adolf Hitler* or that its performance has not be adequately recognized.
If Herr Oberbefehlshaber was of this opinion, he should have conferred with me before conveying my order to the unit.

2). Of the demands which the situation forces me to place on the troops and of their bravery and willingness to sacrifice everything I am too well aware for it to be necessary to speak to me on their behalf.

3). The *Leibstandarte SS-Adolf Hitler*'s successes enumerated in your telegram had not been readily perceptible from the partial results noted by the Heeresgruppe, which is necessarily forced by conditions to give only piecemeal reports. Those successes are now fully recognized.

4). The situation still demands, however, that the *Leibstandarte*, to which the situation has dealt a broad sector in the framework of the defensive mission, wage its battles in a mobile fashion with short strikes. The larger the forces which can be concentrated on each strike, even taking into account the weakening of the rest of the front, the greater the success will be. I ask the Herr Commander of the *Leibstandarte SS-Adolf Hitler* to inform the unit of my opinion in a suitable form.

Oberbefehlshaber of Heeresgruppe Süd
signed, von Manstein
Ia no. 714/43 g.Kdps. II. Angel."

The SS-Panzerkorps, moving to the south, was occupied during the entire day with its attempt to move up to Pawlowgrad. It had to defend itself against continual attacks on its long, stretched-out eastern flank.

In an evening telephone conversation, the Chef of the Generalstab of the Armee (General Dr. Speidel) and the 1. Generalstabsoffizier of the *LAH* (Sturmbannführer Lehmann) agreed that the situation in front of the middle of the Heeresgruppe had developed favorably and that it would be under sufficient control in three or four days for the SS-Panzerkorps with the Division *DR* and the Division *T* to make a thrust to the north toward us.

The Division's orders for 23.2.1943 remained unchanged:

The reinforced III. (armoured)/2., subordinated directly to the Division, was to maintain its hold on Natalino and meanwhile to attempt to establish and maintain contact to the SS-*T*-Division. Combat-strength reconnaissance was to be maintained between the road from Krassnograd over Andrejewka to Dar Nadesdy and the railway line from Krassnograd to Kulikowka as far as the Bogotaja sector.

The reinforced Aufklärungsabteilung and the I./Panzerregiment LAH were to destroy the enemy forces which had been spotted in Paraskowejewskije and to launch an armoured attack against the Orel sector.

The 2. Panzergrenadier-Regiment's orders remained unchanged.

The 1. Panzergrenadier-Regiment was to free the 1./Pionier *LAH* trapped in Borki. Otherwise its mission was unchanged.

23.2.1943: After a peaceful night, the reinforced Aufklärungsabteilung and the I./Panzerregiment *LAH* set out at dawn to make their move on Paraskowejewskije. This thrust led to the destruction of the staff of the Soviet 172nd Rifle Division, elements of the 134th Artillery Regiment, and the 150th Tank Defense Regiment (twenty 7.62-centimeter guns, two 10.5-centimeter guns, four 12.2-centimeter guns, three multiple rocket launchers, and a huge number of men killed).

Untersturmführer Maurer, a Zugführer in the 2./Aufklärungsabteilung *LAH*, reported on this day as follows:

"Our light Feldhaubitze 18, the heavy Züge, and the supply trains were to make a feint to the east while the two Panzerkompanien and the two mounted Kradschützenkompanien were to move between the towns to the

north and then swing around to the southeast in an attack on the rear assembly areas of the Russian forces.
Shortly before dawn, we reached our attack objective, Paraskowejewskije. We could hear our own Artillerie from Jeremejewka, and mortar and machine gun fire started up from there, as well. We attacked on a broad front behind the Panzers to the south. The Russians were caught completely by surprise. A deep anti-tank front stretched out toward our mounted weapons. The house-to-house fighting was easy against a surprised enemy, and we moved about one or two kilometers into the town. At about 10.00 hours, it was ours. The enemy's store of anti-tank weapons and ammunition was destroyed. The enemy had lost probably about 1,000 men and all his heavy equipment. The Russian commander was reported to have been killed.
At about 14.00 hours, as we sat down for a late noon-day meal, we found ourselves back at our starting point. In the 3. Zug there had been no losses, elsewhere only minor ones. But Obersturmführer Bohr, at the time leader of the 1. Kompanie, was badly wounded. We later heard that he died at the main medical clearing station."

On orders from the Division, the thrust against Nishnij-Orel was discontinued after reconnaissance determined that there was a strong and well-organized tank defense in the Orel sector.

The Adjutant of the I./Panzerregiment *LAH*, Obersturmführer Isecke, reported on the preparations for and execution of the Panzer thrust:

"The enemy was installed in a town, the outskirts of which began about three and a half kilometers from us and which stretched several kilometers along a shallow valley. In their conference on the situation, both commanders discussed the possibility of an enveloping or flanking attack. In such a plan, the heavy weapons and supply trains would move frontally on the enemy and provide a feint frontal attack while the Panzers, two mounted Kradschützenkompanien and the light Schützenpanzerwagen-Kompanie of the Aufklärungsabteilung would hurry forward from the flank.
I received orders to reconnoiter the attack terrain, because I was also to lead the attack column into the assembly position.
Ahead of our combat outposts, I left the Panzer accompanying us behind to watch over us. Between the town to be attacked and the next town, lying to the northwest, there was a long plateau. And there appeared to be a ravine running parallel to the town. There were several approaches which favored our intentions. We were so far forward then that we could barely make out the Panzer we had left behind. Our white camouflage provided good cover. We moved carefully forward to the ravine mentioned above and then started back. Our tracks would provide orientation in the night.
My reconnaissance report set the attack preparations in motion. At about 05.00 hours, the assembly of the armoured force was completed. I had a perch built on the extra track links hanging on the front of my Panzer where I could squat and spot our tracks at short range in the dark. Would our surprise succeed? Finding our tracks from the previous evening went without a hitch. When I looked to the side, the next Panzers just looked like shadows. The same was true of the seven or eight Kradschützen sitting

> on them. The column, about one kilometer in length, stopped at about 07.00 hours to the side of the targeted town; only the ravine lay in front of us. The unit commanders went ahead on foot to reconnoiter the descent into the ravine and especially the ascent on the other side. In the approaching dawn, we stood ready. Glancing over the edge, we could see the town only three to four hundred meters away. By radio, we ordered the frontal fire to begin from our support point. Then we fired our volley and gave the order, 'Panzers, march! Drive, drive!' At every house, there were Russians cursing us. The Kradschützen cleared the streets of enemy soldiers to the right and left. They tried to escape across the valley, but we caught them with our machine gun fire. The enemy anti-tank and artillery teams did not even make it to their guns. In the bottom of the valley, we ran into two heavy batteries with their barrels aimed at our frontal support point. With two Panzerkompanien, we pursued the enemy to the east and northeast and destroyed him. Our own Panzer crews suffered no wounds to personnel and only light damage to the equipment. Our thrust hit the Russian divisional headquarters precisely. The division commander was reported killed, and the first officer of the general staff was taken prisoner."

After that action, the commander of the Aufklärungsabteilung *LAH*, Sturmbannführer Meyer, travelled to the Führer's Headquarters to receive the oak leaves to his Ritterkreuz. The command of the Kampfgruppe, consisting of the reinforced Aufklärungsabteilung and the I./Panzerabteilung *LAH*, was taken over by Sturmbannführer Wünsche.

August Zinßmeister, the historian of the Panzerspähkompanie of the Aufklärungsabteilung *LAH*, noted on this day:

> "23.2 (Tuesday). At noon, we were called from our defense position. We conducted reconnaissance toward Kegitschewka; clear of enemy forces; back via Pawlowka. There, we could not make it through the snow. But we did get a few geese from a collective farm."

The III. (armoured)/2. (under Sturmbannführer Peiper), reported by evening that Dar Nadeshdy and Kulikowka were clear of the enemy.

From the left wing of the II./2. Panzergrenadier-Regiment came reports starting at 09.00 hours of constant enemy attacks.

The point of main concentration for the enemy attacks lay on the right wing of the 1. Panzergrenadier-Regiment along the road from Rjabuchino to Nowaja Wodolaga and the road from Merefa to Nowaja Wodolaga. A localized breakthrough in the sector held by the II./1. (under Max Hansen) south of Ordiwka was cleared away with the support of the Panzers of the II./Panzerregiment *LAH* (under Sturmbannführer Groß). A breakthrough in the sector of the unit adjacent to the left, the 320. Infanteriedivision, was also pushed back by the Panzers from our II. Abteilung.

In the late evening, the enemy succeeded in penetrating the positions of the I./1. (under Frey) west of Rjabuchino. In the course of the night, after hasty preparation and with excellent Artillerie support, we were able to repulse this enemy force, as well. In the morning at about 09.00 hours, the Chef of the Generalstab of the Armee was informed of the success of the Paraskowejewskije operation. He in turn informed the Ia of the *LAH* that the Russian advance on

Achtyrka (about one hundred and ten kilometers northwest of Charkow) would necessitate a change in the conduct of the battle. The new plan was to shorten the front by pulling back the *LAH* and the 320. Infanteriedivision to the line Krassnograd — Berestowenka — Paraskoweja — Starowerowka — Nikolskoje — Maidan — Tschutowo. By this move, the Infanterie-Division *Großdeutschland* would be freed up to be used as a mobile reserve force against the enemy forces which had moved far to the west.

The start of the withdrawal was set for 24.2 at 17.00 hours. It was to take place in two stages, first to an intermediate position on 24.2 and then to the newly designated line on 25.2.

On 23.2.1943 at 20.30 hours, Divisionsbefehl No. 6 for this move was issued to the units (see sketch 17). The following is an excerpt:

4) *Orders*:

a) *The reinforced 2. Panzergrenadier-Regiment LAH* is to leave its strong point at Kasatschij Maidan and to occupy the line Wlassowka — Point 171.8 — Point 180.3 — western section of Starowerowka — eastern edge of Popiwka. It is to seek and maintain contact with the 1. Panzergrenadier-Regiment *LAH* at Point 188.1 in order to curve its left wing around toward Jarotin on 25.2. The Artillerie deployed in the Regiment's sector is subordinated to it for the withdrawal.

b) *Kampfgruppe Peiper* is to remain on the southeastern edge of Krassnograd with its previous orders.

c) *The reinforced 1. Panzergrenadier-Regiment LAH* is to occupy the line Point 188.1 — Stanitschnije — road to Walki — Point 195.0 (five hundred meters north of Kadygrobowka) and to establish contact with the 320. Infanteriedivision at Point 195.4 (one kilometer southeast of Monkowka). On 25.2, on orders from the Division, it is then to pull back to the line Jarotin (exclusive of it) — Nikolskoje — Blagodatnoje (exclusive of it). That line must still be reconnoitered. The Artillerie deployed in the Regiment's sector and the II./Panzerregiment *LAH* are to be subordinated to it for the withdrawal.

d) *The Panzerregiment* is to move to Krassnograd with the Stab and the elements not deployed. *The Panzer-Pionierkompanie* is to remain as a defensive force in Ziglerowka.
The I./Panzerregiment is to remain subordinated to the *reinforced Aufklärungsabteilung.*
The II./Panzerregiment is to stand at the disposal of the Division as soon as it has occupied its final position.

e) The Artillerie-Regiment and its Stab are to remain in the area north of Krassnograd. It is to subordinate its Abteilungen to the sector commanders for the withdrawal and to move a Werferbatterie up to serve at the Division's disposal.

f) *The reinforced Aufklärungsabteilung* is to remain in Jeremejewka under the commander of the I./Panzerregiment *LAH* until its own commander returns. It will be used to secure the Division's southern flank in mobile combat.

g) *The Sturmgeschützabteilung* is to leave one Batterie subordinated to the 1. Panzergrenadier-Regiment and one subordinated to Bataillon Peiper. With its Stab and one Batterie, it is then to stand at the disposal of the Division, initially in Jarotin, later in the northern section of Perwomaiskoje.

h) *The Panzerjägerabteilung* is to leave its subordinated elements with the Kampfgruppen and to stand with the bulk of its forces at the dispoal of the Division in Perwomaiskoje.

i) *The Pionier-Bataillon* is to keep the bulk of its forces subordinated to the 1. Panzergrenadier-Regiment *LAH*. The Brückenkolonne is to move to Karlowka and stand at the Division's disposal. It will receive further orders via the Panzerregiment.

k) *The Flakabteilung* with its Stab, 3., 4. and 6. Batterie, is to remain in Poltawa and to leave its subordinated elements as before.

...

10.) *The Divisional headquarters* will be in Krassnograd starting at 15.00 hours on 24.2.1943.

At 21.00 hours, there was an inquiry from the Ia of the *LAH* to the Armee as to whether the area between Paraskoweja and Starowerowka should be kept open. The road itself could not be held, because there was a forest stretching to within fifty meters of it. The road could, however, be seen clearly from the advance line Wlassewka — Jarotin, and heavy weapons could easily fire upon it. The Ia of the Armee, Oberstleutnant I.G. Estor, was to lay this information before the Oberbefehlshaber for his decision.

At 22.15 hours, the Aufklärungsabteilung reported on its findings in the Orel sector: there was an enemy defensive line growing constantly in strength.

At 23.00 hours, the III. (armoured)/ 2. received orders to maintain constant contact with the *T*-Division in Wolny and on the Wshiwaja sector.

24.2.1943: The main concentration for the day was reconnoitering the Division's southern flank. Once again, the following towns were observed to be heavily occupied by the enemy: Nishnji-Orel, Pawlowka, and Andrewjewka. The eastern bank of the Bogotaja, six kilometers north of Kulikowka, and the western entrance into Ssachnowsctschina were heavily mined. Apparently, there were strong security forces protecting the expansion of the Orel positions. In this reconnaissance action, the Chef of the 12./2., Obersturmführer Westrup, was killed.

August Zinßmeister of the Panzerspähkompanie/Aufklärungsabteilung continued his chronicle as follows:

> "24.2 (Wednesday). Early in the morning, we drove off with Steiner to reconnoiter Pawlowka. We came under anti-tank and infantry fire and pulled back. Thereafter, we patrolled the road junction west of Pawlowka. We were the masters of this no-man's land. We got provisions for ourselves from the nearby collective farms. The fog was very thick. In the night between 24.2 and 25.2, we once again patrolled the terrain to provide defense for our Abteilung."

In the early morning, the I./1. was successful in moving one Zug of riflemen with three Sturmgeschütze ahead of the battle line north of Ochotschaje. Four 7.62-centimeter guns and several mortars were destroyed. Sixty prisoners were

6.3.1943: The spearhead of the III. (armoured)/ 2 LSSAH questions a Ukrainian woman near Fedorowka.

7.3.1943: The self-propelled 2-centimeter Flak provides fire support for the 1. Panzergrenadier-Regiment in the attack on Walki.

11.2.1943: The spearhead of the Aufklärungsabteilung has run into mines in front of Jefremowka.

13.2.1943: Dead Russian soldiers in front of Jefremowka.

taken. In the late afternoon, this thrust was repeated, and once again scored the following triumphs: five guns, one heavy machine gun, and thirty prisoners.
In the course of the entire day, the enemy waged heavy attacks from the edges of the forest northwest of Rjabuchino. He was successful in the morning in capturing the strong point of the II./1. in Bulachi. The strong point was recaptured in a counterattack supported by a Panzerkompanie from the II./Panzerregiment *LAH*. In that counterattack, the following enemy forces were destroyed: two T-34's, three American Mark III tanks, fifteen heavy machine guns, five heavy mortars, seven artillery pieces, and four to five hundred soldiers of the Soviet 11th Cavalry Division.
In the afternoon, our former reserve forces arrived and began to occupy the designated intermediate line of scattered strong points.
At 17.00 hours, we began to disengage from the enemy, which operation ran smoothly without the enemy's noticing it.
Between 22.00 and 23.15 hours, the Regimenter reported that they had reached the designated line.
At 23.00 hours, the units received their orders for 25.2.1943 by radio:

> For the *1. and 2. Panzergrenadier-Regiment LAH*, the orders were a continuation of their move to the designated line, beginning at 17.00 hours.
> Additional orders for the *2. Panzergrenadier-Regiment*: continual reconnaissance and defense in front of Losowaja, since Jeremejewka was occupied by enemy forces.
> Additional orders for the *Aufklärungsabteilung and I./Panzerregiment LAH*:
> a) The Kampfgruppe's main objective was to move in mobile combat to prevent the enemy from proceeding on both sides of Jeremejewka toward Krassnograd.
> b) Increased concentration of the reconnaissance into the Orel position in the Dmitrowka — Jeremejewka sector.
> For *Kampfgruppe Peiper*: increased concentration of the reconnaissance against the Orel position in the sector Orelka — Ligowka. Reconnaissance against the Orel south of Ssatschewnilowka and in the area between the road and the railway tracks between Krassnograd and Dar Nadeshdy and Kegitschewka, respectively. The Division wants to know whether the enemy is proceeding across the railway to the west on both sides of Kulikowka and south of Kegitschewka.

In the course of the day, the Division moved its headquarters to Krassnograd.
On 24.2, the SS-Panzerkorps established contact with the 4. Panzerarmee and destroyed the enemy forces in the area around Pawlograd and on both sides of the Ssamara sector. It had orders to proceed to the north, starting in the early morning of 25.2.1943, with Panzergrenadierdivision *DR* moving to the right toward Losowaja and Panzergrenadierdivision *T* to the left toward Panjutina.

25.2.1943: Disengagement from the enemy and the move back to the designated line ran smoothly and according to plan.
At 08.20 hours, the two Regimental forces established contact with each other at the railroad tracks north of Starowerowka.
At 09.00 hours, the Armeeabteilung approved a new line, proposed by the Ia of the *LAH*, running from Wlassowka to Jarotin.

At 12.00 hours, there was an enemy attack on Katygrobowka, supported by four enemy tanks, but the 1. Panzergrenadier-Regiment repulsed it and destroyed one T-34 in the process.

At 13.50 hours, the 1. Panzergrenadier-Regiment reported that twelve T-34's were moving from Peressel toward Minkowka accompanied by several trucks filled with infantrymen. The Division sent four Sturmgeschütze from the 2./Sturmgeschützabteilung *LAH* in Nikolskoje toward Minkowka.

A self-propelled Panzerjägerkompanie was moved to Ljaschewa in order to be able to move on Minkowka, as well, in the night under bright moonlight or in the early morning of 26.2 at the latest.

A Panzer thrust from Jeremejewka in the direction of Jefremowka under the command of Wünsche of the I./Panzerregiment *LAH* ran into enemy attack preparations for a move from the southern tip of Losowaja to the west. Our Panzers defeated the southern attack force of the Soviet 350th Rifle Division, destroyed thirty-seven 7.62-centimeter artillery pieces, ten 4.5-centimeter artillery pieces, and six 12.2-centimeter artillery pieces, recaptured one German light Feldhaubitze, captured three to four hundred sleighs with their horses and oxen, and counted about eight hundred enemy dead.

Obersturmführer Isecke, Adjutant of the I./Panzerregiment *LAH*, reported as follows:

> "Before nightfall on 24.2, our commander, Sturmbannführer Wünsche, held one final briefing on the action. The heavy weapons were to launch an artillery barrage before the start of the attack. The Panzers with mounted Kradschützen were to form a narrow attack wedge until the breakthrough was made. The approach was made through a dip in the valley. The Panzers drove back the enemy anti-tank weapons and made their way through to the enemy artillery standing five to six kilometers back. At daybreak, thirty more Panzers were moved up and began their attack. Because no enemy tanks had been observed, the battle against the enemy anti-tank fire was brought to a quick conclusion with the high-explosive shells from our Panzers. The Russians fled in droves and were easily visible in their brown uniforms against the white ground as soon as they left their snow fortifications.
>
> Our commander urged us on: 'Forward, forward, don't stop to fight their infantry! Their artillery is our goal!' And he was right, for we could soon see that ox-drawn sleighs were being driven into position. Within half an hour, we had destroyed this artillery (fifty-three guns) by blowing it up, tipping it over, and even destroying it as it was being pulled away. Not a single Panzer was hit. They assembled quickly and attacked the enemy infantry in the back. By noon, the Soviet 350th Rifle Division was defeated. To our great joy, our commander, Sturmbannführer Wünsche, the Chef of the 2./Panzerregiment *LAH*, Obersturmführer Beck, as well as Oberscharführer Reimling, a Zugführer in the 2. Panzerregiment *LAH*, received the Ritterkreuz for this operation."

The reconnaissance conducted by the III. (armoured)/2. under Sturmbannführer Peiper revealed enemy trenchwork underway in the line Ssachnowschtschino — Kulikowka — Bessarabowka — Beluchowka — Pawlowka — one kilometer northeast of Ssumzy.

Our losses for 25.2.1943 were as follows:
One officer and six non-commissioned officers and enlisted men killed; two officers and forty-three non-commissioned officers and men wounded; one man fallen ill; three men missing.

At 17.00 hours, the move back to the newly designated line began, and the completion of the move was reported to have been accomplished without exceptional difficulty by 22.00 hours.
The thrust of the SS-Panzerkorps to the north (in the direction of the terrain southeast of our positions) continued as Panzergrenadierdivison *DR* reached Losowaja and SS-Panzergrenadierdivision *T* reached Alexejewka on 25.2.

26.2.1943 (see sketch 18): The I./2. sent out a combat-strength reconnaissance force consisting of the reinforced Krad-Erkundundungszug under Untersturmführer Albers, one Zug from the 1. Kompanie, and half a Zug of 2-centimeter Flak from the 15. Kompanie across Medwedowka and Paraskoweja toward Melechowka. It found that Medwekowka and the hills to the east of there were occupied by enemy forces, as was Berestowaja. An enemy force of about four to five hundred men was on the road from Karawannyi to Starowerowka.
At the same time, strong enemy columns were moving from the east on Jeremejewka. The Flakzug under Armberger (4./Flakabteilung *LAH*), deployed simultaneously toward northern Kotjarowka used mounted Infanterie to attack a weak enemy force in that town and to rout it. Our troops destroyed two 7.62-centimeter guns, twenty sleighs, and counted sixty dead.
At 07.30 hours, there was an enemy attack with tanks on Point 194, but it was repulsed.
At 10.15 hours, the reinforced I./Panzerregiment *LAH* set off from Jeremejewka to the north toward Point 192 (four kilometers south of Jefremowka) with the following success: two 7.62-centimeter guns, one 4.5-centimeter anti-tank guns, and several anti-tank rifles destroyed.
August Zinßmeister of the 4. (Panzerspäh)/Aufklärungsabteilung *LAH* continued his chronicle as follows:

> "26.2. We set off on a reconnaissance trip with Lindloff's [eight-wheel] Panzerspähwagen and a four-wheel Kampfwagenkanone [armoured car equipped with a gun]. We reconnoitered toward Jefremowka. A mounted Russian force escaped us for the most part. Then we saw a group of Russian infantry and artillery limbers which were being ripped apart by two of our dive bombers. We moved close up and let loose on them, as well, with all our weapons and two additional Panzer II's The dive bombers swooped away. We thought we had the situation under control. But then an entire front of anti-tank weapons which we knew nothing about opened up on us. Our eight-wheel Spähwagen was hit and rendered inoperational. The Panzer II next to it tried to take it in tow, but a shell hit the Panzer, too, and it burst into flames. We thought we could make out five Russian anti-tank guns. We and the other Panzer II in front of us drove in a rapid zig-zag to the rear, firing all the way. The Kampfwagenkanone, which had originally been at the end of our little column, joined us. With a great deal of effort, we succeeded in establishing a safe distance between ourselves and the Russians. But the eight-wheeler was on fire. Lindloff, the driver,

> and the gunner were able to jump out and come back to us. The radioman, Wichmann, was missing. Toward evening, our Panzers broke through. We found Wichmann dead beside the eight-wheeler and brought him back to his Kompanie. In the night, we twice acted as liaison reconnaissance force between our unit and the 2. Panzergrenadier-Regiment in Ziglerowka."

At 11.00 hours, on orders from the 1. Panzergrenadier-Regiment, the 6./1. (under Hauptsturmführer Weiher), reinforced by the 1./Sturmgeschützabteilung and one Zug from the self-propelled Panzerjäger stationed in Jarotin, attacked the Wlassowka railway station and destroyed eleven T-34's and one KV I without suffering any losses itself.

At 12.05 hours, the 6./2. (under Hauptsturmführer Scappini) attacked the enemy forces in Wlassowka. The Kompanie achieved the virtual annihilation of the enemy troops. At the same time, the 2./2. (under Haupturmführer Becker) set off once again to take Kotljarowka and was able to throw the enemy out of his positions.

At 14.00 hours, a Kompanie of the III./1. (under Hauptsturmführer Hubert Meyer), reinforced by the 2./Sturmgeschützabteilung (under Obersturmführer Holst), moved out from Nikolskoje to attack Minkowka. Our comrade, F. Kutzner, reported on the move in the periodical "Wiking-Ruf" (no. 7/55, page 16) as follows:

> "Past the collective farm, there was a snow field. The entire Batterie moved forward in a straight line, with five or six Grenadiere from the III./1. Panzergrenadier-Regiment perched on each artillery piece. Despite the fur clothing, they were freezing and swearing mightily. To top it all off, there was an icy north wind blowing across the plain, driving needles of ice into our faces. 'Right face!' A narrow sheltered road led into the village of Bobrowka. The artillery pieces in front halted, and the Grenadiere climbed off to inspect the first houses. Nothing stirred. Neither Ivan nor Germanski. Someone found an old farmer hiding somewhere; in the light from a kerosine lamp, he was supposed to give the Chef information with the map. 'Nje punimai, Pan.' 'Sovietski Soldat?' 'Nema nesnajo.' What direction was the next village? There? Our Chef pointed to a spot on the map. 'Da, da, Pan!' There was not much to be gained from this old fellow. He was either playacting, or he was really stupid. Probably the former. So off we went. Mount the vehicles! 'Panzers, march!' Three more hours passed. Three hours of travel through this wasteland in biting cold and icy wind. Suddenly, figures appeared shovelling snow to the right and left of our road. Russians. Two sentries were with them. They were obviously there to open up the march route. For whom? On we went! The cold penetrated to our bones, and we found not a trace of Russian forces. Then the spearhead suddenly stopped. 'Prepare for combat! Grenadiere dismount!' Finally it had happened! The hatch covers were closed, the breech mechanisms clicked, and the Grenadiere spread out as a line of skirmishers between the artillery pieces as they felt their way forward to the village lying five hundred meters before us. The Grenadiere had just reached the first buildings and were combing the miserable little place when the Sturmgeschütze arrived in open semi-circle formation, already prepared to fire. The first Grenadiere returned. Nothing! The whole place was deserted. This time, it was a thrust

forward into a vaccuum. Either Ivan had not arrived yet, or he was long gone. The whole force assembled and moved back in a hurry, past the Russian column, still shovelling snow."

At 15.00 hours, the Chef of the Generalstab of the Armeeabteilung briefed the Ia of the *LAH* that the 320. Infanteriedivision was to assume a position adjacent to the *LAH* near Landychewo. Sturmbannführer Lehmann reported that the *LAH* had sent a self-propelled Panzerjägerzug to Blagodatnoje to support the weak forces of the 320. Infanteriedivision located there.

The Luftwaffe had provided effective support for the Division's defensive fighting during the entire day.

At 17.30 hours, the Ic of the Armeeabteilung reported that, according to radio reports, the enemy was abandoning all his known battle headquarters away from the area around and to the west of Charkow and moving them to the south. During the day, the Division had dealt the enemy the following losses: thirteen tanks, thirty-six artillery pieces of all types, and numerous heavy and light infantry weapons.

The SS-Panzerkorps and the SS-Panzergrenadierdivision *DR* were still fighting around Losowaja, and Panzergrenadierdivision *T* was able to push forward eight kilometers to the northeast as far as Zavedarowka. The commander of Panzergrenadierdivision *T*, Obergruppenführer Eicke, and his O 1 were shot down in a Fieseler Storch at about 13.30 hours one kilometer southeast of Artlenoje. Oberführer Simon, formerly commander of SS-Panzergrenadier-Regiment 5, assumed command of the Division. Obersturmbannführer Baum took over his position at the head of SS-Panzergrenadier-Regiment 5.

Orders for 27.2.1943:

Hold the designated line with mobile combat in accordance with the situation's development. The 3./Sturmgeschützabteilung *LAH* and the 1./Panzerjägerabteilung *LAH* were only to be deployed with permission from the Division.

27.2.1943: Starting at 03.14 hours, the enemy waged heavy attacks with forces of at least battalion strength from the southeast, east, north, and northwest against the Jeremejewka strong point (held by the reinforced Aufklärungsabteilung and the I./Panzerregimenbt *LAH*). These attacks were supported by isolated, smaller tank thrusts. In repulsing them, we destroyed seven 4.5-centimeter anti-tank guns and four hundred Russian soldiers. The historian of the 4. (Panzerspäh)/Aufklärungsabteilung *LAH*, August Zinßmeister, reported:

"Early on 27.2, we moved forward to Kegitschewka and then made a move toward Selena Dubrowa. There we came under artillery fire.

Aumann then took a reconnaissance force to Tschernoloski and Bessarabowka. Both were clear of enemy forces.

In the evening, another reconnaissance force with Untersturmführer Goltz and Untersturmführer Aumann moved forward to Tschernoloski and back to Kegitschewka. Overnight, we provided defense on the railway embankment one kilometer south of Kegitschewka in conjunction with Aumann's force. That's how it went day in, day out and night after night: reconnaissance duty, security duty, over and over again. We never got out of the Spähwagens any more. We could not even close our eyes at night. And then the orders came again: reconnaissance, security, reconnaissance ...!"

At 07.00 hours, the Sturmgeschütze and the 3./Panzerjägerabteilung *LAH* (under Obersturmführer Woest) had to intervene in the sector held by the unit adjacent to the left, the 320. Infanteriedivision. The enemy was threatening to make a breakthrough there, but the attack was stopped. The enemy, using numerically superior forces and some tank support, began launching well-organized attacks from Paraskoweja, Starowerowka, the Wlassowka railway station, and Minkowka against the positions of the 1. Panzergrenadier-Regiment led by Standartenführer Witt.

The Geschütz under Welser of the 15./1. killed fifteen Russians with a high-explosive shell at a range of fifty meters. The light Infanteriegeschützzug overcame a 7.62-centimeter gun and scored a direct hit on a tank with mounted infantrymen on it.[28]

A localized breakthrough by four enemy tanks south of Starowerowka was pushed back by an immediate counterthrust by the self-propelled 3./Panzerjägerabteilung.

At 08.00 hours, the 1. Panzergrenadier-Regiment reported that the 320. Infanteriedivision had already completed its withdrawal from Blagodatnoje, planned for that evening, and that the enemy had moved infantry and tanks through the resulting hole. His forces were proceeding rapidly toward Olchowatka. The 1. Panzergrenadier-Regiment had first closed the hole using an Infanteriezug supported by Panzers from the II./Panzerregiment *LAH*, and it had then established contact with the 320. Infanteriedivision in Krutaja Balka. In the fighting, two T-34's and eight anti-tank guns were destroyed.

The Ia alerted the Panzers stationed in Karlowka with the vehicle repair team and ordered them to join together under the command of the Adjutant of the Panzerregiment, Obersturmführer Tiemann. They were to prevent the enemy force which had broken through on Olchowatka from severing the Armee's supply route from Poltawa to Krassnograd and, if possible, to destroy that enemy force.[29]

The commander of the 1. Panzergrenadier-Regiment was informed of this measure by the Ia and received orders first to mop up the enemy breakthrough south of Starowerowka by attacking Olchowatka from the east with Panzer support, and then to cooperate with the armoured force under Tiemann to destroy the enemy forces in that town.

Obergruppenführer Tiemann provided the following combat report on 1.3.1943 (excerpt):

"At 09.00 hours, the Kampfgruppe, a light Zug at its head, set out toward Olchowatka. Only two Panzers from the 7. Kompanie were able to go along, and one of them suffered brake damage and had to drop out half-way there. With that, the Kampfgruppe consisted of four Panzer II's, three Panzer III's, and one Panzer IV. The light Zug moved forward to Popowka and set up defenses toward Warwarowka. There, Hauptsturmführer Schürer of the 1. Panzergrenadier-Regiment reported in as a replacement force with sixty men and subordinated them to the Kampfgruppe." (The continuation of this report will be found under the entry for 28.2.1943.)

In several telephone conversations between the Chef of the Generalstab of the Armee and the Ia of the *LAH*, the Division expressed its fear that the enemy's concentrated heavy attacks against both the northern front of the 1. Panzergrenadier-Regiment and the support point at Jeremejewka, located ahead of the eastern front, were an attempt to keep the Division tied up while the enemy moved in from the southeast to capture Krassnograd. The Division's proposal was to use the bulk of the Division to defend the former battle line while moving those forces situated ahead of the positions (namely, the Aufklärungsabteilung and the I./Panzerregiment *LAH*) farther to the south in order to wage the same mobile combat from Kegitschewka as had been waged from Jeremejewka.

The following report on the telephone conversation between the Oberbefehlshaber (General der Panzertruppen Kempf) and Obergruppenführer Dietrich comes from the Kriegstagebuch of the Armeeabteilung, reprinted in "Befehl des Gewissens" (page 172):

> "18.45 hours: after sketching the 4. Panzerarmee's situation and discussing the situation in the *LAH*'s sector, the Oberbefehlshaber expressed the wishes of Generalfeldmarschall von Manstein for combat-strength units to move against the enemy forces in the Orel sector in order to support the thrust of SS-Division *T*. The commander of the *LAH* thought a thrust by his forces, currently to be assembled in Kegitschewka, would be possible and promising, assuming that those same forces were not being held up by engagement with enemy forces from the south or north.
> The Oberbefehlshaber emphasized that all the Luftwaffe forces available would prepare the way for the attack and support it. The Commander of the *LAH* declared himself prepared to lead the attack against the enemy force in the Orel valley as soon as there were results from the early reconnaissance on 28.2 and as long as the forces intended for the attack were not bound up with enemy attacks. He emphasized that he would need to pull back the assault force into their assembly area as soon as the attack operation was completed. The Oberbefehlshaber declared himself to be in agreement with that."

At 16.00 hours, the orders for the night between 27.2 and 28.2 and for the day of 28.2.1943 were issued:

1) *The reinforced Aufklärungsabteilung LAH* (the Aufklärungsabteilung, the I./Panzerregiment, and the 3./Artillerie-Regiment), starting at nightfall on 27.2.1943, is to move back to the railway line on both sides of Kegitschewka. It is to hold the line Wschiweja sector (inclusive of it) — railway line (inclusive of it) — road to Besserabowka. Any advance by the enemy to the west is to be prevented by continued mobile combat movement and reconnaissance along the railway line and along the Bogtaja as far as (and including) Konstantiowka.

The boundary between the reinforced Aufklärungsabteilung and the reinforced III. (armoured)/2. Panzergrenadier-Regiment: Wschiwaja (to the Aufklärungsabteilung) — Kardaschewka (to the III./2.).

2) *The reinforced III. (armoured)/2.* (the 1./Sturmgeschützabteilung *LAH*) is to capture and hold the line Krutojarowka — Lipjanka — Petrowka and to maintain contact with the Aufklärungsabteilung east of Krutojarowka and with the Panzer-Pionierkompanie in Ziglerowka.
For the boundary between the Aufklärungsabteilung and the III.2., see above.
The boundary between the III./2. and the 2. Panzergrenadier-Regiment or the Panzer-Pioniere: Petrowka (to the III./2.) — Kasatschi Maidan (to the III./2.).

3) *The reinforced Panzergrenadier-Regiment* (minus the III./2., reinforced by the 5./Flakabteilung, the 1./Panzerjägerabteilung, and the Panzer-Pionierkompanie) is to hold the designated line and pull back the Kasatschi Maidan support point.
Elements of the greatest strength possible are to be pulled out from the Panzer-Pionierkompanie and to be assembled in Kalinino. The strength of these elements is to be reported.

4) *The reinforced 1. Panzergrenadier-Regiment* (the Pionier-Bataillon and the 2./Sturmgeschützabteilung), the 2. Flakabteilung and the 3. Panzerjägerabteilung are to hold the line Krut. Balka — Now. Grjakowo (northeastern edge) — Point 158.3 — Point 154.8 — Mokrjanka Mokra — Jarotin (exclusive of it). The force is also to clean up the breakthrough at Olchowatka.
...

11) The Divisional headquarters are in Krassnograd.

In the SS-Panzerkorps' area, Panzergrenadier-Regiment *DR* was still fighting around Losowaja, while Panzergrenadierdivision *T* was moving forward toward Krassnopawlowka.

Our losses for 27.2.1943:
Dead: nineteen (one officer among them),
wounded: forty-three (one officer among them), and
sick: eight.

28.2.1943: Before the chronological presentation of this day's events continues, our report on the fighting around Olchowatka, begun in the entry for 27.2 with Obersturmführer Tiemann's words, must be finished. First we will view the action from the vantage point of the 2./Sturmgeschützabteilung, which launched its attack from Olchowatka. The following report came from G. Kutzner:

> "The guns slowly creaked up the steep, ice-covered slope. Without ice studs on their tracks, our poor guns would never have made it. The last Geschütz of the 2. Zug, the only one in the Batterie without ice studs, had to start three times before it reached the top. Each time, when it got half-way up the slope, the tracks lost their hold and it sledded back down.
> Once on top, we deployed from our straight line into the combat formation, the wedge. Combat alert had already been ordered, the turret hatches had

been closed, the Kommandanten were scanning the edge of the village with the telescope in search of some sign of life, and the Grenadiere were fiddling with their weapons with hands stiff from the frost. We moved closer. It was still about five hundred meters to the first cottages. Then it all broke loose: a hellish concert of fire. Machine gun fire punctuated the steady hammering of the Maxims and the blazing volleys from the MG 42's. Mortar shells emerged from somewhere. The Grenadiere dismounted like lightning at the first shot and, gun in hand, went to face the unseen enemy. The fire flashed in front of our eyes unceasingly without our being able to make out where the wolves were hiding. Then there was a tremendous hit, our gun swayed, and we lost hearing and vision. A hit to our left track! It was only a shell from a 4.7-centimeter, but it was enough. Our gunner and the Kommandant stayed in the vehicle. I jumped behind a house to provide cover while the others changed the track at a hellish speed. The Russian resistance intensified. Between the burst of mortar hits and the droning motors, one could now hear the hard bark of the T-34's. All at once, night fell. Signal flares went up, throwing a flickering light over the battlefield. In front of us, the Grenadiere were working in the rock-hard frozen ground, trying to create a little cover from the continuing rain of mortar shells. We stood with the Sturmgeschütze behind them to provide covering fire. Without us, these brave boys would have been in a hopeless situation. Our ammunition drivers arrived with a Schützenpanzerwagen and drove from gun to gun bringing food. Why weren't we moving forward? Then it arrived. From over there behind us, something howled through the air and crashed with an infernal racket into Ivan's camp.
That was a hit! It came from the heavy Infanteriegeschütze of the 1. Regiment, which now began to arrive one after the other. Ivan dug his nose into the mud. We let loose with all the barrels of our 7.5-centimeter guns on the ruins of the village. They must certainly have lost their hearing and vision in there. Now the time had come! To our right, the Regiment's commander was personally urging the troops with his call of 'Forward, boys!' Our motor howled and pushed our twenty-four-tonne assault gun haltingly forward. We rolled over the garden fences closer and closer to this thrice-cursed village, Olchowatka. There was no hurrah from the lips of the men as they moved, bayonets poised, toward the houses, from which gunfire belched forth fire. They were determined, however, to drive out these Soviets. 'Enemy tank to the left,' our on-board radio crackled. Three white-grey boxes rolled toward us. Just in time, we recognized them as German Panzers IV. If only we could warn them! They rolled right in front of the barrels of the T-34. There was a flash; the first one was hit. A man jumped off and threw a violet smoke signal. Enemy tanks! The two others moved back, firing wildly. Our first and second Zug broke through into the village with the Grenadiere. The Geschütz under Wagner took two direct hits from a concealed anti-tank gun. The driver and the gunner were both killed, and Untersturmführer Wagner had to jump, despite a leg half blown-off, with the two ammunition loaders from the Geschütz. The Geschütz under Edelmann moved forward. The same blaze of fire. Hit! The Geschütz was unable to move, but it kept firing on the now-spotted anti-tank gun until it fell silent. Every house was a nest of resistance to be defeated. The Soviets fought to their last bullet. But the resistance was finally broken,

and the Red Army soldiers began to flee in panic. A T-34 with infantrymen riding on it rolled toward the road out of the village at high speed. High-explosive shell! With a blaze from the rear of the vehicle, Soviets went flying to the left and right of us. Tank shells. Direct hits. The last Red Army men saved themselves by fleeing across a frozen swamp, followed by our shells."

The report from Obersturmführer Tiemann, started above, continued:

"Continual reconnaissance reported on 28.2.1943 at 04.00 hours that enemy tanks were moving from Beluchowka toward Olchowatka. At 04.45 hours, the Kampfgruppe launched its attack. The Zug under Janke engaged the enemy with frontal fire on the southwestern edge. The Zug under Stollmayer with infantry moved along the Chalturino — Beluchowka road toward the southeastern edge of Beluchowka.

The town was, for the most part, free of enemy troops. The Kampfgruppe, with the infantrymen riding, moved forward as far as the northeastern edge of town. The Zug under Stollmayer took over providing security at the northeast road out of town, while the Zug under Janke was sent out at 06.30 hours to reconnoiter toward Olchowatka and to establish contact with the Sturmgeschützbatterie under Wiesemann (the 2./Sturmgeschützabteilung) in Krassnosnamenka. On the southern edge of Olchowatka, the reconnaissance force came under heavy anti-tank and tank fire. An armoured car was hit and burst into flames. The gunner and ammunition loaders were killed, and the rest of the crew jumped off with serious burns. The Zug under Stollmayer opened fire on recognized enemy firing positions and destroyed one tank and one anti-tank gun. With mutual fire support, the remainder of Janke's Zug came back, destroying an enemy anti-tank gun on the way. Janke's Panzer received four hits from anti-tank guns and was put out of commission. Stollmayer's Zug opened fire once again from its position on the eastern edge after Janke's return and destroyed one more enemy anti-tank gun.

At 12.00 hours, the Kampfgruppe received a briefing on the situation over the telephone from Standartenführer Witt. Star. Olchowatka was in our hands. The 2./Sturmgeschützabteilung (under Wiesemann) had pushed its way into the southwestern section of Nowo. Olchowatka. The 5./Panzer-regiment *LAH* was to be moved up from the east and, after artillery preparation, was to attack Olchowatka together with the I./1. (under Frey). The Kampfgruppe received orders to open fire on the western edge of Olchowatka as soon as the attack began and to move from Beluchowka toward Olchowatka in the course of the attack. The artillery fire from Olchowatka grew weaker, and at 14.00 hours, the Kampfgruppe saw our Infanterie and Sturmgeschütze move into the southern edge of Olchowatka. The Kampfgruppe used Janke's Zug to open fire on the western edge and sent Stollmayer's Zug around to the right to attack the southwestern edge. By 14.30 hours, one could recognize that about two companies of Russian tanks and infantry were attempting to escape Olchowatka across the marshes to Nagornaja. The two tanks we had spotted got stuck in the marsh and were hit with our fire. The Kampfgruppe suspended its attack and, in accordance with orders, brought the 7./Panzerregiment *LAH* back to the

II. Abteilung. Under orders from Standartenführer Witt, Hauptsturmführer Schürer moved the Infanterie to join the 1. Panzergrenadier-Regiment in Jegorjewka. The light Zug of the Regimentsstab of the Panzerregiment moved back to its billeting area via Beluchowka."

The view of the artillerymen in this fighting offers a complement to the report; here are the words of our comrade Mutterlose:

> "The Russians had broken through near Panzergrenadier-Regiment 1 with tanks. From our observation post, which was set up in a large barn for storing straw, we could clearly see the breakthrough. Our senses were quickly wide-awake, for we recognized that the convoy was moving in the direction of the village in which we had our firing position set up. The danger to our heavy Feldhaubitzen was enormous. We immediately sounded the tank alarm over our telephone connection. The tricky situation was quickly mastered by our young Batterie-Chef, Obersturmführer Topeters. In addition, the Russian tanks gave us a chance by making the mistake of stopping when they spotted the village. Some of the men even climbed out. Did they have to fill up before attacking the village, or was the leader of the convoy getting briefed on the situation?
>
> Our chef swung two Geschütze around one hundred-eighty degrees from their intended firing direction. No sooner said than done, we were once again ready to fire, and the new firing orders were transmitted without a pause. The first shots soon left the barrels. The first hits showed how exactly our Chef and the Kanoniere had calculated. The shells hit almost precisely in the middle of the Russian tanks. Only a tiny correction was necessary in order to bring the tanks' stopping place under completely effective fire. Our tension and nervousness at the observation post gradually lessened, and relief and satisfaction spread. We could see the Russian tank crews panicking as they jumped back into their tanks, and the truck crews attempted to climb into their vehicles. It was too late for two tank crews. One tank evidently had its track hit, for it was turning around in a circle, while others did not move at all. Two or three of our Sturmgeschütze suddenly arrived and got involved in our fighting. Our Batterie did not feel that we could paint the usual "hit rings" around the barrels of our guns; these tanks were easy shots and did not count. But our Batterie did suffer two fatalities. Our food drivers, who had been on the way forward to bring food to the observation post, had not known about the situation and had run into the tanks with their sleighs. Without a shot being fired from our men, the tanks' machine guns just mowed them down."

The Armeeabteilung received the following report on the fighting around Olchowatka: "Olchowatka is firmly in our hands. The enemy escaped with fifty to sixty men, many unarmed, and four tanks. Two tanks were destroyed, and fifty to sixty men taken prisoner."

On the southern and northern wings of our eastern front, the heavy enemy attacks continued, while the enemy conducted only weak reconnaissance thrusts against the middle of the sector. During the night between 27.2 and 28.2, the

Artillerie-Regiment focussed concentrated fire on the heavy column traffic moving to the south via Starowerowka.

On the right wing, the III. (armoured)/2. waged a hard defensive battle for Kegitschewka, which was under attack almost uninterruptedly from the northwest and northeast. In the fighting, three enemy tanks were destroyed.

At 13.10 hours, the Ia of the Armeeabteilung, Oberstleutnant i.G. Estor, reported to the Ia of the *LAH* that aerial reconnaissance had spotted the following: a column of infantry and sleighs about the size of a battalion moving from Nishny Orel to the west; a column of about eight hundred men, two tanks, and fifty motor vehicles moving from Jeremejewka; and a third column of six hundred men and two hundred horse-drawn vehicles moving from the east toward Kegitschewka. The Ia of the *LAH* replied that these columns had probably been hit by the continuous Stuka and dive-bomber attacks being waged at just that moment. Captured enemy radio messages later confirmed this assertion.

At 13.15 hours, the reinforced 11./2. (under Obersturmführer Guhl) set out from Petrowka, moved across Rossoschowatyj, and launched a thrust into the deep flank of the enemy force attacking Kegitschewka, and it thereby brought some temporary relief. A Russian battalion was annihilated in the fighting.

At 16.05 hours, the pressure on Kegitschewka rose considerably, and the Ia agreed by telephone with Sturmbannführer Peiper to pull the Bataillon back to the west bank of the Wschiwaja for the night and to set out the following morning for a thrust to the southeast.

The total success for the day amounted to eighteen enemy tanks destroyed, including one German Panzer IV in enemy hands, as well as the destruction of many heavy and light infantry weapons.

The SS-Panzerkorps stood on the evening of 28.2.1943 with its leading elements in echelon formation in the line Radolje (*DR*) — Ranin (*DR*) west of Krassnopawlowka. Its frontmost forces were therefore about thirty kilometers in front of our battle line. It could be expected that this proximity would influence the enemy's behavior along the right wing of our Division. For the *LAH*, the task basically boiled down to using continuous attacks to keep the enemy on our southeastern and eastern front engaged. In doing so, we would enable our sister divisions, the *DR* and the *T*, to attack him in the rear or flank and then surround him.

Orders for 1.3.1943:

The *LAH* was to attack the enemy north of Kegitschewka. After defeating the enemy, the *LAH* was to continue the attack toward Nishny Orel.

1.3.1943: After a peaceful night, we sent out constant reconnaissance forces along the Divison's entire front. While the seasonal thaw, which had just arrived in full force, and the resulting mud almost thwarted all mobile combat maneuvers, the weather actually favored our reconnaissance activities in the early morning hours.

At 07.00 hours, the 1. Panzergrenadier-Regiment sent the I./1. (under Frey) out from Jarotin for a short-range reconnaissance thrust, and an attack followed at 07.30 hours with Krutaja Balka as its objective. The commander of the I./1. Panzergrenadier-Regiment, Sturmbannführer Frey, was awarded the Ritterkreuz on 5.3.1943 for his consistent bravery and prudent leadership.

On the right wing, to which the Division's commander travelled in the early morning hours, the III. (armoured)/2. waged an armoured attack across Ziglerowka on Jeremejewka and destroyed an enemy column. The thaw did not affect this attack with half-track Schützenpanzerwagens because the move was made across the ridge line of this hilly terrain. The attack ordered on Kegitschewka via the Wschiwaja sector could not be carried out because the muddy terrain, riddled with ravines, prevented it. Making such a thrust with infantry alone did not hold much prospect for success, because it would have been impossible to pursue the enemy on foot as he moved back. The Division therefore ordered our Artillerie to harass the enemy forces in Kegitschewka. The tactic was successful, as intercepted enemy radio tranmissions proved.

An armoured reconnaissance unit from the Aufklärungsabteilung, including August Zinßmeister, was dispatched for some long-range reconnaissance. He reported:

> "We were travelling toward Dar. Nadeshda. Reconnaissance was being sent out from Ssnachnowschschina. A reconnaissance force from the Division's Sicherheitskompanie ran into enemy mines, and its truck got stuck in the mine field. I cleared four of the mines, and we could proceed. We wandered around in the area for a goodly number of kilometers, and in the evening we found billets in a German settlement in Perekulona. On 2.3, we were stuck without fuel. Despite urgent radio messages, it became evening and still no Panzers had arrived bringing gas for us from the Kompanie. It was after dark when we learned by radio that Drawer was six kilometers away from us in his eight-wheeler, with gasoline on board. We took a horse-drawn sleigh and set out, stamping our way through the snow, wading through the muck and mire. After searching for fourteen hours, we finally found Drawer at about 10.00 hours on 3.3. During our search, one of our horses had died, and we had had to find a new team. Loaded up with the fuel, we turned back to Perekulona to our reconnaissance vehicle. Fill 'er up. By evening, Drawer had dug himself free and caught up with us. Aumann, too, returned. Together, we rode via Konstantinowka to Dar. Nadeshda. There, Drawer's eight-wheeler once again got stuck about six kilometers away from the Abteilung's position. I had to climb out and take over this vehicle while the others drove off with mine. We dug and pushed until morning, to no avail. Then to our great good fortune, a Panzer IV appeared and pulled us out. I was finally able to bring the eight-wheeler back to the Kompanie. That was the return from our long-distance reconnaissance trip."

Around noon on 1.3, the *LAH* received the following Armeebefehl:

1) The 4. Panzerarmee has orders to move the bulk of its forces forward and to the east from the line captured on 28.2.1943 (Michailowka — Otrada — Rasdolnje) while sending elements west of the Orel river toward Taranowka and Paraskoweja. The first goal is to destroy the enemy forces located south of the Berestowaja.
2) The *LAH*'s orders:

a) The *LAH* is to destroy the enemy forces between the Orel river and the Berestoweja sector in offensive fighting and thereby relieve the pressure on the advance of the 4. Panzerarmee.
b) It is also to prepare the opening into this sector as the leading elements of the 4. Panzerarmee approach. For this purpose, a strong combat force is to be assembled in the Starowerowka area for deployment toward Taranowka if necessary.
c) To guarantee uniform conduct of the battle, it is possible that the *LAH* may be placed in temporary subordination to the 4. Panzerarmee (of the SS-Panzerkorps) if necessary.

In the course of the afternoon, the Division got the impression that the enemy was making preparations on our right wing, especially in Kegitschewka, to pull back. The Division reported to Armeeabteilung Kempf that it intended to:

1. Send out a combat-strength reconnaissance force toward Jeremejewka and Jefremowka in pursuit of his retreat and to destroy his rear guard, and
2. Make a thrust with the entire reinforced 2. Panzergrenadier-Regiment on Taranowka via Starowerowka and Melechowka north of the Berestoweja sector.

The Chef of the Generalstab of Armeeabteilung Kempf expressed agreement with the plans. He informed us at about midnight that the SS-Panzerkorps was planning for 2.3 to move one force from Jefremowka toward Paraskoweja, another from Bereka toward Ochotschaje, and some elements toward Taranowka. The *LAH* was to seek contact with the left wing of the SS-Panzerkoprs (SS-*T*) by conducting strong reconnaissance.

The III. (armoured)/2. came under the command of the 2. Panzergrenadier-Regiment once again at 22.00 hours on 1.3.

b) 2.3.1943 - 3.3.1943: Jefremowka battle of encirclement. Closing of the encircled area's western front.

2.3.1943 (see sketch 16): By 09.15 hours, the I./Panzerregiment *LAH* had reported that one Panzerkompanie had set out from Gutyrowka via Rojakowka toward Kegitschewka.

The Aufklärungsabteilung reported large motorized enemy columns on the march from Kegitschewka toward Jefremowka.

The reinforced I./2. first overcame weak enemy resistance forces in Wlassowka and Medwedowka, but then found itself locked in fighting with stronger enemy forces in Berestoweja and along the march route from Starowerowka to Paraskoweja.

The 2./Sturmgeschüzabteilung (under Wiesemann), subordinated to the II./2., was engaged in house-to-house combat in Starowerowka.

The reinforced 6./Panzerregiment *LAH*, joined by infantrymen from the 1. Panzergrenadier-Regiment, was fighting near the Wlassowka railway station.

At 10.20 hours, the I./2. and elements from the III. (armoured)/2. captured Berestoweja on both sides of the stream bearing the same name.

13.2.1943: Clearing Jefremowka of enemy forces. The light Panzerspähwagen is providing cover for the Kradschützen.

13.2.1943: Russian prisoners are taken after they have attempted an unsuccessful counterattack.

Generaloberst Hermann Hoth.
Oberbefehlshaber of the 4. Panzerarmee.

At 11.00 hours, the Aufklärungsabteilung reported that the resistance from Kegitschewka was once again growing stronger and that the enemy was digging in between the Kegitschewka railway station and Rossochowatyj. The I./2. (under Kraas) locked up the road to the south between Medwedowka and Losowaja because the enemy was moving strong forces from Kotljarowka to the north to attack our flank. The Bataillon reported the presence of strong enemy columns, several moving alongside each other, moving from Paraskoweja to Jefremowka. The reinforced III. (armoured)/2. had destroyed a fairly strong enemy force west of Paraskoweja and was proceeding toward Medwedowka.

At 13.30 hours, the I./2. reported an attack on Berestoweja by three enemy tank squadrons, an attack which the unit handily repulsed. The bulk of the enemy's forces had been destroyed by two of our Panzers. The road from Paraskoweja to Jefremowka was blocked off just south of Paraskoweja.

At 14.00 hours, the II./2. (under Sandig) reached Karawannyj.

At 15.15 hours, the Aufklärungsabteilung reported heavy enemy truck traffic on the road from Kegitschewka to Beluchkowka. It had already moved through Kegitschewka. A reconnaissance force moving out from that town was pushed back after only two kilometers by our Pak fire.

By 16.00 hours, the reinforced III. (armoured)/2. had moved to follow the large enemy columns as far as seven kilometers north of Melechowka. As night fell, the unit assembled in Melechowka on orders from the Division.

The forward line that evening ran as follows: strong point in Kegitschewka (Aufklärungsabteilung) — south Wlassowka — south Medwedowka — south Berestoweja (I./2.) — north Paraskoweja (elements of the II./2.) — Melechowka (III./2.).

At 16.40 hours, the III./*DF* established contact with the *LAH* in Paraskoweja. On 2.3, the Division destroyed the following: four T-34's, five Mark II's, one armoured reconnaissance vehicle, fifteen 7.62-centimeter guns, fifty to sixty sleighs, and about six hundred Soviet soldiers. The *LAH* reported that it had destroyed one hundred and one Russian tanks since 3.2.1943.

At 17.00 hours, the Chef of the Armee Generalstab informed the *LAH* that, starting at 0.00 hours on 3.3.1943, it would be subordinated to the 4. Panzerarmee (under Generaloberst Hoth) or the SS-Panzerkorps (under Obergruppenführer Hausser). Its orders for 3.3 were to come from the SS-Panzerkorps.

3.3.1943: At 01.00 hours, the SS-Panzerkorps issued its orders for 3.3.1943. It commanded that all forces from the right wing were to assemble in the Starowerowka area as soon as they were free to do so. They were to be added to the SS-Panzerkorps' attack to the north on 4.3.

The Aufklärungsabteilung destroyed the enemy forces northeast of Kegitschewka and then established contact with elements of the SS-Panzergrenadierdivision *T*.

During the entire day, the enemy attacked the Berestoweja sector and attempted to break out of the encirclement around Jeremejewka.

Generaloberst Hausser, at that time commanding general of the SS-Panzerkorps, in his book 'Waffen-SS im Einsatz" described the situation on 3.3.1943:

> "The Armee (the 4. Panzerarmee) was attempting to move its right wing as far as the Donez, while the SS-Panzerkorps was to establish contact with

the right wing of Armeeabteilung Kempf (the *LAH*) ... We later recognized that the result of this fighting was that the newly introduced Soviet forces had marched precisely into the gap between the attack of the SS-Panzerkorps and the defensive front of the *LAH*."

At dawn, Kampfgruppe Meyer (the reinforced Aufklärungsabteilung and elements of the I./Panzerregiment *LAH*) set out from Krutojarowka against the enemy forces pulling back toward Jeremejewka. By 15.00 hours, the Kampfgruppe had established contact with the SS-Panzergrenadierdivision *T* in Jeremejewka. With that, not only was a shoulder-to-shoulder position with Panzergrenadier-Regiment *DF* achieved in Paraskoweja, but a double closing of the encirclement was also accomplished.

According to statements from prisoners, there were in the area around Kotljarowka and Jeremejewka scattered elements of the 52nd Infantry Division, the 118th, 148th, and 350th Rifle Divisions, and the 113. Tank Brigade.

Around noon, the reinforced III. (armoured)/2. assembled in Starowerowka. At the request of the Division, it received orders from the 2. Panzergrenadier-Regiment to set out to the north toward Nikolskoje and the hills east of there. Beginning at 15.25 hours, the Bataillon moved through Nikolskoje. All its forces were through the town by 17.00 hours, and at 18.00 hours it reported the capture of Petscheiwka.

The orders from the SS-Panzerkorps for the *LAH* for 4.3.1943 read as follows:

> "The *LAH* is to capture and hold the high terrain around Ljaschowa. The left wing is to establish start positions for an attack on Walki. The Aufklärungsabteilung/*LAH* is to establish contact with elements of SS-Panzergrenadierdivision *T* and, in conjunction with that Division, destroy the enemy forces in the area south of Jeremejewka.
> SS-Panzergrenadierdivision *DR* is to destroy the enemy forces south of the Msha sector and to establish a bridgehead at Bachmetjewka.
> The Korps headquarters are to be in Krassny."

Orders for the *LAH*'s units for 4.3.1943 read as follows:

> "*The reinforced 2. Panzergrenadier-Regiment* is to take Stanitschnyj and Winnikow and to prepare itself to move forward on 6.3 with the bulk of its forces along the road from Stanitschnyj via Ljaschowa and Peressel to the Msha sector. Elements are to be deployed to the west of this road. Reconnaissance should be conducted on 5.3.1943 as far as the line Ssnameka — Angstenkoff and contact should be established to the *DR*.
> The *reinforced Aufklärungsabteilung and the I./Panzerregiment LAH* are to move to Krassnograd on 4.3.1943. There, the better part of the day is to be used to rest the men and repair the equipment. Both supply trains are already in Krassnograd. Deployment from this area southeast of Krutaja Balka to the north should be expected on 6.3.
> The *reinforced 1. Panzergrenadier-Regiment* is to relieve the III. (armoured)/2. in Nikolskoje on 5.3 and is to send out elements to capture Paschtschinewka. The Regiment should prepare itself to move to the north toward Minkowka on 6.3 within the structure of the Division."

c) 4.3.1943: Regrouping the Division for the thrust to the north.

4.3.1943: After a peaceful night, the III. (armoured)/2. (under Sturmbannführer Peiper) was relieved from its defensive line south of Krutaja Balka by the II./1. (under Sturmbannführer M. Hansen). The III. (armoured)/2. marched in the early morning via Nikolskoje and Jelenowka to Jarotin in order to make a thrust from there to Stanitschnyj.

At 08.15 hours, Stanitschnyj was captured. The Bataillon pursued the enemy forces as far as Jewdokimowka and Ljachowa.

Reconnaissance conducted by the II./2. (under Sturmbannführer Sandig) toward Winnikoff observed strong Russian columns on the march to the north.

At dawn, Kampfgruppe Meyer (the reinforced Aufklärungsabteilung and the I./Panzerregiment *LAH*) launched an armoured thrust into the back of the enemy forces retreating to the north. At 11.00 hours, the Kampfgruppe was able to assemble in Krassnograd for a brief rest.

The reinforced 1. Panzergrenadier-Regiment fought until nightfall to capture its assembly area.

The orders from the SS-Panzerkorps to the *LAH* for 5.3.1943 read as follows:

> "The *LAH* is to wage localized attacks to create favorable start positions for the attack on Walki and the Msha sector."

2) ATTACK ON CHARKOW 5.3.1943 - 31.3.1943

a) 5.3.1943 - 11.3.1943: Thrust across the Msha sector and into the area north of Charkow.

5.3.1943: The situation: In the preceding days, offensive combat on the part of the entire Division along the whole breadth of our defensive front had kept the bulk of the Soviet 3rd Tank Army engaged. These enemy forces were headed for destruction at the hands of elements of Division *Das Reich* and Division *Totenkopf.*

In front of the Division's northern wing, there were reasonably strong enemy forces defending themselves in the line Hf. Ljaschowa — Ssuchaja Balka — Blagodatnoje. These forces were supposed to cover the southern flank of the dangerous thrust by the Soviet 69th and 40th Armies north of Charkow on Poltawa. The leading elements of the Soviet attack crossed the Worskla sector near Kotelwa and moved to a position not far from Sinkiw (ninety kilometers northwest of our left wing.)

On orders from the Panzerarmeeoberkommando 4 (under Generaloberst Hoth), the SS-Panzerkorps was to move SS-Panzergrenadierdivision *DR* to the right and the *LAH* to the left north across the Msha sector in order to build bridgeheads for a later attack to the north and northwest.

Panzergrenadierdivision *Großdeutschland* was to launch an attack on both sides of the Kolomak river on Perekop.

The orders for the *LAH*: "The *LAH* is to set out on 6.3.1943 and to break through the Russian defensive front in order to move forward across the line Hf. Peressel — Anoptschenkoff — Burjakowa as far as the Msha sector."

Divisionsbefehl No. 7, dated 5.3.1943 at 19.00 hours, contained the following orders:

4. a) *The reinforced 2. Panzergrenadier-Regiment* (the Sturmgeschüzabteilung minus the 2. Batterie, the 1./Panzerjägerabteilung *LAH*, the 5. [medium]/Flakabteilung *LAH*, the I. and III./Artillerie-Regiment *LAH* minus one light Feldhaubitze-Batterie) is to position itself in the Stanitschnyj — Winnikoff area and to stand ready to attack to the north on both sides of Road 2 after the enemy resistance in Ljaschowa and Garilowka has been broken.
First attack objective: Belezkowo.
First day's objective: the hills west of Ssnamenka.
Second day's objective: Fedorowka — Hf. Bridok. There, bridgeheads to be established.
The 9. (Panzer-Pionier)/Panzerregiment *LAH* is to be moved back to Beluchowka to join the Stab of the Panzerregiment *LAH*.

b) *The reinforced 1. Panzergrenadier-Regiment LAH* (the II./Panzerregiment *LAH*, the 2. Sturmgeschüzabteilung *LAH*, the II. and IV./Artillerie-Regiment *LAH*, the 2. (heavy)/Flakabteilung *LAH*) is to deploy elements to defend the preparations of the Aufklärungsabteilung *LAH* and to use its subordinated Artillerie to support the Aufklärungsabteilung's attack on Landyschewo and Blagodatnoje. It is then to capture Ssuchaja Balka and to move on Minkowka with a prepared motorized assault force.
First attack objective: Ssuchaja Balka.
First day's objective: Minowka.
Second day's objective: use elements to build bridgehead near Peski; the bulk of the forces are to be positioned in the eastern part of Walki.

c) *The reinforced Aufklärungsabteilung* (the I./Panzerregiment *LAH* with the Tiger-Kompanie, the 3./Artillerie-Regiment *LAH*, the I./Werferregiment 55, the 2./Panzerjägerabteilung *LAH*) is to prepare itself in the area southeast of Krutaja Balka and then to attack the towns of Landyschewo — Blagodatnoje. It is then to move forward toward Sneshkoff Kut.
First attack objective: Landyschewo — Blagodatnoje.
First day's objective: Sneshkoff Kut.
Second day's objective: western part of Walki.

d) *The Artillerie-Regiment LAH* is to use the II., IV., and 3./Artillerie-Regiment *LAH* and the I./Werferregiment 55 to prepare support fire on Landyschewo and Blagodatnoje.
The following are to be subordinated for the attack to the north: the I. and III./Artillerie-Regiment *LAH* (minus the 3./Artillerie-Regiment) subordinated to the 2. Panzergrenadier-Regiment *LAH*; the II. and IV./Artillerie-Regiment *LAH* subordinated to the 1. Panzergrenadier-Regiment *LAH*; and the I./Werferregiment 55 and the 3./Artillerie-Regiment *LAH* subordinated to the Aufklärungsabteilung *LAH*.

e) *The Stab of Panzerregiment LAH* is to stand with the 9. (Panzer-Pionier)/Panzerregiment at the disposal of Division in Beluchowka. The 13. (Tiger)/Panzerregiment *LAH* is to reconnoiter the roads; it is then to be moved to join the I./Panzerregiment *LAH*, to which it is to be subordinated.

f) *The Sturmgeschützabteilung LAH* (minus the 2. Batterie) is to be subordinated to the 2. Panzergrenadier-Regiment *LAH*. The 2./Sturmgeschützabteilung *LAH* is to remain subordinated to the 1. Panzergrenadier-Regiment.

g) *The Panzerjägerabteilung LAH* is to have its Stab and 3. Kompanie stand at the disposal of the Division in Nikolskoje after the 1. Panzergrenadier-Regiment has set out.
The 1./Panzerjägerabteilung *LAH* is to remain subordinated to the 2. Panzergrenadier-Regiment.
The 2./Panzerjägerabteilung *LAH* is to be subordinated to the Aufklärungsabteilung and moved from Jegorjewka.

h) The Pionier-Bataillon LAH is to stand at the disposal of the Division in Karlowka. It is to hold the Karlowka — Nikolskoje road open for traffic and is to prepare itself to move north as the attack progresses.

i) *The Flakabteilung LAH* is to leave the unit subordinations as before. The 1. and 3. (heavy)/Flakabteilung *LAH* are to move into position in the Nikolskoje — Jegorjewka area so that they can defend the air space above the assembly area and so that they can take action against any enemy tanks which might break through on the ground.

5. *Reconnaissance*
   a) *Ground reconnaissance* is to be conducted by each unit in its attack sector. The Aufklärungsabteilung's sector should be reconnoitered on 5.5.1943 by the 1. Panzergrenadier-Regiment.
   b) *Aerial reconnaissance* in the attack sectors has been requested from the Division, and the request has been granted.

6. *The Luftwaffe*
   A Stuka attack on Ssuchaja Balka, Landyschewo, and Blagodatnoje has been requested and promised. The last bomb is to fall at 08.00 hours. Ground attack airplane support has been requested and promised along Road 2.
   Identification marks and swastika flags on the leading vehicle of every attack unit are unconditionally required.

7. - 11.
   ...

12. The Divisional headquarters are in Krassnograd. Starting at 16.00 hours on 6.3.1943, it will be moved to Krestischtsche.

The regrouping and preparations for the attack took the entire day.

6.3.1943 (see sketch 17): from 01.00 hours to 06.00 hours, reports of the completion of preparations reached the Division.
At 05.40 hours, the SS-Panzerkorps informed us that the main point of concentration for the Luftwaffe's actions was in front of SS-Panzergrenadierdivision *DR*. There were only secondary targets in front of the *LAH*.

At 07.00 hours, the reinforced Aufklärungsabteilung reported that four Kampfwagens from the Tiger-Kompanie had arrived. The rest were still on the road between Poltawa and the assembly area.

Because of the catastrophic condition of the roads, the Artillerie's move into its position was considerably delayed in the left sector. For that reason, the reinforced Aufklärungsabteilung and the reinforced 1. Panzergrenadier-Regiment received orders at 07.30 hours to begin the attack at 11.00 hours. The 2. Panzergrenadier-Regiment was to begin at 08.15 hours.

When these orders were given, Hauptsturmführer Diefenthal, Adjutant of the 2. Panzergrenadier-Regiment, reported that the II./2. (under Sandig) had to start at daybreak because its assembly area was open to the enemy's sight.

At 08.20 hours, the 2. Panzergrenadier-Regiment reported the capture of Ljachowa in the face of tough enemy resistance and the occupation of the northern edge of this town by the II./2. The two other Bataillone of the Regiment had started out at 08.15 hours. The I. and II./Panzergrenadier-Regiment had captured Kurganowka and Belezkoje by 11.00 hours after brief, but intense, fighting. The II./2. was sent out against Gawrilowka, while the I./2. held back in order to allow the 1. Panzergrenadier-Regiment to catch up at 11.00 hours.

The reinforced III. (armoured)/2. (under Peiper) started its thrust at 10.00 hours, as soon as the II. Bataillon had opened the way, and by 11.00 hours, it was nearing Peressell. The II./2., moving up behind, was able to observe from its position on the hills south of there the left wing of Panzergrenadierdivision *DR* proceeding on Nowaja Wodolaga.

The III. (armoured)/2. (under Peiper) pursued the enemy forces retreating from Peressell and caught up with some of them. At 14.30 hours, it established a bridgehead over the Msha at Federowka.

The 1. Panzergrenadier-Regiment had as much trouble with the terrible roads as with the tough enemy forces. By 18.00 hours, it had captured, in conjunction with the III. and II./1., the southern edge of Bobrowka and, in conjunction with the I./1., Michailowka.

The reinforced Aufklärungsabteilung and the I./Panzerregiment *LAH*, together with the 1. Panzergrenadier-Regiment, set out at 11.00 hours and by 14.00 hours were only about five kilometers south of Sneshkoff Kut.

The Adjutant of the I./Panzerregiment *LAH*, Obersturmführer Isecke, reported on this day's events as follows:

> "Our Kampfgruppe was on the Division's left wing. For the first time, we were to be supported by the Tiger-Kompanie. Shortly before we set out, the commander brought a war correspondent by the name of Fernau to me. 'Take him along in your Panzer. He would like to go along on an attack.' What should I do with him? We practiced a few times with the crew and found the best spot was inside, alongside the gun.
>
> We set off in one giant concentration of forces. Our breakthrough was successful. Because of the deep snow, the men of the two Kradschützenkompanien sat on our tanks, while the light Schützenpanzerwagen-Kompanie of the Aufklärungsabteilung had to struggle along beside us. The amphibious Volkswagens were being towed. Sturmbannführer Meyer was leading the attack from the Panzer of Obersturmführer Beck (Chef of the 2. Panzerregiment). Sturmbannführer Wünsche was travelling in the middle. To the right was the 2./Panzer-

regiment *LAH* (under Hauptsturmführer Lambrecht), and the 1./Panzer-regiment *LAH* (under Hauptsturmführer Jürgensen) followed along about five hundred meters behind. Two of the Tigers were following behind Sturmbannführer Wünsche. The others had for the most part been put out of operation because parts attached to the armour had been ripped loose and had even injured some of the crew.
To the left and rear, we could hear sounds of combat coming from the sector of the 320. Infanteriedivision. We moved across the level snow fields on a broad front. On the horizon, we could see roofs running across our attack direction. That had to be Sneskoff Kut. During a brief rest commander Sturmbannführer Wünsche gave the 1. Kompanie orders to swing out to the right, attack the spread-out town from the east, and then move toward us. We were to attack in our current direction of travel. In front of the town and to the left of it, a small rise seemed to be occupied. We saw flashes of light from it several times.
On we went. Our companion, Fernau, thought that the headphones he had to wear were a little loud, and that quarters were a bit cramped, but otherwise he found it exciting.
In the meantime, we had come to within two kilometers of that elevated position, which we could now observe better. Now and then, the snow blew up in a cloud and whirled in front of us or beside us. We still had eighteen Panzers, with the two Tigers behind us, with the infantrymen ducked down hiding behind the turret. Shells! Halt! On the gently sloping hill and in front of it, fire suddenly sprang up across a broad front. Damn! It appeared to be an entire anti-tank front. The commander ordered the two Kompanien: 'Faster, speed it up! Forward!' Ahead to the left, the crew of Beck's Panzer was bailing out. What was going on with Sturmbannführer Meyer? The Panzer was not on fire, and I could discern movement behind it. The rapid fire from our Panzers had had its effect on the hill. The lead Panzers were still eight hundred meters from it. To the left and right of us, there were two tanks in flames. We were now in the phase of fighting in which most Panzer attacks become critical. No one moved at that moment. Shortly before, Jürgensen (Chef of the 1. Panzerkompanie) had reported: 'Orion to Merkur (he rolled his R's particularly strongly). Edge of town two kilometers ahead. No resistance.' Answer from the commander: 'Accelerate!' Immediately thereafter: 'Commander to all: Follow!' As Adjutant riding fifty meters to the side and behind the commander's Panzers, I barked to my crew: 'Step on the gas! Straight ahead!' Tensely, I looked through the bullet-proof glass, glancing to the side and the rear.
We had gone about one hundred fifty meters when I saw the commander ahead to the right heading for a barn in order to get some cover from the enemy's view while he took a look at the situation. In a fraction of a second I registered that it was humming all around us. From the hill, now clearly visible, flashes of light were coming with uncomfortable frequency. Apparently, by heading for the barn, we had managed to find a blind spot in their field of fire. Now the other Panzers were finally moving again.
When we reached the hill, with the commander one hundred meters ahead at the barn, I could see the first houses about two to three hundred meters away. Anti-tank fire started up from the first house, and a shell landed right beside us. In the light from the gunfire, I roared: 'To the rear!' Seconds

later there was a second shell. With my cry: 'Bail out!' we found ourselves in the snow beside the Panzer. The wires of our headphone sets were still hanging around our necks. The heat from the blast had given us some serious burns. Instinctively, we buried our heads in the snow. All six of us, fortunately including Fernau, crawled a little bit away from the Panzer. We could not explain why it did not continue burning after the initial flame.
The Panzer rolled back about twenty meters. We later learned that a T-34 had been lying in wait in that first house, and its first shell had caught our drive wheel. In moving back, we had driven over a mine. But at the moment, we did not have much time to ponder the situation, for gunshots told us that the positions were still occupied.
Where were the other Panzers? From the shots and the hits, we could tell that the battle between Panzers and anti-tank guns was in full swing. We could not find the commander's Panzer. About eighty meters to one side of us, a Tiger crawled up the hill. We wanted to draw his attention to the T-34, but he naturally did not see us. What happened next tore our emotions to the heights and depths. As if in a trance, we stared to the left with our gummy eyes, all pain from our burns forgotten. The Tiger had hardly made it up the hill when there was a huge explosion, and light and debris flew all around us. When we looked up, we saw a gouge in the Tiger's turret a meter square in area. But at the same time we saw its 8.8-centimeter gun move and point to the target like a finger. A stream of fire came out of it. We almost stood up to watch what was happening. Half of the house flew away, and we got a clear view of a burning enemy tank with its turret blown off. We embraced each other for joy. Then events came toppling over us. From the edge of the entire town, two dozen T-34's emerged from their hiding places. In the meantime, the second Tiger (under Kommandant Untersturmführer Wendorff; the first Tiger was under the command of Obersturmführer Pezdeuschek) arrived. Eight enemy tanks were destroyed in front of Sneshkoff Kut. After passing through the town, we caught four more, and the rest of the T-34's disappeared to the northeast toward Walki. Sturmbannführer Wünsche had led the Abteilung's advance on the anti-tank front. After the fighting stopped, we counted fifty-six anti-tank guns. Together with the commander of the Aufklärungsabteilung, Wünsche then organized the mop-up operation in the town. After seeing the doctor, I could return to my duties with a bandage around my head."

In the late afternoon, the Ic was able to give the units the results of the aerial reconnaissance: "In Achtyrka (seventy-five kilometers to the northwest), troops are being unloaded and transported to Charkow. There are also apparent movements south of Ssumy. Forces are being moved from the Issjum area (about one hundred forty kilometers to the east) into the Charkow area. The enemy evidently intends to keep his hold on Charkow." By evening, the unit adjacent to us on the right, the SS-Panzergrenadierdivision *DR*, had captured Nowaja Wodolaga and Prossjanoje, while the unit adjacent on the left, initially the 320. Infanteriedivision, had not yet moved ahead.

On 7.3, Panzergrenadierdivision *GD* set out moving across the 320. Infanteriedivision's area toward Kolomak.

Because the choice of this objective for the *LAH* created an open left flank, SS-Panzergrenadierdivision *T* received orders to take over covering the *LAH*'s western flank.

That same evening, the III. (armoured)/2. (under Peiper) expanded the bridgehead as far as Bidok. The Bataillon waged a constant defensive battle against enemy forces attempting to escape from the massive onslaught of the Division and the unit adjacent to the north by fleeing across the Msha. Three T-34's were destroyed in the fighting.

The supply columns had been moved forward during the day into the assembly areas. In tireless action, they acted under orders from the 2. Generalstabsoffizier, Obersturmbannführer Ewert, to provide ammunition, fuel, and provisions to the front during the night. The Armee's failure to assign adequate amounts of fuel seriously endangered the Division's supply lines. The Divisional headquarters moved in the afternoon to Krestischtsche.

The orders for 7.3.1943 remained the same as for 6.3. The reinforced III. (armoured)/2. kept a firm hold on the Federowka and Bridok bridgeheads and provided relief for the advance of the 1. Panzergrenadier-Regiment by attacking Walki from the east.

7.3.1943 (see sketch 18): The Division's three attack groups started off at dawn. The 2. Panzergrenadier-Regiment (under Standartenführer Wisch) sent the I./2. to Ssnamenka and the II./2. to Minkowka to smash the enemy resistance in those towns, a task which they completed by 07.30 hours. By noon the I./2. (under Kraas) had captured Federowka and the II./2. had taken Bridok. The two Bataillone relieved the security forces which the III. (armoured)/2. had left behind.

The bulk of the III. (armoured)/2. set off at 07.45 hours to Tscheremuschnaja (four kilometers northeast of Walki), where it established contact with the leading elements of the Aufklärungsabteilung at 16.30 hours.

Sturmbannführer Kraas, the commander of the I./2., deployed the 3./2. (under Hauptsturmführer Röhwer) in an attack at 09.45 hours on Staraja Wodolaga. At the same time, this town was being attacked by Panzergrenadier-Regiment *DF* from the south. Excellent cooperation between the two units led to the quick capture of the town.[30]

The reinforced 1. Panzergrenadier-Regiment (under Standartenführer Witt) sent the II./Panzerregiment *LAH* and the 2. Sturmgeschüzabteilung to make a thrust on Babirka. From there, after rapid preparation, the Regiment was to deploy the III./1. (on the right) and the I./1. to join the reinforced Aufklärungsabteilung (attacking from the southwest) in the move on Walki. By 14.50 hours, this town had been taken.

Sturmgeschüzmann Kutzner described this attack in the periodical "Wiking-Ruf" (No. 7/55. p. 16 ff.) as follows:

> "The sun, a glowing red ball, had barely mounted the hilltop when a new attack order was given us. The Batterie rolled out into the morning. The leading elements halted on top of a hill, and the other groups followed behind at large intervals. The attack objective lay in a basin below. To reach it, we had about three hundred meters of open terrain to cover at a rapid clip. For the first time, the Batterie was to wage a closed-rank attack in a wedge formation, Panzer-fashion . The first Zug was the spearhead, the

second Zug and third Zug in echelon formation to the right and left in the wedge. Alternating their duties (one moving forward while the other provided cover fire), the guns advanced steadily on the village, from which fire from anti-tank guns and rifles was emanating even at this long distance. We knew Ivan was nervous if he was shooting this far in advance and giving away his positions. His anti-tank guns were shooting wildly inaccurately, mostly too short. Our 7.5-centimeter Kanonen hit all the better for it. The frontmost houses were already burning and the Red Army soldiers who had been hiding in them were leaping from corner to corner, from dung heap to dung heap, in order to escape our machine gun fire. Only down at the collective farm headquarters, where there was evidently a commissar leading the resistance, was there even the weakest attempt at defense. Geschütz 234 moved out toward it, all its weapons firing away. It rolled right over an anti-tank gun, wound its way through the smoldering farm, dead Soviets lying everywhere, and suddenly got stuck in the meter-high snow, which had lifted the track off the drive wheel. The Soviets still had not noticed it. But for how long? The driver slammed it into reverse to pull up the track, which was still resting on the rollers. Exactly the opposite happened. The track fell off the drive wheel completely, and the sticky snow, which had lodged itself between the rollers and the bogie wheels, began to push it off all the way along. Thrown out in front and now lame! Ivan spotted something now. An anti-tank gun began to fire, and the riflemen began to work their way forward in little groups, protected by the ruins of the town. Our men could still defend themselves with high-explosive shells and the on-board machine gun, but the ammunition supply was rapidly dwindling. In addition, those weapons only provided frontal support; once the enemy got into their dead space, the situation would get risky. Support could not be expected, for the radio equipment was out of order. On top of that, no one had noticed in the stormy advance that the Batterie had not followed. The only solution: jump out and try to get back to the Batterie.

The four men jumped out and ran back, stumbling through the smoking farm, followed by the shells of the anti-tank guns. Breathless, they reached the Batterie, which was just being refueled. The Chef, Obersturmführer Wiesemann, made a lightning-quick decision: the Geschütz had to be towed away. The Batterie raced into the basin, where Ivan had once again staked out his position in the ruins. Only their drivers were sitting in the vehicles; all the others were on the fences, firing on all sides with machine guns and submachine guns, shooting at anything moving. The Geschütz stood undamaged on the same spot, but the Russians had reached it and had plundered the clothing storage bin instead of blowing up the Kanone and the motor. At a feverish pace, we tore the track apart and threw it off the wheels. We hooked the Geschütz up on a tow line and tried to pull it along on its road wheels. It took two tries with three other Geschütze pulling, but we finally got it moving. Then we raced off at full throttle. All around us, hell was breaking loose, but we managed it. Our nerves did not settle down until we reached the next town, which the 1. Panzergrenadier-Regiment had in a secure hold. Then the men's faces, black from smoke and powder, broke into smiles; once again, they had given death the slip. Our losses were amazingly minor. There were a couple of men wounded, and those were already on their way to the medical clearing station. And there was one man killed. Yes, only one. But that one weighed heavy on us, for it was an old comrade. One of the many men giving their lives by the hour to spare those at home from what they themselves had to see again and again: want, misery, rape, and death."

Kampfgruppe Meyer (the reinforced Aufklärungsabteilung and the reinforced I./Panzerregiment) set out at the same time and followed the retreating enemy forces through Sneshkoff Kut. North of there, it forced its way through an anti-tank front and, together with the 1. Panzergrenadier-Regiment, pushed through into Walki from the southwest at 13.15 hours. By 16.30 hours, the large town had been captured, and contact with the Peiper Bataillon had been established to the north.

In the morning, before setting out, Panzers from the Panzergrenadierdivision *GD* had established contact with Kampfgruppe Meyer.

Obersturmführer Isecke continued in his report on 7.3.1943 as follows:

"In the early-morning hours of 7.3, I took a tour by motorcycle of the Panzerkompanie, in order to determine the condition of the supplies and to evaluate the combat readiness. Thick fog shrouded the town. On the southern edge, the 2. Kompanie had already begun to get their meal ready. Schnitzel was sizzling in the pan. Pork was often carried on the outside of the Panzers in this freezing weather, and sometimes shrapnel tore it to pieces. But what difference did it make? One could find everything from cigarettes to champagne in the Russians' stock. In our march, we had found plenty of things in the last weeks.

We were still eating when a messenger tore open the door: Tanks to the left and rear!' Wilhelm Beck jumped on his machine, and we were at the outermost Panzers in seconds. Indeed, there was the unmistakable sound of tanks. Beck gave his Panzers orders for the action while I moved back slowly with the motorcycle and stopped one hundred meters back. There was nothing but fog and the drone of the tanks. Suddenly, we spotted ghostly figures two meters tall. After the first fright, we realized they were Germans! We ran to them. Panzer IV's! Which unit? GD! I ran to their Abteilung commander. I informed him of the situation telegram-style and asked him to come along to the Kampfgruppe commander. He did not think much of the idea, but finally accepted my invitation when I informed him that there were ten Panzer IV's waiting for him two hundred meters away. At the headquarters, there was an agreement about the continuation of the battle. *GD* was to move farther to the northwest, and we were to move to the northeast toward Walki. The two commanders warned their comrade from the *GD* about the fog. He said he was not worried about it; they would deal with it. A half hour later, I got a look at two Panzer IV's at the edge of town. They had been scarred by numerous shells. As soon as the fog began to lift, we set out. Once again, the Kradschützen sat on the Panzers and the Schwimmwagens [amphibian Volkswagen vehicles]. We broke through the enemy infantry only to find once again an anti-tank front built up behind it. We had to cross the level terrain quickly. Three Panzers were soon hit. All took direct hits to the turret. Oberscharführer Reimling, recipient of the Ritterkreuz, was killed. The Chef of the 2. Panzerkompanie

was in the fourth Panzer to be hit. This one did not burn. I observed the Abteilung doctor, Dr. Stiawa, rushing to aid with his armoured ambulance car. The Chef of the 2./Panzerregiment, Obersturmführer Wilhelm Beck, was awarded the Ritterkreuz for his daring thrust forward that day.
The one thing we dared not do was stand still. The commander urged us on, ordering: Pursue! Fire with the machine guns as you drive!' In the light of our gunfire and theirs, as we flew back and forth in the fighting, there was only one thought in our minds: it's us or them! Then there was only one hundred meters left to go. Individual figures jumped away from their guns. We rolled right over them: one Panzer even got stuck on an anti-tank gun. The Volkswagens raced past, right into Walki!"

The same fighting can be viewed from the perspective of the Kradschützen in this report from Untersturmführer Maurer, a Zugführer with the 2./Aufklärungsabteilung *LAH*:

"The weather alternated between mud and frost. We had stopped being reconnaissance forces; we had become hood ornaments for every possible Panzerkompanie. The next objective was Walki.
There was fire from anti-tank guns, machine guns, and mortars just before the town. The Russians were offering tough resistance. We jumped off, and our Panzers started fighting with the nests of anti-tank guns. This duel was taking place not a hundred fifty meters in front of us. Obersturmführer Beck from Bitz had been hit twice within a matter of minutes and simply jumped over to the next Panzer right there on the battlefield. Our attack was stuck, and we were lying directly in front of the enemy positions. Suddenly, I saw our commander (Sturmbannführer Kurt Meyer) to the right of me. He climbed out of a Schützenpanzerwagen, shouldered a rifle, and picked off eight men. The spell was broken. We tore loose, broke through their positions, and chased them from foxhole to foxhole with hand grenades. Then we came to the river on the southern edge of Walki. The Panzers took over providing covering fire, and we made a closed-rank jump across the ice and into the town. We fired from all barrels and howled like maniacs. Ivan could not take it. He fled. But we were completely drained. Our faces were streaming with sweat, and our legs just would not hold us anymore. At that moment, four self-propelled 2-centimeter Flak guns arrived and fired high-explosive shells into some isolated nests of resistance to help us out. The enemy could no longer hold on; he had to keep running. We just hopped on the Flak gun, and, without express orders, the Zug pushed on toward the northeast. We ignored the Russians running to our right and left. The men behind us could take care of them. As soon as my boys had caught their breath, they launched into their favorite song: 'Eternal spring is coming, the world is full of sunshine.' We fought for another hour for every foxhole, and then the boys started singing again. I was proud of them and glad that my Zug suffered no casualties in this fight. After a few kilometers, we met up with a Kompanie from the Peiper Bataillon. The Chef of our Kompanie, Obersturmführer Weiser, was awarded the Ritterkreuz for his action."

That evening, the commander of Panzergrenadier-Regiment 5 *T*, Obersturmbannführer Baum, arrived at the headquarters of Kampfgruppe Meyer in Walki. His unit had been deployed to cover the Division's western flank.

The reinforced Aufklärungsabteilung received orders to send out combat-strength reconnaissance forces to establish contact with Panzerregiment *GD* in Schlijach. Panzergrenadierdivision *DR*, the adjacent unit to the right, had taken Pawlowka and Staraja Wodolaga on the Msha sector by evening.

Evidently, there were differences of opinion within the upper leadership about the way to proceed. The Oberkommando of the Heer, the 4. Panzerarmee, and Armeeabteilung Kempf intended to capture Charkow, the Oberbefehlshaber of the Heeresgruppe, Generalfeldmarschall von Manstein, was inclined to force the enemy out of Charkow and to defeat him somewhere to the west. The Oberbefehlshaber of the Armee, Generaloberst Hoth, and General der Panzertruppen Kempf objected that the scarcity of vehicles, coupled with the extraorinarily bad road conditions, would prevent such a large-scale motorized endeavor and would make supplying the troops exceedingly difficult. The Generalfeldmarschall brushed their objections aside with the remark that the enemy had to be defeated despite those difficulties: "For all that, if we get stuck, it doesn't hurt anything."

The Wehrmacht reported on 7.3.1943:

> "In the area south of Charkow, rapidly advancing Heer and Waffen-SS troops broke the enemy's strong resistance and pushed him back to the north. We surrounded and destroyed units of the Soviet 3rd Tank Army consisting of elements of the XIIth and XVth Tank Corps, one cavalry corps, and three rifle divisions. The figures on numbers of prisoners taken and amount of materiel captured can at first only be partially reported. Up to now, over two hundred twenty-five artillery pieces, sixty-one tanks, and over one thousand vehicles have been counted. The Soviets suffered extraordinary numbers of bloody losses."

The Division's orders for 8.3.1943:

> Continuation of the attack on Ogulzy and the towns west of Ljubotin in order to shut down the road to Charkow in the northern part of Ljubotin.

8.3.1943: At 07.30 hours, the Kampfgruppen set off to continue their thrust to the north.

To the right, the reinforced 2. Panzergrenadier-Regiment (under Standartenführer Wisch) proceeded with the III. (armoured)/2. toward Hf. Karasan on the Merefa river. The reinforced I./2. was moving on Odrynka and, left of there, the reinforced II./2. on Ogulzy. The roads, a muddy soup, kept the attack moving at a snail's pace. When our reconnaissance reported Odrynka to be heavily occupied by the enemy, the 2./2. (under Hauptsturmführer Becker) and the Flakzug under Armberger, supported by the light Infanteriegeschütz and the 2./Artillerie-Regiment (under Obersturmführer Luhmann), made rapid preparations behind the hills to the west of Odrynka. They attacked at 11.30 hours and took the entire stream basin north of the town by 12.45 hours. After his first resistance had been broken, the enemy abandoned the town and fled to the north and northeast in a force of at least battalion size. The 3./2. (under

Hauptsturmführer Werner Pötschke.
Received Ritterkreuz on 4.6.1944 as Chef of the 1./SS-Panzerregiment 1 LSSAH.
Killed 14.3.1945 near Vecsprem in Hungary.

The Divisional commander, Oberführer Theodor Wisch, congratulates Michael Wittman and his brave Tiger crew on Wittman's one-hundred-thirteenth enemy tank destroyed. Wittman became the three hundred eightieth soldier to be awarded the Eichenlaub, and Rottenführer Balthasar Woll, his gunner, received the Ritterkreuz.

Having a chat on the edge of battle.
Left to right: Obersturmbannführer Meyer, commander of the Aufklärungsabteilung LSSAH; a Zugführer in the Panzerregiment; Standartenführer Dr. Besuden, the Divisional doctor; Obersturmbannführer Witt, the commander of the 1. Panzergrenadier-Regiment; and Sturmabannführer Wünsche, commander of the I./Panzerregiment 1 LSSAH.

Obersturmführer Röhwer) surrounded and attacked the hills, reaching the stream basin to the north without coming into contact with the enemy.

The II./Panzergrenadier-Regiment *DF*, adjacent to the right, attacked Odrynka from the south and smashed the remaining resistance in the southeastern part of the town by 13.00 hours.

The II./2. entered Ogulzy at 09.00 hours and by evening had made its way into the forest northeast of the town.

The III. (armoured)/2., fighting against enemy troops and the road conditions the entire way, had reached its attack objective by 17.00 hours and was able to establish a bridgehead over the Merefa near Karasan.

The reinforced 1. Panzergrenadier-Regiment set out from Walki at 07.30 hours with the I. Bataillon sitting on the Panzers of the II./Panzerregiment *LAH*. Thanks to better road conditions, it was able to break the weak enemy resistance near Kowalenkoff by 08.45 hours. By 16.00 hours, its leading elements had reached the church in Ljubotin.

The Divisional headquarters were moved first to Minkowka, in order to be able to be more effective in arranging the supply operations. The unit adjacent to the right had closed ranks up to Odrynka. The III. (armoured)/2. was ordered in the late evening to move to Ogulzy.

Kampfgruppe Meyer moved from Walki via Bolgar all the way to the junction of the railway and road at Schljach, arriving there at noon.

Orders for 9.3.1943:

> *The reinforced 1. Panzergrenadier-Regiment* is to move, as soon as the security forces in Ljubotin have been relieved by the 2. Panzergrenadier-Regiment, to the northeast toward Peresstschnaja, meanwhile offering aggressive protection for the eastern flank.
>
> *The reinforced 2. Panzergrenadier-Regiment* is to start as early as possible for Ljubotin, where it is to relieve the elements of the 1. Panzergrenadier-Regiment deployed there. The unit is then to provide defense to the southeast, east, and northeast.
>
> *Kampfgruppe Meyer* (the reinforced Aufklärungsabteilung and the I./Panzerregiment *LAH*) is to move forward on Medweshji and to stand ready there for an attack on Peresstschnaja or Olschany.
>
> *Werferabteilung I/55* is to be moved up to join the Division on 9.3 in Kowalenkoff. It will be subordinated to the Division.

9.3.1943: In the early morning, the Divisional headquarters moved to Litwinowka (two kilometers east of Walki). Because this town was completely destroyed, it was ordered to move at once to Kowalenkoff, arriving there at about 10.15 hours.

At 06.00 hours, the three attack forces continued their movements as ordered.

At 07.30 hours, Kampfgruppe Peiper (the III. [armoured]/2.) moved through the southern part of Ljubotin and established contact with the 1. Panzergrenadier-Regiment. At 11.00 hours, the unit launched its attack on Bogaty along the railway line from Ljubotin to Charkow. It defeated a Russian battalion in the fighting.

The I. and II./2., engaged in clearing Ljubotin and the area around it of enemy forces, reached the eastern edge and relieved the elements of the 1. Panzergrenadier-Regiment deployed there. Both Bataillone could be relieved that afternoon in order to stand ready for their next day's mission.

At 07.30 hours, elements of the reinforced 1. Panzergrenadier-Regiment reached the railway line heading north on both sides of Schpakowo. The Bataillon commander of the III./1., Hauptsturmführer Hubert Meyer, was wounded in the move. Sturmbannführer Weidenhaupt took over the Bataillon.

Kampfgruppe Meyer, deployed to the left, was approaching the railway line west of Peresstschnaja at about this time. The enemy resistance from Peresstschnaja and Schpakowo was intensifying. The Divisional commander, travelling with the attack groups, ordered the Kampfgruppe to move on at 08.30 hours. Obergruppenführer Sepp Dietrich held a meeting with the commanding general, Obergruppenführer Hausser, on the battelfield.

Shortly before 10.00 hours, the 1. Panzergrenadier-Regiment and Kampfgruppe Meyer reported that they had captured Schpakowo and Peresstschnaja and established contact with the *T*-Division in Olschany. When this message arrived, the Chef of the Generalstab of the SS-Panzerkorps, Standartenführer Ostendorf, was at the *LAH*'s Divisional headquarters in Kowalenkoff. He was in agreement with a continuation of the attack on Dergatschi. Standartenführer Ostendorf, while he was staying at the *LAH*'s Divisional headquarters, received briefings on the Armee's orders. Charkow was to be captured, in a surprise attack if that became necessary. He presented the SS-Panzerkorps' plan to move the *LAH* in an initial thrust to the north past Charkow in order to create the preconditions for an attack on 10.3 with the *DR* moving in from the west and the *LAH* from the north to take the city. The *T*-Division was given the task of covering the *LAH*'s flank and rear.

The Ia of the *LAH* requested that the 2. Panzergrenadier-Regiment immediately be released from duty on the eastern edge of Ljubotin. The request was granted and the corresponding orders issued.

The III. (armoured)/2. had in the meantime moved forward on the Bataillon commander's initiative to Nowo Bawaria on the western edge of Charkow. He was ordered to pull back at 14.00 hours.

At 18.40 hours, the Ia of the *LAH* provided the units with preliminary information on the plan of attack for recapturing Charkow.

Kampfgruppe Meyer was subordinated to the commander of the 1. Panzergrenadier-Regiment, and the combined force became known as Kampfgruppe Witt. This Kampfgruppe was to move in the evening of 9.3 forward to the east via Tscherkasskoje (the objective for the 1. Panzergrenadier-Regiment) on Zirkuny (the objective for Kampfgruppe Meyer). There the force was to stand ready to move as soon as the Division ordered. It was to proceed along the following two roads: Tscherkasskoje — Charkow and Zirkuny — Charkow.

The reinforced 2. Panzergrenadier-Regiment was to join the march formation behind Kampfgruppe Witt in Peresstschnaja and move as far as Dergatschi, in order to attack along the road to Charkow as soon as the Division gave the attack order.

Because of the road conditions, including heavy congestion, these moves were hard to commence, and they lasted a seeming eternity. The situation with the roads was particularly difficult to control because the road Poltawa — Walki — Ljubotin — Charkow (Main road no. V) was in the Korps' jurisdiction between Walki and Ljubotin, but then ran right across the combat sectors of three different Panzergrenadierdivisionen. Each one had the right to claim the road for its own use. The Heer's Panzergrenadierdivision *GD* was also using the road.

By 23.00 hours on 9.3.1943, the 2. Panzergrenadier-Regiment had started its march. The leading elements of the reinforced 1. Panzergrenadier-Regiment reached the forests west of Dergatschi by midnight. Combat reconnaissance reported that town to be heavily occupied by the enemy. The Regiment stood ready to attack Dergatschi. The start of the attack was set for dawn.

Kampfgruppe Meyer remained behind Kampfgruppe Witt, in order to move along behind it on Zirkuny after Dergatschi and Tscherkasskoje had been captured.

Pionier-Bataillon *LAH* was deployed to maintain the march route near Kowalenkoff.

To the right of the *LAH*, *DR* closed ranks on both sides of the road from Ljubotin to Charkow. The *T*-Division was attempting to proceed between Olschany and Feski to the east.

10.3.1943: Because of the road conditions, the preparations of the reinforced 1. Panzergrenadier-Regiment lasted well into the morning.

At 11.45 hours, it started its attack on Dergatschi. In the course of the move, it became apparent that elements of the *T*-Division were also in the process of attacking the northern part of Dergatschi. At about noon, the 1. Panzergrenadier-Regiment *LAH* and elements of the *T*-Division jointly captured the town. At about 14.00 hours, Kampfgruppe Meyer moved out from the eastern part of Dergatschi toward Tscherkasskoje and Zirkuny.

Obersturmführer von Ribbentrop, at that time commander of the 6./Panzerregiment *LAH*, reported on the attack on Dergatschi as follows:

> "We were to attack Dergatschi together with the Bataillon under Hansen (the II./1.). After some going back and forth between Sturmbannführer Hansen and Sturmbannführer Groß, the latter ordered a thrust into the town with the Panzers travelling on the village road, since the flooded terrain confined them to it. I rode in the leading Panzer, and we were only able to defend ourselves against the strong Russian infantry because the man behind me, Obersturmführer Stollmeyer (tragically killed two days later), kept shooting the Russian's off my Panzer with high-explosive shells. In spite of this danger, we successfully fought our way through the town and pushed farther into the midst of the retreating Russians."

Obersturmführer Isecke, the Adjutant of the I./Panzerregiment *LAH*, reported as follows on this day:

> "Our burning interest, of course, was how we would make it to Zirkuny. According to the map, there were forests and swamps north of Charkow. Right, happy trails! In pursuit of the enemy, we crossed the two other attack sectors and came into the swamp and forest area between Tscherkasskoje and Zirkuny. The Aufklärungsabteilung was in front of us. Sturmbannführer Wünsche ordered: 'I will take the Panzers along, those which make it through. You mobilize all the forces to get those Panzers going again which have gotten stuck or have slipped off the road. Our objective is known. If you get lost, follow our tracks!' That's when the work began which lasted the entire night and proved unforgettable for all concerned. We got a few, often by pulling with two Panzers and long, long cables, out of the most

difficult places in this swampy, gully-ridden forest terrain. We did not have a clue about the surprise attack which Sturmbannführer Wünsche was pulling off with the Aufklärungsabteilung and three Panzers. We knew nothing about the surprising success of the entrance into Charkow from the northeast. We were still eight kilometers from the decisive junction in Charkow (the road Charkow — Tschugujew)."

The reinforced Aufklärungsabteilung reached Zirkuny in the evening. Commander Sturmbannführer Kurt Meyer was riding with his leading elements, which consisted of only a few vehicles. They encountered an enemy column which had been put into disarray by a Stuka attack. The leading elements dealt with that problem quickly, and the reinforced Aufklärungsabteilung assembled. It then launched its first attack on the city. Kurt Meyer deployed Wünsche's three Panzers in a thrust as far as a brickyard on the northern edge of city. There several enemy tanks were resting and preparing to defend the town. The commander of the Kampfgruppe withdrew this advance detachment of Panzers to Bolschaja Danilowka. There he waited for the Kampfgruppe to close ranks behind him.[31]

The reinforced 1. Panzergrenadier-Regiment, following the rapidly advancing Kampfgruppe Meyer and supported by elements of the II./Panzerregiment *LAH*, had to capture Tscherkasskoje one more time and clear it of enemy forces. In the evening and into the night, it inched up on both sides of the Tscherkasskoje — Charkow attack route as far as the airstrip on the northern edge of the city.

The road conditions held up the advance of the 2. Panzergrenadier-Regiment in Peresstschnaja until 12.00 hours. At 13.00 hours, the I./2. (under Sturmbannführer Kraas) reached Dergatschi. It then moved forward to the south along the road toward Charkow and attacked the enemy columns withdrawing from the southern edge of Podgorodnaja in an effort to break their formation.

The report from Sturmbannführer Krass at 15.30 hours read as follows: "The southern edge of Podgorodnaja and the hills east of the defense line have been captured. Retreating enemy troops have been engaged in fighting along the railway line, and we have scored successes. The enemy is digging in on the edge of the city. He is firing with multiple rocket launchers."

At 17.00 hours, the II./2 (under Sturmbannführer Sandig) destroyed an enemy Batterie at the road out of Malaja to the south.

At 17.00 hours, the Division's orders were issued to the units. They read as follows:

Leibstandarte SS Adolf Hitler
Abteilung 1a *Le./Ga.*

Divisional headquarters
10.3.1943

Divisionsbefehl No. 8

1) *The enemy* has been totally surprised and effectively pushed back by the *Leibstandarte*'s rapid advance.

2) *The SS-Panzerkorps* is to capture Charkow on 11.3.1943 while deploying elements of the SS-Division *DR* to cover the eastern flank along the Merefa and the SS-*T*-Division to cover the northern and northwestern flank in the line Russkoje — Dergatschi — Festiki — Olschany.

3) *The following are to attack:*
The SS-Division DR with a strong Regimental force from the west, the LSSAH with two Regimental forces from the north.
For dividing lines and routes of attack see the map at scale 1:100,000 and the city map.

4) Orders:
   a) *The reinforced 2. Panzergrenadier-Regiment* (Werferregiment I./55., the Sturmgeschüzabteilung minus one Batterie, one 8.8-centimeter Flakbatterie, the I. and III./Artillerie-Regiment, the 5./Flakabteilung) is to move along the western road and attack the northern edge of Charkow, moving forward as far as the dividing line between it and the SS-*DR*. It is to clear this section of the city of all enemy troops.
   b) *The reinforced 1. Panzergrenadier-Regiment* (Kampfgruppe Meyer and the Korps-Nebelwerferabteilung, otherwise as before) is to move along the eastern road into the norteastern section of Charkow. An attack force is to move immediately through the city toward the southeastern road out of it as far as Rogan. It is to clear the center of the city of enemy forces and to set up defenses to the east and northeast. *For the defensive line*, see the map at scale 1:100,000.
   A Bataillon reinforced with Sturmgeschüze is to be moved up behind the Kampfgruppe as far as the bend in the road at Stepanoff. Deployment of that Bataillon is dependent on permission from the Division.
   For this action, the Kampfgruppen are to be moved as close to the edge of the city as possible in the night between 10.3 and 11.3. *The start of the attack is 04.00 hours.*

5) *Reports* are to be given after Charkow has been penetrated according to the designated areas. (Use the map at scale 1:100,000).

6) *Combat reconnaissance* is to be conducted on both sides of the march routes to the east and to the west.

7) *The main medical clearing station* is in Ljubotin.
The wounded and sick should be assembled at the stations in Dergatschi and Tscherkasskoje.

8) *The distribution depot for fuel and ammunition* is three kilometers west of Kowalenkoff at the collective farm along the march route.

9) The Divisional headquarters is to be in *Dergatschi* at the beginning of the attack; with the capture of Charkow, it is to move to *the northeast section of Charkow.*

signed Dietrich
SS-Obergruppenführer and
General der Waffen-SS

Panzergrenadierdivision *DR* had pushed back the enemy forces from the eastern section of Korotischtsche, and it had defeated several counterattacks. Fighting was still under way around Kuraschnoje and the Schpakowka railway station. The SS-*T*-Division, providing cover for our flank and rear, stood in a line from just north of Dergatschi to Feski and on the hills north of Olschany. Together with elements of the Regiment under Baum, it was attacking Russkoje.[32]

The Divisional headquarters moved that night to Dergatschi. There, the Division's commander, Obergruppenführer Sepp Dietrich, received a call from Adolf Hitler, who had traveled that day to the Oberkommando of Heeresgruppe Süd in Saporoshje. Hitler asked Obergruppenführer Sepp Dietrich as to how it was going for "his men." The Ia, who was listening in on the conversation, remembers that Hitler several times expressed his dismay about the losses suffered by "his Leibstandarte" and his concern for Sepp Dietrich's life. Hitler ended the conversation with the words: "If my Leibstandarte attacks with its usual nerve, it cannot fail to tear Charkow from the enemy's hands!"

11.3.1943 (see sketch 19): At 03.10 hours, the I./2. (under Kraas) moved on Alexejewka with the 3. Kompanie (under Obersturmführer Röhwer) and the 1. Kompanie (under Obersturmführer Hausdorf) in the front line. The assault was unsuccessful. The attack got stuck. The 3. Kompanie was pushed back out of the city by a Red Army counterattack with tanks. Only when it reached the ravines north of Alexejewka was the Kompanie able to dig in its heels and stop the retreat.

The II./2. (under Sturmbannführer Sandig), which set out at 04.00 hours from Losowenka to the right, made its way into Ssewerny by 05.30 hours. Its right wing, however, encountered well-defended installations in elevated positions on the northwest edge of Charkow. By 10.15 hours, the II./2. had succeeded in making its way forward from strong point to strong point, finally capturing the Ssewerny railway station and its yards.

At 13.00 hours, the 2./2. (under Hauptsturmführer Becker) received orders to wait for the Stuka attack, and then to launch an assault from the brickyard with the support of four Sturmgeschüze from the 3./Sturmgeschüzabteilung under the command of Untersturmführer Siegel.

At 13.25 hours, the Stuka attack took place, and there was an attack by all our heavy weapons. Exploiting the opportunity, the 2. Kompanie was able to capture the hill in cooperation with the leading elements of the 3. Kompanie. The fighting was slow because the the constant enemy fire which followed the Kompanie the entire way, especially on its flank. Two Sturmgeschüze and two self-propelled 3.7-centimeter Flak guns joined the rest of the 3. Kompanie and elements from the 2. Kompanie in a renewed attempt to penetrate the town. Once again, the attack came to a standstill. One Sturmgeschüz and one Flak gun were destroyed right at the point of breakthrough by fire from a T-34 or a hidden anti-tank gun hiding in the railway watchman's tower. The Sturmgeschüz burned out. Oberscharführer Wolters and his crew were killed inside it.

In this critical situation, Hauptsturmführer Becker took it upon himself to gather a few men together in a hurry and to move west of the hill. Despite heavy fire from the rear and from the elevated position, he was able to penetrate a ravine and move through it to break into the rear of the enemy's front positions. In vicious fighting, the first group of buildings was snatched from the enemy. Two lightning-quick thrusts along the march route and across it to the south expanded the breakthrough point. An enemy counterattack with three tanks was repulsed.

Hauptsturmführer Becker, Chef of the 2./2. was awarded the Ritterkreuz for his courageous and decisive action. The entry in the Kriegstagebuch of the I./2. Panzergrenadier-Regiment *LAH* lists the losses of the Bataillon on 11.3 as follows:

Dead: One officer, twenty-five non-commissioned officers and enlisted men.

Wounded: Five officers (including one who remained with the troops). Untersturmführer Rehm and Untersturmführer Karl Neuner died of their wounds at the medical clearing station.
Eighty-eight non-commissioned officers and enlisted men, twenty-three of whom stayed with the troops.

The III. (armoured)/2., which was equipped for a motorized advance, was moved up to Losowenka in the evening.

The 1. Panzergrenadier-Regiment, which had also set out at 04.00 hours to the left, had skirted the open terrain around the north Charkow airstrip to the right, and it then had to repulse an enemy counterattack against its left flank, waged across the airstrip. Our MG 41's committed terrible slaughter as they fired into the dense Russian ranks.

By afternoon, this center group of the Division's forces had overcome the rough enemy resistance at the rows of houses along the northern edge of the city. The I./Werferregiment 55, assigned to cooperate with the two Panzergrenadier-Regimenter, provided excellent effective cover for the advance by the spearheads of both Regimenter.

Kampfgruppe Meyer, acting as left assault force for the Division, also set out at 04.00 hours. It was accompanied by several Panzers which had arrived in the night (seven Panzer IV's, two Panzers III's and two self-propelled Panzerjägers). The Kradschützen rode mounted on them. Shortly after the unit got underway, the leading Panzer was hit, and immediately thereafter the Schützenpanzerwagen ridden by the Kampfgruppe's commander, Sturmbannführer Meyer. The Zugführer of the Nachrichtenzug of the Aufklärungsabteilung, Obersturmführer Westphal, was killed. But the Kampfgruppe kept its advance going, moving forward house by house. When two T-34's popped up from a gully, they were accidentally fired on by their own comrades. An enemy anti-tank crew was killed by a falling lightpole. The advance began to pick up speed. The Adjutant of the I./Panzerregiment *LAH*, Obersturmführer Isecke, who had remained behind in Bolschaja Danilowka, offered the following report:

> "I had orders from the commander to remain here in order to take care of moving up any elements that fell behind. I was also to provide defense to the east, because being only two kilometers from the edge of the city did not make the commander happy at all. Remaining with me was Obersturmführer Schlauss, the Nachrichtenoffizier of the Panzerabteilung, and two Panzer III's. We got a chance to learn once again how vital good communications are. The technical officers of the Abteillung, the two Kompanie Chefs (Jürgensen and Lambrecht), the Chef of the self-propelled Panzerjäger, and the heavy elements of the Aufklärungsabteilung were all slogging their way through the forests and marshes of the terrain. In the afternoon, our command Panzer, which we had installed in a walled courtyard to watch the east, reported sighting tank movements in Bobrow

(two kilometers to the east). Hell, there were at least thirty of them, some in motion, some already in position, aiming right at us. Schlauss reported that Hauptsturmführer Jürgens [sic] with his seven Panzer IV's and Hauptsturmführer Prinz with his three self-propelled Panzerjägers would shortly make it through. With that, we could show the guys over there that it was not advisable to attack us.

Our tactic was rapid fire from camouflaged positions and immediate shift of position. It was a success. On the other side, there was a shift in position and then rest.

As evening fell, Hauptsturmführer Jürgensen followed the Abteilung commander to the front with five Panzer IV's and picked up fuel, ammunition and supplies for the Aufklärungsabteilung."

For the leading elements of the Aufklärungsabteilung, in the meantime, things were heating up. The commander, Sturmbannführer Meyer, related the events in "Grenadiere" (page 201 ff.):

> "At the moment of our victory, a dangerous crisis arose. Our Panzers had only a little fuel left and could no longer be used. We brought them into hedgehog formation for all-around defense on a large cemetery and thus built a solid bulwark in the center of Charkow. From that position, we sent feelers along the road Charkow — Tschugujew and attempted to block the Soviet's main avenue of retreat. I had had no report since noon from the 2. Kompanie (under Hauptsturmführer Weiser); it had been cut off by enemy forces at the Charkow river. The 1. Kompanie (under Hauptsturmführer Bremer) was fighting for its life, Olboetter (of the heavy Kompanie) was repulsing enemy counterattacks from the east. At the cemetery, we had to defend ourselves against Soviet forces which kept breaking out. As night fell, Hauptscharführer Bruckmann was able to bring through a few truckfulls of fuel."

That afternoon, there was a disagreement between the 4. Panzerarmee and the SS-Panzerkorps. After a preliminary briefing over the telephone, orders arrived from the Armee by telegram at 15.05 hours suspending the attack on western Charkow (*DR*) and pulling back the forces from the northern wing (*LAH*). These forces were to surround Charkow from the east, to attack the enemy's rear in Besljudowka, and to crack open the enemy support point in Smjew from the rear in a wide arc in order to make the enemy's escape to Tschugujew and the east impossible.

The Generalkommando of the SS-Panzerkorps provided the following information about the Korps' situation:

> "In the evening, the Division *DR* stands just outside the western edge of the city facing strongly fortified tank trenches. The Division is in formation for a night attack designed to overcome the trenches. Elements are detailed to provide defense against enemy counterattacks near Korotischtsche and Budy and to clear the areas captured of enemy troops. The *LAH*, moving on a broad front, structured all its available forces for the attack and penetrated the northern part of the city. It is currently engaged in heavy

house-to-house fighting against strong enemy resistance, including some counterattacks."

At 21.00 hours, the Generalkommando of the SS-Panzerkorps responded to an inquiry from the Armee as to its intentions by providing the following evaluation of the situation:

"Starting this evening, we have observed increased signs that the enemy is abandoning Charkow while leaving strong forces behind, especially anti-tank guns and tanks. We expect enemy attacks from Solotschew (to the northwest). The bulk of Division *DR* and Division *LAH* have their weapons aimed at the northeastern, northern, and western edges of the city. The northeastern section has already been penetrated. The road junction Charkow — Woltschansk and Tschugujew is temporarily in our possession. A shift of the *LAH*'s point of main concentration to the eastern wing is in process. The SS-*T*-Division is engaged in defense along a forty-five-kilometer-wide sector with two Regimenter. A Panzerabteilung from the Division is with Panzergrenadierdivision *DR*. The road conditions north of Charkow are such that moving Division *DR* around would require at least a day and a half. Some of the bridges are broken. The ice on the rivers is no longer strong enough to withstand a large weight. The *LAH*'s supply lines are already uncertain. Therefore, the following decision has been made: continuation of the attack in the previous configuration while moving the point of concentration to the eastern wing. After the capture of Charkow, we will assemble the Korps east of the city for a thrust to the south."[34]

b) 12.3.1943 - 15.3.1943: Recapture of Charkow

12.3.1943 (see sketch 19): Armeebefehl No. 34 arrived at the Korps headquarters in excerpts by radio at 01.15 hours and in its complete form by telegram at 02.00 hours. The orders prescribed the details of the restructuring of the SS-Panzerkorps for the attack and described the plan of attack. First there was to be a double encirclement of the enemy by moving around the city to the north and then making one thrust on Wodjannoje (no longer Besljudowka, as it had been in the last orders) and another on Tschugujew to block off the narrow passage there. The units involved in these operations were to be Division *DR* and Division *T*. The Generalkommando of the SS-Panzerkorps enunciated its opinion of the plan in its Kriegstagebuch as follows:

"Two Divisionen of the Armee itself are to be deployed, each with two missions, a defense mission and a pursuit mission. This plan brings all the missions undertaken into danger, because the possibilities for focusing the forces on a single task are diminished."

In the course of the afternoon, the SS-Panzerkorps provided the Panzer-armeeoberkommando 4 once more with a thorough evaluation of the situation, but there was no change of mind. The Armeebefehlshaber insisted on the execution of his previous order in a sharply-worded directive:

> "I hereby make the commanding general of the SS-Panzerkorps responsible for the complete execution of my orders to withdraw SS-Division *DR* from the Charkow fighting and to move it around Charkow to the north onto the eastern wing. A report on the successful completion of the operation is to be provided in complete detail."
>
> The Oberbefehlshaber signed Hoth

This order arrived at the Panzerkorps at 11.50 hours. At 13.50 hours, the Chef of the Generalstab of the SS-Panzerkorps informed the Ia of the *LAH* that Division *DR* was no longer continuing its attack from the west.

The *LAH*, however, had continued its attack in the early morning hours.

At 09.15 hours, the II./2. (under Sturmbannführer Sandig) broke through the field installations at the edge of the city and by 10.15 hours had captured the northern signal box of the main Charkow railway station. For his Bataillon's action in this fighting, Sturmbannführer Sandig was awarded the Ritterkreuz.

At the same time, the I./2. (under Kraas) had once again penetrated Alexejewka. The enemy offered both Bataillone tough resistance from sharpshooters and flat-trajectory guns stationed in buildings with commanding elevations. The Artillerie, Nebelwerfer, and heavy Infanterie weapons moved up behind and provided a fire attack, following which the Bataillone moved in once again at 10.50 hours on the city proper. The enemy continued to resist bitterly. But our attack moved quickly and pursued the retreating enemy forces. In the sections of the city known as Lisa Gora and Pawliwka, we surprised the enemy and forced him into close-range fighting before he could dig himself in in the maze of the inner city. By 16.00 hours, his forces were completely defeated and several of his battalions wiped out. Five officers (including one regimental commander) and one hundred fifty men were taken prisoner.

There was an enemy tank attack against the 1. Panzergrenadier-Regiment in the night. The Chef of the 2. (heavy)/Flakabteilung, Hauptsturmführer Möbius, reported on it as follows:

> "In the evening, all our troops were pulled out and placed in readiness for the attack on the following morning. I placed one 8.8-centimeter Kanone and one 2-centimeter Flak-MG on the road for defense. It was growing dark as the last elements of the Kampfgruppe came to me to report that there were tanks moving our way. They were indeed tanks, T-34's. We fired at extremely close range (tip of the barrel to tank only fifteen meters). A hit. Then the loading mechanism jammed. Our efforts were in vain. The rest of the five T-34's opened fire and we lost our gun. This entire event, of course, lasted only seconds. The gun was reduced to scrap. The next morning, we attacked as far as Red Square."

The 1. Panzergrenadier-Regiment's I. and III. had also set off in the dawn and by 10.00 hours were able to overcome the resistance at the edge of town. Structured into Kompanie groups with individual Panzers, the two Bataillone fought their way forward from one group of houses to the next. As night fell, they had captured a line just two rows of houses north of Red Square.

Horst Mutterlose provided a report on this fighting from the artilleryman's viewpoint:

> "Our Grenadiere were stuck on the elevated cemetery in Charkow, and the attack was not moving forward. The first tall apartment buildings were so close we could touch them. We had to help the Grenadiere. We attempted to aim our Artillerie fire at the street in front of the houses in order to prepare it for the Grenadiere's entrance into the city. Shots rang out to the side and in front. Because of the trees and bushes of the cemetery, we had no line of sight to our right. Ivan was firing with high-explosive shells. We fired our shells so that they exploded above ground in order to see just where they were landing. At least three shots were fired with this corrected trajectory, but we still could not see the where they burst, even though we clearly heard the explosion. It became too much for our Batteriechef to bear. He, who operated his weapon so masterfully, was to delay the attack at its decisive moment? Despite the enemy shots hissing around our Schützenpanzerwagen, Obersturmführer Lehnert jumped out of the vehicle in desperation. He climbed up on a hut to get a better view. Again he ordered us to fire. 'Fired!' I shouted to the Chef, and in seconds the shell's burst was visible right where we wanted it to be. Our Batteriechef was beaming. But at that moment, Lehnert got it. There he lay, still smiling, but we saw at once that he was no longer alive. Those of us in the Schützenpanzerwagen were paralyzed with horror. We, who so loved our young 'old man,' could not speak. At that moment it was incomprehensible that he was no longer in our midst. He, the inspiring example leading us young volunteers, was the one death chose to tear from the Batterie and call home."

The III./1. had sent Unterscharführer Bäumer with the 11./1. into the city on 11.3 as a reconnaissance force. Oberschütze Edgar Börner reported on their actions as follows:

> "Our reconnaissance force moved under cover of darkness as far as Red Square without coming into contact with the enemy. This enormous square lay bright in the moonlight, and a deceptive silence hung over it. Our 2. Regiment was supposed to be at Red Square already. When we asked a few bundled-up infantrymen, 'Are you from the 2. Regiment?', we got no answer except for a shell from a well-hidden tank only one hundred meters from us. It fired over our heads into a building. We crept into a cellar and sent a foot messenger with our report back to the Bataillon commander, Sturmbannführer Weidenhaupt. The messenger returned with the order: 'Stay at Red Square overnight and observe.' We set up telephone lines. In our cellar, we were protected from the night cold. At daybreak, we could not believe our eyes. The entire square was filled with Russian infantrymen getting their morning meal, their rifles hanging on their shoulders. We sat and observed the goings-on until the II./1. with Sturmbannführer Max Hansen arrived and we could climb out of our mouse hole."

The II./1. had set out in darkness. By, in the words of Bataillon-Adjutant Obersturmführer Schuhknecht, "a medium-price miracle," it also made it through the Russian lines without coming into contact with the enemy. Obersturmführer Schuhknecht described the situation as follows:

> "In the tall buildings, there were sharpshooters; they were dealing us considerable losses. Hauptsturmführer Weiher (Chef of the 6./1.) was killed, as was Obersturmführer Richter. At Red Square, the Bataillon divided into groups and moved on, bypassing the square itself. Two Kompanien moved through the park around the zoo as far as the Tschewtschenko monument on Sumskaja street. The Stab and one Kompanie remained in a hotel in the section of town with the tall buildings. Tried-and-true Sturmbannführer Max Hansen was awarded the Ritterkreuz for this decisive thrust through the city.
> From this situation, the commander of the II./1. established contact with the I./1. (under Sturmbannführer Frey). This Bataillon moved forward slowly through the park and suffered heavy losses. The enemy finally began to retreat, however, when he felt us at his back. In the evening, Panzers from von Ribbentrop's Kompanie reached us. One of them was hit when it fired a flare in the dark on Red Square."

The 2. Panzergrenadier-Regiment had in the meantime deployed the III. (armoured)/2. (under Peiper) at 10.30 hours. Sturmbannführer Peiper established contact with the commander of the 1. Panzergrenadier-Regiment (Standartenführer Witt) and then moved along the main thoroughfare. He established contact with Sturmbannführer Hansen (commander of the II./1.) at Red Square and built a bridgehead along Staro-Moskowska street. With two or three Schützenpanzerwagens, Peiper soon established contact with Kampfgruppe Meyer at the Tschugujew road junction.

Kampfgruppe Meyer had moved forward along several different branches of the streets and had managed to capture the important junction of the road Charkow — Tschugujew or Woltschansk. There, it had to defend itself against heavy attacks with an all-around defense.

Two Züge of the 2./Aufklärungsabteilung (under Weiser) were surrounded in a school and were desperately defending themselves against Russian assault troops which had already entered the ground floor. Sturmbannführer Wünsche used several Panzers to launch a counterattack, and the Russian assault force was annihilated. The enemy's pressure on the defenses of the *T*-Division intensified in the Kampfgruppe's rear near Zirkuny.

Back on the right flank with the 2. Panzergrenadier-Regiment, the II./2. managed by the end of the day to capture the main railway station. For the night, the II. and I./2. provided defense along Katerinoslawaska street. The 1. (heavy)/Flakabteilung (under Hauptsturmführer Dr. Loenicker) managed to shoot down two J18 airplanes.

In Regiment 2, Obersturmführer Schmidt, the Ordonnanzoffizier of the I./2., and two Zugführers, Untersturmführer Köhler and Untersturmführer Kaden, were killed.

In the Wehrmacht's report of 12.3.1943, the following appears:

10.3.1943: The motorcycle reconnaissance unit of the 1. Panzergrenadier-Regiment LSSAH has run into enemy troops on the northern edge of Charkow.

14.2.1943: The word "Benzin" [gasoline] has been spelled on the ground with straw pulled off roofs in an appeal to the Luftwaffe for supplies.

14.2.1943:
Supplies from the air. Heating fuel, ammunition, and provisions.

"The Panzer and Grenadier units of the Heer and Waffen-SS broke through the deeply echeloned defensive installations in front of Charkow and penetrated the city from several sides."

In the evening, Baum's pursuit unit of the *T*-Division reached Sowchose Frunse.

Orders for 13.3.1943:

The reinforced 2. Panzergrenadier-Regiment LAH was to exploit the thrust made by Regiment *DR* into the southwestern part of the city and to press on to the southwest. Attack objective: railway yards north of Osnowa.

The reinforced III. (armoured)/2. was to establish solid contact with Kampfgruppe Witt at the road junction Tschugujew — Woltschansk.

Kampfgruppe Witt was to move the II./1. forward to the southeast, keeping it closely adjacent to the 2. Panzergrenadier-Regiment. Attack objective: the eastern railway station. The reinforced III./1. was to cross to the east and attack the Charkow river with the goal of blocking off the road to Woltschansk northeast of the junction. Then it was to proceed toward the tractor factory. The reinforced I./1.'s designation as Division reserve unit was suspended. It was to move forward from the area north of the airstrip into the Schewtschenko settlement in order to move to the southeast left of and adjacent to the III./1. if need be.

The reinforced Aufklärungsabteilung was to hold the road junction and to stand ready to move to the east and capture the tractor factory. It was also to be ready to establish contact with Kampfgruppe Baum or Kampfgruppe Harmel on the road to Tschugujew.

13.3.1943: Since the early morning, the Bataillon forces of the reinforced 2. Panzergrenadier-Regiment had been fighting their way to the southeast. The resistance was extrordinarily tough. Every single group of buildings had to be systematically swept and cleared of enemy foces. Kampfgruppe Peiper, proceeding in the same manner, expanded its little bridgehead across the Charkow river. The Russians were positioned in the houses with machine guns, anti-tank guns, and anti-tank rifles; they fought with unheard-of bravery. Our advance was flanked in every street by enemy tanks placed in every alley and courtyard. The bridges across the Charkow river lay under constant artillery fire from the direction of the North Don railway station. By 12.30 hours, Kampfgruppe Peiper had expanded the bridgehead sufficiently to allow a thrust along Staro-Moskowska street to the east. At 13.00 hours, solid contact was established with Kampfgruppe Meyer at the road junction. The planned clearing of the city between the positions of the I./1., which had moved forward in the meantime to the Woltschansk road, and of the II./1., which was at the point of capturing the North Don railway station, continued in heavy fighting.

At 15.30 hours, the reinforced I./2. (under Sturmbannführer Kraas) crossed the Peiper bridge and made its way toward the church southwest of Michajlowska street. Those of the enemy who had re-occupied the buildings west of the stream were destroyed. One Kompanie of the I./2. was deployed across the bridge on Scharkiwskij street toward the North Don railway station. Sturmbannführer Kraas, whose exemplary action served as a model for the entire Bataillon, was awarded the Ritterkreuz on this day for his careful leadership.

Kampfgruppe Sandig found itself at nightfall fighting to establish a bridgehead on Torgowji street.

In the evening, about two-thirds of the city center was in our hands. The unit adjacent to the right, the reinforced II./*DF* (under Sturmbannführer Bissinger), was fighting weak enemy forces in the southwestern section of the city. East of the city, Kampfgruppe Baum was in bitter combat with Russian forces, including numerous tanks, attacking just north of Rogan. To our rear, the bulk of the *T*-Division had to defend itself in the line Wesseloje — Lipzy against numerically superior enemy forces.

In the report from the Wehrmacht for 13.3.1943, the following passage appears:

> "In Charkow, bitter street fighting is still underway in some sections of the city. The forces of the Waffen-SS smashed the enemy resistance, moved forward to the main railway station and occupied the train yards."

Orders for 14.3.1943:

Essentially unchanged.

The III. (armoured)/2 was to stay adjacent to the Aufklärungsabteilung in moving along Petinska street toward the railway bridge, where it was to provide defense. The buildings south of the street were to be cleared of enemy forces as far as and including Uralska street. If necessary, the agricultural research institute was to be captured.

The reinforced Aufklärungsabteilung was to move ahead toward Tschugujew and to capture the tractor factory.

The reinforced 1. Panzergrenadier-Regiment was to move the I./1. into the northeastern section of the city and to destroy the enemy forces there.

In the SS-Panzerkorps' Kriegstagebuch, it is not difficult to discern barely veiled anger about the withdrawal of Kampfgruppe Harmel from the attack on western Charkow, which had been proceeding so well. The passage reads:

> "The assumption that Charkow would fall on 13.3.1943 was probably justified under the Korps' old plan. Now, however, we could see that the enemy, while leaving strong forces behind, was still able to withdraw most of his troops. It was no longer possible to surround his strongest elements, especially because, as the Korps had foreseen, the units assigned to block their escape were unable to move without supplies."

14.3.1943: In heavy street fighting, the Division moved forward as ordered and cleared the buildings one by one of the enemy, who fought to his last breath.

At 16.45 hours, the Korps received a report that the sections of the city known as Katschaniwka, Plechaniwkij Rayo (as far as the agricultural research institute), Jewgerewka, and Pidgorodnij, that is to say the entire central city, had been captured and were securely in our hands.

With that, Charkow had been recaptured.

Oberführer Staudinger, the commander of the Artillerie-Regiment *LAH*, was given temporary command of the city.

The II./*DF* had captured the southwestern and southern parts of Charkow. Kampfgruppe Harmel and Kampfgruppe Baum were at first stuck for lack of fuel. After receiving fuel supplies at 15.00 hours, they were once again able to set off.

In the afternoon of 14.3.1943, the Großdeutsche Rundfunk [Greater Germany Radio] broadcast the following special report, preceded by the Horst Wessel fanfare:

> "Special bulletin!
> Dateline: field headquarters, 14.3.1943. The Oberkommando of the Wehrmacht announces that Heeresgruppe Süd, which has thrown the enemy back across the Donez in weeks of fighting, joined by the units of the Waffen-SS and valiantly supported by the Luftwaffe, launched a campaign of encirclement and has succeeded in recapturing the city of Charkow after days of heavy fighting. The enemy's losses, in both men and materiel, is incalculable."

In the evening of the same day, the SS-Panzerkorps reported to the Division's commander, Obergruppenführer Sepp Dietrich as follows: "According to information from the Armeeoberkommando, the Führer has recognized your services to the future of the German people by awarding you the Schwerter [swords] to the Eichenlaub of the Ritterkreuz."

That evening, the Oberbefehlhaber of Heeresgruppe Süd, Generalfeldmarschall von Manstein, transmitted to the Oberbefehlshaber of the 4. Panzerarmee, Generaloberst Hoth, to the commanding general of the SS-Panzerkorps, and to the commander of the *Leibstandarte Adolf Hitler*, Obergruppenführer Sepp Dietrich, the following congratulations:

"Appreciation of and thanks for today's success.

signed von Manstein."

Orders for 15.3.1943:
The units were to clear their attack sectors of enemy troops as far as the edge of the city.

15.3.1943: The excellent mood shared by both the leadership and the enlisted men is revealed in the fact that the radio communcation between the Korps and the Division was carried out in rhymes.

The Korps radioed in the morning of 15.3:

"*Leibstandarte heroes, you've done your duty,*
Taken Charkow, now count your booty.
Rake it together in a heap, store it in the *Standarte*'s keep."

The Division answered:

"We bid the Korps, you taunting jerks,
To send us now a hundred clerks.
Your bureaucrats — you've lots of them.
The *Leibstandarte* has only fighting men."

The Divisional headquarters was moved to northeastern Charkow. The individual Kampfgruppen completed their mop-up operations in the city. The reinforced Aufklärungsabteilung pressed forward to western Lossewo and established contact there with Kampfgruppe Harmel.

At 18.00 hours, preliminary orders and descriptions of the missions for 16.3 were issued:

> "*The reinforced 1. Panzergrenadier-Regiment* is to relieve the security forces of the *T*-Division on both sides of the road to Belgorod in the sector from Lipzy (exclusive of it) — Lopan river.
> *The reinforced 2. Panzergrenadier-Regiment* is to set out as soon as possible on 16.3 in the direction of Belgorod via Russkoje and Dementejewka.
> *Mission*: After conducting thorough reconnaissance early in the morning, make a thrust along the road to the north. The first attack objective is Mikojanowka and Warwarowka. In this area, strong enemy forces are expected to be present. An armoured ground/on-board radio transmitter is being subordinated to the Nachrichtenabteilung *LAH*. It is to be moved up. Contact is to be established to the Panzergrenadierdivision *GD*.
> One group from Panzergrenadierdivision *GD* is to set out on 16.3 from Gaiworon via Alexandrowka — Udy toward Belgorod. A second group is to move from Borissowka toward Belgorod.
> The 320. Infanteriedivision and the 167. Infanteriedivision are to reach Prudanka (fifteen kilometers north of Dergatschi) and Solotschew — Alexandrowka on 16.3.1943.
>
> signed Lehmann Sturmbannführer"

The written orders followed this preliminary notice at 19.00 hours. The important thing was to free the forces engaged in local fighting in and to the east of Charkow as quickly as possible in order to push the retreating enemy forces back across the Donez. With that done, it would be possible to construct a defensive front at the Donez and to wait out the muddy season in strong defensive installations. To reach this goal, three Divisionen of the SS-Panzerkorps were to advance next to each other to the northeast and north. On the right was the SS-*T*-Division, which was to capture the Donez in the sector Tschugujew — Werschnij-Ssaltow. In the center was SS-Panzergrenadierdivision *DR* on both sides of Woltschansk. To the left, also serving as cover for the Korps' northern flank, was the *LAH* moving toward Belgorod.

With that, the second conquest of Charkow was completed. The crowning feat of the operation was to be the final closing of a hole three hundred kilometers wide, a hole created by the battle for Stalingrad and its consequences. That final chapter had just begun.

c) 16.3.1943 - 18.3.1943: Thrust on Belgorod (reinforced 2. Panzergrenadier-Regiment)

16.3.1943 (see sketch 20): The 1. Panzergrenadier-Regiment had deployed the reinforced III./1. in the night to relieve the defensive forces of the *T*-Division west of Lipzy on both sides of Mal. Prochody as far as a point just south of Dementejewka. Since early morning, the enemy had been launching intensifying attacks and eventually forced us temporarily to give up our hold on Mal. Prochody.

The reinforced 2. Panzergrenadier-Regiment (under (Standartenführer Wisch) set out at 06.30 hours with the I./2. at its head and reached Russkoje at 07.00 hours.

At 07.15 hours, the 2. Panzergrenadier-Regiment reported the presence of enemy tanks near Bol. Prochody. The Regiment received orders for an immediate attack on the enemy forces there. Other reports had also come in that the enemy was digging in at that location. But the Regiment had already undertaken the attack before the orders came. Attacking without stopping, the II./2. pushed the enemy forces out of Bol. Prochody and the forests to the north. It nevertheless became clear to the Regiment that the enemy resistance along the line Mal. Prochody — Dementejewka could only be broken by a well-organized attack. The Ia travelled to the front and moved the III./1. into the forests northeast of Mal. Prochody. The Regiment moved the II./2. toward Dementejewka and the I./2. toward the hills between Dementejewka and the railway line. After making sure of cover to the rear in conference with the air support officer, the attack was set for 14.20 hours.

After effective fire from the heavy Infanterie weapons, the I. and III./Artillerie-Regiment *LAH*, the I./Werferregiment 55, and the dive bombers, the two Bataillone set out punctually for their attack against these well-fortified installations. They were supported by Panzers from the 5./Panzerregiment *LAH*. The Bataillone moved forward quickly through the deep snow despite dangerous enemy defensive fire. At 18.30 hours it captured the hills, which had been heavily occupied by the enemy. For the night, they stood guard in temperatures around twenty-five degrees below zero. The night passed peacefully.

The orders for 17.3.1943 remained unchanged for the *LAH*. The *T*-Division and the Division *DR* were ordered to move toward Belgorod. 17.3 was to be used to make the preparations for a thrust to the north on the right of the *Leibstandarte*.

17.3.1943: At 05.00 hours, the Bataillone continued their attacks on the designated objectives. At 06.00 hours, Kraas' Bataillon captured the road junction east of Dementejewka and turned the bulk of its forces for an attack on the town to the west.

The II./2. (under Sandig) captured Mal. Prochody and moved onto the commanding hills north of the town.

By 08.30 hours, Kraas had taken Dementejewka and had moved advance security forces into the hills north of the town.

At 12.30 hours, the reinforced III. (armoured)/2. (under Peiper) set out across the sector held by the I./2. for an armoured thrust. By nightfall, the unit had only reached the bend in the road southwest of Nechotejewka; the terrible road conditions had slowed its progress. Just south of there, the armoured force encountered an anti-tank front. Just as night was falling, Peiper's Bataillon, supported by the 7./Panzerregiment *LAH* (under Obersturmführer von Ribbentrop), managed to break through it.

At 17.00 hours, the reinforced II./2. closed ranks level with the III. (armoured)/2. Both Bataillone provided defense for the night along this newly-won line.

Division *DR*, ordered to move up to be adjacent on the right, was to capture Wesseloje and Streletsche on 18.3. The *T*-Division was to move southeast of there and capture, if possible, Saroshnje and Bol. Babka.

The *LAH*'s orders remained unchanged.

Belgorod remained the attack objective for both the *LAH* and the Heer's Panzergrenadierdivision *GD*. The day's objective was the line Andrejewka — Dolbino. Panzergrenadierdivision *GD* had orders to send a strong armoured force from the Arissowka area to the east to close off the railway line and the road from Charkow to Belgorod in the Krassnoje area.

In a private conference between Peiper and the Ia, the idea of a "race for Belgorod" was discussed.

The Ia of the *LAH* arranged with the air support officer and the chief Luftwaffe officer of the Stukas that there would be a Stuka attack on the enemy roadblocks between Krestowo and Naumowka promptly at 07.00 hours.

18.3.1932: At 04.15 hours, the reinforced III. (armoured)/2. *LAH* (under Sturmbannführer Peiper) sent a combat-strength reconnaissance force to observe the enemy defensive lines, discovered the evening before, between Krestowo and Naumowka. The findings were that the enemy line was still occupied by strong enemy forces. The reinforced 2. Panzergrenadier-Regiment *LAH* under the command of Standartenführer Wisch set the III. (armoured)/2. on the march at 06.40 hours. The arranged Stuka attack on the enemy line took place punctually at 07.00 hours, and at 07.10 hours Peiper's Bataillon reported that it had broken through the line and was making a motorized thrust as far as Otradnyj.

The reinforced II./2. had captured Naumowka and Otradnyj by 10.00 hours in light fighting and was in the process of moving along the railway line farther to the east. The Bataillon had to overcome extremely bad road conditions in its attack sector. The reinforced I./2. stood on call in Dementejewka. At 10.00 hours, Kampfgruppe Peiper reached Krassnoje. There it encountered no enemy troops. With that, the attack objective for that day had been left far behind. Sturmbannführer Peiper acted on his own initiative to continue the thrust.

Peiper reported at 11.00 hours:

> "Spearhead eight kilometers southwest of Belgorod on the march route. The Russians are retreating to the west. Two enemy tanks destroyed.
>
> Commander of the III./2."

His next report, arriving at 11.35 hours, read:

> "Belgorod taken in surprise attack. Eight enemy tanks destroyed.
>
> Commander of the III./2."

Untersturmführer Gührs of the 14. (heavy)/2. remembers that day as follows:

> "March 18, 1943. Bright sunlight and snow. Peiper assembled the Kompanieführers and me, as Zugführer of the anti-tank guns, to brief us on the situation. Several Divisionen of the Waffen-SS and Panzergrenadierdivision *GD* had been sent to attack Belgorod. Our attack was to be supported by a Stuka attack on the roadblock at 07.00 hours. The Bataillon was to stand ready to exploit the surpise attack and to drive through the Russian battle line on the road itself. Two or three Tigers were with us. We were attempting to make it through to Belgorod. I was to bring up the rear with my Kanonenzug. Everything went as planned. We made it through. Peiper radioed the spearhead to keep it up at their fastest tempo. The Russians just stood there, rubbing their eyes. Their tanks were still under cover, and men were laying communications cable. They were evidently still going about their regular morning duties as we flew past them through the villages on our way to Belgorod. I did not really get to see how it all went, because our column was so long. But we rolled on without stopping. Gradually the Russians realized what was going on, and I could see the first Russian tanks moving up behind us far to the rear.
> But our tempo was considerable. Down into a basin, across a bridge, and we were suddenly at the town of Belgorod. I did not get to see the visit of the Divisional commander by Storch plane, because my Zug had to provide rear defense at the bridge."

Sturmbannführer Peiper was awarded the Ritterkreuz for undertaking this action on his own initiative.

Obersturmführer von Ribbentrop, supporting this attack with his 7./Panzerregiment *LAH*, remembered that in one of the villages before Belgorod they surprised a Russian tank repair unit and destroyed several enemy tanks without even having to stop. Individual tanks were able to escape because the destruction was not systematic, and these tanks made life hell for the units coming up behind.[35]

At 12.10 hours, Kampfgruppe Peiper repulsed an armoured counterattack on Belgorod from the northwest and destroyed several enemy tanks. The reinforced II./2. dealt with the rest of the Soviet tanks as it moved into the towns of Golonino and Andrewjewka at 15.15 hours and cleared them of enemy forces.

At 12.45 hours, after the arrival of the report that Peiper had taken Belgorod, the reinforced I./2. set out from Dementejewka with orders to provide defense for the march route to the west in the sector from the northern edge of Krassnoje to southern Dolbino.

The reinforced II./2. was providing defense to the east and west for the areas newly captured. It reported at 16.00 hours that it had established contact with the spearhead of *GD* near Dolbino and Nowaja Derewenja.

Kampfgruppe Peiper received orders to provide defense during the night to the north and west for western Belgorod, including the road out to the north.

The report on losses for the III. (armoured)/2. of 18.3.1943 at 1935 hours read as follows:

Enemy losses: ten T-34's, one T-40, one T-60, two General Lee's, sixteen artillery guns, fourteen anti-tank rifles, eighteen heavy machine guns, thirty-four light machine guns, thirty-eight trucks, several flamethrowers and numerous columns of sleighs.

Our losses: one dead, sixteen wounded.

Panzergrenadierdivision *DR* moved Regiment *Deutschland* from the south into the southern section of Belgorod.

The SS-Panzerkorps stood on the evening of 18.3.1943 along the line from the hills southwest of Ternowaja — center of Ternowaja — hills west of Murom — Netschejewka — Botschkowa — Brodok — Tawrowo — all-around defense in Belgorod — western defense on the railway line to Charkow.

d) 19.3.1943 - 26.3.1943: Defensive mission north of Belgorod (reinforced 2. Panzergrenadier-Regiment *LAH*)

Orders for 19.3.1943:

The *LAH* was to defend Belgorod while at the same time moving combat-strength elements forward to Tomarowka. There it was to establish contact with the *GD*. The forward thrust was assigned to the III. (armoured)/2. (under Sturmbannführer Peiper), and the reinforced II./2. took over the defense of Belgorod. The line of defense ran from northern Belgorod including the road to Kursk, through western Belgorod, all the way to the westward-leading roads in the section Bolchowez — Dolbino — Mikojanowka.

The reinforced 1. Panzergrenadier-Regiment received orders to move one reinforced Bataillon up to join the 2. Panzergrenadier-Regiment in Mikojanowka; the Bataillon was to be subordinated to the 2.

The commander of the Artillerie-Regiment, relieved of his duties as temporary town Kommandant in Charkow, received orders to assume the leadership of the Artillerie in the Belgorod area.

It should also be mentioned that the Werfer-Batterie of the *LAH* provided outstanding support for the deployment of the II./2. on that day.

19.3.1943: During the night, the enemy applied constant pressure on the II./2.'s positions in the northern section of Belgorod. In the morning, the Bataillon took over the line of defense held by the III. (armoured)/2. in northern Belgorod.

The commander of the Artillerie-Regiment drew up his plan of fire and cleared it with the commander of Artillerie-Regiment *DR*.

At 13.15 hours, the reinforced III. (armoured)/2., joined by the 7./Panzer-regiment and two Tigers, arrived. At 15.35, it reported engaging in tank combat with Russian tanks near Strelezkoje. In that fighting, seven Russian tanks were destroyed, while we lost not a single Panzer. One Schützenpanzerwagen did take a direct hit. The bridge in Strelezkoje had been destroyed by the enemy, so the Bataillon drew back into the eastern section of the town for the night. On orders from Peiper, Obersturmführer von Ribbentrop went back to the burning Schützenpanzerwagen after the rest of the unit had pulled back. He was to determine whether there were wounded Grenadiere inside to be saved. He was only able to collect soldiers' paybooks and the like; there were no more living men to be found.[36]

In the rest of the Division's sector, there were no particular events.

The enemy's losses: one KV I, one KV II, five T-34's, one T-40, two light American tanks, two armoured reconnaissance vehicles, ten trucks, and numerous infantry weapons, both light and heavy.

Our losses: one Schützenpanzerwagen total. Four men were killed, and one non-commissioned officer and six enlisted men were wounded.

The *T*-Division had in the course of the day captured the line Ssowetskoje — Stariza — Archangelskoje — Gralowka (all of these are villages on the Donez). Elements of Division *DR* had also reached the Donez.

Orders for 20.3.1943 remained as before. The 2. Panzergrenadier-Regiment received orders to move with Kampfgruppe Peiper along the road to Kursk, pursuing the enemy as far as Jakowlewo and feinting an attack. The Kampfgruppe pulled back in the face of heavy resistance. After reaching the designated objective, the unit was to move back to Belgorod. The *GD* armoured force was also to make a thrust from Tomarowka toward Jakowlewo.

On 19.3.1943, Hitler released the following daily order:

The Führer's headquarters 19.3.1943

Daily orders from the Führer

Soldiers of Heeresgruppe Süd and Heeresgruppe Mitte,
of Luftflotte 4 and Luftwaffenkommando Ost!

A few weeks ago, in one of the worse crises of the war (the cause of which is well-known), I turned to you with a plea for you to defend every square meter of ground with fierce determination so that I might have time to move new troops and new weapons to the front, measures necessary to the final smashing of the Soviet onslaught.

Under conditions that demanded great sacrifices on the part of countless officers and soldiers, we were able to create the conditions necessary for our victory, thanks in no small part to our excellent officer corps. It grew increasingly difficult for the Soviets to move forward. More and more, the empty terrain filled up with new German Divisionen, and the enemy faced tougher and tougher resistance. Finally, the time to resist passed and the hour of counterattack arrived. New Divisionen from the Heer and the Waffen-SS came to fight side-by-side with the battle-tested forces from the east. The Russians soon found themselves exposed to a solid onslaught from these ground forces and the continued heroic work of our Luftwaffe at the most vital point of their entire front. Charkow is once again in our hands.

The countless enemy dead, the prisoners, and the huge amount of captured materiel are the visible signs of this triumph. A greater triumph can be found, however, in the fact that the objective of the Soviet offensive, a breakthrough to Dnjepropetrowsk via Charkow, has now finally been thwarted.

Despite all their attempts to shake or break the German front with attacks at other spots, the Soviets have not been able to bring their winter campaign to the conclusion they desired. Their plan was smashed, in the final analysis, when it ran up against the steel-hard German soldier. I give you thanks for that, not only as your Supreme Commander, but first and foremost in the name of the German people, in the name of our homeland, which you are defending and protecting.

Your valor turned the tide of this battle. You have yourselves made it possible for me today to lift the ban on furloughs and to make it possible for you to visit home and your loved ones. Their thoughts, hopes, and prayers have been with you this winter more than ever.

signed, Adolf Hitler

20.3.1943: Kampfgruppe Peiper set out at 06.15 hours in accordance with orders and moved along the road to Kursk. At 08.15 hours, it encountered enemy resistance at the crossing over the stream west of Schopino. It broke the resistance and continued its thrust to the north. Near Gonki, the enemy offered renewed resistance at about 11.00 hours, including tank and artillery fire. The Kampfgruppe withdrew in accordance with orders. For the night, it set up a local defense in Jatschnew-Kolodes and Oskotschnoje (twelve kilometers north of Belgorod).

The enemy suffered the following losses: one T-34 (destroyed by the Panzerkompanie under Eckhardt), one reconnaissance vehicle, five anti-tank guns, four trucks, and forty-nine light infantry weapons.

We lost: five enlisted men killed; one officer (Hauptsturmführer Bohrmann) and eleven enlisted men wounded.

In the night between 20.3 and 21.3, the Ia received a telegram from the Führer's headquarters. It was addressed to Obergruppenführer Sepp Dietrich, and it contained the news that his wife had delivered a baby boy on 20.3 and that both mother and child were in good health. Armed with the last bottle of champagne in the stock, the Ia awakened the commander and congratulated him on the birth of his son. Our boy Sepp sat up in his cot, his face beaming, and said, "Josef, you did that right!" The commander flew to the Führer's headquarters on 21.3.1943 to receive the Schwerter [swords] to add to his Ritterkreuz.

21.3.1943: In the early morning, a Schützenpanzerwagenkompanie in Glinka established contact west of Tomarowka with the Heer's Panzergrenadierdivision *GD*. The line of defense northwest of Belgorod was moved forward to Grinewka and the northern and western edge of Bolchowez.

Orders for 22.3.1943:

The reinforced 2. Panzergrenadier-Regiment *LAH* was to retain its current structure and, with the addition of the III./1. Panzergrenadier-Regiment *LAH*, deploy elements to make a thrust on 22.3.1943 from Belgorod on Strelezkoje. There the elements were to seek, establish, and hold contact with Panzergrenadierdivision *GD*. The Regiment was also to capture and hold the line north Belgorod (as before) — hills north of Strelezkoje.

The subordination of the I./Nebelwerfer-Regiment was suspended. The unit was to be held in readiness for a march. Relief for the III. (armoured)/2. was planned for 23.3.1943.

22.3.1943: At 08.15 hours, the reinforced II./2. began its attack on Strelezkoje. At about 10.00 hours, it reported reaching the hills north of the town without having encountered any enemy resistance worth mentioning. The III./1., subordinated to it, received orders to use its right wing to establish contact with the III./2. at Kasazkoje. It was to clear the towns along the railway line of enemy troops and to provide cover for the Regiment's western flank.

By 10.15 hours, all the designated objectives had been reached. There had been barely any contact with the enemy. Contact with *GD* was established at 10.15 hours at the fork in the stream at Strelezkoje.

For 23.3.1943, the II./2. received orders to send reconnaissance forces toward Beresoff and Jachontoff at dawn.

At 16.00 hours, the Division issued special instructions for the move into the rest areas. That day, a transport train carrying about six hundred non-commissioned officers and enlisted men arrived in Charkow. They were immediately assigned to units.

23.3.1943: In the reinforced 2. Panzergrenadier-Regiment's defensive sector, reconnaissance forces set out in the early morning and reported that there were weak enemy forces in Belomestnaja. The III./2. chased away an enemy scout force from point 190.5. On the southern edge of Schopino and north of the river sector, there were enemy installations with anti-tank guns facing the II./2.

On the march route south of the river sector, there were two enemy 4.7-centimeter anti-tank guns. At 14.00 hours, the left wing of the II./2. set out to occupy a line of defense farther to the north.

By 16.15 hours, the Bataillon had reached this line and began establishing its positions along it. The Regiment's line of defense ran from the hills north of Jatschnew-Kolodes (where it joined that of the *DR*) — northern and western edge of Oskotschnoje — hills to the northeast at the western edge of Kasazkoje (where it joined the line of the III./Füsilierregiment *GD*. The III. (armoured)/2. moved into an advance position on a hill four kilometers south of Skopino.

Losses on 23.3.1943: one non-commissioned officer and one man killed, two one-tonne prime movers destroyed, and one large field kitchen blown up.

During the early evening, there were several heavy enemy bomber attacks.

24.3.1943: After a peaceful night, the II./2. reported that the unit adjacent to the left had abandoned its position in the night without reporting it. One Zug of the 6./2. and the Pionierzug of the 10./2. were immediately dispatched to plug the hole and provide cover for the road to Beressoff. The 2./2. was subordinated to the II. Bataillon with orders to extend the Bataillon's left wing as far as the road to Beressoff.

At 13.00 hours, orders were issued for the reinforced Panzergrenadier-Regiment 5 *T* (under Baum) to relieve the 2. Panzergrenadier-Regiment. In addition to stipulating the time for the move, the order also gave directions for the regulation of traffic on the individual roads from and to the south. The order also instructed that rest periods be allotted such that most of the units would be ready to march within twelve hours.

The 1. Panzergrenadier-Regiment received an indication that soon, possibly in early April, it would receive reinforcements in the form of a mixed Artillerie-Abteilung, a Sturmgeschützbatterie, a self-propelled Panzerjägerkompanie, and a medium Flakbatterie and would be moved into the area southwest of Belgorod to serve as attack reserve force. The Divisional headquarters were in Charkow (Maximiljaniwska) starting at 10.00 hours on 24.3.1943.

25.3.1943: The entire day was quiet along the whole defensive sector. Combat reconnaissance brought back no new information.

At 14.00 hours, the commander of Panzergrenadier-Regiment 5 *T*, established contact and discussed the relief action.

26.3.1943: At 03.45 hours, the III./1. Panzergrenadier-Regiment (under Sturmbannführer Weidenhaupt) pulled out of the defensive sector and set out on its march to Russkoje Losowoje to join its Regiment. The III./2. took over its defense duties. In the morning, the relief units started arriving in the Regiment's sector. At 13.00 hours, the I./Artillerie-Regiment *LAH* was released to join the Regiment, and the III./Artillerie-Regiment *LAH* at 13.30 hours.

At 14.30 hours, the III. (armoured)/2. and all its elements were relieved and began their march to the billeting area.

At 16.00 hours, the last elements of the 2. Panzergrenadier-Regiment *LAH* were relieved by Baum's Regiment of the *T*-Division. Obersturmbannführer Baum assumed responsibility.

At 22.00 hours, all elements of the 2. Panzergrenadier-Regiment reported their arrival in the billeting and rest area northwest of Ljubotin. With that, the battle for Charkow ended for the last unit of Panzergrenadierdivision *LAH*. The Division could devote all its resources to resting and refurbishing its forces.

In the daily orders from the Oberbefehlshaber of the Heeresgruppe, the Oberbefehlshaber of the Armee, and the Oberbefehlshaber of the SS-Panzerkorps, the performance of the men and their leaders was acknowledged and praised.

As early as the first thrust on Belgorod, the graves registration officer of the Division had made conscientious efforts to find all the Division's scattered dead, to identify the bodies, and to provide them with worthy burial places. A report by Jochen Winter of the 15./1. Panzergrenadier-Regiment gives a vivid impression of those efforts' success:

> "The bodies of our comrades killed in the fighting to recapture Charkow and those whose graves were opened by the Russians after we had abandoned the city the first time were assembled in the central park. There they were laid out for identification. Another comrade from the Kompanie and I were detailed to Charkow to assist in that function. There greeted us a terrifying picture, the likes of which I had never seen nor later came to see. All the men were naked and most of the bodies had been mutilated. Many of them, and indeed all of the comrades missing from our unit, had been not only beaten and choked, but their limbs were severed and their eyes gouged out, such that it was hard to identify them. It was bestiality in the truest sense of the word. From that moment on, the fear of being taken prisoner by the Russians haunted us like a ghost. I saw once again the force under Komrowski, which had disappeared while laying a mine barrier near Losewo and was finally declared missing. All of them (Komrowski, Musak, Tümmler, Grügel, Ullrich, and Bukatz) were found in a nearby hangar at the Rogan airstrip, all brutally murdered in the manner described. They had

probably become exhausted in the operation and missed their opportunity to rejoin the withdrawing troops."

The description of the fighting to recapture Charkow would be incomplete without mentioning the charges made by the Soviet Union against the *LAH*.

The state's attorney with the Landgericht Nürnberg-Fürth [Nuremberg Court] who oversees the documents related to this matter provided at the author's request a transcript of the court's judgment of 27.2.1976 under the identification number Az 95 Js 10 100/75. The transcript, provided on 10.10.80, is nineteen typewritten pages long; printing it in its entirety would expand this work beyond a reasonable length. Excerpts of the essential passages are quoted here.

"I. The inquiry has been closed.
II. The inquiry proceedings against the accused NN and other unknown perpetrators have been brought to an end in accordance with Section 170 Abs. 2 StPO."

Reasons:

A.

[There follows here an explanation of the tactical situation.]

B.

In response to a request from the general state's attorney in Frankfurt am Main, the USSR in 1976 provided notarized photocopies of Soviet deposition transcripts and of an exhumation report made in Charkow in September of 1943. The above-named documents contain serious charges against former members of the SS-Panzergrenadierdivision *Leibstandarte SS Adolf Hitler*.

1. According to statements from several witnesses, an officer of the *LSSAH*, known only as NN, was reported to have come into the army's isolation hospital and have ordered wounded prisoners of war to be removed from Building 3 and transferred to Building 8. In the afternoon of the same day, the doors of Building 8 were allegedly locked and the entire building set on fire. About three hundred wounded Soviet soldiers were reportedly killed. About thirty wounded men, who allegedly jumped from the windows to save themselves, were reported by several witnesses to have been shot.
2. The witnesses allege in addition that in the period March 14 - 17, 1943, another four hundred wounded Soviet officers were shot by German soldiers in their beds in several different buildings of the army isolation hospital.
   The Soviet commission from Charkow, charged with the investigation of this crime, named as responsible parties the accused NN and the supposed commander of SS-Panzergrenadierdivision LSSAH, SS-Gruppenführer and Generalleutnant of the Waffen-SS Max Simon. Max Simon, who died on 1.2.1961, was at the time of the alleged crime the commander of SS-Panzergrenadierdivision

Totenkopf, which did not even enter the city of Charkow in March of 1943. The commander of the SS-Panzergrenadierdivison *LSSAH* at the time of the recapture of Charkow was SS-Obergruppenführer and General of the Waffen-SS Sepp Dietrich, who died on 21.4.1966.
The inquiry therefore focusses on the accused NN and the unknown perpetrators.
The witnesses to the crimes described under B.1. and B.2. are identified in the Soviet deposition transcripts as Doctor Katkow Jewgenij Ssewostjanoowitsch, Doctor Dshintschwiladse Georgij Sacharowitsch, Nurse Juchno Anna Ignatjewna, Nurse Dimitrijewa Jelisawjeta Antonowna, Koloslosowa Maija Aleksandrowna, Wladimir Ossadtschuk, and Franzewa Matrena, who were deposed in the summer of 1943. The state's attorney also has a translation of a court report of 7.9.1943 on the exhumation of several bodies found in two mass graves on the grounds of the army isolation hospital. According to the results of the examination conducted by the chief medical expert appointed by the court for the "Steppe Front," Major of the medical service Pritworo M.P., there were in the two graves the bodies of about four hundred Soviet soldiers. Their bodies showed signs of older wounds, which had received treatment. But each showed as well relatively fresh gunshot wounds, mostly in the skull area. The commission reached the conclusion that these were the bodies of Red Army soldiers who had been shot in the hospital by German soldiers. The commission also viewed the burned-out shell of Building 8 and found human remains in the ashes.
Because the USSR did not make these documents available to German authorities until 1967, it is almost impossible to test their veracity. The transcripts of the depositions are relatively brief, the depositions do not appear to have been directed, and it is not always clear whether the witnesses observed the acts they describe first-hand or only heard about them. The exhumation report, too, contains several suppositions, particularly as to the number of the victims and the cause of death. It must also be considered that the hospital complex lay within the attack sector of the 1. Panzergrenadier-Regiment and that an existing situation map shows the Soviet main battle line with gun positions running immediately to the north of the buildings. It is possible that in the fighting, buildings on the grounds of the university and clinic complex were set afire. Karl Meyer, a former member of the *LSSAH*, interviewed as an eye witness, even reports having received fire from one of the hospital buildings during the attack and having broken the resistance there with hand grenades. The state's attorney nevertheless proceeded from the assumption in this inquiry that a large number of wounded Soviet soldiers, who were not taking part in the fighting, were shot by German soldiers. In that case, it could well have been an act of retribution, since several witnesses report that in the course of the eastern campaign, including around Charkow, captured members of the *LSSAH* were found dead with signs of horrible mistreatment having been inflicted on them before death.

C.

In order to reach as complete an explanation of the affair as possible, police conducted an inquiry lasting several years, during which a total of six hundred eighty-eight witnesses were questioned, including six hundred seventy-five former members of SS-Panzergrenadierdivision *LSSAH*. Of the witnesses, two hundred eighty-five participated in the fighting for the recapture of Charkow in March of 1943. The other four hundred three witnesses, who were at the time not with the combat troops, were unable to provide any useful information about the events... All maintained in the questioning that they had never heard of wounded soldiers being shot or burned in Charkow by German soldiers.
Only four of the other two hundred eighty-five witnesses had even heard talk of wounded Soviet soldiers being illegally killed after the end of the fighting... None could provide any further details about the circumstances of that killing or about the persons from whom they had heard about such events. The witnesses also did not know whether they had spoken to eyewitnesses or to others merely repeating rumors. The witness NN was a member of the *LSSAH*'s ambulance unit. He claimed that there were many rumors circulating after the recapture of Charkow.
...
These vague details do little to support the charges made by the Soviet authorities. All the rest of the two hundred eighty-one witnesses who had been in the city of Charkow in March of 1943 maintained throughout their questioning to have no knowledge of any such crimes. They denied not only personal involvement, but categorically rejected the possibility that members of their Division would have shot defenseless wounded men. In the opinion of most of these witnesses, it would have been impossible for a crime of this scope, in which about seven hundred wounded men were killed, to occur without it becoming general knowledge.
Of the witnesses, forty were men of the II. and III. Bataillon/1. Panzergrenadier-Regiment *LSSAH*, ninety-one were soldiers of the I. and III. Bataillon/Panzergrenadier-Regiment *LSSAH*, and thirty-six were members of the *LSSAH*'s ambulance crew. During the fighting and immediately after, they were the forces to occupy Dzerschinskij Square and the hospital located there. To a man, they maintain that the charges made by the Soviet authorities against former members of the *LSSAH* do not square with the truth. Witnesses Wilhelm Weidenhaupt, at that time commander of the III./1. Panzergrenadier-Regiment, and Max Hansen, commander of the II./1. Panzergrenadier-Regiment, denied emphatically that they ordered or even heard about the crimes described. Witnesses Rudolf Sandig, at that time commander of the II./2. Panzergrenadier-Regiment, and Albert Frey, commander of the I./1. Panzergrenadier-Regiment, admittedly did not move with their men directly into Dzerschinskij Square; they do, however, deny any knowledge of such events. Witness Joseph Diefenthal, at that time Hauptsturmführer and Regimentsadjutant in the 2. Panzergrenadier-Regiment, claims that he heard rumors that wounded Soviets were in fact shot by their own compatriots to prevent them falling into German hands. This assertion does not lack credibility, for former General der Panzertruppen Graf von Schwerin confirmed in expert testimony before the state's attorney

that such shootings had taken place, as well as shootings of German prisoners of war and wounded men by Soviet soldiers. It should be remembered that Graf von Schwerin, an active opponent of the National Socialist regime, can be regarded as an objective informant. The statement of witness Waldmar Sch. of the III. Bataillon/1. Panzergrenadier-Regiment is similar in content. He explained that he and his comrades had found the bodies of wounded German soldiers from the *LSSAH*; these were men who had been left behind in the withdrawal from Charkow and who must have been taken prisoner and shot in Soviet prison. Witness Albert Sch. had only heard of German wounded being shot while in Soviet hands, not of any Soviet wounded being killed in Charkow. Witness Georg Preuß, at that time Ordonnanzoffizier in the III. Bataillon/2. Panzergrenadier-Regiment, stated that he had spoken with several Soviet army doctors who were in German POW camps after the capture of Charkow. None of them had told him anything of this alleged killing of wounded Soviet soldiers. Witness Rolf Sch. of the I./2. Panzergrenadier-Regiment, who was cared for by Soviet nurses in a hospital in Charkow for a lengthy period at the end of March, 1943, also claimed to have heard nothing about it, although he reportedly had quite a bit of personal contact with these nurses. Witness Johann Sch. of the I. Bataillon/2. Panzergrenadier-Regiment reported that he could remember the hospital complex on Dzerschinskij Square and the Soviet wounded housed there. They were cared for, in his memory, by his Bataillon doctor immediately after the end of the fighting. More than that he could not say.

Of special significance in this connection is the statement by witness Walentina Knotek, who lived in Charkow in March of 1943 and along with other Russian girls found jobs as nurses' aides with the *LSSAH* after the entry of German troops into the city. She remained with the unit for the rest of the war and came eventually to live in Germany, where she married a former member of the *LSSAH*. In a statement to police, she said that she knew nothing about wounded Soviet soldiers being shot by German soldiers or being killed in any other manner. She did, however, remember that she had heard of a hospital burning down with Soviet wounded inside. The woman who told her this did not know for sure whether the building had caught fire during the fighting or whether the Red Army forces had set it on fire. Ferdinand Reichel, who as Hauptmann in the Heer served in the office of the city Kommandant in southern Charkow from March 19, 1943, until the final withdrawal from Charkow in the fall of 1943, was particularly well-informed about conditions in the city, maintained that he had no knowledge of such a crime. Leopold Swoboda, serving in May of 1943 as an Oberleutnant in a technical section as Kommandant of the Charkow water works, considers it impossible that the crime described could have taken place. According to his statement, he was able to speak good Polish and Russian and had considerable contact with the Russian civilian population. There were in addition numerous Russian POW's serving in his unit. Despite all that contact, he was never told of the alleged killing of wounded Soviet soldiers by German troops.

The statements of the former members of the *LSSAH*'s ambulance unit should also be taken into consideration here, because this unit, comprising two ambulance Kompanien and the field hospital, moved into the intact

buildings of the hospital complex after the storming of Charkow in order to provide medical care for the Division's wounded soldiers.
[Note from the author: When the *LSSAH* withdrew from Charkow at the end of July, 1943, the following Russians joined the ambulance unit as volunteers: the chief surgeon of the Charkow city hospital, a practical physician, and at least ten nurses. They were a positive addition to the staff of the field hospital and remained with the *LSSAH* until the end of the war. Unfortunately, most of them were turned over to the Russians by the Americans at the end of the war.]
Dr. Hermann Besuden, in March of 1943 Obersturmbannführer and Division doctor in the *LSSAH*, reported that he had inspected the hospital buildings and had found no murdered Soviet soldiers. He considered it possible that there had been wounded men killed during the fighting. He had never heard of crimes against wounded Soviets. Dr. Walter Berges, doctor with the 1. Sanitätskompanie, Dr. Robert Brüstle, doctor in the III. Bataillon/ 2. Panzergrenadier-Regiment *LSSAH*, Dr. Werner Kleinebrecht, head doctor in the *LSSAH*'s field hospital, and Dr. Adolf Jackl, at that time head of the 2. Sanitätskompanie, all deny any knowledge of the events contained in the Soviet authorities' charges. Dr. Kleinebrecht even remembers that wounded Soviet soldiers were housed and cared for. Witness Dr. Wilhelm Behre was a doctor in the *LSSAH*'s ambulance unit in 1943. He stated only that he had heard of wounded German prisoners from the *LSSAH* having been burned by Soviet troops before the recapture of Charkow. Witness Fritz NN, SS-Sturmmann in the 1. Sanitätskompanie, gave no credibility to the charges. He himself had seen doctors of the *LSSAH* taking as much trouble with the wounded Soviets as with the wounded Germans ...
The criminal police took great pains to identify any former members of the SS-Panzerkorps with the name NN (phonetic), because according to Soviet documents the perpetrator should have been among them. But this claim, too, is weak at its foundation, for this SS officer by the name of NN was only reported to have ordered the transfer of the wounded Soviets, and not even the Russian witnesses claim that he gave the order to kill. The transfer of wounded soldiers could also have been carried out for other reasons.
Police efforts in this direction produced no results ...

D.

No proof of guilt can be drawn from this scanty evidence. The statements of the Soviet witnesses do not contain enough concrete information about the alleged perpetrators in order for them to be identified. In addition, despite the findings of the medical commission of the Soviet army of 7.9.1943, doubt exists about the correctness of the information given by Russian witnesses. Even if we ignore the fact that Soviet forces brought the hospital complex directly into the battle area and may have thereby caused considerable casualties among wounded soldiers, the statements of six hundred eighty-eight German witnesses must be taken into account. Even though two hundred eight-five of them were in Charkow or its immediate vicinity in March of 1943, all deny having committed or observed crimes against wounded Soviets. Several of the witnesses have reported to the contrary that wounded Soviet soldiers received care from doctors and medical personnel equal to that received by wounded Germans. Other witnesses described their meetings with Russian army doctors, nurses, and civilians in Charkow and pointed out that, despite all their contact with this circle, there had never been a hint of the alleged atrocity. It is of course possible that not all the witnesses told the truth in order to protect themselves or other former members of the SS-Panzergrenadierdivision *Leibstandarte SS Adolf Hitler* from prosecution. But that is merely a suspicion which cannot be proven.

...

Because all our sources have been exhausted, there is no prospect for clearing up the question as to how the wounded Soviets in Charkow were killed and who is responsible for their deaths.

SS-Panzergrenadierdivision *LAH*, acting as part of the SS-Panzerkorps or in subordination to Armeeabteilung Lanz and later Armeeabteilung Kempf, contributed considerably to the efforts to gain control of the crisis created by the fall of Stalingrad. The unit struggled to create the conditions necessary for closing the gaps which stretched hundreds of kilometers within the region held by Heeresgruppe Süd and in the area between Heeresgruppe Süd and Heeresgruppe Mitte.

The Division succeeded in acting as a hundred-kilometer-wide barrier east of Charkow, halting the Russian onslaught and splitting their forward thrust in two, thereby providing cover to the south and southwest of the city for the rear of its sister Divisionen, *Das Reich* and *Totenkopf*, which were initially moving to the south. In cooperation with these two Divisionen, which made a huge circling motion and attacked again from the north, the *LAH* swung its defensive front from its east-west position to north-south, and together they crushed a strong enemy force and then, within the structure of the SS-Panzerkorps, recaptured Charkow.

Generalfeldmarschall von Manstein wrote in his book "Verlorene Siege" (page 466 ff.):

> "It was inevitable that the name Charkow began to have a magical attraction for the men and the mid-level officers. The SS-Panzerkorps wanted to lay the recaptured capital of the Ukraine at the feet of 'their Führer' as a symbol of victory. They therefore pushed their way to Charkow by the shortest route. The Heeresgruppe needed to intervene sharply several times to prevent the Korps from waging a frontal attack on Charkow, which would have kept its forces so occupied that the enemy units fighting west of the city would have been able to escape. The Heeresgruppe was finally able to bring the SS-Panzerkorps around Charkow to the east. The city fell easily, and we succeeded in moving considerable portions of the enemy's escape to the other side of the Donez ... On March 14, Charkow fell into the hands of the SS-Panzerkorps. At the same time, Panzergrenadierdivision *GD* on the northern wing of Armeeabteilung Kempf was proceeding rapidly toward Belgorod. The enemy threw his tank forces at this advance, but the Division smashed them near Gaiworon. The Division continued on toward Belgorod."

The commanding general of the SS-Panzerkorps, Obergruppenführer and General der Waffen-SS Hausser, in his personal notes answered the criticisms leveled by the Generalfeldmarschall, some of them openly expressed, others hidden between the lines. The Obergruppenführer's response is as follows:

> "Naturally the Korps wanted to recapture Charkow. Its commanding general would have had the good sense, however, to put that wish aside if it had conflicted with the Heeresgruppe's overall plan of operation. Just a few days before the attack, it was unclear whether the Korps should be swung around to the east to attack the enemy forces around Charkow or whether it should move to the west against the enemy forces facing Armeeabteilung Kempf.
>
> The somewhat overly-devout language quoted above ('to lay it at the Führer's feet as a symbol of victory') does not suit the Korps' commanding general. Those words do not come from him. I do not know whether anyone else ever used them.
>
> This battle developed in accordance with the instructions of the 4. Panzerarmee by encirclement, without getting the Korps caught up in a frontal attack. The spring weather, it is true, did demand a rapid opening of the streets through the city, for the coming thaw would make them unpassable.
>
> I would like to add the following:
>
> 1) The orders from the 4. Panzerarmee to the Korps are no longer available; I do not have them anymore. [Author's note: they have since been found and are quoted above.]
> But they cannot have been worded as cited by the Generalfeldmarschall. If they had been, the Korps would have acted differently.
>
> 2) Charkow was a city of great importance: it contained a huge network of roads in a low-lying basin, without any by-passes usable by motorized units. The officers at the front were in a better position to evaluate these road conditions. The opening of a march route through the city was of enormous importance. The Korps pointed that out at the time.
>
> 3) It is not devoid of psychological significance for a unit to regain with its own forces an important goal, such as the Charkow region, when they are burning to do so after having held it under severe conditions and only abandoned it to avoid being surrounded (with the specter of the Stalingrad tragedy staring them in the face). That would have been taken into account if there had not been insurmountable disadvantages attached to it. The Generalkommando could not have a clear picture of that. It is possible that this train of thought could have been expressed by one side in conversations between the Stäbe. The commanding general was during this period mostly at the front with the troops and not on the telephone. The only witness to the conversations, his Chef of Stab, was killed.
> The relationship between us and the Oberbefehlshaber of the 2. Panzerarmee (Hoth) was extremely good. There were no objections to his orders."

Elsewhere, Generaloberst Hausser wrote:

> "In reviewing the literature written since the war, one notices that A. Heusinger among others in his book 'Befehl im Widerstreit' failed to mention the events of February and March, 1943, around Charkow in his numerous crisis-situation conversations in the Oberkommando of the Heer. Perhaps the services and successes of the SS-Panzerkorps did not fit into his book's train of thought.
>
> Generalfeldmarschall von Manstein also barely mentioned them in his book 'Verlorene Siege.' He does not say that the Armee's real burden lay on the SS-Panzerkorps' shoulders because the other units had been in constant fighting since the end of 1942 in the attempt to relieve Stalingrad and then in the wearisome retreat."

In the periodical "Der Freiwillige" (Number 1/1856), Hausser wrote in an article entitled "Gedanken zum Buche von Manstein 'Verlorene Siege'" [Thoughts on von Manstein's book 'Verlorene Siege'] as follows:

> "The Feldmarschall, according to his book, knew that the Korps (amazingly) had not abandoned the city against Hitler's orders, but against the instructions of Armeeabteilung Lanz. In one half of one line, he acknowledges that the decision was a correct one. He fails to point out, however, that the Heeresgruppe's operative situation, especially on its northern wing, improved considerably when it received a rested Korps consisting of three Panzerdivisionen ready to stand at its disposal instead of having a Korps surrounded by enemy forces. The author draws the conclusion that if the commanding general had been a general in the Heer, Hitler would have brought him before a court martial.
>
> He is probably remembering the fate of the commander of the 46. Infanteriedivision, Generalleutnant Graf Sponeck, the defender of the Kertsch peninsula at the end of 1941, whose tragedy we all regret. But the situation was entirely different!
>
> The commanding general of the SS-Korps knew clearly that he would assume responsibility for his decision, and that he, as commander of a unit of the Waffen-SS, had to expect the direst consequences. It is true that they did not come to pass. The disgrace was public, the positive signficance was not acknowledged.
>
> The supposition cannot be dismissed that Hitler, who stayed at von Manstein's headquarters immediately afterwards on 19.2.1943, personally recognized the correctness of the decision. A later remark by General Jodl hints at this possibility... The reader cannot escape the impression while reading von Manstein's book that, despite some words of respect for the unit, he harbors in and between the lines a considerable bias against the Waffen-SS, especially against its leadership. This observation, not lessened by my personal experiences, will surely be permitted to a subordinate of his at the time, and to an older soldier."

Other military historians have even written about the recapture of Charkow by the SS-Panzerkorps as follows:

> "The desire to share the glory of recapturing Charkow with no other unit, the difficulty of executing a complicated encircling maneuver with insufficiently trained non-commissioned officers, and the attraction which large cities always exert on an attacking force may all have played a part in this affair."

This unmitigated attack on the SS-Panzerkorps is answered by Generaloberst Hausser in his personal notes to the history of Division *DR*. He writes:

> "That judgment is primitive! ... These criticisms cannot be taken seriously. These are forces which executed extremely difficult attack and retreat operations from east of the Donez and around Charow and which completed the retreat at the last moment, which then attacked through the enemy's forces to establish contact with the former left wing of Heeresgruppe Don, which then turned their front one hundred eighty degrees to the north, and which then made a thrust together with the 4. Panzerarmee on Charkow. These forces have proved that they could execute complicated encircling maneuvers ...
> The commanders were sufficiently trained. I will say nothing of myself, the man in charge."

American historian George Stein wrote in his history of the Waffen-SS about the outcome of this fighting:

> "Although this operation owes a large part of its success to von Manstein's masterly strategy, the three Divisionen of the SS-Panzerkorps (the *Leibstandarte SS Adolf Hitler*, *Das Reich*, and *Totenkopf*) formed the spearhead of this attack and recaptured Charkow. This victory gave Hitler a new drive. This section of the mineral-rich Donez basin, so essential for the German war effort, was kept in German hands. The great Soviet Stalingrad offensive appeared to have been checked. Hitler's policy of never retreating and his trust in the elite divisions of the Waffen-SS appear to have been vindicated ..."

The author finally must comment on the Generalfeldmarschall's sloppy assertion that, "The city fell easily." It is sufficient to point to the reports in this book for the period 11.3. - 14.3.1943 and to the following list of losses in the 2. Panzergrenadier-Regiment *LAH* for the period of the fighting around Charkow:

Dead	14	34	239
Wounded	30	154	615
Missing	1	6	34
Ill or accidentally wounded	2	14	304
	47 Officers	217 NCOs	1,192 Men

e) 27.3.1943 - 29.6.1943: Division rest period in the Charkow area, release of men to form the cadres for the 12. *HJ*-Division and the Generalkommando of the I. SS-Panzerkorps

The Division's commander brought back important news from his visit to the Führer's headquarters:

1. The following new units were to be established immediately from Division *LSSAH*:

   a) A Generalkommando which was to receive the designation I. SS-Panzerkorps Leibstandarte.
   b) A new Division which was to receive the designation SS-Panzergrenadierdivision *Hitler-Jugend*.

2. a) The cadre personnel for the new Generalkommando and the new Division, i.e. the section leaders of the Korpsstab and the commanders and Kompanieführers, were to be drawn from the Division *Leibstandarte*.
   b) The men for the Korps forces and the new Division were to come from the various replacement units of the Waffen-SS or were to be acquired from within the Hitler-Jugend organization. Replacements for Panzergrenadierdivision *LSSAH* were to come primarily from superfluous personnel at the Oberkommando der Luftwaffe.

Considering the considerable toll the last three months had taken on the *LAH*'s forces, its power was decidedly reduced by the additional removal from its ranks of experienced leaders and non-commissioned officers.

To these new losses one must add the bloody losses suffered around Charkow: one hundred sixty-seven officers and 4,373 non-commissioned officers and enlisted men.

That represented forty-four percent of the Division's fighting strength.

The following men were removed from the unit:

From the Divisionsstab:	Divisional commander and General der Waffen-SS, Sepp Dietrich
	O1 Hauptsturmführer Buchstein
	Generalstabsoffizier Sturmbannführer Hubert Meyer (at the time in training)
	Ib Obersturmbannführer Ewert
	O2 Obersturmführer Schmitz
	Ic Hauptsturmführer Maas
	IIa Hauptsturmführer Weiser
	IIb Obersturmführer Ritz
	III Obersturmbannführer Dr. Greineder
	IVa Obersturmbannführer Bludau
	IVb Obersturmbannführer Dr. Besuden
	V Obersturmbannführer Helmut Groß

From the 1. Panzer-grenadier-Regiment:	Regimental commander Standartenführer Witt Kompaniechef Hauptsturmführer Springer Kompaniechef Hauptsturmführer Waldmüller Kompaniechef Hauptsturmführer Urabl TFK Hauptsturmführer Manthey IVb Dr. Rolf Schulz
From the 2. Panzer-grenadier-Regiment:	Regimental commander Standartenführer Wisch (new Divisionsführer of the *LAH*) Kompaniechef Hauptsturmführer Scappini Kompaniechef Hauptsturmführer Kolitz
From the Panzerregiment:	Commander of the I. Abteilung Sturmbannführer Wünsche Adjutant Obersturmführer Isecke the entire I. Abteilung
From the Aufklärungs-abteilung:	Abteilung commander Obersturmbannführer Kurt Meyer the entire 1. Kompanie Kompaniechef Olboeter
From the Panzerjäger-abteilung:	Kompaniechef Hauptsturmführer Prinz
From the Artillerie-Regiment:	Regimental commander Standartenführer Staudinger Abteilung commander Sturmbannführer Schröder the entire II. Abteilung Batteriechef Hauptsturmführer Urbanitz Batteriechef Hauptsturmführer Bartling Batteriechef Hauptsturmführer Willy Müller
From the Flakabteilung:	Abteilung commander Sturmbannführer Krause Batteriechef Hauptsturmführer Fend
From the Nachrichten-abteilung:	Kompaniechef Obersturmführer Krüger Obersturmführer Uibelhack
From the Division supply forces:	Commander Sturmbannführer Siebken
From the replacement Bataillon:	Commander Obersturmbannführer Mohnke

In the period from September, 1943, to February, 1944, the following were transferred from the *Leibstandarte* to the 12. Panzergrenadierdivision *HJ*:

the entire Panzerjägerabteilung, a complete medical clearing station from the Sanitätsabteilung, four Portepeeunteroffiziere [non-commissioned officers above the level of Feldwebel], seven non-commissioned officers, and one hundred twenty-five enlisted men.

On 13.5.1943, the transfer of the former Regiment and Abteilung commanders within the Panzergrenadierdivision *LSSAH* was carried out as planned. The following were given leadership of the following units:

Sturmbannführer Frey of the 1. Panzergrenadier-Regiment
Sturmbannführer Kraas of the 2. Panzergrenadier-Regiment
Sturmbannführer Schiller of the I./1. Panzergrenadier-Regiment
Hauptsturmführer Becker of the I./2. Panzergrenadier-Regiment
Sturmbannführer Mertsch of the Artillerie-Regiment *LAH*
Hauptsturmführer de Vries of the I./Artillerie-Regiment *LAH*
Hauptsturmführer Knittel of the Aufklärungsabteilung *LAH*
Hauptsturmführer Ullerich of the Flakabteilung *LAH*
Hauptsturmführer Stamp of the Division supply troops *LAH*.

Because of the transfer of Luftwaffe personnel to the Division, the commander and the Ia flew in April to the field headquarters of Reichsmarschall Göring. After lengthy negotiations, it was decided that not just Feldwebels (as originally planned by the Luftwaffe), but about twenty-five percent Feldwebels, fifty percent non-commissioned officers, and twenty-five percent service-grade enlisted men would be transferred.

When these approximately 2,500 soldiers arrived in May, they turned out to be overwhelmingly Portepeeunteroffiziere, thus of the Feldwebel rank. The first transport train contained about four or five hundred men, whom the Divisional commander welcomed with an address. The Obergruppenführer undertook the task right then of calling for volunteers for the Panzergrenadiere. The small show of hands was no bigger when he asked for volunteers for the Aufklärungsabteilung. The Artillerie and the other heavy weapons, as well as the Panzerregiment, found a little more favor. The repair section and the Division supply troops were the favorite choices. The Obergruppenführer skipped the receptions for later trainloads. These men's behavior was only too comprehensible to us. The difference between service as maintenance personnel and service in a Panzergrenadierkompanie is enormous. In addition, the way in which these men had been treated played a role. They had all volunteered for the Luftwaffe. All had just been promoted to the Luftwaffe or had just received their Luftwaffe basic training when one day, without explanation, they had been loaded into trucks and delivered to the barracks of the *LAH* in Berlin-Lichterfelde. They had been given uniforms of the *LAH* and been told they had been transferred. After a few days of combat training on the southern exercise grounds of the Cadet Institute, they had been carted off to join field forces. Truly, this was unworthy treatment. When one knows that, one can only be amazed at and respectful of the exemplary manner in which these men performed their service. In retrospect, one can notice how these soldiers joined the individual units willingly and without complaint. In a short time, they were impossible to tell apart from the other members of the *LAH*. But among the troops which came from the various replacement units of the Waffen-SS, there were not only volunteers. These were the first of the draftees, the so-called "yank-alongs." But they, too, were transformed into worthy members of the Division in the brief time available for combat training.

The training guidelines given by the Division demanded various periods of training, depending on the instructions given by the Kommando authorities concerning combat readiness. At first, the Division was subordinated to Armeeabteilung Kempf, which meant that our rest period would end on 20.4.1943. In addition, the reinforced 1. Panzergrenadier-Regiment had to be prepared by 11.4 to march out as an attack force with three hour's notice.

It was relieved between 12.4 and 23.4 by the reinforced 2. Panzergrenadier-Regiment, which was transferred into the north and northwestern section of Charkow for this purpose.

On 20.4, a courier delivered to Adolf Hitler as a birthday present a check for 2,126,512 Reichsmarks for his wartime Winterhilfswerk charity. The Vienna edition of the "Volksblatt" newspaper (no. 112 of 22.4.1943) reported, "This extraordinary sum was collected by the men of the *Leibstandarte* from their own ranks in three months during their campaign in the east."

Starting on 25.4, the Division, within the framework of what was then known as the II. SS-Panzerkorps, was subordinated to the 4. Panzerarmee (under Generaloberst Hoth). As a result of the restructuring of the I. SS-Panzerkorps *Leibstandarte*, the former Generalkommando of the SS-Panzerkorps had been renamed the II. SS-Panzerkorps.

On 26.4, the entire Division, under orders from the 4. Panzerarmee, moved into the area west of Charkow. On 29.4, some elements were transferred again to an area north of the railway line from Charkow to Bogoduchoff. This move had not yet been completed when the 4. Panzerarmee ordered still another transfer into an area about thirty kilometers farther north. The orders for this last move were already part of the overall plan for Operation Kursk, which would later be named "Zitadelle." Because of the postponement of that undertaking, the move was never actually made. During the ensuing rest period, the units undertook a training program ordered by the Division; it lasted five weeks, until 7.6.1943. Another five-week training program was added to the end of it. The second one was to last until 11.7.1943, but the commencement of the march for "Zitadelle" brought it to an end on 28.6.

During this period there was thorough training for officers and non-commissioned officers. In addition, each Bataillon took part in at least two exercises in which it was able to function as a reinforced Bataillon with Panzer and Artillerie support. Orders dated 12.5 from the Division established a Regiments-Aufklärungskompanie and Regiments-Pionierkompanie in each of the two Panzergrenadierregimenter. Obersturmführer Walter Krüger also established the 3. Fernfeldkabelkompanie [field-cable-laying company] in the Nachrichtenabteilung. At the beginning of May, the Reichsführer-SS visited the SS-Panzerkorps and observed firing exercises by a Panzerkompanie of Panzerregiment *LAH*.

On 13.5 the former commanders handed over their units. The Obergruppenführer's birthday provided the opportunity for a ceremonial farewell for the officers leaving the Division. At this birthday celebration, the following officers took part (in addition to those from the *LAH*): the commanding general, Obergruppenführer Hausser; commander of the SS-Panzergrenadierdivision *Wiking*, Gruppenführer Gille; commander of the SS-Panzergrenadierdivision *Totenkopf*, Brigadeführer Prieß; and the commander of the Panzerregiment of Heeres-Panzergrenadierdivision *Großdeutschland*, Oberst Graf Strachwitz.

In the week between 7.6.1943 and 12.6.1943, the elements destined to join the *HJ*-Division were loaded for transport. The former I./Panzerregiment *LAH* handed its Panzers over to the II. Abteilung, which was to stand at the Division's disposal for the Kursk offensive as its sole Panzer unit.

The II./Artillerie-Regiment *LAH* was loaded as a unit. The former III. and IV./Artillerie-Regiment *LAH* were renamed the II. and III./Artillerie-Regiment *LAH*. There was no new IV. established.

The II./Panzerregiment *LAH*, called Kampfgruppe Groß, stood at the disposal of the 4. Panzerarmee from 30.5.1943 to 22.6.1943 as an attack reserve in the forest east of Blichnij. During this period, the Panzerregiment's 8. Kompanie was established. The Panzer drivers from the Kompanie were divided among the 5., 6., and 7. Kompanie because there were not enough Panzers for them all.

The I./Panzerregiment *LAH*, knowing full well that virtually no equipment would be available for reestablishing the force on the homefront, collected from the battlefields of Russia the following to take along: four damaged Panzer IV's, two damaged Panzer III's, two drivable T-34's, six thousand two-liter canisters, forty cows, and twelve prisoner volunteers to maintain the vehicles.[37]

A quotation from the personal diary of Sturmmann Borchers of the Pionierzug of the 5. (heavy)/2. provides information as to the manner in which the Division was received in its rest area northwest of Charkow:

> "9.4.1943: We received billets in Charkow once more. We lived in the old quarter of the city, where we had also fought in the attack. The people were very friendly to us. We soon became very fond of tea from a samovar. We gave them things from our supplies, for there was enough to go around. It was here that I met Johann Vogt from Südende, who was a member of our Flakabteilung. He was later killed. We had our pictures taken in Charkow, and we hardly recognized ourselves.
> Second day of Easter: we moved on. The Russians cried at our departure. Our objective is still unknown."

On 20.6.1943, there was a radio command-post exercise for the armoured force of the *LAH* with enemy position "Zitadelle." It was conducted under the leadership of the Ia in the presence of the future Divisional commander, Standartenführer Wisch, and of the commanding general of the II. SS-Panzerkorps, Obergruppenführer Hausser. During the entire rest period, the Division received entertainment from theatre groups of all kinds. Our Abteilung VI succeeded in getting the Russian theatre in Charkow in operation. There were several performances of Bizet's Carmen.

New equipment as well as personnel replacements arriving to make up the losses of armoured and tracked vehicle drivers necessitated the establishment of a temporary armoured vehicle driving training school at Walki under the leadership of Hauptsturmführer Olboetter.

The II./Artillerie-Regiment's equipment was re-equipped with armoured, self-propelled mounts. Two Batterien received 10.5-centimeter light Feldhaubitzen mounted on Panzer II chassis, designated "Wespe" (Sd. Kfz. 124), and the third Batterie received 15-centimeter heavy Feldhaubitzen mounted on Panzer III/IV chassis, designated "Hummel" (Sd. Kfz. 165). In addition, the heavy Kompanien of the Aufklärungsabteilung and the III. (armoured)/2. received 15-centimeter heavy Infanteriegeschütze mounted on Panzer 38(t), designated as "Grille" or "Bison."

It goes without saying that there were courses for non-commissioned officers in every individual unit on the care and use of weapons of all types.

A "new unit training staff" under Staudinger provided training for beginners or advanced specialists in the Artillerie. The commander of the Pionier-Bataillon, Obersturmbannführer Cissy Hansen, conducted training courses for Infanterie-Pioniere and Panzer-Pioniere.

Even though the official transfer of command for the Division from Obergruppenführer Sepp Dietrich to Standartenführer Theodor Wisch was not to take place until 4.6.1943, the Division's new commander and the officers of his Stab arrived by the end of May to begin the transition.

The imminent departure of Obergruppenführer Sepp Dietrich was hard to bear for the men of his Division, "his boys" as he used to call them all, whether officer or enlisted man. He was connected with every fiber to this unit, which he had set up in 1933, which he had led from its infancy for ten years, and which bore the decisive stamp of his character.

To be sure, our old commander (whom we called Obersepp among ourselves) was no strategic genius. But he was a first-class leader of soldiers and of men. As commanding general or Oberbefehlshaber, he would not be using this gift, and knowing that caused him pain. His forte did not lie in formulating a complete tactical evaluation. But he had an extraordinary sense of a growing crisis and for finding the favorable moment for action. His rare and brief speeches to his men contained no flashes of brilliance, but were palpably heartfelt. And the men took them to heart. His brilliance was in his amazing presence. Anyone who experienced it can only recall with wonder and admiration how he, in the darkest night of a crisis, with everything pushing us back, would face the waves of retreating men, his collar pulled up, his hands shoved in his pockets up to the elbows. Uttering sounds incomprehensible, but full of recognizable rage, he could not only bring the men to stop, but even to turn around and head back in. Unforgettable, too, was his warning to unit leaders of any rank as they set off to battle: "Bring my boys back!"

The incredible human dimensions of this man of simple birth are revealed in the following anecdote:

Generalfeldmarschall von Manstein paid a visit to the Division in March or April of 1943. For some reason, he did not go into the bus used by the commander and clearly marked "Kommandeur," but went instead into the building opposite, labeled "Ia." The Ia saluted him and, at the Generalfeldmarschall's request, began to brief him on the situation. After a short time, the O 1 fetched the Obengruppenführer, who reported to the Generalfeldmarschall with all formality. The Oberbefehlshaber barely took notice of his salute and ordered the Ia to continue with his presentation. When it was over, the Generalfeldmarschall gave a brief description of the larger situation and started to leave. The Obergruppenführer asked him to return to the command bus for a little refreshment, invited the Ia to join them, and asked the Generalfeldmarschall's escort officer to wait with the O1. In the bus, cognac was served, and when the O1 had left us alone, the Obergruppenführer spoke to this effect: "Herr Generalfeldmarschall, I have the impression that you think I have some special line to the Führer's headquarters. I can report to you with all respect that this is not the case. I lead my Division just as all the other commanders do, without going outside of channels." Actually, in mentioning the Führer's headquarters, Sepp Dietrich did not express himself so correctly, but literally said, "a special line to him there," and pointed to his upper lip. The Generalfeldmarschall rose and answered, "Obergruppenführer Dietrich, that was the right word at the right time. I apologize." The author, eyewitness to this exchange, can add nothing to it.

With this brief appreciation of our honored commander, the Charkow chapter of our story finally comes to an end.

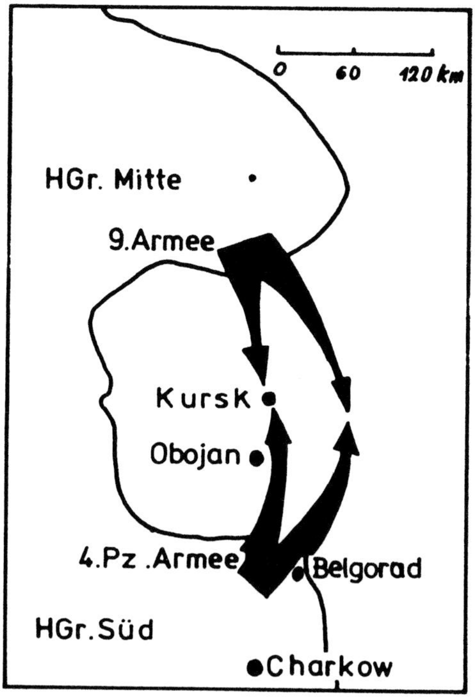

Plan for Zitadelle

Part 7
29.6.1943 - 29.7.1943: OPERATION ZITADELLE

Section I
29.6.1943 - 17.7.1943: THE OFFENSIVE

a) The situation, our intentions, and the orders for Zitadelle

At the end of March, 1943, with the recapture of Charkow and Belgorod at the seam between Heeresgruppe Süd and Heeresgruppe Mitte, the front was stuck in the mud of the spring thaw. Northwest of Belgorod, Heeresgruppe Mitte had not succeeded in moving up to be even with the left wing of Heeresgruppe Süd (Panzergrenadierdivision *GD* and Panzergrenadierdivision *LAH*). As a result, the Russians had a salient two hundred kilometers wide and one hundred twenty kilometers deep west of Kursk.

After Heeresgruppe Süd's defensive success, the OKH planned to undertake an offensive with a limited objective. This operation was to cut off the Russian salient at Kursk, capture a shorter line of defense, and at the same time defeat the enemy's strong forces. The final objective was to render the enemy incapable of a decisive offensive for the entire summer. Hitler and/or the OKH proceeded from the assumption that shortening the front would free up enough units and create such a large reserve that the expected invasion of the western Allies could be repulsed, whenever it came.

The immediate task was to attack the enemy's exhausted troops as soon as the spring muddy period, which severely limited all movement, had passed. There was a series of reasons for the repeated postponement of the attack. To go into them in detail would be outside the framework of this Divisional history.[1]

The author himself remembers with a shudder how the Ic's map of the enemy's position daily grew redder.

The offensive finally began on July 5, 1943, with an attack on enemy forces installed in a well-fortified and deeply echeloned system of positions, with operative reserves at their disposal.

The enemy assessment paragraph of the orders for Operation Zitadelle from the Oberkommando of the 4. Panzerarmee, dated 28.6.1943, read as follows:

> "In front of the Panzerarmee's attack front, we must expect there to be four rifle divisions in the first line and two additional rifle divisions in the second. In addition, there appears to be a tank corps in or just behind the second line, and another tank corps south of Obojan.
> The enemy's behavior shows that he is intending to rely on his deep and well-fortified positions to hold onto his salient at Kursk and is willing to deploy his tank forces close to the front at his first line.

After we break through to the second line, we must expect tank attacks against our eastern flank from several tank corps and attacks against the western flank from three or four rifle divisions."

In the evening of 3.7.1943, one day before the attack was to begin, reconnaissance spotted two hundred twelve enemy tanks south of the Pssel sector, of which one hundred fifteen were west of the road from Belgorod to Obojan, thus squarely in our attack sector. We could safely assume that the enemy knew our intentions, our troop strength, the individual attack forces' orders, and probably even the planned attack date.

All this information resulted in the orders for the 4. Panzerarmee (XXXXVIII. Panzerkorps, LII. Armeekorps):

"*The Panzerarmee-Oberkommando 4* is to begin its attack to surround and destroy the enemy forces in the salient at Kursk within Operation Zitadelle. To this end, the Panzerarmee is to conduct the attack according to plan on X-Day against the first enemy line in the sector from the hills northwest of Belgorod to Korowino, after the XXXXVIII. Panzerkorps has captured the hills on both sides of Butowo and south of Gerzowka on the afternoon of X-minus-One-Day.

The Panzerarmee is quickly to smash all resistance in the second enemy line, destroy the tank forces thrown at it, and to move on Kursk and the area to the east, going around Obojan to the east.

Armeeabteilung Kempf is to provide cover for the Operation to the east. To that end, the left wing of the Armeeabteilung (the 6. Panzerdivision) is to attack from Belgorod via Ssabynino toward Prochorowka.

The II. SS-Panzerkorps is to move on X-Day after Artillerie preparatory and deploy the Panzergrenadierdivisionen *LAH*, *Das Reich*, *Totenkopf*, and one-third of the 167. Infanteriedivision in an orderly attack with Panzer support on the enemy's advance positions in the defensive zone in the sector Beresoff — Sadelnoje. The hills needed for the Artillerie observers should be taken in the night. One Division is to attack in rear echelon formation to the right as far as the Shurawliny area and to open up the road Belgorod — Jakowlewo.

After fighting its way through the enemy's first defensive zone, the Korps is to attack the second one immediately between Lutschki and Jakowlewo. The left flank is to be covered on the Worskla by the third of the 167. Infanteriedivision.

After breaking through the second line, the Korps is to stand ready to move the bulk of its forces in rear echelon formation to the right south of the Pssel sector toward the northeast, with the right wing moving via Prochorowka."

The orders for Panzergrenadierdivision *LAH* in Korpsbefehl No. 17 read as follows:

"*The LSSAH*, reinforced by Grenadierregiment 315 and the II./Artillerie-Regiment 238, is to attack the enemy installations along the road from Tomarowka to Bykowka. Then it is to take Kemenyi Log and Sadelnoje,

provide cover for the flank from that line, and move north to force a breakthrough east of Jakowlewo.
The Division also is ordered to move immediately through to the northeast and capture a crossing over the Pssel in the Michailowka — Kljutschki sector. After the preparation fire is finished, Werferregiment 55 and light Artillerie-Abteilung 861 are to be subordinated to the *LAH*.
The VIII. Fliegerkorps is to use the bulk of its forces to support the attack of the II. SS-Panzerkorps. The first attack objectives in front of SS-Panzergrenadierdivision *DR* are the installations in Beressoff and northeast of there, excluding bridges. The last bomb is to fall at Y + 50.
In front of the *LAH*, the first attack objectives are the installations on both sides of Point 220.5 and north of there. The last bomb at Y + 65.
Ground attack planes will accompany the spearheads of *DR* and the *LAH* from the beginning of the attack."

The Divisionskommando *LAH* prepared the force for the operation by issuing the following orders:
Divisionsbefehl No. 14 on 28.6.1943 for the transfer of the Division from its previous billeting area starting at 02.00 hours on 30.6.
Divisionbefehl No. 15 on 30.6.1943 for preparing the attack in the night between 3.7 and 4.7 and again in the night between 4.7 and 5.7.
Divisionsbefehl 16 on 1.7.1943 for the attack itself.

b) 29.6.1943 - 4.7.1943: March and preparation

29.6.1943: At 09.00 hours, the 1. Generalstabsoffizier in the Divisional headquarters at Charkow held a conference with the Adjutant. Its subject was the transfer of the Division out of its previous billeting area. The emphasis in the order was on camouflaging the movement, both in moving during the night before 1.7 and when reaching the assembly area in the nights before 4.7 and 5.7.

30.6.1943: At 08.00 hours, the Obergruppenführer distributed the orders for the attack at the Divisional headquarters. Taking part in the briefing were all the Regiment, Bataillon, and Abteilung commanders of the Division and its subordinated Heer units.
The Obergruppenführer issued the orders with emphasis on the significance of the attack operation ahead, and he urged the forces to be ready for action. As always on these occasions, he warned the commanders to "bring back his men healthy and in one piece." He handed the floor over to the Ia to explain the exact plan for the battle.
The troops spent the day readying themselves for the march.

1.7.1943: At 08.00 hours, the units which had moved up during the night reported reaching their designated areas. These were the reinforced 1. Panzergrenadier-Regiment (the 4./Flakabteilung *LAH*, the 2./Sanitätsabteilung, the Artillerie-Regiment *LAH* minus the I. Abteilung) and the Flakabteilung *LAH* minus its 4. and 5. Batterie.

2.7.1943: By 08.30 hours, all the units had reached their designated areas. The armoured force (the Panzerregiment *LAH*, the III. (armoured)/2., the Aufklärungsabteilung *LAH*, the bulk of Panzerjägerabteilung *LAH*) was not to be moved up into its assembly area until the night before 4.7.

Number of available Panzers on 2.7.1943:

Panzer II's	4	Command Panzers	15
Panzer III's	12	Motorized Pak Z	18
Panzer IV's	72	Self-prop. Pak	22
Panzer VI's	11	Sturmgeschütze	31

3.7.1943: The march ran according to plan. The forces detailed to capture the enemy's advance outposts before the beginning of the attack (one reinforced Bataillon per Regiment) were already moved up into their start points for the attack in the night before 4.7.1943.

The written Divisionbefehl for the attack reached the units on 3.7.1943.

Its essential points applying to 4.7.1943 read as follows:

6. *Missions:*

I. *Capture of the enemy's advance outposts.*

Beginning of the operation: 4.7 at 23.00 hours

a) One reinforced Kompanie/1. Panzergrenadier-Regiment *LAH* is to proceed through the southern part of the forest and capture the enemy outpost on the hill west of Jachontoff. It is to hold that post until the start of the attack proper. Close contact is to be established and held with Division *DR*, attacking to the right.

b) *One reinforced Bataillon/2. Panzergrenadierregiment LAH* is to move past the forest along its western edge and capture the enemy oupost on Hill 228.6. It is to hold it while providing cover on its left flank against the Stepnoje ravine.

c) *One reinforced Kompanie/reinforced Grenadierregiment 315* is to move through Strelezkoje and capture the enemy posts in the northern part of the town.

Conduct of the battle.

The battle line is to be crossed at 23.00 hours.

The attack is to be conducted as a surprise assault with no preparatory fire.

It is essential the enemy forces not be allowed to filter past us or break through with counterattacks. We must be able to move our main forces into the start position for the assault. We can expect armoured enemy counterattacks. These counterattacks should be exploited as an opportunity to see where they have left trails through their mine fields. Hill 228.6 should be exploited as soon as possible by advance artillery observers.

The Panzer liaison Kommando is to scout the possibilty of marching just south of Hill 228.6 without being visible to ground reconnaissance.

The subordinated *Pioniere*, detailed to cooperate with these forces, are to create and mark paths through the mine fields and crossings over the tank trenches along as broad a front as possible. It is most important for the Sturmgeschütze and the Tigers to be able to move up along the road from Tomarowka via Bykowka to Hill 228.6.

Sturmmann Günther Borchers, member of the 19. (Pionier)/2. Panzergrenadier-Regiment LAH, wrote in his diary:

> "When we reached the assembly area, the attack objective was finally designated. We Pioniere are going to be attached to the individual Infanterie Kompanien in the spearhead. We are supposed to attack with flamethrowers. This is the real suicide squad. We have to get within twenty-five meters of the Russians in order to use the flame throwers. We might just as well be writing our wills now."

As night fell, the units began to arrive in their designated areas. There, the orders from Adolf Hitler for the attack were read to them:

> Soldiers!
> Today, you set out to a great onslaught, the outcome of which could well decide the war.
> Your victory must serve to convince the world more than ever that any resistance to the German Wehrmacht is fruitless. In addition, a new defeat for the Russians can only serve to shake further the already wavering belief among the men in many units of the Soviet army that a Bolshevik victory is possible. Just as in the last war, they will one day be defeated.
> For whatever the Russians have been able to achieve in this victory or that one was due first and foremost to his tanks.
> My soldiers! You now finally have better tanks than he does.
> His apparently inexhaustible supply of manpower has been so reduced by two years of fighting that he was forced to deploy his youngest recruits as if they were old hands. Our Infanterie is far superior to his, as are our Kanoniere, our Panzerjägers, our Panzer drivers, our Pioniere and, as always, our Luftwaffe.
> The mighty blow which will hit the Soviet Armies tomorrow must by definition rock them to their core.
> And you must know that everything depends on the success of this battle. As a soldier myself, I know exactly what I am asking of you. Despite that, we must fight our way to victory, no matter how bitter and difficult it is in the thick of battle. Our German homeland, which is now withstanding the enemy's air raids with greatest valor, those women, boys, and girls fighting tirelessly for victory, look to you with trust.
>
> Adolf Hitler
>
> This order is to be destroyed in front of the Divisionsstäbe after being announced.

In a second daily order, Hitler addressed the commanders. This order, too, was to be destroyed after being issued.

4.7.1943: At 02.30 hours, the 2. Panzergrenadier-Regiment reported reaching its preparation area, as did the 1. Panzergrenadier-Regiment a short time later. The Divisionsstab and the Regimentsstäbe used the night to march ahead to their combat headquarter locations. The Division's headquarters were set up in the patch of forest near Baizury. When he reached the new headquarters, Obergruppenführer Sepp Dietrich handed over the command of the Division to Standartenführer Theodor Wisch.

In the course of the afternoon, there were conferences with the Regiment's officers to brief them on the plan of attack.

The paragraph of the Divisionsbefehl affecting the bulk of the Division's forces read as follows:

> 6. *II. Penetration and breakthrough on X-Day [5.7.1943]*
> Move up in the dark under the cover provided by the advance line of defense.
> The depth of the enemy's defensive zone and the narrowness of our attack sector require us to attack from a deep formation. Penetration itself should be assault-force-fashion, immediately following the Artillerie and Stuka preparation. Cover fire will be provided by the Tigers and Sturmgeschütze.
> *Artillerie preparation* from Y + 15 to Y + 65 [03.15 - 04.05 hours].
> Artillerie preparation should be intensified from Y + 60 to Y + 65 [04.00 - 04.05 hours].
> *Stuka attack* on Point 220.5 starting at Y + 50.
> Last bomb to fall at Y + 65.
>
> *Specifically:*
> a) *The reinforced 1. Panzergrenadier-Regiment LAH* (one Kompanie/Panzerjägerabteilung *LAH*, the 4. [medium]/Flakabteilung *LAH*) is, during the Artillerie preparation from Y + 15 until Y + 65), to work its way forward along the ravine northwest of Jachontoff to its point of departure for the assault. Immediately following the last Stuka bomb, it is to break into the enemy installation.
> Then it is to use the bulk of its forces to continue the attack on the second installation east of Jakowlewo; it is also to send elements to attack the eastern outskirts of Bykowka.
> *First day's objective*: Jakowlewo.
> b) *The reinforced 2. Panzergrenadier-Regiment LAH (minus the III. [armoured]/2., with Sturmgeschützabteilung LAH*, the 13. [Tiger]/ Panzerregiment *LAH*, one Kompanie/Pionier-Bataillon *LAH*, the 5. [medium]/Flakabteilung *LAH*) is to work its way forward during the Artillerie preparation from Y + 15 to Y + 65 as far as its point of departure for the assault. Immediately after the last bomb on Hill 220.5, it is to penetrate the enemy installation under cover of the fire from the Sturmgeschützabteilung and the Tigerkompanie. Then it is to continue its attack on both sides of the road toward Bykowka, clearing the string of towns along the Worskla of enemy forces and preventing our forces being outflanked from the west bank.
> *First day's objective*: Bykowka.
> *One Batterie of the Sturmgeschützabteilung* is, after the breakthrough into the first enemy installation, to be moved up to join the reinforced Grenadierregiment 315, to which it will be subordinated.

Pionierkompanie 627 and Pionier-Bataillon LAH (minus one Kompanie), after the breakthrough, are to be deployed to establish crossings over the tank trenches.
c) *The training columns* of both Panzergrenadier-Regimenter *LAH* are to be held at readiness such that their leading elements, positioned far apart, stand at the road junction 185.7 (one kilometer southeast of Tomarowka) at 08.00 hours on 5.7.
d) *Reinforced Grenadierregiment 315* (the II./Artillerie-Regiment 238, the 1./Pionier-Bataillon 238, one Batterie of Werferregiment 55, later one Batterie/Sturmgeschützabteilung *LAH*) is to move up behind the last attack elements of the reinforced 2. Panzergrenadier-Regiment *LAH*. It is to exploit the Regiment's point of breakthrough to move ahead to the enemy positions to the northwest, then attack Kamenij Log and Sadelnoje. It is to take these towns and hold them, including a bridgehead across to the western bank of the Worskla.
First day's objective: Kamenij Log — Sadelnoje.
e) *Panzergruppe LAH* (provisional composition: Panzerregiment *LAH* minus the 13. [Tiger] Kompanie and minus the I. Abteilung, the III. [armoured]/2. *LAH*, one Kompanie of the Panzerjägerabtilung *LAH*, the II. [armoured]/Artillerie-Regiment *LAH*, the 6. (light)/Flakabteilung *LAH*) is to stand ready to be deployed, as soon as the anti-tank gun strong points have been captured, east of Bykowka and past the town to make a breakthrough east of Jakowlewo to the northeast. The ultimate goal is the capture of a bridgehead across the Pssel.
f) *The Aufklärungsabteilung LAH* and *the rest of Panzerjägerabteilung LAH* are to prepare themselves either to be subordinated to the Panzergruppe or to be deployed for reconnaissance or defense, depending on the situation's development. Until the Panzergruppe begins its attack, they are to remain subordinated to it for the purpose of the march.
g) *the reinforced Artillerie-Regiment LAH* (minus the Meßbatterie and minus the 10-centimeter Kanonenbatterie, with the Artillerie-Abteilung 861), after the completion of the Artillerie preparation, is to assign the following to cooperative relationships in accordance with the Artillerie-Befehl:

I./Artillerie-Regiment *LAH* and Artillerie-Regiment 861 with the 1. Panzergrenadier-Regiment *LAH*
II./Artillerie-Regiment *LAH* with the Panzergrenadier-Regiment 2 of the *LAH* and Grenadierregiment 315
III./Artillerie-Regiment *LAH* is to send advance Artillerie observers to both Panzergrenadier-Regimenter.

The Meßbatterie *LAH* is to be moved back to the Artillerie-Regiment after fulfilling this mission.
The main mission for the Artillerie-Regiment *LAH* will be to defeat the enemy's anti-tank strong points by laying a smoke screen and concentrating fire on them.
The Artillerie-Regiment *LAH* is to prepare itself to switch positions with entire Abteilungen to support the attack on Jakowlewo.

Its positions are to be east of Bykowka.
h) *Werferregiment 55* (minus one Batterie of the II. Abteilung), assigned to cooperate with the 2. Panzergrenadier-Regiment *LAH*, is to provide support for the breakthrough in accordance with the Artillerie orders, and it is to position itself in such a way as to prevent the force from being outflanked from the west bank of the Worskla and so as to provide simultaneous support for the breakthrough into Bykowka.
i) *The Sturmgeschützabteilung* and *the 13. (Tiger)/Panzerregiment LAH* are to reach their assembly area in the night before 5.7. There, they are to be subordinated to the 2. Panzergrenadier-Regiment *LAH*, which will move them along the road to the assembly area south of Hill 228.6.
One Batterie/Sturmgeschützabteilung *LAH* is, after the completion of the breakthrough, to be moved up and subordinated to the reinforced Grenadierregiment 315.
k) *The Flakabteilung LAH* (minus the light and medium Batterie) is to take over the Flak cover for the Division's assembly area from its previous positions and to stand ready to be moved up at the Division's command.
l) *Pionier-Bataillon LAH* (minus one Kompanie) is to stand ready to be deployed for technical assignments in the main enemy battlefield.
m) *The Sanitätsabteilung LAH* is to stand ready in Chworostjanj to establish a medical clearing station in Bykowka on orders from the Division.

7) *Reconnaissance*:
   a) *Ground reconnaisance*:
      conducted by the Grenadierregimenter in their attack sectors, after the breakthrough across the enemy's second line of defense, as far as the line Prochorowka — Malaja Pasinka (nine kilometers north of Prochorowka).
   b) *Aerial reconnaissance*:
      Combat reconnaissance by the VIII. Fliegerkorps ahead of the Division's attack spearheads.
      Tactical reconnaissance as far as the line Staryj Oskol — Korowino-Obojan.
8) Luftwaffe support
   The VIII. Fliegerkorps is to support the attack of the II. SS-Panzerkorps. *The first attack objective* is in front of the *LAH* on the enemy installations on both sides of point 220.5 and to the north.
   Additional Stuka tagets will be found during the course of the attack; inquiry should be made to the Division.
   The officer leading the Stuka action is assigned to cooperation with the 2. Panzergrenadier-Regiment *LAH*.
   Ground attack planes will guard the *LAH*'s attack spearheads.
   Bombers will hit enemy artillery installations, reserves, staffs, and contact points deep in enemy territory.
9) *Flak cover ...*
10) *Traffic regulation ...*
11) *Communications ...*
12) *Reports ...*

13) *Ambulance services.* Medical clearing station in the eastern section of Tomarowka.
A place to stop the ambulances should be set up as soon as possible south of Hill 228.6.
14) *Ammunition distribution depot ...*
Fuel depot ...
15) *Divisional headquarters.* In the patch of forest 2.5 kilometers south of Stepnoje. It is expected that it will move forward to Bykowka.

In the Russian war literature, as quoted here from "The Battle of Kursk" by Reserve Colonel I.I. Markin (published in German as "Die Kursker Schlacht" by the Verlag des Ministeriums für Nationale Verteidigung, Berlin, 1960, page 33), the preparations for Operation Zitadelle are described as follows:

> "On July 2, 1943, one day after Hitler had decided on the date for the start of the offensive, the Soviet High Command informed the commanders of the Army forces on the Central Front and the Woronesch Front that the German offensive against the Kursk salient would begin between July 3 and July 6. All Soviet forces were ordered to assume immediate combat readiness. They occupied their defensive positions ... In the night between July 3 and 4, the German forces between Orjol and Belgorod moved into their start positions for the Kursk offensive. That same night, a Slovene drafted into the German Heer deserted northwest of Belgorod and escaped to the Soviet force. He reported that Hitler's troops were preparing for a move on Kursk."

At 20.30 hours, both Panzergrenadier-Regimenter reported that the elements assigned to capture the enemy's advanced outposts had completed their preparations.

At 21.25 hours, there was an enemy artillery bombardment on the assembly areas of the 1./1. and the II./2., but our losses were minor.

At 23.15 hours, the attack on the enemy's advance outposts on the hill west of Jachontoff and Hill 228.6 began. The night was very dark. The Kompanien, structured as assault forces, felt their way along the terrain, which had been minutely reconnoitered during the day, with the help of their march compasses, and they made it to the enemy's positions. The enemy's fire cut off all our telephone lines; messengers were our only means of communication.

c) 5.7.1943 - 7.7.1943: Penetration and breakthrough

5.7.1943 (see sketch 21): At 01.20 hours, the leading elements of the II./2. (under Sturmbannführer Sandig) reached Hill 228.6 and penetrated the enemy installations. Thereupon commenced close-range combat of unheard-of intensity, with the darkness making it even more difficult to command its progress. Obersturmführer Karck displayed particular valor there. He personally fought at the spearhead of his 8. Kompanie, valiantly stormed and captured Hill 228.6, and held it in close-range fighting against the Russian counterattacks. Taking a wound to the head, he still led his Kompanie as the tip of the attack wedge in an almost superhuman performance and managed to move them on against the enemy's tank trench.

At 01.33 hours, Hill 228.6 was captured, and a little later the northern part of Strelezkoje was occupied.

At 01.33 hours, the 1. Panzergrenadier-Regiment reported the capture of the hills west of Jachontow by the 11. Kompanie under command of Obersturmführer Schmid. Günther Kress reported as follows on the attack:

> "The Russians had dug in in a patch of forest opposite us and established a strong outpost. This was the forest that we were to clear of enemy forces. At 23.00 hours, our 11. Kompanie set out. We got cries of 'Give it to them, boys!' from our comrades in the Heer as we passed the battle line, and soon we were making our way across no-man's land toward the Russian outpost in the forest. We had covered scarcely half of the distance when concentrated fire from Russian artillery hit the battle line behind us. We reached the forest and discovered that the Russians had pulled back their outpost, probably during the artillery fire. So we moved through the forest without a fight. Without firing a shot, we made it to the hill behind the forest and dug in as fast as we could. The Russians did not give away their position, but kept irritating us with loudspeaker announcements urging us to desert. We answered them with short, concentrated blasts of machine gun fire."

Before that, the Regimenter had reported by 00.35 hours that the other Bataillone had reached their assembly areas, The feelings and thoughts of the Panzergrenadiere just before the attack are described by MG-Schütze Pfötsch of the 2./2. Panzergrenadier-Regiment:

> They were trotting to their foxholes through the rain.
> "Funny, how the last night before an attack feels."
> "It doesn't matter a hill of beans whether it's the last night or the last day. It's all shit."
> "Like I asked you on the way, Ernst, you remember, when neither of us felt like talking. I got to thinking about the fear, about the butterflies in the stomach, about the uncontrollable nausea. You want to throw up, hoping that will make it better, but you can't. I thought about the first time I ever had that stupid feeling."
> "And what did you come up with?"
> "Well, first it was my swimming lessons, then the dentist, some assignments for school, and worst of all just before I was drafted."
> "Did it do any good?"
> "No! That's just it. Who gives a shit about this queasy stomach. Also, I realized that everything that's been written about the war is just a pile of crap."
> "I could have told you that without thinking about it for half the night."
> "Bullshit! The other way around! It's crap because the most important thing has been forgotten or purposely left out!"
> "The fear, right?"
> "Right, Ernst. Fear is as much a part of the soldier and the war as mothers and fathers are of your very existence."
> "There are other things."

"I don't mean the heroes! I mean the average guy, the masses! On the way to Berlin to join the replacement Bataillon, different war books kept whirling through my head. In not one of them does the fear get described. I understand that there's no place for it in the so-called patriotic war literature, but even the others don't have it. My grandfather had some books about the wars in classical times, but there's nothing in them about fear. Wills, complaints, resignation, yes. But no writer has ever put down on paper the primitive, knock-knee fear that goes through the head of a soldier, or maybe lots of soldiers, just before action."

"Or through his stomach."

"Just so, Ernst. Like us, squatting in the rain, smoking, knowing tomorrow morning all hell breaks loose, and having butterflies in the stomach. What do we think about? What do we do? Waiting, waiting. What is it? Waiting, hoping, for hours on end, on the outside a camouflaged, pistol-packing youth and on the inside a quivering puddle of fear!"

"Yeah, look, that's how it is with fear."

Ernst starts philosophizing, his second favorite occupation after eating. "It's not so much a question of the fear as a question of why and wherefore."

Whenever he starts to spin a thought, he breaks out in High German. "Primary is the fact of the attack tomorrow. Are you, are we, afraid of the attack itself? No. The unpredictability, the incalculability of the concept 'attack' is the cause. Will it hit me or not, that's the important item. Everything else is nothing. And because our minds cannot answer that question, you're afraid. The indefinable uncertainty is the cause of your tremble-itis. Chance!"

"Do you remember the night before the attack on Charkow?"

"That time we talked half the night away, too, and you came up with the famous theory that fear was a necessary condition for courage and heroism. Anyone who overcame his fear had already earned the Eisernes Kreuz just for that."

"But I also said, the the Ritterkreuz can also be won out of fear, because the guy didn't have any other choice. The born hero had already been killed, or was serving at some cinch job."

The flax-blond soldier laughed softly: "Wisdom of the ages, that most of the heroes are back home. You see them in Berlin on the Kurfürstendamm."

"Drink, that will clear your mind."

They drank, and the vodka helped. After so much water, it restored balance to the stomach. It was now raining only lightly. Ernst lit two cigarettes.

"Funny. Before the attack, a hangover lasts all day. Tomorrow, when it all breaks loose and we're up to our necks in it, the hangover will just vanish."

"You don't have time to think about it."

"I wonder if there are many who aren't thinking now?"

Ernst didn't answer. They smoked in silence. It rained all night.

At 02.15 hours, there was a counterattack by two Russian companies against Hill 228.6, but it was repulsed.

At 03.00 hours, the two Panzergrenadier-Regimenter moved forward. According to the statements of prisoners, the Artillerie's preparation fire starting at 03.15 hours was extremely well-placed.

At 03.15 hours, the Sturmgeschützabteilung and the Tiger-Kompanie moved forward.

13.3.1943: House-to-house fighting in Charkow. Panzergrenadiere move forward in conjunction with a Panzer. The last Grenadier is holding a magnetic anti-tank hollow charge in his hand to take care of enemy

-13.3.1943: Panzergrenadiers from the III./1.Panzergrenadier-Regiment have dug themselves or the night among the ruins of Red Square in Charkow.

13.3.1943: Fighting in Charkow. The commander of the 1. Panzergrenadier-Regiment crosses a street under the cover of a Schützenpanzerwagen.

At 04.05 hours, the 1. and 2. Panzergrenadier-Regiment each sent two Bataillone in the front line to begin the attack.

The entire terrain was riddled with mines, covered with barbed wire, and dotted with well-fortified bunkers and trenches. The main battlefield could be assumed to be about twenty-five kilometers deep.

With the last bomb, the penetration began with full energy. The 2. Panzergrenadier-Regiment managed to make it through as far as a tank trench situated in front of Hill 220.5. The 1. Panzergrenadier-Regiment's I. Bataillon (under Sturmbannführer Schiller), deployed to the left, also made it to the tank trench.

The force first had to dig in under artillery fire to its flank from the western bank of the Worskla. Paths through the mine fields were laid out, crossings over the tank trenches built, and the entire reinforced Artillerie-Regiment *LAH* and Werferregiment 55 concentrated their fire on Hill 220.5. The 2. Panzergrenadier-Regiment began its fight to take the hill. In five hours of tough fighting, with the support of the Sturmgeschütze and the Tigers, the Regiment moved forward meter by meter until the hill was in its hands at 11.45 hours.

In the fighting, Untersturmführer Prczesang of the Sturmgeschützabteilung had both his legs up to the thigh torn off by a high-explosive grenade. It is a tribute to the excellent organization of our medical services and the ability of our doctors that this man was delivered to the Charité in Berlin in the evening of that same day and that from the moment of his injury until his release from the hospital, he never developed a fever. When Obergruppenführer Dietrich presented him with the Eisernes Kreuz on the unit's exercise ground in Berlin, he asked the Untersturmführer how he felt. Prczesang answered, "Thank you, Obergruppenführer, I'm just a little shorter than I was."

The reinforced Grenadierregiment 315 was moved up behind the reinforced 2. Panzergrenadier-Regiment *LAH* at 11.10 hours in order to exploit the point of penetration to establish a bridgehead across the Worskla.

While the 1. Panzergrenadier-Regiment regrouped for its attack on Jakowlewo, the 2. Panzergrenadier-Regiment moved forward and at 12.00 hours captured Hill 217.1, about eight hundred meters northeast of 220.5. From there, it deployed elements to make a thrust to the east in support of the 1. Panzergrenadier-Regiment's attack. Meanwhile, the bulk of the 2. engaged in bitter close-range fighting to capture Hill 215.4, about two-and-a-half kilometers south of Bykowka, at 12.30 hours.

The 1. Panzergrenadier-Regiment set out again shortly before 12.00 hours. Under the personal leadership of the Regiment's commander, Obersturmführer Frey, it crossed the tank trench and captured Hill 224.2 in a well-executed attack.

The two Panzergrenadier-Regimenter were now level with one another. They continued their attack, and by 16.15 hours the 1. Panzergrenadier-Regiment's leading elements had reached the eastern outskirts of Bykowka. The 2. Panzergrenadier-Regiment, meanwhile, broke the weak enemy resistance on the southern edge of this town and pursued the retreating enemy force back through Bykowka. After smashing enemy elements in Kosimo-Demjanowka and east of Belgorod, the forces captured a line from Jakowlewo — one kilometer east of Hill 204.8 (held by the 1.) — Hill 234.8 (at 18.10 hours, the Division moved one kilometer to the north of there and took Kosimo-Demjanowka road) — northern edge of Kosimo-Demjanowka — west of the Worskla facing west as far as Point

214 on the road to Olchowka (held by the 2.) — hills northwest of Kamennyj Log (held by the 315).

Grenadierregiment 315 had been fighting its way through tough enemy resistance to that point.

Division *DR*, adjacent to the right, had captured Hill 233.3 with Regiment *Deutschland* and was now level with the *LAH*.

At 13.00 hours, the subordination of Pionierkompanie 627 was suspended.

At 14.30 hours, Panzergruppe *LAH* received orders to make its way through the second enemy line east of Jakowlewo on that same day (5.7) and to establish a bridgehead across the Pssel.

At 18.00 hours, the Panzergruppe crossed the frontline near Hill 234.8 and, just as night was falling, ran into an anti-tank front near Jakowlewo. The Division ordered the Panzergruppe to stop and to resume its attack in the morning.

The other units received orders to hold the line already captured for the night.[2]

In the course of the day, fifteen enemy tanks and three airplanes had been destroyed and eighty-eight prisoners taken.

The Division suffered the following losses on 5.7.1943: Ninety-seven dead (including three officers), five hundred twenty-two wounded (including seventeen officers), seventeen missing. The officers killed were Obersturmführer von Christen of the 1./1., Untersturmführer Dahlke of the 3./1. and Obersturmführer Kluge of the 2./2.

In the above-mentioned book by Soviet Colonel Markin, he wrote on page 54:

> "The heroic courage and incredible toughness of the Soviet soldier enabled us to move the 28th Anti-tank Artillery Brigade and our engineer units into the sector where the main thrust of the SS-Panzergrenadierdivisionen *Leibstandarte* and *Totenkopf* [author's note: this should read *Das Reich*] had taken place. Five kilometers south of Bykowka, the 1008th Anti-tank Artillery Regiment moved into position. As cover for his medium-sized Panzers, the enemy deployed eighteen Tigers. [Author's note: we in actuality had only eleven.] The Soviet artillerymen hit four Tigers within a matter of minutes, setting them on fire, and two of them were rendered immobile. [Author's note: two Tigers suffered damage to their tracks. They were not made totally unusable.] The 1108th Anti-tank Regiment, joined by elements from the 52nd Guard Rifle Division, repulsed four attacks and destroyed eighteen tanks in one hour. The High Command of the German Heeresgruppe Süd, in order to move forward as quickly as possible, threw all its Luftwaffe forces at the sector, gathered almost three hundred Panzers together in a narrow section of the front, started to make a thrust along the bank of the Worskla, and evidently intended to go around the Soviet center of resistance. In the evening, the German forces formed a small wedge and broke into the villages of Bykowka and Kosimo-Demjanowka.
>
> Under orders from the Corps commanders, the 52nd Guard Rifle Division moved two regiments into position southwest of Bykowka on the west bank of the Worskla. The 3. Regiment of this Division installed itself north of Kosimo-Demjanowka in a defensive posture, and there, together with the 96th Tank Brigade, it checked the enemy's advance. In addition, the High Command of the 6th Guard Army deployed elements of the 51st Guard Rifle Division to move forward from the second echelon. The enemy's advance to the north was stopped."

Orders for 6.7.1943:

"SS-*DR* and *LAH* are to attack the enemy position southeast of Jakowlewo on 6.7 and, after making their breakthrough, are to reach those objectives already ordered for 5.7."

The breakthrough was set to occur at 04.30 hours.

6.7.1943 (see sketch 22): Reconnaissance forces sent out at dawn reported that the hills south of Jakowlewo (held by the 1. Regiment) and west of Kosimo-Demjanowka, the town Olchowka (held by the 2. Regiment), and the Terkowjy ravine south of Bykowka (held by the 315. Regiment) were occupied by strong enemy troops.

At 07.30 hours, the reinforced 1. Panzergrenadier-Regiment, after concentrated fire from the entire Artillerie-Regiment *LAH* and Werferregiment 55, began its attack on Hill 243.2 east of Jakowlewo.

At 09.45 hours, the Regiment was successful in breaking through the well-mined, barbed wire-covered positions near Hill 243.2.

Grenadierregiment 315 pulled its elements back from the Terkowjy ravine in order to made a massive sweep along the Worskla from north to south on Strelezkoje.

At 11.45 hours, the II. SS-Panzerkorps ordered the *LAH* to move through Lutschki. It was not to cross the road north of Lutschki, because the unit adjacent on the left was lagging behind.

By 13.30 hours, the 1. Panzergrenadier-Regiment *LAH* had taken Hill 230.5 in tough fighting for every meter of the trench. With that victory, an important precondition for the deployment of the Panzergruppe had been created.

At 13.00 hours, the Division's commander personally moved the Panzergruppe forward for its breakthrough via northern Lutschki and Teterewino to the Pssel sector.

At 13.15 hours, there was an enemy counterthrust with thirty-eight tanks east of Jakowlewo against the 1. Panzergrenadier-Regiment. Another followed at 14.00 hours with seven tanks from Olchowka against the I./2. The tank attack from Jakowlewo ran into Panzergruppe *LAH*, which had just set out. The Panzergruppe knocked out eight enemy tanks and pushed his counterattack back. Three enemy tanks were spotted by the Stukas as they attempted to escape; they were observed moving from the west toward Pokrowka (three kilometers north of Jakowlewo).

At 14.00 hours, Grenadierregiment 315 was once again subordinated to the 167. Infanteriedivision.

At 14.30 hours, the Panzergruppe received a new shipment of ammunition and set out once again. The entire Panzerjägerabteilung was subordinated to the reinforced 1. Panzergrenadier-Regiment.

At 15.35 hours, an enemy battalion attacked Kosimo-Demjanowka from the west and was beaten back with bloody losses.

At 16.30, the Panzergruppe had moved through Lutschki and was attacking Teterewino. Untersturmführer Gührs, leader of a Kampfwagenkanonenzug [armoured gun platoon] in the III. (armoured)/2., reported on the attack as follows:

"Elements of the Panzers and of the Aufklärungsabteilung were in front of us. We turned northeast and attacked at top speed with all our Schützenpanzerwagens. On a broad front, we rode next to the Aufklärungsabteilung and the Panzers in an attempt to reach the Pssel. Suddenly, it all seemed over for us. There were mines all over the road and the open ground. There were anti-tank guns and tanks behind a tank trench on the hill in front of us. Four of our Panzers hit mines. The air support officer travelling with us in his Schützenpanzerwagen also flew into the air. We could still capture Teterewino. But could we stay there? It was getting darker. We were worried about our flanks, so we set up defenses. I stayed at the Bataillon headquarters for the night. At 01.30 hours, there was a call from the 12. Kompanie (under Obersturmführer Preuß). They had six Russian tanks in front of them. The 13. reported having even more. Remarkably, we hardly got excited. We defended ourselves. In the morning, the Russians took a beating. We destroyed five of his sixteen tanks. Six Russians deserted and came to us. They said that they belonged to a Tank Corps which had only moved out from Moscow on 3.7."

At 19.15 hours, the Chef of the Generalstab of the II. SS-Panzerkorps informed the Ia that a crisis situation was building. The enemy had moved strong tank forces from the northeast into the area Rhoshdestwenka — Krzjukowo — Nowje Losy, and numerous tanks with infantry had been moved across the Donez near Nepchajewo, a fact which had not been noticed at first.

The Korps ordered a reinforced Bataillon under the command of a Regimental commander to set out immediately for northern Lutschki, where it was to provide cover for the march route to the west and northwest and establish contact with the Panzergruppe in Teterewino. For the rest, the Division's orders remained the same.

At 19.30 hours, the 2. Panzergrenadier-Regiment received orders to perform the above-mentioned mission. It was to leave the I./2. in its former sector to provide defense of the Worskla against attack from Ssolnez to the northwest and west while moving the Regimentsstab, the Regiment units, the II./2. and its subordinated elements to perform the Korps' mission. The Regiment ordered the staff cars to move up immediately and at 22.45 hours began the march.

By evening, the following line had been captured: the hills two kilometers west of Lipowyj Donez (held by the *T*) — Petrowski — Kalinin (held by the *DR*) — north Teterewino — north Lutschki — east Pokrowka, two kilometers west of Uljanoff (held by the *LAH*).

Enemy losses: eight tanks, three stationary flame-thrower barriers, twenty-five 7.62-centimeter artillery pieces, two 4.7-centimeter artillery pieces, three 3.7-centimeter artillery pieces, two KV's with 12.2-centimeter guns, thirty-five combat positions, and one hundred ten prisoners.

Our losses: eighty-four killed (including four officers), three hundred eighty-four wounded (including twelve officers), nineteen missing.

7.7.1943: In the night, three Russian tanks with infantrymen sitting on them rode into Teterewino, which was being held by the Panzergruppe. A Panzer VI (Tiger) stationed to provide cover for the road fired at them at close range and knocked out all three.

At 00.50 hours, the 19. (Aufklärung)/2., marching at the head of the Regimental Gruppe of the 2. Panzergrenadier-Regiment, encountered enemy forces with tanks. It moved immediately into defensive position, feeling that a night attack was not advisable.

At 05.00 hours, the 19. (Aufklärung)/2. and elements of the II./2. moved through Lutschki and assumed the designated defensive positions. In the move, they knocked out five T-34's. The enemy continued his attempts to break through to the northeast and the east. The Panzergrenadiere had to defend themselves all day against tank-supported attacks which grew in intensity.

At 06.15 hours, the enemy launched an attack against Lutschki with the support of seven tanks, which we initially repulsed.

A second attack following a short time later, however, succeeded in breaking through into Lutschki. It came from about thirty tanks moving from the northwest.

At 08.50 hours, this enemy force was pushed back in a counterattack by the II./2. The 1. Panzergrenadier-Regiment was able to improve its position considerably by capturing all of Pokrowka and Jakowlewo. Two enemy tank forces with thirty and sixty tanks moving from the northwest out of Obojan were beaten back by the Regiment, with excellent Luftwaffe support, in tough, but successful defensive fighting.

After Stuka preparation, the Panzergruppe *LAH* set out at 06.00 hours along the march route from Teterewino to Prochorowka with Panzergruppe *DR*.

At 07.10 hours, the Panzergruppe was attacked by more than twenty T-34's from the north and northwest. A Panzer battle in cooperation with Panzergruppe *DR* developed, and it lasted until 12.00 hours. Then the enemy finally retreated to the north.

Rolf Erhardt, a Panzer driver for his Zugführer's Panzer in the 7./Panzerregiment *LAH*, saw the fighting like this through his observation window:

> "On a broad front on a hillock stood the 7. Kompanie, or as much of it as was fit for combat after the mine disaster of 6.7. Somewhere lay the town of Teterewino. Behind us lay the smoking ruins of the Russians' first wave of tanks, in front of us stood an inpenetrable wall. Dozens of T-34's from the main tank wave, which we later would defeat in fierce combat. A wall of steel and fire. In the middle, the infantry: our Panzergrenadiere, getting run over; Russians, sitting on the T-34's or being pushed forward in the fighting between the tanks.
>
> The day before, Zugführer Untersturmführer Weiser had climbed into my Panzer IV because his vehicle was still under repair. He was coming back from his honeymoon furlough; he was still wearing his dress uniform, since he had had no chance to get his field uniform. We looked at the pictures from his wedding, everyone crowding around. For me as Panzer driver, my experiences since 5.7 had consisted of one big bang when I ran over a mine on 6.7 and then some insignificant deployments. The day before had certainly not produced anything earth-shattering. The tank trench cost us a lot of time, and by evening we gladly handed over night defensive duty to the Panzergrenadiere of the III. Bataillon of the 2. Panzergrenadier-Regiment not far from our position. We then moved to a slope on the back of the hill and crawled up for the night in our cubby-holes under the Panzers, with the reassuring feeling of twenty-four tonnes of steel above our heads.

We just ignored the fact that more than one tonne of that was highly explosive.
After an extremely early wake-up call, we got orders and were assigned to attack forces: 'Start the motors! Climb in! Ready for attack!' While we were still putting away our bed gear, Untersturmführer Weiser came running in long strides from the direction of the headquarters and yelled, 'Hurry up! Enemy tanks!' Then there was an explosion, and the first T-34 burst into flames, not two hundred meters away. One of the Stab Panzers had hit it with its 5-centimeter gun. Now we did not need orders to know what to do. We moved out and in within minutes had knocked out four T-34's at very close range. The other Panzers of the 7. Kompanie had had similar success. Slowly, we got control of the situation. The radio messages turned back into normal orders. For the moment and for as far as we could see, we were masters of the situation. But what was on its way?
The recitation of detailed orders for a number of shifts in position was suddenly interrupted: we heard 'Georg' talking to 'Irene,' knowing that 'Georg' was the leader of the first Zug, Obersturmführer Hoffmann, and 'Irene' the Chef of the 7. Kompanie, Hauptsturmführer Tiemann. In a few sentences, the following became clear: an infantry messenger had reported that Sturmbannführer Peiper, commander of the III./2., was wounded and surrounded by Russians and was requesting that someone come bail him out. Everyone who heard it knew exactly what had to happen. The wall of smoke and fire was a barrier to both friend and foe. We observed every movement. Any T-34 breaking through would not make it fifty meters without being turned into a sieve by our shells. How deep was the smoke zone? Would it be possible to use it as cover to make it to Peiper's command post? All these questions were going through our heads. What must have been happening to the Chef, Hauptsturmführer Tiemann, who had to decide to whom he should give the order to go fetch him? It was clear to us all that an attempt had to be made. The next message was from 'Irene' to 'Walter.' That was us. 'Your position is the best. Take the messenger into the Zugführer's Panzer and try to save Peiper. Drive like hell, it's your only chance!' With the word 'hell,' I knew what the situation was. That kind of talk just wasn't in our Chef's vocabulary. It showed how upset he was. Untersturmführer Weiser confirmed receiving the message, gave the necessary orders to the Panzers in our Zug, and picked up the messenger. 'Driver, march!' was his order to me. In moments, the smoke was closing in around us; I had to drive slowly so as not to run into things. The images before my window were like pictures from a silent movie: wrecks, flames, ghostly figures with Russian helmets. Shell after shell. Suddenly a heavy hit somewhere. Time to correct the course? How were we supposed to find the command post in this chaos? The messenger had no way of orienting himself, particularly since he was shut up in the turret. Weiser radioed several times, asking for more covering fire, and ordered the other vehicles to stay back. He reported that shells were hitting, and that he would go on alone with his Panzer. Then the final message: 'Am receiving fire from anti-tank rifles and light anti-tank guns. Orientation impossible. Nevertheless, will keep going.' In all the excitement, not one of us noticed that we were not getting any confirmation messages or any orders from outside. When had the antenna given up the ghost? There was no connection to

us anymore from outside. No orders. No end in sight for this hopeless undertaking.
The whole thing probably lasted a shorter time that it takes to read this. The on-board intercom was still working. We were riding right toward the enemy, in the middle of the enemy. Was that a German Schützen-panzerwagen I just saw? German helmets? Gone! Russians once again! Suddenly the alarmed cry: 'T-34 at two o'clock. Load a tank shell! Fire!' The gunner reported that the turret was stuck. It was really becoming serious. 'Driver, aim with the Panzer, turn right!' came the order. I moved up, drove in third gear, really needing to shift gear but knowing I didn't have time. Turned the Panzer around. Suddenly an explosion, then silence! One look at the tachometer told me: the motor was not running. Was it just stalled, or was it hit? Ignition; it ran! I asked, 'What should I do?' The radio operator pulled down my earphones and shouted, 'The gunner is dead. On-board communications are dead.' I yelled back, 'Tell the loader to ask what I should do!' The answer came: 'The commander is dead.' All that ran through my head was, 'Okay, driver, it's up to you.' In the seconds which had passed since the shell had hit our gunner side, I had seen Russians storming toward us. I drove on and suddenly saw our opponent, the T-34, at most one hundred meters away. Was its gun moving? I turned around ninety degrees, and there was an explosion. I was probably only a fraction of a second faster than he. My sixth sense steered me behind a wreck, which served to shield me from him. One more ninety-degree turn, that sure felt like the way home. The messenger had jumped out in the middle of the Russians, I discovered, and our loader was wounded. I was still far from safe. I made it out of the smoke and saw Unterscharführer Harald Stein and his vehicle. The glass in my window was now too shattered to see out of. I drove with my head out of the hatch, and Stein motioned me in the right direction. Hauptsturmführer Tiemann motioned me to drive on; Stein was covering me with his gun at six o'clock. At the tank trench, the radio operator climbed out with the wounded loader and went to the medic's station. I was alone. Someone later counted the direct hits on my Panzer. The men passed around the glass from my observation window to look at. They counted seventeen infantry hits and three from the tanks."

The commander of the III. (armoured)/2., Sturmbannführer Peiper, had in the meantime been brought back by another party safe and sound.

By nightfall, there was still some tank fighting underway. The Panzergruppe was, in the course of it, able to capture the area west of Iwanowski — Wysselok.

The Division used the Panzergrenadier-Regiment to hold the line north Lutschki — Jablotschki (held by the 2.) — hill southeast of Bol. Majatschki — north and east Pokrowka (held by the 1.).

Enemy losses: forty-one tanks (a later, more exact tally brought the number to seventy-five), twelve planes, twenty-three artillery pieces, thirteen deserters, and two hundred forty-four prisoners.

Our losses: twenty-four dead (including one officer), one hundred sixty-four wounded (including two officers), and two missing.

Total number of prisoners and of captured materiel up to and including 7.7.1943: twelve planes, one hundred twenty-three tanks, thirty-seven artillery pieces, thirteen deserters, and two hundred fifty-nine prisoners.[3]

The situation: the massed enemy tank forces had been deployed sooner than expected, and the 4. Panzerarmee stood opposite not just the IInd Guard Corps but two additional Tanks Corps from the 1st Soviet Tank Army. Both flanks of the II. SS-Panzerkorps were threatened. For that reason, the 167. Infanteriedivision, formerly deployed in the southern section of the western flank, was moved to the east to relieve the SS-Panzergrenadierdivision *Totenkopf*. The XXXXVIII. Panzerkorps was also deployed to destroy the enemy forces on our Korps' western flank. Division *Totenkopf* was to be moved up next to the *LAH* to its left to reinforce the attack wedge of the II. SS-Panzerkorps.

Late in the evening, the Panzerarmee Oberkommando decided to concentrate all its available forces for an attack against the strong enemy forces facing the Armee's northern front.[4]

Orders for 8.7.1943:

> "After assembling its attack forces by 06.00 hours with the main point of concentration on the right wing of its sector as far as the road from Belgorod to Obojan, the *LAH* is to move left of Panzergrenadierdivision *DR* and is to establish contact with the XXXXVIII. Panzerkorps north of Nowosselowka.
> Elements should also be moved out of the Lutschki area, turned from the west to the south, and deployed to capture Bol. Majatschki. The completion of the preparations should be reported to the Korps. The start of the attack will be given by order."

d) 8.7.1943 - 10.7.1943: Thrust to the north

8.7.1943 (see sketch 23): At 05.00 hours, the reinforced 1. Panzergrenadier-Regiment *LAH* (Sturmgeschützabteilung *LAH*) left for its attack on Bol. Majatschki. At 07.10 hours, it reported the capture of the town.

At 06.45 hours, thirteen Russian tanks moving out of Mal. Majatschki attacked the positions of the II./2. north of North Lutschki. The attack was repulsed. (See the entry for 11.30 hours.)

At 08.00 hours, the Panzergruppen of Division *DR* and of Division *LAH* set out for their attack to the northwest. Our Panzergruppe ran into at least forty Russians tanks southeast of Wesselyj at 09.20 hours. The skirmish with them lasted until 10.30 hours, when the enemy tanks turned south and attacked the I./2.'s combat outpost in Jablotschki.

The Panzergruppe regrouped and made a renewed thrust at 11.00 hours to the west. Starting at 12.05, it was engaged in serious fighting for Wesselyj. The town appeared to be fortified as the bulwark of the Russian defensive system. There were strong points on Hills 239.6 and 227.4.

At 11.30 hours, four T-34's, which must have somehow slipped through the defenses of Division *DR* near Kalinin, penetrated North Lutschki from the east. They were destroyed in close-range fighting.

11.45 hours: After a conference between the commander of the 2. Panzergrenadier-Regiment (Obersturmbannführer Kraas) and the Division (Sturmbannführer Lehmann) about the new enemy tanks moving out of the area northeast of Teterewino, the Pionier-Bataillon *LAH* was moved up to stand next to the II./2. just east of North Lutschki with its front to the north. This positioning was intended to enable the II. Bataillon to free up its forces. The Sturmgeschützabteilung was moved up to join the 2. Panzergrenadier-Regiment after capturing Bol. Majatschki.

At 15.30 hours, the I./2 launched its attack on northern Jablotschki on orders from the Division. The Division then moved elements from the II./2. to bring the battle line directly in front of the forest north of Lutschki.

In the course of the afternoon, the following locations were cleared of enemy forces; all were spots where enemy tanks had made incursions into our positions: at 06.00 hours six T-34's from the northwest edge of Pokrowka (one T-34 destroyed); at 11.30 hours four T-34's from the northwest edge of Pokrowka (two destroyed); at 12.00 hours four T-34's at the northern edge of Bol. Majatschki (all four destroyed). This defensive triumph was accomplished by the 1. Panzergrenadier-Regiment alone (under Obersturmbannführer Frey) with support from the Sturmgeschützabteilung.

At 14.30 hours, the Panzergruppe diverted some of its elements across Hill 252.5. In doing so, it was attempting on the one hand to relieve the defensive fighting of the II./2. on the northern edge of Jablotschki and on the other to surround Wesselyj from the east and south and to attack it at dusk.

At 17.00 hours, the Korps ordered that the enemy forces in Wesselyj were to be destroyed that same day, 8.7.

At 18.15 hours, the Panzergruppe reported the appearance of numerous enemy anti-tank artillery guns, probably an entire brigade. Two of our Tigers had their tracks damaged. These two had been put out of commission that afternoon east of Hill 252.5. Unterscharführer Staudegger, under attack from the north and east by about thirty enemy tanks, was able to knock out twenty-two T-34's with his own badly damaged Panzer. He was awarded the Ritterkreuz for his action.

The attack on the heavily fortified town of Wesselyj was postponed until 9.7. with the Korps' agreement to the change.

At 20.30 hours, the reinforced 2. Panzergrenadier-Regiment *LAH* received orders to move its right wing up as far as the southwestern edge of Teterewino and to establish a position adjacent to the SS-Panzergrenadier-Regiment *D*. The main line of battle was along the road to Teterewino. The II./2. joined ranks with the I./2. about eight hundred meters southwest of Hill 252.5 along the road. The reinforced I./2. set out at once, but its march was severely hindered by a cloudburst.

In the night, the enemy was quiet.

Losses for the enemy: one hundred forty-two prisoners taken and eighty-two tanks destroyed. Most of the tanks were destroyed by our close-range anti-tank weapons.

Our losses: sixty-six dead (including one officer), one hundred seventy-eight wounded (including one officer) and six missing.

The Korpsbefehl with orders for 9.7.1943 read as follows (excerpt):

The *LAH* is to move forces into the gap between the left wing of *DR* (one kilometer southwest of Teterewino) and its own former right wing. This gap must be secure before the attack can begin.
The Panzergruppe is to pull back behind the main line of battle. The Panzers should be repaired and made fit for battle. The subordination of the III. (armoured)/2. and the II./Artillerie-Regiment is suspended.
The Division is to move a Grenadierregiment out of the area north of Lutschki and pull it up into Ssuch. Ssoltino (including the town). Its right wing should be south of the dividing line between itself and Divison *Totenkopf*. It is to clear the terrain north of the *LAH*'s and 11. Panzer-division's defensive line of enemy forces.
After the *Totenkopf* Division arrives, the defensive line should be called back, and an assault force should be formed in the area around Lutschki.
The dividing line runs as follows, with the *Totenkopf* to the right and the *LAH* to the left: Hill 255.9 (held by the *Totenkopf*) — southern edge of the ravine one kilometer south of Mal. Majatschki — the school in Ssuch. Ssoltino (held by the *Totenkopf*).
The start will be ordered for the *Totenkopf* and the *LAH*. It is now planned for 09.00 hours.

The Divisional headquarters had been moved five kilometers south of Jakowlewo.

9.7.1943: At 04.30 hours, the 2. Panzergrenadier-Regiment reported that it had assumed the line assigned it along the road to Teterewino and that it stood ready for defense.

At 08.00 hours, the reinforced 1. Panzergrenadier-Regiment began to prepare itself in the forked ravine north of Bol. Majatschki.

At 09.30 hours, the Artillerie-Regiment reported that it was ready to provide covering fire for the attack.

At 09.45 hours, the Korps ordered the beginning of the attack for 10.00 hours.

At 10.00 hours, the reinforced 1. Panzergrenadier-Regiment sent its III. Bataillon, positioned adjacent to Regiment Baum of the *T*-Division, and the I. Bataillon, positioned to the left, to begin its attack on Rylskij and southern Ssuch. Ssoltino. The attack moved forward without encountering any enemy resistance worth noting.

At 11.50 hours, the reconnaissance liaison force of the 20. (Aufklärung)/1. established contact with the 11. Panzerdivision about one kilometer south of Ssuch. Ssoltino.

At 12.10 hours, the 1. Panzergrenadier-Regiment reported that it had reached Rylskij without having to fight, and that it had cleared Ssuch. Ssoltino of enemy forces. The crossing over the Ssolotinko river in the center of town had been blown up.

At 11.00 hours, the 2. Panzergrenadier-Regiment received orders to relieve the Pionier-Bataillon.

At 13.30 hours, the Pionier-Bataillon was relieved by the II. and I./2. and found billets in Teterewino.

The Divisional headquarters moved into the forest south of North Lutschki and was in place by 16.00 hours.

At 16.30 hours, the Chef of the Generalstab of the II. SS-Panzerkorps briefed the Ia about the conduct of the battle to be fought on 10.7. Its essential elements were: the *LAH*, adjacent on the right and left, was to move on both sides of the Teterewino—Prochorowka road to the northeast and to capture Prochorowka. The Ia pointed out the ridge of hills north of the Pssel, which had a commanding view over the left flank. The *T*-Division was to attack there.

By 17.00 hours, the Ia had telephoned all the commanders and informed them of the plans for 10.7. The commanders in turn conducted the necessary scouting and made the necessary preparations.

This day, a relatively quiet one for the *LAH*, was described as follows by Soviet Colonel Markin in his book on the battle of Kursk (page 83 ff.):

> "The attack, launched simultaneously along the entire line Werchopenje (held by the 11. Panzerdivision) — Ssuch. Ssoltino (held by the *LAH*) — Kotschewtowka (held by the *T*-Division), was conducted by strong German Panzer forces [author's note: Panzerregiment *LAH* was having a day of rest that day]. It ran into well-organized fire from entrenched Soviet tanks and anti-tank artillery, as well as from massive bombardments from our artillery and mortars firing from hidden positions. The enemy suffered considerable losses from the salvos of Soviet shells, which had been pulled together on the road to Obojan in the night before July 9. The German Panzer crews were not equal to the mighty fire from Soviets forces. Their thrust slowed down, and they began to pull back."

Our losses: twelve dead (including one officer), thirty-four wounded, and two missing.

Divisionsbefehl No. 17 for the attack on 10.7 was issued at 22.15 hours. Because of its fundamental significance for the following days' events, and because it mentions all the Division's units, it is quoted here in its entirety:

"1. *Enemy forces prepared for defense* are equipped with anti-tank weapons and tanks and are standing in a line from the western edge of the forest at Swch. Komssomolez to the railway line at Iwanowskij Wysselok.

2. *The II. SS-Panzerkorps* is to move out at 10.7.1943 with the *LSSAH to the right* and SS-Panzergrenadierdivision *Totenkopf to the left* on both sides of the Pssel and head northeast.
   Attack objective: Prochorowka/East — Hill 252.4 (2.5 kilometers northeast of there) — Beregowoje — Hill 243.5 (two kilometers northwest of Koritnje) — Kartaschewka.

3. *The reinforced LSSAH* is to move out at 06.00 hours on 10.7.1943 after the barrage by the entire Artillerie-Regiment/*LSSAH* and Werferregiment 55. After the Luftwaffe's preparation, the *LSSAH* is to move along the road from Teterewino to Prochorowka, capture the latter town, and hold it.
   First attack objective: Prochorowka — Hill 252.4.
   SS-Panzergrenadierdivision DR is to set out with the *LSSAH* and to capture the high ground two kilometers southeast of Iwanowskij Wysselok.

SS-Panzergrenadierdivision Totenkopf is to move forward from the Kljutschi bridgehead to the northeast.

4. *Dividing lines: To the right* between the *LSSAH* and Division *DR*: Teterewino (held by the *LSSAH*) — forest just east of Iwanowskij Wysselok (held by the *LSSAH*) — Storoshewoje (held by the *LSSAH*) — Jamki (held by the *LSSAH*) — Hill 230.5 (south of Prochorowka and held by the *LSSAH*) — road from Prochorowka to Prisnatschnoje (held by the *LSSAH*).
   To the left between the *LSSAH* and Panzergrenadierdivision *T*: Hill 254.5 (five hundred meters north of Teterewino and held by the *LSSAH*) — Wassiljewka (held by *T*) — the towns in the Pssel basin (held by *T*) — railway line to the northwest (held by the *LSSAH*).
   Between the reinforced 2. Panzergrenadier-Regiment and the reinforced Aufklärungsabteilung LSSAH: northern tip of the forest at Swch. Komssomolez — Swch. Oktabrskij (held by the Aufklärungsabteilung) — Hill 252.4 (held by the Aufklärungsabteilung) — Dumnoje (held by the Aufklärungsabteilung).
5. *To accomplish this, I order the following:*
   a) *The reinforced 2. Panzergrenadier-Regiment LSSAH* (the Sturmgeschützabteilung, the Tigerkompanie, one Kompanie of the Pionier-Bataillon, and the 5. Flakabteilung) is to attack at 06.00 hours on 10.7.1943 after the barrage from the entire Artillerie-Regiment LSSAH and Werferregiment 55 (minus one Abteilung). It is to attack the enemy's installations, penetrate them, and then continue the attack immediately on Prochorowka.
      Attack objective: eastern edge of Prochorowka.
   b) *The reinforced Aufklärungsabteilung LSSAH* (one Kompanie of the Panzerjägerabteilung deployed to cover the left flank) is to start out on 10.7.1943 after the 2. Panzergrenadier-Regiment's successful breakthrough. It is to move around the northern tip of the Swch. Komssomolez forest and is then to move through Swch. Oktabrskij to Hill 252.4. There it is to stop.
   c) *The Panzerregiment LSSAH* (minus the Tigerkompanie) is to stand ready in the area south of the road from Teterewino to Lutschki (excluding the towns) in order to be moved up behind the reinforced 2. Panzergrenadier-Regiment *LSSAH*.
      The subordination of the Tigerkompanie is to end after the successful breakthrough.
      The 6./Flakabteilung *LSSAH* is to be moved up to the Artillerie-Regiment *LSSAH* and subordinated to it.
   d) *The reinforced 1. Panzergrenadier-Regiment LSSAH* (the Panzerjägerabteilung minus one Kompanie and the 4. Flakabteilung) is to stand ready in the eastern part of Bol. Majatschki so that it can be moved up. It should prepare itself to capture and hold the southern edges of the towns Storoshewoje, Jamki, and Prochorowka.
   e) *The reinforced Artillerie-Regiment LSSAH* is to launch a barrage of five minutes' duration to support the attack. Its use in the continuing course of the fighting will be in cooperation with the reinforced 2. Panzergrenadier-Regiment.

Firing should begin as soon as there is daylight.
It should arrange itself so as to support the breakthrough into Prochorowka with at least two Abteilungen.
The 12. (10-centimeter) Batterie is not to take part in the barrage because of insufficient ammunition supplies.

f) *The Werferregiment* (minus the III. Abteilung) is to support the attack on the first position if its ammunition supply allows it. It is to use one Abteilung to support the breakthrough into Prochorowka.
Smoke will probably be used in the forests southeast and northwest of the point of breakthrough.
Firing should begin as soon as there is daylight.

g) *The Pionier-Bataillon LSSAH* is to subordinate one Kompanie to the reinforced 2. Panzergrenadier-Regiment and to stand ready in the area east of Lutschki for expanding the paths through the mine fields.
The commander of the Pionier-Bataillon *LSSAH* is ordered to cooperate closely with the 2. Panzergrenadier-Regiment *LSSAH* in clearing mines and expanding the paths through the mine fields.

h) *The Flakabteilung LSSAH* (minus the light and medium Batterie) is to remain initially in its previous area. The 6./Flakabteilung is to be subordinated to the Artillerie-Regiment *LSSAH*.

6. *Reconnaissance*:
   a) *Ground reconnaissance*:
   by the *reinforced 2. Panzergrenadier-Regiment LSSAH* as far as the line Prissnatschnoje — Skorowka, by the *Aufklärungsabteilung LSSAH* as far as the line Dumnoje — Werchn. Olschanke.
   b) *Aerial reconnaissance*:
   as far as the line Don — Seimiza river.
7. Luftwaffe action has been promised at the main point of concentration in front of the *LSSAH*.
8. Traffic along the march route should be regulated with particular emphasis on the Lutschki — Teterewino sector.
   The *LSSAH* has the right-of-way at intersections over the march of Panzergrenadierdivision *Totenkopf*.
9. *The main medical clearing station* will be ready to accept patients in northern Bol. Majatschki starting at 10.00 hours.
10. *The distribution point for ammunition* for the Infanterie, Artillerie, and Panzers will be *five kilometers southeast of Jakowlewo*.
11. *Fuel distribution point*: Imkerei five kilometers south of Bykowka.
12. *The combat support section of the maintenance Abteilung* is in Bykowka.
13. *Prisoner assembly point*: Bykowka.
14. *Communications* as follows:
    The Nachrichtenabteilung LSSAH is to secure radio communications between the 2. Panzergrenadier-Regiment *LSSAH* and Panzergrenadier-Regiment *Deutschland*.
    The trunk line is to be along the march route.
15. *The Divisional headquarters* are to be in Lutschki starting at 12.00 hours on 10.7.1943.

16. The regulations for keeping information secret are to be observed according to content and distributor.

The commander of the
Leibstandarte SS Adolf Hitler
signed Wisch
SS-Oberführer

10.7.1943: At 00.00 hours, the reinforced 2. Panzergrenadier-Regiment and its subordinated elements, the Sturmgeschützabteilung, the Tigerkompanie, the 1. Pionier-Bataillon, and the 5./Flakabteilung *LAH*, moved into its assembly area southwest of Teterewino.

At 03.00 hours, the 2. Panzergrenadier-Regiment reported the assumption of a new command post location in Teterewino and the completion of its preparations.

At 05.00 hours, the Korps informed the units that the *T*-Division's nocturnal attempt to capture the commanding position at Hill 226.6 north of the bend in the Pssel had been unsuccessful. That failure meant that an essential condition for the Korps' attack to the northeast was lacking. The Korps therefore issued initial orders as follows: "*T* bridgehead not established. Postpone start of attack."

At 09.45 hours, the Korps ordered the attack to begin at 10.00 hours. Because the bad road conditions had delayed the Artillerie's ability to move into position, the Division set the start of its attack for 10.45 hours.

After a short surprise bombardment, the reinforced 2. Panzergrenadier-Regiment sent the I./2. (under Hauptsturmführer Becker) to the right and the II./2. (under Sturmbannführer Sandig) to the left to start the attack. The III. (armoured)/2. stood ready, mounted on its vehicles, in Teterewino; its intention was to exploit the breakthrough as soon as it occurred.

At 11.30 hours, the reinforced I./2., moving rapidly forward, reached the bend in the railway line northeast of Teterewino.

At 11.45 hours, the reinforced II./2. pushed its way through the forest just west of Chomsomolez.

At 11.40 hours, the reinforced Aufklärungsabteilung (one Kompanie/Panzerjägerabteilung *LAH*) set out and attacked the northeast edge of Hill 241.6. The enemy, firmly dug in, offered tough resistance at first, but there were numerous deserters who came over to us.

At 12.45 hours, there was a Russian counterattack with tanks on the right flank of the reinforced I./2., but it was repulsed. Six tanks were destroyed in close-range fighting.

The attack by the I./2. and II./2. suffered extraordinarily from the enemy artillery fire coming from the hills north of the Pssel. The *T*-Division fought an heroic battle there the entire day, and by evening was finally able to establish its bridgehead.

At 13.00 hours, the two Bataillone, proceeding side-by-side, stormed the line from the southwestern tip of the forest in Distr. Sslojewoje to Hill 241.6.

In the late afternoon, there were scattered heavy rains, which limited our movements. The weather began to clear up at 15.00 hours. About that time, the I./2. managed in tough fighting to capture the northern edge of the forest in Distr. Sslojewoje. The II./2. meanwhile was working its way forward with outstanding support from the Sturmgeschütze and the Tigers onto Hill 241.6.

5.7.1943: The 1. Panzergrenadier-Regiment moves forward. The self-propelled Panzerjägers are providing cover for the flank.

5.7.1943: A Kompaniechef of the 2. Panzergrenadier-Regiment leads his men forward through the tank trench.

7.7.1943: The *LAH*'s armoured force advances.

A Panzergrenadier helps a wounded Russian soldier.

This hill was dotted with entrenched enemy tanks, many of which we managed to destroy.

It took the Aufklärungsabteilung and the two Bataillone until 16.30 hours to overcome the enemy installations and to storm and capture Hill 241.6. Localized skirmishes lasted well after darkness. For the night, the 2. Panzergrenadier-Regiment's right wing provided defense from the bend in the railway line along the embankment as far as the northern slope of Hill 241.6. The reinforced Aufklärungsabteilung provided defense on the northwestern slope of 241.6.

The 1./Pionier-Bataillon *LAH* dug up three hundred thirty-six mines in wooden boxes.

Enemy losses: sixty prisoners, one hundred thirty deserters, fifty-three tanks destroyed. Thirty-eight of them were knocked out by the Tigers and Panzerjägers, nine by the Sturmgeschütze, and six in close-range fighting. Twenty-three anti-tank guns were also destroyed.

Our losses: twenty-six killed (including one officer), one hundred sixty-eight wounded (including eight officers), and three missing. Comrade Mutterlose of the 2./Artillerie-Regiment offered the following report on the three missing men:

> "It must have been afternoon when we got a report that one of our self-propelled 3.7-centimeter Flak guns had made a turn into the forest just ahead of us to the right, and that Ivan had captured it there. I did not know what the gun's mission was, but this report touched me somehow. It stuck in my mind.
>
> In October of 1949, I was in a Russian POW camp, the Asbest camp in the Urals. I was working in one of the workshops, when a pleasant, nice-looking fellow prisoner introduced himself to me. (Unfortunately, I have forgotten the name.) He had heard that I was from the *LAH*. As usual, after the first pleasantries came the question: where were you taken prisoner? This man told me that he was one of the crew of that 3.7-centimeter Flak gun with the *LAH*. In July of 1943, in the attack on Kursk, his gun had driven through the fringes of the forest straight into an ambush and had been overcome without even being able to offer any resistance. When I heard that, my mouth went dry. Here was this man telling me the story which had so stuck in my mind.
>
> The tragic part of the story: after taking them prisoner, the Red Army soldiers had approached the gun's crew and asked each his age. The Ivans had then shot one after the other. He alone was allowed to live because he was the youngest. He was allowed to tread the hard path of captivity. It was an uncertain path, and a long one. Only one man from the entire crew of the gun did I meet. Only one!"

For 11.7.1943, the orders were brief: Continue the attack on Prochorowka.

This was the day on which the Western Allies landed in Sicily and set foot for the first time on the European continent.

Karl Wortmann, gunner with the 4./Flakabteilung *LAH*, made the following entry in his personal diary:

"The day was gradually giving way to evening. The march route in front of us was still heavily occupied by other units. The air was thick with swirling clouds of dust. I could not have watched the columns driving by much longer. I looked instead for the last resting place of our comrades, which was said to be someplace nearby. A little bit set back from the march route, I found a simple graveyard built by my comrades' hands. One wooden cross as simple as the next. The names on these crosses were mostly unknown to the other men who stopped to read them. But they meant something to me. These men had died only days ago, at the beginning of this attack. Their 3.7-centimeter gun took a direct hit at close range. Almost the entire crew was put out of action. Some badly wounded, others dead.

A memory came back to me clearly. In my thoughts, I could see the men now beneath me. Oberscharführer Georg Weidner, now resting under the second mound, had been my gun commander since 1940. In the Balkan campaign, we had lived through the heavy fighting at the Klidi Pass together and at Lake Kastoria. Here, in the Belgorod — Kursk battle region, where fierce Panzer fighting had been raging for days, he had stood at the head of his Flakzug and fought his last battle. I knew him all those years as a good comrade and a good leader. I remember those pretty days in Greece when we lay in the streaming sunlight after the fighting, only meters away from the tent of our Divisional commander, Sepp Dietrich.

He loved to talk about his Swabian homeland, about his wife and little son, who was his pride and joy. The pictures passed around in our circle, showed a young wife, smiling and holding the little one on her arm. Joy streamed from her face. It all passed before my eyes, as clearly as if it were yesterday. But the war's demands had put a lot of time between then and now. The war had grown harder and more brutal. Our circle of comrades had been torn open, and there was a gaping wound in it. Where are they all now, all the good buddies from back then?

I stood sunk in my thoughts for a long time before these graves and conversed silently with my dead comrades."

e) 11.7.1943 - 13.7.1943: Panzer battle around Prochorowka

11.7.1943: At 05.00 hours, the two attack Bataillone of the 2. Panzergrenadier-Regiment *LAH* set out, careful to cover themselves against attacks from the forest 1.5 kilometers southwest of Jamki. Bad roads had delayed the start of their attack on Prochorowka.

At 06.25 hours, the attack got stuck in heavy artillery fire from Hill 252.4, from Prelestnoje, and from Petrowka, all falling on the left flank. On the right flank, the Regiment had to defend itself against fierce enemy tank thrusts out of the forest southwest of Jamki. The 2. Panzergrenadier-Regiment reported the discovery of a previously unknown tank trench immediately southwest of Swch. Oktjabrskij.

The line reached by that point ran south of Hill 252.2 for the I./2. and in the basin southwest of there for the II./2.

At 06.30 hours, the 1. Panzergrenadier-Regiment *LAH* received orders to move forward as far as North Lutschki and to prepare itself to make a thrust through the forest north of Storoshewoje in order to prevent the enemy from attacking our right flank from that town or from Jamki.

At 06.45 hours, orders were issued to the reinforced Aufklärungsabteilung to join the northern thrust on Andrejewka and Wassiljewka as soon as the reinforced 2. Panzergrenadier-Regiment was once again in motion.

At 07.05 hours, the Artillerie-Regiment and Werferregiment 55 received orders to concentrate their fire on known targets north of Pssel in support of the move of the 2. Panzergrenadier-Regiment and the Aufklärungsabteilung.

At 08.00 hours, the Division requested a Stuka attack in front of the 2. Panzergrenadier-Regiment, and one was promised for 09.00 hours. A Stuka command officer was sent in a Schützenpanzerwagen to join the 2. Panzergrenadier-Regiment.

At 09.05 hours, the 2. Panzergrenadier-Regiment and the reinforced Aufklärungsabteilung exploited the Stuka attack's effect and made their move.

At 09.50 hours, the reinforced II. Bataillon (under Sturmbannführer Sandig), supported by the Sturmgeschütze and Tigers, penetrated the northern section of Hill 252.2 and, proceeding in an almost textbook-perfect advance, captured trench after trench in fierce close-range fighting. In this attack, the Batterie Chef of the 10. (Werfer)/Artillerie-Regiment *LAH*, Obersturmführer Bartels, and his entire crew were killed when their Schützenpanzerwagen took a direct hit.

Shortly thereafter, the reinforced I./2. under the brave leadership of its commander, Hauptsturmführer Becker, succeeded in breaking into the tank trench and even occupying parts of it. The 1./Pionier-Bataillon (under Obersturmführer Taubert) immediately started constructing crossings over it and marking paths through the mine fields.

At 10.15 hours, the Panzergruppe (under Sturmbannführer Peiper) received orders to advance. At 12.30 hours, it overcame the tank trench and attacked the southern part of Hill 252.2.

At 11.50 hours, the commander of the 1. Panzergrenadier-Regiment reported that his unit had moved ahead as far as the bend in the railway line and was prepared to advance on the forest north of Storoshewoje around noon.

At 12.15 hours, the Regiment's II. (under Sturmbannführer Hansen) and III. (under Sturmbannführer Weidenhaupt), covered in the front line by the I./Artillerie-Regiment *LAH*, set out to clear the forest north of Storoshewoje of enemy forces.

Günther Kress of the 11./1. reported on this endeavor as follows:

> "This was the hottest day of fighting for our Kompanie. We were the spearhead, and we lost contact with the Kompanien following behind in the tricky forest terrain as we advanced so quickly. The Russians succeeded in breaking in behind us, but our first Zug made a lightning-quick counterattack and cleared them away. We reached the edge of the forest with open ground in front of us. We assumed our position."

At 13.10 hours, the Panzergruppe broke the cycle of back-and-forth fighting in which it was caught and captured Hill 252.2. It then made a thrust into Swch. Oktjabrskij, situated in a hollow. The Stuka support for the attack on Swch. Oktjabrskij hit one of our own Schützenpanzerwagens, killing the entire crew, even though there was a Stuka officer riding with the Bataillon commander.

At 13.30 hours, the Russians made a tank thrust into the I./2.'s right flank south of Hill 252.2 but were repulsed.

At 14.40 hours, the reinforced Aufklärungsabteilung had to defend itself against a tank attack from Wassiljewka. Elements of the *T*-Division had just shortly before managed to penetrate the town. The Aufklärungsabteilung was faced with the enemy forces being pushed out of the town.

At 14.50 hours, the Panzergruppe got stuck in front of the numerically superior enemy forces, and both of its flanks were exposed.

By 16.50 hours, the reinforced I./2., proceeding along the railway embankment, had captured the forest southeast of Hill 252.2. The reinforced 1. Panzergrenadier-Regiment had in the meantime been fighting a tough battle, moving forward meter by meter until it had captured the southeast edge of the forest.

The line captured by this point ran Storoshewoje — western and eastern edges of the forest north of there (held by the 1.) — along the road as far as a point 500 meters northwest of Hill 252.2 (held by the 2.) — the hill just west of Swch. Oktjabrskij (held by the Panzergruppe) — eastern edge of Hill 252.2 (held by the Aufklärungsabteilung). That line's position was reported to the Korps, and it was not crossed again that day. The reason for stopping was the positions of the adjacent units on both sides. They were so far behind the Division's advance that we were outflanked on two sides. A frontal attack on Prochorowka would have resulted in heavy losses because of the strong enemy anti-tank and defensive artillery on the southeastern edge of Prochorowka and at the commanding position on Hill 252.4 northwest of the Pssel. This situation was reported to the commanding general at about 17.00 hours at the Divisional headquarters in North Lutschki. A suggestion was made to him to concentrate all the Artillerie available to the Korps and to focus on the *T*-Division's attack on Hill 226.6 on 12.7.1943. Only after the capture of this hill, should the attack by Panzergrenadierdivision *DR* and Panzergrenadierdivision *LAH* on Prochorowka be continued. After conferring on the telephone with the Chef of the Generalstab, Standartenführer Ostendorf, Obergruppenführer Hausser declared himself in agreement with that plan.

The orders for 12.7 were framed accordingly:

> "*The reinforced 1. Panzergrenadier-Regiment* with the Panzerjägerabteilung subordinated to it is to set out at 04.50 hours and capture Swch. Stalinsk and Jamki. It is to establish a position adjacent to the I./2. at the road beside Hill 252.2.
> *The reinforced 2. Panzergrenadier-Regiment, the Panzergruppe, and the reinforced Aufklärungsabteilung* are to stand ready to move in conjunction with elements of the *T*-Division as soon as that Division has neutralized the enemy's attacks on our flank along the Pssel and to capture Prochorowka and Hill 252.4.
> *The Artillerie-Regiment LAH* is to send an Artillerie liaison Kommando to the *T*-Division in order to support the attack by that Division on Hill 226.6."

Enemy losses for 11.7 (from the 2. Panzergrenadier-Regiment's attack only): twenty-one tanks (seven destroyed by Tigers, six by Panzer IV's, five by

Sturmgeschütze, and three by Panzerjägers), thirty-six anti-tank guns, nine artillery guns, and three hundred twenty prisoners and deserters.

Our losses: twenty-one killed (including one officer), two hundred three wounded (including six officers).

Our Panzer strength as of 11.7.1943: four Panzer II's, five Panzer III's, forty-seven Panzer IV's, four Panzer VI's, ten Sturmgeschütze, twenty self-propelled 7.5-centimeter Panzerjägers.

12.7.1943 (see sketch 24): The enemy used two new Tanks Corps (his XVIIIth and XXIXth) to attack the leading elements of the II. SS-Panzerkorps, with the clear intention of destroying them. Because the three Divisionen in the II. SS-Panzerkorps were at the same time setting out for their attack, there developed a tank battle of proportions never before experienced.

Its details:

At 04.00 hours, the I./2. reported an armoured enemy reconnaissance thrust, which was repulsed.

AT 06.00 hours, there was an attack by a force of regimental size across the line Prochorowka — Petrowka. About fifty enemy tanks ran into Panzergruppe *LAH*, which was just beginning its advance. The fighting lasted two hours. Untersturmführer Gührs, the Zugführer of a Kraftwagenkanonenzug [armoured gun platoon] in the III. (armoured)/2., reported as follows:

> "They attacked in the morning. They were around us, on top of us, and between us. We fought man-to-man, jumping out of our foxholes to lob our magnetic hollow-charge grenades at the enemy tanks, leaping on our Schützenpanzerwagens to take on any enemy vehicle or man we spotted. It was hell! At 09.00 hours, the battlefield was once again firmly in our hands. Our Panzers had helped us mightily. My Kompanie alone had destroyed fifteen Russian tanks."

At 09.15 hours, there was an attaack by forty enemy tanks from Jamki against the reinforced 1. Panzergrenadier-Regiment. Hubert Neunzert, a member of Kurt Sammetreiter's Zug of the 3. (self-propelled)/Panzerjägerabteilung *LAH*, reported on this day as follows:

> "It was about 04.00 hours in the early morning when a motorcycle messenger brought us our new orders. We were to provide defense at the collective farm at Stalinsk. We should pay particular attention to the right in the direction of the forest and toward the railway embankment. It was not much longer before we saw about twenty-five or thirty T-34's moving along to our right six or seven kilometers away, heading straight for Division *DR*'s battle line. They were too far away for us, but the Artillerie trained its sights on them and made sure that they did not pass our right flank unscathed. Then there was a silence. But at 08.00 hours, the magic began with a bang. Salvo after salvo from 'Stalin's organs' rained down on our position, with artillery fire and mortar shells in between. All in all, it looked like a preparation for a real attack, and it lasted almost one-and-a-half hours. A German reconnaissance plane fairly deep over the Russian territory, signalled to us with his wings, dropped a message canister, and released two violet smoke flares. That meant tanks. Left of the railway embankment,

there were also violet smoke signals going off, so there must be tanks there too. The enemy fire stopped at the same moment, and over the hill to the left of the embankment came three...five...ten... But what was the use of counting? Racing at full speed and firing from all barrels, T-34 after T-34 rolled over the hill, right into the middle of our Infanterie positions. We opened fire with our five guns as soon as we saw the first tank, and it was only seconds before the first T-34's stood shrouded in black smoke. Sometimes we had to lay off of a target because our infantrymen had jumped up on it to take care of the Russian infantry riding on top of the tank in hand-to-hand fighting.

Then, suddenly, there were forty or fifty T-34's coming at us from the right. We had to turn and open fire on them. All of a sudden, three bold giants among them raced off across the basin toward the collective farm. They captured the road leading to it. I did not have a chance to fire. The gun on the right wing had a jammed loading mechanism, and we could not seem to get it fixed. So we had to shift positions through the farm buildings. I had barely taken aim when I had to fire at my first T-34. My shell went past it, and the shell case got stuck in the gun. I ducked between the houses once again, and I was in front of one when I got the mechanism unjammed. A T-34 appeared right in front of me when my assistant gunner yelled so loud that I could hear him without the headphones, 'Last shell in the barrel.' That on top of everything else! I swiveled around to face the T-34 racing toward us at a distance of about one hundred fifty meters, when the next tragedy struck. The rear support for the gun collapsed, and the barrel swung up to point at the sky. I used the force of swivelling the turret to bring the barrel of my 7.5-centimeter gun down, managed to get the T-34's turret in my sights, and fired. A hit! The hatch opened and two men jumped out. One stayed put, while the other hopped across the road between the houses. About thirty meters in front of me, I hit the T-34 again.

After a shooting match with the Russian infantrymen and the tank crews who had jumped out of their damaged vehicles, in which our Infanterie provided magnificent help, we took off at full speed to get our gun out of the hole we were in. We raced to the forest between burning T-34's. With that, the Russian tank attack, supported by three or four waves of infantry, was broken and pushed back.

Everywhere, there were the shells of burning tanks, standing in a sector about 1,500 meters wide; about ten or twelve artillery pieces were smoldering there, too. One hundred twenty were supposed to have been in the attack, but there could well have been more. Who counted? Oberscharführer Sammetreiter was awarded the Ritterkreuz for his Zug's action in this fighting."

At 09.20 hours, there was a renewed tank attack from Prochorowka. Thirty-five tanks attacked Panzergruppe *LAH*, while forty tanks moved out of Petrowka against the fork in the road one kilometer south-southeast of Swch. Oktjabrskij. These enemy tank attacks received very strong artillery support and were waged at high speed.

In this attack, four of the seven Panzers used by the 6./Panzerregiment *LAH* (under Obersturmführer von Ribbentrop) for defense in front of Swch. Oktjabrskij were put out of commission at a distance of only about two hundred twenty meters. The remaining three Panzers joined the ranks of the advancing Russian tanks and moved with the pack of them into the fire range of the II./Panzerregiment *LAH* (under Sturmbannführer Martin Groß), located about eight hundred meters to the rear. These three could fire at the Russians from a distance of ten to thirty meters and make every shell a direct hit because the Russians could not see through the dust and smoke that there were German tanks rolling along with them in the same direction. There were already nineteen Russians tanks standing burning on the battlefield when the Abteilung opened fire for the first time.[5] Sturmbannführer Groß managed to bring this battle to a successful conclusion despite the crushing numerical superiority of the enemy; he had at that point only thirty-three Panzers. He decided to attack the advancing enemy forces on their flanks from two sides. His Panzers destroyed about sixty-two T-70's and T-34's in a three-hour-long battle which could almost be termed hand-to-hand tank combat. Sturmbannführer Groß and Obersturmführer von Ribbentrop were awarded the Ritterkreuz for this action.

After this heavy attack had been repulsed, which the Divisional commander and the Ia had observed from their advance command post on Hill 241.6, a small enemy tank force managed to penetrate the Aufklärungsabteilung's thin flank defense and to make it through into the Artillerie's positions. There, the enemy force was destroyed, either in the direct fire from the Artillerie or in close-range fighting with the Infanterie.

Comrade Mutterlose, at that time a member of the 8./Artillerie-Regiment *LAH*, wrote his memories of this day:

> "Once again, the turret of a T-34 showed its head. This tank travelled relatively slowly. On its back, clearly outlined against the horizon, rode the Red Army soldiers. Then, twenty or thirty meters behind it, a second, then a third, then a fourth. The crews probably did not believe that our two 15-centimeter guns would be willing to initiate fire. Two lonely artillery pieces faced these agile tanks. But the Russian riflemen on top did not fire a shot from their submachine guns, either. The T-34's reached the edge of the forest. I thought I heard the clear, commanding voice of our Batterie officer, Untersturmführer Protz, and simultaneously the dull boom of our guns resonated. Who could believe it? The Russians tanks just kept going. Not one tank flew in the air or was even hit. Not a single hit! They had not even received a scratch! Even the soldiers still sat on top, now ducking down. With that, the battle was practically lost for our two guns. Fate was against us this time. Before our gunners could reload and fire again, all the tanks turned their turrets and opened fire on our position with their high-explosive anti-tank shells, without pause and without mercy. It was as if they were sweeping their hail of shells into each and every foxhole. Shrapnel flew over our cover. Sand trickled down on us. How protected a hole in the ground can seem! We felt safe, hidden in this Russian earth. Whether friend or foe, the earth took us all in. Suddenly, the fire stopped. There was no command shouted, no orders, not a cry or a groan. Nothing! We jumped out of our hole and were horrified. Death had reaped a rich harvest here. Eight men lay dead. The bodies were horribly torn, two gunners shredded beyond recognition. Any of the gunners still alive were badly wounded. A radio operator and the two of us telephone operators were the only ones in our immediate position who had made it through

> unscathed. Without saying much, we fulfilled our duty to our comrades, helping those still alive, and pulling ground-sheets over those now silenced forever. The short, fatal drama of our firing position was at its end."

At 11.30 hours, there was a localized breakthrough near Hill 252.2, but it was cleared away by 13.15 hours.

In summary, we can say that during the entire afternoon, the Division had to defend itself against enemy attacks from up to forty tanks moving from the north, against an at least regiment-strength infantry force supported by tanks moving from the northeast, and against strong infantry and tank attacks from the east. The attacks from the southeast decreased in intensity with the approach of Panzergrenadierdivision *DR*.

At 14.10 hours, there was, among other actions, an infantry attack on the 1. Panzergrenadier-Regiment's positions. This attack also had strong artillery support and tank accompaniment. It is worth mentioning because the tanks accompanying the attack kept a respectful distance back from the attack spearhead. This attack, too, got stuck in front of the battle line under the concentrated fire from all our weapons.

From 16.00 hours on, the Artillerie was occupied in combatting the tank preparations in the ravine just east of Petrowka and east of Andrejewka, as well as the infantry forces north of Swch. Oktjabrskij.

Heavy rain showers limited movememt during the entire day.

The Chef of the 7./Panzerregiment *LAH* at the time, Hauptsturmführer Tiemann, summarized his impressions of the day in a letter:

> "Then began a period of very hard combat, consisting of an all-around mad defense striking out to all sides, often without resupply for an entire day. The Russians were trying to cut off our Panzer wedge from the east and north with masses of his tanks. There were tanks day and night. Four battles in one day. Then we were pulled back. With only half of my Panzers, and some of them in tow, I returned to the point of departure for this attack in the dark with rain pouring down. I had never experienced war like that, in combat against enemy tank forces outnumbering us by a factor of ten. It was a furious battle of biting in and chewing fast. Our Regiment destroyed sixty-two enemy tanks on this one day. My Kompanie, which made the first contact with the enemy, destroyed twenty by itself. Until today, they had only destroyed forty-three total. But I lost only one Panzer in the Kompanie. The Kompanie has become a pledged brotherhood. There is an esprit de corps and a spirit here; it could pull up trees by the roots. My Panzer was hit once. I got out of it in time, but the radio operator was wounded. Now my Panzer, my trusty 705, is back in the repair shop. I am writing you this letter shortly before a new battle. We have paused on our march behind a hill. The infantry and artillery fighting is boiling on the other side. Around us is the vast expanse of the steppe with its hidden Balkas. There is a wind blowing through the rain, and the sun peeked out for a few seconds. The fighting is moving away from us. In a moment, we will have to wrestle our way out over the infantry lines and thus deep into enemy territory."

In the evening, the Division held the front line: Storoshewoje (where it was adjacent to the *DR*) — eastern edge of the forest north of town (held by the 1.)

— Point 252.2 on the road to Prochorowka — northern and eastern edge of Oktjabrskij (held by the 2. and the Panzergruppe) — support points along a line to Andrejewka (held by the Aufklärungsabteilung), where it joined the *T*-Division.

Enemy losses for 12.7 (including later reports): two hundred fifty-three prisoners, three planes shot down, one hundred ninety-two tanks destroyed, nineteen anti-tank guns demolished. (These totals were contained in the report of 13.7.1943.)

Our losses: forty-eight killed (including three officers), three hundred twenty-one wounded (including fifteen officers), five missing.

It should be added that the commanding general, Obergruppenführer Hausser, was at the *LAH*'s headquarters that evening. He picked up a piece of chalk and declared that he could confirm these highly unlikely figures for the number of tanks destroyed.

Historian Dr. Ernst Klink wrote in his excellent work "Gesetz des Handelns" (page 238 ff.):

> "On the evening of 12.7, Generalfeldmarschall von Manstein was briefed about the 4. Panzerarmee's intentions. He concurred with the opinion of Generaloberst Hoth, that the enemy should be surrounded the next day by making a turn near Prochorowka to the north across the Pssel. The enemy's position seemed to make it impossible to wage a frontal assault on Prochorowka and overcome the strong resistance there. The results of aerial reconnaissance spoke in favor of an enveloping movement from the north. In order to secure the positions of the western flank (the XXXXVIII. Panzerkorps), there should be no further attacks to the north, and all available forces should be used to hit the enemy west and northwest of Beresowka. The enemy was not just to be pushed back."

From the Russian viewpoint, Soviet Marshall Schulkow wrote in his very factual "Memories and Thoughts" about the situation near Prochorowka (excerpted from the German translation, "Erinnerungen und Gedanken," page 172 ff.):

> "The high command at the front moved the 2nd and 5th Guard Tank Corps and several infantry divisions and artillery elements from other directions into the fighting in this threatened sector.
>
> In two days, the enemy lost at least two hundred Panzers and large amounts of other battle equipment. His Infanterie now no longer amounted to fifty percent of its original strength. On July 10, he regrouped his main forces into a narrower sector and threw them toward Prochorowka in hopes of overrunning our weaker forces there. On July 11, there was heavy fighting the entire day moving toward Prochorowka.
>
> By the day's end, a serious crisis had developed in this sector of the Woronesch front.
>
> Headquarters pulled the 5th General Guard Army and the 5. Guard Tank Army from its reserve and moved them systematically into the Prochorowka area. On the morning of July 12, it started the battle. For the fighting, the 5. Guard Tank Army had over eight hundred tanks and self-propelled guns at its disposal. The enemy had around Obojan and Prochorowka no fewer Panzers, but the morale of his troops had been shaken by the long battles with the 6th Guard Army, the 1st Tank Army, and the 7th Guard Army.

On the Woronesch front, an enormous battle of tanks, artillerymen, infantrymen, and planes lasted for the entire day of July 12. The fighting was particularly fiece in the direction of Prochorowka, where the 5th Guard Tank Army under General P.A. Rotmistrow had enormous success.
In the course of the day, the supreme commander called me from his headquarters on the Brjansk front and ordered me to fly to the Prochorowka area and take over the coordination of the fighting on the Woronesch Front and Steppe Front. On July 13, I arrived at the headquarters of the Steppe Front. The high commander of the Steppe Front, I. S. Konew, was also there. Toward evening, I met with Wassilewski at the headquarters of the 69th Army. The supreme commander had ordered him to travel to the Southwestern Front and to organize the attack there, which was to begin as soon as the Woronesch and Steppe Fronts began their counteroffensive. After we had familiarized ourselves with the situation and had gotten to know the enemy's actions and our own forces' response, we decided to continue the counterattack already underway with full force and to stick close to the retreating enemy's heels in order to reach the line in the Belgorod area which he had previously held. Subsequently, the plan was to prepare a force with units from both fronts and to launch an energetic counteroffensive."

The Korps' orders for 13.7.1943:

"The Oberbefehlshaber of Heeresgruppe Süd, Generalfeldmarschall von Manstein, wishes to express his thanks to and admiration for the Divisionen of the II. SS-Panzerkorps for their outstanding successes and exemplary behavior in this fighting.
The II. SS-Panzerkorps is to orchestrate cooperative action between the *LAH* and the SS-*T*-Division in order to destroy the enemy forces which have moved across the eastern and western banks of the Pssel in the area southeast and southwest of Petrowka. It is to hold the line captured by its outer wings against enemy flank attacks.
The DR is to expand the line it has captured to a full-fledged main battle line...
The LAH is to hold the line it has captured. On its right wing and its front, it should be fortified to a full-fledged battle line. The Division is to stand ready to move out as soon as the *T*-Division's attack from the northeast becomes effective, to destroy the enemy on its left flank in cooperation with the *T*-Division.
The T-Division is to continue its right wing's attack in the Pssel valley to the northeast and is to move forces as strong as possible (at least one armoured force) onto the ridge of hills north of the Pssel as far as the road from Beregowoje to Kartschewka. It is to force a crossing over the Pssel to the southeast and to destroy the enemy forces southeast and southwest of Petrowka in cooperation with the *LAH*.
New boundary line: between the *DR* on the right and the *LAH* on the left: northern edge of Iwanowskij Wysselok — northern edge of Storoshewoje — southern edge of Jamki."

13.7.1943: At 05.30 hours, after a peaceful night, two enemy companies moved along the road from Prochorowka to Teterewino, attacking the positions of the 1. Panzergrenadier-Regiment and the I./2. Panzergrenadier-Regiment *LAH* on both sides of Point 252.2. They were repulsed.

At 09.30 hours, the Ia was briefed on the situation by his comrade, the Ia of the *T*-Division (Sturmbannführer Baldur Keller). He learned that the Panzergruppe of the *T*-Division had managed in the night to reach the road from Prochorowka to Kartaschewka as ordered, but that he had to decide whether to pull them back from that position because the enemy had been attacking its left wing since dawn with numerically superior forces moving in from the north. A concentrated attack on Prochorowka could not be expected, as far as the *T*-Division was considered.

At 09.45 hours, after a conference was held with the Korps, the Panzergruppe *LAH* received orders to make an armoured attack with the limited goal of reaching the hills northeast of Swch. Oktjabrskij.

The reinforced Aufklärungsabteilung was to set out at the same time to launch an attack on Michailowka with the intent of solidifying the loose contact it had with the *T*-Division in Andrejewka.

At 10.00 hours, the Panzergruppe and the reinforced Aufklärungsabteilung set out. The Panzergruppe suspended its attack at 10.30 hours, when it captured the hill northwest of Swch. Oktjabrskij in a full-speed attack. But there it ran into a broad anti-tank front installed on the other side of the hill, reinforced with well-entrenched tanks. This installation completely controlled the ridge of the hills.

The reinforced Aufklärungsabteilung succeeded in penetrating Michailowka, but it pulled back to a line 1.5 kilometers north of Point 241.6 after facing fierce fighting in the town and heavy defensive fire from the hills north of the Pssel.

At 12.00 hours, the enemy attacked with one regiment on each side of the road and with strong artillery and air support.

At 12.40 hours, this enemy attack collapsed at our main battle line. Our defensive success is to be ascribed primarily to the Artillerie-Regiment *LAH*, the Werferregiment 55, and the concentrated fire of our heavy Infanterie weapons.

In the afternoon, the enemy's artillery fire decreased in intensity, but it revived with nightfall. The enemy was behaving rather calmly for the most part, but was sending out small forces on constant scouting missions. His particular point of emphasis was on the railway embankment, such that the left wing of the 1. Panzergrenadier-Regiment and the right wing of the I./2. Panzergrenadier-Regiment *LAH* were under constant enemy pressure.

That evening, the Division held the line eastern Storoshewoje — eastern edge of the forest north of the town — Point 252.2 — hills west of Swch. Oktjabrskij as far as the Aufklärungsabteilung's position, 1.5 kilometers north of Hill 241.6 (two kilometers north of Iwanowskij Wysselok).

Our losses for 13.7.1943: sixty-four dead (including four officers), two hundred sixty wounded (including six officers), two missing.

A description of the situation occurs in Dr. Klink's work "Das Gesetz des Handelns" (page 240 ff.):

> "Late in the afternoon of July 13, Generaloberst Hoth (of the 4. Panzerarmee), expressed his opinion to Armeeabteilung Kempf that the Armee saw no chance of continuing the attack to the north. In light of failure of the 2. Armee (the unit adjacent to the 4. Panzerarmee on the left), the situation to the Armee's west was creating considerable problems, since there was

only one weak Division holding a front sixty kilometers wide ... The operation's emphasis thus became defending what had already been achieved on the western and northern front of the 4. Panzerarmee and establishing contact between the II. SS-Panzerkorps (the right wing of the 4. Panzerarmee) and the III. Panzerkorps (left wing of Armeeabteilung Kempf.)"

On July 13, Hitler ordered the Oberbefehlshaber of Heeresgruppe Mitte and the Oberbefehlshaber of Heeresgruppe Süd to come to him in order to decide whether to continue or to suspend Operation Zitadelle. Generalfeldmarschall von Manstein pointed out that the decision really lay within the sector of his Armeen and that the enemy's operative reserves had been hit hard; he wanted to continue the attack under specific conditions. Generalfeldmarschall von Kluge wanted to pull his Armeen back to their departure positions and to suspend the attack. Hitler decided to suspend Operation Zitadelle, but declared that he was in agreement that Heeresgruppe Süd should destroy the enemy forces in front of the 4. Panzerarmee and the 2. Armee south of Kursk.[6]

Orders for 14.7.1943:

1) *Division-DR* is to continue the attack started on 13.7.1943 across the line Iwanowka — Winogradowka. It is to capture the enemy positions on the eastern bank of this sector and is to attaack Praworot as soon as the Panzerregiment has moved up ...
2) *The LAH* is to hold its current line at first and prepare itself to move its right wing via Jamki on Prochorowka as soon as the attack by Division *DR* on Praworot and Prochorowka becomes effective.
3) *The T-Division* is to hold its current position against any and all attacks.

Monument to the Ukrainian national poet Schewtschenko in Charkow.
We did not destroy any monuments.

7.7.1943: Pause in the fighting for the II./2 after capturing Jablotschij.

8.7.1943: The reinforced 1. Panzergrenadier-Regiment has taken Bol. Majatschki and is assembling to continue its attack.

Section II

THE OFFENSIVE IS SUSPENDED

a) 14.7.1943 - 16.7.1943: Holding the captured line.

14.7.1943: Aside from individual reconnaissance thrusts, the enemy remained quiet during the night.

At 10.00 hours, renewed heavy artillery and mortar harassing fire started up along the entire battle line, and it continued the entire day.

At 13.30 hours, the enemy launched a reconnaissance thrust with two companies from Michailowka against the positions of the Aufklärungsabteilung *LAH*, but it got stuck in our Artillerie fire.

Our own combat reconnaissance found more tank preparations underway in Jamki, reinforcement of the enemy positions being undertaken on both sides of the march route to Prochorowka and around Swch. Oktjabrskij, and massing of infantry forces in Michailowka. Surprise fire from the entire Artillerie-Regiment *LAH* on Michailowka temporarily scattered the assembling forces.

At 14.00 hours, the Pionier-Bataillon *LAH* received orders to deploy one Kompanie to occupy a boundary position between the left wing of the Aufklärungsabteilung *LAH* and the right wing of the *T*-Division.

The Panzergruppe assembled at Point 247.6 northeast of Komsomolez.

The *T*-Division had to withstand tough defensive fighting from the enemy for the entire day. The unit adjacent to the right, Panzergrenadierdivision *DR*, set out with its armoured force around noon and by 17.15 hours had captured Iwanowka and was attacking farther to the east.

At 18.00 hours, an inquiry to the Ia of *DR*, Sturmbannführer Maier, revealed that it would still need "a good while" to capture Praworot. The *LAH*'s orders had been to push on to Jamki after the *DR* had captured Praworot.

The Armee's orders for the II. SS-Panzerkorps for 15.7 were that it was to "use all its combat forces, pull together all its Panzers, and drop all other tasks in order to break the resistance of the enemy forces fighting desperately north of Leski in front of the III. Panzerkorps."

The *LAH* once again received orders at 21.00 hours to take Jamki as soon as the *DR* had captured Praworot. Its left wing was to hold its previous position, while an armoured force was to set out at 02.30 hours, move through Iwanowka, and reach the area just west of Point 234.9 (east of Iwanowka).

The armoured force was to be subordinated to the Generalkommando of the II. SS-Panzerkorps, which would deploy it to the south in conjunction with the armoured force of *DR*.

The Generalkommando received information that there were massive concentrations of enemy troops in Jamki and Michailowka. Over one hundred tanks accompanied the troops. It was becoming increasingly clear that the enemy's intention was to cut off the *LAH*'s salient. After evaluating this information, the

Generalkommando finally announced at 06.00 hours on 15.7 that it would not insist on the attack on Jamki.

At 21.30 hours the 3. (self-propelled)/Panzerjägerabteilung *LAH* (under Obersturmführer Woest) received orders to move into position on the western slope of Hill 252.2 to serve as a second line of Panzer defense. On the main battlefield, the heavy Batterien of the Flakabteilung *LAH* had been in position since 11.7 so that they could defend the air space above the *LAH* and repulse a tank breakthrough to the southwest.

Our losses: twenty-one dead (including two officers), one hundred fourteen wounded (including six officers), and sixteen missing.

Our Panzer strength: five Panzer VI's, thirty-two Panzer IV's, six Panzer III's, four Panzer II's, twenty-one Sturmgeschütze, twenty 7.5-centimeter self-propelled guns.

In addition to counting the combat-ready Panzers, we should also point out the devoted and enthusiastic work performed by the repair Abteilung. It had been in action constantly since 6.7.1943. On 10.7, it moved forward to Bykowka and on 12.7 set up a workshop in North Lutschki. The supply services, too, and especially the group under Untersturmführer Koch, must be recognized here. Moving provisions along bombed-out roads, often rendered slippery by the constant rain, demanded not only good driving skills, but also an iron will to help their comrades at the front.

15.7.1943: The preparations for the right wing's move took most of the night. At 06.00 hours, however, the Korps announced that the planned thrust to the south would not take place right away. The *DR*'s attack was stuck on the ridge of hills east of the line Iwanowka — Winogradowka. The rains had washed out the roads and made movement impossible.

Despite this, the preparations for the attack on Jamki had to be made. The enemy had strong artillery and mortar fire on our assembly area, and we suffered real losses. Finally, as has already been mentioned, the Generalkommando of the II. SS-Panzerkorps rescinded the attack order for Jamki at 06.00 hours. By 06.30 hours, all the elements affected had been informed and had been moved back to their previous positions. The Korps insisted, however, that the armoured force had to reach the area east of Iwanowka. After considerable delays in the march, caused by the road conditions, the force (the Panzerregiment *LAH*, the II./Artillerie-Regiment *LAH*, and one reinforced Kompanie of the III./2.) reached the designated area around noon. At 14.30 hours, it was once again released by the commanding general.

By nightfall, it was back with the Division. It moved into the area around Swch. Komsomolez to stand at the Division's disposal.

The enemy sent out reconnaissance feelers all day along the Division's front, with forces up to battalion size. A coherent system of enemy installations could be discerned in a line from 1.5 kilometers east of Storoschewoje — northern tip of Jamki — five hundred kilometers north of Point 252.2 — southern and eastern edge of Swch. Oktjabrskij.

There was an extraordinary amount of aerial reconnaissance during the day. "Franz" Frick, the indefatigable repairman for the bus used by the Ia's command office, wrote to the author:

"Do you remember the time I yanked the bus door open and yelled, 'Air raid! Hit the deck!'? And shrapnel the size of your hand came flying through the front of the bus, right behind your desk. The Russian pilots had spotted us in our patch of forest just before we shifted position. You just said, 'Franz, that was good.'"

Enemy losses: three planes. According to a report from the Ic of the *LAH*, a report which now can no longer be verified, the Division had destroyed five hundred and one Russian tanks up to and including 14.7.1943.

Our losses: twenty-four dead (including one officer), one hundred three wounded, three missing (including one officer).

Panzer strength: eight Panzer VI's, thirty-two Panzer IV's, six Panzer III's, four Panzer II's, twenty-eight Sturmgeschütze, eighteen self-propelled 7.5-centimeter Panzerjägers.

The situation: as has already been mentioned in the entry for July 13, 1943, Hitler decided to suspend Operation Zitadelle, while still ordering Heeresgruppe Süd to destroy the enemy forces in the western part of its salient. The operation's code name was to be "Roland." On July 16, 1943, the regrouping for this new operation began. But Hitler's order of 17.7 to pull the II. SS-Panzerkorps out immediately and to move it west of Belgorod as soon as possible for transport away from the front meant that Operation Roland was doomed from the start.

Orders for 16.7.1943:

1. Fortification of the line already captured to a full-fledged battle line
2. *The 1. and 2. Panzergrenadier-Regiment LAH* and *the Aufklärungsabteilung LAH* were to provide with the Ia's daily report sketches of its position in a scale of 1:25,000 with reconnoitered enemy positions marked.

16.7.1943: During the night and the following day, there was heavy harassing fire from enemy artillery and mortars. There was aggressive enemy assault troop activity and a massive enemy dive bomber attack. The Aufklärungsabteilung *LAH*'s combat reconnaissance reported that the enemy's front ran as follows in front of the Division's left wing:
hills just west of Michailowka as far as the road from Michailowka to the southeast, then following the road.

At 13.30 hours, the Chef of the Generalstaab of the II. Panzerkorps briefed the Ia of the *LAH* about the plans for Operation Roland and the measures to be taken in preparation for it.

At 14.00 hours, the *LAH*'s mission was spelled out in a preliminary order (excerpt):

"1) In the night between 16.7 and 17.7, the battle line should be pulled back to northern edge of Winogradowka — northern edge of the hill two kilometers west of the town — eastern edge of Point 258.2 — eastern edge of Wassylewka.
The LAH is to hold the line from the road between Teterewino and Prochorowka (inclusive) — eastern edge of 258.2 — eastern edge of Wassylewka (exclusive of it).

2) This line is to be reconnoitered on the afternoon of 16.7.1943 by the *Pionier-Bataillon LAH* (minus one Kompanie). It is to be occupied with the main concentration on the road and at the point of contact with the *T*-Division.
The reinforced 1. Panzergrenadier-Regiment is to pull back to this line and hold it. Temporary subordination to the *T*-Division is possible. This line will be held through 18.7.1943 according to current plans.
3) Order of the withdrawal:
right wing of the 1. Panzergrenadier-Regiment *LAH* and the Aufklärungsabteilung *LAH*,
then
left wing of the 1. Panzergrenadier-Regiment and the left wing of the 2. Panzergrenadier-Regiment.
Rear guard: middle of the 2. Panzergrenadier-Regiment.
(Orders for the Division's remaining units will follow.) ...
5) *New areas*: The reinforced 2. Panzergrenadier-Regiment in Netschajewka-Petrowskij,
the Panzergruppe in the area west of Teterewino,
the Artillerie-Regiment *LAH* and Werferregiment 55 in Greater Lutschki,
the Aufklärungsabteilung in the forest south of north Lutschki,
the Panzerjägerabteilung in the forest just north of the road from Greater Lutschki to Pokrowka,
the 1. Panzergrenadier-Regiment (after being released by the *T*-Division) in the forest southeast of Jakowlewo,
the Sturmgeschützabteilung in the forest where the Divisional headquarters previously was south of North Lutschki,
and the Pionier-Bataillon in Ssmorodino.
7) The Divisional headquarters will be north of the tip of the forest four kilometers southeast of Jakowlewo starting at 12.00 hours on 17.7.1943."

The Pionier-Bataillon started at 13.45 hours to occupy and fortify the new battle line.

At 14.30 hours, the Artillerie-Regiment *LAH* and Werferregiment 55 began to shift their position.

At 18.45 hours, the II./1. *LAH* was the first unit to disengage from the enemy, followed by the rest of the units. The operation was conducted without friction. Elements still in contact with the enemy reported having the impression in the first half of the night that the enemy was withdrawing to the east, as well.

Enemy losses: three deserters, three planes.

Our losses: sixteen killed, eighty-six wounded (including three officers), three missing.

The day of rest ordered for 16.7 had done the Panzerregiment some good.

Panzer strength: nine Panzer VI's, forty-two Panzer IV's, five Panzer III's, four Panzer II's, thirty Sturmgeschütze, nineteen self-propelled 7.5-centimeter Panzerjägers.

b) 17.7.1943 - 22.7.1943: Transfer into the area north of Stalino

17.7.1943: By 02.45 hours, all the Division's units had crossed the new battle line.

At 03.00 hours, the reinforced 1. Panzergrenadier-Regiment moved out under orders from the SS-Panzergrenadierdivision *T* and was deployed on that Division's right wing. The Regiment was able in its new position to repulse an attack by an enemy Bataillon supported by ten tanks.

By 03.50 hours, all the Division's units had reached their new billeting areas. The 2. Panzergrenadier-Regiment also reported that it had blown up the bridge over the tank trench and had laid fifty mines.

At 13.00 hours, the Korps informed the units that a significant change could be expected shortly. The Division was instructed as to the particulars.

At 18.00 hours, Divisionsbefehl No. 19 was issued in accordance with the Korps orders; it moved the Division into the area west of Belgorod. The order dictated the move there on two march routes and over two nights. The units were to execute the march in small groups of ten vehicles with fifteen minutes' distance between the groups. Armoured vehicles and Artillerie were only to march at night. Total blackout and total radio silence were ordered.

The Divisional headquarters were in the forest at B. Dolshik starting at 14.00 hours on 18.7.1943.

At 20.30 hours the march began, but it was hindered considerably by the march of Panzergrenadierdivision *DR* across its route.

The subordinations of Werferregiment 55 and Artillerie-Abteilung 861 were suspended. The Division watched these excellent forces leave with great regret. It should be added that the Beobachtungsbatterie came under the command of Gebirgsartillerie-Kommandeur 132 as of 17.7.

18.7.1943: At 03.00 hours, the commander of the 2. Panzergrenadier-Regiment (Obersturmbannführer Frey) reported that the bulk of his Regiment had reached its billeting area in Greater Lutschki.

At 04.30 hours, the 2. Panzergrenadier-Regiment was the last unit to report its arrival in its new billeting area.

At 17.30 hours, orders were issued to continue the march to the Charkow area. The order contained, in essence, instructions for the transfer of the II. SS-Panzerkorps to stand at the Heeresgruppe's disposal. The march was to be along two march routes, with the wheeled-vehicle elements beginning on the evening of 18.7 and moving toward the area just north of Charkow, therefore into the AOK 6's region. The tracked-vehicle elements were to be loaded onto trains at the railway stations in Dolbino and Belgorod.

At the close of Operation Zitadelle, the II. SS-Panzerkorps reported the enemy's losses (prisoners and captured materiel) from 5.7.1943 through 18.7.1943 as follows:

Prisoners	6,441	Personnel carriers	16
Deserters	561	Prime movers	2
Tanks	1,149	Tractors	5
German Panzers in Russian hands	18	Motorcycles	10
		Submachine guns	912

Armoured reconnaissance vehicles	3	Rifles	2,362
Planes	85	Mortars	150
Anti-tank guns	459	Anti-aircraft guns	150
Anti-tank rifles	562	Flame throwers	73
Machine guns	721	Multiple rocket launchers	28
Artillery pieces	47	Trucks	93
		Dead	4,262

Our own losses were not easier to take. The *LAH* suffered:
474 dead (including twenty-one officers), 2,202 wounded (including sixty-five officers), and 77 missing (including one officer).

The Oberbefehlshaber of the 4. Panzerarmee, Generaloberst Hoth, issued the following daily order on the occasion of the II. SS-Panzerkorps' departure from his command region:

The Oberbefehlshaber
of the
4. Panzerarmee

Armee Headquarters
July 18,1943

Daily order

On 18.7, the II. SS-Panzerkorps departs from the 4. Panzerarmee's region.
When the Korps with its three Panzergrenadierdivisionen came under the Armee's command in the second half of March, the great Russian winter offensive was at its peak, and it had torn the German front wide open. Under the most taxing conditions, the SS-Panzerkorps stood shoulder-to-shoulder with the Heer's units and took up the battle, bearing the brunt of the fighting in the great spring battles. With incomparable enthusiasm, the Korps threw back the Russian assault forces and with the recapture of Charkow and Belgorod transformed an imminent catastrophe into a brilliant triumph. After weeks of rest, which were really filled with tough training, the Korps started out again on July 5. It stormed the deeply echeloned enemy positions with a tried-and-true fighting spirit, beat back the Russian counterattack in bloody Panzer combat, and broke the Russians' onslaught.
I can only express my thanks and deepest respect for the II. SS-Panzerkorps for the behavior, toughness, and exemplary valor displayed during its subordination to the 4. Panzerarmee.
If the leadership assigns the Korps other, new, and tougher missions, I am sure that it will also master them as successfully as it did these, in loyalty to the Führer, for Germany's victory.

The Oberbefehlshaber
signed Hoth
Generaloberst

By 05.00 hours on 19.7.1943, the units had reached their designated area without any incidents worth mentioning.

19.7.1943: At 14.45 hours, a Division order for the continuation of the march was issued. There were to be intermediate billeting areas in Alexejewka — Bereka

— Taranowka (Area B), in Ssnamenka — Barwenkowo — Metschebilowka (Area C), and in Gorlowka — Konstantinowka (Area D).

The wheeled-vehicle elements were to set out along two march routes at 19.00 hours on 19.7.1943.

At 17.30 hours, the Chef of the Generalstab issued orders to the Ia of the *LAH* to the following effect: by the time the Division's advance personnel reached the Panzerarmee-Oberkommando in Gorlowka, the Ia was to make sure that the Division's movements out of the two billeting areas could be diverted in another direction.

20.7.1943: By 19.00 hours, all the elements of the Panzergrenadierdivision *LAH* had reached their designated areas.

21.7.1943: At 09.30 hours, there was a conference between the commanding general and the Divisional commanders at the headquarters of the Division *DR*.

The *LAH* received orders to move the units arriving from Area C immediately into assembly area Sslawiansk (exclusive of it) — Ssobolewka (inclusive of it) — Nikolskoje (exclusive of it) — Iwanowskij (inclusive of it) — Schkurky (exclusive of it) — Prelestnoje (exclusive of it). All units were to be through Barwenkowo by 18.00 hours. Any remaining elements should stay in Area C.

This measure was necessary because the Soviet 8th Guard Assault Army had moved out the Ist Guard Mechanized Corps and the XIIIth Guard Tank Corps on 17.7 into the sector west of Isjum and north of Sslawjansk. The Soviet units had made several breakthroughs throughout the frontline and had crossed the Donez at the bend in the river fifteen kilometers north of Sslawjansk, nine kilometers south of Krassny Oskol and south of Isjum.

The XXXX. AK had deployed the 333. Infanteriedivision, the 46. Infanteriedivision and the SS-Panzergrenadierdivision *Wiking* to seal off these breakthroughs.

The II. SS-Panzerkorps was presumably to receive orders to recapture the original battle line.

The assembly areas were to be defended to the north.

At 18.00 hours, the Aufklärungsabteilung and the 1. Panzergrenadier-Regiment reached their designated area and were in the process of assuming their designated line of defense.

The arrival of the 2. Panzergrenadier-Regiment and the elements following it was delayed by a cloudburst of one hour's duration. The units made great efforts to be through Barenkowo by 18.00 hours.

By 16.00 hours, the following had arrived from the tracked-vehicle elements: the 1. and 3./Sturmgeschützabteilung *LAH*, the 11., 12., and 14./2. Panzergrenadier-Regiment *LAH*, the 1. and 3. Panzerjägerabteilung *LAH*, six "Grillen" from the Aufklärungsabteilung *LAH*, the tracked-vehicle elements of the III./Artillerie-Regiment *LAH*, and five newly assigned Panzer VI's.

The Divisional headquarters were in an orchard north of Ssnamenka.

By 21.30 hours, all the Division's wheeled-vehicle elements had reached the designated areas. By this time, the following tracked-vehicle elements had arrived: the 2./Sturmgeschützabteilung, the rest of the III. (armoured)/2., one Zug of the 6./Flakabteilung, the 2./Panzerjägerabteilung, the 1., 2., and 3./Flakabteilung,

The Do-Werfers (Multi-Barrel Rocket Launchers) of the 11./Artillerie-Regiment *LSSAH* firing. Taken from in front.

8.7.1943: The Panzergrenadiere follow the Panzers.

9.7.1943: A personnel truck of the 1. Panzergrenadier-Regiment *LSSAH* has driven onto a mine. The troops riding in it are dismounting for the attack.

9.7.1943: A Panzer IV from the II./Panzerregiment LSSAH attacking Ssch. Ssolotino.

9.7.1943: The armoured force has finished its preparations. The tense faces show that the attack is just about to begin. A Schützenpanzierwagen of the III. (armoured)/2.

the 5./Artillerie-Regiment, twelve Panzer VI's, the 4./Flakabteilung, nine Panzer III's, and five Panzer IV's.

22.7.1943: By 15.00 hours, all the Division's tracked-vehicle elements had arrived except for one traincar-load of Panzer IV's.

The Division had assumed the following line of defense:

one kilometer north of Karpowa — Point 189.3 (three kilometers north of Sslawjansk) — northern edge of Ssobolewka — northern edge of Glubokaja — Makatytka — southern edge of Kolomijzy — northern edge of the pond one kilometer west of the southern outskirts of Kolomijzy — southern edge of Nikolskoje — Point 194.0 — Point 223.0 — northern edge of Wysskij.

c) 23.7.1943 - 25.7.1943: Preparations for the attack on the Russian's bridgehead over the Mius on both sides of Bogoroditschnoje.

The II. SS-Panzerkorps was to deploy the subordinated Panzergrenadierdivision *LAH*, Panzergrenadierdivision *DR*, the 17. Panzerdivision, and the 333. Infanteriedivision on 24.7.1943 to attack the enemy forces which had penetrated the bend in the Prischib and the area on both sides of Bogoroditschnoje on the southern bank of the Donez. While still providing cover over the southern edge of the forest west of Bogoroditschnoje, these units were to destroy the advancing enemy force. Subsequently, the 333. Infanteriedivision and the 17. Panzerdivision were to assume a connecting position in the Prischib bend and also to occupy the old battle line. A quick withdrawal for the Panzergrenadierdivisionen *LAH* and *DR* had to be assured.

That was the Korps' mission.

The Division issued Divisionsbefehl No.23 at 13.00 hours on 23.7.1943, containing details for the preparation and attack.

The 23.7.1943 was used by the commanders for the necessary reconnaissance and scouting. It would be superfluous to expand upon that, for the Division received orders from the Korps at 00.20 on 24.7.1943 as follows:

> "The *LAH* is to report as soon as possible its numbers for combat transport, including its replacement unit. It will be loaded into transport vehicles in the area: Gorlowka, Debalzewo, Stalino, Jassinowataja. The transport groups should be evenly divided among the four stations. A liaison officer must be sent ahead immediately. A second possibility might be a transfer into an area one hundred fifty kilometers away."

Only later would the Korps reveal that this attack, too, was suspended at the Führer's order.

24.7.1943: At 01.30 hours, the last unit of the Division received the orders to cancel the attack and to compile its transport number report.

At 12.00 hours, the Division released on its own authority a preliminary order for the march, which the Korps had indicated would begin at nightfall toward Debalzewo.

At 14.10 hours, a new order arrived from the Korps by telegram:

"The *LAH* and Werferregiment 52 (subordinated for the purspose of the march) is to set out on 24.7.1943 at 20.00 hours from Sslawjansk and to reach the area southeast and northwest of Artemowka. On 25.7.1943, the leading elements are to set out from the junction of the road and the railway line fifteen kilometers southeast of Artemowka and to reach the area Malo — Tschistjakowo — Grjeko — Timofesewkij."

The Division started the march as ordered, but heavy rains hindered it considerably.

25.7.1943: At 12.30 hours, the last unit reported reaching its intermediate billeting area.
The Divisional headquarters were just west of Artemowka.

In the night, Russian bombers attacked the Division's billeting area, but no damage was done.
At 23.55 hours, after the Division was already marching again, a new order arrived:

"Halt the march. Prepare for railway transport! Destination unknown!"

d) 26.7.1943 - 1.8.1943: Loading the Division for "Blitz-Pfeil-Transport" with destination unknown.

26.7.1943: By 00.30 hours, this order to halt was on the way to all the units. Contact was immediately established with the tranport officer of the 6. Armee in charge in Stalino, and a preliminary order for the loading arrived at 06.00 hours.
At 10.30 hours, the details were hammered out at a conference of the commanders. They left with the order for the advance personnel to be in northern Krassnaja Swesda by 18.00 hours on 26.7. The leader of the advance personnel was to be Hauptsturmführer Vögtel, the Division's Ic.

27.7.1943: At 00.00 hours, the Division received the final order for its transport. All usable Panzers of types VI, IV, and III were to be handed over to the Panzergrenadierdivision *DR* and the *T*-Division.[7]
At 01.50 hours, the Division's units received orders to move into the vicinity of the designated railway stations and to prepare for "Blitz-Pfeil-Transport" [lightning-arrow transport]. That meant that the transport trains would not stop to distribute provisions, as was the usual practice, but that the troops would only receive provisions while the locomotive was being switched.
The great mystery, particularly as to why the Panzers were handed over, began.

28.7.1943: By 03.00 hours, all the units had reached their designated stations.

29.7.1943: At this time, the Division's combat forces were loaded as follows:
eight trains to each Panzergrenadier-Regiment
seven trains to the Panzerregiment

two trains to the Sturmgeschützabteilung
one train to the Pionier-Bataillon
one train to the Nachrichtenabteilung and Feldgendarmerie-Kompanie
six trains to the Artillerie-Regiment
two trains to the Aufklärungsabteilung
one train to the Flakabteilung
one train to the Divisionsstab and the rest of the Flakabteilung
one train to the Sanitätsabteilung
two trains to the Division's supply unit and provisions Bataillon.

29.7.1943: The Division received a telegram from Obergruppenführer Dietrich stating that an He 111 plane from the leadership corps with Flugkapitän Dirr in the cockpit would pick up the Divisional commander and the Ia in Stalino on 30.7.

30.7.1943: After the necessary repair of the elevator assembly on the plane, the Divisional commander and the Ia set out around noon and headed toward Berlin. There, they were invited to spend the night with Obergruppenführer Dietrich in the Reichskanzlei.

In Berlin, they learned that the Division would be transferred to Italy because of the threats to the country from both outside and inside. The Divisional commander and the Ia were to report with Obergruppenführer Dietrich to Generalfeldmarschall Rommel in Munich on 31.7.1943. He was there in his private train.

In retrospect, one must admit that Operation Zitadelle was a mistake. The German military command had once again failed to exploit our greatest strength, the combat mobility of our Panzer units, and had instead made these previously well-rested forces run headlong against Russia's incredibly sturdy bulwark. Whether suspending the attack at the height of battle was an additional error, or whether it would have been correct to use the operation as a war of attrition, preventing the great Russian offensive against other parts of the Eastern Front, is a question which cannot be answered today.

In the context of his overall strategy, Hitler's decision to suspend the attack may have been primarily the result of the Allied landing in Sicily. This was the event for which he needed his mobile units free. So he was prepared to pull his especially combat-worthy Division out of the fighting and throw us into Italy.

It must also be noted that we dealt the Russians considerably more losses than we ourselves suffered. To be sure, the Russians could better absorb such losses than we.

But our Division was hit hard. Four hundred seventy-four brave soldiers of the *LAH* gave their lives. They rest in Russian soil, not to be forgotten by us.

Part 8

THE PANZERGRENADIERDIVISION *LSSAH* IN ITALY

Section I
1.8.1943 - 16.8.1943: ASSEMBLY IN THE TYROL AND MARCH OVER THE BRENNER PASS

a) 1.8.1943 - 5.8.1943: Unloading and assembly in the Innsbruck area

On 31.7.1943, Obergruppenführer Sepp Dietrich, Standartenführer Wisch (the Divisional commander), and Sturmbannführer Lehmann (the Division Ia) travelled from Berlin by plane and arrived in Munich in search of Generalfeldmarschall Rommel. After looking in vain at the District Command Post and the Town Kommandant's office, they were finally informed by an Oberfeldwebel in the transport command office that a private train had been standing on a side rail spur near Pasing since the previous day. We were finally able to report there as per our orders. While the Obergruppenführer and the Divisional commander conversed with the Generalfeldmarschall, the Chef of the Generalstab, Generalmajor Gause, briefed the Ia on the situation and the unit's mission.

The collapse of Italy and its departure from the Axis could be expected. The Division was to make an overland march from Innsbruck, where it would be unloaded from the trains, into northern Italy. Its first mission would be to secure the vital road link between the Brenner Pass and Verona and if necessary to disarm the Italian troops in an area yet to be determined, but probably the Po River plain. When asked, the Ic of the Heeresgruppe, Oberstleutnant i.G. Moll, explained that there was no documentation about the structure, strength, or billeting of the Italian troops in the Po region. The Ia's urgent request to move at least the Division's tracked vehicles over the Brenner Pass by rail was refused, even though the vehicles would probably be useless after a march over the mountains. The Italian railway would only take eleven trains a day over from the German railway at the Brenner border station. These trains were vitally needed to supply Heeresgruppe Kesselring, fighting hard in the south of Italy.

Obergruppenführer Dietrich reported to the Oberbefehlshaber of the Heeresgruppe that the Generalkommando of the I. SS-Panzerkorps *Leibstandarte*, still in formation, would be transferred with its troops on orders from the Führer into the southern Tyrol in the course of September and that he would set up a Korps headquarters in Meran.

Toward evening, the Divisional commander and the Ia travelled back to Innsbruck.

1.8.1943: The Division's advance personnel arrived in Innsbruck in the morning. The leaders of the advance detachment were shown their billeting area

12.7.1943: Panzergrenadiere sitting on a Panzer and returning from battle.

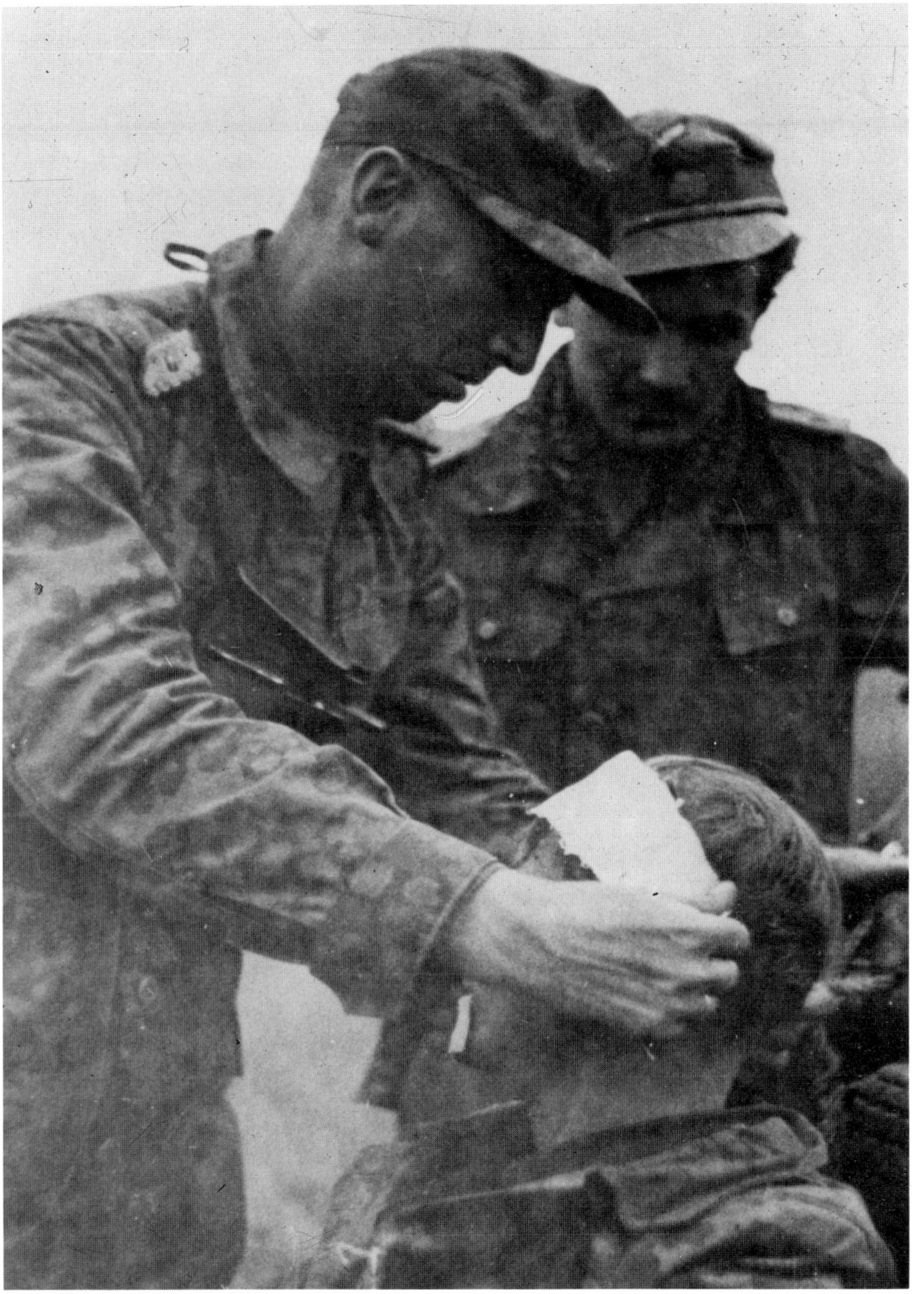

A unit doctor performs first aid.

from the Divisional headquarters in the Otterburg, across from the Inn barracks. The arrangements for unloading at the stations were made with the transport officer in charge.

At 20.50 hours, the following telegram arrived from the "Rest and relaxation staff of the Oberkommando of the Wehrmacht" (the code name for Heeresgruppe B):

1. German units are being transferred to Italy to support the Italian forces against attempted enemy landings.
2. As part of these movements, the SS-Panzergrenadierdivision *LAH* will be marched from its detraining point immediately into the area around Verona. The first day's march objective for the troops arriving on 2.8.1943 will be Trient.
3. Gruppe Feuerstein will be in charge of the march through the Alps and responsible for defending the designated assembly areas.
4. The orders for the continuation of the march and the objective for 3.8.1943, as well as the arrangements for starting later-arriving *LAH* units on their marches, will be issued in a timely fashion.
5. Your attention is drawn to the extraordinary difficulties of travelling on mountain roads.
6. Reports should go via Gruppe Feuerstein.

Because there had been no mention of a Gruppe Feuerstein in the briefing at the Heeresgruppe, it took an ingenious communications officer to discover that the commander of the Gebirgsjäger school in Mittenwald was General Feuerstein. The Ia of the *LAH* reported to him by phone.

General Feuerstein made known the contents of a telegram from Heeresgruppe B, which stated that the first four transport trains of the *LAH* were scheduled to arrive at the Innsbruck railway station in the coming night and that they would probably be subordinated to Gruppe Feuerstein for the trip through the Pass.

At about 22.00 hours, Gruppe Feuerstein issued verbal orders that the first units to arrive should be marched overland immediately upon being detrained to the area Trient — Bozen. There, they were to relieve the force under Major Brand (the remains of the 26. Panzerdivision) in defending that area.

2.8.1943: At 00.15 hours, there was an order issued by telephone from the Ia of Heeresgruppe B, Oberstleutnant i.G. Huhs, as follows:

> "The *LAH* should be stopped immediately. It should not cross the Brenner Pass before 3.8.1943!"

In the course of the day, the following arrived: the Regimentsstab of the 2. Panzergrenadier-Regiment, the III./Artillerie-Regiment *LAH*, and elements of the III./1. Panzergrenadier-Regiment *LAH*.

Divisionsbefehl No. 24 was given to them and to the commanders of the advance detachment. Its essential points were:

"1. German units are being moved to Italy to support the Italian forces against enemy attempts to land.

2. The *LAH* is to be detrained by Gruppe Feuerstein in the Innsbruck area, where it is to stand at the disposal of the OKW.
3. The individual transport groups are to be brought together by the Division into march groups, assembled briefly, and are to be set on the march to Verona.
4. *The first march objective* for the elements unloaded on 2.8.1943 is Trient and Bozen.
   The march objectives for the rest of the march groups will be issued as a supplement to Divisionsbefehl No. 24.
   All commanders are to report immediately upon arrival at the detraining station to the Divisional headquarters in the Otterburg to receive their marching orders.
   March route: Innsbruck — Brenner — Bressanone (Brixen) — Bolzano (Bozen) — Trento (Trient).
5. *March group A*
   Leader: Obersturmbannführer Kraas.
   Units: The elements of the 2. Panzergrenadier-Regiment *LAH* which have already arrived, the III./Artillerie-Regiment *LAH* (minus the 8. Batterie). These are to set out from Schönberg at 06.00 hours on 3.8.1943 and are to reach Trient.
   Immediately upon arrival, one Bataillon is to relieve the force under Brand, deployed on both sides of Bozen to defend the march route and the railway line. (Leader: Major Brand from the Wehrmacht office in Bozen. Unit: Panzer-Pionier-Bataillon 26).
   Mission: Defend the Brenner Pass railway and main highway, including bridges and viaducts, for bringing the rest of the Division over.
   Panzer-Pionier-Bataillon 26 is transferred to Pisa once it is relieved.
   Kommandant for Bozen: Commander of the Bataillon deployed there.
   Kommandant for Trient: Obersturmbannführer Kraas.
   The rest of the march groups will receive their orders upon arrival.
6. *Execution of the march*
   Under no circumstances may damaged vehicles be towed over the Brenner Pass. They should be left at the motor pool in Innsbruck to be repaired. Because of the steep climb up and the equally steep slope down, distance is to be maintained as soon as the Pass has been crossed.
   The top speed for all vehicles is twenty kilometers per hour.
7. *Regulation of traffic* will be performed through the units themselves.
   The *LAH* should establish a traffic-control staff at the German customs house at Brenner.
   Leader: Hauptsturmführer Vögtel.
   The commander of each unit is to report to Hauptsturmführer Vögtel giving his unit's designation, its number of men, and its number of units.
   Supervision of the march should be entrusted to one older, energetic Chef per march group. Stopping on curves is expressly prohibited. Passing individual vehicles is to be avoided. Exception: Generals.
   Every unit commander is to instruct his drivers personally on how to drive in the mountains.

8.-11. ...
   Supplement 1 provides special instructions for the supply units."

At 19.20 hours, Heeresgruppe B issued the following orders:

> "The order stands for the *LAH* elements detrained early on 3.8 to begin marching immediately.
> Objective: the leading elements into area south of Trient. The mood in Italy is growing ugly. Incidents are possible at any time. The troops must be prepared for that. Tactical march!"

This order was transmitted to the march commander by telephone. In the course of the day, the Ia sent his 2. Generalstabsoffizier, Obersturmbannführer Stoltz, to the Italian transport command office outside of Brenner to find out whether a polite request could not be made to bring a couple of additional trains with our tracked vehicles over the Brenner Pass. With cognac and a well-practiced affability, the Ib achieved a promise that starting 4.8.1943, two or three trains could be moved over the Brenner Pass into the area south of Verona. The agreement amazed the transport officer in Innsbruck.

3.8.1943: At 08.00 hours, Obersturmbannführer Kraas reported the arrival of his march group. It passed the traffic-control staff at Brenner at 10.50 hours and reached its march objective in Trient at 18.30 hours without incident.

At 21.00 hours, the Stab of the 2. Panzergrenadier-Regiment *LAH* reported assuming its designated defensive positions.

In the course of the day, more units arrived in Innsbruck. They were set on the march as follows:

March group B
Leader: Sturmbannführer Weidenhaupt
Unit: The elements arriving on 2.8.1943 were to set out on 3.8.1943 and to reach and defend the section of the road from Bressanone (exclusive of it) — Bozen (exclusive of it).

March group C
Leader: Hauptsturmführer Becker.
Unit: The leading elements of the I. and II./2. Panzergrenadier-Regiment *LAH*, the I./Artillerie-Regiment (minus the 2. Batterie), one Zug of the 5. (light)/Flakabteilung *LAH*, and the Division-Sicherungskompanie *LAH* were to set out at 05.00 hours on 4.8.1943 from Schönberg. The group was to reach the area south of Trient.
The commander of the 2. Panzergrenadier-Regiment was to set a Bataillon force marching from there to Verona and then to shift the bulk of the 2. Panzergrenadier-Regiment *LAH* into the area Rovereto — Verona.
Mission: Defense of the road Trient — Verona (including the towns) and of the railway line, including bridges and viaducts, from acts of sabotage.

March group D
Leader: Obersturmbannführer Frey
Unit: The leading elements of the Stab of the 1. Panzergrenadier-Regiment *LAH*, those Regiment units which had already arrived, and the II./1. Panzergrenadier-Regiment *LAH* were to set out from Innsbruck, and the

group was to arrive in the Trient — Bozen area (including the towns) at 11.00 hours on 4.8.1943.
Mission: Defense of the road and railway from Bozen to Trient, as ordered for the 2. Panzergrenadier-Regiment.

The leaders of the march groups were notified in writing that elements of the Italian army might possibly attempt to prevent the execution of the German orders. Emphasizing the necessity of the orders' fulfillments, the command urged the units to reach their designated areas without inciting confrontations. Armed resistance, however, was to be smashed.

At 21.00 hours, Sturmbannführer Weidenhaupt (commander of the III./1.) reported occupying his unit's designated defensive position without incident. The South Tyrolean population greeted the force with enthusiasm.

4.8.1943: At 11.15 hours, the reinforced I./2. (I./Artillerie-Regiment *LAH*, the Divisions-Sicherungskompanie, one Zug of the 5. (light)/Flakabteilung *LAH*) and the reinforced II./2. (the 12./Artillerie-Regiment) were put on the march to Rovereto. The I./2.'s mission was defense of the road and railway line from Ala (exclusive of the town) to Verona (inclusive of the town); the II./2. was to defend the road and railway from Caliano to Ala (inclusive of the towns).
At 21.50 hours, the assumption of the designated defensive positions was reported.

Orders for 5.8.1943:
The 1. Panzergrenadier LAH (minus the I. Bataillon), reinforced by the I./Artillerie-Regiment LAH was to set out from Bozen at 05.00 hours on 5.8.1943 for the Mantua area. Its mission was defense of the road and railway line Mantua — Verona.
The 2./Sanitätsabteilung LAH was to set out at 05.00 hours on 5.8 from Innsbruck for Salorno, and it was to continue its march on 6.8 to the Verona area. A *medical clearing station* was to be set up there.
The advance command of Panzerregiment LAH was to reach Parma on 5.8 and to take possession of the newly assigned Panzers arriving at the Parma and Reggio railway stations.
The III. (armoured)/2. was to move its wheeled vehicles in an overland march to Trient. It was to give the Abteilung's Ia a report on transport needs for the tracked vehicles by 10.00 hours on 5.8. The *Aufklärungsabteilung LAH* was to do the same for its 3./Aufklärungsabteilung and its "Grillen," the Sturmgeschützabteilung LAH for its combat Batterien.
The wheeled-vehicle elements of the Sturmgeschützabteilung were to make an overland march to Verona.
The *Aufklärungsabteilung LAH* (minus the 3. Kompanie and elements of the heavy Kompanie) was to set out from Innsbruck at 11.00 hours on 5.8.1943 and reach the Lavis — Zambana region.
The Divisions-Sicherungskompanie was to set up the Divisional headquarters in Verona.
By 16.00 hours, the units had all reported completion of their orders.

5.8.1943: The leading elements of the Panzerregiment arrived in Innsbruck. Because they had no Panzers, they were put on the march to Parma — Reggio immediately.

Ritterkreuze for Obersturmführer Karck and Untersturmführer Wolff were requested, granted, and announced.

On 6.8.1943, the reinforced 1. Panzergrenadier-Regiment *LAH* was moved from Mantua into the Borgoforte — Parma — Reggio area, and the Pionier-Bataillon *LAH* was moved from Mezzolombarto to Mantua.

Missions: defense of the roads and railway line in the designated area. The Flakabteilung *LAH* (minus its light and medium Batterien) was moved with those wheeled-vehicle elements of the Artillerie-Regiment *LAH* subordinated to it for the purpose of the march; the transfer took place in one uninterrupted march from Innsbruck to the Mantua — Parma — Reggio area. Its mission was to take over active air defense for the region.

b) 6.8.1943 - 7.9.1943: Transfer into the Po River Plain[1]

6.8.1943 - 8.8.1943: These days passed without incident. In Innsbruck, the bulk of the Division was being detrained. The Divisionsstab left a message center behind and moved first to Verona on 6.8 and then to Garda on 8.8. The traffic-regulation staff at the Brenner Pass was relieved by a permanent force from the Feldgendarmerie.

In a briefing, the Adjutanten were shown the areas assigned their units for reconnaissance and scouting. They were also given the following intelligence:

Units and strength of Italian forces in their sectors,
Telephone centrals,
Position of all types of supply depots,
Position and weight capacities of the bridges,
and (of particular interest)
Position of any occupied Italian border fortifications against Germany.

9.8.1943 - 12.8.1943: The units provided constant reports on the results of their reconnaissance activities. It was noted that there were masses of Italian troops on the march or being unloaded from trains along all the roads and railway lines in the sector Brenner Pass — Reschen Pass. The Division therefore determined in a special order dated 9.8 as follows:

1) *General situation*: Despite unequivocal agreements between the Oberkommando der Wehrmacht and the Commando Supremo that the protection of the Brenner — Verona pass over the Alps should be the joint responsibility of the German and Italian forces, the Italians have been moving Alpini forces in (about two Divisionen so far). These forces have been pushing German troops out of the fortifications and have occupied and blocked all the important roads in the Southern Tyrol. Given the swing in the Italian government's political position, possible at any time, this troop presence poses a serious threat to the only effective line of movement for all our forces fighting in Italy.

2) To secure this line of movement, Gruppe Feuerstein, with the 44. Infanteriedivision and the troops of the Hochgebirgschule [high-mountain training school] subordinated to it, has been deployed. It has orders not only to defend the railway and road from Brenner to Bozen against air attack, air landings, and sabotage, but also to spread out along the road on both sides and to occupy all fortifications and installations not occupied by the Italians in order to guarantee adequate protection of them.
3) These steps will not be sufficient in the event of actual confrontation with Italian forces.
4) *The SS-Panzergrenadierdivision LAH* is therefore *not* to move into its designated area Parma — Reggio until more forces, already detailed for the purpose, arrive in Brenner. Instead, the SS-Panzergrenadierdivision *LAH* is to station most of its troops to protect the railway and highway in the Trient — Verona sector. To this end, the following orders are issued:
5) a) The reinforced 2. Panzergrenadier-Regiment *LAH* is to hold its current defensive position and concentrate its forces.
   b) The bulk of the Division is to stand ready to march in the Borgoforte — Parma — Reggion — Mantua area, so that they can be quickly deployed on both sides of Verona.
6) Standing alert status must be guaranteed for all units, and the commanders are to remain with their units.
7) There will be no passes issued to leave the positions except in the most urgent cases.
8) *Communications*
   Radio: as before
   Telephone: Italian network. Watch out for taps in the line!
9) Divisional headquarters in Garda.

On 10.8 Gruppe Feuerstein reported finding seven places where telegraph cables had been cut in the Divisional headquarters' vicinity.

The newly-formed I./Panzerregiment *LAH* (under Sturmbannführer Kuhlmann), equipped with Panzer V's ("Panthers") detrained in Parma — Reggio.

13.8.1943 - 17.8.1943: The Oberkommander of Heeresgruppe B reported on the evening of 13.8 by telephone that the *LAH* was to be subordinated to the Generalkommando of the II. SS-Panzerkorps (under Obergruppenführer Hausser) starting on 14.8. The Korps headquarters were two kilometers southwest of Reggio. With the *LAH*, the 65. Infanteriedivision and the 25. Panzerdivison were also subordinated to the Generalkommando.

At the command of Heeresgruppe B, a Bataillon of the *LAH* was detailed to the meeting between Generalfeldmarschall Rommel, Generaloberst Jodl, and Italian General Roatta, scheduled for 15.8. Schütze Günther Kress reported:

> "It was August 14, 1943. We were in a little village somewhere in upper Italy, a village which appeared to have no name. We did not give our location much thought, for we had enough to do with repairing and taking care of our materiel, such as the uniforms, weapons, etc.

In the middle of this peaceful work, our top sargeant ran up to us, the men of the first Zug of the 11./1., and asked 'Which of you can present arms and goosestep in an orderly fashion?'
At first, I thought of giving him the usual enlisted man's reply, but I swallowed it down and raised my hand, as did several others. All of us had to do a quick change into our grey field uniforms, put on our ammo-belts, grab our rifles and bayonets, and jump in vehicles to be whisked away to the Bataillon headquarters.
There, several other 'field greys' from other Züge of other Kompanien had already been approached by commander Weidenhaupt. Our III. Bataillon had been able to pull together a respectable parade platoon. Weidenhaupt himself took charge of this quickly-thrown-together unit, ran us through our arms presentation, and goosestepped us back and forth across the street. It all went as well as it used to in the old days on the southern training field at Lichterfeld.
It finally occurred to us that we were actually being used for a ceremonial appearance, but none of us had a clue as to for whom or why. Weidenhaupt said that he was satisfied with us and released us to return to quarters. We were to wait there until called for.
Evening came. Then night fell.
Then, suddenly, at 03.00 hours, a motorcycle messenger from the Kompanie came racing up: 'The 11. Kompanie is to march along the street from X to Y in twenty minutes, with full field-march equipment.!'
Twenty minutes later, we were marching along the street toward Y. So where were the orders for the select few chosen for the honor Kompanie? That is what we all were thinking, we who had laboured all afternoon to satisfy our Bataillon commander with arms presentation and orderly marching.
We were now equipped for a field march, so there could be no thought of a ceremonial appearance.
Once again we had thought wrong. It was the motorcycle messenger once again who shouted: 'Those men selected for the honor Kompanie get into the empty vehicles at the head of the column!' We had not had much sleep that night, so we tended to doze in the seats and quickly entered the realm of relaxation. The column's halt shook us awake. As I rubbed the sleep from my eyes, I noticed that a column of Italian soldiers was facing us from the other side of a turnpike gate which was lowered across the road. Next to it was the shield of the city of Bologna. After a brief negotiation, the turnpike was raised, and we crossed the border into Bologna.
It was not long until the column stopped again. The order 'Dismount and march' rang out. We marched in parade formation toward a wide, tall gate of beautiful grillwork, which opened at the last moment. A heavenly picture spread itself before our eyes. There lay before us a wide courtyard with formal gardens, palm trees, and promenade paths. Far to the rear was a broad house facade, but we could not see beyond it.
We swung around the Italian guard house, halted, piled our arms, and ran like lightning into the shade of the buildings on the side. I noticed that our parade unit had grown by now into a Kompanie one hundred twenty men strong, drawn from the entire 1. Regiment. We still did not know on whom we were actually paying this call.

12.7.1943: A Pionier with a flamethrower in a position which has just been captured.
The prisoners are waiting to be taken away.

12.7.1943: The II./Panzerregiment *LSSAH* moves into combat formation near Prochorowka.

Forward Divisional command post on Hill 241.6 on 12.7.1943. Divisional commander Oberführer Wisch and Ia Strumbannführer Lehmann.

12.7.1943: "My foxhole is ready for the night." A Panzergrenadier of the 11./1.

To Italy.

We had already waited for hours when the hoped-for command to march rang out. An Obersturmführer took command of us and ran us through a few test presentation drills. When he was satisfied with our performance, he spoke the first words of explanation we had heard: 'That is how it has to look when the Generalfeldmarschall arrives!' Generalfeldmarschall? That was quite a clue! But which one? When the 'at ease' was given, we thought it over as we watched a plane land behind the buildings in the background. That was our first indication that there was an airstrip behind those buildings. The Bologna military airstrip. Further speculation was diverted by the arrival of an Italian honor company which took up a position on the opposite side of the yard. Their rapid march steps and their trumpeter's eccentric signals did not stir us. We stared as if in a trance at the promenade leading from our position to the buildings in the background. Finally, a swarm of people emerged, moving across the promenade directly toward us with measured steps. Gold and silver sparkled in the Italian noonday sun and blinded our eyes, already strained from the light.

Soon it was upon us. The herd of men, brass one and all, was so close that we could begin to distinguish individuals.

Then I saw which Marschall it was. No less a one than Rommel. The sharp command from our Obersturmführer yanked me from my thoughts.

'Honor Kompanie, halt! Left shoulder, arms! Attention! Present arms! Report to Herr Generalfeldmarschall, face right!'

A pause a second long. The presentation had come off exactly right. Rommel stood before us. Our Obersturmführer marched up to Rommel in perfect form.

'Herr Generalfeldmarschall, I obediently report the arrival of an honor Kompanie from the *Leibstandarte SS Adolf Hitler* to greet you!'

A hearty 'Thanks' from Rommel, an equally hearty handshake for the Obersturmführer, and Rommel started to review the front of the honor Kompanie. He suddenly reconsidered, stood at attention, raised his Marschall's staff, and cried, 'Heil, my honor Kompanie!' We paused only a fraction of a second before answering. We had not been prepared for him to speak nor had we rehearsed our answer. But it rang out clear and in one voice, 'Heil, Hitler!'

Rommel smiled happily and began slowly to review our front line. He looked at each of us closely. He greeted the Zugführers especially. At the end of the review, he once again shook the Obersturmführer's hand briefly and forcefully, then turned and marched to the Italian company.

Once again there sounded that odd trumpet signal. We had barely set our rifles at our feet when a group from the first Zug was ordered into a truck to be taken to 'the castle' for honor guard duty. Later, as we marched away, we also got to see 'the castle' (or the 'castell', as the Italians called it) on a hill in the distance. Rommel was evidently expected there for a conference of some kind.

While most of our Kompanie was stuck with waiting in the airstrip's front courtyard, the honor guard marched past Rommel's vehicle and formed a double-line formation in front of the castle gate. The faces of the Italian soldiers and officers clearly showed that our presence was not exactly appreciated. But we soldiers did not concern ourselves with that and did

our duty. Rommel had arrived at the castle and had joined all the other high German and Italian officers inside.
After a few hours, the process described above repeated itself in reverse. Rommel left the castle, a little hastily, and was driven to the airstrip. Our honor company had once again assumed a position there. This time we were directly facing the Italians, which gave us a chance to make some funny comparisons...
But here, too, Rommel seemed to be in a hurry. He did without any ceremony and moved straight to the airstrip behind the building.
The Rommel adventure appeared to be over for us.
We still did not know anything about the background of Rommel's visit to Bologna, but were fairly surprised to be added suddenly to the vehicle columns of our own units which, it turned out later, had been ordered to follow the honor Kompanie from the beginning.
Returning to my group in the 11. Kompanie, I asked my comrades what they had been doing during our ceremonial appearance. They grumbled that they had been somewhere on the edge of Bologna in the fields on standing alert all day.
It was not for three-quarters of a year that I got a full explanation of the background of Rommel's Bologna visit. That was when I got hold of a copy of the newspaper 'VÖlkischer Beobachter' from September, 1943. There it stood:
'On August 15, 1943, the traitorous Italian General Roatta and his staff planned the assassination of Rommel by taking him prisoner during a conference in the Bologna castle. SS men, tall as trees, were posted in front of the conference site, however, and thwarted any plans for an attempt on Rommel's life by their sheer presence.'
So that was what had happened in Bologna on August 15, 1943.
The Italians should only have known that we were a German honor guard. In accordance with parade regulations, our guns were unloaded and our ammo belts empty..."

During this period, the Oberbefehlshaber of Heeresgruppe Süd, Generalfeldmarschall Rommel, paid a surprise visit to the Divisional headquarters in Garda. He found only the Ia present who, properly attired in swimming trunks, was riding on Lake Garda in an amphibious Volkswagen. Rommel, amused and relaxed, was briefed by the Ia wearing this outfit. The Oberbefehlshaber was impressed with our reconnaissance reports, which had not been expressly ordered, and he announced that the Division could be moved forward into the Reggio region.

On the evening of 17.8.1943, after the Korps had issued its orders, the units received Divisionbefehl No. 25, containing their instructions for closing ranks in the Parma — Reggio — Borgoforte area. They were to expand our reconnaissance into the Italian troops' billeting areas and were to prepare for a surprise occupation of their new area and for disarming the Italian soldiers stationed there. These preparations were to take place under as much secrecy as possible.

The Divisional headquarters remained in Garda until 19.8.1943.

Starting on 17.8.1943, the Oberkommando of Heeresgruppe B had dropped its former code name. Subordinated to it were the II. SS-Panzerkorps with the *LAH*, the 24. Panzerdivision, and the 65. Infanteriedivision; the LXXXIV.

Armeekorps with the 76., 94., and 305. Infanteriedivision; and the LI. Gebirgsarmeekorps with the 44. (*Hoch-und Deutschmeister*) [=Grandmaster of the Teutonic Order] Reichsdivision, the 71. Infanteriedivision, and Brigade Dölla.

The 1. Panzergrenadier-Regiment reported that the Italian army had set up tank traps on the road from Florence to Pisa.

18.8.1943 - 30.8.1943: The reinforced 2. Panzergrenadier-Regiment *LAH* was moved on 19.8 into the area Reggio — S. Polodenza — Schandian.

On 20.8.1943, the Korps informed the units that some elements of the Division might be moved up to the line Aulla — Fivizzano — Bagni di Lucca.[2]

The units received the corresponding reconnaissance missions. The Divisional headquarters were in Felino southwest of Parma starting at 10.00 hours on 22.9.1943. Hauptsturmführer Tiemann reported there to take over the duties of the 1. Ordonnanzoffizier for the Division Stab.

On 27.8.1943, the commanding general, Obergruppenführer Hausser, paid a visit to the Italian General Ruggero, commander of the *Commando Presidio Militare Reggio — Emilia* in Milan.

The Division ordered reconnaissance to be conducted for new places to billet the Panzerregiment and an Artillerie-Abteilung.

28.8.1943 - 30.8.1943: The reinforced Aufklärungsabteilung *LAH* received orders to stand ready at all times to march within two hours. A Korpsbefehl followed on 30.8, ordering the bulk of the Division to stand ready to march within three hours.

On 30.8, the Division issued guidelines for a training course almost like that for war. The main points of focus were:

night-action training,
concentrated fire for all weapons, especially with frequent shift of position,
officer training.

The 1. Generalstabsoffizer conducted a week-long Adjutant training course.

31.8.1943 - 7.9.1943: This period allowed for concentrated reconnaissance training.

An order from the Korps for a possible train embarkation of a reinforced Regimentsgruppe caused some unrest, but the order was rescinded.

On 3.9, the Ia reported to the Chef of the Generalstab of the Korps, Oberführer Ostendorf. Once again, he received guidelines for disarming the Italian forces. At the release of the code word "Nordwind," the disarmament and subsequent internment of the Italian troops was to be carried out. The Division received orders to keep a strong combat force ready to fight to keep the road Verona — Brenner open if necessary.

The Divisional commander travelled to Innsbruck on 7.9 to take care of the Division's supply services.

The *LAH*'s Panzer strength on 7.9.1943:

twenty-three Panzer VI's and four under repair
sixty-five Panzer V's and six under repair
fifty-one Panzer IV's and three under repair
five Befehlspanzer [command tanks] III's and one under repair
three Befehlspanzer II's and one under repair.

Section II
DISARMING THE ITALIAN ARMY
AND DEFENSE OF NORTHERN ITALY AND CROATIA

a) 8.9.1943 - 17.9.1943: Disarming the Italian Army (see sketch 25).

8.9.1943: At 18.00 hours, the 2. Generalstabsoffizier, Obersturmbannführer Stoltz, returned from a drive through Parma. He reported that celebrations were underway among the Italian population over a radio announcement of a peace between Italy and the Western Allies. He brought back a leaflet, the only contents of which we were able to translate were "Pace, pace, pace" [peace, peace, peace].

An interpreter was rushed to the scene and put in front of the radio receiver to listen in on the Italian broadcasts. By late evening, there was still no word. The Korps telephone connections, in the meanwhile, had been disrupted.

At 19.30 hours, the Ia radioed the Korps to inquire about the situation.

When he had received no answer by 20.00 hours, the Ia issued orders in the absence of the Divisional commander:

> "Apparent cease-fire between Italy and Anglo-Americans. Be prepared to march within the hour. Avoid all confrontations."

Finally at 20.25 hours, the following radio message arrived from the II. SS-Panzerkorps:

> "Top alert condition. X-Time is 01.00 hours on 9.9.1943."

The units received the message:

> "*Nordwind*. X-Time 9.9.1943, 01.00 hours."

At 23.00 hours, the Korps informed us that a non-commissioned officer of the Italian Air Force had reported the landing of English-American planes on the Reggio airstrip.

At 23.15 hours, the Korps ordered the Panzerregiment *LAH* to occupy the airstrip.

The Panzerregiment sent a Panzerkompanie there, and it arrived punctually at 01.00 hours.

9.9.1943: At 01.00 hours, the units assembled in front of the Italian barracks and demanded that the troops give up their weapons.

The following units were deployed in this action:

The reinforced I./2. (Sturmgeschützabteilung LAH) in Verona.

The Aufklärungsabteilung in Fonton; it was subsequently deployed to S. Ambrogio, Bussolengo, and Peschiera.

The Pionier-Bataillon in Mantua, with elements in Villafranca and elements sent to defend the bridge over the Po in Borgoforte.

The Wirtschafts-Bataillon in Castelducchio.

The I./Panzerregiment LAH in Reggio with one Kompanie at the military airstrip for La Villa and S. Illono and covering the Italian anti-aircraft guns in Massenzotica.

The III. (armoured)/2. was ordered by the Division at 01.05 hours to support the Panzerabteilung in Reggio; at 09.00 hours, it was ordered to move on to Scandiano.

The Regimentsstab of the 2. Panzergrenadier-Regiment moved out at 07.00 hours from Sassuolo and disarmed the garrison at Albina.

The III./Artillerie-Regiment was moved from Ribbiano to S. Polo.

The II./Panzerregiment LAH was moved from Ribbiano to Cade.

The I./1., reinforced by the I./Artillerie-Regiment moved from the area southwest of the city and reached Parma at 02.00 hours. This was the only place at which any resistance worth mentioning was offered. It came from an officers' training school, but it was broken by 09.30 hours.

The commander of the 1. Panzergrenadier-Regiment *LAH*, Obersturmbannführer Frey, described it as follows:

> "The Italian town commander in Parma proved to be particularly energetic. Even before the disarmament, i.e. when we were still allies, he made an enormous fuss about billeting us. He did not even want to make space for tents available to us in his district. When asked to hand over his weapons, he, like so many of his colleagues, wanted to 'fight to their last drop of blood.' After a single light Feldhaubitze shell was fired straight at his office, however, his courage wafted away with the gunsmoke. In Parma, the Italians also attempted a tank attack, but one of their tanks drove straight into the Parma River."

The Nachrichtenabteilung occupied the vital telephone office and, starting at 17.00 hours, secured a switching station in Lagano.

The reinforced II./1. (Panzerjägerabteilung LAH) marched from Gussola to Casalmaggiore to take its important crossing over the Po. Subsequently, it moved to S. Secondo and Fidenza to intern the Italian soldiers there.

The I. and III./1. were occupied with the large garrison in Cremona from 10.00 hours on. One Kompanie of the III. Bataillon was sent to Manerbio via Robecco.

By early morning, practically the entire day's mission had already been accomplished. Then a radio message arrived from the Korps containing instructions on how to deal with the Italians. The Italian armed forces were to be disarmed by saying that the war was over for Italy. Each soldier was to hand over his weapon and return to his civilian life or enter the German army as a volunteer. The German forces were to use Italian materiel to make themselves fully mobile and to replenish their stocks. Around noon, a second radio message from the Korps declared the Korps' district, minus the South Tyrol, to be an operations area under wartime law. Generalfeldmarschall Rommel was the executive authority for the area.

At 16.22 hours, the Division's Ia released the following daily order:

Telegram

Arrived: 9.9.43, 18.15 hours
Sent: 9.9.43, 16.22 hours
Sent from: *LSSAH* Ia
Mark: KR

To
Generalkommando of the II. SS-Panzerkorps
Ia
Daily report

1) On 9.9.1943, beginning at 01.00 hours and lasting until 13.00 hours, the following garrisons of the Italian army were disarmed and interned:
   Parma,
   Reggio Emilia,
   Guastalla,
   Borgoforte,
   Mantua,
   Villafranca,
   Peschiera,
   S. Ambrogio (sixteen kilometers northwest of Verona),
   Caprino (eight kilometers northeast of Garda),
   Ceraino (ten kilometers east of Garda),
   Casalmaggiore,
   Collechio (ten kilometers southwest of Parma),
   Sala (twelve kilometers south-southwest of Parma),
   Bibano,
   Scandiano.

   Fairly strong resistance was offered in Parma and Mantua, while in the other Garrisons, the disarmament went ahead as planned after a brief exchange of fire.
   In Verona, the disarmament went according to plan, but the size of the forces there made it go slowly.
   Cremona is solidly in our hands.
2) *Headquarters*: Divisional headquarters unchanged,
   Regimental headquarters of the 1. Panzergrenadier-Regiment *LSSAH* in Martignano,
   2. Panzergrenadier-Regiment in Albinea,
   Artillerie-Regiment *LSSAH* is moved for the time being to Cadelbosco,
   Panzerregiment *LSSAH* unchanged.
3) *Information about the enemy*: The behavior of the Italian troops is entirely dependent on the soldierly qualities of the local commander.
4) Our losses will be reported later. Slight so far.
5) Losses of heavy weapons: —
6) Prisoners taken: 333 officers, 7,600 non-commissioned officers and enlisted men.
7) Aerial activity: No flights in.

Panzer strength:

Ready for action		Under repair (fourteen days)	
23	Panzer VI's	4	Panzer VI's
66	Panzer V's	5	Panzer V's
53	Panzer IV's	1	Panzer IV's
6	Panzerbefehlwagen III's	1	Panzer II's
3	Panzer II's		

Sturmgeschütze ready for action: unchanged.
Pak guns reader of action:
7.5-centimeter motorized Z's: unchanged
7.5-centimeter self-propelled: 1 (short repair)

LSSAH
Ia

The subsequent report on our losses came in on 10.9 with the following figures:

5) Our losses: Dead: 9
Wounded: 45 (most of them in Parma)
6) Loss of heavy weapons: 2 self-propelled Pak hit by Italian anti-tank fire in Casalmaggiore.
7) Prisoners: 650 officers, 16,599 non-commissioned officers (without Cremona and Verona)
730 Englishmen
4 Italian tanks destroyed, one driven into the river
20 attack boats voluntarily surrendered.

Leibstandarte SS Adolf Hitler
Abteilung Ia Le/rg

Division headquarters
9.9.1943

Orders for 10.9.1943
(issued in essential points by radio beforehand)
Map: 1:500,000

1. *The LSSAH* is to disarm the following Italian garrisons on the southern edge of Lake Garda in the course of the day: Prescia — Bergamo — Novara — Torino — Airasca-Cuneo — Mondovi — Asti — Alessandria — along the Po as far as Cremona.
The Italian troops disarmed so far should be guarded by the elements which performed the disarmament. All means of transportation (empty trucks, trains) should be used to move them to Mantua. Officers and enlisted men should be transported separately. They are to be handed over to the commander of the Pionier-Bataillon/*LSSAH* in exchange for a receipt.
2. To this end, I order the following:
   a) *The reinforced 2. Panzergrenadier-Regiment/LSSAH*, minus the I./2. (but with the III./Artillerie-Regiment and the 5. Flak), is to set out as early as possible on 9.9.1943 and reach Torino. It is to disarm the garrison there, and then move on to disarm the following garrisons: Barge — Cuneo — Montovi — Ast — Alessandria — Novara (exclusive) — Casabianca.

March route: Parma — Piacenza — Pavia — Mortara — Vercelli — Turin highway. Departure and arrival in Turin should be reported. Contact should be established with the German Luftwaffe at the Airasca airfield (twenty kilometers southwest of Torino) as soon as possible.

b) *The reinforced Panzergrenadier-Regiment/LSSAH*, minus one Bataillon (but with the I./Artillerie-Regiment *LSSAH* [minus one Batterie], one Batterie of 10-centimeter Kanonen, the II./Panzerregiment *LSSAH*, the 4./Flakabteilung, the Stab and two Kompanien of the Panzerjägerabteilung/*LSSAH*), is to execute its missions in the area north of the line Cremona — Piacenza and is then to assemble to depart from there as early as possible on 10.9 to surround and disarm the Milan garrison. Contact should be established as soon as possible with the German Luftwaffe at the Linate airfield. After disarming Milan, the unit should disarm the Italian garrisons in the area Bergamo (exclusive of it) — Trefiglie (exclusive of it) — Codogna (inclusive of it) — along the Po as far as Alexandria (exclusive of it) — Novara (inclusive of it).
For this move, the II./Panzerregiment *LSSAH* is to be moved up behind the march group of the 2. Panzergrenadier-Regiment *LSSAH* in the area north of Piacenza.
March route: all the roads north of the Po.
To reinforce the defense of Parma and Cremona, the following should be moved there and subordinated:
the 2./Sanitätsabteilung *LSSAH* (Cremona) and elements of the Instandesetzungsabteilung *LAH* (Parma).

c) *The reinforced Aufklärungsabteilung LSSAH* (10. and 11./Artillerie-Regiment, one light Feldhaubitze Batterie) is to disarm the garrisons in Brescia and Bergamo as quickly as possible in order to continue this action in the area Bergamo — Trefiglie (inclusive of it) — Creme — Casteleone (inclusive of it) — Cremona (exclusive of it) — Ghedi — Brescia.
March route: Desenzano — Brescia.

d) The reinforced I./2. Panzergrenadier-Regiment LSSAH (Sturmgeschützabteilung minus one Batterie) is to continue the disarmament of Verona.

e) *The reinforced Pionier-Bataillon* (one Sturmgeschützbatterie) is to perform the final disaramament of the Italian garrisons in the area Villafranca — Montova — Borgoforte and is to secure the highway bridges in this area. It is to set up the prisoner assembly point for the entire Division in Mantova.

f) *The combat Stab of the Artillerie-Regiment LSSAH* is to continue guarding the disarmed Italians in its designated areas.

g) *The Flakabteilung LSSAH* is to keep its heavy Batterien providing air defense over Reggio Emilia.

h) *The commander of the Division supply units* is to assume responsibility for defending the roads along the route Parma — Reggio (exclusive of the towns).

i) *The Instandesetzungsabteilung LSSAH* is to station its Stab and additional elements to reinforce the defenses of the I./1. Panzergrenadier-Regiment *LAH* in Parma and to defend the bridge over the Po west of Boretto.

k) *The Sanitätsabteilung/LSSAH* is to reinforce the defense of the III./1. Panzergrenadier-Regiment *LSSAH* in Cremona and to establish a medical clearing station in Pavia.

l) *The Sicherungskompanie/LSSAH* is to move strong elements to Pavia, disarm the garrison there, and to set up a new Divisional headquarters.

m) The Nachrichtenabteilung LSSAH is to send any elements not currently deployed to support the Sicherungskompanie in disarming the Pavia garrison.

The assembly point for English prisoners: the stadium on the southern edge of Mantova. *For disarmed Italians*: Mantova. Hand over prisoners only in exchange for receipt. Once again, it is emphasized that all Italians are to be disarmed and that officers and men are to be housed separately under guard at all times. Italians who wish to volunteer for the German Wehrmacht as Hiwis can be put into use at once.

The population should be notified that no one may walk the streets between nightfall and daybreak.

Windows and doors should be kept closed. Airplanes of the Italian air force may only be shot at if they clearly have attack intentions. After planes land, they should be captured and prevented from taking off again.

Divisional headquarters in Pavia starting on 10.9.1943 at 12.00 hours.

For the *Leibstandarte*
SS Adolf Hitler
1. Generalstabsoffizier
signed Lehmann

10.9.1943: At 00.00 hours, the leading elements of the reinforced 2. Panzergrenadier-Regiment (minus the I. and III. Bataillon, but with the III./Artillerie-Regiment *LAH* and the 5./Flakabteilung *LAH*) set out west of Reggio to march to Turin. The III. (armoured)/2. (under Sturmbannführer Peiper) set out simultaneously to disarm the garrisons in Alessandria and Asti. The Chef of the 19. (Pionier)/2. with elements of the 16. (Infanteriegeschütz)/2. and the 5./Flakabteilung were to perform the same function in Verchelli and Novara.

At 11.15 hours, elements of the 2. Panzergrenadier-Regiment's supply train came under fire in Pavia. Hauptsturmführer Richter of the Division's Sicherungskompanie used Gruppe Schlott (the reinforced 19./2.) to break this resistance.

Our losses: one dead and one wounded.

At 12.00 hours, the leading elements of the 2. Panzergrenadier-Regiment arrived in Settimo, just outside Turin, where they learned from German inhabitants of the city that there were armed Communist demonstrators creating unrest in the city. They had held a conference with the authorities in the city before the German troops had arrived, however, and it had produced promising results.

At 00.00 hours, there was a brief exchange of fire at S. Giugliano.

At 08.00 hours, the reinforced 1. Panzergrenadier-Regiment (minus one Bataillon but with the II./Panzerregiment *LAH*, the I./Artillerie-Regiment *LAH* and its 10-centimeter Kanonenbatterie, the 4./Flakabteilung, and the Panzerjägerabteilung *LAH*) assembled north of Cremona and Piacenza and set off on three march routes toward Milan. By 11.30 hours, the leading elements had reached the outskirts of the city. The Regiment reported extensive field installations on both sides of the road from Triviglio to Milan and from Lodi to Milan. When he arrived there, the commander of the 1. Panzergrenadier-Regiment *LAH*, Obersturmbannführer Frey, established contact with the commander of the Italian *Command Presidio Militare Reggio—Emilia*, General Ruggero. Frey reported that his first impression of the man and indeed the temporary result of the conversation was that General Ruggero had been reasonable in this first openly conducted conference and had declared himself prepared to agree to disarming the garrisons under his command, provided certain conditions were met.

At 14.30 hours, the commander of the 2. Panzergrenadier-Regiment reported from Settimo that the commander in Turin had ordered his men to lay down arms.

At 15.00 hours, the Korps received a radio message that the Italians were fighting openly against Heeresgruppe Süd (under Kesselring) and that the Italian navy had fired at German transports. The following order was therefore given: all Italian soldiers and officers were to be treated as prisoners of war; individual volunteers and whole units up to battalion-size could be conscripted as Wehrmacht attendants and armed with captured weapons. A written order from the Korps regulating the transport of prisoners by train followed.

At 15.10 hours, the II. SS-Panzerkorps ordered from Verona that the garrison in Vicenza be disarmed. Sturmbannführer von Westernhagen and the Sturmgeschützabteilung were deployed for that mission.

The reinforced Aufklärungsabteilung (the 1., 10., and 11./Artillerie-Regiment) had been moved out from Verona to Brescia, and elements had been sent to Bergamo. Sturmbannführer Knittel, commander of the Aufklärungsabteilung, had engaged in conferences with the commanders in the garrisons.

The other elements of the Division reported completion of their assigned missions in accordance with the Divisionsbefehl without particular incident. The Divisional headquarters was moved to Pavia at about 15.00 hours.

The day's negotiations between the 1. Panzergrenadier-Regiment and General Ruggero ended with the General making a radio speech to the population, urging them to maintain peace and order. He said that the Italian force in Milan would disarm the Communist gangs in the city. As recompense, the Italian troops would retain their right to carry arms. An honorable withdrawal from Milan was to be guaranteed them. Shortly after the radio address from the Italian General, one of the English broadcasts over the Italian frequencies urged the population to resist the German soldiers, and there was considerable confusion in the city. Another speech by General Ruggero did a certain amount to restore calm. His announcement that the Italian king had deserted his soldiers and defected to the other side seemed to have a particularly strong effect. The memory of Milan's fate on 18.3.1848, when Austrian Feldmarschall Radetzky had put down a rebellion in several days of bloody street fighting, may also have contributed to the calm.[4]

The reinforced 1. Panzergrenadier-Regiment pulled back by evening to the Milan suburbs. The I./Panzerregiment *LAH* (Panthers) was moved up to join the Regiment and subordinated to it.

The reinforced II./2. Panzergrenadier-Regiment (under Sturmbannführer Sandig) had the key positions in the city of Turin in its hands by 17.00 hours. There was one incident at the railway station. Losses: one man dead, one wounded.

The III. (armoured)/2. had accomplished the disarmament of Asti during the day.

Orders for 11.9.1943: The reinforced 1. Panzergrenadier-Regiment was to continue the disarmament and occupation of Milan. The reinforced 2. Panzergrenadier-Regiment was to complete its occupation of Turin and disarm the Communist demonstrators. The elements from Chivasso were to move to the northeast via Vercelli as far as Novara. The III. (armoured)/2. was to move from Asti to Alba and Bra. The reinforced Aufklärungsabteilung was to continue its Brescia assignment and to determine whether there were Italian troops in Riva. At the same time, it was to disarm Orzinuovi, Soucimo and the towns along the road to Cremona.

11./12.9.1943: At 03.03 hours, the commander of the reinforced 2. Panzergrenadier-Regiment reported that the Italian troops were in the process of disarming the Communist demonstrators. There were loud protests against this action, but no armed resistance. The Regiment moved its vehicles into Turin as planned.

At 04.00 hours, the Adjutant of the reinforced 1. Panzergrenadier-Regiment, Obersturmführer Naujok, reported that his Regimental commander had not returned from Milan, where he had once again been in negotiation. The entire Regiment was to stand ready to march into the city if the negotiations were unsuccessful.

At 04.15 hours, Obersturmbannführer Frey returned from the negotiations with General Ruggero. The result was: we were to march into the city, where the Italian soldiers would still have their weapons. Soldiers with weapons would not be allowed to leave the city, and important sites in the city would be guarded jointly by German and Italian soldiers.[5]

At 04.30 hours, the Panzergrenadiere converged on Milan and by 07.55 hours were at the actual city center.

At 05.37 hours, the Aufklärungsabteilung reported that it had taken Brescia without a fight.

At 07.50 hours, General Ruggero's chief of staff came to Obersturmbannführer Frey with questions regarding the civilian administration of the city.

In driving to the meeting, he had to pass under the barrels of sixty-five Panzer VI's under Sturmbannführer Kuhlmann parked along the street. He appeared mightily impressed.

At 09.50 hours, the Divisional headquarters moved to Forsarmato, four kilometers east of Pavia.

At 10.00 hours, the reinforced Aufklärungsabteilung reported that Riva was not occupied. After breaking considerable resistance, it had disarmed Orzinuovi, Soucino, and the towns along the road to Cremona.

At 10.10, Kampgruppe Schlott (the Regiment units of the 2. Panzergrenadier-Regiment) interned the Italian troops in Vercelli and at 11.00 those in Novara.

At 10.45 hours, there were reports made to the II. SS-Panzerkorps about the events of the day to that point.

At 11.05 hours, the commander of the 2. Panzergrenadier-Regiment reported to the Ia of the *LAH* that he was to subordinate his unit to the German Luftwaffe ground unit stationed at the Italian military airfield in Airasca. The unit was to provide support in Turin.

The III. (armoured)/2. disarmed Alba without particular difficulties. The disarmament in Turin was in full swing. There was resistance at the Fiat factory initially, but it was broken.

The transport of Italian soldiers away from their garrisons by train met with enormous difficulties. Civilians were fleeing from Turin out of fear of Anglo-American air raids. Strict prohibition against anyone's leaving the city became senseless since there were not enough troops to enforce it. It also became counterproductive, since already there were insufficient provisions.

At 12.58 hours, there was a short conference between the commander of the 1. Panzergrenadier-Regiment, Obersturmbannführer Frey, and the Ia of the *LAH*: the occupation of Milan was to proceed according to plan. Forces left at key positions for defense were too weak. The main points to be defended were the main railway station, the main post office, the radio station, the military supply depot, and the airfield.

At 13.00 hours, the Ia requested the Korps to release the forces in Verona and Mantua. The Pionier-Bataillon in Mantua was released, but it was immediately reassigned to guard the prisoner assembly point. The Wirtschafts-Bataillon received orders to move to Mantua and to take over supplying the Italian prisoners of war.

At 15.10 hours, there was a voluntary laying-down of arms in Novara (held by Kampfgruppe Schlott) and in Alba (held by the III. [armoured]/2.). Chiami (twenty kilometers west of Brescia) was occupied by German Luftwaffe forces.

At 16.50, there was a report to the Korps that the transportation of disarmed Italians from Pavia, Turin, Brescia, Cremona, Parma, and Reggio to Mantua had begun.

At 17.00 hours, there was a report from the Aufklärungsabteilung: three hundred inmates at the prison in Bergamo had been released before our troops arrived. Forty of them had been recaptured. The Bergamo garrison had been disarmed.

By 17.45 hours, almost all the units had reported that the transport of Italian prisoners of war was being hindered by civilian resistance. There were small confrontations.

At 18.10 hours, there was a call for a general strike in Turin. The town commander declared martial law.

At 18.30 hours, there was an order from the Korps assigning the tasks for 12.9.1943:

> Disarmament north of Milan and south of Turin to be continued. Italian forces which fight with us against the rebels to be interned with honor.

At 18.35 hours, orders came from the Heeresgruppe directly to the *LAH*:

> "Two Italian divisions (in Milan?) are to disarm immediately under guard. Their field insignia is to be brought under cover to our command post. Italian soldiers who wish to fight with us will be called up later."

At 21.30 hours, orders were given to the 2. Panzergrenadier-Regiment to reconnoiter the railway line from Turin to Susa (French border).

13.9.1943: At 06.50 hours, the Korps transmitted a command from the Führer that one officer from the *LAH* was to be detailed immediately to serve

They rode back and forth across Europe. Wherever they were needed, they went.

Milan under ocupation.
Panzerjägers of the *Leibstandarte* have moved into position on the city's public squares.

as liaison officer to Mussolini's wife. The Division commander appointed Hauptsturmführer Steinert of the Pionier-Bataillon to this service.

The disarmament of the troops in Milan was in full swing by 07.00 hours.

At 07.15 hours, aerial reconnaissance reported strong troop movements via Cuneo to the south. We did not have forces available to march to that area.

At 08.06 hours, elements of the Pionier-Bataillon took control of the engineer depot in Pavia.

At 08.15 hours, the Sturmgeschützabteilung moved through Brescia on its way to Milan.

At 08.20 hours, the Aufklärungsabteilung moved from Brescia, past Milan to the north, and became reinforcement for the 2. Panzergrenadier-Regiment.

09.00 hours: Disarmament in Turin could be completed by the end of the day. The population was to some degree hostile; any threat of violence should be put down immediately.

At 12.00 hours, Gruppe Schlott reached Salucho and moved on to Cavigliano. The forces there had already been disarmed by the Luftwaffe.

The III. (armoured)/2. had scouted from Bra to Fossano and Mondon.

At 11.30 hours, elements of the 11. Kompanie determined that the barracks in Cuneo had been abandoned by the soldiers, and that the population had looted it.

At 16.50 hours, the disarmament in Milan was progressing without incident. In Turin, it was complete. The general strike in Turin was also to be put down on 13.9. The 18. (Aufklärung)/2. (under Obersturmführer Dix), sent out to reconnoiter to the French border, returned without having come into contact with the enemy.

The Regimental command post of the 2. Panzergrenadier-Regiment was moved to Chivasso.

The reinforced I./1. was moved to Varese in the course of the afternoon.

The reinforced II./1. reported at 17.45 hours that Como was only weakly occupied.

The Pionier-Bataillon was moved to Lody, the Flakabteilung (minus the light and medium Batterien) to Binasco.

At 22.10 hours, the reinforced 1. Panzergrenadier-Regiment *LAH* had difficulties stopping the Italian population from looting a weapon, ammunition, and clothing supply depot in the Lombrate section of the city. The Regiment received orders to occupy the depot.

The Korps issued the following report on 12.9:

Generalkommando
II. SS-Panzerkorps
Ic

Kommando headquarters
12.9.1943

Totals of prisoners and captured materiel
(From beginning of the disarmament through 11.9)

A) *Prisoners:*

1) *Italians:*

Area Modena — Bologna	18,010 prisoners
Area Florence	20,000 prisoners

Area Ferrara — Padua — Treviso	10,000	prisoners *LAH*
Area Pistoia	6,000	prisoners *LAH*
Area Reggio — Parma	15,016	prisoners *LAH*
Area Mantua	6,000	prisoners *LAH*
Area Cremona	3,770	prisoners *LAH*
Area Verona	13,250	prisoners *LAH*
Area Milan	14,000	prisoners *LAH*
	106,046	prisoners

2) *Englishmen*:		
Area Bologna	1,077	prisoners
Area Modena	800	prisoners
Area Carpi	5,865	prisoners
	7,742	prisoners

B) *Captured materiel*:	*LSSAH*	*24. Pz.Div.*	*Total*
Railcar-mounted artillery pieces		3	3
Artillery pieces	10	117	127
Artillery pieces minus barrels		144	144
10.5-centimeter barrels		175	175
Anti-aircraft guns	49	10	59
Tanks	27	4	31
Anti-tank guns	46		46
Anti-tank rifles	67		67
Mortars	270	16	286
Machine guns	428	86	514
Rifles	38,591	22,900	61,491
Rifle ammo (rounds)	35,000		35,000
Pistols	320	250	570
Airplanes	391	268	659
Italian airplane motors	22		22
Messerschmitt motors	5		5
Tractors	1		1
Trucks		198	198
Motorcycles		19	19
Submachine guns		12	12
Hand grenades		180	180
Gas masks		100	100

With that, the disarmament of the Italian forces stationed in the Po River Plain could be regarded as essentially completed. The fact that no bloody confrontations of any significance took place between our troops and those of our former ally can be ascribed to the careful and considered actions of our commander. In the case of Milan, one can even speak of diplomatic finesse on the part of Obersturmbannführer Frey.

The orders for 14.9 remained the same.

The Division reported to the Korps its impression that a sizable number of Italian troops had withdrawn into the mountains along the French border southwest of Turin, where capable officers were assembling and structuring these forces.

14.9.1943: At 07.10 hours, the 1. Panzergrenadier-Regiment *LAH* reported Varese and Como to be disarmed by 12.50 hours. There was unrest and shooting in the Lombrate camp in Milan.

At 11.40 hours, the 2. Panzergrenadier-Regiment *LAH* moved up the 19. Pionier/2. to join it in Chivasso. The 15. (Flak)/2. took over the defense of Saluzzo.

At 13.00 hours, orders arrived from the Korps: all Italian generals were to be moved under guard to the airfield at Piacenza.

At 14.05 hours, the III. (armoured)/2. took prisoner a general from the Italian 44th Army.

At 14.30 hours, the commander of the I./2., Hauptsturmführer Becker, received orders to clear the area between Lago Maggiore and the Swiss border of Italian forces.

At 16.00 hours, the 2. Panzergrenadier-Regiment received orders to conduct renewed reconnaissance along the railway line and the highway toward Susa (French border).

At 17.30 hours, the 1. Panzergrenadier-Regiment received orders to reconnoiter the railway stations for captured weapons and equipment. All such weapons and equipment were to be assembled at the stations.

At 17.45 hours, the I./1. was occupied with the disarmament in Gallarate — Busto — Arsicio — Legnano.

The orders for 15.9.1943:

Disarmament in the area west of Milan, west of Lago Maggiore, and south of Cuneo to be continued. The reinforced Aufklärungsabteilung was ordered to reconnoiter Breglio, establish contact with the 19. Armee there, and to disarm the Italian forces along the road Cuneo — Breglio.

15.9.1943: Obergruppenführer Dietrich came from Meran, where he was setting up the Generalkommando of the I. SS-Panzerkorps, and paid the Division a visit. He spent the night at the Regimental headquarters of the 2. Panzergrenadier-Regiment.

At 09.00 hours, the Aufklärungsabteilung set out to the south with the III. (armoured)/2. to disarm Limone (III./2.), Tenda, and Saorgio (Aufklärungsabteilung).

At 19.00 hours, the 18. (Aufklärung)/2. returned once again from the French border without having come into contact with the enemy.

The Division's reconnaissance confirmed that intact Italian troops had pulled back into the area southwest of Cuneo.

At 12.00 hours, a report came from the Korps about large troop massings south of the Splügen Pass, but that they were not being allowed across the Swiss border. The I./1. sent troops to the area, but it was unable to find any Italian forces in the entire region.

At 15.15 hours, the Divisional commander called from the 2. Panzergrenadier-Regiment's headquarters to say that a Kampfgruppe should be sent to Aosta to oversee the transport of a disarmed Italian division.

Orders for 16.9.1943 remained unchanged.

16.9.1943: At 07.00 hours, the reinforced Aufklärungsabteilung reported that it had set out toward Aosta.

At 09.45 hours, the 2. Panzergrenadier-Regiment reported that elements of the III. (armoured)/2. had moved out with heavy Infanterie weapons to crush the Italian forces offering resistance south of Cuneo.

At 13.50 hours, the reinforced Aufklärungsabteilung reported from Aosta that a regiment of the Italian mountain militia had been disarmed by a German Bataillon from France. The area from there to the French border was cleared of Italian forces.

At 17.00 hours, the III. (armoured)/2. was still occupied with the resisting Italian forces.

Orders for 17.9.1943 were unchanged.

17.9.1943: During the night, the disarmament process continued in the area Boves — Chiusa. The leader of the resistance forces, General Pesenti, fled as the Kampfgruppe entered the area.

Numerous military camps were spotted along Lago Maggiore and to the west. They were captured and transported. One company of the Italian border militia subordinated itself to the I./2. and took part in the mop-up operation.[6]

b) 18.9.1943 - 20.10.1943: Defense of the Po River Plain

18.9.1943: The day passed for the most part without incident. The reinforced Aufklärungsabteilung was moved to Brescia at the Korps' order.

An Italian lieutenant colonel appeared at the headquarters of the commander of the III. (armoured)/2., Sturmbannführer Peiper, as official parlementaire for the Italian 4th Army. Under orders from his Army high command, the Italian demanded that Peiper withdraw his Bataillon from the Province of Cuneo. Otherwise, he said, the Bataillon would be destroyed to its last man.

Sturmbannführer Peiper took the following steps:

1. He made an appeal to the populace not to let the troops of the Italian 4th Army incite them to hostilities against the German Armee.
2. He had leaflets printed up inviting the soldiers of the Italian 4th Army to lay down their weapons. The bills were dropped from planes over the mountain valleys southwest and south of Cuneo.
3. He drove to Boves and warned the mayor of that town of the consequences which an uprising among the populace in conjunction with the Italian soldiers would have for the entire civilian population.

19.9.1943: In the course of the day, the barracks of previously disarmed troops were searched again for hidden weapons. This operation yielded no results. At noon, the Italian police in Boves reported that two non-commissioned officers of the 14. (heavy)/2. had been ambushed and kidnapped by Italian soldiers from the 4th Army.

Long after the war, Sturmbannführer Peiper was brought before an Italian court in regard to "the Boves incident." The following was his statement:

> "The Kompaniechef of the 14. (heavy)/2., Obersturmführer Dinse, received orders immediately to retrieve both of the individuals. Dinse drove with a Zug of Schützenpanzerwagens to Boves to rescue them. He fell into an ambush and was surrounded. He radioed back that he had been attacked by numerically superior forces and would not be able to extricate himself without outside help. He feared that the Zug would be annihilated; one man had already been killed. I alerted the forces available to me at once and moved to Boves, riding at the spearhead of my Schützenpanzerwagens, proceeding in combat fashion. In that town, we came under heavy rifle and machine gun fire from the houses and from the hillsides around it. Particularly dangerous to our Schützenpanzerwagens, which had open tops, were the grenades thrown down from the slopes. The unit suffered casualties. In my own Schützenpanzerwagen, a sheaf of machine-gun fire from above hit us, killed a radio operator, wounded another man, shot holes in my tunic, and destroyed my radio. Because we could not see the enemy troops fighting against us from the houses and the terrain, I ordered my unit to pull back to the edge of town, especially since Schützenpanzerwagens are unsuitable for combat action in a town. In prepartion for a rapid thrust through the town to my surrounded comrades, I had the 'Grillen' [15-centimeter heavy Infanteriegschütze on self-propelled mounts] open fire on the front of the town. The shells set several houses on fire. Under the cover of the smoke clouds, the enemy, both uniformed soldiers and civilian-clad individuals, pulled back into a section of the town which was only accessible through a narrow mountain pass and which could not be spotted from our positions. The surrounded force was able to free itself from its encirclement and joined my unit. While the fire, fanned by a strong wind, rapidly climbed up the mountain, we continued our attack into the section of the valley blocked from our view. The enemy resistance had been broken by our heavy weapons, however. Behind the narrow pass previously described, we discovered six artillery guns abandoned at their firing position, and we spotted Italian soldiers and civilians disappearing up the mountainside.
>
> Upon our return into Cuneo, I spoke with the Italian prefect, General Salvi, who expressed the government's deepest regret about the Boves incident and in the name of the government distanced himself from the actions taken, which he claimed were the sole responsibility of the Communists.
>
> The following day, I sent a Kompanie to Peveragno, a town in a region where similar attacks were expected. To my satisfaction, the mayor of that town held considerable influence over those compatriots of his which had not yet been disarmed. He energetically denounced the segments of the town stirred up to rebellion by Allied agents and promised to restore order and prevent further incidents.
>
> I am of the opinion that our action to free our encircled comrades in Boves nipped in the bud the Italian army's attack, for the army fell apart and no

attack ever took place on Cuneo or Turin. However regrettable the consequences of our action was for the affected residents of Boves, it should not be overlooked that our one-time intervention prevented further immeasurable casualties which would have resulted from continued Italian attacks.

signed Peiper."

It should be added that the two kidnapped non-commissioned officers made it back to join the unit which advanced up the valley. They were able to exploit the confusion among the Italians to escape from their guards.

The Italian authorities and nine co-plaintiffs, represented by state's attorneys Dr. Robert Kemper and R.J. Levin, charged Sturmbannführer Peiper, Hauptsturmführer Dinse, and Obersturmführer Gührs with murder in the Stuttgart court. The First Criminal Court ruled on 11.12.1968 that Az. IARs63/68 did not allow for prosecution of the accused.

It is natural that the testimonies of the Italian witnesses for the prosecution differ from the statement by Peiper. The court found, in Section III, Paragraph 3 of its verdict:

> "In respect to the events in Boves on 19.9.1943, there is not sufficient suspicion of criminal activity on the part of any of the accused to warrant prosecution. Despite a considerable number of depositions from witnesses [author's note: one hundred twenty-six members of the III./2. and about seventeen Italians], there is no proof that any of the accused men ordered the incineration of the town or the shootings or that such actions occurred with the approval of any of them.
>
> The fact that Peiper was in charge of the action and Dinse and Gührs took part in their capacity of Kompanieführer does not constitute any criminal responsibility, especially since, as explained above, such transgressions only took place after the accused had withdrawn and without their knowledge. It cannot be concluded merely from the fact the Peiper had threatened acts of retribution against civilians who offered support to the resistance groups that the events of 19.9.1943 constitute such an act. It is noteworthy that not one of the one hundred twenty-seven members of the Bataillon who were deposed for this trial accused any of the defendants with issuing a criminal order, even though some of them did provide details about the laying of the fires. This means that these witnesses cannot be regarded as prejudiced in favor of the accused, especially since a conspiracy among so many witnesses about so complex a series of events appears to be impossible. It cannot, however, be overlooked that the passage of twenty-five years since the events in Boves render a complete explanation impossible."

This excerpt from the Stuttgart court's verdict makes it clear that there was not sufficient suspicion of guilt to warrant prosecution of any of the accused. In stark contrast stands an event which was occurring almost at the same time on Lago Maggiore and which became the subject of a trial before the Osnabrück assize court in 1968.

On September 24 and 25, 1943, members of the I. Bataillon of SS-Panzergrenadier-Regiment 2 (minus the 1. and 2. Kompanie), acting independently, apprehended Jews living in several towns along Lago Maggiore and murdered them in the nights following.

The Osnabrück court found in its verdict that:

1) the troops had strict orders to refrain from any acts of violence against the civilian population (Verdict A page 30),
2) Italian Jews at that time were not being persecuted by German organizations (Charge, page 42; Verdict page 38),
3) the troops were aware that illegal orders were not to be executed (Verdict, page 30),
4) a Kompanieführer who had ordered the shooting of Jews had been called to account for his actions (Transcripts, Vol. I, page 36), and
5) the accused had committed their crime in secret and had hidden it from their superiors (Verdict A, page 30, page 55 ff.).

According to the Osnabrück court (Az: 17 KS 3/67), the evidence gathered contained no indications of a serious nature that members or organs of the Gestapo or the SD took part in the crimes at Lago Maggiore or were reponsible for instigating them. This result was reached after exhaustive investigations in this regard and after following every trace or shred of evidence.

The court also revealed that the Division's court martial, at the request of the Divisional commander, conducted an investigation at the scene of the crime in early October, 1943 (Verdict A, page 216). Unfortunately, due to the Regiment's transfer to Russia soon thereafter and the large-scale fighting which ensued, the investigation could not be complete (taken from the Federal court Verdict of 17.10.1970, Az 5 StR 218/69).

The Osnabrück assize court convicted the five accused men of murder or aiding and abetting a murder. The legal proceedings instituted at the Federal court were finally dropped because the prosecution had exceeded the statute of limitations. All we can say about this crime is that we distance ourselves from it. We must be ashamed of it.[7]

20.9.1943: In the early morning, the 2. Panzergrenadier-Regiment reported its actions in Boves at their end.

At 10.15 hours, the Korps ordered the preparation of a reinforced Regiment for use to the northeast. The tracked vehicles were to be prepared for immediate loading.

At 15.00 hours, the Division reported that the reinforced 1. Panzergrenadier-Regiment (the I./Artillerie-Regiment *LAH*, the Sturmgeschützabteilung *LAH*, one Panzerjägerkompanie on self-propelled mounts, and one medical clearing station) was ready to march and that the tracked vehicles were ready to load.

The II./Panzergrenadier-Regiment *LAH*, reinforced by one Panzerjägerkompanie under the leadership of the commander of the Panzerjägerabteilung *LAH*, took over the defense of Milan.

The Divisional headquarters and the Nachrichtenabteilung prepared to move into the area Parma — Piacenza, a move scheduled for 22.9.

At 22.45 hours, orders were issued for the Regiment's force to march into the Udine area starting at 09.00 hours on 21.9.

For information on the use of this Regimental force, see the following section c) "21.9.1943 - 29.10.1943: The reinforced 1. Panzergrenadier-Regiment in the Yugoslavian guerrilla war."

Most of the Division experienced no confrontations on 20.9.

21.9.1943: At about 18.45 hours, the Generalkommando ordered the Pionier-Bataillon *LAH* to Udine, as well. The Aufklärungsabteilung was also notified that it might possibly be transferred to Udine. In Forli, a Kompanie reinforced with light Flak was to stand ready to receive the Duce on 25.9.1943. A special order was issued for that Kompanie.

The Division detailed the 1./Aufklärungsabteilung (under Obersturmführer Coblenz) and the 6. (light)/Flakabteilung (under Obersturmführer Straubl) to serve in that capacity under the command of Hauptsturmführer Dr. Loenicker.

22.9.1943: The Nachrichtenabteilung *LAH* was moved to Fidenza.

23.9.1943: It remained undecided whether the Aufklärungsabteilung was needed in Forli or would be moved to Udine. The Division set up its Divisional staff quarters in Salsomaggiore.

Special orders from Generalfeldmarschall Rommel:

The Oberbefehlshaber
of Heeresgruppe B

Headquarters
September 23, 1943

Any sentimental second thoughts on the part of German soldiers toward members of Badoglio guerrillas wearing the uniform of our former comrades-in-arms are entirely unsuitable. Any one of them fighting against German soldiers has given up any claim on our mercy and should be treated with the harshness such rabble deserve when they turn their weapons against their friends.

This opinion must immediately become the general understanding of all the German forces.

A corresponding warning should be broadcast to the Italians on all Italian radio stations.

signed, Rommel.

24.9.1943: The Generalkommando replied to an inquiry that the Aufklärungsabteilung would not be moved to Udine for the time being. The Ic of the II. SS-Panzerkorps issued a warning that unrest was building in Milan.

At 23.45 hours, the Division reported that no unrest was known in Milan.

25.9.1943: The Ic of the Generalkommando of the II. SS-Panzerkorps warned that there was a workers' uprising imminent in Turin, but it fortunately did not take place.

At 12.00 hours, Mussolini arrived at the Forli airfield, received by the 1./Aufklärungsabteilung *LAH* and 6. (light)/Flakabteilung *LAH*. He was accompanied to Gargnano, where the force kept him under guard.

There were continual reports from Italian civilians of guerrilla activity in the area around Biella and southwest of Turin. Reconnaissance revealed that bands of guerrillas had assembled in the mountain terrain, which provided ample hiding places, but they did not appear to have become active. The information from the populace often proved to be inconsistent with the facts. The 18. (Aufklärung)/2. reported at 18.00 hours that it had captured fifty-two Australians and Englishmen, in uniform and carrying Italian weapons, southwest of Biella.

26.9.1943: The *LAH*'s field hospital was moved from Castelnuovo to Pavia; one Sanitätskompanie was moved to Chivasso.

27./28.9.1943: Aside from inconsequential transfers for the troops, there were no special events. In the late afternoon, an order was issued to the reinforced 2. Panzergrenadier-Regiment to render the guerrilla bands reported to be east of Pinerolo, north of Avigliana, north of Biella, and north of Varese incapable of fighting. The Division was first to encircle the bands and then to converge upon them and attack, combing the entire area on foot far back from the roads. The order of the areas, as listed above, was to be followed in the action. The Heeresgruppe ordered the French border to be closed down and locked up. The northern areas were to be cleared of enemy forces, starting from the north, in order to prevent any escape over the Swiss border.

29.9.1943 - 4.10.1943: The reinforced 2. Panzergrenadier-Regiment with two reinforced Bataillone and the III./Artillerie-Regiment *LAH* combed the areas designated without achieving any notable results. The few prisoners who were taken gave the impression that most of the so-called guerrillas were hiding in the mountains not for political reasons, but for fear of being forced to be soldiers again. The Regimental and Divisional commanders recommended that leaflets be dropped over the area.

5.10.1943 - 9.10.1943: There were no particular events.

10.10.1943: The Korps ordered the reinforced 2. Panzergrenadier-Regiment to continue defending the Cuneo area, but to stand ready to march. The order was distributed.

The Division received orders to move into the area Voghera — Tortona — Alessandria — Asti and from there to reconnoiter the possibilities for action (march routes) to the southeast, south, and southwest.

In the course of this move, the former subordinations were suspended in order to improve training opportunities.

11./12.10.1943: The Division moved into its new defensive area. The move was completed by the evening of 12.10.

13.10.1943 - 19.10.1943: Most of the Division received at long last some time to rest and to carry out some much-needed training. The newly-arrived replacement troops had to be added to the structure of the units.

Only those forces guarding the Duce were relieved. The reinforced 2./Aufklärungsabteilung under Hauptsturmführer Böttscher took the place of the reinforced 1./Aufklärungsabteilung *LAH*.

20.10.1943: The Heeresgruppe provided information via telephone about the upcoming transport to the east.

The Division issued an order by telegram to all units:

> "The Division is to prepare as quickly as possible for transport to the east. Winter equipment for the vehicles and winter clothing for the men are to be requisitioned immediately from the Ib. The report regulating the transport will be transmitted via the Division. The start of the loading for the tracked vehicles is scheduled for 22.10.1943. The reinforced 1. Panzergrenadier-Regiment will be at the end of the move."

The chronicle of the Division's activities in Italy ends here for the bulk of the Division. It will resume with the loading of the entire Division after the following explanation of the reinforced 1. Panzergrenadier-Regiment's deployment in Istria and Croatia.

Before that begins, however, we must mention the order issued renaming all the units of the Waffen-SS.

A directive from the SS-Führungsamt, Office II, Organisationsabteilung Ia/II, Daily log No. 1574/43 gKdos., dated 22.10.1943, added a number to the beginning of all former Division designations. Our Division thus became:

1. SS-Panzerdivision *LSSAH.*

The Panzergrenadier-Regiment and Schützenregiment were renumbered to correspond with the number of the Division. So the Panzergrenadier-Regimenter of the *Leibstandarte* received the designations:

SS-Panzergrenadier-Regiment 1 *LSSAH* and
SS-Panzergrenadier-Regiment 2 *LSSAH.*

All the other units within the *Leibstandarte* received the number 1.

Because the Division was renamed a Panzerdivision, all the unit designations received the prefix "Panzer." The units were thus now:

SS-Panzer-Artillerie-Regiment 1 *LSSAH*
SS-Panzerregiment 1 *LSSAH*
SS-Panzer-Aufklärungsabteilung 1 *LSSAH*
SS-Sturmgeschützabteilung 1 *LSSAH*
SS-Panzerjägerabteilung 1 *LSSAH*
SS-Panzer-Pionier-Bataillon 1 *LSSAH*
SS-Panzer-Nachrichtenabteilung 1 *LSSAH*
SS-Panzer-Instandesetzungsabteilung 1 *LSSAH*
SS-Sanitätsabteilung 1 *LSSAH*
SS-Wirftschafts-Bataillon 1 *LSSAH*
SS-Panzerdivisions-Nachschubtruppen 1 *LSSAH.*

c) 21.9.1943 - 29.10.1943: The reinforced 1. Panzergrenadier-Regiment in the Yugoslavian guerrilla war (see sketch 25).

The situation: The following "special enemy information sheet" from the Oberkommando of Heeresgruppe B, dated 22.9.1943, provides information on the conditions southeast of Gürz [Gorizia], on the Istria peninsula and in the area south of Laibach (Ljubljana):

Situation in the guerrilla area on the eastern Italian border and evaluation of the guerrillas

Since the collapse of Italy, there has been a daily increase in guerrilla activity in the area around the Istria peninsula — Laibach [Ljubljana] — Gürz [Gorizia]. The bands, most of which are under Communist leadership, have the upper hand there. The "White Guard," which pursues nationalistic goals, has subordinated itself to the Communists. Others stand staunchly opposed to the Communists' goals. Both groups are fighting under the motto: "Fight fascism! Freedom for the people!"

Since 9.9.1943, the guerrilla bands have received considerable additional forces from the Italian army, especially from the Isonzo and Torino divisions. In addition to the reinforcement in personnel, the guerrillas have also received quanitities of weapons and materiel, including artillery pieces and armoured reconnaissance vehicles. We have no estimate as to the extent of this materiel.

In the entire guerrilla area, there appear to be three main concentrations:

a) the area around Gürz,

b) the area south of Laibach, and

c) the Istria peninsula.

In the area around Gürz, which is increasingly appearing as the guerrilla center, there has been back-and-forth fighting since the beginning of the disarmament of the Italian army. It has been growing in intensity. The guerrilla bands have established strong, in some cases fortified, positions all around the city, especially to the east and southeast. They do not tend to attack, but they hold their positions stubbornly. In the last few days, there has been intensified artillery fire up to 15-centimeter calibre in size, particularly harassing fire on the road and the railway along the Isonzo.

The guerrilla area extends along the Isonzo and its tributary valleys as far as the German-Italian border to the north. The strength of the guerrilla bands in this area is estimated to be one to two divisions with about 12,000 to 15,000 men.

A fourth area of guerrilla build-up, which threatens possible contact with the Croatian coastal area to the southeast, could develop in the Fiume [Rijeka] — Susak area. There has also been guerrilla artillery fire here in the last few days, laying harassing fire from the mountains on the coastal road.

The guerrillas' efforts seem right now to be focussed on harassing or possibly capturing the roads. In the course of fighting, they may succeed in swelling their ranks by forced or voluntary recruitment from the countryside and in improving their fighting with better training and more formal structuring. They may be attempting to bring the land bridge between the Dalmatian coast or western Croatia and Upper Italy, with the significant traffic centers of Laibach and Gürz, under their control. It is not impossible that the Anglo-Americans are influencing the guerrilla leadership, since an Allied landing on the Dalmatian coast, already controlled by the guerrillas, would enable the Allies to move across the land bridge into the deep flank of our defensive forces in Upper Italy. This would have strong operational advantages for the Allies. In addition, the capture of the harbors of Triest, Pola, and Fiume would certainly favor a planned Allied landing in this area.[8]

21.9.1943: The reinforced SS-Panzergrenadier-Regiment 1 *LSSAH* (the I./Panzer-Artillerie-Regiment 1 *LAH*, the 1./Panzerjägerabteilung 1 *LAH*, one medical clearing station, elements of the Panzer-Nachrichtenabteilung 1 *LAH*) started out at 08.00 hours on 21.9.1943 with the wheeled vehicles leading the way out of its former billeting area. It took two days to reach Udine. It was reinforced by the Panzer-Pionier-Bataillon 1 *LAH*, which moved up from Mantua on 22.9 to join it.

The tracked-vehicle elements also arrived on 22.9 by railway. Upon arrival in Udine, this reinforced Regiment force left the command area of the 1. SS-Panzerdivision *LAH* and was initially subordinated directly to the II. SS-Panzerkorps.

The Korps, acting upon a directive from Heeresgruppe B, transmitted an order to deceive the enemy. The elements arriving in their new deployment area were involved in these deception maneuvers. Effective immediately, the units carried the following designations, designed to deceive the enemy.

The following units were designated:

Real name	Code designation
a) Generalkommando of the II. SS-Panzerkorps	Oberkommando of the 1. SS-Panzerarmee
b) Stab of the 44. Infanteriedivision	Generalkommando of the XII. Panzerkorps
c) Regimentsgruppe *LAH*	Panzergrenadierdivision *HJ*
d) Elements of the 24. Panzerdivision	18. Panzerdivision
e) Regimentsgruppe of the 44. Infanteriedivision	88. Infanteriedivision[9]

In order to make it easier for the reader, the reinforced Regimentsgruppe *LAH* is referred to in the following pages as Kampfgruppe Panzergrenadier-Regiment 1 *LAH*. The other units will be referred to with their code designations.

22.9.1943: In the course of the day, the Regimentsgruppe assembled in the Udine area. The Regimental commander, Obersturmbannführer Frey, was briefed on the situation by the Oberkommando of the 1. SS-Panzerarmee. The intention was to launch three operations in rapid succession in order to clear the areas east of Gürz, on the Istria peninsula and south of Laibach of guerrilla forces.

23.9.1943 - 24.9.1943: On 23.9, Kampfgruppe Panzergrenadier-Regiment 1 *LAH* received orders to move into the area on both sides of Cervignano with a command post in Ruda. Then on 25.9.1943, subordinated to the XII. Panzerkorps, the Kampfgruppe was to move out of the Monfalcone area toward Rifembergo in order to prevent the guerrilla bands from escaping to the south.

The 18. Panzerdivision farther to the north was to move from the area southwest of Gürz, while the 88. Infanteriedivision moved out of the area north of Gürz. Together, these two units were to surround and attack. At the same time, the 71. Infanteriedivision south of Idria was to prevent guerrillas from fleeing to the east.

25.9.1943: Starting at 06.30 hours, the Kampfgruppe deployed the II. Bataillon to occupy Temenizza and Castagenevizza at 13.00 hours, and by 14.00 hours, the III. Bataillon stood three kilometers northeast of Comeno. The reinforced III./1. moved forward by evening as far as Rifembergo.

Aside from one gap to the northeast, the ring was complete. The enemy avoided engaging in extensive fighting anywhere in the area and sought to escape from his encirclement. Aerial reconnaissance, ground observation, and spy reports revealed that the area was still heavily occupied by the guerrilla forces.

In each village, the partisans alerted those in the next by ringing the church bells. In the mornings, the roads, especially at curves or places with limited visibility, were strewn with obstacles. German soldiers clearing them away were shot at by snipers.[10]

For 26.9, a thorough mop-up operation in the encircled area was planned.

26.9.1943: The elements of the XII. Panzerkorps deployed in the north attempted in vain to close the gap still existing there. Roadblocks and blastings slowed the Korps progress.

Kampfgruppe Panzergrenadier-Regiment 1 spent the day combing the area to the east as far as the line Sistiane (I./1) — Rifembergo (III./1) — Cervizza (II./1).

The enemy fought there, too. For the most part, weak enemy units engaged our forces only briefly. The enemy was successful, however, in using roadblocks to prevent quick advances by our troops. Most of the guerrilla bands were withdrawing to the east and northeast. Some of the larger bands had never stood to fight. The Armee reported the guerrillas' losses to be:

two hundred fifty dead, five hundred twenty-three prisoners, and many weapons and much materiel captured.

On 27.9, the mop-up operation of the area was to continue.[11]

27.9.1943: The reinforced I./1 moved forward as far as Cossovello — Capriva, while the III./1 moved from Rifembergo to the south and occupied S. Daniele.

The II./1 and the Panzer-Pionier-Bataillon 1 *LAH* cleared away guerrilla forces as far as the line Zolla — Aidussina — Slokavi — Predmeia — Carnizza.

Once again, the enemy offered no resistance worth mentioning, but instead attempted to escape through his rathole individually and in small groups. His losses were higher than on the previous day:

Dead: six hundred twenty-eight. Captured: 1,240.

The gap to the north was finally closed.

Orders for 28.9.1943 remained unchanged.

28.9.1943: Panzer-Pionier-Bataillon 1 moved up as far as Villabassa, the reinforced I./1 as far as S. Vito, the III./1 as far as Gradischie. The II./1 mopped up the area on both sides of the road from Aidussina to Zolla.

For 29.9.1943, the Kampfgruppe received orders to close the encircling ring south of the line Vipacco — Preval — Planina, where it had begun to expand.

29.9.1943: At about 13.00 hours, Panzer-Pionier-Bataillon 1 left Villabassa for Senosecchio, the I./1 moved from S. Vito toward Pochrai, and the III./1 from Gradischie toward Senabor. They all reached their day's objectives without encountering significant resistance.

30.9.1943: The units were busy restructuring and preparing for the move on 1.10.1943 into the area on the southern edge of Triest — Cosina.

With that move, the second part of the mop-up action began, the clearing of the Istria peninsula and the area north of Fiume.

1.10.1943: By evening, the units had reached the designated area south of Triest.

The reinforced Regimentsgruppe SS-Panzergrenadier-Regiment 1 *LAH* was to move out on 2.10.1943, push to the south along three separate roads, capture the Quieto river, establish a bridgehead, and block along the line Montone — Pinguente. The other units were to be deployed against the area north of Fiume.

2.10.1943: Without encountering significant resistance, and hindered only by roadblocks or obstacles, the reinforced Regimentsgruppe's Stab and elements of the III./1 reached Isola and Sieciole on the coast of the Gulf of Triest and Castelnuovo. The I./1 reached Cernova, the Pionier-Bataillon San Quirico, and the II./1 Duovi. Special guidelines were given for the clearing of the Istria peninsula. The guidelines touched briefly on the origin of the bands, their activities, and their leadership. In the guidelines, the suspicion was expressed that a high, if not the highest, guerrilla leadership (Tito) was to be found in Pisino. It was also explained that the population, acting under the pressure from the guerrillas, which were predominantly Communist on the Istria peninsula, supported the Communist movement. The Slovenians were to be treated with consideration, if they did not take part in the fight, with an eye toward a latter rapprochement with the country.

3.10.1943: The reinforced Regimentsgruppe Panzergrenadier-Regiment 1 *LAH* used the bulk of the III./1 to capture the section of the Quieto near Cittanova in accordance with orders. Pionier-Bataillon 1 captured the section near Montone, and the II./1 near Pinguente. Elements of the III./1 were still busy mopping up Buie that evening.

4.10.1943: The I./1 was moved around to secure the north-south connection in the section Visinada — Caroiba. The III./1 and the Pionier-Bataillon then moved along two separate roads toward the supposed guerrilla center in Pisino. The II./1 meanwhile, after making a brief reconnaissance thrust into the mountains near Santa Lucia, was moving forward from Pinguente toward Cerraia.

5.10.1943: Tito was rumored to have escaped from Pisino at the last minute. While the Pionier-Bataillon continued to clear the area around that town, the III./1 made a thrust via Gimino to Barbana, which it occupied.

Proceeding in a broad front from Pinguente, the units moved by evening as far as the line Pisino — section of the Borutto — Castel Lupogliano (18. Panzerdivision) and combed the terrain.

The results so far on the Istria peninsula:

six hundred ninety-nine dead, eight hundred thirteen prisoners.

6.10.1943: In the course of the day, the I./1 was relieved by elements of the III./Infanterie-Regiment 191 in the sector Cittanova — Montana.

The I./1's section of road defense was moved farther to the south to the line Caraiba — Pisino.

The Pionier-Bataillon *LAH* was then adjacent to the south as far as and including Barbano. The I./1 swept from Barbano across the Albona area and onto the Istria peninsula to the south.

The II./1 moved from Cerveto via Valdarsa to Rianon, in order to make a move from there toward Moschiena along the coastal road.

Elements of the III./1 swept along the mountains beside the Arsa valley.

7.10.1943: The reinforced Regimentsgruppe regrouped such that it could proceed from the line Barbano — Gimino — Pisino on 8.10 and 9.10, move to the west and south, and finish combing the Istria peninsula.

8.10.1943: The regrouping required an entire day because of the difficult road conditions. The Sturmgeschützabteilung was to be loaded onto trains in Udine on that day and to assemble in the area west of Karlovac for use in clearing the area southeast of Laibach, an operation which received the code name "Wolkenbruch" [cloudburst].

9.10.1943: The reinforced Regimentsgruppe Panzergrenadier-Regiment 1 *LAH*, in performing its mop-up of the western half of the Istria peninsula, reached the line from the eastern edge of Pola — Dignano — Valle — Curilli — Cantanaro. One group of the III./1 occupied Rovigno in a rapid assault.

There was little enemy resistance; the Armee reported thirty-three dead.

10.10.1943: By evening, all the elements of the the reinforced Regimentsgruppe, acting within the framework of the XII. Panzerkorps, had reached the western coast of Istria. In the evening, the Regimentsgruppe began to assemble in the area east of Triest. The reinforced Regimentsgruppe was to be moved into the Gurkfeld area (about one hundred kilometers east of Laibach) to participate in Operation Wolkenbruch. Upon arrival, it was to be subordinated to the 162. Infanteriedivision. The tracked-vehicle elements of the Regimentsgruppe were to be moved to the new assembly area by rail.

11./12.10.1943: The reinforced Regimentsgruppe marched for two days to reach the Laibach area on the evening of 12.10. It found temporary billets there. Because the area west of Gurkfeld was occupied by guerrilla bands, the Regimentsgruppe received orders to continue its march with the bulk of its troops via Litija, Spodlog, Tepe, Preska, and Nzivice to Ratschach. It was to deploy elements immediately into the area St. Janz — Bostanj (about fifty kilometers northeasst of Laibach), from the Save as far as the border of the Reich (today the Austrian border) to clear it of guerrilla forces. Following that, it was to leave defensive forces along the border from St. Janz to Telce, where they would be adjacent to the border patrol.

13.10.1943: The reinforced Regimentsgruppe deployed one reinforced Bataillon for the mop-up operation north of the Save and moved the rest of its forces to Litija on 13.10.1943. From there, it sent out combat reconnaissance forces into the mountainous area held by the guerrillas. This reconnaissance was in preparation for its own continued motorized march. The Sturmgeschützabteilung *LAH*, just arriving in Triest, received orders to move to the Gurkfeld area and to establish contact there with the 162. Infanteriedivision. It was to march via

Laibach, Demzale, Celje, Tuffer, Zidan, Most, Leonica, and Gurkfeld. It was to find intermediate billets on 15.10 northeast of Laibach.

14.10.1943: The reconnaissance showed guerrilla bands on the road from Laibach via Litija to Ratschach.

The Regiment received orders to mop up the areas south and north of the road during its march into the Gurkfeld area.

The Bataillon deployed to the north assumed its designated border defense positions.

15.10.1943: After clearing the area west of Ratschach of guerrillas, the 162. Infanteriedivision issued orders to secure the area Steinbrück — Ratschach — Mrna River — Gurk River.

The Sturmgeschützabteilung moved according to orders into the area northeast of Laibach.

16.10.1943: The Regimentsgruppe occupied its designated defensive positions and conducted reconnaissance into the area south of Gurkfeld.

17.10.1943: The Regiment moved elements into the town of Leskovec and the surrounding area (3.5 kilometers south of Gurkfeld).

The 162. Infanteriedivision had ordered the Regiment to be relieved; elements of Grenadierregiment 314 arrived to do so.

Situation and the mission:

Under the leadership of the Croation guerrilla leader Tito, the Slovenian bands had joined the movement under the slogan of Slovenr freedom.

The bands fought in small groups, aided by the thickly forested, dense mountain terrain. They were hard to catch.

The Armee had as its mission the breaking of guerrilla resistance in a militarily and politically distinct area on both sides of the western Croatian border and well as the Unterkraine area.

The attack was to be conducted primarily by the 162. Infanteriedivision (with the reinforced Regimentsgruppe *LAH*) and the XII. Panzerkorps, while the 71. Infanteriedivision and Artilleriekommando 122 were to hold the designated line south and west of the encircled area. Motorized groups were to make rapid advances, creating smaller encirclements, which were to be mopped up one by one.

18.10.1943: The reinforced Regimentsgruppe of Panzergrenadier-Regiment 1 *LAH* was finally completely relieved.

19.10.1943: The code name "*HJ*-Division" for the reinforced Regimentsgruppe *LAH* was dropped by Heeresgruppe B.

20.10.1943: The reinforced Regimentsgruppe was moved into the area around Landstraß to prepare for the second part of Operation Wolkenbruch.

The Operation was scheduled to begin on 21.10.1943.

21.10.1943: The Regiment set out from Landstraß to the southwest, then turned south. Travelling via Rudolfswerth (Novo Mesto), it reached the town of Semic (ten kilometers northwest of Crnomelj). The enemy offered stronger resistance to this move than previously.

Orders arrived from Heeresgruppe B for the II. SS-Panzerkorps stating that the Führer wished to pull the 1. SS-Panzerdivision *LAH* out of the Operation and to prepare it for transport to the east.[12] The reinforced Regimentsgruppe of Panzergrenadier-Regiment 1 *LAH* was to be added to the structure at the end of the move to the transport area. With that, the Gruppe was still available for use in Wolkenbruch, at least temporarily.

22.10.1943: The reinforced SS-Panzergrenadier-Regiment 1 made a motorized thrust from Zamesko to the south toward Crnomelj and secured the road to the east and west. Elements dismounted and captured the line Pezka — Voda — Gaberje against minor resistance.

23.10.1943: While most of the reinforced Regimentsgruppe of Panzergrenadier-Regiment 1 was securing the line Zamesko — Rudolfswerth (Novo Mesto) — Crnomelj, elements moved from Suhor — Metlika to the east and, near Lovic (eight kilometers east-northeast of Metlika), established contact with the force from 162. Infanteriedivision which was moving west from the Krasic area.

24.10.1943: Because the SS-Panzergrenadier-Regiment 1's coming attack was to be directed toward the northwest, it regrouped (meanwhile combing the terrain) along the line Vivodina — Tupcina road junction — Rudolfswerth.

25.10.1943: By evening, elements of the Regiment had moved from the Rudolfswerth — Gaber area to the soutwest and northwest, had broken the enemy resistance, and had established bridgeheads across the Gurk near Sotesko and Straza.

The Divisionkommando of the 1. SS-Panzerdivision *LSSAH* requested that the reinforced Regimentsgruppe of SS-Panzergrenadier-Regiment 1 and SS-Sturmgeschützabteilung 1 be released. The II. SS-Panzerkorps replied with a request to Heeresgruppe B to retain the Regiment so as not to endanger Operation Wolkenbruch.

26.10.1943: Moving out from the bridgeheads established on the previous day, a motorized force from Panzergrenadier-Regiment 1 moved against tough resistance via Seisenberg and Treffen and captured the town of Mrna. It secured this line to the east and west. In addition, the Regiment extended its line of defense to the south as far as Smuka.

27.10.1943: The roads between Smuka and Seisenberg and between Soteska and Seisenberg were blocked by the Regiment.

28.10.1943: The 162. Infanteriedivision released the reinforced SS-Panzergrenadier-Regiment 1 from its subordination, and the II. SS-Panzerkorps released the entire 1. SS-Panzerdivision *LAH*.

The entire force from the Division deployed in the guerrilla area was to assemble in the Cilli area so that it could be loaded for transport starting on 1.11.1943.

Our presentation of the deployment of the reinforced Regimentsgruppe of the SS-Panzergrenadier-Regiment in the Yugoslavian guerrilla war ends with that. In section d), we will continue with the entire Division's transport.

d) 21.10.1943 - 7.11.1943: Loading the Division for transport to Russia.

20.10.1943: At 16.00 hours the Transport Kommandant for Milan arrived at the Division Stab of the *LAH* in Salsomaggiore to discuss the Division's transport.

He had orders from his higher-ups at the Oberkommando der Wehrmacht to load only the Division's tracked vehicles and to move them to Munich. The wheeled vehicles were to move overland. In Munich, the Division would be issued winter equipment. The date had not yet been set for the beginning of the move.

A lively discussion ensued to persuade him to allow at least the field kitchens and the fuel tanker trucks to travel on the trains.

Further negotiations had to be conducted with the Transport Kommandants for Innsbruck (where the supply services were) and Laibach.

21.10.1943 - 27.10.1943: On 21.10, the advance command group of the Division boarded a train at the Parma station under the assumption that it was to prepare for the Division's billeting in St. Pölten. In the days following, orders for loading the troops were rescinded almost as fast as they were issued.

While the Division was presently in a war theatre under the control of the Oberkommando der Wehrmacht, it was about to be transferred to one for which the Oberkommando der Heer was responsible. This division of command brought with it grotesque arrangements, which eventually worked to the force's disadvantage.

As has been stated, the tracked-vehicle elements were to travel by rail while the wheeled-vehicle elements drove to Munich. Another order followed that one, stating that the wheeled vehicles were to move to Innsbruck, while the I./SS-Panzerregiment 1 without its Panzers would be transported to Kassel, where it would receive new Panzer V's.

Finally, orders came to move the tracked vehicles, including the field kitchens and fuel tankers, and later the wheeled vehicles, all by rail, from Italy, Innsbruck, and Laibach into the area Gmünd — Amstetten — St. Pölten — Stockerau — Horn. There, after a short billeting period while winter equipment was being fitted, the entire unit would be tactically structured and shipped out again.

28.10.1943: Toward noon, the Divisional commander and the Ia arrived in Vienna, reported to the Wehrkreiskommando XVII in the former Royal and Imperial War Ministry, set up an advance message center under Hauptsturmführer Linden, and began the preparatory work for the Division's brief stay in the above-mentioned area.

29.10.1943 - 2.11.1943: In the night before 30.10, the Division received orders to detrain not in the St. Pölten area but to move immediately in present condition into the Ukraine, into the command region of Heeresgruppe Süd.

This meant that the Division would arrive in a new combat area for immediate deployment in a totally unsuitable structure. That structure was (in order of transport trains):

Advance personnel
Tracked vehicles for the entire Division (minus the II./SS-Panzerregiment 1, some of which was equipped with Panzers in Magdeburg and some of which was equipped with Panzers at the detraining station in Russia)
Half-tracked and wheeled vehicle elements of the SS-Panzergrenadier-Regiment 2
Wheeled-vehicle elements of SS-Panzergrenadier-Regiment 2 and Divisionsstab
Wirtschafts-Bataillon
SS-Panzer-Aufklärungsabteilung 1
III./SS-Panzer-Artillerie-Regiment 1 and SS-Sanitätsabteilung 1
The remaining wheeled-vehicle elements of the Division.

SS-Panzer-Nachrichtenabteilung 1 and elements of the Artillerie-Regiment, which had already been detrained in part at Innsbruck and St. Pölten, followed in a second echelon. While the elements deployed in the Laibach area (the SS-Panzergrenadier-Regiment 1, SS-Panzer-Pionier-Bataillon 1, SS-Sturmgeschützabteilung 1) were loaded back in between 2.11 and 7.11 and followed in a third echelon.

This impossible structuring was to have dire consequences.

"From the Eastern Front, over the Brenner Pass, into Upper Italy."

Part 9

THE 1. SS-PANZERDIVISION *LSSAH* IN THE UKRAINE
Fourth deployment on the Eastern Front

Section I
1.11.1943 - 21.1.1944: ALL AROUND SHITOMIR[1]

a) Situation of Heeresgruppe Süd.

Spurred on by their defensive success around Kursk, the Soviet High Command took over the offensive with decisiveness and operational skill. In the second half of 1943, the Soviet Army regained three hundred fifty kilometers and pushed the German forces back across the Dnieper. They owed this triumph to an overwhelming numerical superiority which enabled them to go on the offensive at several places at once and to stay on the offensive. By the middle of October, Soviet General Koniew with his Second Ukrainian Front had captured three bridgeheads across the Dnieper east of Krementschug, from which he could throw his forces at the important industrial area at Kriwoi Rog. We lost Dnjepropetrowsk on October 25. While Heeresgruppe Süd with its 1. Panzerarmee waged a successful counterthrust against Koniew's Second Ukrainian Front, Heeresgruppe A to the south lost Melitopol to General Tolbutkin's Fourth Ukrainian Front and stood in danger of losing the Perekop isthmus. As if that were not enough, on November 3, 1943, Soviet Army General Watutin's First Ukrainian Front launched a counterattack on both sides of Kiev with thirty infantry divisions, twenty-four tank brigades, and ten motorized infantry brigades. Kiev and Fastow (sixty kilometers southwest of Kiev) fell on November 6 and Radomyschl on the Teterew on November 11. On November 13, Watutin's leading tanks were in Shitomir.

The northern wing of Heeresgruppe Süd was hard-hit, and it was in danger of being split from Heeresgruppe Mitte.

For that reason, the two Panzerdivisionen assembling in Kirowograd (in the middle of Heeresgruppe Süd) had to be moved as quickly as possible to the northern wing of Heeresgruppe Süd. Of those forces, the 1. Panzerdivision of the Heer had already arrived in its entirety. Most of the wheeled-vehicle elements of the 1. SS-Panzerdivision *LAH* were also there.

b) 1.11.1943 - 13.11.1943: Battle at the detraining stations, assembly of the Division.

2.11.1943: The advance Kommando of the 1. SS-Panzerdivision *LAH* under the command of the O 1, Hauptsturmführer Tiemann, arrived in Kirowograd and was subordinated to the 8. Armee.[2]

3.11.1943: More wheeled-vehicle elements, including the 2. (Funk)/SS-Panzer-Nachrichtenabteilung 1 and the SS-Panzer-Aufklärungsabteilung 1, arrived. The Divisional headquarters were established in Adshamka (about twenty kilometers east of Kirowograd). The Division was subordinated to the XXXXVIII. Panzerkorps for the purpose of billeting.

4.11.1943: The 1. Generalstabsoffizier of the XXXXVIII. Panzerkorps informed the unit that the enemy forces moving on Kriwoi Rog farther to the south had turned toward Kirowograd. He requested the deployment of fighter commandos along the railway line to the south, especially at the Kuzowka station (about forty kilometers south of Adshamka). The O 1 sent a reconnaissance squad from the SS-Panzer-Aufklärungsabteilung 1 toward Hp. Tschabonowka and one from the SS-Panzer-Pionier-Bataillon 1 toward Nowaja Praga. A fairly weak Russian reconnaissance force was captured in Mitrofanowka and forty Russian soldiers taken prisoner in the southern part of Nowaja Praga. There was no other contact with the enemy. The Korps requested that constant scouting patrols guard the railway line.

5.11.1943: More wheeled-vehicle elements arrived and were detrained. The scouting patrols brought in prisoners, evidently stragglers from their units. The Korps informed us that the arriving heavy Panzers might possibly be moved to Kriwoi Rog and subordinated to the LVII. Panzerkorps.

6.11.1943: The Divisional commander and the Ia arrived at the Adshamka headquarters.

At 18.15 hours, the Chef of the Generalstab of the XXXXVIII. Panzerkorps informed us that the enemy was threatening to capture the railway junction at Fastow (for a description of the situation, see Section Ia) and that orders to march the wheeled vehicles to Biala Zerkwa (about three hundred kilometers away) could be expected in the course of the night. Sturmbannführer Lehmann proposed that the wheeled-vehicle elements of the *LAH* be subordinated to the 1. Panzerdivision for the march, so that the Divisionsstab could move as quickly as possible to the Biala Zerkwa area, where it could unload and assemble most of the Division. The Korps declared itself in agreement.

7.11.1943: At 00.30 hours, the Korps informed us that the railway line near Fastow had been cut and that the rest of the Division would be unloaded in the Berditschew area.

At 03.00 hours, the O 1 was sent to Berditschew (total march: about four hundred kilometers) with an advance detachment, where he was to report to the Panzerarmeeoberkommando 4. The elements of the *LAH* arriving there were to be subordinated to the 4. Panzerarmee.

The elements arriving east of Kirowograd were:

Most of the I./SS-Panzergrenadier-Regiment 2
Elements of the Divisionsstab
Elements of SS-Panzer-Nachrichtenabteilung 1
Elements of SS-Santitätsabtteilung 1
SS-Panzer-Aufklärungsabteilung 1
SS-Verplegungsamt 1
Elements of SS-Flakabteilung 1
III./SS-Panzer-Artillerie-Regiment 1
SS-Panzerjägerabteilung 1
Wheeled-vehicle elements of SS-Panzergrenadier-Regiment 1
SS-Divisions-Nachschubtruppe 1.

Marching behind the 1. Panzerdivision and subordinated to it for the purpose of the march, these units overcame extremely difficult road conditions to reach the area southwest of Fastow on 14.11. There they joined the bulk of the Division, which had already been fighting for days.

The Divisional commander marched away immediately with the operations staff to Kasatin (thirty kilometers southeast of Berditschew), while the Ia travelled to Panzerarmeeoberkommando 4 to be briefed on the situation.

8.11.1943: At 10.00 hours the Chef of the Generalstab of the 4. Panzerarmee, Generalmajor Fangohr, briefed the Ia of the *LAH* on the situation. As has already been mentioned, the First Ukrainian Front had moved numerically superior forces across the Dnieper on both sides of Kiev and was moving rapidly along the road Kiev — Shitomir. Strong elements were also moving to the southwest on both sides of Fastow. The 4. Panzerarmee consisted of eleven Infanterie-Divisionen, but all of them were considerably weakened and were no longer equal to the enemy pressure being exerted on them. In addition, it had been torn into three widely scattered groups. The VII. Armeekorps had been pushed to the southwest, the XIII. Armeekorps forced back to Shitomir, and the LIX. Armeekorps thrown back to Korosten. Although the Chef of Stab had complete understanding for the Division's wish to wait for all its forces to be assembled before deployment, the Armee saw itself forced to deploy each individual element as it arrived. The Division's mission: a counterattack toward Fastow.

At 12.45 hours, the Division's operations staff arrived in Kasatin and established contact with those of its elements which had already arrived or which were currently being unloaded. It discovered that the authorities of the Reichsbahn [German railway] were reporting that the 1. Kompanie of SS-Panzergrenadier-Regiment 2 (under Hauptsturmführer Diefenthal) had been detrained on 8.11 in Kozanka, about eighteen kilometers west of Fastow; it had come under enemy fire during the unloading and was fighting its way along the railway line. It had already captured the railway station at Popielnia.[3] The Kompaniechef was badly wounded in the fighting. The 19. (Aufklärung)/SS-Panzergrenadier-Regiment 1 had detrained in Popielnia, together with the 7. and 9./SS-Panzergrenadier-Regiment 2, and had joined the fighting. Oberscharführer Söllhammer of the 9./2 reported on this combat:

> "Our detraining at the Popielnia station together with the 7. Kompanie was severly complicated by the presence of four T-34's stationed in the vicinity. The vehicles were ordered to withdraw to the west.

We later found the drivers in their vehicles, killed by shots to the head, near Wassylowka. The Kompanie established an all-around defense at the railway station. Shortly after noon, our Kompaniechef (Obersturmführer Karck) realized that we could no longer hold that position. He ordered me to inform the machine gun squad leaders that we would be withdrawing. Just a moment before, two boys from our reserve troops had knocked off two tanks with magnetic anti-tank hollow charges. When we investigated the crippled tanks, we discovered that there were women in the crew. The 7./2 (under Hauptsturmführer Heinze) was to be our rear guard.

Disengaging from the enemy ran fairly smoothly, but those Russian tanks which were still fit for combat immediately pursued us. The goal for our retreat was initially the Browki station. We could see a locomotive with several freight cars sitting there. As we approached the station, five T-34's with about fifty Russian infantrymen sitting on them came charging toward us. There was an exchange of fire, and I heard the Russian commissar shout: 'Don't shoot, SS! There are women and bread waiting for you in Staligrad!' The Russian tanks divided into two groups, surrounded us on both sides, and then advanced on our column from the rear. With that, we were hopelessly surrounded. Some of our men surrendered at once, and I saw Oberscharführer Gratz, Oberscharführer Burgstaller, and Oberscharführer Gantiola shoot themselves with their pistols. The Russian infantrymen hit some of the men with the butts of their rifles. The rest were taken to the railway station and locked in. I myself had lingered at the station at the beginning because I was busy collecting the ammunition boxes from some of the young men who were too weak to follow. So I was heavily loaded down and fell behind the advance. As a result, I was not caught in the encirclement and could observe the events. I took cover in a potato field, covered myself with potato leaves, and waited for a chance to free my imprisoned comrades. The 7. Kompanie behind us was also attacked by tanks with infantrymen mounted on them. The Kompanie retreated across the railway embankment and pulled back into the forest about five hundred meters south of it. Night was falling. I heard the drunken hollers of the Russians, and some pistol shots afterwards. I learned later that the Soldateska were shooting my comrades in the back of the neck. I waited for dawn and used its light to make my way along the embankment to the west. I was shot at by the Russian guards and took a hit to the left heel. For two days I walked along the tracks with the Russian spearhead often catching up with me or even passing me. Each night, I marched on and put a little distance between me and the Russians. At about noon on the third day, I finally reached the German position. I came under fire from my comrades as I approached. I had to pull off my more-or-less white undershirt and wave it. The Kompanieführer of this Heer unit had me driven in his car back to the field kitchen, where the rest of the Kompanie was. Our field cook had managed to sneak away from the railway station and to spirit his field kitchen away, as well. He had set himself the task of feeding a starving Kompanie. He was extremely disappointed that he had put seventy chickens into the soup, and only myself and one comrade (Hoffmann), who showed up after me, were alive to benefit from them. This was all that was left of the 9. Kompanie."

Farther to the west, elements of the II./SS-Panzergrenadier-Regiment 2 had detrained in Browki and Czarnorudka and, under the leadership of the returning Hauptsturmführer Heinze (Chef of the 7./2), were securing the towns of Browki (the 1. and elements of the 7./2) and Wczerajsze (elements of the 7./2) and the Czarnorudka railway station (the 5./2) with all-around defenses. Elements of the 6., 10., 14., and 18./SS-Panzergrenadier-Regiment 2 were also deployed there.

At 13.10 hours, Hauptsturmführer Wiesemann, Chef of the 2./SS-Sturmgeschützabteilung 1 reported that his unit was ready for detraining in Berditschew. He received orders to unload in Kasatin instead and to move his Batterie along the railway line to join Kampfgruppe Heinze in Browki. The 1. Batterie/SS-Sturmgeschützabteilung 1 (under Obersturmführer Gaschnitz) arrived and received orders to unload in Berditschew, from where it was to march to Czarnorudka. The 3./SS-Sturmgeschützabteilung 1 (under Hauptsturmführer Rettlinger) was moved up to Kasatin to stand at the Division's disposal.

At 13.40 hours, the commander of the III./1, Sturmbannführer Weidenhaupt, reported that his troops were unloaded at Skwira, farther to the east. He received orders to reach Wczerajsze, proceed to Browki, and provide defense on both sides of the railway line.

The I./1 (under Obersturmbannführer Schiller) was detrained in the Berditschew — Kasatin area and proceeded to Rozyn, where it provided defense. Finally, the elements of the Pionier-Bataillon arrived and were ordered to set up all-around defenses in Kaszperowka, twelve kilometers west of Czarnorudka.

At 14.15 hours, the first elements of SS-Panzerregiment *LAH* to arrive received orders to unload in Berditschew because of the good ramps available there, and to march in groups no smaller than a Kompanie. These groups were to conduct road reconnaissance beforehand toward Kasatin and Czarnorudka.

At 15.30 hours, the Ia inquired at Heeresgruppe Süd about the situation and the measures to be taken.

At 18.40 hours, there was a call from Oberst i.G. von Mellenthin. The *LAH* was to be subordinated to the XXXXVIII. Panzerkorps under General der Panzertruppen von Knobelsdorff. Its intended mission: to make a thrust along the railway line on Fastow with whatever forces had already arrived.

At 21.30 hours, the 1./SS-Sturmgeschützabteilung 1 (under Obersturmführer Gaschnitz) reported from Czarnorudka that it had assumed its designated defensive position and that it had sent out forces to establish contact with Kampfgruppe Heinze in Wczerajsze. In Czarnorudka, the men separated from the 19./2 were picked up.

At 20.10 hours, the Ia informed the Chef of the Generalstab of the Korps that the Division could set out on 9.11 with only two Bataillone and one Sturmgeschützbatterie. The reason was that most of the Division had been unloaded in Shitomir at the Armee's command. There were no fuel supplies there, and the road was completely congested with the retreating supply trains, the Luftwaffe's ground forces, and more. In addition, no communications equipment had arrived. The Chef of the Generalstab of the Korps ordered all elements which had arrived (except for those in Wczerajsze) to move on 9.11 into the Biala Zerkwa area and to the north of there (about one hundred twenty kilometers to the east).

At 20.30 hours, the shift in the Division's position was set in motion with the issuance of individual orders.

9.11.1943: The Division's march was made extrordinarily long and difficult by the muddy roads.

At 17.30 hours, the new Divisional headquarters were set up in Biala Zerkwa.

The headquarters of the SS-Panzergrenadier-Regiment 1 were in Ssokolow. Elements of the Regiment had also arrived there. The commander of the I./SS-Panzerregiment 1, Sturmbannführer Kuhlmann, reported the arrival of the Abteilung's Stab with one Kompanie of Panzer V's in Wczerajsze. An eighty-watt radio station from the Korps-Nachrichtenabteilung was to report there, according to the Korps' orders, and was to be handed over the Division. Two additional Kompanien from the I./SS-Panzergrenadier-Regiment 1 had been detrained in Skwira and were at the time on the march toward Biala Zerkwa.

At 22.05 hours, orders came from the Korps. All at the time in Wczerajsze were to fuel the Panzers and to set out immediately in the dark for Fastow without waiting for the arrival of other elements.

At 22.10 hours, this order was transmitted to Sturmbannführer Kuhlmann with instructions that the refueling was to be done by means of an armoured train holding about sixty cubic meters of fuel. Obersturmbannführer Stoltz, the Division's Ib, and his co-workers had found this way to solve the problem.

On 10.11.1943, the *Leibstandarte* was to relieve the elements of the 25. Panzerdivision deployed near Fastowez (twelve kilometers east of Fastow).

10.11.1943: At 03.00 hours, one Bataillon from SS-Panzergrenadier-Regiment 1 set out from Sokolowka toward Fastowez. Reconnaissance reported that the railway embankment south of Fastowez was occupied by enemy troops.

By 08.30 hours, the I./1 had pushed the enemy away from the railway embankment south of Fastowez and was attacking to the north.

At 11.45 hours, SS-Panzergrenadier-Regiment 1 reported its intention to go around Fastowez and to attack the town from the north. The Sturmgeschützabteilung and one Pionier-Kompanie were moved up to Hrebionki and subordinated to the Regiment.

At 14.05 hours, the Ia of the 2. SS-Panzerdivision *DR* reported that enemy tanks were attacking from Kischtschenzi toward Kowalowka. An Artillerie-Abteilung from SS-Panzer-Artillerie-Regiment 2 *DR* was subordinated to the SS-Panzergrenadier-Regiment 1 *LAH*. The 2. SS-Panzerdivision *DR* had orders to cover the eastern flank of the planned attack by the XXXXVIII. Panzerkorps.

About noon, the Chef of the Generalstab of the Korps, Oberst i.G. von Mellenthin, had informed the Ia that the enemy was preparing himself in the area northeast of Fastow with three tank corps, evidently with the intention of moving on Berditschew. The Korps intended to move north into the flank of this enemy attack in order to interrupt his march route from Kiev to Shitomir.

For this purpose, the 2. SS-Panzerdivision *DR* stayed to the right in its former position with orders to cover the eastern flank, while the 25. Panzerdivision moved to the left with orders to attack Fastow from the south. The *LAH* was to deploy elements to cover the 25. Panzerdivision's attack.

By 14.00 hours, the I./1 had penetrated Fastowez, and the II./1 was moved up to that town as reinforcement.

At 14.15 hours, the commander of SS-Panzergrenadier-Regiment 1, Obersturmbannführer Frey, reported that there was an attack by at least an entire enemy regiment from the northeast, supported by at least five tanks. Because the enemy's situation and strength to the east was unclear, the III./1 and its subordinated Pionier-Kompanie were to halt in Sokolowka in order to provide cover for the deep flank.

At 14.40 hours, the Chef of the 2. (Panzerspäh)/SS-Panzer-Aufklärungsabteilung 1 reported to Biala Zerkwa and received orders to billet his forces there and to hold two combat-strength reconnaissance forces ready for 11.11.

At 15.09 hours, the Ia of the Generalkommando reported that elements of Division *DR* had been forcefully attacked in Winnizkija Stary. Orders were issued to the *LAH* to take over the defense of this town without losing sight of its mission to attack to the north.

At 15.15 hours, orders went out to the SS-Panzergrenadier-Regiment 1 to deploy a Grenadierkompanie reinforced by Sturmgeschütz to clear Winnizkija Stary of enemy forces and to defend the town.

At 16.15 hours, the reinforced SS-Panzergrenadier-Regiment 1 received its orders for 11.11:

> "The reinforced SS-Panzergrenadier-Regiment 1 is to capture its first intermediate objective, the line Klechowka — Snatinka, on 11.11 and to hold it."

At 16.30 hours, there was a call from the Chef of Stab: "The attack of the 25. Panzerdivision has not made it through. Regrouping will be necessary. The *LAH* is to capture and hold the designated line Snatinka — Klechowka and is to provide cover for our flank. The unit adjacent to the right is unable to start its advance on 11.11."

At 16.35 hours, the commander of the SS-Panzergrenadier-Regiment 1, Obersturmbannführer Frey, informed us that the I./1 had reported from Fastowez that the enemy was launching heavy attacks, which it had so far repulsed. In Winnizkija Stary, the 16. (Flak)/1 and the 20. (Pionier)/1 together with subordinated elements of the SS-Panzer-Artillerie-Regiment 2 *DR* were defending the town. The leading elements of the reinforced II./1 were at the railway embankment south of Fastowez. The reinforced III./1 (one Sturmgeschützbatterie and one Pionier-Kompanie) stood at the Division's disposal level with Hrebonki.

At 18.30 hours, the Ia ordered the Kommandant-Stabsquartier (under Hauptsturmführer Korsemann) to use the subordinated 4./SS-Panzer-Aufklärungsabteilung 1 (minus one reconnaissance group) to reconnoiter toward Ustynowka and to secure a new Divisional headquarters.

At 19.15 hours, the reinforced SS-Panzergrenadier-Regiment 1 (minus the III./1) was defending Fastowez. The reinforced III./1 remained in Hrebonki with orders to keep the supply route open. SS-Panzer-Pionier-Bataillon 1 received orders to move forward to Hrebonki.

At 22.15 hours, the Ia of the Generalkommando, Oberstleutnant i.G. Estor, expressed his opinion in a briefing that a thrust by the armoured force under Kuhlmann (the reinforced I./SS-Panzerregiment 1) along the railway line toward Fastow could contribute to the success of the endeavours planned for 11.11.

For that reason, we present here that force's attack:

At 11.40, after receiving fuel from the armoured train, the Kampfgruppe had set out with twenty-two Panzer V's, two Panzergrenadierkompanien and one Panzer-Pionierkompanie.

At 12.40 hours, the first contact with the enemy occurred. The weak enemy resistance in front of and inside of Parypsi was broken. Three T-34's were destroyed. The unit's intention was then to regroup and to set off via Kamionka toward Popielnia. The difficult terrain meant that fuel consumption was high and the advance slow.

At 21.15 hours, Sturmbannführer Kuhlmann reported that the Kampfgruppe could not make an organized attack on Popielnia, which was occupied by strong enemy forces. The Kampfgruppe pulled back to Kamionka. The armoured train being used to provide fuel derailed north of Browki, and fuel had to be moved up by truck.

11.11.1943: At 09.35 hours, Kampfgruppe Kuhlmann set out at dawn and made a successful attack on Popielnia. It destroyed four enemy tanks.

At 11.30 hours, the Korps ordered the armoured force standing in front of the enemy stronghold at Kozanka to turn to the north toward Woliza and to have its forces capture the high ground west of Fastow.

By 12.05 hours, Kampfgruppe Kuhlmann had reached the forest north of Slawizce after a few small skirmishes. There it was to wait for the armoured fuel train. That train was stopped in Popielnia because the tracks had been blown up.

In Fastowez, an enemy attack on the southern edge of the town had been repulsed at 08.55 hours.

At 11.00 hours, the reinforced I./1 (under Obersturmbannführer Schiller) set out for Klechowka, and the reinforced II./1 (under Sturmbannführer Max Hansen) moved on Snetinka at 11.30 hours.

At 12.15 hours, the leading attack elements of the I./1 were involved in hard fighting for the commanding position on Hill 210. 6.

At 15.25 hours, Obersturmbannführer Frey reported the capture of Klechowka.

At 15.30 hours, preliminary briefings took place by the commanding general and the Chef of the Generalstab, and preparations began for the "great attack" on Fastow planned for 12.11.1943. The preparations ceased at 19.00 hours when a call came from the Ia of the Generalkommando: "Orders will probably change."

At 19.30 hours, orders came through the Chef of the Generalstab:

> "Stop preparations. Disengage from present sector in the night and assemble near the armoured force. The armoured force is to move at dawn via Dmitrowka toward Kornin. The Panzers of the VII. Armeekorps are to move from Chodorkow to the east. The VII. Armeekorps will attack frontally. Around Shitomir, our weak forces have been pushed back. The Russian cavalry attack on Shitomir is being fought on the eastern edge of the town."

At 19.47 hours, the Ia briefed the commander of the SS-Panzerregiment 1. The commander expressed concern that the relief of the forces in the Fastowez area be performed in time and with forces of sufficient strength. The Korps ordered at 23.25 hours that one reinforced Bataillon remain in Fastowez, which was to be subordinated to the 25. Panzerdivision starting at 05.30 hours on 12.11. Because these measures meant that the assault power of the Division, of which only elements were present already, was greatly reduced, the Ia rejected a march starting on 12.11.

The Generalkommando approved postponement of the beginning of the attack and ordered the Fastowez sector to change hands in the evening of 21.11.

At 21.10 hours, the Division ordered SS-Panzergrenadier-Regiment 1 to move along the reconnoitered road Biala Zerkwa — Fyrsy — Piszczyki — Dunajka and to reach Zydowieckie, where it was to establish a bridgehead. It was to seek and maintain contact with Kampfgruppe Kuhlmann. The reinforced 2./Sturmgeschützabteilung 1 (under Hauptsturmführer Wiesemann) formed the rear guard and disengaged when SS-Panzergrenadier-Regiment 1 had passed Winnizkija.

12.11.1943: At 01.00 hours, the commander of SS-Panzergrenadier-Regiment 1 (Obersturmbannführer Frey) reported in person at the Divisional headquarters that the disengagement had begun at 00.00 hours. The 1./SS-Panzer-Pionier-Bataillon 1 (under Obersturmführer Karstens) had been sent ahead to repair the designated march route. The reinforced III./1 followed with Poczujki as its provisional objective. The Divisional headquarters were supposed to be established in Dunajka.

At 11.25 hours, The Ia gave the Generalkommando a report from the Kommandant-Stabsquartier of the *LAH* that Parypsy was occupied by enemy forces and that the reinforced III./1 had orders to attack the town from the area two kilometers south of Dunajka. The new Divisional headquarters were in Dunajka. The Generalkommando responded that Panzer-Aufklärungsabteilung 25 was conducting reconnaissance toward Poczujki and Popielnia. The VII. Armeekorps had captured Lipki and was moving to the south on Kotljarka.

At 15.15 hours, the Generalstab's tactical group arrived in Dunajka and established contact with SS-Panzergrenadier-Regiment 1. Combat reconnaissance had revealed that Poczujki was free of enemy troops and that the bridge there was destroyed. Swch. Ssofijewka was occupied by enemy troops. The 1./SS-Panzer-Pionier-Bataillon 1 was on the way to Poczujki, and an assault troop had been deployed to capture Swch. Ssofijewka.

At 17.10 hours, Sturmbannführer Weidenhaupt, commander of the III./1, reported that the bridge in Poczujki was not capable of carrying Sturmgeschütze. They were being diverted to the crossing at Sawarce.

At 20.05 hours, orders were given to the SS-Panzergrenadier-Regiment 1: the reinforced III./1 was to start out immediately that night to Kornin because Kuhlmann was just before the town and needed fuel and ammunition. His supply elements had set up an all-around defense on the railway embankment south of Czarnowka.

At 22.40 hours, the III./1 was proceeding on Zydowce, while the I./1 was being relieved by the 25. Panzerdivision in Fastowez and was beginning its march to Dunajka.

At 23.00 hours, the armoured force reported that it was making no progress toward Kornin from the east because of the difficult terrain. Kuhlmann attempted to swing around to the south.

13.11.1943: At 03.30 hours, the reinforced III./1 (under Sturmbannführer Weidenhaupt) encountered enemy forces on the southern edge of Czernarowka and along the railway embankment to the south. He attempted to move around Czernarowka to the west and to advance on Zydowce.

By 10.05 hours, the reinforced III./1 had taken Zydowce and had established a bridgehead north of the Unawa sector.

At 10.10 hours, there was a visit from General der Panzertruppe Balck, who introduced himself at the Divisional headquarters as the next commanding general of the XXXXVIII. Panzerkorps. He informed us that the 1. Panzerdivision was southwest of Kornin and that he had seen German Panzers in the town. Those probably belonged to the armoured force under Kuhlmann.

At 10.15 hours, the reinforced SS-Panzergrenadier-Regiment 1 with two Bataillone set out for Karnin and reported at 10.47 hours the capture of Hill 218 (ten kilometers south of Kornin).

By 10.30 hours, the armoured force of the *LAH* and the armoured force of the 1. Panzerdivision had established contact near Balki, seven kilometers southeast of Kornin.

SS-Panzer-Pionier-Bataillon 1 received orders to secure the line Poczujki — Sawarce and to conduct reconnaissance along the railway line to the east toward Salwiszce and Kozanka and to the northeast toward Romanowka.

At 11.10 hours, the commanding general reported from the headquarters of SS-Panzergrenadier-Regiment 1 that the assumption was that the enemy had tanks and infantry of at least battalion-strength in Kornin. The situation in Paryspsy was unclear. He asked that the reinforced Panzergrenadier-Regiment 1 be moved up quickly.

The Ia of the 1. Panzerdivision, Oberstleutnant i.G. Zitzewitz, reported that the enemy had broken through with tanks from the west in Strokow (twelve kilometers west of Dunajka). Our Schützenpanzerwagenkompanie was fighting there.

At 11.15 hours, the armoured force under Kuhlmann became involved in the fighting around Kornin.

At 11.55 hours, the Oberbefehlshaber of the 4. Panzerarmee, Generaloberst Hoth, arrived at the Divisional headquarters to be briefed by the Ia on the situation. The Oberbefehlshaber also gave his impressions of the larger picture. A short time later, commanding General von Knobelsdorff arrived and brought along information that enemy infantry columns were marching southeast of Kornin from Mochnatschka toward Balki. A Sturmgeschützbatterie from the 1. Panzerdivision was moved out of Rudo and deployed against the enemy force attacking our deep flank and the rear of the 1. Panzerdivision in the area Parypsy — Pawolocz — Strokow.

At 13.00 hours, the Chef of the Generalstab, Oberst i.G. von Mellenthin, informed the Ia personally at headquarters that there were essentially no combat actions taking place on the Korps' defensive front east of Fastow. The 25. Panzerdivision had cleared the southern bank in Kamionka of enemy forces, captured Trylisy, and was moving forward against the railway line.

At 15.50 hours, there were reconnaissance reports from SS-Panzer-Pionier-Bataillon 1 to the following effect:

Romankowka, Slawiszcze, Czernowka, and Kozanka were free of enemy troops. The Bataillon was engaged in improving the two highway bridges between Poczujki and Zydowce.

At 16.50 hours, the Divisional commander, Oberführer Wisch, returned from Kornin and Balki. Both towns were under constant attack from the east by a force between battalion and regiment strength.

At 21.14 hours, the orders for 14.11.1943 were given:

> "The Generalkommando assumes that the enemy is assembling strong forces in the area east and north of Fastow in order to attack our right flank. The *LAH* is to deploy a Regimental force to secure the Irpen line from the fork in the river southwest of Mochnatschka as far as the western edge of Kornin. The Kornin bridgehead is to be expanded to the north and held.
> The dividing line between the *LAH* and the 25. Panzerdivision to the right: western edges of the towns Kozanka — Dmitrowka — Goljaki.
> Between the *LAH* and the 1. Panzerdivision to the left: Strokow (1.) — Zydowce (*LAH*) — church and north-south street in Kornin (1.)."

To accomplish this task, Kampfgruppe Heinze (the 6., 7., 10., 15., and 18./SS-Panzergrenadier-Regiment 2) was subordinated to SS-Panzergrenadier-Regiment 1.

SS-Panzer-Pionier-Bataillon 1, reinforced by one Batterie from SS-Sturmgeschützabteilung 1, cleared the towns of Pawolocz and Strokow of enemy forces.

The Divisional headquarters were in Zydowze starting at 11.00 hours on 14.11.

By 22.15 hours, all the Division's elements which had arrived had been informed of their missions.

At 23.30 hours, the Ia of the 1. Panzerdivision informed us that we could expect the arrival of the elements being moved up from Kirowograd on 14.11.1943.

c) 14.11.1943 - 25.11.1943: Fighting around Brusilow (see sketch 26)

14.11.1943: By 04.50 hours, the designated defensive positions had been assumed.

At 07.30 hours, Sturmbannführer Sandig, who had moved up the wheeled-vehicle elements from Kriwoi Rog, reported to the Divisional headquarters. In the course of the day, he reported, these elements could be expected to arrive. Obersturmbannführer Kraas, commander of SS-Panzergrenadier-Regiment 2, reported back from his furlough and applied himself at once to assembling and regrouping his unit.

At 08.45 hours, Hauptsturmführer Linden reported from the railway stations at Biala Zerkwa and Berditschew that the 5. and 6./SS-Panzergrenadier-Regiment 1 *LAH* had arrived. Additional elements were being detrained fifty kilometers west of Biala Zerkwa and were on the march toward Zydowce; among them were two heavy Flak-Batterien and one Vierlings-Flak-Batterie [four-barrelled anti-aircraft gun battery].

At 09.30 hours, the I./1 occupied Lipky, ten kilometers west of Kornin.

At 10.00 hours, SS-Panzer-Pionier-Bataillon 1 reported having cleared the towns of Strokow, Pawolocz, and Popielnia of enemy forces.

By 13.10 hours, the Divisional headquarters had been moved to Zydowce. The new commanding general arrived with his Ia and informed us of the plans for 15.11.1943. There was to be an attack, with the *LAH* to the right and the 1. Panzerdivision to the left, moving north along the route Kiev — Shitomir. The 25. Panzerdivision and elements of the 2. SS-Panzerdivision *DR* were to cover the right flank. The time planned for the start of the attack was 05.30 hours.

At 17.50 hours, the Chef of the Generalstab provided additional details concerning the next day's attack.

At 18.30 hours, the commanding general, General der Panzertruppen von Knobelsdorff, took his leave from the Divisional commander and from the Division. His successor, as has already been stated, was General der Panzertruppen Balck.

At 22.15 hours, Divisionsbefehl No. 34 was issued, giving the orders for the *LAH*'s units for 15.11:

> "The *XXXXVIII. Panzerkorps* is to move out of the Kornin area at 05.30 hours on 15.11.1943 with two Panzerdivisionen, the spearheads of which are to be held close together. The force is to make a thrust into the flank and rear of the enemy forces attacking Shitomir.
>
> The *25. Panzerdivision* is to use one Regimental force to provide cover for the flank in the Dmitrowka sector (including the town).
>
> The *attack objective*: the Korostyschew area. Bridgeheads are to be established across the Teterew on both sides of Korostyschew.
>
> The *march route* for the *LAH*: Kornin — Ssolowjewka — Wodotyi — Boljatschew — Sdwishka — Wilnja — Korostyschew.
>
> The *dividing line* between this unit and the 1. Panzerdivision: North Kornin — Gnilez (1.) — Center of Boljatschew — Ssemenowka (*LAH*) — Schtscheglijewka (1.) — Korostyschew (*LAH*).
>
> *Missions*:
>
> a) The *reinforced SS-Panzergrenadier-Regiment 1* (consisting of Sturmgeschützabteilung 1, the I./SS-Panzerregiment 1, the I., II., and 9./SS-Panzer-Artillerie-Regiment 1, the 1. and 3. of SS-Panzerjägerabteilung, and the 1./SS-Panzer-Pionier-Bataillon 1 *LAH*) is to wait until the II. and III./1 have been relieved by the I./2 and Kampfgruppe Heinze and then to set out at 05.30 hours on 15.11.1943 to break through the enemy installations north of Kornin in order to make a thrust along the designated march route with a pursuit group held in readiness for that purpose.
> The unit must provide cover against the main roads leading to the march route from the north and northeast near Ssolowjewka, north of Wodotyi and north of Wilnja.
>
> b) *Elements of SS-Panzer-Aufklärungsabteilung 1 LAH* are to capture Ssolowjewka and then move across Chomutez, Brusilow, Priworotje, and Wojtaschewka toward Gorodsk to cover the northern flank. Once west of Kotscherowo, they are to provide cover for the Division's rear by turning their front to the east. The commander of the reinforced

SS-Panzergrenadierregiment 1 *LAH* is to put them into formation behind the pursuit force for this deployment.

c) *SS-Panzer-Pionier-Bataillon 1 LAH* (minus the 1. Kompanie), reinforced by one-half of the 12./SS-Panzer-Artillerie-Regiment 1, is to move into formation behind reinforced SS-Panzergrenadierregiment 1 and is to stand ready to repair the bridges along the march route. Starting immediately, it is to move up during the night into the southern part of Kornin.

d) *Kampfgruppe Heinze* (consisting of the 6., 7., 10., 14., and 18./SS-Panzergrenadierregiment 2 *LAH*, the 5./SS-Panzerregiment 1, and the 3. and 8./SS-Panzer-Artillerie-Regiment 1, with the II./SS-Panzer-Artillerie-Regiment 2 assigned to cooperate with it) is to relieve the III./1 from its positions around Kornin in the night before 15.11.1943.
The *I./2* is to relieve the I./1 from its positions in the night before 15.11.1943.
The *Regimentsstab of SS-Panzergrenadierregiment 2* is to assume command immediately over the defensive sector running from the East Balki railway line (inclusive of it) to a point 1.5 kilometers northwest of Kornin. The II./SS-Panzer-Artillerie-Regiment 2 and the 11./SS-Panzer-Artillerie-Regiment 1 are to be subordinated to it for this move. The Regiment should prepare itself to move one Bataillon forward to protect Ssolowjewka from the southeast, east, and north.
Contact should be established and maintained with the Regimental force of the 25. Panzerdivision near Lytschi.

e) The *I./SS-Panzerregiment 1*, subordinated to SS-Panzergrenadierregiment 1, should be moved behind Kampfgruppe Heinze to Kornin in the night for purposes of arranging the march.
Support from the Luftwaffe will be provided by fighter planes and Stuka units in front of the spearhead and on the flanks. The Stuka liaison officer must be at the Divisional headquarters rather than with the attack force because of the lack of communication equipment. For that reason, the leading elements should report continually."

15.11.1943: At 05.00 hours, Sturmbannführer Kuhlmann reported that his Abteilung would not reach the assembly area until 08.00 hours because of difficulties with the roads and bridges.

At 06.00 hours, the I. and II./2. relieved the III. and I./1.

At 07.30 hours, reinforced SS-Panzergrenadierregiment 1 launched its attack on Solowjewka.

At 08.05 hours, the Chef of the Generalstab of the Korps informed us that elements of the 1. Panzerdivision had occupied Chodorkow and Skotschisk.

At 08.25 hours, the attack spearhead of Regiment 1 reached the southern edge of Lisowka and encountered strong enemy forces outflanking it from the forest southeast of Lisowka.

At 08.35 hours, the commander of SS-Panzer-Aufklärungsabteilung 1, Sturmbannführer Knittel, reported to the Divisional headquarters. He received orders to cover the Division's open right flank by launching an attack with Turbowka as its first objective. The Chef of the 13. (Tiger)/SS-Panzerregiment 1, Hauptsturmführer Kling, arrived immediately after him. His unit was subordinated to SS-Panzerregiment 2 *DR*.

At 08.40 hours, a Russian radio message was intercepted with the following content:

"German Panzer spearhead has advanced a large distance. I am attempting to cut it off. I need ammunition and fuel. If I fail here, I am finished."

At 09.45 hours, there was a visit from the new commanding general, General der Panzertruppen Balck. A period of harmonious cooperation marked by mutual trust began. His Chef of the Generalstab was Oberst i.G. von Mellenthin, whose service brilliantly complemented Balck's leadership. Von Mellenthin later wrote his well-regarded book "Panzerschlachten," which attracts attention in international circles. In that work, he wrote:

> "Just before the start of our counterattacks, General Balck, to my great joy, was given the command of the Panzerkorps. With that, the Korps received one of the best Panzer commanders alive. Indeed, if Feldmarschall von Manstein is regarded as Germany's greatest strategist of the Second World War, so too, I believe, must General Balck receive his due recognition as the best field commander of the Wehrmacht!"

Oberst von Mellenthin continued as he described the Generalkommano's mission:

> "For our counterattack west of Kiev, no fewer than six Panzerdivisionen and one Infanterie-Division were subordinated to the XXXXVIII. Panzerkorps. I was proud to learn that we were regarded as an elite corps and that our Generalkommando was being entrusted with the leadership of especially difficult and significant operations.
> The following units now belonged to our Panzerkorps:
> the 1. Panzerdivision (under Generalleutnant Krüger)
> the 7. Panzerdivision (under Generalleutnant Hasso Manteuffel)
> the 1. SS-Panzerdivision *LAH* (under Oberführer Wisch)
> the 19. Panzerdivision (under Generalleutnant Källner)
> the 25. Panzerdivision (under Generalleutnant von Schell)
> the 2. SS-Panzerdivision *DR* (under General der Waffen-SS Walter Krüger)
> and the 68. Infanteriedivision.
> The unit adjacent to the left was Armeeabteilung Mattenklodt with the XIII. Armeekorps and various alert units ...
> Our proposal, to make a lightning-quick surprise thrust with Panzers deep into the rear of the enemy troops positioned on both sides of Shitomir, was rejected in favor of an operation more orthodox in nature. General der Panzertruppen Raus, who took over the command of the 4. Panzerarmee at Shitomir and who made the decision for the second plan, was a glorious and experienced Panzer commander. But the events of the coming weeks were to show that even our great tactical successes did not make it possible to destroy the huge enemy bridgehead west of Kiev by attacking it frontally from the west. There is naturally no proof to be offered that the opposite plan would have worked, but I point out its existence here because the experience of Panzer warfare shows that great triumphs can only be achieved by speed, daring, and maneuver ...
> Forced to weaken our plan to fit the directions of the 4. Panzerarmee, the XXXXVIII. Panzerkorps decided to conduct the battle as follows: the

reinforced 25. Panzerdivision was to proceed on the right and the reinforced 7. Panzerdivision on the left wing of the Korps. In the center, at the Korps' main point of concentration, the 1. Panzerdivision and the 1. SS-Panzerdivision *LAH* were deployed, both of them old, fast Divisionen with plenty of combat experience and adequately manned; they were to proceed from Chernorudka and the area north of Skwira toward the Kiev — Shitomir railway line."

At 10.10 hours, the commanding general announced his intention to use the 25. Panzerdivision to move across Skragilewka or via Mochnatschka — Suschtschanka to attack the rear of the enemy forces advancing from the east toward the *LAH*'s march route.

At 10.35 hours, the advance force setting up the telephone lines reported from Lisowka that SS-Panzergrenadier-Regiment 1 was standing ready on the northern edge of the town for an attack on Solowjewka and was only waiting for the Artillerie to announce its preparedness to fire. Enemy anti-tank guns and tanks were offering considerable defense from the north and from Turbowka.

At 10.40 hours, there was a visit from Generaloberst Hodt, the Oberbefehlshaber of the 4. Panzerarmee.

At 10.45 hours, orders were issued to SS-Panzer-Aufklärungsabteilung 1 to move as quickly as possible on Turbowka to relieve the right flank of Regiment 1. The 5./SS-Panzerregiment 1 was moved up and subordinated to the SS-Panzer-Aufklärungsabteilung to provide support.

At 11.10 hours, there was a report from Obersturmbannführer Frey, the commander of SS-Panzergrenadier-Regiment 1, that he would be moving out at 11.50 hours with the I./1 to the right, the III./1 to the left, and the II./1, mounted, moving behind.

At 11.15 hours, there was a briefing by the Korps with a request for Luftwaffe support for the attack on Solowjewka. The unit adjacent to the left was attacked by enemy tanks near Sapadnja.

At 13.05 hours, reports came in that the I./SS-Panzergrenadier-Regiment had penetrated Solowjewka, but that heavy anti-tank fire had damaged some of our Panzers.

At 13.25 hours, the commanding general departed, issuing a statement recognizing the exemplary combat waged by SS-Panzergrenadier-Regiment 1.

At 13.40 hours, the reinforced SS-Panzer-Aufklärungsabteilung 1 set out for Turbowka.

At 13.45 hours, Obersturmbannführer Frey reported the capture of Solowjewka and the destruction of at least seven T-34's. A large quantity of captured materiel was also reported. Later, the actual number of T-34's destroyed was determined to be nineteen. The Chef of the 2./Sturmgeschützabteilung *LAH*, Hauptsturmführer Wiesemann, personally bore a large part of the responsibility for this success. He was killed in the fighting and was awarded the Ritterkreuz posthumously.

At 13.55 hours, SS-Panzergrenadier-Regiment 2 received orders to move the I./2 up to Solowjewka immediately and to use it to defend the town against attacks from Diwin and Brusilow and to keep the supply road open.

At 14.10 hours, SS-Flakabteilung 1 received orders to move a heavy Batterie into firing position northwest of Kornin to be used against targets both on the ground and in the air. The 3. Batterie was so deployed.

At 14.55 hours, reinforced SS-Panzergrenadier-Regiment 1's I. and II. Bataillon moved forward. The III./1 and the I./Panzerregiment 1 remained in Solowjewka to hold that town until the arrival of the I./2.

At 15.55 hours, the Chef of Stab informed us that the 25. Panzerdivision would be making its move on Suschtaschanka during the coming night.

At 16.53 hours, the commander of SS-Panzer-Pionier-Bataillon 1 reported and received orders to repair the march road.

By 17.10 hours, SS-Panzer-Aufklärungsabteilung 1 had fought its way through the forest south of Turbowka.

At 17.25 hours, SS-Panzergrenadier-Regiment 1 captured Wodotyi and reported that enemy forces were growing in strength in front of Boljatschew. There was an especially strong Pak front.

At 17.45 hours, SS-Panzer-Aufklärungsabteilung 1 received orders to station a reconnaissance force at the bridge in front of Mochnatschka.

At 17.55 hours, the commander of the reinforced III./1, Sturmbannführer Weidenhaupt, reported an enemy tank attack from Turbowka on Solowjewka.

At 20.55 hours, SS-Panzergrenadier-Regiment 2 reported the arrival of the I. Bataillon in Solowjewka. It received orders to defend the town and to conduct combat-strength reconnaissance missions toward Turbowka in order to support the Aufklärungsabteilung's attack from the south.

At 21.45 hours, a general order was issued stating that the units' mission remained unchanged for 16.11.1943.

At 23.55 hours, the I./2 (under Hauptsturmführer Becker) moved on Turbowka with one reinforced Kompanie.

16.11.1943: By 02.30 hours, the I./2 had reached the northwestern edge of Turbowka. It still had no contact with SS-Panzer-Aufklärungsabteilung 1. A reconnaissance force with the strength of one Zug sent out feelers into the town. There were enemy tanks retreating to the north. One of our men was wounded, but we destroyed two T-34's and captured four anti-tank guns.

At 03.15 hours, SS-Panzer-Aufklärungsabteilung 1 took possession of Turbowka and at 07.00 hours launched its attack on Diwin. The attack became stymied in front of the superior enemy forces. It was to regroup with Panzer support and to set out anew from Solowjewka. By 03.00 hours, SS-Panzer-Aufklärungsabteilung 1 had repulsed an enemy tank attack in its rear from Lutschin. Reinforced SS-Panzergrenadier-Regiment 1, moving from Wodotyi via Pokryschew, Sememowka, and Sdwishka, had to break enemy resistance in all those towns. By 09.30 hours, it had moved as far as the western edge of Wilnja in hard house-to-house fighting.

Günther Kress on the 11./1 provided a dramatic short report on this thrust:

> "Once again our 11. Kompanie drove straight into the enemy territory without pausing. Our exemplary Kompanienchef, Obersturmführer Schmid (we lovingly called him 'Schmidchen') was once again the first out of his vehicle when the shooting began. He gave his orders clearly and succinctly. The Kompanie was not yet properly structured for an attack when Schmidchen was killed by a shot to the head. The 11. Kompanie erupted in one unified cry of horror. With the help of the Tigers, which Kompanie-Truppführer Rudi Renger called to the scene, we succeeded in carrying out

our attack. Schmidchen was no more. Our beloved, respected, and revered Chef had been irrevocably torn from us."

Following that action, this Kompanie was surrounded by Russian infantry for a short time near Wodotyi. It was able to liberate itself in tough close-range fighting from foxhole to foxhole.[4]

In the course of the morning, the 2./SS-Panzer-Pionier-Bataillon 1 repulsed an enemy attack on Lisowka with the support of the 3./SS-Panzer-Pionier-Bataillon 1 from Kornin and a few of the I./SS-Panzerregiment's Panzers from Solowjewka.

The attack of SS-Panzer-Aufklärungsabteilung 1 on Diwin got underway at 17.00 hours after the deployment of a Kampfgruppe from the I./2. At 18.40 hours, that Kampfgruppe established contact with SS-Panzer-Aufklärungsabteilung 1 in Diwin. The town was solidly in our hands.

At 12.00 hours, enemy preparations southwest of Lutschin were destroyed by our Artillerie fire. At 13.00 hours, an enemy preparation area north of Solowjewka was blown to pieces by a Panzer attack.

Another attack from Brusilow on Wodotyi was successful in temporarily interrupting our march route. This enemy breakthrough and one by an enemy battalion near Mascharina were both cleared away, and six enemy tanks were destroyed. In both cases, the Russian forces were from the 894th Rifle Regiment of the Soviet 211th Rifle Division. In a night attack on Wodotyi, the divisional staff of the 211th Rifle Division was destroyed.

At 18.00 hours, the unit adjacent to the right, the 25. Panzerdivision, reached the area east of Suschtschanka and was engaged in defending itself against attacks from the north. The unit adjacent to the left, the 1. Panzerdivision, had its right-wing force in Nikolajewka (after capturing Kropiwnja); its left-wing force was attacking Produbowka.

The missions for the night and for 17.11.1943:

Reinforced SS-Panzergrenadier-Regiment 1 was to move farther along the road Kiev — Shitomir and was to block the road off.

Reinforced SS-Panzergrenadier-Regiment 2 and *SS-Panzer-Pionier-Bataillon* were to cover the Division's northern flank from the line Solowjewka — Wodotyi in offensive fighting. In the event that the 25. Panzerdivision's attack provided some relief on the western flank, reinforced SS-Panzergrenadier-Regiment 2 was to attack Brusilow.

Reinforced SS-Panzer-Aufklärungsabteilung 1 was to clear Diwin of enemy forces and to move on Romanowka in order to shift its position via Priworotje onto the march route Kiev — Shitomir. It was to block off that road and to establish contact with reinforced SS-Panzergrenadier-Regiment 1.

17.11.1943: Reinforced SS-Panzergrenadier-Regiment 1 (the I./Panzerregiment 1, Sturmgeschützabteilung 1, the I. and II./Panzer-Artillerie-Regiment 1, the 1. and 3./Panzerjägerabteilung 1, and the 1./Panzer-Pionier-Bataillon 1) had set out from Wilnja for Woitaschewka at 23.40 hours on 16.11.1943.

At 01.35 hours, a narrow bridgehead over the Roschtschewka was established in hard fighting. At 07.00 hours, the Division got the impression that the enemy had succeeded in establishing a continual defensive front along the southern edge of the large forest between Kotscherowo and Korostyschew. Orders were therefore issued for a small force to defend the bridgehead near Woitaschewka while an attack was launched immediately on Kotscherowo. There the march route was to be blocked.

At 08.30 hours, the reinforced II./1 (under Sturmbannführer Max Hansen) encountered enemy troops digging in north of Kamenzi. It threw them back and pursued them as far as the hills southwest of Kotscherowo.

At 12.30 hours, the I./1 (under Schiller) followed behind. It made quick preparations and attacked the enemy defensive installations in Kotscherowo and captured the town by 13.30 hours. The enemy force, including ten tanks, pulled back to the northwest. The commander of SS-Panzergrenadier-Regiment 1, Obersturmbannführer Frey, was awarded the Oak Leaves to his Ritterskreuz for his careful and decisive leadership. He was the three hundred fifty-ninth soldier of the German Wehrmacht to receive this honor.

In aggressive flank defense, the following operations were undertaken on 17.11.1943:

a) A thrust by the II./Panzerregiment 1 (minus two Kompanien) under Sturmbannführer Martin Groß from Solowjewka to the northeast across the Ulschka — Chomutez road back toward Diwin to disrupt the Russian supply traffic.
b) A thrust by one Panzerkompanie from Diwin on Ulschka.
c) Continual reconnaissance by the II./1 toward Mochnatschka, by the I./2 from Solowjewka to the north, and by the III./2 with the 14./2, reinforced by Tigers (under Hauptsturmführer Dinse), from Turbowka toward Lutschin to the south around the forest. Five T-34's were destroyed in the fighting, and by 15.40 hours, Lutschin was in our hands.
d) At 12.50 hours, the 1. and 2./2, reinforced by Sturmgeschütze, attacked Tissniwka and captured it.
e) The reconnaisance showed, in brief, that:
There were scattered enemy positions stretching from the Irpen sector over East Lutschin — Goljaki — Ulschka — Chomutez — Krakowtschina — Karabatschin — Piliponka. There was strong artillery in Ulschka and Chomutez. There were tanks and anti-tank guns in all these towns.
The Divisional headquarters was in Solowjewka.

At 20.00 hours, orders arrived for 18.11.1943:

Reinforced SS-Panzergrenadier-Regiment 1 (in its previous configuration) is to use the bulk of its forces to block off the march route on both sides of Kotscherowo. It is to deploy the III./1 in a night attack to make an enveloping movement to the north and to capture Priworotje. It is to hold this town and to leave a force to secure the bridge near Wojtaschewka in the Roschtschewka sector.

Reinforced SS-Panzergrenadier-Regiment 2 (minus the III. [armoured]/2 and the III./Panzer-Aufklärungsabteilung 1) is to conduct renewed reconnaissance forays against the western edge of the forest west of Suschtschanka. It is to leave a small force to hold the covering front and is to prepare itself to launch a night attack to capture Brusilow together with Panzer-Aufklärungsabteilung 1 and the II./SS-Panzerregiment 1 on 18.11.1943. In the early morning on 18.11.1943, an armoured thrust is to be made by the

III. (armoured)/2 in cooperation with the II./Panzerregiment 1 from Solowjewka to destroy the enemy force in Morosowka.
SS-Panzerregiment 1 (minus the I. Abteilung) is to use its II. Abteilung in a cooperative Panzer thrust with the III./2 on Morosowka.
Kampfgruppe Kling (elements of the 13. [heavy]/Panzerregiment 1 and elements of the 14. [armoured]/2) is to hold Lutschin until relieved by elements of the 25. Panzerdivision. The Kampfgruppe is to pull back to Turbowka in the event of heavy enemy attack.
Reinforced Panzer-Aufklärungsabteilung 1 (the 5./Panzerregiment 1 and the 11./Panzer-Artillerie-Regiment 1) is to provide offensive flank cover while conducting combat reconnaissance against the line Goljaki — Ulschka — Chomutez. It is to prepare itself for deployment together with Panzergrenadier-Regiment 2 on Brusilow.
Flakabteilung 1 is to move into position in the area Wodotyi — Pokryschew — Romanowka so that it can hold the march route open. The weak enemy force in the southwestern part of Wodotyi is to be destroyed, and Boljatschew is to be cleared of straggling enemy troops.
Panzer-Pionier-Bataillon 1 (minus the 1.) is to maintain the road Kornin — Solowjewka — Wodotyi. It is also to scout for and improve a march route from the Pokryschew — Romanowka area to Priworotje.

18.11.1943: During the night, Kampfgruppe Kling had to fend off an enemy reconnaissance attack in battalion strength from Fedorowka on Lutschin.

At 06.45 hours, the reinforced II./2 left its position east of Kornin and headed toward the forest two kilometers east of there to clear it of enemy forces.

At 10.10 hours, the reinforced 18. (Aufklärung)/2 relieved the II./2 (under Sturmbannführer Sandig) from its positions east of Kornin in order to free the unit up for the night attack on Brusilow. The Bataillon received orders to move forward toward Solowjewka.

At 11.30 hours, the reinforced I./2 (under Sturmbannführer Becker) reported capturing Morosowka (six kilometers south of Brusilow) and clearing it of enemy forces. The Bataillon held Morosowka with the 1. Kompanie on the northeastern edge, the 2. Kompanie on the northern edge, and the 3. and 4. Kompanie on the northwest edge.

At 11.35 hours, there was an attack from numerically superior enemy forces moving out of Goljaki on Lutschin. The attack succeeded in pushing Kampfgruppe Kling into the western part of Lutschin.

At 12.00 hours, the enemy continued its attack on Lutschin with a regiment-size force. For that reason, Panzergrenadier-Regiment 2 received orders to keep its II./2 (at the time marching to the north) as a mobile reserve in Lisowka. This move was especially necessary because strong enemy forces were attempting to go around Lutschin to the north in order to threaten the Division's flank. The Oberbefehlshaber of the 2. Panzerarmee, Oberst Hoth, happened to be at the Division's headquarters at the moment and agreed with that measure. These enemy attacks were supported by tanks and by strong artillery and anti-tank gun fire from open positions southwest of Goljaka. Southweast of Diwin, too, the enemy inched closer. All his attacks were repulsed. In the Division's northern fighting area, the reinforced III./1 (under Weidenhaupt) had orders to capture Priworotje, but it had to yield to the superior resistance coming from the town and pull back into the forest three kilometers to the west. The bulk of Panzergrenadier-Regiment 1 (under Obersturmbannführer Frey) was surrounded in Kotscherowo. Between 06.30 and 15.30 hours, it had to defend itself, sometimes by launching counterattacks, against eight enemy attacks in regiment-size from the southeast, east, northeast, north, and northwest, all with tank and strong artillery support. Thirteen enemy tanks were destroyed in the fighting. In the early morning, the Regiment was resupplied with ammunition and fuel under the cover provided by the 11./1.

The Division's frontmost elements by 19.00 hours were the 2. and 18./2, which were one-and-a-half kilometers east of Kornin; Kampfgruppe Kling, which was in the western section of Lutschin; reinforced Panzer-Aufklärungsabteilung 1 in the line Turbowka — Diwin; the Division's supply trains under the Stab of Panzergrenadier-Regiment 2 in Solowjewka; the I./2 in Morosowka; Flakabteilung 1 in the Wodotyi — Pokryschew — Romanowka area; and the II./2 as reserve in Lisowka.

Reinforced Panzergrenadier-Regiment 1 was in Kotscherowo in an all-around defensive position. The Divisional Stab was in Solowjewka.

The following report on the action as seen from the 8./1 provides an idea of this battle's bitterness and of our soldiers' toughness:

> "Kampfgruppe Frey had orders to hold Kotscherowo at any price. It was not the first time in the course of this war that this order had been given: 'Hold at any price!' Any time that this order was given in the German Wehrmacht, the man giving the order weighed in his mind what it really meant. And he who received the order knew that it was necessary. It required that final, highest dedication; it required that final consequence of a soldier's existence, the sacrifice of the individual for a greater need, sensed by all. One thing was clear: the Russians we had just pushed back would come again and attempt to recapture Kotscherowo. We had cut off their supply line here. And the ring encircling us had closed behind our last Panzer.
>
> On the eastern edge of our all-around defenses, the 8./1 moved into position on both sides of the march route from Kiev. Rottenführer Schneidereit, a twenty-four-year-old East Prussian, set up his anti-tank rifle at the side of the road. Now morning and Ivan could come whenever they wanted to.
>
> And they came. Punctually at 06.30 hours, the fire attack from the Russian artillery set in on the village. There followed the salvos from 'Stalin's organs,' which rang out at regular intervals well until evening. The air was filled with the incessant whistling, hissing, and screaming of enemy shots of all calibres. After the artillery attack, the Soviet infantry arrived on all sides with tank support and stormed our position. Rottenführer Schneidereit had his work cut out for him. Within a half an hour, he had destroyed two T-34's with his anti-tank rifle and had damaged two others, which pulled back in a hurry. Over the rise directly in front of the Kompanie came the grey figures of the Soviet infantrymen. We opened fire on them with our hammering machine guns, and they hit the ground. Their hoarse battle cry of 'Urräh' fell silent again. In the second attack, once again supported by tanks, the Kompanie was pushed back and Rottenführer Schneideit wounded. Unassisted, he bound the wound opened up by the shrapnel. He knew that the T-34's would try to come through here again.

He was one of those old, unflappable Rottenführers to whom years of combat experience had given an infallible instinct for each situation in a changing battle. Nothing in the world could shake him, and you could depend on him in any situation. The Soviet onslaught did not let up. New waves stormed toward us without a pause, new tanks churned the earth, new artillery explosions sprayed fountains of dirt over our Grenadiere. The Kompanieführer of Schneidereit's Kompanie, Untersturmführer Müller, was killed. One Zugführer after the other, including Untersturmführer Branstätter, was wounded. At about noon, the enemy succeeded in breaking through. There was the real danger that the Soviets would make it across the road to attack from the rear our comrades on the other side of our all-around defenses. Rottenführer Schneidereit pulled a few men together and got a machine gun which was still firing. This little band made a counterattack, captured Schneideit's old position, and regained possession of his undamaged anti-tank rifle. But the artillery and 'Stalin's organs' kept drumming at us without a pause and the Russian infantry kept coming. By evening, the 8. Kompanie's resources were exhausted. There were no officers or non-coms left. The mechanized weapons were almost all out of operation, and our Artillerie had fired almost all of its ammunition. Even Schneidereit's gun was not working anymore. He had tried to move it in a shift of position, and it had taken a direct hit. The gun was blown apart, and he lost a couple of fingers from his left hand. A bandage, quickly put on, could do nothing to stop the bleeding. His comrades urged him to go back.

Then came the order that the Kompanie had to hold out until the morning and that there would be no reinforcements. The Kompanie? The men lying there in the mud looked at each other. It was at most two groups, without leadership. Rottenführer Schneidereit stayed. When the Russians sent out feelers again and the first wave started, he grabbed a machine gun with his right hand, jumped from cover, and took over the leadership of the last few men left of his Kompanie. He pulled them forward, where they repulsed the attack and took control of the road once again. One machine gun had been brought along, and another was found. There was also ammunition. They fired away with the machine guns the entire night, fooling the enemy as to the size of their force. That position stayed in the hands of those few remaining Panzergrenadiere of the 8. Kompanie. The fire gradually slackened off. They brought Schneidereit to the medical clearing station, where he fell into deep unconsciousness. For his decisive, exemplary behaviour, Rottenführer Schneidereit was awarded the Ritterkreuz. When he was killed in the fighting around Berlin in April of 1945, he had reached the rank of Unterscharführer."

The 25. Panzerdivision, deployed to the right, fought for the northern section of Mochnatschka, while the 68. Infanteriedivision on the left made it to the march road between Kotscherowo and Korostyschew by evening. The 1. Panzerdivision's leading elements were fighting fifteen kilometers east of Shitomir.

Orders for 19.11.1943:

The *25. Panzerdivision* is to take over the defense of the Korps' eastern flank and is to relieve the elements of the *LAH* in the sector Kornin — Lutschin.
The *LAH*, after its elements in the Kornin — Lutschin sector have been relieved, is to capture Brusilow. Kotscherowo is to be held at all costs.
The *1. Panzerdivision*'s mission regarding Shitomir is unchanged. After destroying the enemy forces in Shitomir, it is not to wait for further orders but is to turn around and march as quickly as possible (day and night march) toward the enemy forces northwest of Kotscherowo. It is to destroy these forces.

19.11.1943: At 00.30 hours, the reinforced III./1. arrived in Kotscherowo. There was harassing fire from enemy artillery during the night.

At 03.30 hours, the enemy focussed considerable artillery on the I./2 and then broke into Morosowka. With the support of the II./Panzerregiment 1, the incursion was cleared away by 10.15 hours, and the old positions were assumed once again. Four T-34's were destroyed in the action.
At 09.22 hours, Panzer-Aufklärungsabteilung 1 reported repulsing an enemy attack of regimental size north of Diwin. At 09.30 hours there was another attack, this time of battalion size, from the northwest against reinforced Panzergrenadier-Regiment 1 in Kotscherowo.
At 11.00 hours, the relief action by the 25. Panzerdivision was going very slowly.
At 13.00 hours, the Divisional commander and the Ia met with the unit commanders at the headquarters of Panzergrenadier-Regiment 2 in Solowjewka to confer about the night attack on Brusilow:

1. Situation of the enemy:
The enemy forces advancing on the area around Shitomir and to the east and southeast of the city have suffered a serious set-back from the XXXXVIII. Panzerkorps' attack. The Soviet 3rd Guards Tank Army with two tank corps and one mechanized corps and the 40th Army with seven rifle divisions have been defeated and in part completely destroyed. With the units of the 3. Guards Tank Army (some of them severely reduced in number) and new forces being brought up from the area east of Fastow, the enemy is attempting to establish a defensive front approximately along the line south of Fastow — Wel. Goljaki — Brusilow — Priworotje — Wilija sector — Teterew sector — Studeniza. In an attempt to push back the incursion made by the *LAH* in this front at Kotscherowo, the enemy rushed forces (the Vth Guards Tank Corps and the Ist Guards Cavalry Corps) to the scene and launched desperate counterattacks on 18.11. After those attacks collapsed, he appeared to loosen up his attack force to the northwest and to move to a defensive posture. In the area Fastow — Brusilow — Kotscherowo, we must assume that the following forces are present:
four or five rifle divisions, six rapid-advance units, in part severely reduced in number (the Vth, VIth, and VIIth Guards Tank Corps, the IXth Mechanized Corps, and the VIIIth and Xth Tank Corps), as well as the bulk of the Ist Guards Cavalry Corps. The forces standing at the enemy's disposal would permit him to carry out an aggressive defense and further attacks to the

southeast in an attempt to overrun the *LAH* and to hit the XXXXVIII. Panzerkorps' rear and flank.
The 7. Panzerdivision captured Shitomir in the course of the night before 19.11 in cooperation with the 1. Panzerdivision.
The 1. Panzerdivision has already turned some of its elements around and is making an attack to the northeast.
The *1. SS-Panzerdivision LAH* with Werferregiment 57 and the I./Panzer-Artillerie-Regiment 2 *DR* subordinated to it is to attack in the night leading up to 20.11.1943 as soon as its elements have been relieved from the Kornin—Lutschin—Diwin area. It is to move from the line Morosowka—Wodotyi and, while still maintaining an aggressive defense on the flank, it is to attack Krakowschtschina and capture and hold Brusilow.
For this action, the following is ordered:

a) *Reinforced SS-Panzergrenadier-Regiment 1* (the I./Panzerregiment 1, the I. and II./Panzer-Artillerie-Regiment 1, the 1. and 3./Panzerjägerabteilung 1, Sturmgeschützabteilung 1, and the 1./Panzer-Pionier-Bataillon 1 *LAH*) is to block the road Shitomir — Kiev in Kotscherowo. The Regiment is to prepare itself to move across Oserjany toward Brusilow to join the bulk of the Division as soon as it is relieved by the 1. Panzerdivision.
b) *Reinforced SS-Panzergrenadier-Regiment 2* (the II./SS-Panzerregiment 1 assigned to cooperate with Artillerie-Gruppe Mertsch and Werferregiment 57) is to ready itself along the line Morosowka — Wodotyi on 19.11.1943 for an attack so that it can start out at 01.00 hours on 20.11.1943 to capture and hold Brusilow.
c) *Reinforced Panzer-Aufklärungsabteilung 1* (one Tiger-Gruppe) is to stand in the area south of Morosowka ready to attack so that it can set out at the Division's order to capture Krakowschtschina and Chomutez and thereby to cover the Division's eastern flank.
d) *Artillerie-Gruppe Mertsch* (the I./Panzer-Artillerie-Regiment 2 *DR*, the III./Panzer-Artillerie-Regiment 1 *LAH*, the 10. 11, and 12./Panzer-Artillerie-Regiment 1, and Flakabteilung 1 *LAH*) is to move into position in the area Solowjewka — Wodotyi so that it can fulfill its missions.
   Werferregiment 57 is to move into position in the Tesnowka area so that it can fulfill its separate missions.
   Panzer-Pionier-Bataillon 1 LAH (minus the 1. Kompanie) is to use its 3. Kompanie to defend the II./2's prearations and its 2. Kompanie to reconnoiter toward Priworotje. If that town is free of enemy forces, it is to occupy it immediately. Some forces should be deployed to repair the Lisowka bridge.
   Panzerregiment 1 LAH is to moved up to join Kampfgruppe Kling as soon as it has been relieved. The Stab of Panzerregiment 1 is assigned the organization of the defense of Solowjewka. The Panzers assigned to the maintenance and repair units should assemble there for new deployment.

Conduct of the battle:
a) The Panzergrenadiere, Panzer-Artillerie, and Werfer are to assume their preparation positions in such a way that their movements are concealed from enemy sight.

b) The attack of Panzergrenadier-Regiment 2 should be waged in such a way that the II. Bataillon attacks with the bulk of the Panzers along the road from Wodotyi to Brusilow. As soon as the southwest entrance into Brusilow has been captured, the I./2 is to move from the northern edge of Morosowka to the southeastern entrance into Brusilow. At the same time, reinforced Panzer-Aufklärungsabteilung 1 is to set out from the southern part of Morosowka and attack Krakowschtschina. Depending on the development of the enemy's situation, the unit is then to continue its attack to capture Chomutez or is to hold the northeastern edge of Krakowschtschina.

At 15.30 hours, Sturmbannführer Peiper reported his arrival at the Biala Zerkwa railway station with the rest of the III. (armoured)/2, of which only the 14. (heavy) Kompanie had arrived before that moment.

20.11.1943: At 01.00 hours, reinforced Panzergrenadier-Regiment 2 (minus the III./2) started its attack with the reinforced II./2 moving along the road from Wodotyi to Brusilow.

By 03.05 hours, the reinforced II./2 (under Sturmbannführer Sandig) had penetrated the enemy positions near Hill 185.6 (three kilometers southwest of Brusilow) and was fighting its way forward against tough enemy resistance.

By 03.15 hours, the I./2 and Panzer-Aufklärungsabteilung 1 had repulsed an enemy tank attack from the east and northeast onto Morosowka, but they were unable to prevent the enemy from getting a firm foothold in the northeastern section of Morosowka.

By 04.15 hours, the reinforced II./2 had fought its way through two more enemy installations and was only one-and-a-half kilometers southwest of Brusilow. Its advance was stopped by a tank trench dug in the forest, with its two ends in the marshes on either side. Dawn was breaking as the unit finally overcame this trench, and the enemy's superior artillery and anti-tank fire pinned down the attacking spearhead.

At 04.30 hours, the Bataillon under Sandig set out to go around the tank trench to the east. This advance got stuck at 05.30 hours in the swamp and under the enemy's artillery fire.

At 05.30 hours, Panzergrenadier-Regiment 2 reported that Morosowka had been cleared of enemy forces by the I. Bataillon.

At 05.45 hours, the Division ordered the attack to be suspended.

At 08.00 hours, Sturmbannführer Kuhlmann, commander of the I./Panzer-regiment 1 *LAH* reported the capture of the line Piliponka — Priworotje.

At 15.00 hours, Panzergrenadier-Regiment 1 was relieved in Kotscherowo by the 1. Panzerdivision, which immediately moved along the road to the east. Panzergrenadier-Regiment 1 received orders to move into the area Pilipowka — west of Priworotje and to prepare itself to move on 21.11.1943 through Priworotje, Oserjany, and Ossovzy, then around Kostowzy to the north, and to capture Brusilow from the north.

Reinforced Panzergrenadier-Regiment 2 was to set out with Regiment 1 at 08.30 hours on 21.11.1943, move across the northern edge of Morosowka, consolidate its forces on its inner wing, and attack Brusilow from the south.

Reinforced Panzer-Aufklärungsabteilung 1 was to attack the enemy in Krakowschtschina in order to pin him down.

The Artillerie had orders to cooperate with the I. and III./Panzer-Artillerie-Regiment 19 to knock out the enemy artillery in Chomutez.

The 1. Panzerdivision was to break through the enemy's defensive front east of Kotscherowo, turn to the south, advance across Kostowzy, and attack Brusilow from the northeast. The 19. Panzerdivision was charged with the capture of Chomutez. At about noon, the commander of SS-Panzerregiment 1 *LAH*, Obersturmbannführer Schönberger, was killed when the enemy scored a direct hit on his headquarters. The command of Panzerregiment 1 passed to Sturmbannführer Peiper. Obersturmbannführer Schönberger was awarded the Ritterkreuz posthumously. Hauptsturmführer Guhl took over the command of the III. (armoured)/2.

21.11.1943: At 04.00 hours, Panzergrenadier-Regiment 1 reported that the road conditions resulting from the previous days' continuous rains would prevent it from moving before 08.30 hours.

At 07.45 hours, the frontmost Bataillon of Panzergrenadier-Regiment 1 moved into attack right out of its march and captured Priworotje.

At 08.30 hours, Regiment 1 began its attack on Oserjany.

At 10.30 hours, the enemy's forward position, well supported by artillery, mortars, and a strong concentration of anti-tank guns, was finally broken. Our attack then got stuck in the enemy's defensive fire four hundred meters southwest of Oserjany. After we had repulsed an enemy tank attack from the north, our Panzers and Sturmgeschütze moved around the town to the north and launched an attack. This one, too, collapsed against the strong enemy tank defense.

At 15.00 hours, Regiment 1 moved again, this time moving around to the south, but it ran into an overwhelming defensive front there, as well. With the Division's permission, the attack was suspended at 13.30 hours.

Reinforced Panzergrenadier-Regiment 2 moved out at 09.30 hours for a frontal attack on Brusilow from the south. The I./2, deployed to the right, could hardly move out of its start position, but the II./2, attacking to the left, had made its way as far as the triangular forest southwest of Brusilow by 10.25 hours.

At 11.00 hours, the II./2 overcame tough enemy resistance and pushed its way through the enemy's position. It began its attack on Hill 182.2, just south of Brusilow, and it began to receive heavy fire to its flank from Karabatschin.

At 12.20 hours, the attack was stuck, and the Korps agreed that it should be suspended.

At 13.20 hours, orders came for Panzergrenadier-Regiment 2 to leave a small defensive force while disengaging the bulk of its troops from the enemy so that they could attack Ulschka once more.

At 15.00 hours, the III. (armoured)/2, coming from the station where it had been unloaded, arrived in Solowjewka.

Orders for 22.11.1943:

The *LAH* was to leave a thin defensive screen in its current position and move the bulk of its southern force (Panzergrenadier-Regiment 2) over Diwin and Ulschka in a thrust on Jastrebenka. After capturing that town, it was to take Brusilow from the east on 22.11 and to hold it.

The northern force (Panzergrenadier-Regiment 1) was to leave Oserjany to its left as it moved south of the Oserjany — Brusilow road toward West Brusilow.

The *1. Panzerdivision* was to move on Brusilow from the north. The 19. Panzerdivision was to move from Ulyschka to the north and was to capture Chomutez from the northeast.

22.11.1943: After a peaceful night, the last elements of Panzergrenadier-Regiment 2 were finally put on the march toward Ulschka. Between Diwin and Ulschka, there was an extraordinarily difficult piece of road to overcome.

At 04.30 hours, the commander of Panzerregiment 1, Sturmbannführer Peiper, reported that the II. Abteilung would only be available after the salvage work to recover the Panzers which had been put out of operation on the previous day south of Brusilow. That work was scheduled for completion at 14.00 hours.

At 05.55 hours, reinforced Panzergrenadier-Regiment 2 set out from Ulschka with the I./2 in the front line and the II./2 in echelon formation to the right and rear and with three Tigers supporting it for its attack on Jastrebenka. The III. (armoured)/2 stood ready in Diwin to act as a pursuit force for a move on Jastrebnja after the breakthrough into Jastrebenka.

At 06.45 hours, Hill 297.7 was captured.

At 07.00 hours, the enemy launched a heavy bomber attack on Regiment 2's attack.

At 08.15 hours, the Regiment reported good progress despite the strong anti-tank fire from the front and the flank.

At 10.05 hours, the attack got stuck in the enemy's overwhelming fire from weapons of all calibres. The two Bataillone dug in five hundred meters south of Hill 186.3 (1,500 meters south of Jastrebenka).

At 11.30 hours, Panzerregiment 1 reported that it had twenty-five Panzer IV's of the II. Abteilung ready for action in Diwin.

Obersturmführer Kraas, commander of Panzergrenadier-Regiment 2, to whom these Panzers were subordinated, set out at 13.05 with the support of this newly-formed force.

At 14.30 hours, Hill 186.3 was captured. In the fighting, the Panzers were entrenched and disguised as haystacks. The came under anti-tank fire not just from the flank, but also from the rear out of Chomutez and Jarowka.

At 14.50 hours, the attack was launched on the main enemy position on the southern edge of Jastrebenka and along the road to the town. The enemy defended his positions from deeply echeloned field installations with the support of artillery firing from an elevated position.

At 16.15 hours, the Panzergrenadiere managed to break into Jastrebenka, and at 18.00 hours Panzergrenadier-Regiment 2 reported that the town was in our hands following fierce house-to-house fighting. Panzergrenadier-Regiment 2 set up defenses on the eastern edge of the town; elements of Infanterie-Regiment 73 were moved up to defend its western edge.

We had destroyed or captured two enemy assault guns and twenty-four tanks.

Reinforced Panzergrenadier-Regiment 1 got the impression from reconnaissance at 08.00 hours that the enemy in Oserjany was preparing for a retreat. For that reason, the Divisional commander decided, in variance with the orders from the Korps directing him to move the Regiment into the Solowjewka area, to make one more attack on Oserjany.

At 10.15 hours, Panzergrenadier-Regiment 1 moved against Oserjany, advancing rapidly to within about one hundred meters of its southern edge, where it got stuck in the massive defensive fire from enemy anti-tank guns, artillery, mortars, and ground-attack planes.

The Regiment received orders to disengage from the enemy and to move via Pilipowka and Semenowka into the area east of Solowjewka. The Korps received a report that reinforced Panzergrenadier-Regiment 1 would be prevented by the road conditions from reaching the designated area before 07.00 hours on 23.11.1943.

Orders for 23.11.1945 arrived at 21.15 hours:

> The *LAH* was to close ranks around Jastrebenka and then attack to the northwest. It was to capture Lasarowka. Elements of the Division were to provide cover for its eastern and northern flank from northern Ulschka over Hill 186.3 (one kilometer south of Jastrebenka). The weak defenses in the sector Wodotyi — Priworotje were to be left there until further notice.
>
> The *1. Panzerdivision* was to move through Kostowzy from the west toward Lawarowka, establish contact with the *LAH* there, and then attack Brusilow from the northeast.
>
> The *19. Panzerdivision* was to set out from the southern part of Jastrebenka in an attack on Chomutez from the north and northeast.

The *LAH* intended to use the elements of Panzergrenadier-Regiment 1, which were arriving so slowly because of the road conditions, for its defensive missions. Reinforced Panzergrenadier-Regiment 2, supported by the armoured Gruppe, would fulfill the attack mission.

23.11.1943: The Division had at this point twenty-three Panzer IV's, fifteen Panzer V's (Panthers), and four Panzer VI's (Tigers) at its disposal and ready for action. During the night, there was scattered harassing fire from the enemy artillery. The rain continued, making the road conditions all the more difficult.

At 00.10 hours, there was an attack on the western entrance into Jastrebenka, but the 14./2 cleared it away in a counterthrust.

At 06.00 hours, there was an enemy tank attack from Stavizkaja against the northern edge of Jastrebenka. The III./2 repulsed it. One T-34 was destroyed.

The attack on Lasarewka which had been ordered had to be postponed. The defensive forces originally planned in the orders proved to be too weak for the enemy pressure being applied from the north. In addition, the road conditions had prevented the timely completion of the shift in position for the armoured Gruppe. The Schützenpanzerwagens of the III./2 moved the III./1 up in order to accelerate the III./2's combat preparations.

At 11.30 hours, the III./1 (under Weidenhaupt) completed its relief action.

At 11.35 hours, the Chef of the Generalstab informed us that the 1. Panzerdivision had penetrated Brusilow from Kostowzy at 10.00 hours and that it had diverted a Kampfgruppe to the northeast from Brusilow toward Mestetschko.

At 12.30 hours, the armoured Gruppe (the II./Panzerregiment 1 and the III. [armoured]/2) set out under the command of Sturmbannführer Peiper. It was to move through Dubrowka toward Lasarowka.

At 12.35 hours, the Korps ordered the armoured Gruppe to turn north immediately, advancing through Starizkaja and Marjanowka on Fasowaja.

At 14.00 hours, Dubrowka was captured. From there, the armoured Gruppe was ordered to turn its attack on Starizkaja and Fasowaja. The Gruppe refueled in Mestetschko and moved out again.

Jupp Steinbüchel, a member of the 2./Panzer-Nachrichtenabteilung 1, was the radio operator in the Divisional commander's Schützenpanzerwagen. He recalled the following:

> "The Divisional commander needed a radio operator for his Schützenpanzerwagen. So that is what I did. Every morning I went with the Oberführer to the front. The roads were unmercifully muddy. But our vehicle got us everywhere. Often we were extremely glad that our vehicle was armoured, because the commander went right where the action was. Sometimes to Peiper, other times to Kraas or Kuhlmann. Whatever the situation demanded. On my birthday (23.11), we drove along in a pretty heavy attack with Peiper's force. The Russians suffered heavy losses. We pushed right past Brusilow, but the swamps made us stop, unfortunately."

At 12.30 hours, reinforced Panzer-Aufklärungsabteilung 1 set out from Morosowka via Krakowschtschina and Chomutez to reach the armoured Gruppe.

The bulk of Panzergrenadier-Regiment 1, with the I./Panzer-Artillerie-Regiment 1 and Sturmgeschützabteilung 1, was scattered all along the road between Priworotje and Diwin because of the appalling roads and the catastrophic condition of our vehicles.

At 12.35 hours, Panzer-Pionier-Bataillon 1 received orders to reinforce the crossing over the river at Jastrebenka and Starizkaja.

At 12.40 hours, Falkabteilung 1 shifted to Brusilow and set up defenses on the northern edge.

At 13.45 hours, the Ia of the 19. Panzerdivision (the unit adjacent on the right) reported large enemy forces advancing to the west in the area southeast and northeast of Jastrebenka.

At 13.50 hours, the commander of Panzergrenadier-Regiment 1, Obersturmbannführer Frey, received orders to move elements of the II./1 into the sector Ulschka — Jastrebenka to defend it. The I./1 (under Sturmbannführer Schiller) was involved in the attack on Karabatschin (four kilometers west of Brusilow), and the III./1 was proceeding to Ulschka.

At 17.30 hours, as it was being refueled in Mestetschko, the armoured Gruppe reported having captured Lasarowka. An attack across the Sdwish, it reported, would only be possible after the bridge had been reinforced.

At 18.05 hours, the Chef of the Generalstab informed us that the 1. Panzerdivision was just about to establish a bridgehead across the Sdwish north of Mestetschko and that the 19. Panzerdivision was busy clearing Brusilow of enemy forces.

Orders for 24.11.1943:

> The *LAH* is to advance on 23.11 with all its available forces to the northeast via Marjanowka toward Fasowaja. It is still responsible for defending our flank in the sector Ulyschka (exclusive of the town) — Jastrebnja. The elements still deployed west of Brusilow are to be moved up via Oserjany and Brusilow.

Panzergrenadier-Regiment 1 received orders to use its elements in the order of their arrival to relieve the Kompanien of Panzergrenadier-Regiment 2 deployed in the Division's defensive sector Ulyschka — Jastrebnja. Panzergrenadier-Regiment was to move the elements being relieved immediately to join the armoured Gruppe.

The armoured Gruppe was to move on Marjanowka and Fasowaja via Starizkaja as soon was the Sdwish crossing had been prepared.

With that move, the Korps' five Panzerdivisionen found themselves side-by-side in an attack to the northeast with the objective of hitting the Russian bridgehead across the Dnieper west of Kiev. The Division no longer considered a successful breakthrough possible, considering the superiority of the enemy forces, and the leadership expressed this opinion clearly in conversations with the Korps. The leadership knew that this opinion was shared by the Divisionskommando of the 1. Panzerdivision (Generalleutnant Krüger and Oberstleutnant i.G. von Zitzewitz).

Enemy materiel losses on 23.11.1943: nine T-34's destroyed, twenty-four artillery pieces and twelve American trucks captured.

24.11.1943: After a peaceful night, the 2./Panzer-Pionier-Bataillon 1 arrived at the bridgehead east of Kostowzy at 10.00 hours.

At 11.30 hours, the bridge was ready, and the armoured Gruppe moved forward into its bridgehead.

At 12.30 hours, the armoured Gruppe set out. Its leading elements encountered a strong anti-tank front on the western edge of Starizkaja. At the same time, the Gruppe was attacked from the north by enemy tanks coming from Mal. Karaschin. The Gruppe lost some Panzers, but it did manage to repulse the attack and destroy six enemy tanks while continuing its thrust into the center of Starizkaja. In that fighting, Oberscharführer Dauser, a Zugführer in the 1./Panzerregiment 1 exhibited outstanding valor and was awarded the Ritterkreuz.

At 15.40 hours, the commander of the armoured Gruppe, Sturmbannführer Peiper, reported that he had succeeded in pushing forward to the edge of Starizkaja. There his attack got stuck in front of the enemy's well-fortified installation on Hill 185.4.

On the Division's defensive front, Panzergrenadier-Regiment 1 had been able to use its III. and elements of its II. Bataillon to relieve the elements of Panzergrenadier-Regiment 2 deployed there. The I./1 was still on the march, so there were elements of the I./2 which could still not be relieved.

At 17.40 hours, the Division issued an order by radio to Panzergrenadier-Regiment 2:

> "Regiment 2, minus the I. Bataillon, is to take Hill 185.2 in nocturnal attack in order to enable the armoured Gruppe to make a breakthrough. All Artillerie and Werfer stand at your disposal. Report the start of your attack."

After the 1. Panzerdivision had gotten stuck in front of Mal. Karaschin, the Korps ordered it to conduct a thorough preparation for execution of the attack on 25.11.

At 22.55 hours, an order was issued to the unit commanders to report to Panzergrenadier-Regiment 2's headquarters in Lasarewka at 08.00 hours on 25.11.1943 to receive their orders.

25.11.1943: At 00.00 hours, the Divisional headquarters moved to Brusilow.

At 08.00 hours, the orders were issued in Lasarewka for the attack to the north. Because this attack never actually took place, we will not go into the plans laid out at that time.

The day was peaceful except for some harassing artillery fire, especially on the bridge.

In the course of the morning, Panzergrenadier-Regiment 73 (19. Panzerdivision) relieved Panzergrenadier-Regiment 1 *LAH* in Jastrebenka. The Regiment assembled in Dubrowka.

In the course of the afternoon, the I./1 moved forward to relieve the III. (armoured)/2. It had to move through Lasarewka over terrible roads and under the constant harassing fire on the right wing of the expanded bridgehead.

At 17.15 hours, orders came from the Korps: "Suspend attack preparation. Adopt defensive positions. Orders to follow."

With that, the battle for Brusilow can be regarded as at its end.

The Division reported the following figures for materiel captured in the period 19.11.1943 - 24.11.1943: eight T-34's, two American Mark II tanks, three General Shermans, fifty-four artillery pieces and countless light infantry weapons.

Orders for 26.11.1943:

> "The *XXXXVIII. Panzerkorps* is to suspend its attack to the east temporarily and move into defensive position to hold the line reached in the sector Jastrebenka — Starizkaja — Shmurowka — Rakowischi. The Korps is to regroup so that it can set out early on 27.11.1943 with a strong force to destroy the enemy forces between Teterew and Belka.
>
> The *LAH* is to hand over its sector to the 1. Panzerdivision and to set out at 06.30 hours on 26.11.1943 along two march routes to reach the area south of Negrebowka and east of Sabelotschje. On 27.11.1943, it is to cross the line Negrebowka — West Sabelotschje and move its point of concentration to the right on Radomyschl. There it is to attack the flank of the enemy forces moving south. After the completion of this operation, the Division is to be pulled back into the area Brusilow — Solowjewka.

d) 26.11.1943 - 16.12.1943: Fighting around Radomyschl (see sketch 27).

26.11.1943: At 06.30 hours, the Division, divided into march groups, started its march. By 13.00 hours, all units had reached the designated area.

From 11.30 hours, the new Divisional headquarters were in Sabelotschje, where orders for the attack of 27.11.1943 were given orally at 14.00 hours:

> The Division is to position *reinforced SS-Panzergrenadier-Regiment 2* (the II./Panzerregiment 1 and the 2./Panzer-Pionier-Bataillon 1) so that, when the attack begins, it can send elements around to the south to capture the crossing west of Negrebowka in a surprise attack and then immediately move the bulk of its forces toward Werbowka (while maintaining cover against attacks from Rajewka). The II. and III./Panzer-Artillerie-Regiment 1 are assigned to cooperate.

Reinforced SS-Panzergrenadier-Regiment 1 (Sturmgeschützabteilung 1 and the 1. and 3./Panzerjägerabteilung) is to position itself in the Sabelotschje area ready for the attack so that it can send elements around to the east to force a crossing over the Belka River north of Sabelotschje and then move the bulk of its forces via Sabelozkaja across the line Gardow — Rudnja. Elements are to be sent to establish contact with Panzer-Aufklärungsabteilung 1 in the Sobolow area, later on the southwest edge of Rudnja. The I./SS-Panzer-Artillerie-Regiment 1 and the I./SS-Panzer-Artillerie-Regiment 2 *DR* are assigned to cooperate.

Reinforced Panzer-Aufklärungsabteilung 1 (one Abteilung of Panzer-Artillerie-Regiment 73 and one Abteilung of Panzer IV's from the 1. Panzerdivision) is to position itself in the Kotscherowo area ready to attack so that it can move the bulk of its forces across the line captured on 26.11.1943 and have them proceed along the road Kotscherowo — Radomyschl toward Rudnja. Elements are to move via Stanizkaja Sloboda in order to establish contact with the 68. Infanteriedivision near Lenino (west of Litwinowka).

Start of the attack:

for SS-Panzergrenadier-Regiment 1 and 2:	27.11.1943, 04.30 hours
for Panzer-Aufklärungsabteilung 1:	27.11.1943, 05.45 hours

SS-Panzer-Artillerie-Regiment 1 was to move into the area east of Negrebowka and north of Sabelotschje.

27.11.1943: Once again, the adverse road conditions forced a two-hour postponement of the beginning of the attack.

At 06.00 hours, assault forces from SS-Panzergrenadier-Regiment 1 and 2 crossed the Belka River with orders to open up crossings near Negrebowka and near Point 170.3 (three kilometers north of Sabelotschje) in a surprise attack. This operation was badly outflanked on the north, where the I./2 was deployed, by enemy forces moving out of the northern section of Negrebowka, and the unit failed to take its crossing. The I./1, however, was able to capture the bridge at Point 170 in a surprise attack at 08.10 hours. The small bridgehead captured there was expanded by an attack on the woods in front of it; the fighting lasted until 11.00 hours. The III./1 then crossed over and made a frontal attack on the hill southwest of Guta Sabelozkaja. The hill was taken from a weaker enemy force, and at 11.30 hours the attack on Guta Sabelozkaja itself began.

At 15.30 hours, the III./1 (under Sturmbannführer Weidenhaupt) was engaged in bitter house-to-house fighting, with a large number of enemy tanks involved, in Guta Sabelozkaja. Untersturmführer Nowotnik, the Kompanieführer of the 14./1, destroyed six Russian artillery pieces there and was awarded the Ritterkreuz for his personal valor and for his leadership of his Kompanie.

By 12.00 hours, the II./1 (under Sturmbannführer Max Hansen), had made its move against the enemy forces in the forest northwest of Sabelotschje.

At 18.30 hours, the town was solidly in our hands. There we spotted the 174th Soviet Anti-Tank Regiment.

By 08.40 hours, the I./SS-Panzergrenadier-Regiment 2 had moved into the river basin. At 08.50 hours, it came under fire as it was capturing the road Negrebowka — Radomyschl from the north and northeast. The II./2 had already crossed the river at 08.15 hours, but it then got stuck under enemy fire one and eight-tenths kilometers west of Negrebowka.

By 09.30 hours, the II. Bataillon, despite the intensifying enemy fire, had managed to penetrate the forest two kilometers west of Negrebowka. Its success was due in large part to the excellent support it received from our Artillerie.

At 11.00 hours, the I./2, stuck on the road between Negrebowka and Radomyschl, repulsed an enemy counterattack from the north. The Bataillon commander was wounded and replaced by Obersturmführer Schnell. The Bataillon suffered considerable losses. The 19. (Pionier)/2 was deployed near the I./2 to cover to the northeast.

Regiment 2 moved the III. (armoured)/2 across at 13.30 hours. It set out at 14.00 hours from there to make an armoured thrust on the multiple road junction north of Guta Sabelozkaja. After capturing this junction without encountering much enemy resistance, the Bataillon was pulled back to Guta Sabelozkaja.

At 07.30 hours, the subordinated, reinforced Panzer-Aufklärungsabteilung 1 (Heer) had moved out of the area north of Kotscherowo, broken the enemy resistance in Potaschnaja, and moved forward as far as the edge of the forest north of there. At 18.30 hours, it was still there, stymied in front of strong enemy forces. Its left assault force managed to push forward as far as Litwinowka on the Teterew.

The enemy launched several attacks in the course of the day against the unit adjacent on the right, the 2. SS-Panzerdivision *DR*. Some of these were supported by tanks, and all were with forces ranging from two to four hundred men in size. They were attempting to make localized breakthroughs on both sides of Rakowitschki and just north of Negrebowka. To reinforce this defensive front, the Korps issued orders on 28.11 at 22.40 for the *LAH* to send one Pionierkompanie there to be subordinated to the Division until the arrival of troops to relieve the 2. SS-Panzerdivision *DR*.

The Division had the impression that the strong enemy forces north and west of Negrebowka and northwest of Sabelotschje had intended to attack, but they had been surprised by our attack and had moved the bulk of their forces to the north and northwest. There were enemy forces with a large number of anti-tank guns facing Panzer-Aufklärungsabteilung 1, which made a frontal thrust along the road impossible. The Panzergrenadiere, worn down by ceaseless fighting and exhausted by the weather-ruined roads, were simply unable to keep up with the enemy as he pulled back.

28.11.1943: In the early morning, Panzer-Pionier-Bataillon 1 began to build a bridge north of Sabelotschje. By 09.15 hours, it was completed.

At 09.15 hours, the reinforced III. (armoured)/2 (under Hauptsturmführer Guhl) moved across the bridge for its attack on Gardow. After breaking fairly weak resistance north of Guta Sabelozkaja, the unit rolled over several well-built field installations lying one behind the other.

At 10.45 hours, the attack was pinned down by fire from the well-fortified installations at the southeast entrance to Gardow. The unit finally had to be pulled back because the Bataillon's rear was being threatened from the enemy positions it had moved across but which were now coming back to life.

The armoured force (Panzerregiment 1, SS-Panzer-Aufklärungsabteilung 1 *LAH*) set out under the command of Sturmbannführer Peiper at 11.20 hours. It crossed over to the other bank and proceeded to the west. Elements of Panzer-Aufklärungsabteilung 1 were to capture the road Kotscherowo —

Radomyschl and to keep the road to the north open while the bulk of the troops moved north on Radomyschl.

By 15.40 hours, the bulk of the armoured force had moved through the enemy's infantry, his tanks, and his anti-tank guns as far as the road junction just south of Radomyschl. The elements moving south along the road (the I./Panzerregiment 1) broke through a number of enemy positions, cleared away countless mines, and at 14.00 hours established contact with reinforced Panzer-Aufklärungsabteilung 1 (Heer) in Potaschnja. Sturmbannführer Kuhlmann, commander of the I./Panzerregiment 1, was able to capture and hold the line Guta Sabelozkaja — Sobolew (inclusive of it) in the course of the morning. Two Bataillone of Panzergrenadier-Regiment 2, meanwhile, were able to hold the line Negrebowka North — Sobolew in back-and-forth fighting.

At 16.45 hours, at the highway junction south of Radomyschl, the armoured force turned toward Gardow. By nightfall, it had captured the edge of the town and had set up all-around defenses for the night.

Starting at 16.00 hours, the enemy launched attacks on the II./2 of regimental size, and some enemy elements succeeded in making a breakthrough. The I./2 made a counterattack in the dawn hours of 19.11 and cleared up the incursion.

At 23.00 hours, the commander of the 2. Fallschirmjägerdivision reported to us. The Division was to be subordinated to the 1. SS-Panzerdivision *LAH* for the purpose of combing the forest between the Belka and the Teterew; later it was to relieve the *LAH* in the line Gardow — Teterew (two kilometers north of Marjanowka) as soon as that line was captured.

29.11.1943: At 05.30 hours, the reinforced III. (armoured)/2 moved out to make an attack on the edges of the forest west of Kol. Tolstoje. At the same time, the enemy attacked from Kol. Tolstoje. The enemy was repulsed in a meeting engagement, after which the assault force returned to its starting point because the Bataillon still had one more attack to launch that morning, with the support of the I./Panzerregiment 1.

The I./2 had, at the same time, undertaken a thrust with Sturmgeschütz support to clear the forest south of Sobolew of enemy forces. Two hundred prisoners were taken; they surrendered without a fight.

By 09.00 hours, Sturmbannführer Peiper had continued his armoured force's assault on Gardow; he reported at 10.00 hours that the town had been taken against tough enemy resistance. At the same time, the left wing of Panzergrenadier-Regiment 1 swung around from Sobolew to the southern edge of Gardow.

At 10.15 hours, the III. (armoured)/2 sent out the I./Panzerregiment 1 under the command of Sturmbannführer Kuhlmann for a new thrust on the forest west of Kol. Tolstoje. By 16.00 hours, it was able to destroy the enemy's preparation of two battalions which it spotted there.

Panzer-Aufklärungsabteilung 1 (Heer) reached Marjanowka at about 10.00 hours. The town had been abandoned by the enemy in the course of the night. The unit received orders to secure the line from Marjanowka to the ox-bow in the stream north of there (inclusive of it).

At 15.00 hours, SS-Panzer-Aufklärungsabteilung 1, returning with Peiper's armoured Gruppe, was moved into the defensive line to the left next to Panzergrenadier-Regiment 1.

By 17.50 hours, the Division held the following line:

November, 1943: The 5. Kompanie of Panzerregiment 1 *LSSAH* in action west of Teterew.

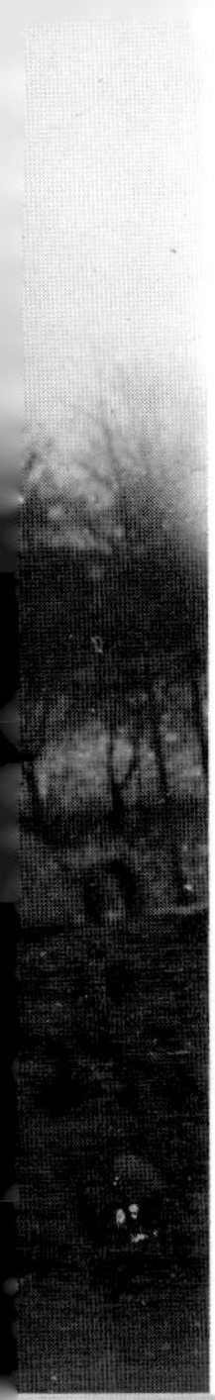

November, 1943: The leading elements of the *LAH* and of the 1. Panzerdivision meet in a joint Panzer attack near Kovnin.

Men of the *Leibstandarte*

A nameless, but important, helper in the fight.

Panzergrenadier-Regiment 2 held from the bridge at Negrebowka along the road to the west as far as the junction at Guta Sabelozkaja; Panzergrenadier-Regiment 1 held as far as the junction at Gardow (exclusive of the town).
SS-Panzer-Aufklärungsabteilung 1 held from Gardow (inclusive of the town) as far as the road Kotscherowo — Radomyschl (inclusive of the road).
Panzer-Aufklärungsabteilung 1 (Heer) held from the road as far as the ox-bow in the stream three kilometers north of Marjanowka.

At 18.00 hours, the Ia of the 2. Fallschirmjägerdivision reported that some of his troops had arrived in Kotscherowo. The Division received orders to prepare for the *LAH* to be relieved.

At 20.00 hours, the Korps ordered 30.11 and 1.12 to be spent in clearing the forest between the Belka and the Teterew of enemy forces. Following that, defenses were to be established in the newly-captured line. Preparations were to be made for relief by the 2. Fallschirmjägerdivision on 2.12 and a move in the night between 2.12 and 3.12 into the area Studeniza — Werressy — Wazkow — Lewkow — Strischewka. Subordinated reinforced Panzer-Aufklärungsabteilung 1 of the 1. Panzerdivision was to be relieved by 1.12.1943 at 06.00 hours. It was then to be divided into small march groups and put on the road to the area north of Shitomir.

30.11.1943: After a peaceful night, the enemy's artillery and mortar fire started up again with renewed vigor in the course of the morning. In the Gardow sector, it intensified by about 14.00 hours to the point of one-hour-long fire for effect.

In the sector to the right, the enemy moved to within four hundred meters of us and began to dig in.

In the sector to the left, all was quiet. The enemy had occupied the forest on the western bank of the Teterew with combat outposts. Between our left wing near the bend in the Teterew two kilometers north of Marjanowka and the right wing of the 68. Infanteriedivision, there was a gap.

At 06.00 hours, elements of the 2. Fallschirmjägerdivision crossed the line Potaschnja — Rudenka and began their designated mop-up operation. At 11.00 hours, they penetrated the forest.

In the course of the morning, the Division's units were moved into the new area under individual orders, beginning with the supply trains. The 2. Fallschirmjägerdivision would not be able to relieve it completely until 1.12. Panzer-Aufklärungsabteilung 1 (Heer) was the exception.

At 17.15 hours, the commander of the 2. Fallschirmjägerdivision reported the arrival of Fallschirmjägerregiment 2 in Sobolew. The start of the move to relieve Panzer-Aufklärungsabteilung 1 (Heer) was on the morning of 1.12.1943.

The IIa of the *LAH* reported:

Losses up to and including 30.11.1943:

363 dead
1289 wounded
33 missing

Trench strength of SS-Panzergrenadier-Regimenter 1 and 2 on 30.11.1943:

SS-Panzergrenadier-Regiment 1

	Officers	Non-coms	Men
I. Batl.	4	32	138
II. Batl.	5	15	148
III. Batl.	9	20	193
Stab and Rgt. units	9	20	202
	27	87	681

SS-Panzergrenadier-Regiment 2

	Officers	Non-coms	Men
I. Batl.	3	10	90
II. Batl.	3	16	92
III. Batl.	8	24	131
Stab and Rgt. units	18	37	315
	32	87	628

1.12.1943: At 11.50 hours, the relief maneuver began, and it was completed for Panzer-Aufklärungsabteilung 1 (Heer) by 15.00 hours. The Divisional commander bid farewell to the brave Abteilung, to which a true brotherhood-in-arms had joined us for several days, and he thanked the Abteilung commander for the good cooperation.

At 20.00 hours, Fallschirmjägerregiment 7 assumed responsibility for Panzergrenadier-Regiment 1's former sector. With that, the entire *LAH* sector was handed over to the 2. Fallschirmjägerdivision.

In the Wehrmacht's report of 30.11.1943, the combat just described was evaluated as follows:

> "In offensive and defensive fighting in the area around Kiev and Shitomir, the forces of the Heer and the Waffen-SS under the command of Generaloberst Hoth intercepted the enemy armies making an attempt to break through our lines. In mobile combat and a counterattack to the east, they pushed the enemy back. The Soviets suffered 20,000 dead. 4,800 Soviet soldiers were taken prisoner. 603 tanks and 1,305 artillery pieces were destroyed or captured."

By means of their thrust into the flank of the First Ukrainian Front (the force which had broken through at Shitomir), the Panzerdivisionen of the XXXXVIII. Panzerkorps had succeeded in denying the enemy access to his system of roads south of the Pripjet swamp. By Russian standards, these were good roads. But the German assault power had not been enough to destroy those forces which the enemy had rushed to his defense. The Soviet 60th Army was assembled in the area northeast of Shitomir and was threatening to move through the gap in our lines north of Shitomir. The Oberkommando of the Heeresgruppe ordered the XXXXVIII. Panzerkorps to make a surprise thrust against the forces posing this threat; this thrust was to be against the enemy troops facing the XIII. Armeekorps between the Teterew and the road Shitomir — Korosten. That move was intended to allow the XIII. Armeekorps to swing around against the Teterew and to establish contact with the LIX. Armeekorps to the north.

The situation between Shitomir and Korosten, from which area our thrust was to be made, was for the most part unknown. Because there were only weak Infanterie forces holding it at that point, no adequate ground reconnaissance could be conducted. The continuing bad weather meant that no reliable aerial reconnaissance could be gathered, either. Oberst i.G. von Mellenthin wrote in his book "Panzerschlachten":

> "Regardless of those facts, we decided to conduct no tactical ground reconnaissance. Sending out any such reconnaissance forces would have immediately alerted the Russians that we had something in mind here. To add to our difficulties, it now appeared from several reports that all the bridges in the area between Shitomir and Korosten had been destroyed."

2.12.1943: Informed of the new intentions noted above, the leadership group of the *LAH* reached the new Divisional headquarters in Gorodischtsche at 08.40 hours. In the course of the day, the Division's units arrived in their designated areas. They were given orders for specific road reconnaissance in the Shitomir area and to the north.

In the afternoon, Obergruppenführer and General der Waffen-SS, Sepp Dietrich, arrived at the Divisional headquarters to be briefed on the condition of his old Division. In the following days, he visited the *LAH*'s units and paid a visit to the Generalkommando of the XXXXVIII. Panzerkorps.

3.12.1943 - 5.12.1943: The days were used to improve our combat readiness and to scout the roads. The Division formed a march group from the supply trains and from any elements not needed for combat. This march group was set on the road on 3.12.1943; it marched by day as a diversion to fool the enemy, moving via Shitomir to the southeast into the area Skwira — Shamrajewka.

The Korps and Division used 4.12 and 5.12 for careful preparation of their march, which was to be an enveloping move to the west. The Korps moved its three Panzerdivisionen in a night march (5.12-6.12) to avoid detection by the enemy as much as possible. Starting from the left, the 7. Panzerdivision, the 1. Panzerdivision, and the 1. SS-Panzerdivision *LAH* moved into the area north of Tschernjachow in order to be able to make a thrust from there across the road Shitomir — Korosten to the east. For that purpose, the 7. Panzerdivision made a wide enveloping move to the west into the Wolodarsk area. The 1. Panzerdivision did not have to swing out so wide to get into the Fedorowka area (south of the 7. Panzerdivision), and the 1. SS-Panzerdivision *LAH* moved into the Siljanschtschina area.

The *LAH* was to begin its move on 5.12 at 15.00 hours. On 6.12 it was to cross the line Mokrentschtschina — Pekarschtschina to the east and to attack the flank of the enemy forces facing the XIII. Armeekorps. Its first attack objective was the high ground on both sides of Styrty. Partial elements were to be turned from the north toward Tschernjachow and were to capture the town in cooperation with the 208. Infanteriedivision.

Combat-ready Panzers on 4.12.1943:

		Combat-ready	Under short-term repair	Under long-term repair
Panzer VI		4	12	9
Panzer V		28	41	11
Panzer IV		30	39	5
Panzer III		4	1	
Sturmgeschütze:	7.5-cm	11	18	8
	10.5-cm	1	7	1
Pak:	7.5-cm (mot. Z)	6		
	7.5-cm (self-propelled)	9		

At 16.00 hours, the new Divisional headquarters were set up in Sorokow. The intention was to move the Division's armoured tactical group to Klitischtsche at nightfall.

The units received the following orders for the battle:

Reinforced Panzer-Aufklärungsabteilung 1 (the II./Panzer-Artillerie-Regiment 1 and the 10./Panzer-Artillerie-Regiment 1) is to move through Sorokow to the west at 15.30 hours and make a rapid march via Siljaschtschina, Pekarschtschina, and Andrewjew onto the high ground around Styrty. Enemy resistance around Siljanschtschina is to be surrounded from the east and broken.

Reinforced SS-Panzer-Aufklärungsabteilung 1 is to be subordinated to the armoured force under Peiper (new designation: Kampfgruppe Peiper) after reaching Pekarschtschina.

Kampfgruppe Peiper (Panzerregiment 1, the III. (armoured)/2, the 2./Panzer-Pionier-Bataillon 1 with bridging equipment of type K, the 5. (light)/Flakabteilung 1; formerly armoured force under Peiper) is to follow Panzer-Aufklärungsabteilung 1 with the Panzers in a spread-out formation. It is to capture Siljanschtschina (this town could be by-passed if necessary), Pekarschtschina, Andrejew, and Styrty in order to move from there immediately across the high ground north of Bystrijewka on Radomyschl.

First attack objective: Styrty.

Second attack objective: Radomyschl.

The Division is to move through the line Mokrentschtschina (exclusive of it) — Pekarschtschina to the east in a broad front and to win as much ground as possible without paying attention to the threat to its flank. The road Shitomir — Korosten is to be blocked at Andrejew until the fall of Tschernjachow.

March group A Leader: Obersturmbannführer Frey

Force: Regimentsstab of Panzergrenadier-Regiment 1
one reinforced Bataillon from Panzergrenadier-Regiment 1
Sturmgeschützabteilung 1
the bulk of Panzergrenadier-Regiment 1

March group A is to reach the Pekarschtschina area behind Kampfgruppe Peiper. It is then to destroy the enemy forces in Mokrentschtschina in order to move from there in a broad front with the assault force of the 208. Infanteriedivision to capture Tschernjachow. The Regiment is also responsible for reestablishing contact with the bulk of the Division in Styrty and is to follow behind the Division as it moves to the south to smash the enemy forces in the string of towns along the Bystrijewka. That move to the south is intended to permit the XIII. Armeekorps to advance to the northeast.
First intermediate objective: Mokrentschtschina.
First attack objective: Tschernjachow.
Second attack objective: Bystrijewka River in the sector Kiselewka — Kamenyj.
The XIII. Armeekorps is asked to detail elements from its Artillerie to support the attack of the 208. Infanteriedivision by preventing any outflanking from the high ground north and northwest of Kiselewka. The XIII. Armeekorps is also to keep the enemy engaged in front of it by increasing its reconnaissance and assault activities and by feigning Artillerie bombardments.

March group B *Leader:* Obersturmbannführer Kraas
Force: Regimentsstab of Panzergrenadier-Regiment 2
Panzergrenadier-Regiment 2 (minus the III./2)
The III./Panzer-Artillerie-Regiment 1
Stab of Panzer-Artillerie-Regiment 1

This group is to reach the Pekarschtschina area behind March group A in order to move from there immediately and to seek contact with Kampfgruppe Peiper. In close cooperation with the Kampfgruppe, March group B is to capture Kortschewka and Tortschin and make a thrust on Radomyschl.
First attack objective: Kortschewka.
Second attack objective: Tortschin.

March group C *Leader:* Sturmbannführer Ullerich
Force: Flakabteilung 1 (minus the 5. Batterie)
Panzer-Pionier-Bataillon 1 (minus the 2. Kompanie)
Combat group of Sanitätsabteilung 1
Main medical clearing station: Gogoljewka

6.12.1943 (see center of sketch 27): By 02.10 hours, reinforced Panzer-Aufklärungsabteilung 1 had crossed the road between Mokrentschtschina and Pekarschtschina and was moving east toward Andrejew.

At 02.30 hours, the traffic-control officer at Weresy, Sturmbannführer Besch, reported that all the Division's elements had passed his traffic-control point.

By 04.40 hours, the spearhead of the armoured force, the III.(armoured)/2., had captured Pekarschtschina, and it was moving on Andrejew by 05.00 hours. The Bataillon commander (Hauptsturmführer Guhl) and Untersturmführer Sterl were wounded in the fighting. Hauptsturmführer Guhl received the Ritterkreuz for his decisive attack.

By 06.30 hours, reinforced Panzer-Aufklärungsabteilung 1 had moved through Andrejew and was regrouping on the eastern edge of the town in order to advance on Stryty.

At 06.45 hours, the I./Panzerregiment 1 caught up with Panzer-Aufklärungsabteilung 1 in Andrejew, and the III./2 moved up somewhat later.

At 09.40 hours, Panzergrenadier-Regiment 2's leading elements reached Andrejew. The enemy forces there were scattered. They wandered about and could only summon up some disorganized defensive strikes.

By 09.45 hours, Panzergrenadier-Regiment 2 had started its move on Mokrentschtschina, and the Division's advance headquarters moved to Siljanschtschina at the same time.

At 10.10 hours, the enemy forces appeared to be assembling in Tschernjachow.

At 10.30 hours, the armoured Gruppe captured Styrty. There, the enemy finally offered organized resistance. Our Panzers and Panzergrenadiere advanced without a pause and by 11.00 hours had managed to take possession of the high ground outside of Kortschewka and by 11.15 of the town itself.

By 11.15 hours, the leading elements of Panzergrenadier-Regiment 2, which had followed behind with the men riding, reached Styrty. Scattered enemy groups hit the motorized column with some localized gunfire. The battlefield was covered with many dead and with a rich assortment of materiel. The enemy made futile and disorganized counterattacks out of the string of villages south of our march route. Elements of Regiment 1 were turned to the southeast toward Beschew, and they captured the town at 12.30 hours. They then moved to the southwest on Kiselewka.

At 11.55 hours, Kampfgruppe Peiper was engaged in fighting for Point 204. The Korps was informed immediately and tried to move the XIII. Armeekorps up at once, so that it could destroy the enemy forces in the string of villages south of the march route.

At 13.25 hours, the Divisional headquarters moved to Pekarschtschina.

By 13.45 hours, the III./1 (under Sturmbannführer Weidenhaupt) had turned from the area east of Mokrentschtschina and was moving south toward Tschernjachow.

At 14.15 hours, the Chef of the Generalstab informed us as follows:

the 7. Panzerdivision at 13.30 hours in Majanowka, the 1. Panzerdivision at 13.30 hours in Wydybor,
the 208. Infanteriedivision fighting southeast and east of Tschernjachow,
the XIII. Armeekorps moving from the south in an attack on Sliptschizy and Golowin.

The Korpsbefehl for 7.12.1943 read as follows:

1. *The enemy* has been defeated in front of the XIII. Armeekorps.
2. *The XXXXVIII. Panzerkorps* is to pursue, catch, and destroy the enemy forces retreating west of the Teterew and south of the Irscha. It is to block crossings over the Irscha and the Teterew in this area.
3. *The LSSAH* is to give pursuit across Tortschin, Tschaikowka, Ljachowaja, Sabolot, Mal. Ratscha, and Wel. Ratscha. Elements are to turn toward Radomyschl and clear that town of enemy forces in cooperation with the XIII. Armeekorps.
   All crossings over the Teterew between Tschudin and Wel. Ratschka are to be destroyed, and all fording places are to be mined.

The 1. Panzerdivision is to proceed via Gorbuleff, Sanki Minkowka, Chordory, Mirtscha, and Weprin.

Generalkommando of the
XXXXVIII. Panzerkorps
Abteilung Ia, No. 2465/43 geh.

At 14.30 hours, Kampfgruppe Peiper captured the railway line west of Tortschin and planned to make a stop for provisions and supplies.

The Ia, who wanted to encourage Peiper to continue the attack across Tortschin toward Tschaikowka, discovered that the radio operator in the operations staff's Funkpanzer III [radio-equipped tank] did not have the Panzerregiment's call signal. But the commander of this Panzer, Unterscharführer Steinbüchel, knew what to do. He later wrote:

> "We did not have a call signal. Upon orders from the Ia, we radioed 'Jochen from Rudi, come in please' right into the middle of the armoured force, and sure enough, Sturmbannführer Peiper's Panzer answered. From the radio conversation between Sturmbannführer Peiper and Sturmbannführer Lehmann we gathered that their communication was extremely important, and we were pretty proud of having made the contact."

The author was Ia at the time and can add that it was extremely difficult to convince Peiper of the need for continuing the attack at once. Because of the friendly relationship between them, the Ia wanted to avoid a direct order and asked Peiper a question which Peiper later characterized in a letter from his prison cell in Landsberg as "arrogant": was he stopping because he was tired? The angry reply came back: "I am attacking, over and out." The answer was preceded by a challenge quoted from Goethe's play "Götz von Berlichingen." This radio conversation was sharply censured by the Armee's radio communications overseers, not just for the non-standard call signal, but also for its content. Rightly so, but the end justifies the means.

At 14.55 hours, aerial reconnaissance reported that the enemy was pulling out of Tschernjachow to the west.

At 15.00 hours, the 2./Panzer-Pionier-Bataillon 1 set out with several Panzerjägers on self-propelled mounts which happened to be available, moving from Mokrentschtschina into these enemy forces' flank.

At 15.05 hours, Panzer-Pionier-Bataillon 1 received orders to block the roads leading out of Tschernjachow to the west along the line Klitschtsche — Slawow.

At 15.10 hours, reinforced II./2 under Sturmbannführer Max Hansen reached the fork in the road one-and-a-half kilometers north of Tschernjachow. The Bataillon halted in order to allow the unit adjacent on the left, the I./1 under Obersturmbannführer Schiller, to close ranks.

At 15.20 hours, reinforced Panzergrenadier-Regiment 1 moved forward into Tschernjachow and Kampfgruppe Peiper captured Kaetanowka.

At 15.30 hours, the Ajutant of Panzergrenadier-Regiment 1, Obersturmführer Naujock, reported that the Regiment had broken through into Tschernjachow. The Regiment received orders to let the 208. Infanteriedivision clear the town of enemy troops and instead to move as quickly as possible via Styrty, Kortschewka, Kaetanowka, and Tschaikowka in an attempt to establish contact with the Division. In the thrust on Tschernjachow, the Sturmgeschützabteilung under Hauptsturmführer Heimann provided outstanding support.

At 15.55 hours, Flakabteilung 1 was moved up to Styrty and received orders to reinforce the weak defensive forces of Panzergrenadier-Regiment 2 left behind there and to provide defense to the south and west.

At 16.30 hours, Kampfgruppe Peiper reported that Panzerregiment 1 and Panzer-Aufklärungsabteilung 1 were proceeding across Tortschin toward Tschaikowka.

At 17.00 hours, the Divisional commander returned to the Divisional headquarters and allowed the Ia to brief the armoured force on the battlefield.

At 19.00 hours, the Ia met the commander of the armoured force as it was engaged in the mop-up operation in Tortschin. Combat reconnaissance sent out toward Tschaikowka reported that there were sizable enemy forces there in well-fortified installations. The Ib, Obersturmbannführer Stoltz, encountered on the way, reported that the supply column for the armoured force could not be expected to arrive before morning. It had been halted by the XIII. Armeekorps' Feldgendarmerie in Shitomir in order to give the right-of-way to other units. For that reason, the armoured force's thrust was promised to proceed from the west via Gorbulew after a preparatory attack by Panzergrenadier-Regiment 2 on Tschaikowka.

The author remembers standing with Sturmbannführer Peiper in a hut on the eastern edge of Tortschin and observing the attack terrain. A clever driver had set up a Wehrmacht radio receiver in the hut. Out of it, the voice of Herbert Ernst Groh provided an accompaniment to the heavy Russian artillery and mortar fire. He intoned: "Friends, life is worth living!"

At 19.30 hours, the commander of Panzer-Pionier-Bataillon 1 reported that he had attacked and scattered the enemy column moving from Tschernjachow east of Klitschtsche.

At 23.40 hours, the combat forces received their missions in individual orders:

Reinforced Panzergrenadier-Regiment 1 is to move forward immediately. It is to move each Bataillon to Tortschin in the order of its arrival as the Bataillone close ranks. The attack of the XIII. Armeekorps is to be supported by turning to the south from the line Tortschin — Kortischewka against the Bystriewka sector.

Reinforced Panzergrenadier-Regiment 2, after the first elements of Panzergrenadier-Regiment 1 have moved through Kortschewka, is to follow the armoured force to Tortschin in order to capture Tschaikowka and thus to open up the road via Ljachowaja amd Sabolot toward Mal. Ratscha and Wel. Ratscha for the armoured force. The attack objective is the Teterew sector between Mal. and Wel. Ratscha.

7.12.1943: At 06.15 hours, the Divisional headquarters were moved to Kortschewka.

At 07.50 hours, the reinforced III./1 arrived in Kortschewka and deployed elements to take over the defensive positions of Panzergrenadier-Regiment 2 and then moved the bulk of its forces via Tortschin to Kamenyj Brod.

At 08.30 hours, Panzergrenadier-Regiment 2, with the 18. and 19./2 moving ahead, continued the march toward Tortschin.

At 9.10 hours, the 18. and 19./2 pushed weak enemy forces out of the forest east of Kortschewka.

At 10.15 hours, the II./2 (under Sturmbannführer Sandig), which had moved up in the night, began its attack on Tschaikowka and came under heavy defensive fire from the hills north of Tortschin.

At 12.30 hours, the Panzerregiment moved from the south on Tschaikowka in order to assist the II./2's attack forward. This attack, too, got stymied in the heavy anti-tank fire from the hills south of Tschaikowka.

At 13.00 hours, the Divisional headquarters moved to Tortschin.

At 14.00 hours, the Divisional commander ordered Panzergrenadier-Regiment 2 to surround and attack Tschaikowka while the armoured force moved around that town and launched an attack to the northwest via Point 213, circumventing Ljachowa on the south.

At 19.00 hours, the II./2 started a new attack on Tschaikowka and was able to take the town in hard fighting by 21.30 hours. The Regiment received orders to follow the armoured force. Its leading elements caught up with the armoured force at about 21.30 hours.

At 19.00 hours, the armoured forced reported reaching the fork in the road three kilometers southeast of Ljachowaja. It received orders to move east towards Wel. Ratscha and to block the crossing over the Teterew at that point. A small force was to be deployed to Radomyschl to support the thrust of the XIII. Armeekorps on that town.

At 21.15 hours, the armoured force reported that it was four kilometers southeast of Sabolot under heavy anti-tank fire. It was being outflanked from the northwestern section of Mal. Ratscha and from the hills to the north. It set up an all-around defense for the night.

8.12.1943: At 02.15 hours, reinforced Panzergrenadier-Regiment 1 set out toward Ljachowaja.

At 03.45 hours, the armoured force captured Chodory north of Sabolot, turned to the south, and penetrated the northern section of Sabolot at 08.15 hours.

At 10.15 hours, the armoured force reported that Sabolot was firmly in our hands.

At 06.00 hours, Panzergrenadier-Regiment 1 was able to capture Ljachowaja after brief fighting. It then moved immediately forward to the southwest until it got stopped at about 07.15 hours by strong enemy forces along the river northwest of Gluchow.

At 13.00 hours, the Regiment deployed the II. and III./1 in the front line and was able to take the town of Gluchow by 14.15 hours. The Regiment received such outstanding support from the 2./Sturmgeschützabteilung 1 that the Kompaniechef, Hauptsturmführer Rettlinger, was awarded the Ritterkreuz, an award long overdue that valiant officer.

The leading elements of reinforced Panzergrenadier-Regiment 2 had reached the area south of Ljachowaja by 02.00 hours in a night march. The marching column was stretched out and full of gaps because of the terrible road conditions. The Regimental commander ordered the unit to halt and assemble its forces.

At 06.00 hours, the Regiment, burdened by constant enemy air attacks and considerably harassed by enemy artillery fire, continued its march.

At 08.30 hours, it was reported that Kotowka (northeast of Ljachowaja) was occupied by the enemy.

At 09.30 hours, the 18./2, sent out on a reconnaissance mission, launched a surprise attack on the western outskirts of Kotowka and captured them.

At 13.15 hours, Regiment 2, with the I. Bataillon to the right and the II. Bataillon to the left, began its attack on Kotowka. The attack proceeded well even though the enemy offered stubborn resistance from well-fortified installations. Our well-placed Artillerie, Pak, and Flak fire forced him finally from his positions, and he took flight.

The reinforced II./2 was to establish contact with the armoured force in the eastern section of Sabolot. This thrust was to clear the way for the armoured force's supplies to come through.

At 16.00 hours, the Division's leading elements stood as follows:

Panzergrenadier-Regiment 1 in Gluchow, reconnaissance sent out toward Radomyschl.

Panzergrenadier-Regiment 2 in Sabolot.

The bulk of the armoured force in Sabolot and elements in Chodory.

At 19.00 hours, the commanding general gave an oral command to clear the terrain of enemy forces all the way to the Teterew in the area Radomyschl — Meschiritschka — Krasnoborki. The Kampfgruppen received written orders as follows:

Reinforced Regiment 1 was to attack Radomyschl on both sides of the road as soon as possible. It was to seek and hold contact with the XIII. Armeekorps.

Regiment 2 and the armoured force were to start at 24.00 hours to move from Sabolot on Wel. Ratscha.

During the entire day, there was fire from heavy Russian artillery weapons on Sabolot. The Divisional headquarters moved from there to Kotowka.

9.12.1943: The Division halted reinforced Panzergrenadier-Regiment 1's attack two kilometers northwest of Radomyschl after the Ia became convinced of the strong enemy resistance there.

At dawn, the III. (armoured)/2 captured the ravine northwest of Meshiritschka without encountering serious enemy resistance.

At 10.30 hours, the bulk of Regiment 2 closed ranks with the III./2.

At 12.15 hours, the Division received the following order from the Korps:

> "The *LSSAH* is to suspend the attack by Panzergrenadier-Regiment 1 and is to concentrate all the forces available to it southeast of Medelewka in order to force a breakthrough with the entire Division using all its Artillerie, Werfer, Flank, Panzers, and Sturmgeschütze on the enemy bridgehead from the north and to capture Meshiritschka. Preparation, structure, attack direction, and intended time of start all to be reported.
>
> Generalkommando of the XXXXVIII. Panzerkorps
> Abteilung Ia, No. 2481/43 geheim."

At 15.30 hours, the II./2 started its preparatory attack on the hills north of Meshiritschka.

At 17.30 hours, the enemy was thrown out of the hills. An enemy attempt to surround our forces from the east was repulsed by the 15./2.

At 18.00 hours, the bulk of the Regiment waited for the completion of a preparatory attack by the Artillerie, heavy weapons, and Panzers, and then launched its attack.

At 19.30 hours, the attack was making good progress despite heavy resistance. The leading elements were able to enter the town and by 20.00 hours had pushed the enemy back to the Teterew.

The enemy attempted to make immediate counterthrusts, later counterattacks, to regain the town, but all attempts were repulsed.

At 22.00 hours, the Divisional commander ordered Panzergrenadier-Regiment 2 to move ahead with the armoured force west of the Teterew, attacking from the north toward Wel. Ratscha in order to capture the town.

In the meantime, Panzergrenadier-Regiment 1 had assumed a line of defense stretching from just west of the Gluchow—Radomyschl road. It received orders to capture Hill 187, flanking this position, and then to establish contact with the 68. Infanteriedivision. During the day, the Regiment had to repulse a number of enemy attacks.

At 17.30 hours, the Regimental commander, Obersturmbannführer Frey, received the following informational order from the Korps:

> The 68. Infanteriedivision had penetrated Radomyschl from the south and west and had come as far forward as the three churches. A small force from the Division was moving to the west on Hill 178, while the mass of the Division was moving along the road to the northeast with its right wing on the Teterew. The *LAH* was to send reinforced Panzergrenadier-Regiment 1 to join this attack on the left wing of the 68. Infanteriedivision and was to capture Mal. Ratscha. It was to await orders from the Division before starting.

Panzers available for combat on 9.12.1943:

		Combat-ready	Under short-term repair	Under long-term repair
Panzer VI		4	10	10
Panzer V		6	53	17
Panzer IV		8	47	15
Panzer III		2	2	2
Sturmgeschütze:	7.5-cm	7	20	10
	10.5-cm	1	7	1
Pak:	7.5-cm (mot. Z)	6		
	7.5-cm (self-propelled)	7		

10.12.1943: Harassing artillery fire rained down on the positions of Panzergrenadier-Regiment 1 northwest of Radomyschl the entire night. Because the unit adjacent to the right, the 68. Infanteriedivision, was not planning a thrust to the north, according to the statements of the two first Generalstab officers, Panzergrenadier-Regiment 1 stayed in its positions for the time being. Reinforced Panzergrenadier-Regiment 2 was under constant counterattack from enemy units up to a regiment in size, with a heavy barrage of artillery fire coming from east of the Teterew.

At 04.00 hours, Panzer-Aufklärungsabteilung 1 and the III. (armoured)/2 were to the west of the road from Meshiritschka to Wel. Ratscha and the reinforced I. and II./2 were east of it. Both groups set out to the south for their attack. The numerically superior enemy forces were in field installations and had the support of strong artillery. In crossing the first hill south of Meshiritschka, the leading elements came under extraordinarily heavy defensive fire from all weapons.

At 07.30 hours, the enemy launched a surprise preparatory artillery fire and followed it with a counterattack against the left flank of the II./2 and on Meshiritschka. The Divisional commander, at the time in the town, ordered our forces to suspend their attack.

At 08.00 hours, the armoured force had barely left Meshiritschka when it came under heavy anti-tank fire from the eastern edge of Krasnoborki. This attack, too, had to be broken off.

At 10.00 hours, the Korps was briefed on the Division's situation. The Chef of the Generalstab reported that the 1. Panzerdivision would on the following day move on Krasnoborki from the north; he proposed that the armoured force of the *LAH* set out at the same time over Hill 170 against Wel. Ratscha or Krasnoborki. Because he shared our opinion that the enemy forces near Radomyschl had no intention of attacking us, while those in Wel. Ratscha and north of there clearly had such intentions, he agreed with our plan to move the I./Artillerie-Regiment and Sturmgeschützabteilung (currently stationed with Panzergrenadier-Regiment 1) to Meshiritschka to join Panzergrenadier-Regiment 2. Starting at 11.15 hours, the units were informed of the intentions for 11.12.1943 and the corresponding orders were issued.

The Divisional commander returned from the battlefield and declared himself dissatisfied with the last days' attacks. He had the Ia issue a "Directive for the conduct of the attack on 11.12.1943" (included here as Appendix No. 6). The rest of the day was needed for the careful preparation of the attack scheduled for the following morning.

11.12.1943: The night was quiet except for the fact that the enemy focused artillery fire for the destruction of Meshiritschka on the town between 21.00 and 22.00 hours.

At 04.00 hours, the Division's attack force deployed in the ravine northwest of Meshiritschka in preparation for the attack on Krasnoborki as follows:

the I. and II./2 were in the first line,

to the right of the I./2 was Sturmgeschützabteilung 1,

to the left of the II./2 was the armoured force (Panzerregiment 1, the III. (armoured)/2).

Reinforced Panzer-Aufklärungsabteilung 1 (the 2./Panzer-Pionier-Bataillon 1, elements of the 13. and 18./2) assumed the responsibility for defense of Meshiritschka to the east.

From 11.55 - 12.00 hours, there was a sudden concentration of fire from the heavy weapons. At 12.00 hours, the units drove out with the men mounted for their attack on the eastern section of Krasnoborki. From there they were to turn to the southeast to attack Wel. Ratscha over Hill 170.

At 12.00 hours, the attack began. It made smooth progress.

At 12.50 hours, the leading elements of the Grenadiere, with outstanding support from the Sturmgeschütze, broke into the eastern edge of Krasnoborki and found themselves entangled in house-to-house fighting. The armoured force turned to the southeast.

At 13.15 hours, the armoured force penetrated the forest at Point 170.

At 13.50 hours, Hill 170 and the forest around it were captured.

Twenty-one enemy anti-tank guns had been destroyed to this point. There were enemy tanks on the western edge of Wel. Ratscha.

By 15.00 hours, Panzergrenadier-Regiment 2 had moved up from behind, reached the stream bed south of 170, and worked its way forward to within one thousand meters of Wel. Ratscha.

At 15.05 hours, the Korps Arko was requested to fire upon and destroy the enemy flanking movements from the western bank of the Teterew.

At 16.50 hours, the Adjutant of Panzerregiment 1, Obersturmführer Wolff, reported that the armoured force had broken into Wel. Ratscha. It then received orders to capture and hold Tschudin.

At 16.55 hours, Panzergrenadier-Regiment 2 received orders to move on after the capture of Wel. Ratscha and to capture Badjelowka (two kilometers north of Tschudin). Panzer-Aufklärungsabteilung 1 was to swing forward with its right wing onto the hill south of Meshiritschka.

At 18.00 hours, the units deployed in front reported the towns of Tschudin and Badjalowka heavily occupied by enemy forces as far as the hill south of Meshiritschka. The effect of the enemy weapons situated on the elevated and thickly forested eastern bank of the Teterew was particularly unpleasant.

At 20.30 hours, the enemy waged an organized counterattack with a force larger than a regiment from the southwest on the weakly occupied positions of the II./2 on the southeastern edge of Wel. Ratscha. Personally led by the Bataillon's commander, Sturmbannführer Sandig, our forces managed to clear away a local enemy breakthrough and restore the old battle line. The Sturmgeschütze provided vital support there. In the course of the cold, dry night, strong enemy attacks were repulsed.

The XXXXVIII. Panzerkorps intended to use the *LAH* and the 1. Panzerdivision on 12.12.1943 to surround the enemy forces still on the western bank of the Teterew and to destroy them. For this purpose, Werferregiment 1 was subordinated to the *LAH*.

12.12.1943: At 04.05 hours, after repulsing several enemy attacks, elements of Panzergrenadier-Regiment 2 managed to pursue the retreating enemy and move forward until approximately the center of Badjalowka. Reasonably large groups of enemy troops, separated from their units, kept trying to break out of the forest south of Krasnoborki to the northeast.

At 06.30 hours, Panzergrenadier-Regiment 1 and the Flakabteilung received the following orders: the III./1 with its subordinated heavy Flak-Batterien was to act as a blocking unit on the northern edge of Wischewitschi. Its mission was to defend against any enemy forces breaking through from the north in the sector Wischewitschi — Sarudje (inclusive). There it was to be adjacent to the 1. Panzerdivision, also acting as blocking unit.

At 10.12 hours and again at 10.35 hours, a telephone construction unit and the commander of the Pionier-Bataillon reported that the enemy was retreating in droves from the forest near Gluchow toward the forests south of Krasnoborki.

All available elements were deployed to "gather up" these enemy elements. The heavy weapons focused harassing fire on the forest. The commander of Werfer-regiment 1 reported that the heavy Abteilung had run out of ammunition. The medium Abteilung was subordinated to Panzer-Artillerie-Regiment 1.

At 10.25 hours, the commander of Panzergrenadier-Regiment 2 reported that there were constant enemy attacks from Tschudin and the south.

At 10.45 hours, Panzergrenadier-Regiment 1 received orders to join the attack of the 68. Infanteriedivision to the north with the forest south of Krasnoborki as its objective.

At 14.30 hours, a small armoured force under the command of Hauptsturmführer Dinse attacked in Badjalowka with the intention of forcing its way as far as the bank of the Teterew and blowing up the crossing there. The attack was successful in breaking through the enemy position immediately opposite it, but in moving through the city it began to feel the effects of the many anti-tank and heavy weapons firing from the eastern bank of the Teterew. For that reason, Kampfgruppe Dinse was pulled back to its point of departure on the western edge of Badjalowka.

At 15.30 hours, Panzergrenadier-Regiment 1 received orders to assemble after capturing the forest south of Krasnoborki and to prepare to march.

At 16.10 hours, Sturmbannführer Weidenhaupt, commander of the III./1, reported that the Russians had forced their way into Wischewitschi from the east immediately upon their arrival there.

At 17.00 hours, Panzergrenadier-Regiment 1 reported that the bulk of its forces had assembled near Sabolot.

At 22.15 hours, a fairly large contingent of enemy troops separated from their units attempted to break through our line near Wel. Ratscha and to move to the east. The III./2 defeated them and took them prisoner.

At 23.30 hours, the Ia of the 1. Panzerdivision requested the left wing of the blocking unit at Wischewitschi to extend to the west as far as Medelewka. The Russians, he reported, had moved strong forces across the line Krugli — Point 163.

At 23.35 hours, reinforced Panzergrenadier-Regiment 1 received orders to set out immediately and to capture the line Wischewitschi — Medelewka (exclusive of it), then to occupy it with its front to the north, and to hold it. The III./1 returned to the Regiment, but the Flakabteilung remained subordinated. A Panzerkompanie of ten Panzer IV's was moved up and temporarily subordinated to the Regiment for the purpose of capturing this line.

At 23.45 hours, the commander of the Pionier-Bataillon, Hauptsturmführer Steinert, received orders to move the 1. and 3. Kompanie up and to extend the left wing of the 2./Panzer-Pionier-Bataillon 1 from Meshiritschka as far as Passika on the Teterew (exclusive of it).

13.12.1943: At 01.00 hours, the units received their orders for the day.

At 00.30 hours, reinforced Panzergrenadier-Regiment 1 had already moved out, and it reported at 10.15 hours that it had captured the designated battle line. The enemy forces in the easteern section of Wischewitschi were thrown out. The following were deployed: from right to left, the II./1, the I./1, and the III./1.

At 10.30 hours, the commanding general briefed us at the Divisional head-quarters on the plans for 14.12.1943. The *LAH*, the 7. Panzerdivision, and the 1. Panzerdivision were to launch an attack to the north against the Irscha sector.

The Flakabteilung had moved its heavy Batterien into position, with the 1. Batterie north of Wischewitschi, the 2. Batterie west of there, and the 3. Batterie on the edge of the forest between Wischewitschi and Medelewka. There was an extraordinary amount of enemy air combat activity the entire day. There were at any moment fifteen to twenty ground attack planes with fighter escort above the Division's area. The planes launched numerous attacks on our positions and the march roads leading to them.

The Divisional commander, Oberführer Wisch, held a birthday party for himself at the headquarters in Kotowka at 16.00 hours. The new Oberbefehlshaber of the 4. Panzerarmee, General der Panzertruppen Raus, joined the group briefly for coffee. Shortly after his departure, an amusing event occurred. The commander of the I./Panzerregiment 1, Sturmbannführer Kuhlmann, had ordered two broken-down Panthers standing nearby to fire two shots in the air. The Divisional commander recalled:

> "Robert Arthecker, the Chef of the baking Kompanie, was just putting the birthday cake on the table. Suddenly, there were shots outside the door. Everyone took cover, grabbed his weapon, and evaluated the situation. Rudi Lehmann had grabbed the cake and brought it to safety with one great leap through the window. Then, when the fear had subsided, he appeared at the door, beaming with joy, and the cake was still intact."

The Wehrmacht report for 13.12.1943 contained the following:

> "...In the combat area northeast of Shitomir, the Soviets undertook heavy counterattacks with newly-introduced forces, but they were repulsed. Our forces renewed their attack and defeated an enemy counterattack on the western bank of the Teterew."

14.12.1943: The preparations for the planned attack began during the night before. The II./1 was relieved from its positions on the northern edge of Wischewitschi, and it occupied new ones south of Iskra in order to provide cover for the preparations of Panzergrenadier-Regiment 1.

The previous days had given us the impression that the enemy forces in the triangle formed by the Teterew and Irscha rivers were attacking the XXXXVIII. Panzerkorps with the intention of protecting the railway line from Kiev to Korosten and to win time and ground for the arrival of sizable forces. For this reason, the enemy needed to maintain an operative bridgehead across the Irscha and Teterew at all costs. The Soviet forces involved were: the 14th Guards Tank Brigade and the 3rd Guards (motorized) Rifle Brigade of the IVth Guards Tank Corps, elements of the VIIth Guards Tank Corps, the remaining units of the defeated 60th Army, and the newly introduced 161st and 348th Rifle Divisions.

> *Orders for the LAH*: "The 1. SS-Panzerdivision *LAH* is to ride along the road from Radomyschl to Sarudja and capture as its first attack objective Irscha. Immediately thereafter, it is to turn to the northeast and capture the edges of the forest near Belyj Bereg. The Division will also be required to turn to the southeast from there and to make a thrust through the forest area to reach the railway bridge over the Teterew. The bridge is to be destroyed beyond repair."
>
> *Reinforced Panzergrenadier-Regiment 1* (the III. [armoured]/2) is to move out of the area just east of Medelewka and proceed, in close cooperation with *Panzergrenadier-Regiment 1*, via Iskra and Wyrwa to capture Irscha

as its first attack objective. After a brief pause to order the ranks, it is to proceed to the north and is to block the bend in the railway line from Kiev to Korosten. The Panzers are to be moved via Krasnoselki into the assembly area such that they can set out immediately after only a brief pause in their march. The Panzer attack is to be in two waves.
Reinforced Panzergrenadier-Regiment 2 (minus the III./2 but with the Sturmgeschützabteilung) is to leave its positions east of Wel. Ratscha in the night between 13.12 and 14.12 and is to stand ready in the Krasnoborki area to be moved up behind Panzergrenadier-Regiment 1 via Medelewka into the area north of Iskra. From there, it is to turn to the east to attack and capture Weprin and Hf. Kodinka.
For this move, it is assigned to cooperate with Werferregiment 1.
Panzer-Artillerie-Regiment 1 is to move into position in the area southeast of Medelewka so that it can aim its concentrated fire in front of the attack of Panzerregiment 1 and Panzergrenadier-Regiment 1, with which it is assigned to cooperate.
Flakabteilung 1 is to subordinate its light and medium Batterien to Panzer-Aufklärungsabteilung 1. The heavy Batterien are to remain in their positions for the time being.
Reinforced Panzer-Aufklärungsabteilung is to cover the Division's eastern flank in the sector from the southeastern edge of Meshiritschka to the northeastern edge of Wischewitschi. It is assigned to cooperate with the Division Artillerie of the 68. Infanteriedivision.
Panzer-Pionier-Bataillon 1 is to detail one Pionier assault group each to the two Panzergrenadier-Regiment's attack forces. Acting independently of each other, one is to move along the Teterew and the other along the railway line; both are to reach the railroad tracks west of the Teterew station. These tracks are to be destroyed beyond repair.
The *advance headquarters of the Division* are to be north of Medelewka starting with the beginning of the attack.

At 11.30 hours, the armoured force, followed by Panzergrenadier-Regiment 1, began its attack.

At 12.25 hours, the enemy forces were thrown out of Iskra, and the first wave of the Panzer attack pursued them. By 13.40 hours, the Panzers had reached the road from Weprin to Fedorowka, where they encountered strong defense from field installations. They turned to the west and proceeded along the stream bed to reach the fork in the road one kilometer south of the eastern section of Fedorowka, which they captured at about 15.00 hours. Once there, however, they became enmeshed in fighting with Soviet tanks. We lost two Panzers but managed to destroy three T-34's. When the armoured force turned to the west, Panzer-Artillerie-Regiment 1 aimed its concentrated fire on the edges of the forest southeast of Fedorowka.

At 15.00 hours, the 1. Panzerdivision informed us that the spearhead of the Panzer force was one kilometer south of Fedorowka, while the attack force to the left was fighting around Ostroff, four kilometers southwest of Fedorowka.

At 16.00 hours, Panzergrenadier-Regiment 1 was fighting its way to the north. By about 18.00 hours, it was involved in wearisome combat as it proceeded toward Wyrwa.

At 18.30 hours, Panzergrenadier-Regiment 2, still mounted in its vehicles, reached Iskra and proceeded on both sides of the road to Krugli, which it reached at 19.25 without having encountered enemy resistance. The Regiment continued its attack toward Weprin.

At 19.30 hours, the Adjutant of Panzerregiment 1 reported that there were no places to cross the river before Wyrwa; the armoured force would therefore have to use the crossing on the eastern edge of Fedorowka.

At 19.35 hours, an order from the Korps reached the Division suspending the attack. The Korps was to disengage from the enemy in the night before 15.12 and stand ready for a new mission.

The *LAH* was to disengage from the enemy and move via Medelewka, Krasnoselki, and Sabolot to reach the area Sabolot — Chodory — Golubowka — Detinez — Ljachowaja.

Panzer-Aufklärungsabteilung 1 was to be the last unit to pull back. The 1. Panzerdivision's march route was to be the road from western Medelewka — Mirtscha — Chodory — Minkowka. There, the *LAH* was not allowed to use or cross the march route until the 1. Panzerdivision had moved through.

Starting at 19.50 hours, the units were given their new assignments, march routes, and billeting areas individually.

The order of the retreat march: Panzer-Pionier-Bataillon, armoured force, Panzergrenadier-Regiment 1, Panzer-Aufklärungsabteilung 1, Panzergrenadier-Regiment 2.

Panzergrenadier-Regiment 2 had taken up a position around Iskra and Medelewka for the night.

The Ib received orders to keep the supply units and the repair Abteilung ready for immediate action in the Kotowka — Ljachowaja area.

15.12.1943: At 03.45 hours, the Division reported to the Korps that the withdrawal had been in progress since 21.00 hours. By 03.00 hours, the last units had left the towns of Meshiritschka, Wischewitschi, and Medelewka. In each of these three towns, one Kompanie of Panzer-Pionier-Bataillon 1 was deployed to mine the roads and destroy the bridges.

Starting at 06.00 hours, the units began reporting their arrival in the designated billeting areas.

At 06.15 hours, the last element of Panzer-Aufklärungsabteilung 1 passed through Medelewka. The disengagement was not hindered by the enemy .

At 08.20 hours, Panzergrenadier-Regiment 2 reported that Medelewka had been abandoned.

At 10.15 hours, the Divisional headquarters were moved to Ljachowaja.

At 12.15 hours, the commanding general arrived at the Divisional headquarters with the news that the Russians had broken through a part of the positions of our 68. Infanteriedivision and had pushed through to Krasnoborki and Mal. Ratscha.

At 12.17 hours, Panzergrenadier-Regiment 2 received orders to move out of its current billeting area and to launch a counterattack with Sturmgeschütz support to recapture Krasnoborki.

At 12.20 hours, Panzer-Aufklärungsabteilung 1 received corresponding orders to support the attack.

At 12.25 hours, Panzer-Aufklärungsabteilung 1 received orders to launch a counterattack from Sabolot on Mal. Ratscha. The II./Artillerie-Regiment 1 was subordinated to it for this purpose.

At 14.15 hours, the Chef of the Generalstab informed us that the enemy had also penetrated Litowka. The force deployed against Mal. Ratscha was to proceed immediately against Litowka.

At 14.20 hours, the enemy was thrown back from Hill 170 northwest of Wel. Ratscha. At 14.30 hours, Panzer-Aufklärungsabteilung 1 captured the northeastern edge of Mal. Ratscha and by 14.45 hours had moved through the city to the south. The arrival of darkness quieted both sides down. For his leadership in this attack, the commander of Panzer-Aufklärungsabteilung 1, Sturmbannführer Knittel, was awarded the Ritterkreuz.

The Generalkommando of the XXXXVIII. Panzerkorps ordered the Division to find billets in the designated area in such a way that the attack groups were already in place and could set out from all sides upon short notice.

16.12.1943: During the entire night and morning, the former battle line was restored with the close cooperation of the 68. Infanteridivision. In the fighting, Panzer-Aufklärungsabteilung 1 destroyed four of five enemy tanks which attacked it near Mal. Ratscha.

At 13.45 hours, the Korps issued a new order for thorough road reconnaissance as far as the march route from Kiev to Shitomir. The assignment went to Panzer-Pionier-Bataillon 1.

The III./1 reported that it still had a combat strength of one hundred fifty-seven men. With that, the fighting west of Radomyschl came to an end.

> "The bulk of the Russian 16th Army was completely destroyed. Judging from the stores of ammunition and the outstanding network of roads we found prepared by the enemy, we could not doubt that we had prevented an extensive offensive on the part of the Russians," observed the Chef of the Generalstab of the XXXXVIII. Panzerkorps, Oberst i.G. Mellenthin, in his book "Panzerschlachten."

The new plan for the Panzerdivisionen was for them to regroup in preparation for a thrust across Korosten and through the area south of there in order to destroy the enemy forces gathering northwest of Malin.

e) 17.12.1943 - 23.12 1943: Fighting around Tschepowitschi

17.12.1943 - 18.12.1943: In order to realize the intention stated above, the Korps was to move the 7. Panzerdivision out of the Janowka — Budilowka area to the north; at the same time, it was to swing the 1. SS-Panzerdivision *LAH* and the 1. Panzerdivision around to the northeast. Later, this second assault force was to turn to the southeast in order to establish contact with the 7. Panzerdivision in the area east of Tschepowitschi.

To that end, the 1. Panzerdivision and the *LAH* were moved in two nights of marching into their designated assembly areas; for the *LAH* that was the area two-and-a-half kilometers west of Meleni. Both Divisionen were to stand ready to attack early in the morning on 19.12.1943.

On 18.12.1943, the Divisional commander and the Ia scouted the assembly area and the attack terrain in the morning. At 12.00 hours, the commanding general held a briefing at the headquarters of the 291. Infanteriedivision. Each Division's part in the planned attack was presented.

Before we describe this attack, let us turn first to a report from the trusty Hauptsturmführer Rettlinger, at that time the Chef of the 3./Sturmgeschützabteilung 1, concerning those prisoners of war who chose to serve with us, our Hiwis:

> "Probably all the units in our Division had volunteer Russians serving in their ranks. My Batterie alone had twelve of them. We had nothing but good experiences with them. They were almost all the same age as we were and therefore as fond of jokes as anyone. They all came from the area around Charkow and had offered their services to our Batterie willingly and without any pressure from us. They served with the repair and maintenance crews and as riders in the ammunition and fuel supply trucks. They had come to us in July of 1943, got to know central Europe and Italy, and then travelled back to their homeland with us in November of 1943. We detrained at the Biala-Zerkwa station. We moved forward and had to pull right back; that was a familiar pattern. In this back-and-forth fighting, Rottenführer Ihsen and his Hiwi, Kraszielnik, received orders right after getting off the train to fetch fuel for the Batterie in their tanker truck. Shortly after they set out, the Batterie got caught in fighting and began moving from town to town. Our two tanker drivers could not find us again. A full three weeks later, we were in the Korosten area when the door to the communications room flew open one night. A bundled-up figure snapped to attention and reported: 'Hiwi Kraszielnik reporting in. Truck kaputt. Planes. Ihsen wounded. Hospital.' He had brought back his own gun and Ihsen's and both their packs. He had searched for the Batterie until he found it. What would have prevented our friend Kraszielnik from going over to the partisans' side? I often think of these brave boys, of Basch and Krupp and VW and Magirus and whatever their other names were. Are they still alive? They all deserve a kind thought from us."

Back to the events of 18.12.1943:

The Division's plan was to assemble and make its preparations in and south of the forest two-and-a-half kilometers to the south of Meleni, then to launch a concentrated Artillerie attack, and finally to set out in a broad front to the north at 09.05 hours. The first attack objective was to be the road from Malin to Korosten north of Schw. Gemüse. The Division intended to wage the attack from the left wing (Panzergrenadier-Regiment 2) with the Panzerregiment moving in closed ranks and the Sturmgeschützabteilung making two surges. Panzergrenadier-Regiment 1, deployed to the right, was to capture the area just northwest of Schw. Gemüse, then to move along the gravel road with the subordinated III. (armoured)/2 to capture territory to the southeast. Panzergrenadier-Regiment 2, deployed to the right, was to capture its first attack objective and then to make a mounted thrust along the road (with the

1. Panzerdivision moving along the railroad tracks) into the area just northeast of Tschepowitschi.

Under this plan of attack, Tschepowitschi would be attacked from both the north and the northeast and captured. Later, the units were to seek contact with the 7. Panzerdivision, attacking from the south.

At 16.05 hours, the Divisional commander and Ia returned from the briefing with the commanding general and proceeded to brief the individual unit commanders on the Division's plan of attack in a meeting at the Divisional headquarters in Kowaliwschtschina.

At 22.10 hours, the Korps issued an addendum to the plan of attack stating that Meleni was to be captured and held.

In the evening, the able 1. Ordonnanzoffizier of the Division, Hauptsturmführer Tiemann, handed over his unit's position to Hauptsturmführer Taubert, formerly Chef of the 1./Panzer-Pionier-Bataillon. Hauptsturmführer Tiemann was detailed to the general staff training course in preparation for joining the Generalkommando of the XIII. Armeekorps.

19.12.1943: After a heavy preparatory barrage from thirty Batterien and from the concentrated Nebelwerfers, reinforced by the Panzers from the I./Panzer-regiment 1 (Heer) under Hauptmann von Krauß, elements of Panzergrenadier-Regiment 1 launched an attack late in the night on 18.12 in order to capture its assembly area on the other side of the Steditsch river.

At 05.55 hours, the Division informed the Korps that the difficult road conditions would delay the prepartions of the entire Division. The attack could begin at 10.00 hours at the earliest, but preferably at 11.00 hours. In the meantime, the tireless communications squads were working around the clock to establish the necessary telephone connections.

At 09.00 hours, the Division was able to report that it would be able to begin the attack with all its forces at 10.05 hours. It had at its disposal seven Panzer VI's, twelve Panzer V's, thirty-three Panzer IV's, thirteen 7.5-centimeter Sturmgeschütze, five 10.5-centimeter Sturmgeschütze, and twelve 7.5-centimeter Panzerjägers on self-propelled mounts.

At 10.05 hours, the Division began its attack.

At 11.15 hours, the two Panzergrenadier-Regimenter broke through the first enemy installation along the road from Meleni to Garbuy.

At 13.20 hours, the enemy was thrown back out of his second installation near Hf. Meleni.

By 13.35 hours, the leading elements of the attack were west of Schw. Gemüse.

At 14.30 hours, Panzergrenadier-Regiment 1 captured the line Stremigorod — Chotirowka.

The enemy forces in the first and second battle positions had certainly been surprised and offered no organized resistance to our attack. But the fighting, which had proceeded through the thickly overgrown terrain since we left our bridgehead, could almost be called bush warfare. We were therefore forced to clear away individual nests of resistance, even though it cost us valuable time.

At 14.30 hours, the armoured force, followed by Panzergrenadier-Regiment 1, set out toward Hf. Baljarka. At 14.55 hours, it was engaged in combat with tanks and infantry in the southeastern part of Stremigorod. It turned to the south and by 15.20 hours had captured Hf. Baljarka. In the fighting, two T-34's were destroyed.

At 15.30 hours, the 18., 15. and elements of the 17./Panzergrenadier-Regiment 2 set out from the south and southwest toward Swch. Gemüse. The enemy forces in that town offered such tough resistance that the Kompanien were only able to penetrate as far as the first row of houses and were forced to assume defensive positions there for the night.

At 18.30 hours, the spearhead of the armoured force penetrated Peremoga, but the attack got stuck in front of a well-fortified anti-tank front on both sides of the road junction one-and-a-half kilometers south of Peremoga.

Panzergrenadier-Regiment 2 moved up as far as Peremoga and positioned the II./2 to the right and the I./2 to the left to take over the defense.

Panzergrenadier-Regiment 1 was fighting strong enemy forces on both sides of the railway line near Hf. Lipjany.

Panzer-Aufklärungsabteilung 1 provided cover for the Division's eastern flank along the line Scherschni — eastern edge of the forest west of Meleni — road from Meleni to Garby (inclusive of it).

The Flakabteilung's heavy Batterien had held Meleni from their position in Tschubarowskije under harassing fire from the enemy. Untersturmführer Breinersdorfer of the 1. Batterie, deployed as the advance artillery observer, and Rottenführer Werner took eleven prisoners.[5]

The 7. Panzerdivision, moving from the south, fought against strong enemy forces but succeeded in capturing the area to the east of Ustinowka.

Results of reconnaissance revealed that it was possible that the enemy was attempting to build a linking position along the line west Tschepowitschi — Ossefowka — Lipljany — Distr. Koschary — Gorbatschi.

The XXXXVIII. Panzerkorps expressed its opinion in the enemy evaluation section of Korpsbefehl No. 14 that the enemy forces had been pushed back. The evaluation continued:

> "The *LAH*'s rapid advance means that the enemy's forces in the Meleni — Tschepowitschi area will be surrounded shortly."

In his book "Panzerschlachten," Oberst i.G. von Mellenthin writes as follows about the leadership of the battle within the XXXXVIII. Panzerkorps:

> "Cooperation such as this, in an attack from several directions, could only be accomplished by combat units of high quality. The two Panzerdivisionen attacking there (the 1. Panzerdivision and the *LAH*) belonged without doubt to the best German Divisionen."

20.12.1943: In the course of the night, the spearhead of the Panzer forces was pulled back behind Panzergrenadier-Regiment 2's line.

At 07.30 hours, Swch. Gemüse was captured from enemy forces offering only weak resistance. Flakabteilung 1 was moved up via Swch. Gemüse to Hf. Baljarka and moved into position there with the six 8.8-centimeter Kanonen it possessed which were still capable of firing.

At 08.50 hours, a Russian cavalry troop attacked the positions of the II./2 south of the road and was beaten back in bloody fighting.

At 13.30 hours, the armoured force and Kampfgruppe Bradel of the 1. Panzerdivision set out in their vehicles along the road to the southeast. By 14.45 hours, they were involved in fighting for the Tschepowitschi railway station.

15.11.1943: Zydouce. The commanding general of the XXXXVIII. Panzerkorps, General der Panzertruppen Balck, with the commander of the 1. SS-Panzerdivision *LSSAH*, Oberführer Wisch, and the Ia of the 1. SS-Panzerdivision.

November, 1943: Sturmbannführer Peiper, commander of the III. (armoured)/2. Panzergrenadier-Regiment *LSSAH*, issuing orders south of Brusilow.

At 13.45 hours, reinforced Panzergrenadier-Regiment 1 had set out from the road junction south of Hf. Lipjany for its attack on Hill 185.3. The patches of forest around it were heavily occupied by enemy troops. Six T-34's were destroyed in the fighting. Because of the thick undergrowth and the numerous enemy mines, the attack gained territory very slowly. After the capture of Hill 185.3 at about 17.30 hours, the attack was halted. One Bataillon was left behind there as a security force, and the bulk of the Regiment received orders to move into the area north of the Tschepowitschi railway station. There, it was to secure the junction of the highway and the railroad tracks one-and-a-half kilometers south of Ossefowka.

By 18.00 hours, the armoured force, working in conjunction with Kampfgruppe Bradel, had captured the spread-out Tschepowitschi railway station and was defending the crossing of the highway with the railway north of the town. The III. (armoured)/2 had assumed responsibility for defense to the east and south at this position.

At 20.45 hours, the two other Bataillone of Panzergrenadier-Regiment 2 moved out of their former defensive positions in front of Peremoga under the command of Hauptsturmführer Bormann with orders to relieve the armoured force.

The enemy had, after the armoured group's breakthrough, reoccupied the line of houses just south of the railway line with a sizable force. The II./2, engaged in penetrating the western part of the town, came under heavy fire from mortars, anti-tank guns, and tanks. Each building had to be stormed individually. In the fighting, the Bataillon was forced to defend itself against enemy counterattacks with tanks and mounted infantry.

At 23.45 hours, Hauptsturmführer Bormann reported:

> "23.30 hours: We reached the eastern exit from the Tschepowitschi railway complex. The town is occupied by enemy forces to within one hundred meters south of the road in front of the station. Moves to clear away enemy forces proceed very slowly. Russian tanks are attacking the railway from the north. Two of our Pak guns are out of commission because the crews have been wounded, and one has been destroyed by a mine. We have caught up to the armoured force, but we are unable on my side to maintain contact. The armoured force is presently at the crossing over the railroad tracks two kilometers east of the Tschepowitschi station. One Panzer is north of the tracks even with the station. Request armour-piercing weapons.
>
> signed Bormann,
> Hauptsturmführer."

Panzer-Pionier-Bataillon 1 was pulled back to Hf. Baljarka. The following number of Panzers were fit for combat at that moment:

Panzer VI's	3
Panzer V's	8
Panzer IV's	9

Enemy losses in materiel for 20.12.1943: seventeen T-34's, four assault guns, and forty-four artillery pieces were destroyed. The 13. (heavy)/Panzerregiment

1 played a considerable role in this success. Kompaniechef Hauptsturmführer Kling was awarded the Ritterkreuz for this action.

At 17.30 hours, the Ic of the Division, Hauptsturmführer Vügtel issued the following report to the Korps:

"Telephone transcription 20.12.1943
Received at 17.30 hours by 1./SS-Panzerdivision *LSSAH* 01 — Oberfeldwebel Kremer

The 1./SS-Panzerdivision LSSAH has in the one hundred and five days of its 1943 Russian campaign destroyed one thousand and three enemy tanks. In detail:

1) Winter battle around Charkow from 28.1.1943 to 20.3.1943: two hundred forty-one tanks
2) Operation Zitadelle from 5.7.1943 to 17.7.1943: five hundred and four tanks
3) Fighting east of Shitomir from 8.11.1943 to 20.12.1943: two hundred and fifty-eight tanks

These figures do not include armoured personnel carriers or other armoured vehicles."

Orders for 21.12.1943:

The XXXXVIII. Panzerkorps was to continue its attack to the southeast, driving along the road and the railway line from Korosten to Malin. It was to capture the area east and northeast of Tschepowitschi. Thereafter, the intention was to provide cover to the east and north, to surround the enemy forces in Tschepowitschi and Meleni, and to destroy them one after the other."

21.12.1943: In the course of the night, the bulk of Panzergrenadier-Regiment 1, reinforced by several Panzers, captured the crossing of the railroad tracks and the highway one-and-a-half kilometers south of Ossefowka. The Regiment spent the morning fending off constant enemy tank attacks. Obersturmbannführer Frey, the valiant Regimental commander, managed to destroy twenty-one enemy tanks with his six combat-ready Panzers.

At 12.13 hours, the Regimental commander pulled back to the eastern edge of the Tschepowitschi railway station area with the one Panzer in his possession which was still fit for combat.

The remaining elements of Panzergrenadier-Regiment 2 were moved up to the southern part of the Tschepowitschi railway station in the early morning hours and deployed to join the heavy defensive fighting to the south on the southern edge of the railway station complex.

In the evening of 21.12.1943, Panzer-Aufklärungsabteilung 1 was fighting along the line Schwerschny — Budnja Schwerschnewskaja — two kilometers west of Meleni — road from Meleni to Grabuy.

The Divisions-Sicherungskompanie was on the eastern edge of Swch. Gemüse, which was where the Divisional headquarters were also located.

The 2./Panzer-Pionier-Bataillon 1 was one and two-tenths kilometers south of Hf. Baljarka.

Elements of Panzergrenadier-Regiment 1 were on the southern edge of Hill 185.3.

The 3./Panzer-Pionier-Bataillon 1 was on the high ground southeast of Peremoga.

Panzergrenadier-Regiment 2 and most of Panzergrenadier-Regiment 1 were on the southern and eastern edges of Tschepowitschi.

Results of combat reconnaissance:

a) Enemy positions: southeastern section of Schwerschny and the patch of forest at Budnja Schwerschewskaja heavily occupied by enemy forces.
From the southeastern edge of Meleni to Hill 178.2, trenches and mines.
Hill 189.5 east of Meleni heavily occupied by the enemy.
Enemy positions from three kilometers south of Hf. Baljarka — road junction three kilometers south of Peremoga — march route one kilometer south of Tschepowitschi with an advance outpost on the edge of the forest south of Peremoga.

b) Enemy weapons: In Meleni, one heavy infantry weapon. Between Meleni and Tschepowitschi twenty-four enemy tanks counted (from the 1290th Tank Regiment). In Tschepowitschi in the course of the afternoon, according to reports from prisoners, a heavy battery and multiple rocket launchers arrived.
North of the Tschepowitschi railway station, considerable reinforcement in the Mostwa position in the form of artillery pieces and multiple rocket launchers. Numerous enemy tanks in the Tschepowitschi and Ossefowka area.

The Korps' evaluation of the enemy: a captured map confirmed the presence of the Soviet XXVth Tank Corps and the 149th and 140th Rifle Divisions. The map also revealed that the enemy had formed a new point of concentration in the Tschepowitschi — Meleni area with the newly-arrived forces in order to attack with a strong western wing from the line Malin — Meleni toward Shitomir (to the southeast). Our forces appeared to have anticipated the Russian attack by a few days, as the move forward of the Soviet XXVth Rifle Division's command posts revealed.

The Division reported the results of its reconnaissance and closed its daily report from the Ia as follows at 18.00 hours on 21.12.1943:

> "There is constant reinforcement for the enemy from the east. The fact that we are being outflanked on both sides makes it impossible to hold on to our decision to make a forward thrust on both sides of the march route. It is possible for the Korps to attack on both sides of the Perogorschtsch river to the southeast. The following actions must, however, be taken before such an attack is possible:
> 1. Meleni be cleared of enemy troops beforehand, and
> 2. All elements of the Division currently at the Tschepowitschi railway station and Peremoga must be relieved."

Panzers ready for combat service as of 18.00 hours on 21.12.1943:

Panzer VI's	2	Panzer III's	1
Panzer V's	4	Sturmgeschütze	14
Panzer IV's	6	Pak (self-prop.)	6

Enemy losses: twenty-three T-34's and two anti-tank guns destroyed.

The light Flak weapons of the 1. and 3./Flakabteilung 1 shot down an enemy plane of the Type IL II.

Our losses for 16.12.1943 - 21.12.1943 (for Panzergrenadier-Regiment 1 and Panzergrenadier-Regiment 2):

Dead: five officers, twelve non-commissioned officers, and twenty-three men.

Wounded: twenty officers, thirty-two non-commissioned officers, and two hundred fifty men.

The officers killed were:

Obersturmführer Glados and Untersturmführer Korten of Panzer-Artillerie-Regiment 1,

Obersturmführer Michalsky, Untersturmführer Wagner, and Untersturmführer Beckmann of Panzerregiment 1.

The officers wounded included:

Unterarzt Dr. Schneider of Panzerregiment 1 and

Hauptsturmführer Rettlinger, Chef of the 3./Sturmgeschützabteilung 1.

Orders for 22.12.1943:

The *LAH* was to begin at 00.00 hours pulling its forces out of the Tschepowitschi railway station. It was to be relieved by the 1. Panzerdivision. The *LAH* was then to stand ready at Point 180.3 (two-and-a-half kilometers southwest of Peremoga) to be able to move its left wing along the road from the Tschepowitschi railway station via Kipjaschtsche toward Meleni starting at 09.00 hours. The Division's elements stationed at the Tschepowitschi railway station were to be subordinated to the 1. Panzerdivision for the withdrawal until they crossed the 1.'s new defensive line.

Panzer-Aufklärungsabteilung 1 was to be relieved by Pionier-Bataillon 70.

The following were to be subordinated to the *LAH* for its attack:

Arko 144

Commander of the Nebeltruppen 1 [chemical troops] with Werfer-Regiment 57

Reserve-Grenadier-Regiment 212.

This last unit was to be reinforced with heavy weapons for the attack on northwestern Meleni.

22.12.1943: At 00.05 hours, there was a local attack from the forest south of Peremoga. The 2./2 repulsed it.

At 2.10 hours, there was a renewed enemy tank attack from the southeast on Peremoga, but it was brought to a halt by the I./2 after a lengthy fight.

At 06.00 hours, Panzer-Aufklärungsabteilung 1 was relieved by Pionier-Bataillon 70 and prepared itself, as ordered, for the attack.

At 11.05 hours, most of the Division began its attack on Meleni with the subordinated Reserve-Grenadier-Regiment 212 on the right, Panzer-Aufklärungsabteilung 1 in the middle, and Panzergrenadier-Regiment 1 on the left. Meanwhile, those elements of Panzergrenadier-Regiment 2 freed up by being relieved by the 1. Panzerdivision had been assembling since 09.00 hours east of Baljarka in order to be moved up behind Panzergrenadier-Regiment 1 to cover the deep eastern flank. The Stab of Panzerregiment 1 was pulled out, and the command over the remaining Panzers was given to the commander of the I./1, Sturmbannführer Kuhlmann.

From the beginning, the attack gained ground only slowly and did not manage to break through. As a result of strong enemy defense on the front and especially from the eastern flank into our rear, the attack was stymied. The leading elements of the attack were stopped in a line from before Hill 179.2 — the ridge one-and-a-half kilometers east of Hill 189.5 — eight hundred meters southwest of Hill 185.3.

In the late afternoon, the enemy began launching battalion-strength counterattacks with tank support from the southeast against Hill 185.3. Panzergrenadier-Regiment 2, intended to serve as cover against attacks from Tschepowitschi, was able to launch a counterattack and stop the enemy advance. Weak enemy elements which had succeeded in penetrating the forest were thrown back in an immediate counterattack. Ten enemy tanks were destroyed in the bloody fighting.

Panzergrenadier-Regiment 2 suffered the following losses on 21.12 and 22.12:

Killed: one officer (Obersturmführer Dix), five non-commissioned officers, and fifty-one men.

Wounded: eight officers, fifteen non-commissioned officers, and one hundred twelve men.

Missing: one officer (Obersturmführer Lamberts) and ten men.

The wounded officers were Hauptsturmführer Richter of the 16./2, Hauptsturmführer Bormann of Panzergrenadier-Regiment 2's Stab, Obersturmführer Gührs of the III./2 (who remained with his unit), Obersturmführer Dinse of the III./2, Obersturmführer Schnelle of the 5./2, Untersturmführer Kammerer, Untersturmführer Sievers, and Untersturmführer Babick of the III./2.

Panzers ready for combat:

Panzer VI's	2	Sturmgeschütze	14
Panzer V's	9	Pak (self-prop.)	7
Panzer VI's	12		

Enemy materiel losses: 13 T-34's destroyed.

Orders for 23.12.1943:

The XXXXVIII. Panzerkorps was to suspend its attack on Meleni and to adopt a defensive stance for 23.12.1943.

The *LAH* was to remain in the line captured on 22.12. It was to maintain close contact with the 1. Panzerdivision. at Hill 185.3.

Reserve-Grenadier-Regiment 212 and Pionier-Bataillon 70 were to remain subordinated to the *LAH* in their current positions. An armoured assault group was to stand ready even with the Divisional headquarters for deployment in our unit's sector or in the sector held by the 291. Infanteriedivision.

23.12.1943: The Division arranged its units along the main battle line as follows for its defense:

The Pionier-Bataillon held the line from the northwestern part of Schwerschny — eastern edge of Budnja Schwerschewskaja — the eastern edge of the forest west of Meleni.

Reserve-Grenadier-Regiment 212 held the line from Hill 212.3 east of Grabuy — Hill 189.5 — three kilometers south of Hf. Baljarka.

Panzer-Aufklärungsabteilung 1 and Panzergrenadier-Regiment 1 held the southern edges of the forest southwest of Peremoga.

The armoured force consisting of three Panzer VI's, seven Panzer V's, sixteen Panzer IV's, and the remaining elements of the III. (armoured)/2 stood ready in Swch. Gemüse.

In the early morning, the enemy made a cautious reconnaissance thrust right at the seam between Reserve-Grenadier-Regiment 212 and Panzer-Aufklärungsabteilung 1 along the road from Meleni to Hf. Baljarka.

In the course of the afternoon, the armoured assault force's Panzers were engaged in repulsing an enemy tank attack on the 291. Infanteriedivision's sector. Four T-34's were destroyed in the fighting.

Panzergrenadier-Regiment 2 received a day of rest in the area around Hf. Meleni.

The Divisional headquarters were moved to Slobitschi at 15.00 hours.

An enemy tank suddenly appeared near Bf. Berkoff in the 291.'s sector. Flakabteilung 1 hit it and set it on fire.

Because the enemy had succeeded in making several incursions into the LIX. Armeekorps' territory and had pushed his way forward as far as the railway line between Malin and Korosten, the XXXXVIII. Panzerkorps wanted to pull back the 1. Panzerdivision's and the *LAH*'s front, which was forming a salient. Pulling the front back would also make forces available to intervene in the LIX. Armeekorps' crisis. The Korps therefore ordered reconnaissance for a new battle line to begin.

The Korps also ordered all the combat-ready Panzers of the 1. Panzerdivision and the *LAH* to assemble in Sobolowka starting at 06.00 hours on 24.12.1943 to stand at the Korps' disposal.

At 17.00 hours, the enemy forces advancing on Hf. Baljarka along the march route were surrounded on both sides by our I./1 (the infantrymen mounted on the Sturmgeschütze). The enemy unit was routed.

At nightfall, Panzergrenadier-Regiment 1 pulled its battle line back to the road from Meleni to Baljarka. Reserve-Grenadier-Regiment 212 and Pionier-Bataillon 70 remained in their previous positions.

Panzer-Aufklärungsabteilung 1 stood at the Division's disposal three kilometers west of Hf. Baljarka.

f) 24.12.1943 - 21.1.1944: Transfer to the south and defensive fighting west of Berditschew

24.12.1943: By 05.30 hours, the withdrawal was complete.

At 10.00 hours, The I. (armoured)/Panzergrenadier-Regiment 113, supported by twenty-five Panzers from SS-Panzerregiment 1 *LAH* (under Hauptsturmführer Kling), set out under the command of Oberst i.G. von Mellenthin. With Panzers from Heeres-Panzerregiment 1 covering its eastern flank, the Regiment moved north via Schewtschenko into the area south of Schatrischtsche. There it destroyed numerous enemy units and thereby caused considerable confusion in the enemy ranks. In the southern part of Grosin, contact was reestablished with the elements of the LIX. Armeekorps deployed there. After this brief, but highly successful, Panzer raid, Hauptsturmführer Kling returned to Sobolewka with those Panzers still fit for combat.

At 15.30 hours, the Korps ordered another pull-back of the front to start at 17.00 hours. The new battle line was to be east of Swch. Gemüse.

Pionier-Bataillon 70 was to remain subordinated.

Reserve-Grenadier-Regiment 212 was to come under the command of the 291. Infanteriedivision starting once again at 07.00 hours on 25.12.1943.

These orders had scarcely been issued when a new Korpsbefehl arrived at 18.45 hours. That order revealed that enemy troops had attacked the XXXXII. Armeekorps along a broad front east of Shitomir and that they had succeeded in making a number of breakthroughs. The enemy's leading tanks were already northeast of Kotscherowo.

On 24.12.1943 at 18.00 hours, the XXXXVIII. Panzerkorps turned over command of its former sector to the LIX. Armeekorps and the XIII. Armeekorps and moved, with the 1. Panzerdivision and the *LAH*, into the area south of Shitomir.

Orders for the *LAH*:

> The 1. SS-Panzerdivision *LAH* is to pull its last elements out of battle on 25.12.1943 and to start a march away at noon. Moving behind the 1. Panzerdivision, it is to march first into the area Shitomir (excluding the city itself) — Tschernjachow (including the city). Pionier-Bataillon 70 is to remain in its sector and to be subordinated to the 291. Infanteriedivision.

The Chef of the Generalstab of the XXXXVIII. Panzerkorps, Oberst i.G. von Mellenthin, wrote in his book "Panzerschlachten" (page 213):

> "The XXXXVIII. Panzerkorps, in evaluating its accomplishments to this point, had the satisfaction of knowing that it had anticipated another carefully planned and prepared enemy offensive against the Shitomir — Korosten area and had thoroughly smashed all the enemy's preparations for the operation. Had it taken place, that attack would probably have been able to overcome and destroy the northern wing of our 4. Panzerarmee, the weakened XIII. and LIX. Armeekorps."

On page 214 of the same book, he continued:

> "In any case, our counterattacks dealt the enemy heavy losses. During this time, the Panzerarmee-Oberkomanndo 4 (of which we had been the spearhead during six hard weeks) captured more than seven hundred enemy tanks and six hundred sixty-eight artillery pieces. Of the three enemy forces which had crossed the Dnieper in November, the first had been hit at Brusilow and wiped out. The second had been defeated in the area Radomyschl — Shitomir. The third group had been so badly hit southeast of Korosten that it was initially incapable of undertaking any attack operations whatsoever. The LIX. Armeekorps, fighting around Korosten, only had to be pulled back to the west later as a result of the developing crisis to the south, which left the Armeekorps totally isolated."

Feverish activity filled this Christmas Eve for the entire Division. The many damaged Panzers and tracked vehicles, which had to be transported out of danger beyond the reach of the enemy, gave us particularly heavy work. A reserve unit of two hundred fifty Panzergrenadiere was divided between the two Panzergrenadier-Regimenter. The pull-back of the front ran according to plan.

25.12.1943: At 08.00 hours, the march began to the south. First came the Division's operations staff, then Panzergrenadier-Regiment 2, and finally Panzer-Aufklärungsabteilung 1. The march advanced quickly until the northern edge of

Shitomir. There, the Division received orders to accelerate its march into the area Woliza — Iwniza — Staraja Kotelnja and to close ranks for a thrust to the east.

The march through Shitomir was a disaster. The city was hopelessly congested.

The Ia's operations staff and elements of the Divisions-Sicherungskompanie reached Iwanokowo at about midnight and waited there for the other elements.

26.12.1943: At 02.00 hours, the commander of Panzergrenadier-Regiment 2 received orders to occupy a line of defense from Woliza to Stepok and to conduct reconnaissance along the march route toward Popelnja. With that move, the Division was once again in the same deployment area which it had occupied at the beginning of this winter campaign.

At 04.30 hours, the Regiment was in the process of assuming the designated line, with the II./2 on the right and the I./2 on the left.

By 07.00 hours, the enemy-occupied town of Woliza had been captured by the II./2. At the same time, the I./2 had cleared Stepok of enemy forces.

At 08.00 hours, the enemy began a series of constantly intensifying attacks across the line Trojany — Kortschmischtsche. These were waged by forces of Regimental size, with support from up to eighty tanks.

By 11.45 hours, Panzer-Aufklärungsabteilung 1 had assembled and was moving on Iwniza.

At 13.40 hours, Panzer-Aufklärungsabteilung 1 reported that the town was occupied by a large enemy force. The Abteilung received orders to lock up all roads on both sides of the railway line and to keep Iwniza covered. It was then to establish contact with Eisenbahn-Panzerzug 31 [armoured train], which was subordinated to the Division.

At 13.45 hours, Panzergrenadier-Regiment 1 reported that it was arriving unit by unit in its new area and was starting to occupy its designated line along the route from Gardyschweka to Woliza. Sturmgeschützabteilug 1 was deployed in the sector held by Panzergrenadier-Regiment 1, and the rest of the Panzers were placed with Panzergrenadier-Regiment 2.

The reconnaissance force sent out by Panzergrenadier-Regiment 2 reported at 10.00 hours that large enemy motorized and tank columns were approaching; their leading elements were already four kilometers southeast of Woliza.

Soon thereafter, there was another enemy attack on Woliza by only two tanks. The 5-centimeter Pak positioned there scored direct hits on the tanks and forced them to turn back. At 12.30 hours, a T-34 with mounted infantry broke into Woliza. It was repulsed in close-range fighting by the men of the III. (armoured)/2.

At 12.35 hours, twelve newly-arrived Panzer V's set out on a short thrust to the southeast and destroyed ten enemy tanks while losing two of their own number.

At 14.00 hours, we lost Stepok to an enemy attack supported by eight tanks with infantrymen mounted on them. In the opinion of the commander of Panzergrenadier-Regiment 2, Obersturmbannführer Kraas, the newly-arrived men began to display signs of "tank shock."

At 21.00 hours, a new Korpsbefehl was issued:

> "The *LAH* is to abandon Woliza and Gardyschewka but is to hold the sector Minkowzy — Andruschewka — Starosselje. A thrust should be made to the southeast in order to gain a firm hold on Andruschewka and to capture Minkowzy. Contact should be established there with the 20. Panzergrenadierdivision."

The 19. Panzerdivision, deployed farther to the left, was in the process of fighting its way back to Lewkow on the Teterew.

The 1. Panzerdivision pulled back behind the Teterew in the sector Koscharischtsche — Korostyschew — Hf. Krassnyj Jar. There it was to establish contact with the Kampfgruppe of the 2. SS-Panzerdivision *DR*.

During the march, the units used the long involuntary pauses to restructure. This restructuring had been made necessary by the losses they had suffered. So, for example, the former II./1 was reformed into a Kompanie consisting of:

I.	Zug	=	remainder of the 6./1
II.	Zug	=	remainder of the 7./1
III.	Zug	=	remainder of the 8./1
heavy	Zug	=	9. and 10./1.

The Kompaniechef was Hauptsturmführer Maier.

This Kompanie was deployed on 26.12 at about 17.00 hours at the Guiwa bridge in Staraja Kotelnja.

27.12.1943: The I./Panzerregiment 1 had been ordered to make a attack with Panzergrenadiere from Panzergrenadier-Regiment 1 mounted on the Panzers. The attack was to move via Gardyschewka and Ljassowka on Andruschewka. It was launched in the night, but the numerically superior enemy forces on the northern edge of Ljassokwa pushed it back.

While this force was stymied in front of Andruschewka, Gardyschewka in its rear was occupied by enemy forces. It had to fight its way through to Starosselje.

Flakabteilung 1, arriving in the early morning, received orders to capture Bolschije Moschkowzy (ten kilometers southwest of Starosselje) in order to provide cover for the Division's rear and deep flank.

Panzer-Aufklärungsabteilung 1 was pulled back on the northern wing under orders from the Korps. It left an armoured reconnaissance force stationed in Turowez and proceeded to capture and hold Tscherwonoje (seventeen kilometers southwest of Starosselje). While holding this town, it was to conduct reconnaissance to the southeast, east, and northeast.

At 12.45 hours, the 1./Panzer-Pionier-Bataillon 1 was moved into the former position of Panzer-Aufklärungsabteilung 1.

The enemy waged attacks with forces of company-and regiment-strength across a broad front during the entire day.

At 13.00 hours, there was an attack by an enemy regiment, supported by thirteen T-34's, which was finally repulsed. Four of the T-34's were destroyed.

At 19.30 hours, the enemy forces moving from Stepok to attack the III./2 in Staraja Kotelnja succeeded in breaking into the buildings on the east side of town. This incursion was pushed back by 21.00 hours with the help of Sturmgeschütze and flamethrowers. More attack preparations taking place in the small valleys to the east of the town were destroyed by Werferregiment 1.

At 18.00 hours, the following were deployed:

the newly subordinated Kavallerie-Regiment Süd in Kryliwka;
Panzer-Aufklärungsabteilung 1 with its leading elements in Tscherownoje;
Kampfgruppe Scheler (the 2./Panzer-Pionier-Bataillon 1, the 14. [Panzer-Pionier]/Panzerregiment 1, nine Panzer IV's) in Mal. Moschkowzy;
Panzergrenadier-Regiment 1 from Hill 239.0 — Antopol Bojarka — southern Starosselje — Hill 238.9;

Panzergrenadier-Regiment 2 from the eastern edge of Starosselje — eastern edge of Staraja Kotelnja — railway line (inclusive of it);
the 1./Panzer-Pionier-Bataillon 1 on both sides of the railway line;
and north of there the standing armoured reconnaissance force of Panzer-Aufklärungsabteilung 1 in Turowez.

The result was a line of defense thirty-five kilometers long and full of gaps.

Losses for these days (to the extent reported):
Dead: one officer, one non-commissioned officer, seven men.
Wounded: one officer, thirteen men.

Panzers ready for combat:

Panzer VI's	5	Sturmgeschütze	12
Panzer V's	13	Pak (self-prop.)	5
Panzer IV's	11		

Orders for 28.12.1943:
The *LAH* is to prevent the enemy from advancing to the west and southwest across the line Kryliwka — Bol. Moschkowzy — Starosselje — Borok.
The 19. Panzerdivision, with the subordinated 8. Panzerdivision and the Kampfgruppe from *DR*, is to move north of there as far as Studeniza.
The 1. Panzerdivision is to be moved up via Shitomir and Beritschew onto the Korps' right wing behind Panzer-Aufklärungsabteilung 1.

28.12.1943: At 02.30 hours, the armoured reconnaissance force at Turowez reported that it was pulling back in the face of about ten enemy tanks and a column of trucks moving south toward the Divisional headquarters.

At 03.00 hours, these enemy forces approached our march route north of Iwankowo. The armoured force received orders to make a thrust into the enemy's flank. The attack objective was Tschubarowka.

At 05.00 hours, thirteen Panzer V's (Panther) set out.

At 05.30 hours, the enemy attacked across the railway line west of Tschubarowka with thirty-five to forty tanks and a strong infantry force. The Panzer V's making the attack on Tschubarowka caught this enemy force in the flank. In the ensuing tank battle, nineteen T-34's were destroyed. The enemy attack was halted just north of our march route. The Russian infantry pulled back across the railway line.

His valiant and tactically brilliant leadership of the Panzers on this day was the cause for Hauptsturmführer Pötschke's recommendation to receive the Ritterkreuz. He finally received the medal on 4.6.1944.

The enemy undertook renewed battle preparations. In the area southeast and east of Staraja Kotelnja — Iwniza, two regiments equipped with forty tanks assembled. In the area Tschubarowka — Turowez — Jusofowka, two more regiments assembled with about twenty tanks. At 12.30 hours, the enemy moved out once again.

By 16.00 hours, he had advanced as far as our march route in the section from north of Wolossowo to Luka and had made a breakthrough into Starosselje, capturing the bridge by the four churches. Fortunately, we had demolished the bridge just in time.

On the Division's southern wing, Kavallerie-Regiment Süd had to be pulled back in the face of an attack by an enemy regiment with about twenty tanks moving from Kryliwka toward Tscherownoje.

At 15.30 hours, the Division was holding the following line:

Panzer-Aufklärungsabteilung 1 and Kavellerie-Regiment Süd on the southern and eastern edges of Tscherwonoje with an armoured reconnaissance force stationed in Gadomzy;

Kampfgruppe Scheler on the eastern and northern edges of Mal. Moschkowzy;

Flakabteilung 1 on the eastern edge of Bol. Moschkowzy;

Panzergrenadier-Regiment 1 at the road out of Antopol-Bojarka to the southeast as far as Hill 238.9, with the Regimental headquarters in Leonowswkij;

Panzergrenadier-Regiment 2 on the eastern edge of Staraja Kotelnja as far as the march route near Hill 228.7;

the Divisions-Sicherungskompanie providing all-around defense in Iwankowo;

elements of the Fernsprechkompanie on the northern edge of Leschtschin;

elements of the Quartiermeisterstaffel in Golubjatin;

Divisional headquarters in Raskopana Mogila.

Panzergrenadier-Regiment 2, deployed on the left wing, had orders to cross the Guiwa river at nightfall and to pull back to the line Nowaja Kotelnja — Leschtschin — Golubjatin.

At 16.00 hours, the enemy intensified his pressure on Panzergrenadier-Regiment 2's positions. The move back could not be carried out under this pressure. The Regiment was forced to create some breathing space for itself by conducting localized counterattacks with tank support. Oberscharführer Grebarsche of the 3./2 distinguished himself with particular valor in this fighting and was awarded the Ritterkreuz.

At 17.30 hours, the I./Panzergrenadier-Regiment 1, deployed on the left wing, launched a counterattack to camouflage our disengagement from the enemy. We completed an orderly withdrawal across the river. In the middle of Panzergrenadier-Regiment 2's section, the designated line of defense could not be captured, because enemy troops had already taken the town of Leschtschino.

At about 19.30 hours, Panzergrenadier-Regiment 2 reported assuming the following line of defense:

the III./2 along the river south of Iwankowo;

the II./2 one kilometer southwest of Leschtschino over Hill 235.3;

the I./2 along the road from Leschtschino to Golubjatin.

The Regimental headquarters were in Worschin.

Panzergrenadier-Regiment 1 also received orders to pull its left wing back as far as Point 228.9, one kilometer north of Stawischtsche. The I./1 deployed there had a few Sturmgeschütze subordinated to it, but they got stuck in the swampy ground around Nowaja Kotelnja after the counterattack mentioned above. They did not reach the position of 2./1 (under Untersturmführer Rink) until dawn. Once there, they immediately became involved in the fighting around the northern edge of Antopol-Bojarka and were able to destroy two T-34's.

Trench strength of the 1. SS-Panzerdivision *LAH* on 28.12.1943:

(The number in parentheses is, by way of comparison, that of the 1. Panzerdivision for the same day.)

	Officers	Non-comm.	Men	Total	(Comp.)
Panzergrenadier-Regiment 1	14	49	379	442	(551)
Panzergrenadier-Regiment 2	11	21	249	281	(387)
Panzer-Aufklärungsabteilung 1	8	14	56	78	(395)
Pionier-Bataillon 1	5	22	198	225	(221)

Men put out of action: 12.12.1943 - 18.12.1943: 2742 (2558)
19.12.1943 - 22.12.1943: 495 (481)

Panzers ready for action:

Panzer VI's	4	Sturmgeschütze	15
Panzer V's	8	Pak (self-prop.)	4
Panzer IV's	17		

Losses dealt the enemy: twenty-one enemy tanks destroyed.

29.12.1943: As has already been mentioned, the 2./1 had to defend itself against an enemy attack on Antopol-Bujarka at dawn.

At 08.10 hours, there was a strong enemy attack on the I./2's positions southwest of Leschtschino.

At about 09.00 hours, a thrust along a broad front was made toward Antopol-Bujarks against the positions of the I. and III./1. In repulsing this attack, the heavy Flakbatterie in its installations near Bol. Moschkowzy performed with particular distinction. One enemy tank was destroyed. In the course of this fighting, thirty to forty T-34's made a sudden appearance; twelve of them were destroyed by two Sturmgeschütze. Oberscharführer Henke of the 3./Sturmgeschützabteilung 1 bore the major responsibility for this success, and he was awarded the Ritterkreuz. One of the Panzer VI's (Tiger) deployed there had to leave the battlefield because of damage to its barrel, but not until it had put eight enemy tanks out of commission. The 2./1 suffered four dead and six wounded during this day's hostilities.

In the early afternoon, a crisis developed in Panzergrenadier-Regiment 2's sector. The enemy made a breakthrough just north of Borschino, and the Regimental commander, Obersturmbannführer Kraas, was able to launch a counterattack with only two Panzer V's and the few men of the Regimentsstab still able to fight. In brave personal engagement, Kraas led the force in clearing away the enemy incursion. The commander, at the head of the force, was then able to catch up with our retreating troops and lead his men back to their old positions.

At 14.15 hours, an enemy attack by sixteen tanks south of Antopol-Bujarka made a breakthrough to the west toward Raskopana-Mogila. At the same time, six T-34's with infantrymen mounted on them broke through two kilometers west of Woroschino in an attempt to reach the Divisional headquarters in Raskopana-Mogila. The Ia was able not only to hold the town until nightfall with only those elements of Panzer-Nachrichtenabteilung 1 which happened to be present, two tanks which were under repair, and the Divisionsstab's writers and drivers, but also to provide cover for the Divisional elements which had broken through farther to the east.

Flakabteilung 1 was able to repulse another attack on Bol. Moschkowzy.

At about 15.10 hours, the enemy was able to move ten tanks around the Division's left wing near Mlinischtsche. They attacked Kodnja at 19.00 hours from the east. There, the enemy was able to unite that force with another force of about thirty-five tanks proceeding along the railway line from Shitomir to Berditschew. At that moment, we had only our subordinated Eisenbahn-Panzerzug 69 to put into action at that spot.

At 17.00 hours, the Korps issued the following orders:

The *LAH* was to move back at nightfall to the line Polowezkoje — Solotwin — Kodnja and to hold that line. Contact was to be established to the unit adjacent to the right (the 1. Panzerdivision) near Hill 271.8 (just northeast of Berditschew).

The armoured force was to destroy the enemy forces which had penetrated as far as the march route from Shitomir to Berditschew. The armoured force was then to make a thrust to the north to establish contact with the right wing of the XIII. Armeekorps south of Shitomir. The intention was to have the 7. Panzerdivision attack from the Shitomir area to the south in order to close the gap between the XIII. Armeekorps and the XXXXVIII. Panzerkorps once and for all.

At 18.15 hours, the Ia in Raskopana Mogila was able to inform the commanders of the two Panzergrenadier-Regimenter of the new orders affecting their units while they were moving their units through the town. The Divisional commander, meanwhile, was busy reconnoitering the new battle line and mopping up the situation around Kodnja. Because we expected the enemy's main attack to come from the northeast toward Berditschew, Solotwin was chosen as the pivot point of the new battle line, and the town was occupied with a correspondingly strong force. Flakabteilung 1 and Kampfgruppe Scheler (the 2. and 3./Panzer-Pionier-Bataillon 1, the 14. [Panzer-Pionier]/Panzerregiment 1, and later the Division-Sicherungskompanie under Hauptsturmführer Linden) were deployed there.

On 29.12.1943, the Division destroyed fifty-nine Russian tanks.

The heavy defensive fighting of 29.12.1943 received the following evaluation in the Wehrmacht report of 31.12.1943:

> "...In the heavy defensive fighting around Shitomir, the 1. SS-Panzerdivision *LAH* under the leadership of Oberführer Wisch distinguished itself by its exemplary fighting spirit..."

The commander of SS-Panzergrenadier-Regiment 2, Obersturmbannführer Kraas, was awarded the Oak Leaves for his extraordinary personal valor and for his Regiment's defensive success during this period. Sturmbannführer Lehmann received the Ritterkreuz for "his personal bravery and his outstanding performance as a leader."

30.12.1943: The Division had occupied its designated line of defense by 05.30 hours, as follows:

Panzer-Aufklärungsabteilung 1 from the northern edge of Berditschew up to and including Point 271.8.

Sturmgeschütz ready to fire.

December, 1943: Gorodischtsche. Divisional commander Oberführer Wisch, Ia Sturmbannführer Lehmann, and O 1 Hauptsturmführer Tiemann.

The Kradmelder [motorcycle messenger]

Pionier-Kampfgruppe Scheler from the eastern edge of Galtschinez as far as Hill 237 south of Solotwin. Flakabteilung 1 and a Panzer group under the command of Untersturmführer Sternebeck around Solotwin.

Panzergrenadier-Regiment 1 north of Solotwin as far as and including Hill 235.8 and the railway line.

Panzergrenadier-Regiment 2 as follows: the I./2 along the railway line with its right wing at the crossing of the highway and the railroad tracks two-and-a-half kilometers west of Kodnja; the II./2 adjoining the I./2 as far as a point just south of the Kodnja railway station; the III./2 from Point 225.6 near the station as far as the bridge four hundred meters northwest of the place where the railroad tracks crossed the river.

The Divisional headquarters were in Polowezkoje.

At 06.30 hours, two T-34's with infantrymen mounted on them made a raid into the territory held by the 1. and 2./Flakabteilung 1, but they were repulsed. One of the tanks was destroyed.

At 09.00 hours, there was a heavy attack by eight T-34's and one enemy assault gun on the positions of the 14. (Panzer-Pionier)/Panzerregiment 1 and the 3./Flakabteilung 1. Our Panzers, situated just right in Solowtin under the command of Untersturmführer Sternebeck, were able to wipe out all the attacking Russian tanks.

At 11.00 hours, a small armoured force set out from the southwest for the Kodnja railroad station. It was able to force the enemy forces out of the station and thus bring the II./2 into its designated position in the line of defense.

At 15.45 hours, an enemy battalion attacked from Skussilowka and Kodnja with a small tank force. At the same time, about twelve enemy tanks attacked the junction of the railroad tracks and the highway west of Kodnja. The I./2 was able to repulse both attacks. Two enemy tanks broke through the battle line but were destroyed in close-range combat.

At 16.00 hours, the armoured force which had set out from a point southwest of Dworez (itself southwest of Perwomaiskij) to attack the enemy field installations on the railway embankment northeast of the town found itself in hard fighting once again.

At 16.15 hours, the brave men of Flakabteilung 1 and the Pionier-Kampfgruppe under Scheler were once more caught up in heavy defensive fighting in Solotwin. They succeeded in destroying nine T-34's and one KV I. The enemy began to dig in in front of Solotwin.

In the early evening, there was another heavy attack with artillery and mortar support, but it was repulsed after about one hour of fighting. The Division's last reserve force, the Divisions-Sicherungskompanie under Hauptsturmführer Linden, was moved up to join Flakabteilung 1 and subordinated to it. The 7. Panzerdivision, moving forward from the north toward Shitomir, had by then reached Singury (six kilometers north of the II./2's positions).

The unit adjacent to the right, the 1. Panzerdivision, had deployed a Regiment force to fight on the eastern edge of Semenowka and had sent its Panzer-Aufklärungsabteilung 1 to the eastern edge of Berditschew.

In the course of the day, a replacement force of twenty non-commissioned officers and three hundred men arrived and was divided up between the Regimenter.

The Division's orders for 31.12.1943 remained unchanged.

31.12.1943: In general, the night passed quietly except for an enemy force which attempted repeatedly to get closer to our installations along the sectors held by Panzer-Aufklärungsabteilung 1, the Pionier-Kampfgruppe under Scheler, and reinforced Flakabteilung 1. Individual enemy riflemen did manage to sneak into Solotwin. One of our assault groups combed the city repeatedly. It rounded them up and took them prisoner. There was a fairly serious enemy breakthrough in the territory held by the unit adjacent to the left, Panzergrenadier-Regiment 1, and a reserve Zug was requested, but it did not need to be used.

In the early morning, Hauptsturmführer Scheler and Hauptsturmführer Dr. Loenicker reported sizable enemy preparations underway among the enemy forces southwest of Solotwin. Panzer-Artillerie-Regiment 1 and one Abteilung from its subordinated Werferregiment 1 (in position in the western part of Solotwin) opened fire on these preparations with the small stores of ammunition at their disposal.

At 10.30 hours, the enemy launched a large-scale attack across the Division's entire front. Panzer-Aufklärungsabteilung 1 and the Pionier-Kampfgruppe under Scheler came under attack from a battalion each, at least a regiment apiece attacked Flakabteilung 1 and Panzergrenadier-Regiment 1, and two regiments attacked the positions of Panzergrenadier-Regiment 2.

The Kodnja railway station was abandoned, and the II. and III./2 pulled back in an orderly retreat to a line from the edge of Pawliniwka — Point 225.6 — southern Dworez (exclusive of the town).

Other than that, however, all the attacks were repulsed, and twenty-five Russian tanks were destroyed.

At 18.30 hours, the Korps issued the following orders:

> "The *LAH* is to begin at 22.00 hours to pull back to the line from the northern edge of Berditschew — Kateriniwka — Gwasdawa — Trajanoff. It is to place a force in the Trajanoff area prepared to make a thrust to the north on the eastern bank of the Gnilopjat early in the morning of 1.1.1944 in order to prevent the enemy from moving west out of Schumsk. The road from Dworez to Trajanoff should be kept free during the pull-back for the movements of the 7. Panzerdivision.
> Contact with the battle command headquarters in Berditschew should be secured at the road out of Berditschew to the north toward Shitomir."

The following are two first-hand reports which show the situation our men found themselves in during these nights.

In his private notebook, the Schützenpanzerwagen squad leader of the III. (armoured)/2, Helmut Krauß, noted:

> "On New Year's Eve, there were Russian tanks right in front of our quarters. They drove by without seeing my Schützenpanzerwagen, which was full of provisions and ammunition. They drove west. We made a hasty retreat to the southeast. My accompanying driver, a Russian Hiwi, wanted to shoot at the Soviets with my submachine gun. I stopped him, because we would only have given ourselves away. In the dark, we crossed a Russian truck column without being noticed. At dawn I could see some Russian tanks firing at our march column about one kilometer from us. I got away, hidden by the drifting snow. I have not felt healthy since Shitomir, can't eat. No German soldiers to be seen on the way. Our hospital was standing empty

and must have been looted by the Russians. On 3.1.1944 I found a doctor, and he sent me to the medical clearing station. I have jaundice."

Rottenführer Werner Müller of the 1./Flakabteilung 1, wrote:

"On New Year's Eve between 1943 and 1944, I moved into position with a force of about twenty-five men around a cemetery outside a village in order to provide cover for the withdrawal of our heavy Batterie. In the night, Ivan moved in on our flank and occupied the village we had abandoned behind us. We were picked up shortly after midnight by three Panzer IV's."

Panzers ready for combat:

Panzer VI's	2	Panzer IV's	12
Panzer V's	7	Sturmgeschütze	9

At 22.00 hours, we began to disengage from the enemy. Bu 01.00 hours, the operation was completed.

1.1.1944: By 05.30 hours, the Division had occupied the new battle line as follows:

Kampfgruppe Knittel (Panzer-Aufklärungsabteilung 1) from one kilometer south of the workhouse just north of Berditschew — eastern edge of Agatowka.

Reinforced Panzer-Pionier-Bataillon 1 (Flakabteilung 1) from one-and-a-half kilometers east of Kateriniwka — Gwasdawa (exclusive of it).

Panzergrenadier-Regiment 1 from the east edge of Gwasdawa — Point 241.5 — Point 238.1 (exclusive of it).

Panzergrenadier-Regiment 2 from Point 238.1 (inclusive of it) — Trajanoff (inclusive of it).

The Divisional headquarters in Schweikowka.

This withdrawal took place without trouble from the enemy except on the left wing, where the II. and III./2 were closely pursued.

At 06.45 hours, eight enemy tanks attacked along the road from Woliza to Trajanoff. Our Panzer V's, standing ready, destroyed four of them.

Attacks started at 09.45 hours along a broad front, but the focal points were against the Aufklärungsabteilung from Ossykowka, Panzer-Pionier-Bataillon 1 in Kateriniwka, the I. and III./1 in Gwasdawa, and Trajanoff. Untersturmführer Wendorff, a Zugführer in the 13. (heavy)/Panzerregiment 1, destroyed five T-34's with his Tiger and was awarded the Ritterkreuz for his actions.

At 15.20 hours, Panzergrenadier-Regiment 2 reported coming under pressure from the enemy from the north and northeast. The enemy managed to break through in the territory of the unit adjacent to the left and to advance as far as the eastern bank of the Gnilopjat. The enemy was able to force a crossing over onto the western bank by evening. Because of the shortage of forces, the Regiment was only able to defend its northern flank by defending the western edge of Tranjanoff. Under orders from the Generalkommando, the armoured force had to be deployed to push back an incursion on the northeastern edge of Berditschew.

Reconnaissance to the northwest revealed that Buki and Deneschi (twenty-five kilometers to the north) were clear of enemy troops. Men separated from their

units in Divisionen of the XIII. Armeekorps were found there and were ordered to assemble in Tschudnoff (thirty kilometers to the west).
At 21.00 hours, Panzergrenadier-Regiment 2 was pulled back to Gorodischtsche.

Enemy materiel losses: nine T-34's destroyed and eight artillery pieces wiped out.

Panzers ready for combat:

Panzer VI's	0	Sturmgeschütze	8
Panzer V's	6	Pak (self-prop.)	5
Panzer IV's	10		

2.1.1944: At 05.20 hours, Panzergrenadier-Regiment 2 occupied the northern and western edges of Gorodischtsche with the I. and II./2. The III./2 was held in Gorodischtsche as a reserve.
In the course of the night and at dawn, enemy tanks managed to make local breakthroughs into the territory held by Panzer-Pionier-Bataillon 1 and on the right wing of Panzergrenadier-Regiment 1.
Flakabteilung 1 deployed two Züge under Obersturmführer Straubl to reestablish its battle line. While this fighting was underway, there was another enemy infantry attack with tank support. The 1./Flakabteilung 1 was able to destroy one enemy tank. In the fighting, two Panzer IV's returning from a reconnaissance mission suddenly found themselves on a hill with enemy tanks, although somewhat apart from them; unfortunately, the thick fog kept the 2./Flakabteilung 1 from distinguishing among the tanks, and our two Panzer IV's were destroyed by friendly fire. Untersturmführer Sternebeck remembers that morning with a shudder to this day.
At 10.00 hours, there was the first attack of the day (with tanks and infantrymen mounted on them) against the previously unmolested positions of the II./1. The enemy tanks turned back under the fire from our Sturmgeschütze only five hundred meters from our position.
At 13.00 hours, there was a second attack on the II./1's left wing, where the 8. Kompanie was stationed. The attack also hit the right wing of Panzergrenadier-Regiment 2. At the same time, the III./1 was attacked again in Gwasdawa.
At 12.40 hours, there was exceedingly intense enemy pressure on the II./2. A Panther was destroyed by Russian anti-tank fire. Obersturmführer Dinse, the Bataillonführer of the III./2, and Obersturmführer Schid, Chef of the 11./2, were wounded. Obersturmführer Schlott, the Chef of the Pionierkompanie, was badly wounded and died at the medical clearing station.
At 14.10 hours, the III./2 and the right wing of the 68. Infanteriedivision pulled back to the southern edge of Gorodischtsche.
At 15.30 hours, an enemy regiment attacked Panzer-Aufklärungsabteilung 1, which was able to hold its position only by exerting its last forces. The II./Panzer-Artillerie-Regiment 1, positioned behind it, joined in the fighting, sometimes with its barrels absolutely horizontal. It contributed considerably to the defensive success.
At 17.30 hours, this attack was finally repulsed.
During the entire day, there were attacks from enemy planes, and our Luftwaffe did not interfere with them at all. Sizable enemy groups, some of them armed

with anti-tank guns, began to show up in the supply train's assembly area in the forest north of Mazebinze.

At 15.00 hours, the units received orders as follow:

"The *LAH* is to pull back behind the Gnilopjat sector between Stragliwka and Olschanka as soon as ordered to do so on 2.1.1944.
Combat outposts are to be set up in the line Stbr. (two kilometers northeast of Skragliwka) — 228.4 (two kilometers east of Schajkiwka) — 270.9 — eastern edge of Bobrik.
Reinforced Panzer-Aufklärungsabteilung 1 (Kavallerie-Regiment Süd, III. [heavy]/Werferregiment 1) from Skragliwka (where it is to have contact with the battle command headquarters in Berditschew) — patch of forest north of there (inclusive of it).
Reinforced Panzer-Pionier-Bataillon 1 (14. [Panzer-Pionier]/Panzerregiment 1, Kanonengruppe/Artillerie-Regiment 1) from Raiki (inclusive of it) to Schajkiwka (exclusive of it).
Reinforced Panzergrenadier-Regiment 1 from Schajkiwka (inclusive of it) — Olschanka (inclusive of it). There it is to have contact with the 68. Infanteriedivision.
Reinforced Panzergrenadier-Regiment 2 is to be the last unit to leave the former position and is to assemble in the Pjatki area immediately thereafter to stand at the Korps' disposal.
Panzerregiment 1 is to leave former subordination for 2.1.1944 and is to cross the Gnilopjat and assemble all its tanks in the Pjatki area to stand at the Division's disposal.
Road reconnaissance should be conducted to the south and north. It should begin as soon as the repair service units have been moved out of Pjatki on 2.1.1944.
Panzer-Artillerie-Regiment 1 is to move into position on 2.1.1944 west of the Gnilopjat so that it is able to accomplish the following main assignments:

a) concentration of fire from at least two Abteilungen on Ossykowka, Kateriniwka, Gwasdawa, Gai Perschij, and Bobrik;
b) placement of advance artillery observers in the combat outposts;
c) establishment of the following cooperative relationships:
II. and III./Panzer-Artillerie-Regiment 1 with Panzer-Aufklärungsabteilung 1 and Panzer-Pionier-Bataillon 1;
I. and III./Panzer-Artillerie-Regiment 1 with Panzergrenadier-Regiment 1.

Werferregiment 1 is to scout for positions west of the Gnilopjat on 2.1.1944 which will enable it to accomplish the following main assignments:

a) deployment of the III. Abteilung against the eastern sections of Dmitriwka and Rajki;
b) concentration of the fire from the I. and II. Abteilung on Schajkiwka and Porochownja;
c) focus of the II. Abteilung's fire on Bobrik.

For the withdrawal, the Abteilungen are to remain subordinated as before.
Flakabteilung 1 is to establish the following anti-tank defense points deep in the battlefield:

260.2 (two kilometers east of Malaja Tatarinowka)
258.2 (two kilometers southwest of Schweikowka)

287.7 (one kilometer south of Pilipy)

Pioniere: One Kompanie of Pionier-Bataillon 70, subordinated to the Division for the purpose of destroying the bridges over the Gnilopjat, is to prepare and to leave demolition teams at the bridges. The commanders are responsible for giving the command to blow up the bridges within their sectors. The crossing for Panzergrenadier-Regiment 1 is Schajkiwka. The Pioniere are then to assemble immediately in Mal. Tatarinowka.

Supply trains: Sturmbannführer Hanreich, the commander of Panzerjägerabteilung 1, is hereby named the leader of the supply trains. He receives the disciplinary authority of a Regimental commander. All the Division's supply trains are subordinated to him in every respect. He is to assemble the supply trains in the area Tereszpol — Semki — Kaszanowka — Wojdowce — Kumanowce by 4.1.1944.

Panzerinstandesetzungsabteilung 1 [Panzer repair battalion] in Starokonstantinow.

Operations group in Januschpol.

Wirtschaftsbataillon 1 in Starokonstantinow area.

Panzer-Divisions-Nachschubtruppe 1 in Krassnopol area.

Operations group in Bol. Korowinzy.

Field hospital in Starokonstantinow.

Main medical clearing station in Tatarinowka.

Quartiermeisterstaffel in Pilipki.

Divisional headquarters in Ratschki."

In the sector held by Panzergrenadier-Regiment 2, the enemy had already crossed the bridge near Gorodischtsche by 15.00 hours and made a thrust into the left flank and rear of the III. and I. Bataillon.

At 16.00 hours, the enemy was in Bobrik and simultaneously launched an attack from the northeast with the support of four T-34's.

At 16.00 hours, the Division ordered the units to disengage from the enemy starting at 18.00 hours.

At 18.00 hours, the II./2, supported by one Panzer, had to fight its way house-by-house through Bobrik to pull back across the Gnilopjat. The doctor of the II./2, Hauptsturmführer Dr. Radda, was killed in the fighting. Other units also were forced to disengage while under considerable pressure from the enemy.

Under these conditions, the line of combat outposts designated in the order became cover for the Division as it conducted an emergency establishment of the new battle line.

At 23.30 hours, the commander of Panzergrenadier-Regiment 2 reported that the last elements of his unit had finally disengaged from the enemy under extreme pressure. The demolition squad of Pionier-Bataillon 70 could not fulfill its assignment because of a shortage of explosives; instead it set the wooden bridge on fire.

The abandonment of Berditschew meant that we had lost a second cornerstone (Shitomir was the first) of the Eastern Front's southern section.

Panzers ready for combat:

Panzer V's	4
Panzer IV's	4

3.1.1944: At 03.00 hours, all of the outposts east of the Gnilopjat were in direct contact with the enemy. Our comrade Knäbke of the 8./1 was stationed at one of those outposts and reported:

> "Defensive duty north of Sosnowka. It was early morning and the Kompanie had just finished the construction of the necessary installations when strong enemy forces attacked, supported by tanks. The enemy succeeded in breaking through the gaps in our broad defensive sector, and he made an incursion on the Kompanie's left wing. It was accordingly pulled back onto the western bank. At about 11.00 hours, there was another large-scale attack from the east and north. This time the enemy broke through on the right wing. At 11.30 hours, the Kompanie escaped the intense pressure from the enemy by pulling back to the southwest. The Kompanie had fulfilled its mission as combat outpost in an exemplary fashion. It reached Pilippi and had a few hours of rest. In the action, four were killed, nine wounded, and six comrades were found to be missing."

During the pullback, Panzergrenadier-Regiment 2 was outflanked, and elements of it were temporarily cut off from the bulk of the unit.

At 05.20 hours, the last elements of the Regiment reached Pjatki. The Regimental commander had to go to the medical clearing station because of a wound to his hand.

At 14.00 hours, there was an enemy incursion from the north at the seam between Panzergrenadier-Regiment 2 and the 68. Infanteriedivision. For the purpose of clearing away this incursion and closing the gap between the two units, the remainders of the I. and II./2 were combined to form Kampfgruppe Bormann, which was subordinated to Panzergrenadier-Regiment 1. The rest of Panzergrenadier-Regiment 2 stayed in Pjatki to serve as Divisional reserve.

At 15.30 hours, Kampfgruppe Bormann, supported by Sturmgeschütze, began its attack. By midnight, it had restored the situation on the left wing and dealt the enemy heavy losses. Six T-34's were destroyed. Artillery fire of all calibres rained down during the day on the Division's other sectors.

Panzer-Aufklärungsabteilung 1, Panzer-Pionier-Bataillon 1, and Panzergrenadier-Regiment 1 all had to repulse repeated enemy attacks.

At 16.00 hours, Kavallerie-Regiment Süd, deployed on the right wing of Panzer-Aufklärungsabteilung 1, was subordinated to the battle operations commander in Berditschew.

The 1. SS-Panzerdivision *LAH* was subordinated to the XIII. Armeekorps at the same time. The Division was ordered to prepare to be relieved in the night between 4.1 and 5.1 and moved south for a new mission.

At 23.45 hours, the Generalkommano of the XIII. Armeekorps (under commanding general General der Infanterie Hauffe and Chef of Generalstab Oberst i.G. von Hammerstein) issued the following order:

> "The *LAH* will be relieved in its right-hand sector by the 1. Panzerdivision and in the left-hand sector by the 208. Infanteriedivision. The move will begin in the night 4.-5.1.1944 upon an orally transmitted command. At 09.00 hours, an armoured force is to set out from the area south of Knjashin to destroy, in cooperation with the SS-*Reich* and the 340. In-

fanteriedivision, the enemy forces which have broken through at Chutor Petrowskogo."

An inquiry over the radio, asking the Korps where fuel could be obtained, was answered as follows: "Fuel should be taken from the countryside. Chef." The Division answered: "Our Tigers and Panthers don't eat hay. Ia." When telephone communications were restored, the Chef of Generalstab proved to be displeased with that answer.

4.1.1944: The 8./1's log (kept by Willi Knäbke) reported the following about this section of the front:

> "At 03.00 hours in the morning, the Kompanie was sitting on three Sturmgeschütze and heading for a new assignment. In crossing a bridge, one of the Sturmgeschütze broke down. The Kompanie proceeded on foot and set up defenses facing the east in Olschanka. The enemy launched a mighty fire preparation on our neighbor to the left (the 68. Infanteriedivision) and followed it with a large-scale attack. He succeeded in breaking through. The Kompanie was therefore forced to disengage from the enemy during an attack. We made a counterattack and dealt him heavy losses. In the course of the afternoon and evening, we reached a new battle line along the march route from Tschudnoff to Pjatki."

In the course of the night and the next day, the Division found itself engaged in mobile combat at the "hot spots" south of Skragliwka (Panzer-Aufklärungsabteilung 1), west of Schajkiwka (Panzergrenadier-Regiment 1), north and northwest of Sw. Tatarinowka (elements of Panzergrenadier-Regiment 1), and north of Ratschki (Kampfgruppe Bormann/Panzergrenadier-Regiment 2).

The enemy was waging his attacks with forces of battalion and regimental strength and had the support of both the heavy calibre weapons and his tanks. He was successful in outflanking individual combat units and forcing them to pull back. In pulling back from Olschanka, the 3. (heavy)/Flakabteilung 1 was faced with such a rapidly-advancing enemy force that it was unable to bring one of its heavy artillery pieces along. The unit blew up the gun with explosives before leaving.

At about 17.00 hours, the Division assumed the following strong points:

Panzer-Aufklärungsabteilung 1 from Skragliwka (inclusive of it) — Rajki (exclusive of it);

Panzer-Pionier-Bataillon 1 from Rajki (inclusive of it) — Point 260.2 (east of Mal. Tatarinowka);

the last remaining artillery piece of the 3. (heavy)/Flakabteilung 1 was also situated at Point 260.2;

Panzergrenadier-Regiment 1 from northern Mal. Tatarinowka — Point 258.2;

Panzergrenadier-Regiment 2 (with the Divisions-Sicherungskompanie) at the road junction north of Raitschki;

the armoured force engaged in fighting in and to the west of Pjatki.

Direct contact with the unit to the left could not be established that day or the following night. The Russians were holding eastern Bol. Korowizy, which had been designated in the order as the point of contact between the two units, and were also holding Michailenki, three kilometers to the west.

Panzer-Aufklärungsabteilung 1 was relieved by Kavallerie-Regiment Süd and redeployed to serve the battle operations commander at Berditschew.

At 24.00 hours, the XIII. issued the following order:

"The *208. Infanteriedivision* is to attack from Bol. Korowinzy to the northwest early in the morning of 5.1 in order to close the hole on both sides of Mal. Korowinzy.

The *armoured force of SS-Reich* is to attack at 07.00 hours from Korotschenki and the *Sturmgeschütze of the 340. Infanteriedivision* from Schewtschukoff; both are to attack Mal. Korowinzy.

The *armoured force of the LAH* (four Panzers) is to cross the western edge of Bol. Korowinzy at 07.00 hours and proceed via Michailenki and Korowinzy on Mal. Korowinzy.

After completing this assignment, the force is once again to stand at the Division's disposal."

5.1.1944: The events of this day are best described by reprinting the radio messages from the *LAH* and the XIII. Armeekorps. Telephone communications were not reestablished until 23.00 hours on 5.1, and then it was to the XXXXVIII. Panzerkorps.

02.23 hours, *LAH* to the XIII. Armeekorps:

Road Ratschki — Januschpol west of Lessnaja Sslobadka blocked by Russian tanks.

03.25 hours, *LAH* to the XIII. Armeekorps:

Enemy incursion cleared away in counterattack. Eighteen enemy tanks launch new attack from west.

04.20 hours, XIII. Armeekorps to Panzerarmee-Oberkommando 4:

[Excerpt from *LAH*'s morning report.] Enemy incursion in area north of Slobodischtsche. Fighting underway to clear it.

13.10 hours, XIII. Armeekorps to the *LAH*:

SS-*Reich* making thrust on Korowinzy. *LAH* with all forces available make thrust to northwest to close gap. Then subordination once again to XXXXVIII. Panzerkorps.

15.25 hours, *LAH* to the XIII. Armeekorps:

Part 1: Relief of Panzer-Aufklärungsabteilung 1 completely destroyed. Constant attacks in regimental strength on Mal. Tatarinowka and Ratschki.

Part 2: Terrain just south of railroad not passable for Panzers. Enemy presence to north prohibits use of Panzers.

Panzer attack as per order not possible until 6.1, because unit tied up frontally.

15.30 hours, XIII. Armeekorps to Panzerarmee-Oberkommando 4:

[Excerpt from daily report.] 1. SS-Panzerdivision repulsed regiment-strength attack on Mal. Tatinowka and with Panzer support pushed enemy breakthrough into Ratschki back to north.

15.50 hours, *LAH* to the XIII. Armeekorps:

Enemy breakthrough in battalion strength from north into Mal. Tatarinowka. Counterattack in progress.

16.15 hours, *LAH* to the XIII. Armeekorps:

Enemy broken through at Golodki. Proceeding rapidly on Demtschin.

16.35 hours, *LAH* to the XIII. Armeekorps:

Enemy attack three kilometers wide from Pjatki to south and on both sides of railway to east toward Ratschki. Obersturmführer Kraas, commander of Panzergrenadier-Regiment 2, wounded. Battle commander now Sturmbannführer Kuhlmann, commander of the I./SS-Panzerregiment 1.

17.55 hours, *LAH* to the XIII. Armeekorps:

Incursions at Mal. Tatarinowka and Ratschki cleared away in counterattack. New attacks in progress. Request order to relieve Panzer-Aufklärungsabteilung 1 (east of Berditschew).

18.30 hours, *LAH* to the XIII. Armeekorps:

At 18.15 hours, renewed attack on Mal. Tatarinowka and Ratschki, now in regimental strength with tanks.

20.00 hours, *LAH* to the XIII. Armeekorps:

Renewed massive attacks on Mal. Tatarinowka from northeast and north. Left wing of Kavallerie-Regiment Süd pulled back to 268.2. Is being assembled by Panzer-Aufklärungsabteilung 1 in Demtschin and moved back up.

22.00 hours, *LAH* to the XIII. Armeekorps:

Situation restored in Mal. Tatarinowka and Ratschki by counterattack. Point of contact on right returned to former position. 20. Panzergrenadierdivision had orders for new battle line.

23.00 hours, telegraphic orders from the XXXXVIII. Panzerkorps the *LAH*:

> "The *LSSAH* is to be subordinated to the Panzerkorps immediately. It is to retreat starting at 24.00 hours to the line from eastern Demtschin — northern Ratschki and is to hold that line. Point of contact with 1. Panzerdivision: eastern Demtschin.
> The Division is to stand ready by 07.00 hours on 6.1 in Ratschki to set off toward Bol. Korowinzy on both sides of the railway line at 10.00 hours after the Stuka attack.
> *The assault force SS-Das Reich* is to move simultaneously from Michailenki on Bolschije Korowinzy with its right wing along the railroad."

6.1.1944: At 02.40 hours, Panzergrenadier-Regiment 1 was able to clear away the enemy incursion in Mal. Tatarinowka and to advance as far as Point 258.8. Immediately thereafter, the Sturmgeschütze with riflemen mounted on them moved to the southeast straight into the flank of the enemy forces moving out of Rajki to the west.

At 02.45 hours, Panzergrenadier-Regiment 1 pulled its I. Bataillon, deployed on the right wing, back to the northern edge of Demtschin under intense enemy pressure. Panzer-Pionier-Bataillon 1 was freed up by this shortening of the front, and it was moved into the town of Pilipki south of Ratschi to stand at the Division's disposal.

The Kriegstagebuch of Flakabteilung 1 reported on this retreat as follows:

> "At 02.15 hours, the Abteilung received word from the commander of Regiment 1 that the Infanterie was to disengage from the enemy. A Flak combat force under the leadership of Obersturmführer Graul was formed, consisting of one heavy artillery piece each from the 1. and 3. Batterie, one 2-centimeter piece from the 3. Batterie, and two 3.7-centimeter pieces from the 4. Batterie. Its mission: to move into position immediately on the northern edge of Demtschin to provide defense against tank attacks. A second Flak combat force was formed from the two remaining heavy

artillery pieces of the 1. Batterie and one 2-centimeter self-propelled gun from the 2. Batterie. This second force was moved into position east of Ratschki near Point 248 to offer tank defense. Two 2-centimeter guns from the 2. Batterie were moved into position on the northern edge of Ratschki to reinforce our Infanterie."

Panzergrenadier-Regiment 2's Kampfgruppe Bormann, deployed on the left wing of Panzergrenadier-Regiment 1, had to repulse eight enemy tank attacks between 03.30 and 12.00 hours, sometimes with counterattacks. The assembly in preparation for the attack order on Bol. Korowinzy did not take place because the forces designated for it (the armoured force, Panzer-Aufklärungsabteilung 1, and Panzer-Pionier-Bataillon 1) were either tied up by enemy attacks or engaged in counterattacks.

At 08.40 hours, the enemy started a pincer attack. On our right wing, it led to an incursion in the territory held by the unit adjacent to the right along a broad front between Mal. Radsiwilowka and Kustin. In the middle of our sector, there was a breakthrough across the line Mal. Tatarinowka — Pjatki to the southwest.

At 08.55 hours, the enemy attacked from Korowinzy (which supposedly we were to attack) with tanks, and he broke through into the western part of Ratschki.

At 09.35 hours, the Division therefore issued the following: Start of the attack only possible after current enemy attacks repulsed.

At 10.50 hours, there was an enemy breakthrough from the west into the southern part of Ratschki, and an attack followed in regimental strength from Kustin on Gardyschewka in the territory held by the unit adjacent on the right.

Lessnaja Sslobodka was occupied by enemy troops. The Division's supply route was blocked south of Osadowka. The Flak combat force under Graul deployed against the enemy forces blocking the road was not able to reach the position assigned it because heavy enemy mortar fire from the forest west of the Gnilopjat made it impossible to approach the hill.

At 12.10 hours, the armoured force found itself locked in Panzer warfare around Ratschki. Five enemy tanks were destroyed.

At 12.45 hours, the Korps issued the following orders: Attack assignment to the west unchanged. Sector Buraki (exclusive) — southwest edge of Januschpol — Dubrowka — Troschtscha (exclusive) to be thoroughly reconnoitered for deployment of *LAH* with subordinated Kampfgruppen from the 68. and 208. Infanteriedivisionen.

At 12.50 hours, the Division reported to the XXXXVIII. Panzerkorps: Holding Demtschin and Ratschki with last reserves. Supply route blocked. Heavy burden on Infanterie.

At 14.30 hours, the units received orders by telephone to begin a withdrawal at nightfall. They were to move via Kostepalnja (enemy-occupied), Osadowka, Marzynowka (enemy-occupied), and Raigorodok to reach the new line of resistance at Buraki (exclusive of it) — Hf. Selenyj — 267.7 — Dubrowka — Troschtscha. This line was to be captured and held. The Kampfgruppen of the 208. and 68. Infanteriedivision were subordinated to the *LAH*. The unit adjacent on the left was Kampfgruppe SS-Panzerdivision *DR*, on the right remained the 20. Panzergrenadierdivision. The point of contact was northwest Buraki.

At 15.00 hours, Panzer-Aufklärungsabteilung 1 was fighting on the northern edge of Garyschewka with open wings.

At 16.00 hours, the withdrawal began.

At 20.00 hours, the Regimental commander of Panzerregiment 1 opened up Osadowka from the south with his own Panzers and kept the Division's retreat road open until 24.00 hours.

At 23.00 hours, there was a report from the Korps: "Bulk of Division penetrated from Osadowka to south. Russian tanks all around. Situation clear aside from that. Divisional headquarters in Smela starting at 07.00 hours. Weak security forces are already north of Shersbki."

7.1.1944: At 00.00 hours, Sturmbannführer Peiper waited for Panzer-Aufklärungsabteilung 1 to move out of Gardyschewka, then moved his Panzer rear guard out of Osadowka.

At 00.35 hours, the enemy roadblock north of Marzynowka was opened by a couple of Panzers.

At 06.35 hours, the rear guard passed Buraki. The reinforced Division occupied its designated line of resistance as follows:

Kampfgruppe 208. Infanteriedivision (Grenadierregiment 337, Grenadierregiment 338, Landesschützen-Bataillon 375, Artillerie-Regiment 208, one Kompanie of Panzer-Zerstörer-Bataillon 473) from Buraki — the road between Pelewaja and Januschpol (inclusive);

Panzergrenadier-Regiment 1 from 294.4 (inclsuive) — road between Sherebki and Januschpol (exclusive);

Panzergrenadier-Regiment 2 from 276.7 (inclusive) — Dubrokwa (exclusive);

Kampfgruppe 68. Infanteriedivision (Grenadierregiment 188, 196, 169, 245, 172, Pionier-Bataillon 168, Panzerjägerabteilung 168, Aufklärungsabteilung 168, Artillerie-Regiment 168, one Kompanie of Panzer-Zerstörer-Bataillon 473) from Dubrokwa (inclusive) — Troschtscha;

Flak force Graul on the road from Pelewaja to Januschpol;

The rest of the Flakabteilung assembled in Sherebki and in the course of the day reinforced the line of resistance within the framework of the Division's anti-tank defense plan;

Panzerregiment 1 assembled in Ssmela;

Panzer-Aufklärungsabteilung 1 in Pelewaja and Panzer-Pionier-Bataillon 1 in southern Sherebki standing at the disposal of the Division;

Divisional headquarters in Ssmela.

At 06.45 hours, reconnaissance discovered enemy forces on Hill 276.7. A T-34 destroyed one Schützenpanzerwagen of the III./2, and Untersturmführer Tomhardt was wounded.

At 08.00 hours, Sturmbannführer Kuhlmann led elements of Panzergrenadier-Regiment 2 and several Panthers in capturing Hill 276.7. The III./2 then moved in an occupied it. Three T-34's were destroyed in the fighting.

Starting at 11.00 hours, there were enemy reconnaissance attacks from forces up to company strength along the Division's entire front.

At 16.00 hours, the commanding general, General Balck, appeared at the Divisional headquarters and reported that there had been a breakthrough by two enemy battalions moving from the north into the forest west of Dubrowka in the territory held by Kampfgruppe 68. Infanteriedivision.

At 16.05 hours, Panzer-Pionier-Bataillon 1 was ordered to move in and clear away this incursion west of Dubrowka. The Bataillon was then to occupy the line Dubrowka (exclusive) — Troschtscha (inclusive).

Panzers ready for combat:

Panzer VI's	2	Sturmgeschütze	5
Panzer V's	11	Pak (self-prop.)	3
Panzer IV's	6		

Evaluation of the enemy: Enemy attempting on 6.1.1944 to surround and break our cornerstone at Ratschki in order to open a gap in the Armee's front which could not be closed.

The *LAH* had, during the retreat, faced about sixty to eighty enemy tanks and a rifle corps. Nine of the tanks were destroyed. On 7.1, the enemy regrouped and reconnoitered in order to launch his new attack on 8.1.1944. He conducted aerial and ground reconnaissance and moved new forces toward the southwest. In Januschpol stood the Soviet VIIth Guards Tank Army, with the IVth Guard Tank Corps following behind. Many of the prisoners we took and deserters who came to us were sixteen years old and even younger.

> "Our conclusion that the Russian's store of human resources was rapidly dwindling, too, and must sometime come to an end appeared to be justified. That finding strengthened our resolve to hold on."

That was the evaluation of Oberst i.G. von Mellenthin, Chef of the Generalstab for the XXXXVIII. Panzerkorps. It accorded with our estimation of the quality of the enemy infantry.

Orders for 7.1.1944:

> "The *LAH* with subordinated Kampfgruppen 208. and 68. Infanteriedivision is to hold its positions and is to work in cooperation with Kampfgruppe SS-Panzerdivision *DR* to clear up the situation near Jassopol. The Division is to reconnoiter and to expand its second position in accordance with the special orders." (See sketch 29.)

8.1.1944: At 00.00 hours, the Ia was at the Bataillon command post of the III. (armoured)/2, deployed at Point 276.7. The Bataillon commander reported that there had been loud tank sounds on the southwestern edge of Januschpol in the first hours of the night. The armoured force in Ssmela was put on alert and given orders to move forward as far as the southern edge of Stepok.

At 05.15 hours, thirty to forty enemy tanks with infantrymen mounted on them crossed our battleline at the seam between Panzergrenadier-Regiment 1 and Panzergrenadier-Regiment 2. In Regiment 1's area, they pushed forward as far as the ravines north of Stepok; in the III./2's area they broke through into Sherebki. At that point, the concentrated fire from Panzer-Artillerie-Regiment 1 halted their advance, and the valiant commander of Panzergrenadier-Regiment 1, Sturmbannführer Peiper, led the armoured force in a pincer attack in cooperation with Panzerzerstörer-Bataillon 473. The attacking force was destroyed.

By 09.00 hours, the situation had been cleared up. In the fighting, thirty-three T-34's and seven assault guns belonging to the Soviet 54th Guards Tank Brigade were destroyed. Our Panther force deployed in and to the east of Sherebki took care of eight of those T-34's and two of the assault guns.

The battle line was moved to run along the road three miles north of Sherebki; in the move, Point 276.7 was abandoned.

To reinforce our anti-tank defenses, a Flak force was organized under the command of Untersturmführer Seemann. It consisted of an 8.8-centimeter Geschütz, one 2-centimeter Geschütz each from the 1. and 3. Batterie, and the two remaining 3.7-centimeter Geschütze of the 4. Batterie. It was deployed in the northeast section of Ssmela.

At 11.00 hours, the enemy began applying pressure once again, this time with a battalion from the north attacking just east of Point 272.9 in the forest west of Dubrowka. He aimed his attack at Dubrowka and had support from automatic weapons firing from the east and west. Our Panzer-Pionier-Bataillon, deployed to make a counterattack, had insufficient forces to clear the forest of enemy troops. It was only able to engage them in fighting and keep them tied up.

Additional attacks against the positions of the Panzergrenadier-Regimenter from enemy battalions were nipped in the bud by timely Panzer attacks.

At 16.00 hours, there was another battalion attack, this time with support of eight T-34's moving out of the forest southeast of Januschpol toward our march route and the positions of Kampfgruppe 208. Infanteriedivision. Six of the T-34's broke into Podoroschnja. The armoured force was able to clear away the enemy forces by 23.00 hours.

On the left wing, the battle line was moved back (avoiding the forest) to the line Pewna — Kortschunezkij.

Paragraph 8 of the Ia's daily report for 8.1.1944 read as follows:

> "Untersturmführer Michael Wittmann, a Zugführer in the Tiger-Kompanie of the 1. Panzerdivision *LAH*, distinguished himself in a Panzer counterattack on 8.1.1944 and in the action destroyed his sixtieth enemy tank."

The commanding general of the XXXXVIII. Panzerkorps, General der Panzertruppen Balck, in a radio address expressed his congratulations and admiration to the commander of Panzerregiment 1 for his Regiment's success that day.

The Divisional headquarters were moved to Lipjatin.

The Division's mission remained unchanged. The *LAH* subordinated one Panzerkompanie to the 7. Panzerdivision. Untersturmführer Köchlin was put on the march with four Panzer V's and eight Panzer IV's.

9.1.1944: From 00.00 to 03.00 hours, the enemy attempted in vain to attack the positions of Kampfgruppe 208. Infanteriedivision with forces of varying sizes. At about 04.00 hours, the enemy did manage to make a breakthrough at the seam between the 208. Infanteriedivision and Panzergrenadier-Regiment 1. At daybreak, the 3. (armoured)/Panzer-Aufklärungsabteilung 1, supported by two Tigers under Untersturmführer Wittmann, made a counterattack and pushed these enemy forces back across our march route. Twelve T-34's were destroyed in the fighting.

At 10.40 hours, there were enemy attacks with infantry and eight to ten tanks on the right wing of Panzergrenadier-Regiment 2. The enemy did penetrate as far as the northern edge of Sherebki. The Panthers stationed there made a counterattack, sealed the point of breakthrough, and destroyed six T-34's.

At 12.45 hours, there was an enemy attack along a broad front across the line Buraki — Januschpol toward the southwest. Enemy forces broke through our lines south of Hf. Selenlyj (Kampfgruppe 208. Infanteriedivision), at the junction with the march route (Panzergrenadier-Regiment 1), and north of Sherebki (Panzergrenadier-Regiment 2).

Panzer-Aufklärungsabteilung 1 managed to seal off the breakthrough near Hf. Selenyj. The two Panzergrenadier-Regimenter received orders to make counterattacks in order to disguise a newly-ordered withdrawal to a new line of defense.

Total losses for the enemy: nineteen T-34's, three assault guns.

Untersturmführer Wittmann, a Zugführer in the 13. (heavy)/Panzerregiment 1, destroyed his sixty-sixth enemy tank in the counterattack on 9.1. This triumph was reported in the Wehrmachtsbericht of 10.1.1944.

Starting with that day, individual Kompanien were pulled out of action despite the constant defensive fighting and moved behind the front to rest, warm up, and receive medical attention.

At 19.00 hours, the Korps issued the following order:

> "The *LAH* with subordinated Kampfgruppe 208. Infanteriedivision and Kampfgruppe 68. Infanteriedivision is to disengage from the enemy and to assume a new position in the line from north of Petrikowzy — Ssmela — Bespetschna (inclusive). The point of contact with the unit to the right is Point 299.6 (two kilometers northeast of Petrikowzy), to the left with Kampfgruppe SS-Panzerdivision *DR* the western end of the row of houses one-and-a-half kilometers north of Bespetschna. The Panzerkompanie detailed to the 7. Panzerdivision is to remain there for the time being. The Division is to prepare to release Kampfgruppe 208. Infanteriedivision in the night between 10. and 11.1.1944. It is then to be put on the march toward Nowaja Ssinjawka. The withdrawal is to begin at 22.00 hours."

The withdrawal from the position was accomplished without trouble from the enemy on the left wing, where a counterattack had been launched to cover our intentions. On the right wing, the enemy gave pursuit with reconnaissance forces.

10.1.1944: The Division gave orders for 10.1.1944 to the following effect:
The following are deployed:
Panzer-Aufklärungsabteilung 1 from Point 299.6 (inclsuive) — eastern edge of Ssmela.
Kampfgruppe 208. Infanteriedivision from the northern edge of Ssmela — Swch. techn. Gewächse (inclusive).
Panzergrenadier-Regiment 1 from the western edge of Swch. techn. Gewächse — ravine three kilometers west of there.
Kampfgruppe 88. Infanteriedivision as far as Chutor Woroschilowa.
Panzergrenadier-Regiment 2 in Chutor Woroschilowa.
Panzer-Pionier-Bataillon 1 is to relieve Kampfgruppe 208. Infanteriedivision at nightfall. The Kampfgruppe is to receive provisions in Lipjatin and then be loaded into trucks for transport to the Panzergrenadier-Regiment 1 in Nowaja Ssinjawka.
The armoured force is to stand in Ssmela at the Division's disposal.
Positions are to be prepared between Petrikowzy and Ssmela as well as on the northern edge of Lipjatin and Ssalniza.
The Panzerwerkstattkompanie is to be in Tereschpol.
Panzerinstandesetzungsabteilung 1 is to be in Nowo Konstantinow.
The rest of Flakabteilung 1 is to remain in Lossowa (east of Proskurow) from 9.1. - 16.1.1944 to repair its weapons and equipment.

At 15.00 hours, the enemy continued his attacks across the line Pelewaja — Stepok — Sherebki against Panzer-Aufklärungsabteilung 1 and Kampfgruppe 208. Infanteriedivision; he had the support of tanks and heavy-calibre artillery.

Seven T-34's were destroyed.

In Panzergrenadier-Regiment 1's and Kampfgruppe 68. Infanteriedivision's sector, the enemy was quiet. In front of Panzergrenadier-Regiment 2, the enemy was digging in with weak infantry forces. There was heavy column traffic from Januschpol to Krassnopol, and farther to the west there were signs of the enemy's build-up of a main point of concentration to the west.

Orders for 11.1.1944 remained unchanged.

Panzers ready for combat:

Panzer VI's	4	Sturmgeschütze	7
Panzer V's	8	7.5-cm Pak	7
Panzer IV's	8	Pak (self-prop.)	5

11.1.1944: In the course of the night, the enemy conducted reconnaisance toward Ssmela, Swch. techn. Gewächse, and Chutor Woroschilowa. Otherwise, there was no action along the Division's front outside of harassing fire.

The Division was in the following defensive positions:

Panzer-Aufklärungsabteilung 1 from Point 299.6 — ravine east of Ssmela.

Panzer-Pionier-Bataillon 1 as far as the eastern edge of Smela.

Panzergrenadier-Regiment 1 from the northern edge of Ssmela — Swch. techn. Gewächse (inclusive).

Kampfgruppe 68. Infanteriedivision (under Oberst von Künsberg) from Swch. techn. Gewächse (exclusive) — two kilometers west of there.

Panzergrenadier-Regiment 2 on the northern edge of Chutor Woroschilowa.

Kampfgruppe 208. Infanteriedivision was relieved in accordance with orders. It received provisions from the Division and was transported away.

The armoured force under Untersturmführer Köchlin, subordinated to the 7. Panzerdivision on the Korps' left wing, was deployed as part of an armoured attack into the enemy forces.

The following report on the unit's combat and trench strength gives a good picture of the personnel and materiel situation of the 1. SS-Panzerdivision *LAH*:

1. SS-Panzerdivision *LAH* — 11.1.1944, 16.00 hours

Ia

To

Generalkommando of the XXXXVIII. Panzerkorps Ia

Re: today's combat and trench strength

Ref: none

Unit:	*Combat strength*	*Trench strength*	*Combat-ready weapons:*
SS-Panzergrenadier-Regiment 1 *LSSAH*	19/71/471	13/40/329	37 light MG 3 heavy MG

Unit:	*Combat strength*	*Trench strength*	*Combat-ready weapons:*
			2 heavy Gr.Wf. 2 2-cm Flak (self-prop.) 1 2-cm Flak (mot. Z) 1 7.5-cm Pak 3 5-cm Pak 2 heavy IG 1 light IG
SS-Panzergrenadier-Regiment 2 *LSSAH*	9/43/330	7/20/174	20 light MG 1 5-cm Pak 2 heavy IG 2 light IG 5 2-tonne SPW
SS-Panzerregiment 1 *LSSAH*	15/68/313	7/29/140	4 Panzer VI 8 Panzer V 8 Panzer IV 5 2-cm Flak 8 light MG
SS-Panzer-Artillerie-Regiment 1			
I. Abteilung	5/18/93		9 light FH 10 light MG
II. Abteilung	8/56/320		6 Wespe 4 Hummel
III. Abteilung	11/67/390		4 heavy FH 2 10-cm Kan. 2 5-cm Pak 15 light MG
Regimental units	6/22/124		5 21-cm Wf. 8 15-cm Wf. 2 2-cm Flak 2 5-cm Pak 11 light MG
SS-Panzer-Aufklärungs-abteilung 1 *LSSAH*	8/42/247	8/38/159	1 7.5-cm Pak (mot. Z) 6 7.5-cm Pak (self-prop.) 1 5-cm Pak (self-prop.) 1 heavy IG (mot. Z) 31 light MG

Unit:	*Combat strength*	*Trench strength*	*Combat-ready weapons:*
			9 1-tonne GPW 1 SPW 1 medium PW
SS-Sturmgeschütz-abteilung 1 *LSSAH*	7/46/137	1/6/21	6 7.5-cm Gesch. 1 10.5-cm Gesch.
SS-Panzer-Pionier-Bataillon 1 *LSSAH*	2/18/139	2/17/108	15 light MG
SS-Flakabteilung 1 *LSSAH*	1/7/65		1 8.8-cm Gesch. 2 3.7-cm Gesch. 2 2-cm Gesch.
Kampfgruppe 68. Infanterie-division von Künsberg	17/82/347	8/43/166	23 light MG 3 heavy Gr. Wf. 5 light IG 3 heavy IG 1 7.62-cm Pak
Panzerzerstörer-Bataillon 473	5/22/161	5/20/146	6 light MG
Artillerie-Regiment 208 (and 168)	30/128/701		21 light FH 3 heavy FH
Werferregiment 1			
I. Abteilung	3/11/52		6 15-cm Wf. 2 light MG
II. Abteilung	9/52/297		13 30-cm Wf. 2 light MG
III. Abteilung	13/37/217		12 30-cm Wf. 6 light MG

1. SS-Panzerdivision *LAH*
Ia

12.1.1944: At 02.00 hours, there was an armoured attack by seven enemy tanks against the left wing of Kampfgruppe 68. Infanteriedivision. The tanks deposited the Russian infantrymen mounted on them behind our lines and then moved off to the north.

At 03.45 hours, there was a second tank assault on the same spot. A first wave of twelve enemy tanks moved past Lipjatin to the east and broke through into Ulanoff, where it blocked our supply route. The second wave was forced to turn back under fire from our Sturmgeschützabteilung 1; three T-34's were destroyed. The Sturmgeschützabteilung pursued the enemy as far as the southern edge of Chutoryski Hf., causing a panic among the enemy troops stationed there and forcing them to pull back to the north. Fourteen enemy anti-tank guns were destroyed.

At 09.15 hours, the gap in the battle line was closed once again. Repeated concentrated fire from our two Artillerie-Regimenter caused considerable disruption in the enemy preparations around Chutoryski Hf. The commander of the Sturmgeschützabteilung, Sturmbannführer Heimann, was awarded the Ritterkreuz for his unit's action.

Of the enemy tanks which had broken through early that morning at Ulanoff, ten or twelve turned east. The rest were attacked in Ulanoff by two of the *LAH*'s Tigers which just happened to be returning from repairs under the command of the Regiments-Ingenieur [engineer] of Panzergrenadier-Regiment 1, Hauptsturmführer Gilles. The *LAH* destroyed two of the enemy tanks, and Panzer-Zerstörer-Bataillon 473 took care of two. Two additional enemy tanks were damaged. The *LAH* Panzers detailed to the 7. Panzerdivision under Untersturmführer Köchlin were constantly in action there.

Seven bunkers were fitted out as living quarters in the third line of defense. The roads were iced over, and the snow was drifting strongly.

The commanding general issued a directive to the Division's commanders about the measures to be taken to get provisions to the troops. (See appendix no. 7.)

13.1.1944: At 00.30 hours and again at 02.30 hours, there were enemy attacks at the seam between Kampfgruppe 68. Infanteriedivision (Kampfgruppe von Künsberg) and Panzergrenadier-Regiment 2. In the fighting, Panzer-Zerstörer-Bataillon 473 destroyed two T-34's in close-range fighting.

At 08.30 hours, the enemy attacked from Chutoryski Hf. with strong tank forces and assault guns. He hit the middle of Panzergrenadier-Regiment 1's defensive sector, broke through, and advanced his troops as far as Tschessnowka. His tank unit was completely wiped out by a counterattack by the armoured force under Peiper. Thirty-seven T-34's and seven assault guns were destroyed. Untersturmführer Wittmann destroyed his eighty-eighth enemy tank and his gunner, Rottenführer Balthasar Woll, his eightieth. Both were awarded the Ritterkreuz.

At 15.30 hours, there was another attack by two enemy regiments with artillery support from a number of heavy batteries against the left wing of Panzergrenadier-Regiment 1 and the right wing of Kampfgruppe 68. Infanteriedivision (Kampfgruppe von Künsberg). The Kampfgruppe and its officers held Bespetschna. The Divisions-Sicherungskompanie (under Hauptsturmführer Linden) was sent to the spot to seal off the enemy incursion and close the gap. Kampfgruppe 68. Infanteriedivision (Kampfgruppe von Künsberg), consisting for the most part of Oberst von Künsberg's Infanterie-Regiment 188, was considerably weakened by its losses in this fighting and by its shortage of non-commissioned officers. The 68. Infanteriedivision issued an urgent request for more non-coms to be transferred to it.

With this deployment of the Divisions-Sicherungskompanie, the Division had no more reserves at all available to it.

In Comrade Knäbke's (8./1) diary, the following entry appears:

"The day began with a Russian attack. It was supported by about twenty T-34's. The focus point was on the unit adjacent to us on the left. In the Kompanie's sector, one T-34 was destroyed by the Pak assigned to us. The attack got stymied before our positions. The Kompanie suffered severe losses. Two men were killed and ten wounded. The Kompanieführer, Untersturmführer Gewellhoff, was wounded. He was succeeded by Untersturmführer Poss. Toward evening, the enemy succeeded in penetrating our position. We were only able to seal off the point of breakthrough."

Oberst von Künsberg, commander of the Infanterie-Regiment 188, wrote to the author as follows:

"My good friend Peiper sent two Tigers into my sector, where Untersturmführer Wittman destroyed countless enemy tanks and the other Tiger gunner about twenty during that Russian attack. Wittmann did, however, suffer a broken front tooth on the edge of his turret. I was extremely pleased with the willing and selfless cooperation among our commanders."

The commanding general, General der Panzertruppen Balck, congratulated Michael Wittmann in a radio message addressed personally to him.

At 16.00 hours, an enemy battalion attacked the right wing (Panzer-Aufklärungsabteilung 1) and was repulsed.

At 23.20 hours, the armoured force, together with elements of Kampfgruppe 68. Infanteriedivision (Kampfgruppe von Künsberg) and Panzergrenadier-Regiment 1, launched a counterattack. By 02.10 hours on 14.1.1944, they had succeeded in driving the enemy out of Bespetschna and in restoring the old battle lines.

14.1.1944: After the armoured force returned, it grew quiet along the entire Divisional front in the course of the morning. The enemy was observed to be withdrawing forces from Chutorysko Hf. in the early morning, and new forces were seen moving into the town at about 11.00 hours. He appeared to be relieving his troops.

The armoured group decided to risk a Panzer raid.

At 12.30 hours, Sturmbannführer Peiper was ordered to move all the Panzers and Schützenpanzerwagens available to him and the subordinated II. (armoured)/Panzer-Artillerie-Regiment 1 from the area west of Ssmela. In an attack to the northwest, he was to destroy the enemy forces in Chutorysko Hf. and to capture the march route from Berditschew to Ljubar. In cooperation with the armoured force *DR*, he was then to capture Krassnopol.

At 12.55 hours, the armoured force moved out. It penetrated the relief maneuvers underway in Chutorysko Hf., destroying at least two enemy regiments, and by 14.00 hours was able to capture the northern edge of Krassnopol. At 16.30 hours, it had turned to the west and stood at the bridge in the middle of Molotschki. The enemy fled, abandoning his weapons, to the northeast, east, and northwest. The armoured force *DR* was by this time fighting in the southern part of Molotschki. This advance destroyed countless enemy vehicles, twenty anti-tank guns, and two T-34's.

15.1.1944: At 03.45 hours, the spearhead of our Panzer units was locked in battle at the march route south of Matrunki. Defensive forces on the northern edge of Krassnopol had established contact there with the armoured force *DR*. In the course of the early morning, Panzergrenadiere from SS-Panzerdivision *DR* took over the defensive positions on the northern edge of Krassnopol, while the *LAH* armoured force closed ranks west of Molotschki. For his valiant and prudent leadership in this advance and for the triumphs of his Regiment, Sturmbannführer Peiper became the three hundred seventy-seventh soldier of the Wehrmacht to receive the Oak Leaves to his Ritterkreuz.

At 10.00 hours, the XXXXVIII. Panzerkorps ordered the armoured forces of the *LAH* and the *DR* to be combined under the command of Panzerdivision *DR* for an attack to the northwest on Ljubar.

At 13.15 hours, Division *DR* was forced to pull back its defenses from the northern section of Krassnopol with heavy losses.

At 15.00 hours, the armoured force set off via Stetkowzy for another thrust. The attack failed in the face of heavy fire from anti-tank artillery and multiple rocket launchers. After losing four of our Panzers, the force pulled back to Stetkowzy.

The rest of the front was quiet.

Panzers ready for combat:

Panzer VI's	5	Panzer IV's	5
Panzer V's	9	Sturmgeschütze	21

Orders for 16.1.1944 remained unchanged. The Panzerregiment remained subordinated to the 2. SS-Panzerdivision *DR* for 16.1. It was to move with the armoured force *DR* in front of our battle line in a feigned continuation of the Panzer attack from Stetkowzy to the northwest; the intention was to tie up the sizable enemy force in Ljubar.

Panzergrenadier-Regiment 2 used its day of rest to regroup. The I. and II. Bataillone were combined to form Kampfgruppe Schnelle.

16.1.1944: At 08.00 hours, the four Panthers subordinated to Panzergrenadier-Regiment 2 set out under the command of Sturmbannführer Kuhlmann for a thrust on Krassnopol. They succeeded in penetrating the southern part of the city. Six Russian tanks were destroyed, and the enemy suffered serious losses in manpower. Otherwise, the day passed quietly.

At 15.00 hours, the Division moved its headquarters to Ssalniza.

Panzergrenadier-Regiment 1 was moved back to join the Division, to which it was subordinated. Panzer gunner Simon, the driver of a Panzer V, reported to Panzergrenadier-Regiment 1 with his radio operator; both of them were wounded. Their Panther had taken several direct hits to its steering mechanism and was only partially drivable. Steering with one hand, Simon had travelled about fifteen kilometers through heavily occupied enemy territory to bring the Panzer back to our position. Both soldiers were mentioned in the Heer's honor roll.

Toward evening, the Division received orders to extend its line about one kilometer to the west. Panzergrenadier-Regiment 2 extended its III./2's sector by a kilometer. A heavy Werfer-Batterie from Werferregiment 1 was subordinated to it for this purpose.

2.12.1943: Obergruppenführer und General der Waffen-SS Sepp Dietrich pays a visit to his old Division. From right: Hauptsturmführer and Adjutant Weiser, Sepp Deitrich, Oberführer Wisch. With back to the camera: Sturmbannführer Lehmann.

13.12.1943: The new Oberbefehlshaber of the 4. Panzerarmee, General der Panzertruppen Raus, with Oberführer Wisch.

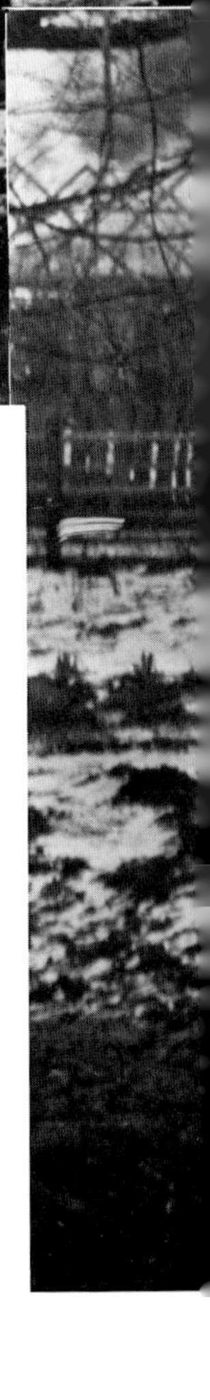

22.12.1943: The last shot from Panzer 504. Shortly thereafter, it took a hit itself and was disabled.

12.12.1943: A Panzer IV under command of Untersturmführer Sternebeck just south of the railway line from Kiev to Korosten.

19.12.1943: Panzers and Sturmgeschütze preparing west of Meleni.

January, 1944: Pulling out a stuck Panzer south of Krasnopol.

At 23.30 hours, the new position was occupied, and contact was established with Division *DR*.

17.1.1944: A quiet day followed an equally quiet night. At 08.00 hours, the Panther force under Sturmbannführer Kuhlmann made a renewed thrust on Krassnopol. The attack received outstanding support from the heavy Werferabteilung and from the I./Panzer-Artillerie-Regiment 1, and the enemy was driven out of his positions. Five enemy heavy anti-tank weapons were destroyed.

At 10.00 hours, the Panther force returned behind our lines without having suffered any losses.

Our radio reconnaissance force (composed of Hiwis operating equipment captured from the Russians; they had been providing us with excellent service since November) reported that our suspicion that a Russian staff was located in the western outskirts of Sherebki had been confirmed by an intercepted radio message. The message was a call for a conference of the Russian commanders there at 13.00 hours. Two heavy artillery barrages were arranged with the commanders of our Werferregiment 1 and Panzer-Artillerie-Regiment 1, scheduled to hit this tiny section of town at 13.10 and 13.35 hours, provided that ground observations confirmed this radio intelligence. After the completion of the first fire attack, we observed a panicked abandonment of that section of town. Other radio messages intercepted contained reference to "many lights being extinguished," which we interpreted to mean the loss of many commanders.

18.1.1944: The night and following day were quiet. Werferregiment 1 was withdrawn and put on the march to Chmelnik. Toward evening, a Korpsbefehl arrived ordering two Infanterie-Regimenter of the 371. Infanteriedivision to relieve the 1. SS-Panzerdivision *LAH* and its subordinated Kampfgruppe 68. Infanteriedivision (Kampfgruppe von Künsberg) in the nights between 19.1 and 20.1 and between 20.1 and 21.1.

For this change, the following was ordered:

At nightfall on 19.1.1944, Grenadierregiment 671 was to relieve Panzer-Aufklärungsabteilung 1, Panzer-Pionier-Bataillon 1, and Panzergrenadier-Regiment 1. Artillerie-Regiment 371 was to relieve Panzer-Artillerie 1 on 19.1. At nightfall on 20.1.1944, Grenadierregiment 669 was to relieve Kampfgruppe 68. Infanteriedivision and Panzergrenadier-Regiment 2.

After being relieved, the Division was moved into the area Chmelnik (exclusive of it) — Konstantinoff (exclusive) — Djakowzy (exclusive) — Ssandraki (inclusive). Panzergrenadier-Regiment 1 moved six combat-ready Panzer V's into the new assembly area on 19.1 and the rest on 20.1. It moved the 1. Batterie of Sturmgeschützabteilung 1 on 19.1 and the 2. Batterie on 20.1. Artillerie-Regiment 208 and Panzer-Zerstörer-Bataillon 473 came under the command of the 371. Infanteriedivision.

In the assembly area, the Division was deloused at the *LAH*'s field hospital in Chmelnik.

The Divisional headquarters were in Koschuchoff starting at 14.00 hours on 21.1.1944.

The document "Number of Enemy Tanks Destroyed Between 25.12.1943 and 18.1.1944" (see appendix no. 8) can be seen as a sign of the quiet period then setting in.

The commander of the 1. SS-Panzerdivision *LAH*, Oberführer Wisch, was rewarded for his high personal valor in battle by becoming the three hundred ninety-third soldier of the German Wehrmacht to receive the Oak Leaves to the Ritterkreuz.

19.1.1944 - 21.1.1944: During this period, the relief maneuvers on the front and the assembly in the newly designated area took place with no particular friction. The command responsibility in the defensive sector was handed over from the 1. SS-Panzerdivision *LAH* to the 371. Infanteriedivision at 09.00 hours on 21.1.1944.

Our Panzer strength in the assembly area:

		Combat-ready	Under short-term repair	Under long-term repair
Panzer VI		1	2	6
Panzer V		22	7	7
Panzer IV		25	4	4
Panzer III		2	1	1
Sturmgeschütze:	7.5-cm	25	3	2
	10.5-cm	2	2	—
Pak:	7.5-cm (mot. Z)	6	—	—
	7.5-cm (self-propelled)	6	—	—

Of the Panzers subordinated to the 7. Panzerdivision, Untersturmführer Köchlin brought none back in combat-ready condition.

The Oberbefehlshaber of the 4. Panzerarmee, General Raus, issued the following daily order:

Armee headquarters,
January 21,1944

The soldiers of the 4. Panzerarmee

At Christmas, enemy infantry and tank forces far superior to us in number attacked our front in an offensive of unusual proportions. They intended to destroy our Armee and to cut the Heeresgruppe off from its lines of supply.

In three weeks of hard fighting, you have frustrated the enemy's intentions by your tough resistance and mighty countermoves. The enemy suffered terrible losses, and his massive attack came to a halt. More than one thousand enemy tanks out of commission, many thousands of Soviets dead, and huge amounts of enemy materiel destroyed all bear witness to the enormity of our Armee's triumph.

I wish to express to all officers and troops my deepest respect and sincerest thanks for this outstanding performance.

The enemy is, however, filling in the gaps in his ranks and will shortly resume his attacks with the same intentions. I expect that the 4. Panzerarmee will repulse the enemy onslaught and destroy his forces.

Raus,
General der Panzertruppen

The Generalkommando of the XXXXVIII. Panzerkorps evaluated the defensive fighting west of Berditschew in its daily report of 22.1 as follows:

> "The XXXXVIII. Panzerkorps in its offensive fighting on 14.1 and 15.1 and the subsequent battle to close the gap between the Panzerkorps and the LIX. Armeekorps not only dealt the enemy heavy losses in personnel and materiel, but also pulled away and tied up forced from the north, thereby weakening the enemy advance on Rowno and Ostrog. (The Soviet 336th Rifle Division and XXVth Tank Corps.) The XXVth Tank Corps also suffered heavy losses in the fighting around Labun. It can be assumed that the Corps' 175th Tank Brigade lost most of its combat-ready tanks in that fighting. Radio reconnaissance has determined that our restructuring in the last few days has not escaped the enemy's attention, and that it has caused some uncertainty for him as to our intentions. The continued strong enemy presence in the area Ljubar — Wel. Derewitschi and the presence of the 3rd Guards Tank Army at rest so close to the front lead us to the conclusion that, after the completion of a rest period, the enemy will attempt to continue his offensive at the same focal points: both sides of the road from Berditschew to Chmelnik and from Ljubat to the west."

Appendix 1

List of sources

German-language sources:

Balck, Hermann	"Ordnung im Chaos." Osnabrück, 1980.
Bauer, E.	"Der Panzerkrieg." 1965.
Carell, Paul	"Unternehmen Barbarossa." Berlin, 1963.
Cerff, Karl	"Die Waffen-SS im Wehrmachtsbericht." Osnabrück, 1971.
Dahms, H.G.	"Der 2. Weltkrieg." 1968.
Domarus, Max	"Hitler." Wiesbaden, 1973.
Fraschka, Günter	"Mit Schwertern und Brillianten." Wiesbaden, 1977.
Freund, M.	"Geschichte des 2. Weltkrieges in Dokumenten," Vol. III. 1956.
Fricke, Gert	"Fester Platz Tarnopol 1944." Freiburg, 1969.
Gehlen, Reinhard	"Der Dienst." Berg, 1971. "Geschichte der 3. Panzer-Division", 1967
von Gersdorff, U.	"Geschichte und Militärgeschichte." Frankfurt am Main, 1974.
Greiner	"Die Oberste Wehmachtführung." Wiesbaden, 1971.
Guderian, Heinz	"Erinnerungen eines Soldaten." Heidelberg, 1951.
Halder, Franz	"Kriegstagebuch," Vol. III. Stuttgart, 1964.
Haupt, Werner	"Heeresgruppe Süd." Bad Nauheim, 1968. "Krim-Kaukasus-Stalingrad." Friedberg, 1977.
Hausser, Paul	"Waffen-SS in Einsatz." Göttingen, 1953. "Soldaten wie andere auch." Osnabrück, 1966.
Hermann, K.-H.	"Deutsche Militärgeschichte." 1968.
Höhne, Heinz	"Der Orden unter dem Totenkopf." Essen, 1972. "Canaris." Munich, 1976.
Hubatsch, W.	"Hitlers Weisungen für die Kriegsführung 1939/1945." 1962.
Husemann, Fr.	"Die guten Glaubens waren." Osnabrück, 1975.
Klietmann, K.G.	"Die Waffen-SS." Osnabrück, 1965.
Klink, Ernst	"Gesetz des Handelns: Operation Zitadelle." Freiburg.
Lange, W.	"Korps-Abteilung C."
von Manstein, E.	"Verlorene Siege." Bonn, 1955.

von Manteuffel, H. — "Die 7. Panzerdivision." Friedberg, 1978.

von Mellenthin, F. W. — "Panzerschlachten." Neckargemünd, 1963.
"Deutschlands Generale des 2. Weltkrieges." Bergisch-Gladbach, 1980.

Meyer, Kurt — "Grenadiere." Munich, 1973.

Munin-Verlag — "Der Kessel von Tscherkassy." Osnabrück, 1969.
"Wenn alle Brüder schweigen." Osnabrück,, 1973.

Oswald, W. — "Kraftfahrzeuge und Panzer." Stuttgart, 1970.

Pemler, G. — "Der Flug zum Don." Leoni, 1981.

Philippi, Hein — "Der Feldzug gegen Sowjet-Rußland." Stuttgart, 1962.

Pottgießer, H. — "Die Deutsche Reichsbahn im Ostfeldzug." Neckargemünd, 1960.

von Seemen, G. — "Ritterkreuzträger." Friedberg, 1976.

Seraphin — "SS-Verfügungstruppe und Wehrmacht." In "Wehrwissenschaftliche Rundschau." 1955.

Scheibert, Horst — "Panzer zwischen Don und Donez." Friedberg, 1979.

Schneider, Jost W. — "Verleihung genehmigt." San Jose (California), 1977.

Schröter, Heinz — "Stalingrad." Lengerich.

Speidel, H. — "Aus unserer Zeit." Berlin, 1977.

Stadler, S. — "Die Offensive gegen Kursk." Osnabrück,, 1980.

Steenberg, S. — "Wlassow." Cologne, 1968.

Stoves, Rolf — "Die 1. Panzerdivision."

Streit, Christian — "Keine Kameraden." Stuttgart, 1978.

von Tippelskirch, Kurt — "Geschichte des 2. Weltkrieges." Bonn, 1954.

Thöle, K. — "Befehl des Gewissens." Osnabrück, 1976.

Weidinger, Otto — "Division *Das Reich*," Vol. I. - IV. Osnabrück, 1967 - 1979.

Zentner, Chr. — "Der große Atlas zum 2. Weltkrieg." Munich, 1974.

Foreign-language sources:

Butcher — "My Three Years with Eisenhower."

Clark, Allan — "Barbarossa."

Fuller — "Der 2. Weltkrieg."

Irving, David — "Hitler und seine Feldherren." Berlin, 1975.
"Rommel." Hamburg, 1978.

Liddel, Hart — "Geschichte des 2. Weltkrieges." Vienna, 1972.

Lucas and Cooper — "Hitler's Elite." London, 1975.
"Panzer: The Armoured Force of the Third Reich." New York, 1976.

Markin, I.I. — "Die Kursker Schlacht." East Berlin, 1960.

Müller, Janus — "Hitlers Werk."

Pospelow — "Die Geschichte des großen vaterländischen Krieges der Sowjet-Union."

Shilin — "Die wichtigsten Operationen des großen vaterländischen Krieges, 1941 - 1945."

Shukow — "Erinnerungen und Gedanken."

Telpuschowskji — "Die sowjetische Geschichte des großen vaterländischen Krieges."

Weingartner, James — "Hitler's Guard." Edwardsville, 1968.

de Zayas, A. — "Die Wehrmachtuntersuchungsstelle." Munich, 1979.

Unpublished sources:

Personal diaries from:
Günther Borchers
Karl Hahn
Josef Steinbüchel
Oberscharführer Hübner

Daily log and documents from the 2. Panzergrenadierregiment *LSSAH* from 5.7.1942 through 17.4.1944

West Point Atlas of American Wars

Archival material from:
The Bundesarchiv-Militärarchiv [Federal military archives] in Freiburg
The archives of Jost W. Schneider
The Vopersal archives

Daily log from the SS-Flakabteilung 1 *LSSAH*, December 1943 - January 1944.

Photographs:

Archives of Jost W. Schneider, Wuppertal	15
Bibliothek für Zeitgeschichte, Stuttgart	1
Albert Frey, Heilbronn	1
Martin Groß, Bad Laer	1
Paul Guhl, Renningen	1
Max Hansen, Niebüll	1
Fritz Henke, Podendorf	1
Hans-Hinrich Karck, Kiel	1
Dr. Herbert Knoll, St. Margarethe	1
Hugo Kraas (deceased), Selk	4
Günther Krätschmer, Ottobrunn	4
Erwin Kurz, Nürtingen	9
Rudolf Lehmann (author)	4
Gerhard Maurer, Sindelfingen	7
Munin-Verlag	12
Walter Ott, Gettorf	7
Karl Rettlinger, Gunzenhausen	1
Rudolf von Ribbentrop, Düsseldorf	1
Rudolf Sandig	1
Oswald Siegmund, Cologne	3
Gerhard Stiller, Stuttgart	3
Alfred Tamm, Lüdenscheid	1
Marga Weiser, Ludwigsburg	1
Theodor Wisch, Norderstedt	9
Peter Witt, Hagen	1
Karl Wortmann, Nienburg	2
Dietrich Ziemssen (deceased), Tübingen	1

Appendix 2

Comparison of the service ranks Heer — Waffen-SS

Heer rank	SS rank
Schütze, Kanon.	Schütze
Oberschütze	Oberschütze
Gefreiter	Sturmmann
Obergefreiter	Rottenführer
Unteroffizier	Unterscharführer
Unterfeldwebel	Scharführer
Fähnrich	Standartenjunker
Feldwebel	Oberscharführer
Oberfeldwebel	Hauptscharführer
Oberfähnrich	Standartenoberjunker
Stabsfeldwebel	Sturmscharführer
Leutnant	Untersturmführer

Heer rank	SS rank
Oberleutnant	Obersturmführer
Hauptmann	Hauptsturmführer
Major	Sturmbannführer
Oberstleutnant	Obersturmbannfführer
Oberst	Standartenführer
	Oberführer
Generalmajor	Brigadeführer
Generalleutnant	Gruppenführer
General der Infanterie, etc.	Obergruppenführer
Generaloberst	Oberstgruppenführer after 1942

Appendix 3

Key to German words and abbreviations used in this volume

German (plural form in parentheses where applicable)	Abbreviation	English equivalent
A-Tag		A-Day (secret or as-yet-undetermined day for beginning of an attack)
Abteilung (-en)	Abt.	Battalion (in reference to military unit); section (in reference to administrative office)
Adjutant (-en)	Adj.	Adjutant
Allgemeines Heeresamt	AHA	General Army Office
Allgemeines-SS		General (non-combat) SS
Arbeitsstab (Arbeitsstäbe)		Work staff
Armee (-n)	A	Army
Armeebefehl		Army order
Armee-Hauptquartier	AHQu.	Army headquarters
Armeekorps	AK	Army corps
Armee-Oberkommando	AOK	Army High Command
Artillerie	Art.	Artillery
Artillerieabteilung (-en)	AA	Artillery battalion
Artillerie-Bekämpfungsgruppe (-n)		Anti-artillery group or unit
Artillerie-Kolonne (-n)		Artillery column
Artillerie-Kommandeur	Arko	Artillery commander (artillery officer within a corps)
Artillerie-Regiment	AR, Art.Reg.	Artillery regiment
Artillerie-Verbindungskommando (-s)	AVK	Artillery liaison command post
Aufklärungsabteilung (-en)	AA	Reconnaissance battalion
Aufklärungsgruppe (-n)	Aufkl.Gr.	Reconnaissance group
Aufklärungsstaffel	Aufkl.-Staffel	Reconnaissance squadron (Luftwaffe)
Ausbildungs-Bataillon	A-Bataillon	Training battalion
Ausbildungs-Kompanie	A-Kompanie	Training company
Ausbildungs- und Ersatz-Bataillon	A.-u.E.-Batl.	Training and battalion
außer Dienst	a. D.	Retired
Bataillon (-e)	Batl.,Btl.	Battalion
Batterie (-n)	Bttr., Battr.	Battery
Befehlshaber		Commander
Befehlshaber des Ersatzheeres	BdE	Commander of the Replacement (and Training) Army
Befehlspanzer		Command tank
Begleitkommando (see Führerbegleitkommando) Beiwagen-Kraftrad	B-Krad	Motorcycle with sidecar
Beobachtungsbataillon	Bb	Observation battalion
Beobachtungsoffizier	B-Offz.	Observation officer (artillery)
Beobachtungsstelle der Artillerie	B-Stelle	Artillery observation unit
Bergezug		Recovery or salvage platoon
Beritt		Cavalry unit
Betriebsstoff-Kolonne	B-Kol.	Fuel column
Bevollmächtiger Transportoffizier	BvTO	Transport officer in charge

German (plural form in parentheses where applicable)	Abbreviation	English equivalent
Blinktrupp (-s)		Signal-lamp team
Brückenkolonne	Brüko	Bridge column
Bundesarchiv - Militärarchiv	BA - MA	Federal military archives
Bundeswehr	Bw	Post WW II army of the Federal Republic of Germany
Chef		Chief, leader, or commander
Examples:		
Chef des Generalstabes	Chef d.Gen.St.	Chief of the General Staff
Chef des Heeres-Rüstungswesens	Chef H-Rüstung	Commander of the Army Armament Office
Chef des persönlichen Dienstes	Chief of Personal Service (to Hitler)	
Chef des XXXX. Panzerkorps	Chef des XXXX. Pz.Kps.	Commander of the XXXXth Panzerkorps
der Reserve	d.R.	Of the Reserves
Deutsches Rotes Kreuz	DRK	German Red Cross
Division (-en)	Div.	Division
Divisionsbefehl		Divisional order
Divisionskommandeur	Div.Kdr.	Divisional commander
Divisions-Nachschubführer	Div. Nachsch.Fhr.	Divisional supply officer
Divisions-Stabsquartier	Div.St.Qu.	Divisional staff quarters
Divisions-Gefechtsstand	Div.Gef.St.	Divisional headquarters
Do (-Werfer)		Multiple-barrel rocket launcher
Druckereitrupp (mot.)		Motorized printing unit
Durchgangsstraße	Dg	Transit thoroughfare (with number)
Eichenlaub	EL	Oak Leaves (decoration)
Eisenbahn-Panzerzug		Armoured railway train
Eisernes Kreuz (Eiserne Kreuze)	EK	Iron Cross (medal)
1. or I. Klasse	EK I, EK 1. Kl.	Iron Cross First Class
2. or II.Klasse	EK II, EK 2. Kl.	Iron Cross Second Class
Ersatzbataillon	E-Btl., Ers.Btl.	Replacement battalion
Ersatzkompanie	E-Kp., Ers.Komp.	Replacement company
Ersatzregiment	E-Rgt., Ers.Reg.	Replacement regiment
Fallschirmjägerregiment		Parachute regiment
Feldartillerie		Field artillery
Feldgendarmerie		Military police
Feldhaubitze (-n)	FH	Field howitzer
Feldjägerkorps		Field rifle corps
Feldmarschall (Feldmarschälle)	FM	Field marshall
Fernfeldkabelkompanie	FF	Field cable-laying company
Fernsprecher	Fe	Telephone
Feuerwerker	FW or TF	Technical officer
Flakabteilung	Flak-Abt.	Anti-aircraft artillery battalion
Flak-Trupp (-s)	Flak-Tr.	Anti-aircraft artillery unit
Flammenwerfer	Fw	Flame-thrower
Type 41	FmW 41	
Fliegerdivision		Airborne division
Fliegerkorps		Airforce corps
Fliegerverbindungsoffizier	Flivo	Airforce liaison officer
Flugabwehrkanone (-n)	Flak	Anti-aircraft gun
Flugabwehr-Maschinengewehr	Fla.MG	Anti-aircraft machine gun
Führer	Fhr.	Officer or commander

German (plural form in parentheses where applicable)	Abbreviation	English equivalent
der Führer		Hitler, the Führer
Führer-Flakabteilung	FFA	The Führer's anti-aircraft artillery battalion
Führerbegleitkommando		Führer bodyguard commando
Führerschutzkommando		Führer protection commando
Führerkorps		Officer corps
Führungsstaffel		Headquarters operations staff
Fürsorge- und Versorgungsabteilung		Care and welfare section
Funk	Fu	Radio
Funkzug	Fu.-Zg.	Radio platoon
Gasschutzoffizier		Chemical defense officer
Gauleiter		District Party leader
Gauparteitag		District Party rally
Gebirgsartillerie	Geb. Art.	Mountain artillery
Gebirgsbrigade	Geb.Brig.	Mountain brigade
Gebirgsdivision	Geb.Div.	Mountain division
Gebirgsjäger-Regiment	Geb.J.Rgt., Geb.Rgt.	Mountain infantry regiment
Gebirgs-Pionier-Bataillon	Geb.Pi.Btl.	Mountain engineers battalion
Gefallen	gef.	Killed in action
Gefechtsstaffel		Combat-trained echelon
Geheim	geh.	Secret
Geheime Feldpolizei	GFP	Secret field police
Geheime Kommandosache	g.Kdos.	Secret command document
Geheime Staatspolizei	Gestapo	Secret state police
Generalfeldmarschall	GFM	Field marshal
Generalität		Generals' corps
Generalkommando	Gen.Kdo.	General command
Generalstab	Gen.St.	General staff
Generalstab des Heeres	Gen.St.d.H.	General staff of the Army
Generalstabsoffizier	Gen.St.Offz.	General staff officer
Gepanzert	gep.	Armoured
Gerichtsabteilung		(Military) court section
Geschützwagen		Gun car (railroad)
Granatwerfer (-)	Gr.Wf.	Mortar
Granatwerferzug	Gr.Wf.Zg.	Mortar platoon
Großdeutschland	*GD*	"Greater Germany" (Elite unit of the Heer) Grenadier-Panzerdivision
	GPW	Armoured personnel carrier
Grille		15-centimeter heavy infantry weapon on self-propelled mount (literally: "cricket")
Gruppe	Gr.	Group or force (often combined with name of commander, e.g. Gruppe von Kleist = von Kleist force)
Gruppenbefehl (see Heeresgruppenbefehl)		
Gruppenkommando		Group commando
Gruppenstab		Group staff
Haubitze (-n)		Howitzer
Haubitze-Batterie		Howitzer battery
Hauptkadettenanstalt	HKA	Central cadet academy
Hauptkampffeld	HKF	Main battle field
Hauptkampflinie	HKL	Main battle line
Hauptquartier	HQu.	Headquarters
Hauptverbandsplatz	HVP	Main medical clearing station
Heer		H

German (plural form in parentheses where applicable)	Abbreviation	English equivalent
		Army
Heeresdienststelle		Army command headquarters
Heeresgruppe	HGr.	Army group
Heeresgruppe Nord		Army Group North
Heeresgruppe Süd		Army Group South
Heeresgruppenbefehl		Army group order
Heeresleitung		Army leadership
Heeres-Musikinspizient		Army music director
Heeres-Rüstungswesen	HRüstung	Army armament office
Heereswaffenmeisterschule		Army armory school
Heimat-Kraftfahr-Park	HKP	Homefront motor transport park; homefront motor pool
Hilfswilliger	Hiwi	Captured prisoner who volunteered to serve with the Germany army
Hitler-Jugend	HJ	Hitler Youth
Hochgebirgsschule		High-mountain training school
Hummel		Heavy field howitzer on self-propelled mount
im Generalstab	i.G.	On the general staff (additional designation for officers assigned to the general staff)
Infanterie	Inf.	Infantry
Infanterie-Bekämpfungsgruppe		Anti-infantry group
Infanterie-Division	Inf.Div., I.D., ID	Infantry division
Infanteriegeschütz (-e)	IG	Infantry gun
Infanteriegeschützbatterie		Infantry gun battery
Infanteriegeschützkompanie	(IG-)Kompanie	Infantry gun company
Infanteriekolonne	IK	Infantry column
Infanterie-Regiment	Inf.Reg., Inf.Rgt., I.R., IR	Infantry regiment
Infanterie-Regiment *Großdeutschland*	IR *GD*	Infantry Regiment *Großdeutschland*
Infanteriezugführer		Infantry platoon leader
Ingenieur	Ing.	Engineer (civilian title with nominal military rank)
Instandesetzungsabteilung	Inst.Abt.	Repair battalion
Instandesetzungszug	Inst.Zg.	Repair platoon
Intendant		Leader of the Indentantur (q.v.)
Intendantur		General staff administrative section dealing primarily with supply matters
Kampfgruppe	KGr.	Combat group
Kampfwagen		Combat car
Kampfwagenkanone	KwK	Armoured car with gun
Kampfwagenkanonenzug		Armoured gun platoon
Kanonenabteilung		Cannon battalion
Kanzlerschutzdienst		Chancellor protection service
Kartenstelle		Cartographic unit
Kavallerie		Cavalry
Kavallerie-Division	Kav.Div., KD	Cavalry division
Kommandant		Commander (of camp or region)
Kommandeur	Kdr.	Commander (of military unit)
Kommandierender General	KG	Commanding general (of a corps)
Kommandosache	Kdos.,Kds.	Command document
Kompanie (-n)	Komp., Kp.	Company
Kompaniechef		Company commander

German (plural form in parentheses where applicable)	Abbreviation	English equivalent
Kompaniefeldwebel		Company technical sergeant
Kompanieführer		Acting company commander
Kompanietrupp (-s)	Kp.Tr.	Company unit
Kompanietruppführer		Company unit commander
Korps	K	Corps
Korpsbefehl		Corps order
Korpshauptquartier	KHQu.	Corps headquarters
Krad-Erkundungszug		Motorcycle reconnaissance platoon
		Kradmeldezug
		Motorcycle messenger platoon
Kradschütze (-n)		Motorcycle riflemen
Kradschützen-Bataillon	Kradsch.-Btl.	Motorcycle rifle battalion
Kradschützengruppe	Kradsch.Gr.	Motorcycle rifle group
		Kradschützenkompanie
	Kradsch.Kp.	Motorcycle rifle company
Kradschützenzug	Kradsch.Zg.	Motorcycle rifle platoon
Krad-Spähtrupp		Motorcycle reconnaissance unit
Kraftfahrabteilung		Motor vehicle unit
Kraftfahrkompanie		Motor vehicle company
Kraftfahr-Pionierzug		Motorized engineer platoon
Kraftfahrzeug	Kfz.	Motor vehicle
Kraftfahrzeugkompanie		Motor vehicle company
Kraftfahrzeugoffizier	TFK	Motor vehicle technical officer (See "Technischer Feuerwerker" for explanation of abbreviation.)
Kraftfahrzeugstaffel		Vehicle section
Kraftrad (Krafträder)	Krad	Motorcycle
Kraftwagenkanone	KwK	Gun mounted on motor carriage
Kraftwagenkanonenzug	KwKZg.	Platoon of guns mounted on motor carriages
Kraftwagenkolonne	Kw.Kol.	Motor vehicle column
Kraftwagenkompanie	Kw.Kp.	Motor vehicle company
Kraftwagenwerkstattzug		Vehicle maintenance platoon
Krankenkraftwagenzug	Kr.Kw.Zg.	Ambulance truck platoon
Kriegsberichter		Accredited war correspondent
Kriegsausrüstungs-nachweisung	KAN	Table of equipment (TOE)
Kriegsmarine		(Wartime) Navy
Kriegsstärkenachweisung	KstN	Table of organization
Kriegstagebuch	KTB	War diary or combat log
Ladungswerfer		Spigot mortar
Landespolizei		State police
Landespolizeigruppe	LPG	State police force
Landesschützeneinheit		Regional defense unit (mainly for guard duty)
Examples:		Landesschützenbataillon
Landesschützendivision		
Landesschützenkompanie		
Landesschützenregiment		
Landser		Infantryman, common soldier
Lastkraftwagen	Lkw	Truck (cargo)
Lastwagen-Division	Lw.Div.	Truck division
Lehrsturm		Training division
Leibstandarte SS Adolf Hitler	*LSSAH,LAH*	"SS Body Guards, Adolf Hitler"
Leibwache		Body guard
Leicht	Le. or l	Light (applied to weapons or units, e.g. le. FH, lGr.Wf., lIG, etc.)

German (plural form in parentheses where applicable)	Abbreviation	English equivalent
Leiter des Nachrichtendienstes	LDN, L.D.N.	Leader of communications services
Lichtmeßbatterie		Flash-ranging station
Lichtmeßzug		Flash-ranging platoon
Luftlandedivision		Air Landing division
Luftwaffe		Airforce
Mannschaftstransport-Wagen	MTW	Personnel carrier
Marine		Navy
Maschinengewehr	MG	Machine gun
Maschinengewehr-Bataillon	MG-Btl.	Machine gun battalion
Maschinenpistole	MPi	Submachine gun
Meßbatterie		Artillery survey battery
Minenwerfer (-)	MW	Trench mortar
Minenwerferkompanie	MW-Kp.	Trench mortar company
Mittlerer Panzerwagen	mPW	Medium armoured car
Mörser (-)	Mö	Howitzer of 210 millimeters or larger
Motorisiert	mot.	Motorized
Motorsturm		Motor company
Musikkorps		Music corps
Musikzug		Music platoon
Nachkommando		Replacement staff
Nachrichtenabteilung	NA, Nachr.Abt.	Signals battalion
Nachrichtenführer	NF	Signals officer
Nachrichtenkompanie		Signals company
Nachrichtenoffizier		Signals officer
Nachrichtenstaffelführer		Signals section leader
Nachrichtenzug		Signals platoon
Nachschubführer		Supply officer
Nachschubkompanie		Supply company
Nachschubtruppe		Supply unit
Nationalsozialistische Deutsche Arbeiterpartei	NSDAP	National Socialist German Workers' Party
Nationalsozialistisches Kraftfahrkorps	NSKK	National Socialist Motor Corps
Nebelabteilung	Neb.Abtl.	Smoke-producing unit
Nebel-Lehr-Regiment	(see Nebelwerfer-Lehrregiment)	
Nebeltruppen		Chemical troops, smoke-generating units
Nebelwerfer		Multiple Rocket Launcher
Nebelwerfer-Batterie		Multiple Rocket Launcher battery
Nebelwerfer-Lehrregiment	Nb.-Lehr.-Rgt.	Multiple Rocket Launcher training regiment
Nebelwerfer-Regiment		Multiple Rocket Launcher regiment
O 1 - 5	(See table of position designations below)	
Oberbefehlshaber	OB	Commander-in-Chief
Oberbefehlshaber des Heeres	Ob.d.H.,	Commander-in-Chief of the Army
Oberfeldkommandantur	OFK	Office of Field Commander
Oberkommando	Obkdo.	High command
Oberkommando des Heeres	OKH	Army High Command
Oberkommando der Wehrmacht	OKW	Armed Forces High Command
Oberquartiermeister	OQ	General staff officer
Oberst beim Stabe		Headquarters adjutant
Oberster Befehlshaber		Supreme Commander

German (plural form in parentheses where applicable)	Abbreviation	English equivalent
Operationsabteilung	Op.Abt.	Operations section
Ordonnanzenkommando		Orderly unit
Ordonnanzoffizier	Ord.Offz.,OO	Special-mission staff officer
Ortsunterkunft	O.U.	Town billets
Panzer (-)	Pz.	Tank
Panzerabwehrabteilung		Anti-tank battalion
Panzerabwehrkanone (-n)	Pak	Anti-tank gun
Panzerabwehrkompanie	PzAbw	Anti-tank company
Panzerarmee		Tank army
Panzerbefehlswagen		Armoured command car
Panzerbrigade	Pz.Brig.	Tank brigade
Panzerbüchse		Anti-tank rifle
Panzerdivision	Pz.-Div., PD	Tank division
Panzergrenadier (-e)		Armored infantry rifleman
Panzergrenadierdivision		Armored infantry division
Panzergrenadier-Regiment		Armored infantry regiment
Panzergruppe	Pz.Gr.	Tank group or force (consisting of several Panzerkorps and often named after the commander, e.g. Panzergruppe Guderian)
Panzerjägerabteilung	Pz.Jg.Abt.	Anti-tank battalion
Panzerjägerkompanie	Pz.Jg.Kp.	Anti-tank company
Panzerkorps	Pz.K.	Tank corps
Panzerkorps-Kommando	Pz.K.Ko.	Tank corps command
Panzerkampfwagen		Tank
Panzerregiment	Pz.Rgt.	Tank regiment
Panzerspähtrupp (-s)	Pz.Sp.Tr.	Armored reconnaissance car section
Panzerspähwagen	Pz.Sp.W.	Armored reconnaissance car
Panzerspähzug	Pz.Sp.Zg.	Armored reconnaissance platoon
Panzersturmbatterie		Tank assault battery
Panzertruppe (-n)		Tank units
Panzerwagen	PW	Armoured car, combat car, tank
Panzerwaffe		Armored command
Panzerzerstörer		Tank destroyer
Panzerzerstörer-Bataillon		Tank destroyer battalion
Parteigenosse	PG	Party member of NSDAP
Parteitag		Party rally
Personalbefehl		Personal order
Personalabteilung		Personnel section
Personenkraftwagen	PKW, Pkw	Passenger vehicle
Pionier (-e)	Pi.	Engineer
Pionier-Bataillon	Pi.Btl.	Engineer battalion
Pionierkompanie	Pi.Kp.	Engineer company
Pionierzug	Pi.Zg.	Engineer platoon
Polizeiabteilung		Police battalion
Portepeeunteroffizier	Portepee-Uffz.	Non-commissioned officer above the level of Feldwebel
Quartiermeister	Qu.M., QM	Quartermaster
Quartiermeisterabteilung	Qu.M-Abt.	Supply group of staff section
Quartiermeisterstaffel	QM-Staf.	Qaurtermaster staff
Rata (-s)		Russian fighter plane of type Polikarpov I-16
Regiment (-er)	Reg., Rgt.	Regiment
Regiment SS-*Deutschland*	Rgt. SS *D*	SS Regiment *Deutschland*
Regiment SS-*Der Führer*	Rgt. SS *DF*	SS Regiment *Der Führer*
Regiment SS 11	Rgt. SS 11	SS Regiment 11

German (plural form in parentheses where applicable)	Abbreviation	English equivalent
Regimentsbefehl		Regimental order
Regiments-Gefechtsstand	Rgt.Gef.St.	Regimental headquarters or command post
Regimentsstab		Regimental staff
Reichsführer-SS	RSFF	SS Commander for the Reich
Reichführung-SS		SS Headquarters
Reichsheer	RH	Army of the Reich
Reichskanzler		Reich chancellor
Reichskanzlei		Reich chancellery
Reichsminister		Minister of the Reich
Reichspräsident		President of the Reich
Reichssicherheitsdienst	RSD	Reich security service
Reichswehr		Reich Armed Forces
Richtkanonier		Gunner
Ritterkreuz (-e)	RK	Knight's Cross
Rollbahn		Runway (of airstrip) or March route
Rückwärtige Dienste	Rückw.Dienste	Supply services
SA-Befehl		SA order
Sanitätsabteilung	San.Abt.	Ambulance battalion
Sanitätskolonne		Ambulance column
Sanitätskompanie	San.Kp.	Ambulance company
Sanitätskraftwagen	Sankra	Ambulance
Sanitätsstaffel		Ambulance section
Schallmeßbatterie		Sound-ranging battery
Schallmeßkompanie		Sound-ranging company
Schallmeßzug		Sound-ranging platoon
Schießschule		Firing school
Schnelle Gruppe	Schn.Gr.	Rapid-advance group
Schutzpolizei	Schupo	State police
Schutzstaffeln	SS	Elite guard of NSDAP
Schützenbrigade		Rifle brigade
Schützenkompanie		Rifle company
Schützenpanzerwagen	SPW	Armored personnel carrier
Schützenregiment	SR	Rifle regiment
Schwer	s	Heavy (applied to weapons or units, e.g. sFH, sGr.Wf., sIG, sMG)
Schwimmlastkraftwagen		Amphibian truck
Schwimmpanzerkampfwagen		Amphibian tank
Schwimmvolkswagen		Amphibian Volkswagen vehicle
Selbstfahrlafette	SFL	Self-propelled mount
Sicherungsdivision		Security division
Sicherungskompanie		Security company
SMKA-Munition		Infantry ammunition capable of piercing armour
Sonderkommando		Special commando
Spähtrupp(-s)		Reconnaissance unit
Sperrkreis		Blockade circle
Spielmann (Spielleute)		Bandsman
Spielmannszug		Bandsmen platoon
Sportpalast		Sports palace
SS-Sportgemeinschaft Lichterfelde		SS Sport Association
SS-Verfügungsdivision	SS-V-Div.	SS reserve division
SS-Verfügungstruppen	SS-VT	SS reserve units
Stab		Staff
Stabschef		Chief of staff
Stabswache		Headquarters guard
Standarte		Regiment (in the SS only)

German (plural form in parentheses where applicable)		Abbreviation	English equivalent
Standarte	(see *Leibstandarte SS Adolf Hitler*) Standartenbefehl		Order from the *Leibstandarte*
Standartensonderbefehl			Special order from the *Leibstandarte*
Stellvertreter			Deputy
Storch			Fieseler "Storch" ["stork"] airplane used for liaison missions
Stoßtrupp (-s)			Assault troops
Sturm (Stürme)			Company (in the SS only)
Sturmabteilungen		SA	Storm trooper units of the NSDAP
Sturmgeschütz (-e)			Assault gun
Sturmgeschützbatterie		Stu.Gesch.Bttr.	Assault armored vehicle battery
Sturzkampfflugzeug		Stuka	Dive bomber
Tagebuch		Tgeb., Tgb.	Diary, daily log
Tambourmajor			Baton major
Tankkommandant			Tank commander
Tankwaffe			Tank command
Technischer Feuerwerker		TF	Technical officer
—Kraftfahrzeuge		TFK	Motor vehicles technical officer
—Nachrichten		TFN	Signals technical officer
—Pioniere		TFPi	Engineering technical officer
—Waffen		TFW	Weapons technical officer
Teileinheit		TE	Basic element of a unit
Tonne		t	Metric ton
Totenkopf-Division		*T*-Div.	SS "Death's Head" Division
Tross (-e)			Supply train
Unteroffizier		Uffz.	Non-commissioned officer
Verfügungsdivision		V-Div.	Reserve division
Verfügungstruppen		VT	Reserve units
Verfügungstross		V-Tross	Reserve supply train
Verkehrsreglungsbataillon			Traffic control battalion
Vermessungstrupp (-s)			Survey unit
Vermessungszug			Survey platoon
Vermißt		verm.	Missing in action
Verpeflegungsamt			Ration supply office
Verpflegungswagen		V-Wagen	Ration supply vehicle
Verteidigungsgruppe (-n)			Defensive force
Vertreter	(see Stellvertreter)		
Verwundet		verw.	Wounded in action
Vierlings-Flak			Four-barreled anti-aircraft gun
Vorausabteilung		VA	Advance battalion
Vorausbefördertes Personal		VP	Advance personnel
Vorgeschobener Beobachter		VB	Advance artillery observer
Vorhutbataillon			Advance guard battalion
Wachbataillon			Guard battalion
Wachkommando			Guard commando
Wachkompanie			Guard company
Wachtmeister			Sergeant-major (police)
Waffen-SS			Combat SS
Waffen und Munition		WaMun	Weapons and munitions
Wehrkreis			Military district
Wehrmacht			Armed Forces
Wehrmachtbericht			Armed Forces report
Wehrmacht-Heer		WH	Armed Forces Army
Werfer		Wf.	Smoke-shell projector (see also Nebelwerfer)

German (plural form in parentheses where applicable)	Abbreviation	English equivalent
Werferbatterie (see Nebelwerfer-Batterie)		
Werfer-Lehrregiment (see Nebelwerfer-Lehrregiment)		
Werfer-Regiment (see Nebelwerfer-Regiment)		
Werkstattkompanie	WK	Vehicle maintenance company
Werkstattzug		Vehicle mainteance platoon
Wespe		Light field howitzer on self-propelled mount (literally: "wasp")
Wettertrupp (-s)		Meteorological unit
Winterhilfswerk		Compulsory charity ostensibly to relieve hardship during the winter months
Wirtschafts-Bataillon	Wi-Btl.	Supply battalion responsible for producing foodstuffs (contains baking and butchering companies)
X-Zeit		X-Time (secret or as-yet-undetermined time for beginning of an attack)
Zug (Züge)	Zg.	Platoon
Zugführer		Platoon leader
Zugkraftwagen	Zkw	Half-track carrier
zur besonderen Verwendung	z.b.V, ZBV	Special-missions

Abbreviations for position designations

Abbreviation	German term	English equivalent
Ia	1. Generalstabsoffizier (Führung)	First general staff officer (Leadership)
Ib	2. Generalstabsoffizier (Versorgung)	Second general staff officer (Supply)
Ic	3. Generalstabsoffizier (Feindlage, Abwehr, Sicherheit)	Third general staff officer (Enemy position, defense, security = intelligence)
IIa	Adjutant beim Stabe	Staff adjutant
IIb	Personalabteilung	Personnel section
III	Gericht	Court
IVa	Verwaltung	Administration
IVb	Arzt	Doctor
VI	Weltanschauliche Schulung	Philosophical indoctrination
O 1	1. Ordonnanzoffizier (bei Ia)	First special-missions officer (to Ia)
O 2	2. Ordonnanzoffizier (bei Ib)	Second special-missions officer (to Ib)
O 3	3. Ordonnanzoffizier (bei Ic)	Third special-missions officer (to Ic)
O 4	4. Ordonnanzoffizier (bei Ia)	Fourth special-missions officer (to Ia)
O 5	5. Ordonnanzoffizier (Begleitoffizier des Divisions-Kommandeur)	Fifth special-missions officer (Accompanying officer for the Divisional commander)

Examples of method of unit designation employed

II./SS-AR	II. Abteilung of the SS Artillery Regiment
3./SS-AR	3. Batterie of the SS Artillery Regiment
IV. (s)/SS-AR	IV. heavy Abteilung of the SS Artillery Regiment
II./*LSSAH*	II. Bataillon of the *Leibstandarte SS Adolf Hitler*
II./*LAH*	II. Bataillon of the *Leibstandarte SS Adolf Hitler*
5./*LAH*	5. Kompanie of the *Leibstandarte SS Adolf Hitler*
I./1.	I. Bataillon of the 1. Panzergrenadier-Regiment
I./1	I. Bataillon of Panzergrenadier-Regiment 1

Appendix No. 4

Divisional headquarters
2.2.1943

SS-Panzergrenadierdivision
Leibstandarte Adolf Hitler
Abteilung Ia Le./Ga.

Divisionsbefehl No. 1

1) *Numerically superior enemy forces* have launched a massive attack with tanks and artillery against our defensive front on the Don and have broken through. Today, 2.2.1943, they stand with infantry and cavalry units (as well as some tanks and weak artillery) along the general line from the eastern bank of the Oskol east of Ssenkowo and Kupjansk — western bank of the Oskol north of Kupjansk — Dwuretschnaja. Numerically superior forces are waging a strong attack on Regiment *Deutschland*, deployed on the high ground southeast and northeast of Olchowarka. Between Kupjansk and Olchowatka, a small unit of the Panzergrenadierdivision *Großdeutschland* is defending itself against an attack from the south against Welikij Burluk. An enemy column has crossed the railway line near the Burluk station and is moving toward the west.
We can expect the enemy forces to continue to move to the west and to reach the road between Kupjansk and Tschugujew in the night between 2.2.1943 and 2.3.1943.
2) *SS-Panzergrenadierdivision LAH*, subordinated to the Generalkommando of the SS-Panzerkorps, is to assemble in the area southeast of Charkow and to stand at the disposal of the Oberkommando of the Heer so that it can be deployed at short notice if need be to defend the Donez sector between Smijew and Chotomlja.
3) *SS-Panzergrenadierdivision LSSAH* is to position itself in order to be able to defend the forces assembling in the designated Donez area. The defensive positioning should be as follows:
The Pionier-Bataillon/*LSSAH*, the 2. Panzergrenadier-Regiment *LSSAH*, the Aufklärungsabteilung/*LSSAH*, and the 1. Panzergrenadier-Regiment *LSSAH* in the front line.
The Division is to delay the enemy's advance by using mobile forces to engage the enemy in front of our position.
The main battle line (map 1:100,000): southern and eastern edge of Smijew — southern edge of Sidki — western edge of the forest west of Genijewka — eastern edge of Scheludowka — eastern edge of Skripai — southeastern edge of the forest west of Malinowka — southeastern edge of Malinowka — Donez line three kilometers south of Kizewka — southern and eastern bank of the Donez as far as and including Chotomlja.
Borders of the sector:
Between the Pionier-Bataillon and the 2. Panzergrenadier-Regiment LSSAH:
Railway bridge at Sidki (held by the Pioniere) — northern tip of the forest near Kostjukowka — Hf. Omeltschenkow — western bank of the Ssuchoj Liman — road to Isjum (held by the 2. Panzergrenadier-Regiment *LSSAH*).

Between the 2. Panzergrenadier-Regiment LSSAH and the Aufklärungsabteilung:
Northern tip of Nowopokrowskoje — northern tip of the forest southwest of Malinowka — bend in the railway line at the southern tip of Malinowka (held by the 2. Regiment) — Point 136.7 (2. Regiment) — southwestern tip of Grakowo — road to Isjum (Aufklärungsabteilung).
Between the Aufklärungsabteilung and the 1. Panzergrenadier-Regiment LSSAH:
Southern edge of Kamennaja Jaruga — southwestern and southeastern tips of the forest east of Kamennaja — Donez riverbed north of Point 98.6 and Point 106.5 (Aufklärungsabteilung) — southwestern tip of Puschkarnoje — southern edge of Wassilenkowo — northern edge of Otratnoje — northern edge of Arkadijewka — northern edge of Kupjansk.
A line of combat outposts is to be reconnoitered by the sector commanders and their position reported.

4) *Combat missions*:
   a) The reinforced Pionier-Bataillon (minus one Kompanie, reinforced by the 2./Flakabteilung) is to establish defenses on the southern and eastern edge of Smijew and on the southern edge of Sidki as far as and including the railway bridge. Until the arrival of the commander of the Pionier-Bataillon, it is to be led by the Chef of the 1./Pionier-Bataillon *LSSAH*.
   b) *The reinforced 2. Panzergrenadier-Regiment LSSAH* (the 5./Flakbteilung, the 2./Panzerjägerabteilung, further subordinations as the situation develops) is to offer defense in the sector from the forest west of Genijewka (inclusive of it) — railway stretch southwest of Malinokwa (inclusive). At the same time, it is to hold back combat-strength reserve forces. In the event of an enemy advance across the line Isjum — Kunje, the Regiment is to delay the enemy's movement by sending one reinforced Kompanie to engage him in battle in the Balaklaja area.
   c) *The reinforced Aufklärungsabteilung LSSAH* (the 3./Artillerie-Regiment, one-third of the 1./Panzerjägerabteilung) is to provide defense in the sector Malinowka — bend in the Donez south of Kizewka. It is to use one Kompanie to delay the enemy's advance along the road from Kupjansk to Tschugujew in the Schewtschenkowo region. The Division must make sure that the Malinowka bridgehead remains firmly in our hands for the deployment of the Panzerregiment. (Reinforcement by two Kompanien if the situation develops.)
   d) *The reinforced 1. Panzergrenadier-Regiment LSSAH* (the I./Artillerie-Regiment, the 3. and 4./Flakabteilung) is to offer defense in the sector from the bend in the Donez — Chotomlja (inclusive of it). It is to hold back combat-strength reserves.
   e) *Artillerie-Regiment LSSAH* (minus the I. and II. Abteilung) is to assign the following for cooperation:
   The III./Artillerie-Regiment (two heavy Feldhaubitzen-Batterien) with the reinforced 2. Panzergrenadier-Regiment; the IV./Artillerie-Regiment (two heavy Feldhaubitzen-Batterien and one 10-centimeter Kanonen-Batterie) with the 1. Panzergrenadier-Regiment; the Werfer-Batterie at the Division's disposal.

It is to move into position in the main battle field so that it can accomplish the following principal missions:

I. covering the units as they move into their defensive positions;

II. supporting the fighting of the combat outposts;

III. supporting the assembly of the units deployed in front of our positions;

IV. concentrating the fire from one heavy and one light Abteilung in front of the section of the battle line held by the Aufklärungsabteilung and the 1. Panzergrenadier-Regiment *LSSAH* and in front of the northern wing of the 2. Panzergrenadier-Regiment *LSSAH*; concentrating fire from one heavy Abteilung in front of the Pionier-Bataillon's battle line;

V. barrage fire in front of the main battle line;
barrage fire areas are to be arranged in agreement with the sector commanders.
Until the Regimental commander arrives, the oldest commander present will be in charge.
The Batterien are to be moved into the reconnoitered positions as soon as they are unloaded from transport.

f) *The Panzerregiment* is to remain in its billeting area to stand at the Division's disposal. It is to reconnoiter a march route and possibilities for deployment in the event of an enemy breakthrough into the positions of the Aufklärungsabteilung and the reinforced 1. Panzergrenadier-Regiment *LSSAH.*

g) The Sturmgeschützabteilung is to stand in its billeting area at the Division's disposal and is to reconnoiter march routes and possibilities for action in the event that the enemy makes a breakthrough into the positions of the Pionier-Bataillon and the 2. Panzergrenadier-Regiment *LSSAH.*
The 1./Sturmgeschützabteilung is to be moved to Tschugujew until the Panzerregiment arrives.

h) *The Panzerjägerabteilung* is to provide one Kompanie each as reinforcements to the 2. Panzergrenadier-Regiment *LSSAH* and the Aufklärungsabteilung. Those Kompanien which have arrived at this point are to remain for the time being in Kotschelok to stand at the Division's disposal.
The Chef of the 1. Kompanie is to establish contact with the Aufklärungsabteilung and the 1. Panzergrenadier-Regiment *LSSAH*; the Chef of the 2. Kompanie with the 2. Panzergrenadier-Regiment *LSSAH.*

i) *The Flakabteilung* is to deploy the following Batterien to the units indicated, to which they will be subordinated:
the 2. Batterie to the Pionier-Bataillon,
the 3. and 4. Batterie to the 1. Panzergrenadier-Regiment *LSSAH*, and
the 5. Batterie to the 2. Panzergrenadier-Regiment *LSSAH.*
the 1. and 6. Batterie are to be brought by the Flakabteilung into position in the Tschugujew area.

5) Reconnaissance:
   a) Ground reconnaissance should be conducted along the borders of the sector as far as the line Ssawinzi — Powelkowka (sixteen kilometers southwest of Kupjansk) — railway line near the Gusinka railway station (twenty kilometers north west of Kupjansk) — railway line as far as the Burluk station. The *Aufklärungsabteilung* is to reconnoiter in the direction of the railway line Gusinka — Burluk (across the line Petschenegi — Artemowka) at dawn on 3.2.1943.
   b) Aerial reconnaissance has been requested and is being conducted in the area Tschugujew — Kupjansk — Wolokonowlka — Woltschansk.
6) *Terrain fortifications*:
   a) *Trench digging* should be performed as quickly as possible by conscripting the populace and by personal involvement of all the commanders and the Chefs. All works are to be camouflaged from enemy aerial reconnaissance.
   b) *Roadblocks*: Mines are to be laid on the main march routes and in the terrain in front of the main battle line. *Make maps of your mines!* Mine distribution is planned to be done by the Ib on the night between 2.3.43 and 3.3.43.
   The bridges in front of the battle line should be prepared for demolition.
7) *Traffic control*:
   Heavy retreat traffic can be expected on the east-west road. The sector commanders are to make the preparations necessary to avoid traffic congestion.
   Those elements of the Feldgendarmerie-Kompanie *LSSAH* which have already arrived are to be deployed by Untersturmführer Buschhausen to keep Thoroughfare V (Dg. 5) open. A team of horses should be moved into position to assist in overcoming the steep climb on the eastern edge of Tschugujew.
8) *Communications*: The Nachrichtenabteilung is to establish:
   a) telephone communications to all fighting units,
   b) free radio access while in contact with the enemy, otherwise radio preparedness.
9) *Light signals*:
   Single white flare = Here we are!
   Single red signal flare = Enemy attacking!
   Single green signal flare = Move fire forward!
   Violet or blue smoke grenade = Tank warning!
   The main recognition signal for German troops on the ground is the orange smoke signal.
10) *Ambulance services*:

Wounded assembly point I	western edge of Tschugujew
Wounded assembly point II	northern edge of Samostje Sidki
Main medical clearing station	Tschugujew (elements of Sanitätsabteilung *Das Reich*)

Starting at 16.00 hours on 3.2.1943.

Until the arrival of the ambulance services, the Regimental doctor of the 1. Panzer-grenadier-Regiment and the Regimental doctor of the 2. Panzergrenadierregiment are to prepare the medical clearing station.

11) *Munitions depot*: Lossewo.
Until the arrival of the Divisions-Nachshubtruppe, ammunition should be requested from the Abteilung Ib and, upon instructions, picked up from the *main ammunition depot in Magdeburg*, on the eastern edge of Charkow.
12) The Divisional headquarters: Tschugujew.

Commander of the SS-Panzergrenadier-Regiment *LSSAH*
i.V.

signed
SS-Standartenführer

Appendix No. 5

Remarks on Hans Speidel's book "Aus unserer Zeit" (Berlin: Propyläen Verlag, 1977. Page 142 ff.)

Generalleutnant (Bundeswehr) Professor Dr. Hans Speidel, in his above-mentioned book, deals with the factual course of events in a rather loose fashion, as the events around Charkow demonstrate. The present author rests this statement on the Kriegstagbuch of Armeeabteilung Lanz, later called Armeeabteilung Kempf, and finally known as Armeeoberkommando 8. Dr. Speidel was responsible for the content of that combat log, because he served as Chef of the Generalstab of these command bodies.

On page 142 of "Aus unserer Zeit," Dr. Speidel writes:

> "In the evening of February 6, General Lanz called me from the Führer's headquarters to say that Hitler would not budge from his decision to have the SS-Panzerkorps attack to the east and to defend Charkow as a fortress: 'Charkow remains a fortress which must be defended to the last man.' Upon his return, Lanz was briefed on the new situation. He then flew immediately to the Divisional commander of SS-Division *Das Reich* and, on his own initiative, altered this senseless attack order."

The Kriegstagebuch has the following to say about this "initiative" on the part of the Oberbefehlshaber to change the senseless attack order:

> "On 7.2.1943, at 16.00 hours, the SS-Panzerkorps gave a written evaluation of the situation. It ended with the decision: suspension of the attack toward Artemowka. Attack with Panzers against Rudki and south of Welikij Burluk.
>
> At 16.00 hours, there was a discussion of the situation among the Oberbefehlshaber (General Lanz), General Hausser, Chef Cramer, General Korten, and General Waver (city Kommandant for the city of Charkow).
>
> The result of General Lanz's visit to the Führer's headquarters: [details omitted here].
>
> The Oberbefehlshaber summarized the Korps' mission as follows:
>
> > The SS-Panzerkorps was to cooperate with the Divisionen *LAH* and *Das Reich* to destroy the enemy forces in Artemowka. To this end, *Das Reich* was to deploy as strong a force as possible. The *Leibstandarte* was to join the attack by *Das Reich* at an appointed time.
>
> At 19.30 hours, the Chef of the SS-Panzerkorps reported the result of the attack of the day:
>
> The attack on Artemowka could not be carried out because the snow drifts prevented fuel from being delivered and the Schützenpanzerwagen-Bataillon from arriving...
>
> At 21.30 hours, the Chef pointed out the general sense expressed in the SS-Panzerkorps' daily report that the attack on the following day would not be made. Oberbefehlshaber Generalfeldmarschall von Weichs had ordered, however, that the attack by SS-*Das Reich* should be carried out under all circumstances just as had been discussed with General Hausser. Objections would no longer be entertained. Generalfeldmarschall von Weichs had

committed himself personally to the attack before the Führer. The SS-Panzerkorps was made aware of this.

At 21.55 hours, the Chef of the SS-Panzerkorps reported:

1. There are sizable enemy forces starting today at the seam between the *LAH* and *Das Reich* in the Chotomlja river valley. This is a sign that a new enemy force is moving in this direction.
2. ...

   The report from Division *Das Reich* had not yet been received. It is requested that it be given to us first and then immediately telephoned to the Chef of the Generalstab of the Heer.

At 00.45 hours on 8.2.43, the Ia of the SS-Panzerkorps received word that the attack was to be executed, under orders from both the Heeresgruppe and the Armeeabteilung. Orders from the Führer!

At 00.45 hours, there was a call from the Chef of the Generalstab of the SS-Panzerkorps saying that after a conference with the Chef of the Generalstab of the Heer, the thrust on Artemowka would not be carried out. The Chef of the Armee answered that he could not acknowledge that instruction. General Lanz insisted expressly on the Führer's order.

At 02.45 hours, the Oberkommando of the Heer issued the following order: the order for SS-Division *Das Reich* to attack remained in force... This order was subsequently transmitted to the SS-Panzerkorps."

These entries prove beyond any doubt, first, that it was not the Divisional commander who lodged his objection with Hitler, as Speidel claims, but the Chef of the SS-Panzerkorps; second, that the Chef of the SS-Panzerkorps did not complain directly to Hitler, but to the Chef of the Generalstab. Finally, this unusual step was not taken to report, as Speidel claims, that Lanz was unwilling to execute an order from the Führer; rather, it was an attempt to have the Chef of the Generalstab of the Heer withdraw an order from the Führer. In addition, General Zeitzler, the Chef of the Generalstab of the Heer, had given Obergruppenführer Hausser permission at the conference at the Führer's headquarters to approach him directly "if he should have any concerns whatsoever."

The rescinding of the attack order is justified in the next entry in the Armeeabteilung's Kriegstagebuch:

> "At 11.00 hours, there was a telephone conference between the Chef of the SS-Panzerkorps and the Chef [Speidel himself]. The strong enemy pressure on the northern flank (Belgorod) was making a new decision necessary. Belgorod can no longer be held with the weak forces there. Infanteriedivision *Großdeutschland* wants to withdraw to Woltschansk, because the line Jefremowka — Pankoff can no longer be held. The SS-Panzerkorps must therefore be pulled back, as well. The thrust to the southwest is no longer possible, because the events in Belgorod are destroying the northern flank of the SS-Panzerkorps."

Speidel's version: "Generalfeldmarschall von Manstein, to whom we were subordinated on February 13 [it was actually the 14th!], had vainly attempted to prohibit use of this channel of reporting." This statement is very misleading, because von Manstein during the period in question (6.2 - 8.2) did not have any authority whatsoever over Armeeabteilung Lanz.

Speidel continues in his description of the abandonment of Charkow:

"Hitler demanded that both the Feldmarschälle (von Manstein and von Weichs) account for what had happened. On February 17, he came with Generaloberst Zeitzler to Feldmarschall von Manstein in Saporoshje. Lanz was also sent there, and Hitler expressed his extreme displeasure to him."

This "demand for an account" and this "extreme displeasure" are not found anywhere in von Manstein's "Verlorene Siege" or in the Kriegstagebuch of Armeeabteilung Lanz.

There, the entry reads only:

"At 13.00 hours, there was a conference of commanders in Walki. The Oberbefehlshaber related an excerpt from the conference with the Führer at the Oberkommando of Heeresgruppe Süd on 17.2.1943. The Führer did not intend to withdraw in a great leap; rather he wanted to continue the current type of combat.

The Oberbefehlshaber, when asked about the abandonment of Charkow and the area to the east, explained that the reasons for it were the facts that the 298. and 320. Infanteridivision were surrounded, the flanks were in grave danger, and the threat existed that all our troops in Charkow would be surrounded.

The Oberbefehlshaber related to the Führer his concern about the threat to the Armeeabteilung's flank resulting from the large gap betwen the unit and the Panzerarmeeoberkommando 1 and Armeeoberkommando 2."

Finally, it should be noted that Kampfgruppe Peiper of the SS-Panzergrenadierdivision *LAH* was the unit which captured Belgorod and not, as Speidel maintains, Panzergrenadierdivision *Großdeutschland*. According to the Kriegstagebuch of Armeeabteilung Lanz (entry of 18.3.1943, 15.10 hours), the armoured force of *Großdeutschland* was engaged in heavy tank combat in the area around Orlowka, twenty-five kilometers southwest of Belgorod, under the command of Oberst Graf Strachwitz. Clearly, it was not in Belgorod when Peiper captured it (18.3.1943 at 11.25 hours).

In conclusion, we would like to point out that the SS-Panzergrenadierdivision *LSSAH* was directly subordinated to the Armeeabteilung of which Speidel was the Chef of Generalstab from 21.2.1943 to 3.3.1943, with no Generalkommando standing between them. (See section II, Part Ia of this volume, entry for 21.1.1943.) The author to this day has not changed his opinion of the harmonious tenor of this period.

Appendix No. 6

Telegram No. 96

11.12.1943

Directive for Conduct of the Attack on 11.12.1943:

Attacking across a wide plain, devoid of any cover, against a fortified town demands a careful coordination of all the movements of the Infanterie and Panzers with the firing plan of all the heavy weapons. In particular, the balance must be carefully considered between the subduing effect of the fire from Artillerie and Werfer and the immediacy of the breakthrough after it. It will be necessary to have reached the start point for the assault by the time the artillery barrage begins.

The attack will be divided into the following phases:

1. Scouting of the approach from the preparation area to the assault starting point. Keep well in mind that the armoured force must make the move at high speed and in one fell swoop. Calculate the time needed exactly.
2. Briefing all the unit leaders on the terrain. Moving all the 8.8-centimeter, light, and medium Flak into position to defend against anti-tank guns attempting to outflank our move and in order to cover our flanks. Careful aiming of all heavy weapons, Artillerie, and Werfer.
3. Capturing the assault starting point with the armoured force (Panzers, Sturmgeschütze, Schützenpanzerwagen-Bataillon, and the armoured Artillerie) in one move at as high a speed as possible. During the move, smoke screening of the attack wing by release of smoke candles. Infanterie mounted on the Panzers; Artillerie and heavy weapons support by firing on recognized anti-tank positions (firing a combination of smoke and explosives).
4. Fire attack by the Artillerie and Werfer. Immediately following, breakthrough by the armoured force at high speed. Structured in two waves:

   First wave: Thrust deep into enemy territory.

   Second wave: Defeat of the enemy defense at the point of breakthrough in cooperation between the Schützenpanzerwagens, the Grenadiere, and the Infanterie advancing on foot. If necessary, fire cover should be provided for the advance of the Infanterie.

Ia

Appendix No. 7

To Divisional commanders of the *LSSAH*, *SS-Das Reich*, 19. Panzerdivision, 7. Panzerdivision, Qu./IVb as information

January 12, 1944, 22.05 hours

To
Divisional commanders
of the *LSSAH*
SS-Das Reich
19. Panzerdivision
7. Panzerdivision
Qu./IVb as information

I have discovered that a Divisional doctor with a faulty understanding of the situation has entered a general request for his Division to be relieved for purposes of health but has failed to inform the Korps doctor in a sufficiently bureaucratic and statistical manner of the actual illnesses affecting the men. It was left to my personal observation to determine the horrifying extent to which stomach and intestinal disorders have increased in the unit. I request the medical officer of each unit not only to be completely informed on the condition in the unit assigned to his medical care, but also to report on it to his superiors in a factual manner in keeping with the conditions. Above all, I ask each one to take all conceivable and possible steps to improve conditions.

I request all commanders to inspect their medical officers' activities personally to determine what they are doing in the areas of disease prevention and health maintenance; the officers must be monitored constantly in these areas.

In order to contain the stomach and intestinal diseases currently so prevalent, I order the following:

1) The consumption of freshly-slaughtered meat is prohibited. I have no objections if the units are given meat to roast which has been refrigerated and stored.
2) Every unit doctor must make sure that sufficient quantities of specially prepared foods are cooked for those ill with stomach and intenstinal diseases.
   Resistance on the part of the Intendantur [general staff administrative section dealing mostly with supply] to requests for special foods should be taken care of in each case by the unit commander.
3) Each unit doctor is to make sure that abdominal belts are issued properly and distributed correctly.
4) Our current position on the front allows the establishment of warm-up rooms and wash facilities. I direct your attention to my order for our subordinated construction Pionierkompanie to be deployed only for the building of warm-up facilities in the battle area.
5) The Zahlmeister [paymaster officials] and Hauptfeldwebel [first sergeants] must establish wash facilities with the assistance of the civilian population in order to ensure that the fighting troops receive regular changes of clean linen.
6) Wherever the troops deployed at the front are missing winter clothing or are wearing worn-out clothing, the needed items should in all cases be taken from the supply trains.

Appendix No. 8

Number of enemy tanks destroyed from 25.12.1943 through 18.1.1944

	LSSAH	SS-*Reich*	Panzerdivision Källner	7. Panzer-division	1. Panzer-division	Total
1. Disabled by Panzers	184	12 1 damaged 1 assault gun	44	53	140	435 = 64 %
2. Disabled by Sturmgeschütze	40	22	—	6	—	68 = 10 %
3. Disabled by self-propelled Pak	5	14	7	10	8	44 = 6 %
4. Disabled by Pak (mot. Z)	5	12	7 by 8.8-cm Flak	14 3 by 8.8-cm Flak	5 5 by 8.8-cm Flak	51 = 7.5%
5. Destroyed by Artillerie	31	5	1	4	7	48 = 7 %
6. Destroyed by mines	2	—	—	1	—	3 = 0.5%
7. Destroyed by magnetic anti-tank hollow charges	4	2 1 assault gun	—	—	3	10 = 1.5%
8. Destroyed by Faust patronen	1	—	—	—	4	5 = 1 %
9. Destroyed by bazookas	5	—	—	—	—	5 = 1 %
10. Destroyed by other weapons	11	1	—	1	—	13 = 1.5%
						682

Appendix No. 9

Generalkommando XXIV. Panzerkorps
—Abteilung Ia—

Korps headquarters
7.4.1944

Supplement to weekly report

Combat force 1. SS-Panzerdivision LSSAH

1) a) five battle-weary Panzergrenadier-Bataillone,
immobile;
one battle-weary Panzergrenadier-Bataillon (armoured),
5% mobile;
I./SS-Panzergrenadierregiment 1 *LSSAH*:
twelve light MG, two heavy MG;
II./SS-Panzergrenadierregiment 1 *LSSAH*:
ten light MG, one heavy MG;
III./SS-Panzergrenadierregiment 1 *LSSAH*:
eleven light MG, three heavy MG;
I./SS-Panzergrenadierregiment 2 *LSSAH*:
five light MG;
II./SS-Panzergrenadierregiment 2 *LSSAH*:
Four light MG, one heavy MG, two medium Granatwerfer:
III. (armoured)/ SS-Panzergrenadierregiment *LSSAH*:
two light MG;
one battle-weary Panzer-Aufklärungsabteilung immobile:
five light MG.

b) one weak Panzer-Pionier-Bataillon immobile:
eighteen light MG.

2) Two light Feldhaubitzen-18 100% mobile;
one light Feldhaubitze-18 (on self-propelled mount) 100% mobile;
one 15-centimeter Werfer and one 21-centimeter Werfer 100% mobile.

3) Infanteriegeschütze — — — — —

4) One medium Grenadier-Panzerwagen ready for action;
two Panzer VI's ready for action;
nine 7.5-centimeter Sturmgeschütze ready for action.

5) The force's communications equipment is insufficient.
Wire and radio stations are missing.
The radio stations the unit does have are not fully mobile and can only be transported and used under very limited conditions in rough terrain.
Repair equipment is missing altogether. Repairs have been made to this point with whatever materials could be found and under emergency conditions.
Replacement parts have been patched together; there is an insufficient supply of them.

Appendix No. 10
List of those holding posts SS-Panzergrenadierdivision *LSSAH* (Divisionsstab) (From 22.10.1943 called 1. SS-Panzerdivision *LSSAH*)

	Feb. - Mar., 1943	July, 1943	Oct., 43 - Apr., 44	July, 1944	Dec., 1944	Feb. - May, 1945
Divisional commander	SS-Ogruf. u. Gen. d. Waffen-SS Dietrich	SS-Oberführer Theodor Wisch	SS-Brig.Fhr. u. Gen.Mj. d. W-SS Theodor Wisch	SS-Brig.Fhr. u. Gen.Mj. d. W-SS Theodor Wisch	SS-Brig.Fhr. u. Gen.Mj. d. W-SS Mohnke	Brig.Fhr. Mohnke Brig.Fhr. Kumm
Führungsabteilung Ia (Administrative section) 1. Generalstabsoffizier	Stbf. Lehmann	Stbf. Lehmann	Stbf. Lehmann	Ostbf. Grensing Stbf. Ziemssen	Stbf. Ziemssen Stbf. Tiemann	Ostbf. Ziemssen
Ordonnanz-Offizier 1 (O 1)	Hst. Buchsein	Hst. Buchsein	Hst. Tiemann Hst.Taubert	Hst. Taubert	Hst. Taubert	Hst. Bernard
3. Generalstabsoffizier Ic (intelligence) Ordonnanz-Officier (O 3)	Hst.Maas Ust. Härtel	i.V.Ust. Härtel	Hst. Vögtel †	Hst. Bernhard Ost. de Groof	Hst. Bernhard Ost. de Groof	Ust. Walter Ost. de Groof
Divisional Cartographic unit Ia mess	Ust. Tamm	—	—	—	—	—
Leader of communications services (L.D.N.)	Ost. Liebrich	Ust. Fritsche	Ust. Fritsche	Ost. Fritsche	?	?
Divisions-Sicherungskompanie Feldgendarmeriekompanie	Hst. Richter Hst. Hildebrand	Hst. Richter Ost. Rosenstengel	Hst. Linden Ost. Rosenstengel	? ?	? ?	? ?
Abteilung VI (Philosophical indoctrination) Care of the unit	Ust. Hannig	Ust. Pröschold	Ust. Pröschold	Ost. Pröschold	?	?
Adjutant: IIa	Stbf. Schiller	Stbf. Junge, Max	Stbf. Junge, Max	Stbf. Junge, Max	Hst. Meyer Hst. Kioer	Hst. Lange, Fritz Hst. Dinse
Abteilung IIb Acompanying officer for commander	Ost. Ritz, Ost. d. R. Jungell, Ost. d. R. Frhr. v. Waldenfels					
Abteilung III (Division Court)	Stbf. Dr. Greineder Hstuf. Jochum	Hst. Jochum	Stbf. Jochum	Stbf. Jochum	?	?
Kommandant of Stab quarters	Hst. d. R. Korsemann	Stbf. Korsemann	Hst. Linden	Hst. Scheeler	?	?
Graves registration officer	Ust. Hanisch	?	?	?	?	?

Continuation of Divisionsstab of SS-Panzergrenadierdivision *LSSAH* (From 22.10.1943 called 1. S-Panzerdivision *LSSAH*)

	Feb. - Mar., 1943	July, 1943	Oct., 43 - Apr., 44	July, 1944	Dec., 1944	Feb. - May, 1945
Quartiermeisterabteilung Ib 2. Generalstabsoffizier	Ostbf. Ewert	Ostbf. Stoltz	Ostbf. Stoltz	Ostbf. Stoltz	Hst. Stegemann	Hst. Stegemann
Ordonnanzoffizier 2 (O 2) WaMun (Weapons and ammunition)	Ust. Schmitz Ust. (F) Schlömer	Ust. Stegemann Ust. (F) Schlömer	Ost. Stegemann Ust. (F) Schlömer	Ost. Stegemann Ust. (F) Schlömer	Ost. Kröger Ost. (F) Schlömer †	Ost. Kröger Ust. (F) Lange
Abteilung IVa Divisions-Intendant	Stbf. Bludau	Stbf. Tauber	Stbf. Tauber	Stbf. Tauber	Stbf. Dr. Grunert	Stbf. Dr. Grunert † Hst. Wülze
Abteilung IVb Division doctor, Division Dentist	Ostbf. Dr. Besuden Ostbf. Dr. Wagner	Stbf. Dr. Liebrich	Stbf. Dr. Liebrich	Stbf. Dr. Liebrich	Ostbf. Dr. Jackl	Ostbf. Dr. Jackl
Abteilung V Divisions-Ingenieur	Ostbf. (Ing) Groß, Heln	Ostbf. (Ing) Groß, Heln	Stbf. Gilles	Stbf. Gilles	Stbf. Gilles	Stbf. Gilles

SS-Panzergrenadierregiment 1 *LSSAH*
(Stab and Regimental Units)

	Feb. - Mar., 1943	July, 1943	Oct., 43 - Apr., 44	July, 1944	Dec., 1944	Feb. - May, 1945
Regimental commander	Staf. Witt	Ostbf. Frey	Ostbf. Frey; starting Feb. 1944, Kampfgruppe under Hst. Meier	Ostbf. Frey Stbf. Hansen, Max	Ostbf. Hansen, Max	Ostbf. Hansen, Max Ostbf. Neumann
Adjutant	Ost. v. Christen	Ost. Naujork	Ost. Gevellhoff ?	?	Ost. Mackensen	Ost. Lange
Ordonnanzoffizier	Ost. Breinlich	?	Ost. Walter Ust. Zaag	?	?	?
Administrative officer	Hst. Reichenbach	Hst. Reichenbach	Hst. Knoll	?	Hst. Krämer	Hst. Krämer
Doctor	Hst. Dr. Schulz, R.	Ost. Dr. v. Paternos Hst. Dr. Hentschel	Ost. Dr. v. Paternos Hst. Dr. Hentschel	Hst. Dr. v. Paternos	Hst. Dr. Williams	?
Motor vehicle technical officer (TFK)	Hst. Wiggers	Hst. Manthey	?	?	Ost. Hannes	Ost. Hannes
Signals officer	Ost. Schmaloer	Ost. Schmaloer	Ust. Schäfer	?	?	?
Stabskompanie	Hst. Schuch †	?	?	?	Ost. Gummersbach	?
16. (Flak)/1 (starting May, 1944, called 14. [Flak]/1)	Ost. Ball	?	Ost. Kunde	Ost. Schmitz Hst. Teich	Ost. Stuna	Ost. Stuna
17. (light Infanteriegeschütz)/1 (starting May, 1944, called 13. [light Infanteriegeschütz]/1)	Ost. Najork	?	Ost. Krause	?	Ost. Voss	?
18. (Panzerjäger)/1 (dissolved May, 1944)	Hst. Graetz	Hst. Graetz	Hst. Graetz	–	–	–
19. (Aufklärung)/1 (dissolved May, 1944)	Starting May, 1943	?	Ust. Poss	–	–	–
20. (Pionier)/1 (starting May, 1944, called 15. [Pionier]/1)	Starting May, 1943	?	?	Ust. Lenski	?	?
Reinforced Kompanie	Starting July, 1944	–	–	Ost. Kummert	?	?

I. Bataillon of SS-Panzergrenadierregiment 1 *LSSAH* (I./1)

	Feb. - Mar., 1943	July, 1943	Oct., 43 - Apr., 44	July, 1944	Dec., 1944	Feb. - May, 1945
Bataillon commander	Stbf. Frey	Stubaf. Schiller	Stbf. Schiller Hst. Lotter	Ostbf. Schiller Hst. Lotter[1]	Hst. Karst † Hst. Rink (1.1.44)	Hst. Rink Hst. Wandt (6.4.45)
Adjutant	Ost. Troschier †	?	Ost. Gevellhoff	Ost. Lange Ost. Gevellhoff[1]	?	Ust. Jehle
Ordonnanzoffizier	?	?	?	Oscha. Auerbach[1]	?	?
Administrative officer	Ust. Markows	?	?	?	?	?
Doctor	Ost. Dr. v. Paternos	?	?	Ost. Dr. Ehrlinger[1]	?	?
Motor vehicle technical officer (TFK)	Ust. Uhde	Ust. Uhde	?	?	?	Ost. Uhde Ust. Nellis
Kradmeldezug	Hscha. Meder	?	?	–	–	–
1. Kompanie	Hst. Springer	Ost. v. Christen †	?	Ost. Grathwohl[1]	?	?
2. Kompanie	Ost. Peinemann	Ost. Wolter	Ost. Rink	Ost. Rink Ust. Wrabetz[1]	Ost. Ulmer	Ost. Ulmer Ost. Vögler
3. Kompanie	Ost. Geßner	Ost. Dahlke Ust. Zaag	Hscha. (Fa) Hüser	Hst. Maurer Hst. Harrer[1]	Hst. Griese	
4. (MG) Kompanie (dissolved May, 1944)	Hst. Waldmüller	?	Ost. Lotter	–	–	–
5. (heavy) Kompanie (starting May, 1944, called 4. [heavy]/1)	Hst. Besch	Ost. Rosenstock	Hscha. Spelsberg	Ust. Kruse	Ost. Lotter	?

1. According to original documents of 16.7.1944 (Bundesarchiv-Militärarchiv file number BA-MA RS 4/1242)

II. Bataillon of SS-Panzergrenadierregiment 1 *LSSAH* (II./1)

	Feb. - Mar., 1943	July, 1943	Oct., 43 - Apr., 44	July, 1944	Dec., 1944	Feb. - May, 1945
Bataillon commander	Stbf. Hansen, Max	Stbf. Hansen, Max	Stbf. Hansen, Max KGr.	Ostbf. Hansen, Max	Hst. Unterkofler †	?
Adjutant	Ost. Meier, Heinz Ost. Schuhknecht	?	?	?	Ust. Gummersbach	?
Ordonnanzoffizier	Ost. Gruhlig	?	?	?	?	?
Administrative officer	Ost. Schulzer	?	?	?	?	?
Doctor	Ost. Dr. Slonek	Ost. Dr. Slonek	?	?	?	?
Motor vehicles technical officer(TFK)	Ust. Gude	Ost. Gude	?	?	?	?
6. Kompanie (Starting May, 1944, called 5./1)	Hst. Weiher	?	Ust. Förster	?	?	Ust. Stauß
7. Kompanie (starting May, 1944, called 6./1)	Ost. Denecke	Ost. Denecke	Ost Denecke Ust. Herfort	?	?	Ust. Lenski
8. Kompanie (starting May, 1944, called 7./1)	Hst. Friedrich	Ost. Müller	Ost. Schuhknecht Ust. Brandstätter Hst. Meier	Ost. Bruckmann	Ust. Sievers	Ost. Gummersbach
9. (MG) Kompanie (dissolved May, 1944)	Ost. Anderlik	?	?	—	—	—
10. (heavy) Kompanie (starting May, 1944, called 8. [heavy]/1)	Ost. Pinter, Rup.	?	?	Ost. Banasch	?	?

III. Bataillon of SS-Panzergrenadierregiment 1 *LSSAH* (III./1)

	Feb. - Mar., 1943	July, 1943	Oct., 43 - Apr., 44	July, 1944	Dec., 1944	Feb. - May, 1945
Bataillon commander	Ostbf. Weidenhaupt	Ostbf. Weidenhaupt	KGr.Rgt.1	Ostbf. Weidenhaupt Hst. Graetz	Hst. Böttcher Hst. Haft	?
Adjutant	Ust. Bode Ust. Rink	Ust. Banasch	Ust. Banasch	Ust. Kaiser Ust. Bode	?	?
Ordonnanzoffizier	Ust. Wessel			?	?	
Administrative officer	Ost. Bartling	Ust. Olbrich	Ust. Olbrich	?	?	Oscha. Arnold
Doctor	Ost. Dr. Ludwig	Ost. Dr. Ludwig Hst. Dr. Knoll	Hst. Dr. Knoll		?	?
Motor vehicle technical officer (TFK)	Ust. Rathey	?	?	?	?	?
Kradmeldezug	Ust. Hasse	?	?	–	–	–
11. Kompanie starting May, 1944, called 9./1)	Hst. Albrecht	Hst. Albrecht Ost. Schmid, Rud.	Ost. Schmid, Rud. † Ust. Schäfer	?	?	?
12. Kompanie (starting May, 1944, called 10./1)	Ost. Jürgensen	?	Ost. Günsche Ost. Hüttner	Ust. Nowotnik	?	?
13. Kompanie (starting May. 1944, called 11./1)	Hst. Urabl	?	Ost. Hasse	Ost. Hasse	?	Hst. Neuberth
14. (MG) Kompanie (dissolved May, 1944)	Hst. Timmermann	?	Ust. Haft	–	–	–
15. (heavy) Kompanie (starting May, 1944, called 12. [heavy]/1)	?	?	Ost. Glaser	?	?	?

SS-Panzergrenadierregiment 2 *LSSAH*
(Stab and Regimental Units)

	Feb. - Mar., 1943	July, 1943	Oct., 43 - Apr., 44	July, 1944	Dec., 1944	Feb. - May, 1945
Regimental commander	Staf. Wisch	Ostbf. Kraas	Ostbf. Kraas Stbf. Sandig KGr.	Ostbf. Sandig	Ostbf. Sandig	Ostbf. Siebken
Adjutant	Ost. Diefenthal	Ost. Hildebrandt ab 25.9.43	Ost. Lange Ost. Schermeng	Ostf. Hildebrandt Hst. Becker, Fritz	Hst. Bremer	Ust. Herrmann
Ordonnanzoffizier	Ust. Günsche Ost. Westemeyer	Ust. Klein	Ust. Schellmacher	Ust. Schellhammer	Ust. Schellhammer	?
Administrative officer	Hst. Lange	Hst. Löbig	Hst. Thiering Ost. Löbig	Hst. Thiering	?	?
Doctor Dentist	Hst. Dr. Vieweg Ust. Dr. Schmitt	Hst. Dr. Sauer Hst. Dr. Rudolph	Hst. Dr. Houtrow	Hst. Dr. Houtrow Hst. Müller, Wilh.	Hst. Dr. Houtrow	?
Motor vehicle technical officer (TFK) Weapons technical officer (TFW)	Stbf. Stoltz Ust. Röntgen	Ost. Lotz Ost. Schulze, Wilh.	Ost. Lotz ?	Hst. Bossen ?	? ?	? ?
Signals officer	Ust. Schermeng	Ost. Schermeng	Ost. Schermeng	Ost. Schermeng Ust. Fritsche	?	?
Stabskompanie	Ost. Wandt	?	?	?	?	?
15. (Flak)/2 (starting May, 1944, called 14. [Flak]/2)	Ost. Boysen	Hst. Boysen	Hst. Boysen Ost. Kunde Ost. Duppel	Ost. Duppel	Ost. Duppel	Ost. Duppel
16. (Infanteriegeschütz)/2 (starting May, 1944, called 13. [Infanteriegeschütz]/2)	Hst. Wiest	Ost. Brosch † Ust. Noth	Hst. Richter Ost. Noth	Hst. Wiest	Ost. Koch	?
17. Panzerjäger)/2 (dissolved May. 1944,)	Hst. Linden	Hst. Linden	Ost. Heiger † Ust. Graf †	?	?	?
18. (Aufklärung)/2 (dissolved May, 1944,)	Ost. Dix	Ost. Dix	Ost. Dix † Ost. Schmidt, Rud.	—	—	—
19. (Pionier)/2 (dissolved May, 1944)		Ost. Schlott	Ost. Schlott † Hst. Radon Ust. Haensel	?	—	—
Versorgungskompanie (Supply company formed May, 1944)				Hst. Bormann	?	?

I. Bataillon of SS-Panzergrenadierregiment 2 *LSSAH* (I./2)

	Feb. - Mar., 1943	July, 1943	Oct., 43 - Apr., 44	July, 1944	Dec., 1944	Feb. - May, 1945
Bataillon commander	Stbf. Kraas	Hst. Becker	Hst. Becker Hst. Röhwer Hst. Richter KGr.	Stbf. Becker †	Stbf. Richter	Stbf. Möllhof
Adjutant	Ust. d.R. Bolz	Ust. Sachse	Ust. Moldenhauer Ust. Boldt.	?	?	Ust. Sterl
Ordonnanzoffizier	Ust. Schmidt, R.	Ust. Schlee Ust. Boldt	?	?	?	Ust. Pollmann
Administrative officer	Ust. Thieming	Ost. Beutin	Ust. Löbig Ust. Alexander	?	?	Ost. Behrendt
Doctor	Ost. Dr. Necker	Hst. Dr. Necker	Hst. Dr. Necker Hst. Dr. Radda †	?	?	Ust. Dr. Rüther
Motor vehicles technical officer (TFK)	Ust. Lotz	?	Ust. Gail	Ust. Gail	Ost. Gail	Ost. Gail
1. Kompanie	Ost. Hausdorf Ost. Kalcher †	Ost. Dr. Fiedler † Ust. Sterl	Hst. Diefenthal Ust. Sterl	?	?	Ost. Teis †
2. Kompanie	Hst. Becker, Hans	Ost. Meir	Ost. Meir Ust. Salamon	?	?	?
3. Kompanie	Hst. Röhwer	Ust. Teich Ost. Kluge † Ost. Krüger	Ost. Krüger? Ost. Teich	?	?	Ust. Langer †
4. (MG) Kompanie (dissolved May. 1944)	Ost. Waldow	Ost. Bremer	Ost. Bremer	—	—	—
5. (heavy) Kompanie (starting May, 1944, called 4. [heavy] Kompanie)	Hst. Kaschula	Ost. Schnelle	Ost. Schnelle	—	Ost. Leissner Hscha. Weber	Ost. Fiedler
Versorgungskompanie (Supply company formed May, 1944)				?	?	?

II. Bataillon of SS-Panzergrenadierregiment 2 *LSSAH* (II./2)

	Feb. - Mar., 1943	July, 1943	Oct., 43 - Apr., 44	July, 1944	Dec., 1944	Feb. - May, 1945
Bataillon commander	Stbf. Sandig	Stbf. Sandig	Stbf. Sandig Hst. Bormann Hst. Karck, Pfeiffer	Stbf. Junge, Max Hst. Karck †	Hst. Schnelle	Stbf. Junge, Max † Stbf. Rau Stbf. Eberhard †
Adjutant	Ust. Stehr	Ust. Klein †	Ust. Kirchner † Ust. Sander	Ust. Urban StOj. Flacke	Ost. Urban	Hst. Schmidt
Ordonnanzoffizier	Ust. Klein, Willy	Ust. Clausen	?	?	?	?
Administrative officer	Ost. Laue	Ost. Laue	Ust. Seebauer	Ust. Seebauer	Osts. Seebauer	Ost. Seebauer
Doctor	Ost. Dr. Houtrow	Hst. Dr. Schmidbauer	Hst. Dr. Schmidbauer	?	?	?
Motor vehicles technical officer(TFK)	Ust. Wehrmeyer	Ust. Wehrmeyer Ust. Krämer	Ust. Seipp Ust. Krämer	Ost. Mielke	?	?
6. Kompanie (Starting May, 1944, called 5. Kompanie)	Hst. Scappini	Ost. Gaerthe	Hst. Gaerthe Ost. Pfeiffer †	Hst. Gaerthe	Ost. Schmidt † Ust. Kühne	?
7. Kompanie (starting May, 1944, called 6. Kompanie)	Hst. Bormann	Hst. Heinze †	Ust. Kürner Ost. Schmidt, Hans Ost. Kleiner	?	?	Ost. Bieder
8. Kompanie (starting May, 1944, called 7. Kompanie)	Hst. d.R. Junge, M.	Hst. Diedrich Ust. Zingel	?	Hst. Junge, Max † Ost. Kübler	Ost. Kübler	Ost. Kübler† Ost. Schellhammer
9. (MG) Kompanie (dissolved May, 1944)	Ost. Weitzel †	Ost. Karck Ust. Keil	?	—	—	—
10. (heavy) Kompanie (starting May, 1944, called 8. [heavy] Kompanie)	Hst. Vögtel	Ost. Hampel Ust. Schmidt	Ost. Keil	Ost. Keil	Ost. Keil	Ost. Keil
Versorgungskompanie (Supply company formed May, 1944)				Ost. Seebauer	Ost. Schmidt	Ost. Seebauer

III. (armoured) Bataillon of SS-Panzergrenadierregiment 2 *LSSAH* (III. [armoured]/2)

	Feb. - Mar., 1943	July, 1943	Oct., 43 - Apr., 44	July, 1944	Dec., 1944	Feb. - May, 1945
Bataillon commander	Stbf. Peiper	Stbf. Peiper	Stbf. Peiper Hst. Guhl Hst. Dinse, Preuß	Stbf. Wandt Hst. Dinse Hst. Diefenthal	Hst. Diefenthal	Hst. Preuß Hst. Rink
Adjutant	Ost. Dinse	Ost. Wolff	Ust. Kobler Ost. Gührs	Ost. Gührs	Ost. Flacke	Ust. Enders Ust. Gräber StOj. Morczek
Ordonnanzoffizier	Ust. Möhrlein Ust. Kindermann	Ust. Hülsen † Ust. Möhrlin	Ust. Kern	?	Ust. Kindermann	?
Administrative officer	Ust. Moldt	Hst. Moldt †	Ust. Verboot	Ust. Ogertschnik	?	?
Doctor	Ost. Dr. Brüstle	Hst. Dr. Brüstle	Ost. Dr. Breme	Hst. Dr. Brüstle Hst. Dr. Lorenz	Hst. Dr. Brüstle Ost. Dr. Dittmann	?
Motor vehicle technical officer (TFK) Weapons technical officer (TFW)	Ost. Ratschko Ust. Bloch	Ost. Ratschko Ost. Bloch	Ost. Ratschko ?	Ost. Ratschko Ost. Maiwald	Ost Maiwald ?	Ost. Maiwald ?
Pionierzug	Oscha. Haberstroh	?	?	?	Ust. Hofbauer	?
11. (armoured) Kompanie (starting May, 1944, called 9./2)	Ost. Guhl	Hst. Guhl	Hst. Guhl Ost. Schmitt	Ost. Schmitt	Ust. Leike	Hst. Rink Ost. Gölling Ost. Kowallik
12. (armoured) Kompanie (starting May, 1944, called 10./2)	Ost. Westrup †	Ost. Preuß	Ost. Preuß	Hst. Preuß	Hst. Preuß	Ost. Schlee Ost. Krüger Ost. Düke
13. (armoured) Kompanie (starting May, 1944, called 11./2)	Ost. Pinter	Hst. Wandt	Ost. Möhrlin Ust. Tomhardt	Ost. Tomhardt Ust. Babick	Ost. Tomhardt	Ost. Tomhardt † Ost. Vögler Ust. Käding
14. (heavy armoured) Kompanie (starting May, 1944, called 12. [heavy]/2)	Hst. Kolitz Ost. Dinse	Ost. Dinse	Hst. Dinse	Hst. Dinse Oscha. Thiele	Ust. Thiele	Ost. Thiele Ust. Wagner
Versorgungskompanie (Supply company formed May, 1944)					Ost. Lüdecke	Ost. Lüdecke

SS-Panzerregimental 1 *LSSAH*
(Stab and Regimental Units)

	Feb. - Mar., 1943	July, 1943	Oct., 43 - Apr., 44	July, 1944	Dec., 1944	Feb. - May, 1945
Regimental commander	Ostbf. Schönberger	Ostbf. Schönberger †	Ostbf. Schönberger Stbf. Peiper	Ostbf. Peiper	Ostbf. Peiper	Ostbf. Peiper
Adjutant	Hst. Tiemann	Hst. Nüske	Hst. Gruhle	Hst. Gruhle Hst. Nüske[1]	Hst. Gruhle	Ost. Köchlin
Ordonnanzoffizier	Ust. Junker	?	Ost. Rümmler	St.Obj. Adam[1]	Hst. Nüske	?
Administrative officer	Hst. Wellershaus	Hst. Wellershaus	?	Hst. Zimmermann[1]	?	?
Doctor	Hst. Dr. Peters	Hst. Dr. Peters	Hst. Dr. Peters Hst. Dr. Sickel	Hst. Dr. Sickel	Hst. Dr. Sickel	Hst. Dr. Sickel
Motor vehicle technical officer 1(TFK 1) Motor vehicle technical officer 2(TFK 2)	Hst. Giles ?	Hst. Giles Ost. Strohschön	Ost. Strohschön ?	Hst. Strohschön ?	Ost. Gülden	? ?
Signals officer	Ost. Jahn	Ost. Jahn	Ost. Jahn	?	Ust. Krause	?
Chef of the Stabskompanie	Hst. d.R. Füß	Stbf. d.R. Füß	Stbf. Füß †	Hst. Sachse Oscha. Neilsen	Ost. Maule † Hst. Dr. Sickel	?
9. (Panzer-Pionier) Kompanie	Hst. Nüske		Ost. Rumpf	Hst. Rumpf	Hst. Rumpf	Hst. Rumpf
13. (heavy) Panzerkompanie	Hst. Kling	Hst. Kling	Hst. Kling Ust. Wittmann	Komp. to schw. Pz. Abt. 101	–	–
10. (Panzer-Flak) Kompanie (formed in Dec., 1944)					Ost. Vögler	Ost. Vögler
Panzer repair Kompanie	Hst. Gilles	Hst. Gilles	Hst. Kluge	Hsts. Kluge	Ost. Ratschko	Ost. Stöckel
Versorgungskompanie (Supply company)				Ost. Höcker	Stbf. Unger	Stbf. Unger

1. According to the original documents (Bundesarchiv-Militärarchiv file number BA-MA-RS 4/1242).

I. Abteilung of SS-Panzerregiment *LSSAH* (I./Pz. Rgt. 1)

	Feb. - Mar., 1943	July, 1943	Oct., 43 - Apr., 44	July, 1944	Dec., 1944	Feb. - May, 1945
Abteilung commander	Stbf. Wünsche	See below	Stbf. Kuhlmann Hst. Pötschke	Hst. Pötschke	Hst. Pötschke	Stbf. Pötschke † Hst. Birnschein
Adjutant	Ost. Isecke		?	?	Ust. Fischer Ust. Reiser	?
Ordonnanzoffizier	?		?	?	Ust. Kramm	?
Administrative officer	?		?	Ust. Möfle [1]	Ust. Sethean Ust. Harms	?
Doctor	Ost. Dr. Stiawa		?	?	Hst. Dr. Neumeier	?
Motor vehicles technical officer (TFK)	Ust. Klein		Ust. Sachse	Oscha. Oeltjen	Ust. Diefental	?
Signals officer	Ust. Schlauß		Ust. Schleif Ust. Bönisch †	Oscha. Nielsen	?	?
Stabskompanie	Hst. Weibgen		Ost. Gruhle Ust. Jahn	?	Hst. Otto Ust. Buchheim	?
1. Panzerkompanie	Hst. Jürgensen, Arno		Hst. Pötschke	?	Ost. Kremser Ust. Hennecke	?
2. Panzerkompanie	Ost. Beck, Wilh.		Ost. Stübing	Hst. Malkomes	Ost. Christ Hst. Malkomes	Hst. Malkomes
3. Panzerkompanie	Hst. Lambrecht		Ost. Kleist	Hst. Sachse[1]	?	Ost. Sternebeck
4. Panzerkompanie			Ost. Otto	Ost. Otto[1]	?	?

The Abteilung did not take part in Operation Zitadelle (July, 1943). Equipped with Panzer V's, it rejoined the field units in Italy in August of 1943.

1. According to the original documents (Bundesarchiv-Militärarchiv file number BA-MA-RS 4/1242).

II. Abteilung of SS-Panzerregiment 1 *LSSAH*
(II./Pz. Rgt 1)

	Feb. - Mar., 1943	July, 1943	Oct., 43 - Apr., 44	July, 1944	Dec., 1944	Feb. - May, 1945
Abteilung commander	Stbf. Groß, Martin	Stbf. Groß, Martin [2]	Stbf. Groß, Martin Hst. Schmidt, Manf. Hst. Streipart	Stbf. Kling	Stbf. Guhl [3]	Stbf. Guhl
Adjutant	Ust. Sprunk	Ost. Sprunk		Ost. Wendorff [4] Ust. Dr. Richert [4]	Ust. Köchlin	?
Ordonnanzoffizier	Ust. Bohnenberg	Ust. Michalski	?	Ust. Mühlenbach [4]	Ust. Reiser	Ost. Reiser
Administrative officer	?	?	?	Ost. Christke [4]	Ost. Kröger, Tim	Ost. Kröger, Tim
Doctor	Ost. Dr. v. Guelfenberg	Ost. Dr. v. Guelfenberg	?	Fehlstelle [4]	Ost. Dr. Neumaier	Ost. Dr. Neumaier
Motor vehicles technical officer (TFK) Repair platoon	Ust. Grundmann Ost. Bache	Ust. Grundmann ?	Ost. Grundmann ?	Fehlstelle [4] ?	Hst. Scherer ?	Hst. Scherer ?
Signals officer	Ust. Beckmann	Ust. Beckmann	?	?	?	?
Stabkompanie	Ost. d.R. Dieweige	Hst. Unger	Hst. Unger Ust. Habermann	Ost. Vollert [4]	Ust. Wettach	Ust. Wettach
5. Panzerkompanie	Hst. Schmidt	Ost. Scharke	Ost. Scharke † Ust. Schäfer	Hst. Streipart [4] Ost. Sternebeck	?	?
6. Panzerkompanie	Hst. Pfeiffer	Ost. v. Ribbentrop	Ost. Malchow	Ost. Junker [4]	Ost. Junker Ust. Steiniger	?
7. Panzerkompanie	Ost. Astheger Ost. Alt	Hst. Tiemann	Ost. Sprunk †	Ost. Wolff [4] † Ust. Stiller	Hst. Klingelhöfer	Ust. Stiller
8. Panzerkompanie	—	Ost. Armberger [1]	Ost. Armberger Ost. Sternebeck	Hst. Armberger [4] †	Hst. Christ	?

1. The 8. Kompanie did not take part in Operation Zitadelle because of an insufficient number of Panzers.
2. In the move from Russia to Italy, the II. Abteilung was forced to give up its Panzers. In the move back into Russia at the end of October, 1943, it was equipped with new Panzer IV's in Magdeburg and at the station where it was unloaded.
3. The Stab of the II./SS-Panzerregiment 1 and the 5. Panzerkompanie remained in the Rahden-Lübbecke area in December of 1944 and January of 1945 without Panzers.
4. According to the original documents (Bundesarchiv-Militärarchiv file number BA-MA-RS 4/1242).

SS-Panzer-Aufklärungsabteilung 1 *LSSAH* (Pz.AA/Pz. Rgt. 1)

	Feb. - Mar., 1943	July, 1943	Oct., 43 - Apr., 44	July, 1944	Dec., 1944	Feb. - May, 1945
Abteilung commander	Stbf. Meyer, Kurt	Stbf. Knittel	Stbf. Knittel	Stbf. Knittel	Stbf. Knittel	Hst. Wawrczinek
Adjutant	Ost. v. Büttner	Ust. Leidreiter	?	Ost. Oetter †	Ustf. Wagner Ust Kugel	Ust. Lenz
Administrative officer	Hst. Kukatsch	Ust. Wegener	Ost. Wegener	?	?	?
Doctor	Hst. Dr. Gatternig	Hst. Dr. Gatternig	Hst. Dr. Gatternig	?	?	?
Motor vehicles technical officer(TFK)	Ost. Eggers	?		?	?	?
Signals officer	Ost. Westphal	?	Ust. Gerlach Uscha. Wiesner	Ust. Eggers ?	?	?
Stabskompanie	Ost Reuß	Ost. Reuß	Ost. Reuß	Ost. Reuß	Ost. Goltz	?
1. Aufklärungskompanie (equipped with VW's)	Hst. Bremer	Ost. Coblenz	?	Ost Leidreiter	Ust. Rentsch	?
2. Aufklärungskompanie (equipped with VW's)	Ost. Weiser	?	Hst. Böttcher Ust. Kasper Oscha. Galart	Ost. Coblenz	Ost. Leidreiter	?
3. Aufklärungskompanie [3] (equipped with light Schützenpanzerwagens)	Hst. Knittel	Ost. Wawrczinek	Ost. Lindenberger	Hst. Wawrczinek	Ost. Coblenz	?
4. (Panzerspäh) Kompanie	Hst. Böttcher	Ost. Goltz	Ost. Goltz	Ost. Goltz	Ust. Fritsch	?
5. (heavy) Kompanie	Hst. Olboeter	?	Ost. Junghans	Ost. Junghans	Ost. Wegner	?
Versorgungskompanie (Supply company)				Oscha. Koppel	Ost. Reuß	?

3. The 3./SS-Panzer-Aufklärungsabteilung 1 was partially equipped with bicycles starting in December of 1944.

SS-Sturmgeschützabteilung 1 *LSSAH*
(Starting Oct., 1944, Called SS-Panzerjägerabteilung 1 *LSSAH*)

	Feb. - Mar., 1943	July, 1943	Oct., 43 - Apr., 44	July, 1944	Dec., 1944	Feb. - May, 1945
Abteilung commander	Stbf. v. Westernhagen	Stbf. v. Westernhagen	Hst. Heimann	Stbf. Heimann † Hst. Rettlinger	Hst. Rettlinger	Stbf. Rettlinger
Adjutant	?	Ost. Gaschnitz	Ost. Gaschnitz Ost. Tischendorf	Ust. Bröcker, J.	Ust. Bröcker, Jochen	Ust. Milles
Ordonnanzoffizier	?	?	?	Ost. Eder	Ost. Zoglmann	Ost. Zoglmann
Administrative officer	Ost. Johanisson	Ost. Johanisson	Ost. Johanisson	Ust. Orth	Hst. Schreier	
Doctor	Ost. Dr. Raabe	Hst. Dr. Raabe	Hst. Dr. Raabe	Ost. Dr. Strametz	Ost. Dr. Strametz	Hst. Dr. Strametz
Motor vehicles technical officer(TFK)	?	Hst. Eggers	?	Hst. Eggers	?	Ost. Sievert
Signals officer	Ust. Tischendorf	Ost. Eder	Ost. Eder	Ust. Maurer	Ost. Eder	Ost. Herzog
Stabsbatterie	?	Ust. Persson	Ust. Grinda	Ust. Paulsen Ust. Schaschek	Ost. Schaschek	?
1. Batterie/kompanie	Hst. Heimann	Hst. Heimann	Ost. Gaschnitz † Ost. Holst	Ost. Holst	Hst. Holst	Hst. Holst Ost. Stark
2. Battr.	Ost. Holst	Hst. Wiesemann	Hst. Wiesemann † Ust. Kründer Ust. Wagner	Ost. Wagner	Ost. Giesicke †	Ost. Piegler
3. Battr.	Hst. Rettlinger	Hst. Rettlinger	Hst. Rettlinger Ust. Schulz W.	Ost. Bröcker, Br.	Ost. Bröcker, Bruno Ost. Schulz, W.	Ost. Bröcker, J.

SS-Panzerjägerabteilung 1 *LSSAH*
(Starting January, 1944, joined the 12. SS Panzerdivision *HJ* as its SS-Panzerjägerabteilung 12 *HJ*)

	Feb. - Mar., 1943	July, 1943	Oct., 43 - Apr., 44	July, 1944	Dec., 1944	Feb. - May, 1945
Commander	Stbf. Hanreich	Stbf. Hanreich	Stbf. Hanreich			
Adjutant	Ost. Tirschler	Ost. Hurdelbrink	Ost. Hurdelbrink Ust. Winkler			
Ordonnanzoffizier	?	Ust. Walter	Ust. Walter			
Administrative officer	?	?	?			
Doctor	Ost. Dr. Preissl	?	?			
Motor vehicles technical officer(TFK) Weapons technical officer (TFW)	Ost. Aus der Wiesche	Ust. Bartel	Ust. Bartel			
Signals officer	Ost. Siegert	?	?			
1. Kompanie	Hst. Prinz	?	Ost. Miegel †			
2. Kompanie	Ost. Sörensen	?	Ost. Tirschler			
3. Kompanie	Ost. Woest	Ost. Woest	Hst. Woest			

SS-Panzer-Artillerie-Regiment 1 *LSSAH*
(SS-Pz.AR 1)
(Stab and Regimental Units)

	Feb. - Mar., 1943	July, 1943	Oct., 43 - Apr., 44	July, 1944	Dec., 1944	Feb. - May, 1945
Regimental commander	Staf. Staudinger	Ostbf. Merstch	Ostbf. Merstch Stbf. Sedlaczek	Ostbf. Steineck	Ostbf. Steineck	Stbf. Sonnenstuhl Stbf. Dr. Kohler
Adjutant	Ost. Preuß	Ost. Queißer	Ost. Queißer	?	Ost. Kosch	Ost. Kosch
Special-missions officer (z.b.V.)	Hst. Bartling	?	?	?	?	Hst. Bernhard
Administrative officer	Hst. Wittesch	Ost. Zunker	Ost. Zunker	Hst. Zunker	Hst. Zunker	Hst. Zunker
Doctor	Hst. Prof. Mündnich	Hst. Dr. Walzel	Hst. Dr. Walzel	?	?	?
Motor vehicles technical officer(TFK) WaMun (Weapons and ammunition)	Ost. Riedl Ost. Taut	Ost. Riederle Ust. Hannes	Ust. Marchand Ust. Hannes	Ust. Marchand Ust. Hannes	Ost. Marchand ?	Ost. Marchand ?
Signals officer	Ost. Krüger, W.	Ust. Kubatsch	Ust. Kubatsch	Ost. Kubatsch	Ust. Siefert	Ust. Siefert
Stabsbatterie	Ost. Krüger, W.	?	?	?	?	?
Beobachtungbatterie (Observation battery dissolved May, 1943)	Hst. Müller, Willy	—	—	—	—	—
10. (10-cm) Kanonenbatterie (formed May, 1943)		Hst. Urbanitz	Hst. Urbanitz	?	?	?
11. (Werfer) Batterie (Formed May, 1943, and dissolved May, 1944)		Ost. Bartel †	Ost. Oertel	—	—	—

I. Abteilung of SS-Panzer-Artillerie-Regiment 1 *LSSAH*
(I./Pz.AR 1)
(Starting June, 1944, called the II. Abteilung of SS-Panzer-Artillerie-Regiment 1 *LSSAH*)

	Feb. - Mar., 1943	July, 1943	Oct., 43 - Apr., 44	July, 1944	Dec., 1944	Feb. - May, 1945
Abteilung commander	Stbf. Steineck	Hst. de Vries	Hst. de Vries	Stbf. Dr. Köhler	Hst. Schlett	Hst. Schlett
Adjutant	Ust. Schulz †	Ost. Einert	Ost. Einert	?	?	?
Administrative officer	Ust. Müller	?	?	?	?	?
Doctor	Ust. Dr. Dreier	?	?	?	?	?
Motor vehicles technical officer(TFK)	Ust. Magunna	?	?	?	?	?
Stabsbatterie	Ust. Kurth	?	Ust. Eisenblätter	?	?	?
1. Batterie (Starting June, 1944, called 4. Batterie)	Hst. de Vries	?	Ost. Rademacher	?	?	?
2. Batterie (Starting June, 1944, called 5. Batterie)	Hst. Luhmann	?	Ost. Guß	?	?	?
3. Batterie (starting June, 1944, called 6. Batterie)	Ost. Haack †	Ost. Gohlke	Ost. Funk	Hst. Funk	?	?

II. (armoured) Abteilung of SS-Panzer-Artillerie-Regiment 1 *LSSAH*
(II [armoured]/Pz.AR 1)
(Starting June, 1944, called I. [armoured]/SS-Artillerie-Regiment 1)

	Feb. - Mar., 1943	July, 1943	Oct., 43 - Apr., 44	July, 1944	Dec., 1944	Feb. - May, 1945
Abteilung commander	Stbf. Luhmann	Stbf. Luhmann	Stbf. Luhmann	Stbf. Luhmann	Hst. Kalischko	Stbf. Sonnenstuhl Hst. Funk
Adjutant	Ost. Balchuweit	?	?	?	?	Ust. Scheuermann
Administrative officer	?	?	?	?	?	?
Doctor	?	?	?	?	?	?
Motor vehicles technical officer(TFK)	?	?	?	?	?	?
Signals officer	Ost. Kästner	Ost. Kästner	?	?	?	?
4. (armoured) Batterie (Starting June, 1944, called 1. [armoured] Batterie)	?	?	Ost. Henssler	?	Ost. Buschek	?
5. (armoured) Batterie (Starting June, 1944, called 2. [armoured] Batterie)	?	?	?	?	?	?
6. (armoured) Batterie (Starting June, 1944, called 3. [armoured] Batterie)	?	?	Ost. Kalischko	Hst. Kalischko		?

III. Abteilung of SS-Panzer-Artillerie-Regiment 1 *LSSAH* (III Pz.AR 1)

	Feb. - Mar., 1943	July, 1943	Oct., 43 - Apr., 44	July, 1944	Dec., 1944	Feb. - May, 1945
Abteilung commander	Stbf. Schröder	Hst. Sedlaczek	Stbf. Sedlaczek	?	?	Stbf. Luhmann
Adjutant	Ost. Bernhard	Ost. Bernhard Ust. Butschek	Ust. Butschek	?	?	?
Ordonnanzoffizier						
Administrative officer	?	?	?	?	?	?
Doctor	Hst. Dr. Vogt	?	?	?	?	?
Motor vehicles technical officer(TFK)	?	?	?	?	?	?
Signals officer						
Stabsbatterie	Ost. Forck	?	?	?	?	?
7. Batterie	Ost. Rauh	Ost. Forck	Hst. Forck Ust. Oertel	?	?	?
8. Batterie	Hst. Sedlaczek? Ost. Lehnert	Ost. Flemmes Ost. Schlett	Ost. Bernhard	?	?	?
9. Batterie	Ost. Glasl	?	Ost. Gladoss	?	?	?

IV. Abteilung of SS-Panzer-Artillerie-Regiment 1 *LSSAH*
(IV./Pz.AR 1)
(Stab was dissolved May, 1943)

	Feb. - Mar., 1943	July, 1943	Oct., 43 - Apr., 44	July, 1944	Dec., 1944	Feb. - May, 1945
Abteilung commander	Hst. Sedlaczek					
Adjutant	?					
Ordonnanzoffizier						
Administrative officer	?					
Doctor	?					
Motor vehicles technical officer(TFK)	?					
Signals officer	?					
10. (Werfer) Batterie (Starting May, 1944, called 11. Batterie)	Ost. Bartels	—				
11. (heavy Feldhaubitze) Batterie	?					
12. (10-cm) Kanonenbatterie (Starting May, 1944, called 10 Batterie)	Hst. Urbanitz					

SS-Flakabteilung 1 *LSSAH*

	Feb. - Mar., 1943	July, 1943	Oct., 43 - Apr., 44	July, 1944	Dec., 1944	Feb. - May, 1945
Abteilung commander	Stbf. Krause, Bernh.	Stbf. Ullerich	Stbf. Ullerich Hst. Dr. Loennicker	Stbf. Ullerich	Stbf. Ullerich	Hst. Kleemann
Adjutant	Ust. Brinkmann	Ust. Vögler	Ost. Vögler	Ost. Vögler	Ost. Thielbar	Ust. Sellner Ust. Schmorte
Ordonnanzoffizier	Ust. Plöbsch	?	?	?	Ust. Kniest	?
Administrative officer	Hst. Dietrich	Hst. Bentlin	Hst. Bentlin	Hst. Bentlin	Ost. Bentlin	Hst. Bentlin
Doctor Dentist	Hst. Dr. Hattler Hst. Dr. Achtel	Hst. Dr. Hattler	Hst. Dr. Hattler †	Hst. Dr. Meixner	Hst. Dr. Hohmann	Hst. Dr. Hohmann
Motor vehicles technical officer(TFK) Weapons technical officer (TFW)	Ost. Trinkhaus Ost. Thiemig	Ust. Lieder Hst. Thiemig	Ust. Lieder Hst. Thiemig	Ost. Lieder Ust. Gabler	Ost. Lieder Ost. Gabler	Ost. Lieder Ost. Gabler
Signals officer	Ust. Persson	Ust. Persson	Ust. Persson † Ust. Galler	Ust. Galler	Ust. Galler	Ost. Galler
Stabsbatterie	Ust. Persson	Ust. Persson	Ust. Persson † Ust. Galler	Ust. Galler	Ust. Galler	Ost. Galler
1. (8.8-cm) Batterie	Hst. Dr. Loennicker	Hst. Dr. Loennicker	Hst. Dr. Loennicker	Hst. Dr. Loennicker	?	?
2. (8.8-cm) Batterie	Hst. Möbius	Ost. Kleemann	Ost. Kleemann	Ust Thielbar	Hst. Kleemann	Ost. Thielbar Ost. Sellner
3. (8.8-cm) Batterie	Hst. Ullerich	Ost. Graul	Hst. Graul	Ost. Seethaler	Ost. Breinersdorfer	Ost. Breinersdorf
4. (3.7-cm) Batterie (self-propelled)	Hst. Mendryk	Hst. Mendryk	Hst. Mendryk	Hst. Mendryk	Hst. Mendryk	?
5. (3.7-cm) Batterie (self-propelled)	Ost. Assbach	Ost. Assbach	Ost. Straubel	Ost. Straubel	Ost. Straubel	Ust. Leiberts
6. (light) Batterie (self-propelled)	—	Ost. Straubel [1]	—	—	—	—

1. The 6. (light) Batterie was transferred as a unit to the Generalkommando of the I. SS-Panzerkorps to act as Flaskkompanie in November of 1943.

SS-Panzer-Pionier-Bataillon 1
(SS-Pz. Pi. 1)

	Feb. - Mar., 1943	July, 1943	Oct., 43 - Apr., 44	July, 1944	Dec., 1944	Feb. - May, 1945
Bataillon commander	Stbf. Hansen, Christian	Hst. Steinert	Hst. Steinert	Stbf. Steinert	Stbf. Scheler	Stbf. Scheler
Adjutant	Ust. Spitzer	?	?	?	Ust. Felsinger	Ust. Felsinger
Administrative officer	Ost. Leibezeder	Hst. Leibezeder	?	?	?	?
Doctor	Ost. Dr. Kaiser	Hst. Dr. Kaiser	Hst. Dr. Kaiser	Hst. Dr. Kaiser	Hst. Dr. Kaiser	Hst. Dr. Kaiser
Motor vehicles technical officer(TFK) Engineering technical officer (TFPi)	Ust. Bossen Ust. Schmitt, Karl	? ?	? ?	? ?	? ?	? ?
	—					
1. Pionierkompanie	Hst. Steinert	Hst. Taubert	Hst. Taubert Ost. Karstens	Ust. Leifheit	Ost. Leifheit	Ost. Leifheit Ust. Kühne
2. Pionierkompanie	Hst. Wendler	Ost. Scheler	Hst. Scheler	?	?	?
3. Pionierkompanie	Hst. Tschöltsch	Ost. Schütte	Ost. Schütte Ust. Fellhauer	Ust. Fellhauer ?	Ost. Sievers	?
4. (Heavy) Kompanie (dissolved May, 1943)	Ost. Keck	—	—	—	—	—
Bridge-building column	Ost. Wendt	Ost. Wendt	Ost. Wendt	?	?	?
Light Pionier column	Ost. Weitzel	Ost. Weitzel	?	?	?	?

SS-Panzer-Nachrichtenabteilung 1 *LSSAH*
(SS-Pz.NA 1)

	Feb. - Mar., 1943	July, 1943	Oct., 43 - Apr., 44	July, 1944	Dec., 1944	Feb. - May, 1945
Abteilung Commander	Stbf. Metz	Stbf. Metz	Stbf. Metz	Stbf. Metz	Stbf. Berg Hst. Stieglitz	Stbf. Stieglitz
Adjutant	Ust. Uibelhack	Ost. Uibelhack Ust. Tschampel	Ust. Schäfer Ust. Wunderlich †	?	?	?
Administrative officer	Ost. Zunker	Ost. Zunker	Ust. Brunner	Ust. Brunner	?	?
Doctor	Ost. Dr. Waleczek	Ost. Dr. Waleczek	Hst. Dr. Weigt	?	?	?
Motor vehicles technical officer(TFK) Signals technical officer (TFN)	Hst. Smolinski Ust. Slawski	Ust. Heuer Hst. Smolinski	Ost. Heuer ?	?	?	?
1. (Fernsprecher) Kompanie	Hst. Hermanns	Hst. Hermanns	Hst. Hermanns Ust. Schäfer	Hst. Schäfer	?	?
2. (Funk) Kompanie	Ost. Liebrich	Ost. Preußer	Ost. Liebrich	Hst. Liebrich	Hst. Liebrich	Hst. Liebrich
3. (Fern and Funk) Kompanie (May to July, 1943)		—	—	—	—	—
light Nachrichtenkolonne	Hscha. Petersen	Hscha. Petersen	Hst. Petersen	Hscha. Petersen	?	?

SS-Panzerdivisions-Nachschubtruppen 1 *LSSAH*

	Feb. - Mar., 1943	July, 1943	Oct., 43 - Apr., 44	July, 1944	Dec., 1944	Feb. - May, 1945
Abteilung commander (Division Nahrung und Fütterung = Provisions and Feed)	Stbf. Siebken	Hst. Stamp	Stbf. Stamp	Stbf. Stamp	Stbf. Stamp	Stbf. Stamp
Adjutant	Ost. Jürgens	Ust. Sander	Ust. Sander	Ost. Jürgens	?	?
Administrative officer	Ost. Furch	Ost. Furch	Ost. Furch	?	?	?
Doctor	Ost. Dr. Schneller	Ost. Dr. Schneller	Ost. Dr. Schneller	?	?	?
Motor vehicles technical officer(TFK)	?	Ost. Meens	Ost. Meens	?	?	?
Nachschubkompanie	Hst. Stamp	Ost. Jungekrüger	Ost. Jungekrüger	Ost. Jungekrüger	Ost. Puhlmann [1]	Ust. Moosmann
1. Krafwagenkompanie 2. Krafwagenkompanie	? ?	? Ost. Koch	Ust. Huber Ost. Koch	?[2] ?	?[3] ?	?[4] ?
3. Krafwagenkompanie 4. Krafwagenkompanie	? ?	Ost. Deiß Hst. Karge	Ost. Deiß Hst. Karge	? ?	? ?	? —
5. Krafwagenkompanie 6. Krafwagenkompanie	? ?	Ost. Sander Ost. Kummert	Ost. Sander Ost. Kummert	? —	— —	— —
7. Krafwagenkompanie 8. Krafwagenkompanie	? ?	Ost. Puhlmann Hscha. Lehmann, F.	Ost. Puhlmann Hscha. Lehmann, F.	— —	— —	— —

1. On 3.4.1945, the 1. Zug of the Nachschubkompanie (under Hauptscharführer Kirme), was transferred to the Divisions-Begleitkompanie.
2. In June, 1944, the 6. - 8. Krafwagenkompanie was dissolved.
3. In December, 1944, the 5. Krafwagenkompanie was dissolved.
4. In January, 1945, the 4. and 5. Krafwagenkompanie were dissolved.

SS-Panzer-Instandsetzungs-Abteilung 1 *LSSAH*

	Feb. - Mar., 1943	July, 1943	Oct., 43 - Apr., 44	July, 1944	Dec., 1944	Feb. - May, 1945
Abteilung commander	Stbf. Groß, Helm.	Ostb. Groß, Helm.	Stbf. Linnbrunner † Stbf. Gilles	Stbf. Gilles	Stbf. Gilles	Stbf. Gilles
Adjutant	Ust. Weiß	?	?	?	?	?
Special-missions officer (z.b.V.)	Hst. Diedrich	?	?	?	?	?
Administrative officer	Oscha. Merkel	?	?	?	?	?
Doctor	Ost. Dr. Hann	?	?	?	?	?
Motor vehicles technical officer(TFK)	?	?	?	?	?	?
1. Werkstattkompanie (Wheeled vehicles)	Stbf. Linnbrunner	Ost. Kempka	Hst. Kempka	Hst. Kempka	Hst. Weitzel	Hst. Weitzel
2. Werkstattkompanie (Wheeled vehicles)	Ost. Bossen	Ost. Wiechmann	Hst. Weichmann	Hst. Weichmann	Hst. Weichmann	Hst. Weichmann
3. Werkstattkompanie (Tracked vehicles)	Ost. Linz	Ost. Bossen	Hst. Bossen	Ost. Weitzel	Ost. Linz	Hst. Linz
4. Werkstattkompanie (Weapons)	Hst. Walther	Hst. Schulze, W.	Hst. Schulze, W.	Hst. Schulze, W.	Hst. Schulze, W.	Hst. Schulze, W.
Ersatzteil-Kolonne (Replacement parts column) (Starting May, 1943, called 5. [Ersatzteil] Kompanie)	Ost. Rosenögger	Hst. Rosenögger	Hst. Rosenögger	Hst. Rosenögger	Hst. Rosenögger	Hst. Rosenögger [1]

1. In April, 1945, the 5. (Ersatzteil) Kompanie was transferred to SS-Panzerregiment 1 *LSSAH* to serve as a Panzergrenadierkompanie.

SS-Verwaltungstruppen-Abteilung 1 *LSSAH* (Administrative supply battalion, also known as Wirtschafts-Bataillon *LSSAH*)

	Feb. - Mar., 1943	July, 1943	Oct., 43 - Apr., 44	July, 1944	Dec., 1944	Feb. - May, 1945
Abteilung commander	Stbf. Bludau	Stbf. Tauber	Stbf. Tauber	Stbf. Tauber	Stbf. Tauber	Stbf. Dr. Gruner † Hst. Wulze
Adjutant	Ust. Kellermann	Ust. Freudenberger	Ust. Emmerling	Ust. Olbrich	Ost. Kellermann	?
Administrative officer	?	?	Hst. Pflaum †	Ust. Kellermann	Ost. Marx	Ust. Jürgens
Doctor Veterinarian	Ost. Dr. Moritz Hst. Zander	Ost. Dr. Weber Hst. Zander	Ost. Dr. Weber Hst. Zander	Ost. Dr. Weber Hst. Zander	Ost. Dr. Weber Hst. Zander	Ost. Dr. Weber † Ost. Dr. Moritz Hst.Zander
Motor vehicles technical officer (TFK)	Ost. Meier	Hscha. Wolf	Ust. Meier	Ust. Wohlgehagen	Ust. Wohlgehagen	Ost. Wohlgehagen
Baking Kompanie	Hst. Arthecker	Hst. Arthecker	Hst. Arthecker Hst. Lewerenz Ust. Brettschneider	Ust. Brettschneider	Ust. Brettschneider	Ost. Gottselig
Butchering Kompanie	Hst. Zander	Hst. Zander	Hst. Zander	Hst. Zander	Hst. Zander	Hst. Zander
Divisions-Verpflegungsamt (Division supply office)	Hst. Lewerenz	Hst. Lewerenz	Hst. Lewerenz	Dissolved	—	—
Field post office	Feldpostmstr. Ebert	Feldpostmstr. Ebert	Feldpostmstr. Ebert	Feldpostmstr. Ebert	Feldpostmstr. Ebert	Feldpostmstr. Ebert
Verpflegungskolonne (Supply column formed June, 1944)	—	—	—	Ost. Hilgemann	Ost. Hilgemann	Hst. Hilgemann

SS-Sanitätsabteilung 1 *LSSAH*

	Feb. - Mar., 1943	July, 1943	Oct., 43 - Apr., 44	July, 1944	Dec., 1944	Feb. - May, 1945
Abteilung commander	Ostbf. Dr. Besuden	Stbf. Dr. Liebrich	Stbf. Dr. Liebrich	Stbf. Dr. Leibrich	Stbf. Dr. Vieweg	Stbf. Dr. Vieweg
Adjutant	Hst. Lang	?	?	?	?	?
Administrative officer	Hst. Zimmermann, R.	?	?	?	?	?
Motor vehicles technical officer (TFK)	?	?	?	?	?	?
1. Sanitätskompanie	Hst. Dr. Liebrich	Hst. Dr. Stenzl	Hst. Dr. Stenzl	Hst. Dr. Stenzl	?	?
2. Sanitätskompanie	Hst. Dr. Jackl	Hst. Dr. Luchesi	Hst. Dr. Luchesi Stbf. Dr. Meyer	Hst. Dr. Luchesi	?	?
Division field hospital	Hst. Dr. Jatzlauk	Stbf. Dr. Niedner	Stbf. Dr. Niedner	Transferred to Generalkommando of I. SS-Panzerkorps to serve as Korps Field Hospital 501	—	—
1. - 3. Krankenkraftwagenzug	?			Ust. Kapahnke	Ust. Kapahnke	Ost. Kapahnke
Field Dentistry laboratory	?	?	?	?	?	?

Appendix 10a

Abbreviations for Rank Designations used in Appendix 10

Brig.Fhr.	Brigadeführer
Brig.Fhr. u. Gen.Maj. der W-SS	Brigadeführer und Generalmajor der Waffen-SS
Gen.	General
Gen.Maj.	Generalmajor
Hscha.	Hauptscharführer
Hst.	Hauptsturmführer
Hst. d.R.	Hauptsturmführer der Reserve
Ogruf.	Obergruppenführer
Ogruf. u. Gen. der Waffen-SS	Obergruppenführer und General der Waffen-SS
Oscha.	Oberscharführer
Ost.	Obersturmführer
Ost. d.R.	Obersturmführer der Reserve
Ostbf.	Obersturmbannführer
Schaf.	Scharführer
Stbf.	Sturmbannführer
Staf.	Standartenführer
Uscha.	Unterscharführer
Ust.	Untersturmführer

Appendix No. 11

NOTES

Abbreviations of repeated source citations

BA-MA	Bundesarchiv-Militärarchiv (archive file number follows).
KTB	Kriegstagebuch (designation of unit follows).
SS-FHA	SS-Führungshauptamt [SS leadership headquarters] (file number follows).

Introduction and Part 5

1. BA-MA 31 783/3.
2. SS-FHA 890/42 geh.
3. SS-FHA 8141/42 geh.
4. BA-MA 31 783/3.
5. Husemann's "Guten Glaubens."
6. Report from Miehe.
7. Husemann.
8. Report from Burghardt.
9. Husemann.
10. Report from Wolf.
11. BA-MA 31 783/3.
12. Report from Miehe.
13. Report from Wolf.
14. Report from Miehe.
15. Husemann.
16. Diary of Hübner.
17. Diary of Hübner.
18. Report from Krötz.
19. Report from Krötz.
20. Husemann.
21. Husemann.
22. Diary of Hübner.
23. BA-MA 31 783/3.
24. Husemann.
25. Diary of Hübner.
26. Diary of Hübner.
27. Husemann.
28. von Mellenthin's "Panzerschlachten."
29. Husemann.
30. Husemann.
31. Husemann.
32. Husemann.
33. Husemann.
34. Scheibert's "Panzer zwischen Don und Donez."
35. Scheibert.
36. Husemann.
37. Scheibert.
38. Report from Miehe.
39. Husemann.
40. von Manstein's "Verlorene Siege."
41. Diary of Hübner.
42. von Manstein.
43. Husemann.
44. Husemann.
45. Husemann.
46. Diary of Hübner.
47. Husemann.
48. Husemann.
49. Husemann.
50. BA-MA 31 783/3.
51. ibidem.
52. ibidem.
53. ibidem.
54. ibidem.
55. Weidinger's "Division *Das Reich*," Volume III.
56. BA-MA 31 783/3.
57. Husemann.
58. BA-MA 31 783/3.
59. Husemann.
60. Weidinger.
61. Husemann.
62. ibidem.
63. ibidem.
64. ibidem.
65. BA-MA RH 21-1/87.
66. Husemann.
67. BA-MA RH 21-1/87.
68. Husemann.
69. Weidinger.
70. Husemann.

Part 6

1. BA-MA RH 31 IX 20-23.
2. KTB 2. Panzergrenadierregiment *LAH* (KTB 2). Because this Kriegstagebuch and all its supporting documents are extant, it served as the single most important source for the presentation here of the fighting through April of 1944. Those entries with dates and times are extracted from it, and it will not be cited as a source henceforth.
3. BA-MA 31 IX 20-23.
4. ibidem.
5. "SS-Panzerkorps zwischen Donez and Dnjepr."
6. Ia's daily report of 3.2.1943. All the Ia's daily reports and special reports are extant among the supporting documents to the KTB's of the responsible command authorities. They served as the main source of information for

the depiction here of the daily course of the battle. They will not be cited individually.
7. BA-MA RH 31 IX 20-23.
8. ibidem.
9. Meyer's "Grenadiere."
10. Ia's daily report of 5.2.1943.
11. von Manstein's "Verlorene Siege."
12. Report from Linden.
13. KTB SS-Panzerkorps.
14. Report from Tamm.
15. Meyer.
16. BA-MA RH 31 IX 20-23.
17. Report from Springer.
18. KTB No. 1 AOK 8, 14.2.1943, 08.25 hours.
19. KTB SS-Panzerkorps.
20. Meyer.
21. Weidinger's "Division *Das Reich*," Volume IV.
22. Ia's daily report of 11.2.1943.
23. Weidinger, Volume IV.
24. Diary of Hahn.
25. Report from Isecke.
26. Weidinger, Volume IV.
27. Meyer.
28. Report from Winter.
29. Report from Tiemann.
30. Weidinger, Volume IV.
31. Meyer.
32. KTB SS-Panzerkorps.
33. ibidem.
34. ibidem.
35. Report from von Ribbentrop.
36. Report from Isecke.

Part 7

1. Klink's "Gesetz des Handelns."
2. KTB II. SS-Panzerkorps, reprinted in its entirety in Stadler's "Die Offensive gegen Kursk," served as an essential document for Part 7 of this chronicle.
3. Ia's daily report.
4. Klink.
5. Report from von Ribbentrop.
6. Klink.
7. OKH Ia 36 659 geh. of 29.7.1943.

Part 8

1. RH 19 IX/16 Oberkommander Heeresgruppe B served as the basis for Part 8 of this chronicle.
2. BA-MA RS 2-2/20 KTB II. SS-Panzerkorps.
3. Original situation map of Italy for the *LAH* from 9.9.1943 to 19.10.1943 in the possession of Ralf Tiemann served as the basis for information about the unit's local deployments.
4. Report from Frey.
5. ibidem.
6. BA-MA RS 2-2/20.
7. Osnabrück Schwurgericht [Osnabrück court] Az: 17 KS 3/67; Bundesgerichtshof [Federal court] Az: 5 StR 216/69.
8. RH 19 IX/16.
9. RS 2-2/21 T2.
10. Report from Wortmann.
11. The KTB of the II. SS-Panzerkorps BA-MA RS 2-2/20 served as the documentary evidence for the writing of Part 8, Section Ic, of this chronicle.
12. BA-MA RS 2-2/20.

Part 9, Section I

1. The essential documents for Part 9, Section I, were the KTB of SS-Panzergrenadierregiment 2 *LAH*, BA-MA RS 4/1141, the history of the 1. Panzerdivision written by Rolf G. Stoves, and the daily reports from the Ia of the 1. SS-Panzerdivision *LAH*. This last group of reports are archived in the documents supporting the KTB of the XXXXVIII. Panzerkorps (BA-MA 51 393 and 51 956).
2. Telephone log of the O 1, Hauptsturmführer Tiemann.
3. Pottgießer's "Die Reichsbahn im Ostfeldzug."
4. Report from Erwin Kurz of the 11. Kompanie/SS-Panzergrenadier-Regiment 1.
5. KTB SS-Flakabteilung 1 *LAH*.